IBN's International Trade and Business Guide

How to Profit in the 16
Top African and Caribbean Basin Countries

Franklin Brown

Editor-in-Chief

IBN PUBLICATIONS, LTD.
Research Triangle Park, North Carolina

IBN's International Trade and Business Guide

How to Profit in the 16 Top African and Caribbean Basin countries

Franklin Brown
Editor-in-Chief

Published by:
IBN Publications, Ltd.
Post Office Box 14765
Research Triangle Park
Durham, NC 27709-4765 U.S.A.
This book is available at quantity discounts for bulk purchases
For information, contact the above address or send email to order@ibn-online.com
Visit us on the Web at www.ibn-online.com

Publisher's Cataloging-in-Publication
(Provided by Quality Books, Inc.)

IBN's international trade and business guide : how to
    profit in the 16 top African and Caribbean Basin
    countries / Franklin Brown, editor-in-chief. -- 1st ed.
    p. cm.
    LCCN: 2001087655
    ISBN: 1-931516-06-5

    1. International business enterprises--Africa.
    2. International business enterprises--Caribbean Area.
    I. Brown, Franklin.

HD2755.5.I26 2001   338.8'8
                QBI01-200311

PRINTED IN THE UNITED STATES OF AMERICA

Notice: Every effort has been made to make this guide as complete and accurate as possible. However, there may be mistakes, both in typography and in content. Therefore this text should be used only as a general guide and not as the ultimate source of international trade information. Furthermore, this guide contains information on international trade that is current only up to the printing date.

This book is designed to provide accurate and authoritative information on international trade for the top African and Caribbean Basin countries. It is sold with the understanding that the publisher and the editorial team are not engaged in rendering legal, accounting, or other professional services. If legal or other expert assistance is required, the services of a competent professional should be sought. The editorial team and IBN Publications, Ltd. shall have neither liability nor responsibility to any person or entity with respect to any loss or damage caused, or alleged to have been caused, directly or indirectly by the information contained in this book.

CONTENTS

Each market information contains: **Country Profile, Political Outlook, Economic Outlook, Trade, Marketing Tips, Foreign Investment, Finance, Communications, Transportation, Work Week, Holidays, Business Travel and Contacts.**

ABOUT THE EDITOR-IN-CHIEF

Franklin Brown has held senior technical and management positions in new product development and commercialization with Ford Motor Company and Bausch & Lomb. He has also consulted with several global companies including: GE, 3M, Xerox, and Osram-Sylvania. He has studied, lived, worked, and traveled extensively in Africa, Europe, Asia, and the Americas and these experiences have enabled him to gain insights that led to his career in global business development. Mr. Brown received an MBA in global business administration from the Fuqua School of Business, Duke University, and completed an Executive Management Program in Leading Product Development for senior executives at Harvard Business School.

PUBLISHER'S ACKNOWLEDGEMENTS

The publisher wishes to thank government officials from the United States and overseas nations for their input and expertise. We especially appreciate and thank the many foreign embassies and consulates, the U.S. Department of Commerce, and the U.S. Department of State for their assistance.

The publisher would like to give special thanks to the following individuals without whom this book would not have been possible.

EDITORIAL TEAM

Franklin Brown, MBA, Global Business Administration, Duke University
Shehu Farinwata, PhD Electrical Engineering, Georgia Institute of Technology
Renu Bora, BA, Cornell; PhD English (in progress), Duke University
Paul Graeve, BA, Dartmouth; PhD English Literature (in progress), Duke University
Adriane Brown, MBA, Management Information Systems, SUNY Binghamton
Robert Fiske, President, Vocabula Communications Company, Lexington, MA

CONSULTANTS

Clayton H. Osborne, MSW, CSW, VP of Human Resources, Bausch & Lomb, Rochester, NY
Raphael T. Tshibangu, M.D., Managing Partner, Southeast OB/GYN, P.C., Rochester, NY
Tom I. Lyon, Attorney at Law, Maupin Taylor & Ellis P.A. Raleigh, NC
Richard A. Bynum, Attorney at Law, Maupin Taylor & Ellis P.A. Raleigh, NC
William B. Gwyn Jr., Attorney at Law, Maupin Taylor & Ellis P.A. Raleigh, NC
Thomas Woll, President, Cross River Publishing Consultants, Inc., Katonah, NY
Alice Allen, Alice Allen Communications, New York, NY
Helen Allen, Alice Allen Communications, New York, NY

DESIGN

Website Development, BookZone, Scottsdale, AZ
Cover and Text Layout and Design, Graphics Ink, Durham, NC

Major breakthroughs in transportation and communications in the last century have brought the nations of the world closer. Technological advances have created a boom in international trade and, as the World Trade Organization (WTO) expands its role in international commerce, membership in such global organizations is increasing. As progressive companies increasingly realize that the global marketplace provides bigger and better business opportunities than domestic markets, developing countries worldwide are concluding trade agreements that will allow unprecedented access to their markets.

In May 2000, the U.S. Senate passed the Trade and Development Act of 2000 and President Clinton signed the Act into law. This historic Act will help the developing countries of sub-Saharan Africa and the Caribbean Basin create viable markets while strengthening commercial ties with the United States. A copy of the Trade and Development Act of 2000, Public Law 106-200, May 18, 2000 (H.R. 434) is available at http://thomas.loc.gov.

Title I of The Trade and Development Act of 2000, or the African Growth and Opportunity Act (AGOA), provides reforming and developing African countries with greater access to the U.S. market than any other country or region with which the United States does not have a Free Trade Agreement. The AGOA also provides improved access to U.S. credit, technical expertise, and markets, while initiating a dialogue on trade and investment, the U.S.-Sub-Saharan Africa Trade and Economic Forum. By creating tangible incentives for African countries to implement economic and commercial reform policies, AGOA contributes to better market opportunities and forges stronger commercial partnerships in Africa for U.S. companies. This Act should, in theory, help create stronger commercial ties between Africa and the United States. U.S. firms may find new opportunities in privatizations of African state-owned enterprises, or in partnerships with African companies in infrastructure projects.

Title II of The Trade and Development Act of 2000, also called the Caribbean Basin Trade Partnership Act, seeks to expand the benefits provided under the Caribbean Basin Initiative (CBI). It will, in effect, restore the margin of preferences CBI countries enjoyed prior to the implementation of the North American Free Trade Agreement (NAFTA) as well as improve the range of economic opportunities available to these countries.

Secretary of State, Colin L. Powell stated in his confirmation hearing that improving relations with Africa and the Caribbean Basin Countries (CBC) will be a priority for the Bush administration.

IBN's International Trade and Business Guide: How to Profit in the 16 Top African and Caribbean Basin Countries contains comprehensive and essential economic, political and cultural information critical to firms interested in identifying business opportunities in these countries and provides detailed information that is key to operating successfully in these markets.

This book also provides marketing information to help international businesses and trade organizations succeed and build profitable, quality relationships with customers, business partners and suppliers. The guide is designed as a "one-stop source" to be used by businesses of all sizes, students studying international marketing or international relations, trade consultants, and investors doing business in Africa and the CBC. As international trade is a long-term investment, the information provided is designed to make business trade information gathering efficient and convenient.

The Editorial Team of IBN Publications, Ltd.

A Special Note to Readers

IBN's international trade and business information is compiled from several U.S. and foreign government sources and private organizations worldwide. Our in-house proprietary data collection and analytical tools are used to continually enhance accuracy and completeness and update our database.

IBN's editorial team took great care in compiling the information in this guide. Numerous international trade and business organizations in the United States and abroad were contacted and letters were sent to foreign embassies and consulates requesting information on the most recent investment and trade regulations, documentation requirements, trade prospects and procedures for their respective countries. IBN's research team used the services of international trade professionals for foreign market information and reviewed hundreds of U.S. and foreign governmental and private publications for relevant information.

As numerous sources were referred to - departments of the federal government, libraries, industrial institutions, periodicals, private organizations and individuals - we have not attempted to cite all the authorities consulted in the preparation of this guide.

We wish to thank the many government officials, both from the United States and overseas nations, and the many foreign embassies and consulates, the U.S. Department of Commerce, and the U.S. Department of State for their assistance in the preparation of this guide.

IBN's information is evolving and expanding and we will continue to provide accurate, current, complete and relevant information in print and downloads. The authors, reviewers, editors, and publisher have made extensive efforts to ensure that the information provided herein conforms to the standards accepted at the time of publication. Changes in information due to continual changes in investment and trade regulations, documentation requirements, trade prospects and procedures, and the possibility of human error in preparing an extensive text require that the reader exercise judgment when making decisions, consult and compare information from other sources, and discuss information obtained in this book with international trade specialists to obtain the most current data available. The authors, reviewers, editors, publisher, editorial team and IBN Publications, Ltd. cannot assume liability for the accuracy of this material. Any errors detected will be corrected in the next edition.

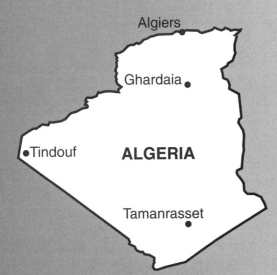

A L G E R I A

TRADE AND BUSINESS GUIDE

Official Name:	Democratic and Popular Republic of Algeria
Official Languages:	Arabic, with French, Berber dialects
Population:	31.2 million (2000 est)
Population Growth:	1.74% (2000 est)
Age Structure:	0–14 years: 35%, 15–64 years: 61%, 65 years and over: 4% (2000 est)
Location:	Northern Africa, bordering on the Mediterranean Sea, between Morocco and Tunisia
Area:	2,381,740 sq. km. Slightly less than 3.5 times the size of Texas
Type of Government:	Republic, bicameral parliament. National People's Assembly (by popular vote for four-year terms) and Council of Nations (one-third by president, two-thirds by indirect vote for six-year terms). President by popular vote for five-year term (next in 2003)
Head of State:	President Abdelaziz Bouteflika
Cabinet:	Council of Ministers appointed by prime minister
Religion:	99% Sunni Muslim, 1% Christian and Jewish
Major Cities:	Capital: Algiers (1.5 million), Oran (663,504), Constantine (448,578), Annaba (348,322), Blida (191,314), Sétif (186,978), Sidi-Bel-Abbès (186,978)
Climate:	Mild, wet winters with dry, cold summers on coast. Dry with cold winters and hot summers on high plateau. Sirocco (hot dusty, sandy wind) common in summer
Time:	The entire country is +1 GMT (Greenwich Mean Time), six hours ahead of EST (Eastern Standard Time)
GDP:	Purchasing power parity (PPP): 147.6 billion (1999 est); real growth rate: 3.9% (1999 est); per capita PPP: $4,700 (1999 est); composition by sector: agricultural = 12%, industry = 51%, services = 37% (1997 est)
Currency:	1 Algerian dinar (DA) = 100 centimes
Exchange Rate:	US$ 1 = 76.6 DA (2000 est), 66.5 DA (1999 est), 59.0 DA (1998 est)
Weights & Measure:	Metric system
Natural Resources:	Petroleum, natural gas, iron ore, phosphates, uranium, lead, zinc
Total Trade:	In billions US$ [exports (fob)/imports (cif)]: 1997 est (14.6/10.2), 1998 est (10.2/9.4), 1999 est (12.1/9.9)
Trade with US:	In millions US$ [exports (fob)/imports (cif)]: 1997 est (2,439/695), 1998 est (1,656/713), 1999 est (1,775/905)

Major Trade Partners: Imports and exports: France, Italy, Spain, United States, Germany

Membership: AfDB, IBRD, IDB, IFC, IMF, MIGA, ISO, OPEC, UN, UNCTAD, WCO and WIPO. See membership description in appendix.

Sources: *CIA World Facts, United Nations World Statistics, the World Bank, Algerian Statistics Office, Algerian Customs, U.S. Department of Commerce, U.S. Department of State.*

POLITICAL OUTLOOK

②

Relationship with the U.S.

Algeria is an important trading partner in the Middle East and North Africa (fifth largest export market for U.S. in Arab world in 1996). The U.S. supports economic reform for Algeria, with the IMF and World Bank. The improvement of living standards is seen by the U.S. as key to long-term stability and social peace. Terrorist violence discourages investment. The U.S. encourages Algeria to participate in regional discussions such as creation of Middle East/North Africa Development Bank, antiterrorism summit, and general peace efforts. The U.S. Department of State advises Americans not to travel to Algeria. See **Business Travel**.

Influences on Business

Armed Islamist groups target not just security services but civilians, including journalists, intellectuals, and government officials. Hydrocarbons industry people have been threatened. Two legal Islamist parties form the large parliamentary minority group, and members of one are ministers of (Government of Algeria) GA. The fairness of legislative elections is sometimes seen as questionable..

Profile

System: The Legislature has 380-member National People's Assembly and 144-member Council of Nations. The National Assembly seats by party: RND (Democratic National Rally), 156; MSP (Movement of a Peaceful Society), 69; FLN (National Liberation Front), 62; Nahda Movement, 34; FFS (Socialist Forces Front), 20; RCD (Rally for Culture and Democracy), 19; others, 4 or less. Council of Nations seats by party RND (Democratic National Rally), 80; FLN (National Liberation Front), 10; FFS (Socialist Forces Front), 4; MSP (Movement of a Peaceful Society), 2; remaining 48 seats appointed by president.

Schedule for Elections: President in 1999, 2003. National Assembly in 1997, 2001. Two-thirds of Council of Nations in 1997, 2003.

Major Parties: The FIS (Islamic Salvation Front, fundamentalist) party, banned by the government, seeks to replace secular government with Islamic law (sharia).

Political Violence: Terrorism is a persistent problem. See **Business Travel.**

Corruption: Many cases of corruption are argued in courts. Senior officials, of state-owned companies, have been accused of abuse of public trust, misappropriation of company funds, aiding and abetting and overcharging of company suppliers. Over 2,000 public company officials have been accused or convicted of charges varying from petty crime to grand larceny. Algerian business people claim some are being punished for bad business decisions. The U.S. Embassy believes fear of being punished encourages companies to avoid business risk.

ECONOMIC OUTLOOK
③

Trends

The Government of Algeria (GA) seeks industrial reforms and privatization. Tax incentives, deferred payments, and stock ownership encourage the sale of state companies. Problems include: oil prices, weather (has a great effect on the economy), unemployment (exceeds 28%), and terrorism.

Major Growth Sectors

Hydrocarbons, vital for Algeria, are still immune from terrorism. Sonatrach (the state-owned hydrocarbons company) is expanding pipelines and production aggressively. Sonatrach is also in agreements with many foreign oil companies for oil and gas exploration. There is a 20-year, $3.5 billion agreement with British Petroleum to develop the In Salah gas field, which is expected to produce nine to ten billion cubic meters of natural gas per year starting in 2002. Also planned is a $1.3 billion Arco–Sonatrach output agreement using in-fill drilling and miscible gas injection technology. U.S. firms such as Anadarko, Arco Mobil, and Louisiana Land & Exploration are pursuing Algerian projects. Agriculture is promising since Algerian farmers need U.S. farm equipment and supplies to raise productivity. GA is making land easier to own and sell, and medium- and long-term financing more available. There is a huge housing shortage, but GA is financing and mortgaging a large real estate market for developers and construction materials.

Key Economic Indicators

Income, Production and Employment *(millions of U.S. dollars unless otherwise indicated)*			
	1997	1998	1999[1]
Nominal GDP[2]	47,100	48,300	51,400
Real GDP Growth[3]	1.1	5.1	4.0
GDP by Sector[2]			
Agriculture	4,497	5,756	6,171
Manufacturing	4,405	4,765	5,129
Construction	4,616	4,731	5,028
Hydrocarbons	13,717	10,700	12,042
Services	10,771	11,794	12,707
Government	8,922	9,670	10,323
Real Per Capita GDP (US$)	1,596	1,610	1,620
Labor Force (millions)	8.07	8.10	8.3
Unemployment Rate (pct)	27.8	28.0	28.0
Fiscal Deficit/GDP (pct)	2.4	-3.50	-4.5

1. 1999 figures are all estimates based on most recent data available. 2. GDP at factor cost.
3. Percentage changes calculated in local currency.
Source: Bureau of Economic and Business Affairs; U.S. Department of State

- Infrastructure
Algeria has a relatively well-developed transport and telecommunications infrastructure. However, terrorists sometimes disrupt power and telecommunications networks, railways, and roads. See **Communications** and **Transportation**.

- Labor
U.S. firms have few union problems because of good work conditions and salaries. About 28 percent of the workforce is unemployed. About 4 percent of the workforce has at least 12 years of schooling. Average wages are $190 per month. (Some foreign companies pay a portion in hard currency.) Employers pay social security tax, which covers retirement and unemployment compensation at 24 percent of gross salary. There are no restrictions on expatriate supervisory personnel.

Money and Prices (annual percentage growth)			
	1997	**1998**	**1999**[1]
Money Supply (M2)	18.5	19.0	21.5
Consumer Price Index	5.7	5.0	3.5
Exchange Rate (dinar/US$ annual average)			
Official[2]	57.7	59.5	65
Parallel[3]	65.0	70.0	71

1. 1999 figures are all estimates based on most recent data available. 2. Bank of Algeria and embassy estimate. 3. Embassy estimates.
Source: Bureau of Economic and Business Affairs; U.S. Department of State

Balance of Payments and Trade (millions of U.S. dollars unless otherwise indicated)			
	1997	**1998**	**1999**[1]
Total Exports	14,640	10,213	12,100
Oil/Gas	13,700	10,100	11,000
Exports to U.S.[2]	2,439	1,656	1,775
Total Imports CIF	10,190	9,403	9,900
Imports from U.S.[2]	695	713	905
Trade Balance	4,450	810	2,200
Trade Balance with U.S.	1,744	943	870
Current Account Deficit/GDP (pct)	6.45	-1.00	-1.6
External Public Debt	31,050	30,261	28,960
Debt Service Payments/GDP (pct)	8.9	11.1	11.3
Gold and Foreign Exchange Reserves	8,500	8,300	6,510
Aid from U.S.[3]	156	209	325
Aid from All Other Sources[3]	392	N/A	N/A

1. 1999 figures are all estimates based on most recent data available.
2. 1999 data, based upon nine-month statistics. 3. In thousands of dollars, IMET and USIA exchanges.
Source: Bureau of Economic and Business Affairs; U.S. Department of State

Government Influence on Business

The GA is seeking WTO membership and agreement with the European Union. State-owned banks sometimes are unwilling to give crucial documentation to new luxury goods exporters. The GA is giving incentives to increase non-hydrocarbon exports. The Algerian Foreign Trade Promotion Agency has created a Foreign Trade Promotion Fund, an export credit insurance agency, and a Special Export Promotion Fund for financial and logistic support. State-owned enterprises (SOE) have debt problems that are being restructured. The World Bank and GA are seeking privatization, but investors are needed. Privatization law offers flexibility in pricing and payment terms, authorizes sale of non-autonomous public enterprises, and allows sale of equity to public. Workers (with vouchers, coupons, or cash) may own up to 30 percent of the company being privatized. Public land titles may be offered to farmers, which would encourage agricultural investment. The GA monopoly over transport will be ending. State-owned companies are increasingly contracting with private management firms, with success in two hotels and city water distribution. Waste water systems, water treatment, building materials, and agriculture will soon privatize production management.

TRADE
④

Leading Imports and Exports

Imports: Capital goods, food and beverages, consumer goods, grain and feed

Exports: Oil, natural gas

Foreign Trade (Exports and Imports in US$M)			
	1997	1998	1999[1]
Total Exports	14,640	10,213	12,100
Oil/Gas	13,700	10,100	11,000
Exports to U.S.[2]	2,439	1,656	1,775
Total Imports CIF	10,190	9,403	9,900
Imports from U.S.[2]	695	713	905

1. 1999 figures are all estimates based on most recent data available.
2. 1999 data, based upon nine-month statistics.
Source: U.S. Department of Commerce, U.S. Department of State

Best Prospects Analysis

Best Prospects for Nonagricultural Goods and Services

Oil and Gas Field Machinery (OGM)

	1996 $M	1997 $M	1998 $M
Total Market Size	420	520	650
Total Local Production	80	90	100
Total Exports	0	0	0
Total Imports	340	430	550
Imports from the U.S.	150	250	340

Water Resources Equipment (WRE)

	1996 $M	1997 $M	1998 $M
Total Market Size	282	332	387
Total Local Production	25	25	25
Total Exports	8	8	8
Total Imports	265	315	370
Imports from the U.S.	66	85	100

Computers and Peripherals (CPT)

	1996 $M	1997 $M	1998 $M
Total Market Size	107	142	182
Total Local Production	2	2	4
Total Exports	0	0	0
Total Imports	105	140	178
Imports from the U.S.	47	65	82

Telecommunications Equipment (TEL)

	1996 $M	1997 $M	1998 $M
Total Market Size	250	300	380
Total Local Production	100	100	100
Total Exports	0	0	0
Total Imports	150	200	280
Imports from the U.S.	30	45	70

Food Processing and Packaging Equipment (FPP)

	1996 $M	1997 $M	1998 $M
Total Market Size	218	260	315
Total Local Production	8	10	15
Total Exports	0	0	0
Total Imports	210	250	300
Imports from the U.S.	20	37	65

Drugs and Pharmaceuticals (DRG)

	1996 $M	1997 $M	1998 $M
Total Market Size	440	520	515
Total Local Production	40	55	85
Total Exports	0	0	0
Total Imports	400	465	430
Imports from the U.S.	12	27	45

Building Products (BLD)

	1996 $M	1997 $M	1998 $M
Total Market Size	312	344	385
Total Local Production	40	45	65
Total Exports	8	6	10
Total Imports	280	325	330
Imports from the U.S.	10	20	40

Mining Industry Equipment (MIN)

	1996 $M	1997 $M	1998 $M
Total Market Size	110	135	180
Total Local Production	0	0	0
Total Exports	0	0	0
Total Imports	110	135	180
Imports from the U.S.	8	12	35

Best Prospects for Agricultural Products

Grain and Feed (Wheat, Barley, Oats, Corn)

	1996 MT ('000)	1997 MT ('000)	1998 MT ('000)
Total Market Size	8,000	8,200	8,400
Total Local Production	3,000	1,050	2,000
Total Exports	0	0	0
Total Imports	5,000	7,000	6,400
Imports from the U.S.	1,300	1,800	1,500

Vegetable Oil and Other Oilseeds Products (Soybean, Sunflower Seed, Rapeseed, Palm Oil)

	1996 MT ('000)	1997 MT ('000)	1998 MT ('000)
Total Market Size	675	690	700
Total Local Production	35	40	50
Total Exports	0	0	0
Total Imports	640	650	670
Imports from the U.S.	440	450	460

Dairy Products (Non-fat Dry Milk, Whole Milk Powder, Butter Oil, Butter, Cheddar Cheese

	1996 MT ('000)	1997 MT ('000)	1998 MT ('000)
Total Import Market	410	420	480
Total Local Production	185	190	180
Total Exports	0	0	0
Total Imports	225	230	300
Imports from the U.S.	98	100	100

The above statistics are unofficial estimates. Exchange rate: US$ 1.00 = DA 54 (1996), DA 59 (1997), DA 64 (1998)
N/A - Not Available, E - Estimate
Note: MT ('000) = Thousand Metric Tons

Extracted from the U.S. Department of Commerce USA Trade 2000 Country Commercial Guide for Algeria.

Import and Export Tips

- ## Regulations

    Customs: Few barriers exist to U.S. exports. Trade is being increasingly liberalized to appease WTO and the European Union. Algeria is a member of the Arab League. The Anti-Israel boycott was not perceived as affecting U.S. trade. Though customs are being modernized, some cases of burdensome administration remain. Restricted imports include firearms, explosives, narcotics, and pork products (for security or religious reasons). Algeria's Post, Telephone, and Telecommunications Ministry has a monopoly on all telecommunications services (including telephone, telex, telegraph, fax network, mobile telephone system, public data communications network, and maritime radio). Telecommunications equipment, however, is open to private production, importation, and distribution. See **Business Travel (Currency Exchange).**

    Tariffs: Algeria uses Harmonized System of product classification. Custom duties on imports range from 3 to 40 percent. Equipment and machinery temporarily brought for a specific project are exempt from duties and taxes. Bellara (wilaya of Jijel, new port of Djendjen) is a free trade zone. There are no taxes and duties in free trade zones, which may be used by foreign suppliers as customs depots to stock goods for Algerian sale. Algiers International Fairgrounds may become free trade zone. See **Trade Zones and Free Ports.**

    Import Taxes: There is a VAT (value-added tax) at 7, 14, or 20 percent on purchase price plus customs duties. An additional TSA (Taxe Spécifique Additionelle) import tax from 20 to 110 percent on the purchase price, primarily on luxury goods, also exists.

    Exchange Rate: With hydrocarbon exports making up well over 90 percent of export earnings, the price of oil is the major determinant of the exchange rate. A government board implements a managed float system for the dinar, which is convertible for all current account transactions. Private and public importers may buy foreign exchange from five commercial banks for commercial transactions provided they can pay for hard currency in dinars. Although commercial banks may buy foreign exchange from the Bank of Algeria at regular weekly auctions, at which they set the dinar's exchange rate, they are no longer required to surrender to the Bank of Algeria the foreign exchange they acquire, and may trade these resources among themselves. However, since the Central Bank buys the foreign hydrocarbon export proceeds of the national oil company, Sonatrach, the bank plays the dominant role in the foreign exchange market. The primary objective of its intervention policy is to avoid sharp fluctuations in the exchange rate.

- ## Documentation

    Exports: There are almost no export restrictions though palm seedlings, sheep, and historical or archaeological artifacts are restricted. Non-hydrocarbons exports are encouraged by the GA. The Algerian Export Insurance and Guarantee Company, created by the GA, offers various types of insurance.

    Imports: No import licenses are required. Some items, especially luxury items, require documents from state-owned banks, which sometimes refuse to provide them. Temporary equipment and machinery require a form for duty or tax waiver, which must be shown to customs authorities when goods are re-exported.

    Labeling: All imported products, particularly consumer goods, must be labeled in Arabic. Imported drugs must have prior authorization from the Ministry of Health and Population, and must have been marketed first in country of origin. Customs Service has strict controls over food imports. A minimum validity period of food products must be specified.

Standards: No information is available at this time.

• Payment

Terms: Usual terms are 90 to 120 days. Confirmed irrevocable letters of credit are recommended.

Currency Exchange: Foreign exchange available to Algerians if they have dinar equivalent of the hard currency cost of the imports. Local importers have access to foreign exchange through five state-owned commercial banks. The Central Bank estimates foreign exchange reserve at $6.2 billion (1995 est) See **Business Travel (Currency Exchange).**

Fund Transfer: The average foreign exchange delays are reported to be about three months. Local delays are about one month. The GA prohibits Algerians from holding real and financial assets abroad.

Offshore Loans: No information is available at this time.

MARKETING TIPS ⑤

Agents and Distributiors

The U.S. government encourages the use of agents, distributors, or joint-venture partners to become active in Algeria's market. Under the 1993 Investment Code, foreign suppliers don't need to invest in Algeria to set up distributorships. One can use one's own distribution companies or use local agents and distributors. Algerian law prohibits foreign firms from using commercial agents to bid on government tenders.

Establishing an Office

U.S. firms must prioritize security for any presence in Algeria. The U.S. government recommends relying on experienced Algerians rather than expatriates. U.S. oil companies are model examples of quick expansion.

Distribution and Sales Channels

The Algerian distribution system is well developed. Primarily private entrepreneurs run an extensive network of wholesale and retail outlets. State-owned wholesale marketing firms sell imported foodstuffs, pharmaceuticals, and industrial supplies and equipment. Private wholesalers are increasingly active in these sectors. The GA is privatizing state-owned distribution outlets. Algeria's import market is becoming increasingly liberalized, with new private stores, which stock mainly imported foodstuffs and household equipment. The retail trade is controlled almost 100 percent by private businesspeople.

Direct Marketing

No information is available at this time.

Leasing/Joint Ventures

The GA invites foreign investors to modernize state-owned manufacturing plants. Algerian companies want technical expertise from foreign partners, who can share equity in Algerian joint ventures in regional, national, and global markets. These partnerships can be used to better understand the local market and reach solid wholesale and retail distribution channels.

Leasing: Algerian companies may lease foreign-made equipment. Private firms are showing increasing interest in leasing, particularly construction equipment. Air Algérie was soliciting offers for the lease of nine large passenger aircraft. The Agricultural Mutual Bank, in partnership with a large insurance company and the Union Bank (private), operates an agricultural equipment leasing company.

Franchising

Franchising is not common, but private firms are growing interested. Coca-Cola and a private Algerian food processing company run a very successful bottling operation.

Advertising and Promotion

Direct advertising of equipment and machinery has minimal impact on local end users. Because state-owned companies import via international tenders, they are not affected by advertising. With the opening of Algeria's import market, advertising is becoming effective for consumer products. Algeria's Radio and Television Service accepts advertisements. The Algiers International Fair, normally held every June, is the main event of Algerian trade promotion. The Algerian Fair Authority, SAFEX, and a private company, Group ABH, have organized several fairs centered on industry sectors. The U.S. Embassy in Algeria is ready to share information on fairs once security is feasible for U.S. firms.

Selling Factors

No information is available at this time.

Selling to the Government

GA institutions (ministries, other public agencies, and local government units) buy foreign-made goods via tenders open to all potential suppliers. The Law on Public Tender governs Algerian government procurement: a 2 percent bid bond and a 5 percent performance bond are required. Foreign bidders must deal directly with client agency. Tender documents (listing procedures and requirements) are available by local representatives or embassies. Although state-owned companies are not required to use tenders by Law on Public Tender, many do. Government agencies and public companies can work directly with foreign suppliers in limited consultations (consultations restreintes) with at least three suppliers. Government entities and state-owned companies routinely request financing in their tenders.

Pricing

No information is available at this time.

Customer Support

Suppliers of capital goods to the Algerian market must provide sales service and customer support. Free sales service is usually required for a one-year period. Suppliers may then sell customers sales service, which Algerians call "technical assistance." Distributors of foreign products must provide a 6–18 month warranty (depending on types of goods), stock parts in Algeria, and provide customers after-sales service. Foreign suppliers provide customer support via liaison offices in Algeria. Liaison offices are prohibited from engaging in commercial activities, so they cannot import or distribute equipment and spare parts. These items must be imported by Algerian end users either directly or via distributors

Intellectual Property Rights (IPR)

U.S. trade is unhindered by Algeria's intellectual property practices. The U.S. Embassy knows no instance of U.S. export or investment opportunity loss due to imported or domestic counterfeited or pirated goods.

Patents: Patents are protected by the law of December 7, 1993, which is administered by the Institut Algérien de Normalisation et de Propriété Industrielle (INAPI). Algeria follows the Paris Convention and its revisions. The INAPI grants 20-year patents for all types of technology.

Trademark Protection: Trademark protection is specified by the laws of March 19, 1966, and July 16, 1976. The Centre National du Registre du Commerce (CNRC) has trademark authority, but the INAPI may have it soon.

Copyright Protection: Algeria has ratified the 1952 Convention on Copyrights in 1973. Algerian law has copyright protection for books, plays, musical compositions, films, paintings, sculptures, and photographs. Authors have the right to control commercial exploitation or marketing of these products. The law will also provide protection for video, radio, and Internet programs. The Office National du Droit d'Auteur (ONDA) manages copyright protection.

Attorney

Exercise caution before exporting to Algeria. Some Algerian commercial laws and regulations can be complex. The U.S. Embassy maintains a list of experienced Algerian lawyers who have worked with U.S. companies.

FOREIGN INVESTMENT 6

Openness: The GA welcomes foreign investment to diversify and modernize the Algerian economy. The GA doesn't distinguish between investments made by Algerians or foreigners. The Algerian investment code grants new investors three-year exemption from VAT on goods and services acquired locally or imported; exemption on property taxes; two-to-five-year exemption from corporate income taxes; only 3 percent customs duties on 30 products (usually 25 to 45 percent); no more than 7 percent of gross wages as employer contribution to social security (normally 24.5 percent); firms exporting 100 percent of production are completely tax-exempt; firms exporting 50 percent of production are 50 percent tax exempt. The APSI (Agence de Promotion de Soutien, et de Suivi des Investissements) registers investment applications and determines which advantages are legally given to investors. The CALPI (Comités d'Assistance à la Localisation et la Promotion des Investissements) helps investors obtain land and deal with local authorities. Most foreign company personnel receive a flat income tax of 20 percent.

Regulatory System: Algeria is moving from a centrally planned economy to a free market system. The GA is focusing on a regulatory role and providing public services rather than production. Recent laws reduce government controls of economy, apply market principles to state-owned firms, and give debt relief to the private sector.

Investment Agreements: Bilateral agreements are in place with France, Italy, Belgium, and Spain. Agreements are also being forged with Turkey, Indonesia, Romania, Canada, Russia, Portugal, and India. Most agreements have clauses against double taxation.

Trade Zones and Free Ports: Algeria, Tunisia, Morocco, Mauritania, and Libya form the Arab Maghreb Union (UMA). Algeria is negotiating a free trade zone with the European Union and plans to join WTO.

Performance Requirements/Incentives: Foreign firms that receive advantages from the GA are expected to perform well enough to justify keeping those benefits. To determine benefits given to investors, the APSI considers whether the investor has a foreign partner; the extent of self-financing (over 30 percent yields maximum advantages); the use of local inputs (over 50 percent yields maximum advantages); and the extent of technology transfer and job creation. The U.S. Embassy in Algiers maintains a list of lawyers to help with APSI registration.

Capital Markets and Investment: There are no capital markets outside the banking system in Algeria. The Central Bank is initiating open market operations. Government bonds are financing part of the deficit. The stock exchange trades state-owned company stocks.

Private Ownership: Foreign and domestic private entities may establish and own businesses and engage in all forms of business activity.

Expropriation and Compensation: The U.S. Embassy in Algiers knows of no recent expropriation of U.S. or other foreign firms.

OPIC and Investment Insurance: OPIC (The Overseas Private Investment Corporation) offers insurance against political violence, expropriation, currency inconvertibility, wrongful calls of bid performance or advance payment, and losses due to unresolved contractual disputes with foreign buyers. Special insurance for oil and gas sectors is also available. Projects must be registered with OPIC prior to investment or commitment. Registration with OPIC is free and treated as privileged information. Various financing is also available from OPIC.

Dispute Settlement: The GA is part of the convention of the International Center for Settlement Disputes. Algeria is also a member of the Multilateral Investment Guarantee Agency (MIGA). The GA Code of Civil Procedure allows for international arbitration. Algerian contracts may contain international arbitration clauses. The U.S. Embassy in Algiers knows of no recent case of U.S. or foreign firms seeking arbitration.

FINANCE ⑦

Algeria has a Central Bank (Banque d'Algérie), six state-owned banks, one public development bank, and one private bank (mainly merchant banking). An Islamic bank is owned jointly by a state bank and the Saudi Al-Baraka Group. The GA would like reputable private foreign banks established.

Export Financing: The GA gives small subsidies indirectly to Algerian firms doing market research on non-hydrocarbon exports. The Export-Import Bank (EXIM) cover is open for short-term transactions (180 days or less) with 5 state banks and Sonatrach. The EXIM exposure as creditor is estimated at

$2.2 billion. The EXIM guaranteed a $150 million Citibank loan for Halliburton Company services to Sonatrach. The Coface (French Export Credit Guarantee Agency) covers about $1 billion of imports, as do Spain and Germany. Other guarantors of credit to Algeria include Belgium, Italy, Netherlands, and the United Kingdom.

Project Financing: Both the World Bank and the African Development Bank finance infrastructure and social projects for Algeria. The World Bank is funding Algeria's economic restructuring, and the European Union and European Investment Bank are funding major investments. All state-owned banks maintain correspondent banking relations with several U.S. banks. Banque Extérieure d'Algérie and Banque Nationale d'Algérie maintain banking relationships with Bank of New York, American Express Bank, BankAmerica International, Bank of America, Bankers Trust, Bank of New York, Chase Manhattan Bank, Bankers Trust, Chemical Bank, Citibank, First Chicago, CoBank Denver, and First Interstate Bank. Crédit Populaire d'Algérie maintains banking relationships with Citibank Mellon Bank, Arab American Bank, Pittsburgh National Bank, Chemical Bank, United Bank for Africa, and Mellon Bank. Banque de l'Agriculture et du Développement Rural and Banque de Développement Local maintain banking relationships with Citibank, Bank of America NY, Crédit Lyonnais, CoBank Denver, Rabo Bank, Citibank. United Bank for Africa: Bankers Trust, and First Chicago.

COMMUNICATIONS 8

Phone

The Algerian Post and Telecommunications (PTT) Ministry operates telephone, telex, telegraph, and facsimile networks; a maritime radio service; a mobile telephone system; a public data communications network. There were 1.66 million telephone lines installed in 1996. PTT subscribers in 1995 totaled 1.25 million (41 per 1,000 vs. world average of 100 per 1,000). Eighty percent of the national telecommunications net is digital. Domestic and international telephone network links often malfunction, but PTT is improving their performance. There are promising markets for U.S. goods and services. The international access code is 011, and the Algerian access code is 213. City codes for major cities are Algiers (2), Adrar (7), Ain Defla (3), Bejaia (5), Oran (6). Seek operator assistance for other city routing codes.

Internet

No information is available at this time.

Mail

The postal mailing system is reasonably developed although street names and numbers may not be well defined. Express Mail International Services are available between Algeria and the U.S.

TRANSPORTATION
9

Land

Algeria is about one-third the size of the U.S. Algeria has relatively well-developed transport and telecommunications infrastructure. Terrorists sometimes disrupt power and telecommunications networks, railways, and roads. The GA is amid a 20-year road development project. The road network is approximately 100,000 kilometers (26,000 are trunk roads and highways, 23,000 are provincial roads, or "wilaya"). The railway network is found mainly northern Algeria. There are 4,200 kilometers of tracks (3,060 standard gauge and 1,140 narrow gauge).

Sea

There are 13 multipurpose ports, 2 hydrocarbons terminals, and 19 smaller ports for fishing and sailing. Port flow (1994) exceeds 82 million tons of merchandise and 282,512 passengers. Ports at Algiers, Oran, Annaba, and Djendjen are equipped to handle containers.

Air

There are 29 domestic airports (12 are international airports). Passenger flow (1994) is 6.9 million. Cargo flow (1994) is 36,187 metric tons. National carrier, Air Algérie, serves 37 destinations in Europe, Africa, and the Middle East. For security reasons, few international airlines serve Algeria. There are no direct flights between Algeria and the U.S. The U.S. Department of State warns U.S. citizens not to use Algerian airports without prior and proper security arrangements. The Civil Aviation Code may change to enable proposals for private air transport companies.

WORK WEEK
10

Business Hours: 8:00 a.m. to 12:00 p.m. and 2:30 p.m. to 5:30 p.m. Sunday through Thursday.

Bank Hours: 8:30 a.m. to 4:30 p.m. Sunday through Thursday. Banks are closed on Friday and Saturday.

Government Hours: 8:00 a.m. to 12:00 p.m. and 1:00 p.m. to 5:00 p.m. Sunday through Thursday.

HOLIDAYS 2001

New Year's Day, January 1
First day of Id al Adha, March 5
Islamic New Year, March 25
Ashura, April 3
Labor Day, May 1
Prophet Mohammed's Birthday, June 3
Recovery Day, June 19
Independence Day, July 5
Revolution Day, November 1
First day of Id El Fitr, December 26

Some holidays may be observed on different dates depending on the day of the week on which it falls. Certain holidays are based on the lunar calendar and change every year.

BUSINESS TRAVEL

Business Customs

Business customs still show French influence in major cities. Greetings accompanied by a handshake are considered cordial in Algeria. The use of first names is usually reserved for close friends and family.

Travel Advisory and Visas

Passports and visas are required of U.S. citizens. Visas of up to one year are available from the Algerian Embassy. Heavy security against terrorism is crucial. See **Security**. Local agents and distributors are alternatives to travel.

Business Infrastructure

Entry Requirements (personal and professional goods): To obtain additional and updated information on entry and exit requirements, travelers can contact the Consular Section of the Embassy of Algeria.

Currency Exchange: The Algerian dinar is the main currency: $1 = 61.2 DA est. All foreigners must purchase $200 of local currency when entering Algeria. Documentary proof of legal currency exchange required when leaving Algeria.

Taxes: See **Regulations** and **Labor**.

Labor Costs and Legislation: U.S. firms have few union problems because of good work conditions and salaries. About 28 percent of the workforce is unemployed. About 4 percent of the workforce has at least 12 years of schooling. Average wages are $190 per month. (Some foreign companies pay a portion in hard currency.) Employers pay social security tax, which covers retirement and unemployment compensation at 24 percent of gross salary. There are no restrictions on expatriate supervisory personnel.

Literacy: Age 15 and over can read and write. Total population: 61.6%, male: 73.9%, female: 49% (1995 est.)

Travel Notes

The following travel notes have been supplied by the U.S. government. For the most recent general travel and consular information, see the U.S. Department of State travel publications or call the Traveler's Telephone Hotline at (202) 647-5225.

Security: The crime rate in Algeria is increasing. Pick pocketing, mugging, assaults, and scams of all types are common in urban areas. Serious crimes such as armed robbery against foreigners and armed carjackings have been reported. If possible, consider meeting Algerian trade and investment partners in the U.S. or Europe. Business travelers should arrange for armed protection in advance that starts from the moment of arrival.

Health Precautions: Adequate medical services are available although specialized care and treatment may not be. Hospitals and doctors expect immediate cash payment for services. U.S. travelers may want to consider supplemental medical insurance to cover medical evacuation as well as care outside the U.S. Current information on health matters may be obtained from the Centers for Disease Control and Prevention's international travelers' hotline at (404) 332-4559.

Embassy Assistance

To obtain additional and updated information on entry and exit requirements, travelers can contact the Consular Section of the Embassy of Algeria at 2118 Kolarama Road, N.W., Washington, D.C. 20008; Tel: (202) 265-2800. Travelers may also contact the Algerian consulate, which is located in New York.

CONTACTS
13

U.S. and Country Contacts

Corresponding with U.S. and Country Contacts

All written correspondence to Algerian entities should be in Arabic or French. Correspondence to ministries should be addressed to Le Directeur des Relations Extérieures. Correspondence to public companies regarding the sale of products should be addressed to Le Directeur des Approvisionnements.

Algerian Ministries

Ministry of Finance
Palais du Gouvernement
Algiers, Algeria
Tel: (213-2) 732340
Fax: (213-2) 735472

Ministry of Commerce
Palais du Gouvernement
Algiers, Algeria
Tel: 732340
Fax: 733091

Ministry of Industry and Restructuring
Immeuble le Colisée
Algiers, Algeria
Tel: 592440
Fax: 604584

Ministry of Small and Medium Industry
Immeuble le Colisée
Algiers, Algeria
Tel: 592232
Fax: 592658

Ministry of Energy and Mines
80 Avenue Ghermoul
Algiers, Algeria
Tel: 673300
Fax: N/A

Ministry of Equipment
Ex-Grand Séminaire
Kouba
Algiers, Algeria
Tel: 689503

Ministry of Post and Telecommunications
4 Boulevard Krim Belkacem
Algiers, Algeria
Tel: 711220
Fax: 711771

Ministry of Transport
119 Rue Didouche Mourad
Algiers, Algeria
Tel: 747506
Fax: 656637

Ministry of Agriculture
4 Rue des Quatre Canons
Algiers, Algeria
Tel: 711712
Fax: 612542

Investment Promotion Agency

APSI
(Agence de Promotion, de Soutien
et de Suivi des Investissements)
Boulevard du 11 décembre 1960
El Biar
Algiers, Algeria
Tel: 924269
Fax: 924647

Customs Office

Direction Générale des Douanes
Avenue du Dr. Saadane
Algiers, Algeria
Tel: 711616
Fax: 746974

CNIS
(Centre National de l'Informatique et des
  Statistiques)
Avenue du 1er novembre
Algiers, Algeria
Tel: 715600
Fax: 715640

Commercial Banks

**BADR (Banque de l'Agriculture et du
  Développement Rural)**
17 Boulevard Colonel Amirouche
Algiers, Algeria
Tel: 746117
Fax: 615551

Al Baraka (Algerian-Saudi bank)
12 Boulevard Colonel Amirouche
Algiers, Algeria
Tel: 745627
Fax: 745629

BDL (Banque du Développement Local)
5 Rue Gaci Amar
Staoueli
Tipaza, Algeria
Tel: 392850
Fax: 392351

BEA (Banque Extérieure d'Algérie)
11 Boulevard Colonel Amirouche
Algiers, Algeria
Tel: 605241
Fax: 602253

BNA (Banque Nationale d'Algérie)
8 Boulevard Che Guevara
Algiers, Algeria
Tel: 713540
Fax: 713623

CPA (Crédit Populaire d'Algérie)
Boulevard Colonel Amirouche
Algiers, Algeria
Tel: 740528
Fax: 641179

Union Bank (private bank)
5 bis chemin Macklay
El Biar
Algiers, Algeria
Tel: 914552
Fax: 914548

Large Public Sector Enterprises

Sonatrach (hydrocarbons)
10 Rue du Sahara
Hydra
Algiers, Algeria
Tel: 607000
Fax: 601949

Sonelgaz (electric power and natural gas)
2 Boulevard Krim Belkacem
Algiers, Algeria
Tel: 644555
Fax: 611314

ENIP (petrochemicals)
Zone Industrielle
BP 215, Skikda
Skikda, Algeria
Tel: (8) 958862
Fax: (8) 756146

SIDER (steel)
Chaiba, Commune Sidi Amar
BP 342, Annaba
Annaba, Algeria
Tel: (8) 851011
Fax: (8) 838957

SNVI (industrial vehicles)
BP 153, Rouiba
Boumerdes, Algeria
Tel: 851970
Fax: 857345

Chamber of Commerce

CACI
(Chambre Algérienne de Commerce et
 d'Industrie)
Palais Consulaire
Place des Martyrs
Algiers, Algeria
Tel: 574444
Fax: 577025

Private Sector Employers Associations

ACE
(Association des Chefs d'Entreprise)
Route d'Ouled Fayet
Cheraga
Algiers, Algeria
Tel: 365154
Fax: 365155

CAP
(Confédération Algérienne du Patronat)
Hotel Aurassi
Niveau C, Bureau 7
Algiers, Algeria
Tel: 647030
Fax: 647020

CGOEA
(Confédération Générale des Opérateurs
Economiques Algériens)
27 Rue Ferhat Abdelkader
Staouéli
Tipaza, Algeria
Tel: 392145
Fax: 392146

CNPA
(Confédération Nationale du Patronat Algérien)
39 Rue Rahmoune Dekkar
El Biar
Algiers, Algeria
Tel: 922495
Fax: 922498

U.S. Embassy Trade

U.S. Embassy Algiers
BP 408, Alger-Gare
16000 Algiers, Algeria or
Amembassy Algiers
Department of State
Washington, D.C. 20521-6030
Tel: (213-2) 693973
Fax: (213-2) 693979

U.S. Consulate General Casablanca
8 Boulevard Moulay Youssef
Casablanca, Morocco
Tel: (212-2) 264550
Fax: (212-2) 220259

U.S. Embassy Rabat
2 Avenue de Marrakech
Rabat, Morocco
Tel: (212-7) 762265
Fax: (212-7) 765661

Washington-Based Country Contacts

U.S. Department of Commerce
Algeria Desk Officer
Washington, D.C. 20230
Tel: (202) 482-1860
Fax: (202) 482-0878

**MDBO, Multilateral Development
  Bank Operations**
14th and Constitution, NW
Washington, D.C. 20007
Tel: (202) 482-3399
Fax: (202) 482-5179

**TPCC, The Trade Promotion Coordinating
  Committee**
TPCC Trade Information Center
Tel: 1-800-USA-TRADE

U.S. Department of State
Room 5250
Algeria Desk Officer
Washington, D.C. 20520
Tel: (202) 647-4680
Fax: (202) 736-4458

U.S.-Based Multipliers

EXIM, Export-Import Bank
811 Vermont Ave, NW
Washington, D.C. 20571
Tel: (202) 566-8945
Fax: (202) 566-7524

TDA, U.S. Trade and Development Agency
Africa and Middle East Region
SA-16, Room 309
Washington, D.C. 20523-1602
Tel: (703) 875-4357
Fax: (703) 875-4009

**OPIC, Overseas Private Investment
  Corporation**
1100 New York Ave, NW
Washington, D.C. 20527
Tel: (202) 336-8575
Fax: (202) 408-5142
Registration for Political Risk Investment
  Insurance/OPIC Financing
Tel: (202) 336-8700

U.S. Department of Agriculture
Foreign Agricultural Service
Trade Assistance and Promotion Office
Tel: (202) 720-7420

Algerian Embassy
2118 Kalorama Road N.W.
Washington, D.C. 20008
Tel: (202) 265-2800

Advertising Agencies

ANEP
(state-owned agency)
1 Avenue Pasteur
Algiers, Algeria
Tel: (213-2) 737678
Fax: (213-2) 739559

HIWAR-COM
(private agency)
Maison de la Presse
Place du 1er mai
Algiers, Algeria
Tel: 667204
Fax: 654501

Major Newspapers

Liberté (independent French-language daily)
37 Rue Larbi Ben M'Hidi
Algiers, Algeria
Tel: 736480
Fax: 730487

El Khabar (independent Arabic-language daily)
1 Rue Bachir Attar
Place du 1er mai
Algiers, Algeria
Tel: 653224
Fax: 652280

El Watan (independent French-language daily)
1 Rue Bachir Attar
Place du 1er mai
Algiers, Algeria
Tel: 681987
Fax: 681988

La Tribune (independent French-language daily)
1 Rue Bachir Attar
Place du 1er mai
Algiers, Algeria
Tel: 685424
Fax: 68685423

El Moudjahid (government-controlled French-language daily)
20 Rue de la Liberté
Algiers, Algeria
Tel: 737678
Fax: 739559

Patents

la Protection Industrielle, 42 Rue Larbi Ben M'Hidi, Algiers
Tel: 213-2-735581
Fax: 213-2-73-55-81

Trademark Protection

Marques, CNRC, R.N. 24, BP 18, Bordj El Kiffan, Algiers
Tel: 702303

Copyright Protection

la Répartition et de la Documentation, 6 Boulevard du 11 Décembre 1960, Algiers
Tel: 921308
Fax: 790381

Diplomatic Representation in the U.S.

Chief of mission:
Chancery: 2118 Kalorama Road NW, Washington, DC 20008
Tel: (202) 265-2800
Fax: (202) 667-2174

Diplomatic Representation from the U.S.

Chief of mission:
Embassy: 4 Chemin Cheikh Bachir El-Ibrahimi, Algiers
Mailing address: B. P. Box 549, Alger-Gare, 16000 Algiers
Tel: (213-2) 69-11-86; 69-12-55; 69-18-54; 69-38-75
Fax: (213-2) 69-39-79

CÔTE D'IVOIRE

Abidjan

CÔTE D'IVOIRE
(IVORY COAST)

TRADE AND BUSINESS GUIDE

Official Name:	Republic of Côte d'Ivoire
Official Language:	French
Population:	15.98 million (2000 est)
Population Growth:	2.58% (2000 est)
Age Structure:	0–14 years: 46%, 15–64 years: 51%, 65 years and over: 2% (2000 est)
Location:	Western Africa, bordering the North Atlantic Ocean, between Ghana and Liberia
Area:	322,460 square kilometers, slightly larger than New Mexico
Type of Government:	Unitary republic
Head of State:	Gen. Robert GUEI (since 25 December 1999); note — took power following a military coup against the government of former President Henri Konan BEDIE. President is both chief of state and head of government.
Cabinet:	The appointed Council of Ministers consists of 33 ministers, minister-delegates, and high commissioners, sworn in January 1996
Religion:	60% Muslim, 22% Christian, 18% Indigenous
Major Cities:	Capital: Yamoussoukro (365,522), Administrative Center: Abidjan (2.6 million), Daloa (1 million), Man (957,706), Bouake (816,945), Korhogo (732,390), San Pedro (644,805), Dimbokro (556,565), Bouafle (538,824), Bondoukou (513,220), Divo (505,478), Agboville (440,995), Seguela (353,659), Aboisso (328,165), Abengourou (298,566), and Odienne (169,433)
Climate:	Tropical along coast, semiarid in far north. Three seasons: warm and dry (Nov. to March), hot and dry (March to May), hot and wet (June to Oct.)
Time:	The entire country is 0 GMT (Greenwich Mean Time), five hours ahead of EST (Eastern Standard Time), four hours ahead during daylight savings time
GDP:	Purchasing Power Parity (PPP): $25.7 billion (1999 est); real growth rate: 5% (1999 est); per capita PPP: $1,600 (1999 est.); composition by sector: agriculture = 32%, industry = 18%, services = 50% (1998 est)
Currency:	1 Communaute Financiere Africaine franc (CFAF) = 100 centimes
Exchange Rate:	Average exchange rate: CFA francs (CFAF) per US$ 1 = 617.39 (July 1999 est), 734.76 (2000 est)
Weights & Measure:	Metric system; 220 v 50 mHz cycles for electricity
Natural Resources:	Petroleum, diamonds, manganese, iron ore, cobalt, bauxite, copper

Total Trade:	In millions US$ [exports (fob)/imports (cif)]: 1997 (4,147/2,755), 1998 (4,395/2,991), 1999 est (4,499/3,224)
Trade with U.S.:	In millions US$ [exports (fob)/imports (cif)]: 1997 (289/151), 1998 (397/151), 1999 est (365/104)
Major Trade Partners:	Imports: France, Nigeria, Japan, United States, Germany, Italy, Ghana. Exports: France, Germany, Italy, Burkina Faso, Mali, United States, United Kingdom, Netherlands
Membership:	AfDB, ECOWAS, IBRD, ICC, IFC, IMF, MIGA, UN, UNCTAD, WCO, WIPO, and WTO. See membership description in appendix

Sources: *CIA World Facts, Financial database of the National Statistics Institute of Côte d'Ivoire, United Nations World Statistics, U.S. Department of Commerce*

POLITICAL OUTLOOK ②

Relationship with the U.S.

Ties with the U.S. have been excellent. Since its independence in 1960, Côte d'Ivoire has maintained close ties to France in particular and the West in general. These ties have promoted a remarkable degree of political stability until 1999 when soldiers ousted the democratically elected government in a bloodless coup d'etat. Former President Bédié was the Ivoirian ambassador to the U.S., and hundreds of younger Ivoirians study in America. Most non-humanitarian assistance has been suspended in compliance with U.S. law.

Influences on Business

Problems such as terrorism and strong ethnic tensions do not cast shadows over the business environment. Côte d'Ivoire began to move peacefully from a single-party to a pluralistic system in 1990. There have been minor challenges to the country's long track record of political stability, including minor party boycotts of the 1995 elections. The future of Côte d'Ivoire will depend on whether the Ivoirian society will maintain the political stability, investor confidence and economic development. Other future challenges to the political status quo may stem from the problems of population growth, crime, AIDS, illiteracy, and ethnic and religious differences.

Profile

System: General Robert Guei and his National Committee for Public Salvation (CNSP) now dominate the political system. Key political, economic and military decisions are made bt the CNSP. Before the coup, the president dominates the ruling party as well as the legislature, judiciary, and regional administration. President Felix Houphouet-Boigny served from independence in 1960 to 1993. Since then, Henri Konan Bedie has held the presidency until the coup in 1999. The legislative branch consists of the unicameral, 175-seat National Assembly. The legal system is based on the 1960 constitution and the Napoleonic Code.

Schedule for Elections: The president is elected to a seven-year term, whereas Assembly members are elected by popular vote to five-year terms. Although the next election was scheduled for October 2000, General Robert Guei and his National Committee for Public Salvation (CNSP) dominate the political system.

Major Parties: Although there are 26 registered political parties, Parti Democratique de Côte d'Ivoire (PDCI-RDA) dominated, holding roughly 84 percent of the seats in the National Assembly. Significant minor parties include Front Populaire Ivoirien (FPI) and the Rassemblement des Republicains (RDR).

Political Violence: There have been several civil disturbances in the past few years, and Côte d'Ivoire has become less predictable since the December 1999 coup. Following the coup, properties of the former president and his family were destroyed. Other disturbances include widespread looting, even by uniformed soldiers, beating and even killing of suspected criminals, and the use of violence to prevent political demonstrations.

Corruption: With liberalization and privatization, incidents of corruption should be reduced, yet the problem will remain an obstacle to business. Particularly, concerns lie in the judiciary, customs, contract awards, and tax enforcement.

Media: Independent newspapers were legalized in 1990.

ECONOMIC OUTLOOK 3

Trends

Côte d'Ivoire offers one of the top markets for U.S. exports in sub-Saharan Africa. Since the CFA franc was devalued in 1994, GDP growth has been consistently strong. Inflation remains low, and solid economic policies have built commercial confidence. The Ivoirian economy's outlook is strong, although the economy remains dependent on agriculture and related industries. Côte d'Ivoire produces about 40 percent of the world's cocoa for the production of chocolate each year. Efforts are underway to diversify the economy by promoting extractive industries, the services sector, other agricultural crops, and the cocoa processing industry. The country also faces a serious debt problem, although major steps were taken in the late 1990s on this issue. Challenges exist in the areas of the environment, medicine, demographics, and education. Further challenges that reduced economic growth include lower coffee, palm oil, rubber, and especially, cocoa prices that continue to the present. Commodity prices may not bounce back to historic levels. Rural incomes are down, earnings for shippers and handlers are off, and government export tax revenues are depressed. Considering the slump in traditional exports, cuts in foreign assistance because of the military coup, and no IMF structural adjustment budget assistance, the post-coup transitional government adopted a severe austerity budget. Côte d'Ivoire has a chance to return to respectable growth rates when elections are completed. The return to civilian government will reduce uncertainty and boost investor confidence. The path of future progress depends in large part on Côte d'Ivoire's continued adherence to its adjustment policies.

Major Growth Sectors

Sectors of major interest to U.S. business include agriculture and food processing, offshore oil and gas development, telecommunications, pharmaceutical products, reconditioned industrial equipment, cosmetics, franchising, and used clothing. However, strong competition from French firms must be expected.

Key Economic Indicators

Income, Production and Employment (millions of U.S. dollars unless otherwise indicated)			
	1997	**1998**	**1999**[1]
Nominal GDP	10,817	10,585	12,001
Real GDP Growth (pct)[2]	6.6	6.0	4.7
GDP by Sector (pct)			
Agriculture	N/A	33	N/A
Industry	N/A	20	N/A
General Government	24	N/A	N/A
Per Capita GDP (US$)	690	735	744
Labor Force (millions)	N/A	N/A	N/A
Unemployment Rate (pct)	N/A	N/A	N/A

1. 1999 data are projections from Institut National de Statistique. 2. Percentage changes calculated in local currency.
Sources: U.S. Department of Commerce, EIU Country Reports, World Bank, and IMF

- **Infrastructure**
  In comparison with other developing countries, Côte d'Ivoire has an outstanding infrastructure. Reliable systems are in place for utilities and telecommunications (including internet providers). The country has over 8,000 miles of paved roads. There are two modern seaports, two international airports, rail links, modern real-estate developments, supermarkets, hotels, international banks, and a small but functional regional stock exchange. Abidjan is one of the most modern cities in the region, and the country's networks make it an excellent base from which to conduct operations in West Africa. The government's plan to privatize the management of infrastructure should further promote the quality of services, while also increasing capital investment.

- **Labor**
  By regional standards, Côte d'Ivoire has a highly trained and highly capable workforce. About one third of the population is non-Ivoirian, most of whom are immigrant workers from neighboring countries. Expatriate managers dominate the upper ranks of the business community. The new labor code has fewer restrictions on recruitment and dismissal. The guaranteed minimum monthly wage (SMIG) is approximately $75. Employers must pay social insurance premiums of 9.9 percent; health insurance; and a number of mandatory allowances, including those for meals, transportation, housing, and seniority. Employees receive 2.5 days of paid vacation per month of work. Base salaries for certain occupational salaries are as follows: semiskilled worker, $120; skilled worker, $135–$150; bilingual skilled office worker, $800–$1,000; typist, $130–$150; bilingual receptionist, $500; secretary, $600; bilingual accountant/MBA, $1,600–$2,700.

Money and Prices *(annual percentage growth)*			
	1997	1998	1999[1]
Money Supply Growth (M2)	N/A	N/A	N/A
Inflation	5.2	2.1	0.7
Exchange Rate (CFA Franc/US$ annual average)			
Official	584	588	608.04

1. 1999 data are projections from Institut National de Statistique.
Sources: U.S. Department of Commerce, EIU Country Reports, World Bank, and IMF.

Balance of Payment and Trade *(millions of U.S. dollars unless otherwise indicated)*			
	1997	1998	1999[1]
Total Exports FOB[2]	4,147	4,395	4,499
Exports to U.S.[2]	289	397	365
Total Imports CIF[2]	2,755	2,991	3,224
Imports from U.S.[2]	151	151	104
Trade Balance[2]	1,392	1,404	1,275
Balance with U.S.	138	246	261
Foreign Debt (US $B)	17.7	14.6[3]	N/A
Current Account Deficit/GDP (pct)	N/A	N/A	N/A
Debt Service Ratio (pct)	22.9	23.3	13.8[3]
Gold and Foreign Exchange Reserves	708	N/A	N/A

1. 1999 data are projections from Institut National de Statistique. 2. Merchandise Trade
3. Merrill-Lynch after Paris Club rescheduling
Sources: U.S. Department of Commerce, EIU Country Reports, World Bank, and IMF.

- **Balance of Payments**
  Despite Côte d'Ivoire's situation in regard to the balance of payments and total debt, currency availability and convertibility are not grave problems. Côte d'Ivoire is a member of the West African Economic and Monetary Union (WAEMU, or UEMOA in French). The CFA franc is guaranteed by the French Treasury and is convertible at a fixed rate against the French franc. The French Treasury, in turn, requires strict controls on the creation of new money. The current balance of payments situation deteriorated sharply in the late 1980s. By the early 1990s, account deficits consistently ran at approximately $1.2 billion. Total external debt grew to more than twice the size of GDP. In 1994, currency devaluation allowed Côte d'Ivoire to turn this situation around. Since then, exports and trade surpluses have grown significantly. The debt picture has improved greatly, and current account balances may well improve beginning in 2000 or 2001.

Government Influence on Business

The old French tradition of strong government involvement in the economy retains its influence. However, the IMF and World Bank have actively encouraged structural adjustments, and Côte d'Ivoire has liberalized almost all sectors of its economy. A privatization program, begun in 1990, has succeeded in moving 54 of 60 targeted enterprises to the private sector, although the government still often holds minority stakes.

TRADE
④

Leading Imports and Exports

Imports: Food, consumer goods, capital goods, fuel, transport equipment

Exports: Coffee, cocoa, tropical woods, petroleum, cotton, bananas, pineapples, palm oil, cotton, fish

Foreign Trade (Exports and Imports US$M)			
	1997	1998	1999[1]
Total Exports FOB[2]	4,147	4,395	4,499
Exports to U.S.[2]	289	397	365
Total Imports CIF[2]	2,755	2,991	3,224
Imports from U.S.[2]	151	151	104

1. 1999 data are projections from Institut National de Statistique. 2. Merchandise trade
Sources: Department of Commerce, EIU Country Reports, World Bank, and IMF.

Best Prospects Analysis

Best Prospects for Nonagricultural Goods and Services

Machines, Mechanical Apparatus, Engines (Air Conditioning, Refrigeration Equipment, Computer Equipment and Peripherals, Food Processing Equipment) (CPT, ACR, FPP)

	1998 $M	1999E $M	2000E $M
Total Market Size	395	460	478
Total Local Production	0	0	0
Total Exports	0	0	0
Total Imports	395	460	470
Imports from the U.S.	22	25	30

Automobile, Agricultural, and Mining Equipment (AUT, AGM, MIN)

	1997 $M	1998 $M	1999E $M
Total Market Size	237	229	234
Total Local Production	0	0	1
Total Exports	17	13	0
Total Imports	254	228	233
Imports from the U.S.	10	11	12

Building Construction Equipment and Materials (BCE)

	1997E $M	1998 $M	1999E $M
Total Market Size	212	239	267
Total Local Production	100	120	140
Total Exports	77	81	86
Total Imports	189	200	213
Imports from the U.S.	11	15	19

Energy and Oil and Gas Field Services (OGM)

	1997E $M	1998E $M	1999E $M
Total Market Size	N/A	N/A	N/A
Total Local Production	N/A	N/A	N/A
Total Exports	N/A	N/A	N/A
Total Imports	N/A	N/A	N/A
Imports from the U.S.	N/A	N/A	N/A

Drugs and Phamaceuticals Including Generic Drugs (DRG)

	1997 $M	1998 $M	1999E $M
Total Market Size	104	107	113
Total Local Production	6.2	7.0	7.5
Total Exports	0.1	0.4	0.5
Total Imports	98	100	105
Imports from the U.S.	0.2	0.3	1

Plastic Materials and Resins (PMR)

	1997E $M	1998 $M	1999E $M
Total Market Size	105	116	118
Total Local Production	70	85	90
Total Exports	80	90	95
Total Imports	115	121	123
Imports from the U.S.	21	19	11

Paper and Paper Board (PAP)

	1997 $M	1998 $M	1999E $M
Total Market Size	148	152	160
Total Local Production*	70	70	75
Total Exports	49	47	48
Total Imports	78	82	85
Imports from the U.S.	11	12	12

Agricultural Chemicals (AGC)

	1997 $M	1998 $M	1999E $M
Total Market Size	69	80	86
Total Local Production	50	65	67
Total Exports	54	59	62
Total Imports	61	74	81
Imports from the U.S.	15	20	16

Cosmetics and Toiletries (COS)

	1997 $M	1998 $M	1999E $M
Total Market Size	64	74	84
Total Local Production	88	105	120
Total Exports	47	65	80
Total Imports	25	34	44
Imports from the U.S.	1	1	1

Telecommunications (TEL)

	1998 $M	1999E $M	2000E $M
Total Market Size	41	56	65
Total Local Production	0	0	0
Total Exports	10	14	13
Total Imports	51	70	78
Imports from the U.S.	6	8	15

Professional Services (Advertising, Engineering, Consulting, Financial Services)

	1998 $M	1999E $M	2000E $M
Total Market Size	44	48	40
Total Local Production	30	30	28
Total Exports	1	1	1
Total Imports	14	14	12
Imports from the U.S.	1	1	1

Used Clothing (CLT)

	1997 $M	1998 $M	1999E $M
Total Market Size	6.0	8.5	7.5
Total Local Production	0	0	0
Total Exports	0	0	0
Total Imports	6.0	8.5	7.5
Imports from the U.S.	3.7	5.0	4.5

Franchising (FRA)

	1997E $M	1998E $M	1999E $M
Total Market Size	N/A	N/A	N/A
Total Local Production	N/A	N/A	N/A
Total Exports	N/A	N/A	N/A
Total Imports	N/A	N/A	N/A
Imports from the U.S.	N/A	N/A	N/A

Best Prospects for Agricultural Products

Rice

	1998/99 MT (000)	1999/00 MT (000)	2000/01 MT (000)
Total Market Size	1044	971	998
Total Local Production	504	514	520
Total Exports	0	3	2
Total Imports	540	460	480
Imports from the U.S.	15	10	10

Wheat

	1998/99 MT (000)	1999/00 MT (000)	2000/01 MT (000)
Total Market Size	280	290	300
Total Local Production	0	0	0
Total Exports	0	0	0
Total Imports	300	245	320
Imports from the U.S.	25	8	10

Corn

	1998/99 MT (000)	1999/00 MT (000)	2000/01 MT (000)
Total Market Size	757	788	805
Total Local Production	766	795	810
Total Exports	10	9	8
Total Imports	1	2	11
Imports from the U.S.	0	0	7

Whole Milk Powder

	1998/99 MT (000)	1999/00 MT (000)	2000/01 MT (000)
Total Market Size	12	12	12
Total Local Production	0	0	0
Total Exports	2	2	3
Total Imports	14	14	15
Imports from the U.S.	0	0	0

Alcoholic Beverages

	1999 MT (000)	2000 MT (000)	2001 MT (000)
Total Market Size	233	236	240
Total Local Production	0	0	0
Total Exports	4	4	5
Total Imports	235	241	251
Imports from the U.S.	48	50	55

Variety Meats

	1999 MT (000)	2000 MT (000)	2001 MT (000)
Total Market Size	17	20	24
Total Local Production	9	10	12
Total Exports	0	0	0
Total Imports	8	10	12
Imports from the U.S.	6	8	9

Canned and Dry Goods for Groceries

	1998 MT (000)	1999 MT (000)	2000 MT (000)
Total Market Size	N/A	N/A	N/A
Total Local Production	N/A	N/A	N/A
Total Exports	N/A	N/A	N/A
Total Imports	N/A	N/A	N/A
Imports from the U.S.	N/A	N/A	N/A

The above statistics are unofficial estimates.
Exchange rate (1998): US$ 1 = CFA franc 588
N/A - Not Available, E - Estimated
Note: MT– Metric Tons

Extracted from the U.S. Department of Commerce USA Trade 2001 Country Commercial Guide for Côte d'Ivoire.

Import and Export Tips

- ## Regulations

Customs: BIVAC International, a subsidiary of the French company Bureau Veritas, handles the import inspection duties in Côte d'Ivoire for general merchandise, having replaced Societe Generale de Surveillance (SGS) Inspection on July 1, 2000. COTECNA Inspection Ltd. performs services related to temporary importation, and exportation of petroleum products and forestry products. All exports worth more than CFA/F 1.5 million (approximately $2,145) are inspected by the inspection company at the point of origin. An inspection certificate is then issued as the basis for custom valuation. Imports valued between 500,000 and 1,500,000 F/CFA are controlled at entry. BIVAC and COTECNA inspection fees are 0.75 percent of the f.o.b. value of the merchandise, subject to a minimum fee of 100,000 F/CFA. Export licenses are required for restricted exports. Licenses are issued by the Ministry of Commerce and Industry, except for export licenses for coffee and cocoa, which are issued by Nouvelle Caisse de Stabilization et Soutien des Prix de Produits Agricoles (la Nouvelle CAISTAB). Regulatory agencies: Taxation Direction Generale des Importations; Ministere de l'Economie, des Finance et du Plan (the tax department of the Ministry of Economy, Finance and Plan); Transactions Direction des Finances Exterieures et de Credit du Ministere de l'Economie, des Finances et du Plan (the international finance and credit department of the Ministry of Economy, Finance and Plan); Agence d'Etude et de Promotion de l'Emploi (AGEPE, the labor department); Ivoirien de Droits d'Auteurs (BURIDA, Ivoirian Bureau of Author's Rights, the copywright bureau).

Tariffs: The tariff structure consists mainly of a fiscal duty and a customs duty. Together they may not exceed 35 percent.

Import Taxes: A statistical tax of 2.6 percent is paid on all declarations. The value-added tax (VAT) rate is 20 percent. There are special compensatory levies on meat and poultry imports as well as specific excise taxes on tobacco products and alcoholic beverages. Most duties are based on ad valorem rates, which are imposed on the current export price from the country of sale or origin plus any shipping or insurance expenses incurred. The method of value assessment is based on the Brussels Definition of Value (BDV). Côte d'Ivoire is a voting member of the Customs Valuation Code (CVC).

Exchange Rate: Côte d'Ivoire is a member of the Communaute Financiere Africaine (CFA Franc Zone and the Banque Centrale des Etats de l'Afrique l'Ouest, or BCEAO). BCEAO is a central bank of West African states, headquartered in Dakar, Senegal, and acts as a central bank for Benin, Burkino Faso, Côte d'Ivoire, Guinea Bissau, Mali, Niger, Senegal, and Togo. The CFA franc is linked to the euro under the EMU treaty and is guaranteed by France through an operations account linking the BCEAO and the French treasury. The BCEAO controls the liquidity within the zone and within each country by granting rediscounting facilities and money market advances. Import operations exceeding CFAF 500,000 conducted with foreign countries must be domiciled with an authorized bank. Import operations of lower value must also be domiciled with an authorized bank if a financial transaction is required before customs clearance. Importers with import licenses or import attestations are entitled to purchase the necessary foreign exchange.

- Documentation

  Exports: For most exports the following are required:

  a) Commercial invoice: two copies, in French. All invoices must include the names of the exporter and consignee, the number and types of packages, the marks and numbers on the packages, the net and gross weights, the cif value, the terms of sale, and a thorough description of the merchandise.
  b) Certificate of origin: two certified copies.
  c) Packing list: not required but essential to speed the customs process.
  d) Bill of lading (or air waybill): should include clear marks of identification and the name and address of the consignee of the goods.
  e) Pro-forma invoice: six copies attached to the application for an import license and/or the intent to import.
  f) SGS inspection certificate: issued at the point of origin and delivered to the importer in Abidjan.

  Imports: The government has recently liberalized the importation of goods and services. Import licenses are no longer needed for most products. Ineligible or restricted goods include live animals and genetic material (veterinary preapproval by the Ministry of Agriculture), live plants and seeds (sanitary approval by the Ministry of Agriculture), arms or munitions, plastic bags, distilling equipment, pornography, saccharin, narcotics, explosives, illicit drugs, and toxic waste. Temporary entry of goods is available to new businesses and for goods that will be re-exported. New investments may apply for a priority agreement. Petroleum products, livestock, and animal products (including hides and skins) are still subject to prior authorization from the Ministry of Agriculture.

Labeling: The bill of landing must include clear marks of identification and the name and address of the consignee of the goods. Packages containing U.S.-produced merchandise must be clearly labeled "MADE IN THE U.S.A." High-tech equipment such as photocopiers, telecommunications equipment, computers and software must be adapted to run as specified by European electric and metric standards. Generally, consumer product labels must be in French to attract the interest of importers and consumers. Manufactured food products must have an expiration date and labeled in French.

Standards: Côte d'Ivoire uses the metric system and 220 v 50 mHz cycles for electricity. Standards usually follow the French or European norm.

- Payment

Terms: Foreign competition often grants credits of 90 to 120 days for consumer goods and 24 months for machinery and equipment. Payment via confirmed irrevocable letter of credit is desirable for U.S. exporters. However, such terms may limit market penetration since European suppliers effectively use buyer financing to accommodate customers and capture market share.

Currency Exchange: There are no limitations to the importation of U.S. currency although amounts must be declared upon entry. The importation and exportation of Ivoirian currency is strictly prohibited. Funds may be exchanged at local banks, hotels, and at the airport. French francs can be exchanged at the fixed rate of 1 French franc = 100 CFA/F.

Fund Transfer: Côte d'Ivoire is a member of the CFA Franc Zone. Thus the convertibility of the CFA franc is guaranteed by the French Treasury. Prior permission is required and routinely granted for investments coming into the zone. The same is true for the remittance of dividends, for the repatriation of capital, and for many routine transactions. Occasionally, there have been delays of one to three months in the relevant processes. A somewhat more liberalized foreign exchange regime should be on the horizon in accord with a 1998 West African Economic and Monetary Union agreement.

MARKETING TIPS

Agents and Distributors

The use of one or more resident agents or distributors is strongly recommended. In many sectors, one distributor supplies a majority of the market while smaller agents vie for niche markets. Fluency in French on the agent's part is crucial. A common problem for U.S. exporters is the failure to clarify terms and conditions in agreements with agents and distributors. The issue of after-sales support is especially important since many European competitors boast of their geographic proximity as a competitive advantage. The U.S. Commercial Service offers the Agent Distributor Service (ADS) program and its Gold Key Service, a custom-tailored service for firms planning to visit a country. Services include office support, in-depth briefing, and potential contacts at an estimated $120 per day. Contact at least three weeks before embarking.

Establishing an Office

1. Contact the Ivoirian investment promotion center (Centre de Promotion des Investissements en Côte d'Ivoire, or CEPICI), which has been active in promoting joint-venture operations and foreign investment. CEPICI figures itself as the one-stop shop, offering guidance and handling the necessary registration formalities. Fast-track registration is also provided

2. Consult a local attorney before establishing a business entity. The Commercial Service maintains updated lists.

There are four common forms adopted by businesses. In any of these, the foreign identity may hold more than 50 percent of the company's assets.

1. Joint venture (Association et Participation).

2. Branch of a foreign company (Succursale): must first be registered with the Tribunal de Premiere Instance, when the branch then becomes an Ivoirian judicial entity that is legally independent of the parent company.

3. Limited liability company (Societe Anonyme and Responsabilite Limitee, or SARL): must have a minimum capital of CFA/F 1 million (approximately $1,600) and at least one shareholder. Share certificates are not issued.

4. Stock corporations (Societe Anonyme, or SA): only one shareholder is now required. The minimum capital requirement is CFA/F 10 million (approximately $14,250) for closely held Sas and CFA/F 100 million for publicly traded companies. For corporations with capital valued below approximately CFA/F 2.5 billion (approximately $3.6 million), a stock registration tax of 0.6 percent of the value of the stock applies. The registration tax is reduced for corporations with capital valued above CFA/F 2.5 billion.

Other business forms include regional offices, sole proprietorships, and local agency or distributorship arrangements.

Distribution and Sales Channels

Principal means of selling are through wholesalers, retail outlets (local market or an established chain), a direct sales force, and an agent or distributor. Foreign firms also sell directly to the government, cooperatives, and other indigenous organizations. The major trading centers, with population estimates in millions, are Abidjan (2.6), Daloa (1.0), Man (1.0), Bouake (0.8), Korhogo (0.7), San Pedro (0.6), Dimbokro (0.6), Bouafle (0.5), Bondoukou (0.5), Divo (0.5), Agboville (0.4), Yamoussoukro (0.3), Seguela (0.4), Aboisso (0.3), Abengourou (0.3), and Odienne (0.2).

Direct Marketing

Many areas, including tobacco products, pharmaceuticals, rice, wheat, and flour, are served by large exporting trade companies, some of which are oligopolies. Most wholesale establishments and modern retail outlets are concentrated in major cities. Most owners of small shops and retailers are sole-proprietor operations with limited management capability. The Lebanese community dominates the retail business and is more connected to the countrywide wholesale network.

Leasing/Joint Ventures

See **Steps to Establishing an Office.**

Franchising

Except for car rental agencies and a few small fast-food restaurants, franchising is not common. Lack of financing and limited understanding of this business concept have limited its growth. However, there is a strong demand for American brands, and the potential for franchising arrangements is growing rapidly. Specific opportunities lie in the business-to-business area: there is a need for medium-sized companies to provide quality products and services to larger businesses, particularly in a subcontracting arrangement.

Advertising and Promotion

A wide variety of advertising agencies and services are available. Major agencies include Lintas, Nelson McCann Erickson, Young and Rubicam, and Olgivy. Advertising has increased in recent years. Radio and TV commercials are commonly used, as are posters, point-of-sales displays, coupons, and billboards. Suppliers of imported products are expected to provide advertising and promotional support. International trade fairs and smaller exhibitions are also effective ways to get the word out. Packaging is important. Colorful designs, blister packs, and small, reusable containers appeal to the consumer. Extended shelf life in a humid climate is also an important requirement.

Selling Factors

Ivoirians are certainly open and hospitable to trade and investment from the U.S. However, traditional ties to France (and Europe), the almost exclusive use of the French language, and geographic distances have created some predisposition to French and European goods and services. A high level of personal contact and presence is thus required not only to meet Ivoirian habits but also to overcome pro-European biases. Ivoirians are formal and extremely polite. Business is conducted in a slower, more personal mode. The Lebanese make up an important business community, in which French is still the dominant language.

Selling to the Government

Government procurement tenders are published in local newspapers and sometimes in international magazines and newspapers. The implementing agency is usually the responsible ministry making the request. Procurement is typically financed by a multilateral lending institution such as the World Bank or the AfDB. Commercial Service Abidjan has been providing "Fast Track Bidding Services" to reduce the time for U.S. bidders to obtain bidding documents. Payment by the government is now centralized through a one-stop

paying agency, the Caisse Autonome d'Amortissement (CAA), a government agency that acts like the government's bank.

Pricing

Pricing in French francs is more effective than pricing in U.S. dollars. Competitive credit terms are an important factor in purchasing decisions and may be part of an effective marketing strategy in the Côte d'Ivoire. Risk may be limited by insuring foreign receivables through the Export-Import Bank of the United States (EXIM) or through many private firms. The Commercial Service provides information on sound credit policies, and the ICP (International Company Profile) program has information on specific Ivoirian firms.

Customer Support

Weakness in after-sales support and service has been a main reason for limited U.S. marketing success. Support is especially critical for high-tech or heavy industrial equipment. Many local firms use a central service telephone number and radio-dispatched technicians. French-language service manuals, frequent personnel training, and a reasonable inventory of spare parts are also crucial.

Intellectual Property Rights (IPR)

Côte d'Ivoire is a party to the Paris Convention, its 1958 revision, and the 1977 Bangui Agreement grouping thirteen Francophone African countries in the African Intellectual Property Organization (OAPI). Rights registered in one OAPI country are valid in all. Patents are valid for ten years with two five year extensions, trademarks are valid for ten years and renewable indefinitely and other intellectual property rights are valid for five years with various renewal periods. Literary copyrights are protected for fifty years after the author's death. Local and international legal strides give increasing protection. Côte d'Ivoire is a member the World Intellectual Property Organization (WIPO). In 1999, fifteen member countries of OAPI adopted revisions of the Bangui Accords to conform with the WTO on Trade Related Intellectual Property Issues (the TRIPS).

Attorney

A local attorney is advisable to ensure compliance with employment laws and other

matters. Lawyers, "huissiers," and "notaires" are part of the judicial system and often are used for commercial matters. Labor laws are more burdensome than those in the U.S., and procedures for establishing a business presence are more costly and involved. For the most part, the French corporate and commercial laws that were in force prior to independence in 1960 are still in effect.

FOREIGN INVESTMENT ⑥

Openness: Generally, there are no efforts to restrict foreign investment, participation, or control of local industry. In 1995, the government stepped up its already active encouragement of foreign investment. An Investment Promotion Center—CEPICI by its French acronym—was designed to provide investment information and assistance for entrepreneurs. Meanwhile, the Investment Codes of 1985 and 1995 provide incentives to investments of all sizes. There are also additional incentives for investments outside established urban regions. Regulations are on the books to control land speculation by foreigners, but foreigners may and do own significant amounts of land.

Regulatory System: The Ivoirian government is working with the IMF and the World Bank to make improvements in this area. A centralized Office of Public Bids in the Ministry of Finance has been created to ensure compliance with international bidding practices. Regulatory bodies have been created for the increasingly liberalized telecommunications and electricity sectors.

Investment Agreements: The U.S. does not have bilateral investment or tax treaties. Côte d'Ivoire has double taxation treaties (based on the OECD model) with France, Belgium, Germany, Great Britain, Norway, Canada,

Italy, and, in Africa, with Benin, Burkina Faso, Congo, the Central African Republic, Gabon, Mauritius, Mali, Mauritania, Niger, Rwanda, Senegal, and Togo. These treaties relate to both personal and corporate income taxes.

Trade Zones and Free Ports: There are no foreign trade zones since high port costs and maritime freight rates have inhibited the development of in-bond manufacturing. Bonded warehouses serve mostly for transshipment of goods to Mali and Burkina Faso. Bonded zones within factories are allowed.

Performance Requirements/Incentives: No general performance requirements are applied to investments. Incentives available to new investments were described earlier.

Capital Markets and Investment: Côte d'Ivoire's financial system, though limited in scope, is sound and functional. Government policies encourage the free flow of capital, and the government now holds only small shares in the country's banks. Bonds and stocks have traded on the stock exchange since the 1970s. Accounting systems in Côte d'Ivoire are well developed and approach international norms. The total assets of the country's banking system were CFA 1.9 trillion (approximately USD 2.7 billion) at year-end 1997, the most recent year for which data are available.

There are no private sector or government efforts to restrict foreign investment, participation or control of local industry.

Private Ownership: Generally, foreign investors do not face special restrictions.

Expropriation and Compensation: The country's general-purpose public expropriation law is similar to that in the U.S. There are no specific cases of the expropriation of private property by the Ivoirian government.

OPIC and Investment Insurance: OPIC does insure a number of U.S. investments in Côte d'Ivoire, but exposure is relatively small. The African Project Development Facility (APDF), the African Investment Program of the International Finance Corporation, and the Africa Growth Fund are other sources of information for interested investors. Côte d'Ivoire is a member of the Multilateral Investment Guarantee Agency (MIGA).

Dispute Settlement: The judicial system is slow and costly. Some judgments have seemed arbitrary and even corrupt. The government has taken a number of steps to improve the system and promote accountability. Alternatively, businesses may now go to an arbitration tribunal, which is under the auspices of the Chamber of Commerce, to settle commercial disputes. Côte d'Ivoire is a member of the international center for the settlement of investment disputes (ICSID).

Protection of Property Rights: Property rights, including intellectual property rights, do exist, and they are respected. However, enforcement falls under the vagaries of the legal system. Côte d'Ivoire is implementing the terms of the WTO TRIPS agreement (Trade-Related Aspects of Intellectual Property Rights).

FINANCE ⑦

Côte d'Ivoire has 15 commercial banks, a regional stock exchange, over 30 insurance companies, and the headquarters of the African Development Bank (in Abidjan). The World Bank and the International Finance Corporation also maintain regional offices. Financing is generally available for short-term private-sector projects (one year or less). Commercial lenders typically rely more on collateral than on prospective cash flow. Lending rates range from 15 to 17 percent. Banking supervision for the eight UEMOA countries is the responsibility of the Banking Commission, headquartered in Abidjan.

Export Financing: The associated fees are high for traditional trade finance instruments such as letters of credit, collections, and funds transfer. If a letter of credit is chosen, the exporter should require an irrevocable, confirmed letter of credit to ensure prompt, reliable payment. The OPIC/Citibank African Trade Facility of $100 million is available. The GSM-102 and GSM-103 Credit Guarantee Programs guarantee payment to U.S. exporters for various agricultural goods for 90 days to 1 year.

Project Financing: Finance and insurance products for exporters are available from the Overseas Private Investment Corporation (OPIC). The Export-Import Bank of the U.S (EXIM) supports short-, medium-, and long-term private-sector financing. The U.S. Trade and Development Agency, the World Bank, and the African Development Bank offer funds to finance feasibility studies and loans to finance Ivoirian government-sponsored procurement.

COMMUNICATIONS (8)

Phone

The telephone system is well developed by African standards, with 200,000 subscribers, a number that is expected to double in three years. CI-Telcom services include mobile radio telephone, telex, telegraph, and facsimile services. Paging, cellular, and other wireless services are available through private local companies. Cellular and other wireless services are also available from private carriers since 1996. The international access code is 011, and the Côte d'Ivoire access code is 225. City codes are not required. The local telephone number is six digits.

Internet

Government authorities have strongly encouraged Internet connectivity, which has been available commercially since 1996. More recently, the number of Internet users has substantially increased, and growth rates are expected to remain high. In 1997, an 11-member council, the Conseil National des Autoroutes de l'information (CNAI), was established to advise the government on issues related to Internet development. Côte d'Ivoire is also funded under the Leland initiative, a five-year, $15 million USAID project to install full Internet connectivity in up to 20 African countries. The project has helped to increase the number of Internet service providers and to reduce subscription costs to about $35 to $40 per month for a full service package

Mail

International postage rates to U.S.: Ordinary airmail letter to the U.S. at CFA/F 400 up to 20 grams; at CFA/F 850 up to 40 grams; post cards at CFA/F 400. Large hotels sell stamps and accept mail from guests.

TRANSPORTATION (9)

Land

The road network is well developed, with 43,000 miles of paved roads. Starting three years ago, the railway company, SITARAIL, along with multilateral and bilateral donors, began to invest $68 million to upgrade its system. Most large shipments within and from Côte d'Ivoire can be managed. For transportation around major urban areas, it is advisable to hire a car and driver for visits of a week or more. Buses are not recommended for reasons of safety and reliability. City taxis (orange-red in color) are available day and night on main streets. Rates are reasonable, but make sure the driver does know where you want to go.

Sea

There are ports at Abidjan (mainly petroleum products) and San-Pedro (mainly timber and other agricultural products), as well as Aboisso and Dabou. Total freight traffic in 1997 exceeded 14 million tons. Ninety percent of international trade is through sea transportation. The Port of Abidjan is modern, but you can expect paperwork delays. Use of a freight forwarder (transitaire) is mandatory. With the Maersk Line's new bulk service, rates from the

U.S. have decreased considerably. Côte d'Ivoire has three national shipping lines: Sivomar, Comarco, and CMGI.

Air

About 19 international airline companies serve Abidjan's Felix Houphouet Boigny International airport, which handled more than 1.2 million passengers and over 25,000 tons of freight in 1998. The other international airport is located in Yamoussoukro. Aeroport International d'Abidjan (AERIA) began a major renovation project of the Abidjan airport valued at $20 million.

WORK WEEK

Business Hours: 7:30 a.m. to 12:30 p.m. and 3:00 p.m. to 6:00 p.m. Monday through Friday.

Bank Hours: 9:30 a.m. to 1:00 p.m. and 2:00 p.m. to 5:30 p.m. Monday to Friday.

Government Hours: 7:30 a.m. to 12:00 p.m. and 2:30 p.m. to 6:00 p.m. Monday through Friday.

Shops: Some shops are also open on Saturday from 7:30 a.m. to 12:30 p.m. and 3:00 p.m. to 6:00 p.m.

HOLIDAYS 2001

New Year's Day, January 1
End of Ramadan, Jan./Feb. or March*
Easter Monday, April 16
Labor Day, May 1
Ascension Day, May 24
Tabaski, May*
Pentecost Monday, May
Whit Monday, June 4
Independence Day, August 7
Assumption Day, August 15
Prophet Mohammed's Birthday, August*
All Saint's Day, November 1
National Peace Day, November 15
Houphouet Boigny Day, December 7
Christmas Eve, December 24
Christmas Day, December 25
First day of Eid al Fitr*, December 26
New Year's Eve, December 31

*Business travelers should verify the dates of these holidays prior to undertaking their trip. These holidays vary from country to country and depend on the sighting of the moon. Business establishments are normally closed on public holidays in Côte d'Ivoire.

Some holidays may be observed on different dates depending on the day of the week on which it falls. The Embassy will be closed on U.S. and Ivoirian holidays. It is recommended that business travelers do not schedule trips to Côte d'Ivoire immediately before or immediately after local or U.S. holidays.

Business Customs

Business customs are similar to those of the U.S., particularly at the management level, but somewhat more formal. Titles and firm names are used frequently, as are business cards (cartes de visite). Tropical-weight suits are necessary throughout the year, as is an umbrella during the rainy season. Personal contact and connections are also of greater emphasis. French is the dominant business language. Visitors should show respect for the national flag, the president, and all that he symbolizes.

Travel Advisory and Visas

A valid U.S. passport and an international health certificate showing current yellow fever and cholera immunizations are the required documents. Ensure that Ivorian officials stamp the passport at the port of entry. U.S. citizens do not need a visa for visits of less than 90 days. Long-term visas are issued by the Embassy of Côte d'Ivoire. See **Contacts**. Malaria prophylaxis and inoculation against typhoid, tetanus, diphtheria, and typhus are advised. Visitors should keep their passports with them at all times.

Business Infrastructure

Entry Requirements (personal and professional goods): Personal baggage and effects, including portable computers, are free of duty. Temporary entry permission is available for exhibition items and samples. Visitors deposit what would be the duty fee and file a claim for temporary exemption at the point of importation. The deposit is refunded once the items are re-exported within the declared time period.

Currency Exchange: Funds may be exchanged at banks, hotels, and at the airport. French francs can be exchanged at a fixed rate of 1 = 100 CFA/F. There are no limitations on the importation of dollars or travelers checks as long as they are declared upon entry. Permission from an authorized Ivoirian bank is required to export dollars. The importation and exportation of Ivoirian currency is strictly prohibited

Taxes: Corporate taxes: corporate profits, 35 percent; national contribution tax, 1 percent; personal property, 6 percent of income for foreign subsidiaries, 12 percent of income for Ivoirian firms; payroll taxes, 2.5 percent for local workers, 16 percent for foreign workers; workers compensation, 5 percent for family allowances, 2 to 5 percent toward industrial injury costs, and 1.8 percent pension contribution. Personal income taxes: subject to numerous adjustments. Other taxation: a value-added tax (VAT) of 20 percent for domestic or imported goods. A filing fee is assessed on documents and legal transactions. Real estate taxes may be levied depending on the nature of the building or property.

Hotels and Restaurants: Major hotels in Abidjan include Hotel Ivoire, Hotel Sofitel, and Golf Hotel. The number of restaurants is large, their prices by U.S. standards are quite reasonable, and the selection is varied, with many French and international options. Luncheon is usually served from 12:30 to 3:00, and dinner from about 7:30 onward. Expectations for tipping are not clear, but it is recommended that you leave at least 10 percent for normal service. Many hotels and restaurants as well as nightclubs and supermarkets provide security for clients and their vehicles. However, armed robberies have occurred at some restaurants, usually after 9:30 p.m.

Rent: In Abidjan, residential housing is good, with the availability of apartments, duplexes, and single-family homes. Presently, there is a shortage of expatriate housing, which has caused rental rates to increase sharply. Expatriate residential rent averages $12,000 per year. A downtown office lease averages $4.30 per square meter (for a lease of three years or more).

Business Services: Abidjan offers a wide range of professional business services, including but not limited to accountants, tax advisors, appraisers, architects, lawyers, engineers, computer consultants, real estate managers, and construction contractors. The Commercial Service aids with recommendations.

Labor Costs and Legislation: The guaranteed minimum monthly wage (SMIG) is approximately $65. Employers must pay social insurance premiums of 9.9 percent; health insurance; and a number of mandatory allowances, including those for meals, transportation, housing, and seniority. Employees receive 2.5 days of paid vacation per month of work. Base salaries for certain occupational salaries are as follows: semiskilled worker, $105; skilled worker, $120–$140; bilingual skilled office worker, $750–$900; typist, $110–$140; bilingual receptionist, $450; secretary, $550; bilingual accountant/MBA, $1,400–$2,500.

Education: Abidjan boasts of an excellent American-curriculum international school and several excellent French schools. Literacy rate is 41.1 percent (1995 est).

Insurance: Business travelers should examine their insurance needs prior to their departure from the U.S. Several U.S.-based companies provide very reasonably priced accident, sickness, and liability insurance. Because there are limitations in the types of medical care available in Côte d'Ivoire, all visitors should obtain medical evacuation insurance before arrival.

Travel Notes

The following travel notes have been supplied by the U.S. government. For the most recent general travel and consular information, see the U.S. Department of State travel publications or call the Traveler's Telephone Hotline at (202) 647-5225.

Security: Common sense precautions as one would take in any large, U.S. city are generally enough to ensure one's safety in Abidjan. However, crime remains at critical levels. Street theft, robbery, pick-pocketing, carjacking, and house break-ins are frequent.

In December 1999, Côte d'Ivoire experienced its first coup d'état, and a military government came to power. Although a timetable for the transition back to democracy was established in early 2000, there are numerous contentious issues facing the country pending the completion of elections.

Health Precautions: Vaccinate against typhoid, tetanus, diphtheria, and typhus before arrival. The use of malaria prophylaxis before and after travel is encouraged. New visitors are often overwhelmed by the heat and the sun. It is necessary to slow down and drink quantities of bottled water. Tap water and ice should be avoided (except in major hotels). Uncooked vegetables are not safe. Abidjan's inner lagoons are badly polluted, and the surf and undertow at its beaches are dangerous. Sexually transmitted diseases are prevalent in the local population. Health facilities in Abidjan are good, with many doctors who have had training in France. Current information on health matters may be obtained from the Centers for Disease Control and Prevention's international travelers' hotline at (404) 332-4559.

Embassy Assistance

To obtain additional and updated information on entry and exit requirements, travelers can contact the Consular Section of the Embassy of the Republic of Côte d'Ivoire at 3421 Massachusetts Avenue, N.W., Washington, D.C. 20008; Tel: (202)

797-0300. Travelers may also contact the nearest Côte d'Ivoire consulate. They are located in Detroit, New York, and San Francisco. Business travelers are encouraged to obtain a copy of the Key Officers of Foreign Service Posts: Guide for Business Representatives, available for sale by the Superintendent of Documents, U.S. Government Printing Office, Washington, D.C. 20402; Tel (202) 512-1800; Fax (202) 512-2250.

Prior to traveling to Côte d'Ivoire, U.S. business visitors are encouraged to contact their nearest U.S. Department of Commerce District Office or the Regional Commercial Service located at Immeuble Ecobank/Paribas (5th floor), Plateau, Abidjan, or the Foreign Agricultural Service located at Immeuble Tropique Trois, Mezzanine Level, Plateau, Abidjan (across the street from the U.S. Embassy).

CONTACTS 13

U.S. Embassy Personnel

U.S. Department of Commerce Commercial Service
Unit 2508
APO, AA 34020 9508
SApartado 185-2120 Guadalupe
San Jose, Costa Rica
Tel: (506) 256-3956
Fax: (506) 256-3955
U.S. Embassy - Abidjan
Department of State
Washington, D.C. 20521-2010
Tel: (225) 21-09-79
Fax: (225) 22-32-59
www.usis/posts/abidjan

The local mailing address is:
Ambassade des Etats Unis d'Amerique
01 B.P. 1712 Abidjan 01, Côte d'Ivoire

Trade Associations and Chambers of Commerce

American Chamber of Commerce of the Côte d'Ivoire (AMCHAM)
01 B.P. 3394 Abidjan 01, Côte d'Ivoire
Tel: (225) 21-46-16 (Executive Secretary)
Fax: (225) 22-24-37

Chambre de Commerce et de l'Industrie de (CCI-CI)
(Ivoirian Chamber of Commerce and Industry)
6, Avenue Joseph Anoma - Plateau
01 B.P. 1399 Abidjan 01, Côte d'Ivoire
Tel: (225) 33-16-00
Fax: (225) 32-39-42

Centre de Promotion des Investissements de Côte d'Ivoire (CEPICI)
CCIA Building (5th floor), Plateau
01 B.P. V 152, Abidjan 01, Côte d'Ivoire
Tel: (225) 21-40-70
Fax: (225) 21-40-71

Federation Nationale des Industries de Côte d'Ivoire
CCIA Building (13eme Etage), Plateau
Tel: (225) 21-71-42; 21-77-27
Fax: (225) 21-72-56

Conseil National du Patronat Ivoirien (CNPI)
Immeuble CCIA, (13eme etage) - Plateau
01 B.P. 1340, Abidjan 01, Côte d'Ivoire
Tel: (225) 22-69-37; 22-70-33
Fax: (225) 22-70-37

Cour d'Arbitrage de Côte d'Ivoire (CACI)
01 BP 1399 Abidjan 01
Phone: (225) 3314 14
Fax: (225) 33 14 13

**Bureau National d'Etudes et de
  Developpement (BNETD)**
Bld de la Corniche, Cached
01 B.P. 1345 Abidjan 01, Côte d'Ivoire
Tel: (225) 44-2805
Fax: (225) 44-0567

Ivoirian Publicity and Marketing
  Research Firms

Lintas Abidjan
16 B.P. 1340 Abidjan 16, Côte d'Ivoire
Tel: (225) 21-46-78; 21-80-04; 21-88-91
Fax: (225) 22-81-82

Nelson McCann Erickson
Near Institut Goethe, Abidjan-Cocody
B.P. 3420 Abidjan 01
Tel: (225) 48-6500
Fax: (225) 48-9418

Panafcom Young Rubicam
51, Bis Bld Achalme, Marcory Residentiel
01 B.P. 3067 Abidjan 01
Tel: (225) 26-659; 26-2525
Fax: (225) 26-1529

Publicite Ocean
01 B.P. 7759 Abidjan 01, Côte d'Ivoire
Tel: (225) 21-84-51; 22-02-72
Fax: (225) 21-86-90

Dialogue Production (video productions)
M. Cyril Durand
Residence les Capucines, Rue Canebiere,
  Cached
01 B.P. 2081 Abidjan 01
Tel: (225) 44-18-49
Fax: (225) 44-61-30

Contact Information for Advertising on
Radio and TV

RTI-Publicite
Television Chaines 1 and 2
Tel: (225) 32-27-71
Fax: (225) 32-41-86

Canal+ Horizons
01 B.P. 1132 Abidjan 01
Tel: (225) 21-9999
(Presence Regie for advertising)
Tel: (225) 25-5225

Cinema

Les Studios
01 B.P. 4280
Abidjan 01
Tel: 21-38-97

Societe Ivorienne De Cinema (SIC)
01 B.P. 304
Abidjan 01
Tel: 44-01-45

Publicite Côte d'Ivoire
Immeuble Fraternite Matin (220 Logements)
01 B.P. 1807, Abidjan 01, Côte d'Ivoire
Tel: (225) 37-04-66
Fax: (225) 37-16-67

Bus/Billboards

Publicite Côte d'Ivoire
Immeuble Fraternite Matin (220 Logements)
01 B.P. 1807, Abidjan 01, Côte d'Ivoire
Tel: (225) 37-04-66
Fax: (225) 37-25-45

Publistar
Avenue Lamblin, Residence Lamblin
  2eme Etage
01 B.P. 3760 Abidjan 01, Côte d'Ivoire
Tel: (225) 32-1138; 32-1139
Fax: (225) 32-1140

Weekly and Monthly Press

Abidjan le Griot 7 Jours
Tel: (225) 35-39-39; 35-72-23

Daily Papers

Fraternite-Matin
Boulevard du General de Gaulle (220
  Logements), Adjame
01 B.P. 1807, Abidjan 01, Côte d'Ivoire
Tel: (225) 37-06-66
Fax: (225) 37-25-45

Notre Voie
Cocody les II Plateaux
09 B.P. 254 Abidjan 09
Redacteur en Chef
Tel: (225) 42-63-27; 42-63-29
Fax: (225) 42-63-32

Le Jour
26, Avenue Chardy, Abidjan Plateau
01 B.P 2432 Abidjan 01
Tel: (225) 21-95-78
Fax: (225) 21-95-80

Soir Info
Rue Louis Lumiere, Zone 4C
10 B.P. 2462 Abidjan 10
Tel: (225) 25-32-77
Fax: (225) 35-85-66

Commercial Banks and Financial Services Institutions in Côte d'Ivoire

Citibank
28, avenue Delafosse, Plateau
01 B.P. 3698 Abidjan 01, Côte d'Ivoire
Tel: (225) 21-46-10
Fax: (225) 21-76-85

Banque Internationale pour le Commerce et l'Industrie de la Côte d'Ivoire (BICICI)
Avenue Franchet d'Esperey
01 B.P. 1298 Abidjan 01, Côte d'Ivoire
Tel: (225) 20-16-00; 20-16-02
Fax: (225) 20-17-00

Societe Generale de Banques en Côte d'Ivoire (SGBCI)
M. Pascal Bernard-Mettil, Administrator-
  General Manager (speaks fluent English)
01 B.P. 1355, Abidjan 01, Côte d'Ivoire
Tel: (225) 20-12-34
Fax: (225) 20-14-92

Societe Ivorienne de Banque (SIB)
M. Jean Pierre De Pellecome
01 B.P. 1300 Abidjan 01, Côte d'Ivoire
Tel: (225) 20-00-00; 20-00-80
Fax: (225) 21-97-41

BIAO- Côte d'Ivoire
01 B.P. 1274 Abidjan 01, Côte d'Ivoire
Tel: (225) 20-07-20
Fax: (225) 20-07-00

Ecobank
M. Amin Uddin, General Manager (speaks
  fluent English)
01 B.P. 4107, Abidjan, Côte d'Ivoire
Tel: (225) 21-10-41
Fax: (225) 21-88-16

Banque Paribas
17 B.P. 9, Abidjan 17, Côte d'Ivoire
Tel: (225) 21-30-32; 21-86-86
Fax: (225) 21-88-23

HSBC Equator Bank
M. Rizwan Haider, Senior Vice-President
  (speaks fluent English)
15, avenue Joseph Anoma, 12eme etage
04 B.P. 815, Abidjan 04, Côte d'Ivoire
Tel: (225) 33-62-11
Fax: (225) 33-62-10

Network Financial Services (agent of First International Bank of Hartford Connecticut, specialists in securing EXIM Bank financing)
M. Yaw Adu Poku, Vice-President (speaks
  fluent English)
06 BP 6092 Abidjan 06
Tel: (225) 35-16-44
Fax: (225) 35-16-42

Multilateral Financial Institutions in Côte d'Ivoire

African Development Bank (AFDB)
01 B.P. 1387 Abidjan 01, Côte d'Ivoire
Tel: (225) 20-40-15; 20-42-18
Fax: (225) 33-14-34

The World Bank
01 B.P. 1850, Abidjan 01, Côte d'Ivoire
Tel: (225) 44-22-27
Fax: (225) 44-16-87

The International Finance Corporation
01 B.P. 1850, Abidjan 01, Côte d'Ivoire
Tel: (225) 44-22-27; 44-32-44
Fax: (225) 44-16-87; 44-44-83

Africa Project Development Facility (APDF)
01 B.P. 8669, Abidjan 01, Côte d'Ivoire
Tel: (225) 21-96-97
Fax: (225) 21-61-51

Washington, D.C. Contacts for Côte d'Ivoire

U.S. Government Agencies

U.S. Department of Commerce
14th and Constitution Ave., N.W.
Washington, DC 20230
Tel: (202) 482-4836
Fax: (202) 482-5179

The Trade Information Center (TIC)
Office of Export Promotion Coordination
International Trade Administration
U.S. Department of Commerce
14th and Constitution Ave., N.W. HCHB 7424
Washington, DC 20230
Tel: (202) 482-0543
Fax: (202) 482-4473
http:/www.ita.doc.gov/tic

Multilateral Development Bank Operations
HCHB Room H1107
Tel: (202) 482-3399
Fax: (202) 273-0927

U.S. Department of State
Africa Bureau-AF/W, Room 4250
Desk Officer for Côte d'Ivoire
Tel: (202) 647-1540
Fax: (202) 647-4855

U.S. Department of Treasury
1500 Pennsylvania Avenue, N.W.
Washington, DC 20220
Office of the Assistant Secretary of Int'l
 Affairs
IDB Room 5400
Tel: (202) 622-1231
Fax: (202) 622-1228

U.S. Department of Agriculture
Foreign Agricultural Service
14th & Independence Ave., S.W.
Washington, DC 20250
Trade Assistance and Promotion Office
Tel: (202) 720-7420
Fax: (202) 690-4374

USAID AFR/ONI
1111 N. 19th Street, Rm. 210
Rosslyn, VA 22209
Tel: (703) 235-9082
Fax: (703) 235-5423

Overseas Private Investment Corporation (OPIC)
1100 New York Avenue, N.W.
Washington, DC 20527
Tel: (202) 336-8799
Fax: (202) 336-8700

U.S. Trade and Development Agency
1621 North Kent Street
Arlington, VA 22209
Tel: (703) 875-4357
Fax: (703) 875-4009

Export-Import Bank of the United States (EXIM Bank)
Ms. Annmarie Emmett
Coordinator/Counselor for Africa
811 Vermont Avenue, N.W., 7th Floor
Washington, DC 20571
Tel: (202) 566-8008
Fax: (202) 566-7524

U.S.-Based Multilateral Financial Institutions

The World Bank
1818 H Street, N.W.
Washington, DC 20433
Tel: (202) 477-1234
Fax: (202) 477-6391

The International Finance Corporation
1818 H Street, N.W.
Washington, DC 20433
Tel: (202) 477-1234
Fax: (202) 477-3112

Multilateral Insurance Guarantee Agency (MIGA)
1818 H Street, N.W.
Washington, DC 20433
Tel: (202) 473-3075
Fax: (202) 477-6391

Africa Growth Fund
1850 K Street, N.W., Suite 390
Washington, DC 20006
Tel: (202) 293 1860
Fax: (202) 872-1521

Other U.S.-Based Contacts

Business Council for International Understanding (BCIU) Inc.
420 Lexington Avenue
New York, NY 10170
Tel: (212) 490-0460
Fax: (212) 697-8526

Corporate Council on Africa (CCA)
1660 L Street, N.W., Suite 301
Washington, DC 20036
Tel: (202) 298-7800
Fax: (202) 333-5792

SGS Government Programs, Inc.
(preinspection of exports to Côte d'Ivoire)
42 Broadway
New York, NY 10004
Tel: (212) 482-8700
Fax: (212) 363-3316

Embassy of Côte d'Ivoire
2424 Massachusetts Ave.
N.W., Washington, D.C. 20008
Tel: (202) 797-0300
Fax: (202) 387-6381

U.S. Embassy
5, rue Jesse Owens on the Plateau
(Abidjan's central district)
Web site: http://www.usis.doc.gov/post/abidjan

The Côte d'Ivoire Mission to the United Nations
46 East 74th Street
New York, NY 10021
Tel: (212) 717-5555
Fax: (212) 717-4492

List of Banks with Correspondent U.S. Bank Arrangements

SGBCI Societe Generale (SoGen)
BIAO Credit Commercial de France (CCF)
BICICI Banque Nationale de Paris (BNP)
SIB Credit Lyonnais
Citibank Citibank
Paribas Paribas
BHCI None
Ecobank Chase Manhattan, and Bankers Trust
Bank of Africa None
HSBC Equator Bank HSBC Group

Alexandria

Cairo●

EGYPT

Aswan ●

E G Y P T .

TRADE AND BUSINESS GUIDE

Official Name:	Arab Republic of Egypt (Jumhuriyah Misr al'-Arabiyah)
Official Languages:	Arabic, English, and French widely understood by educated classes
Population:	68,359,979 (2000 est)
Population Growth:	1.72% (2000 est)
Age Structure:	0–14 years: 35%, 15–64 years: 61%, 65 years and over: 4% (2000 est)
Location:	North Africa bordering the Mediterranean Sea, between Libya and the Gaza Strip
Area:	1,001,450 square kilometers, slightly more than three times the size of New Mexico
Type of Government:	Democratic republic, presidential/parliamentarian
Head of State:	President Mohamed Hosni Mubarek
Cabinet:	By presidential appointment
Religion:	Sunni Muslim 90%, most of the others are Coptic Christians
Major Cities:	Capital: Cairo (6.4 million), Alexandria (3.1 million), Giza (2.1 million), Shubra Al Khayma (811,000), Port Said (461,000), Suez (390,000), Mahalla Al Kubra (358,844), Tanta (334,505), Hulwan (328,000), Mansura (316,870)
Climate:	Tropical. Cairo's hottest months are from May to October, with temperatures reaching as high as 107 degrees F. Cairo's cool season is from November to April, with average temperatures ranging between 55 and 70 degrees
Time:	The entire country is +2 GMT (Greenwich Mean Time), seven hours ahead of EST (Eastern Standard Time) but six hours ahead during daylight savings time
GDP:	Purchasing power parity (PPP): $200 billion (1999 est); real growth rate: 5% (1999 est); per capita PPP: $3,000 (1999 est); composition by sector: agricultural = 17%, industry = 32%, services = 51% (1999 est)
Currency:	Egyptian pound (£E 1 = 100 piastres; £E 3.4 = US$ 1)
Exchange Rate:	Egyptian pound per US$ 1 = 3.4375 (2000 est), 3.4353 (1999), 3.4175 (1998)
Weights & Measure:	Metric system
Natural Resources:	Petroleum, natural gas, phosphates, manganese, and coal
Total Trade:	In millions US$ [(Exports (fob)/Imports (cif)] 1997 (5,345/15,565), 1998 (5,128/16,899), 1999E (4,445/16,969)
Trade with U.S.:	In millions US$ [exports (fob)/imports (cif)]: 1997 (695/3,840), 1998 (698/3,060), 1999 est (660/3,000)

Major Trade Partners: Imports: European Union countries, United States, Japan.
Exports: European Union countries, United States, Japan

Membership: AfDB, COMESA, EBRD, IBRD, ICC, IDB, IFC, IMF, MIGA, ISO, UN, UNCTAD, WCO, WIPO, and WTO. See membership description in appendix

Sources: *CIA World Fact Book, United Nations World Statistics, Central Bank of Egypt Statistics, U.S. Department of State, U.S. Department of Commerce*

POLITICAL OUTLOOK ②

Relationship with the U.S.

Egypt and the U.S. share a strong political relationship, which Hosni Mubarak has supported throughout his presidency. The two countries work to promote regional peace, develop the Egyptian economy, and strengthen trade ties. In 1994, President Mubarak and Vice President Al Gore launched The U.S.–Egypt Partnership for Economic Growth and Development, through which the U.S. supports Egypt's economic transformation. Other recent initiatives are meant to promote free trade, political risk insurance for foreign enterprises, and project feasibility studies. Egypt also has substantial relationships with the European Union, COMESA (the Common Market for Eastern and Southern Africa), and the Arab League.

Influences on Business

Since 1992, extremist groups have targeted government officials, security forces, and foreign tourists. The attacks do not threaten the government's stability, but they have affected business, particularly the important tourism industry. A November 1997 attack in Luxor killed 58 foreign tourists. Since then, security has been strengthened, and the wave of terrorism has receded. The first half of 1998 saw the fewest tourist attacks since 1993. Correspondingly, the tourism industry has shown signs of revival.

Profile

System: The Egyptian Constitution provides for a strong president, who appoints vice presidents, the prime minister, the cabinet, and the governors of Egypt's 26 provinces. The People's Assembly (454 members) is popularly elected, and the last round of elections took place in 2000. The Shura (Consultative Council, 254 members) has an advisory role on public policy but no legislative power. The political system has made great progress since the Nasser era of the 1950s and 1960s. Citizens enjoy a substantial degree of freedom of expression, and the judiciary has established its independent powers. However, the government's antiterrorism campaign has raised questions about human rights abuses. Furthermore, Egypt officially has been under Emergency Law since 1981, the year of President Sadat's assassination.

Schedule for Elections: President Hosni Mubarak was reelected in September 1999 to a fourth 6-year term. Next election to be held in October, 2005.

Major Parties: Although Egypt has more than a dozen authorized opposition political parties, the great dominance of the National Democratic Party (NDP) threatens the actual practice of representative government. The NDP has been in power since its establishment in 1978, and it commands large majorities in the Assembly and the Shura. Only 12 seats are held by opposition parties in the 454-member People's Assembly.

Political Violence: Egyptian extremist groups began their attacks in the mid-1990s. These hostilities have not threatened the stability of the government though they have had serious effects on Egypt's important tourism industry.

Counterterrorism activities have been stepped up, and there were no attacks on foreign tourists in 1998.

Corruption: The level of corruption in Egypt is below average for a developing country. U.S. firms occasionally report corruption by lower-level government officials, but they do not identify corruption as a significant obstacle to foreign investment.

Media: The NDP effectively controls the mass media as well as local governments, organized labor, and the large public sector. Furthermore, the media have recently been the target of increased government scrutiny.

ECONOMIC OUTLOOK
③

Trends

The government achieved solid macroeconomic performance and stabilization through its reform program. The achievements include positive growth rates averaging 4-5% in recent years, low inflation, large foreign currency reserves, a stable currency and sustained fiscal discipline. There is an upward trend in foreign exchange reserves in key sectors such as tourism and oil and gas. The government is committed to continuing budget discipline and desires to hold the deficit to around 3.4% of GDP for FY 2000/01.

Challenges

The trade deficit has grown, exports are lagging, and foreign exchange earnings have been squeezed. Such concerns have cast some doubt on the exact course of further economic reform. Furthermore, transaction costs and a difficult regulatory environment present barriers to trade. Egypt's private savings and investment rates are relatively low, and its unemployment rate is high. Strong job creation is thus necessary, particularly since Egypt's population and labor force are quickly growing.

Major Growth Sectors

Egypt can boast of significant economic success over the past ten years. Growth has been strong, and the government's reform program has greatly opened the Egyptian market. Privatization has transferred a large number of companies to the private sector. Important trade relations have deepened. Many tariffs have been reduced, and the burden of bureaucracy has been lightened. Meanwhile, inflation remains under control, the political situation is stable, the country holds a substantial reserve of foreign currency, and the rate of foreign investments in the capital markets has increased. Finally, in 1999 a new Commercial Law was passed to modernize the legal environment for business. Looking ahead, the Egyptian government has set aggressive goals. One is the maintenance of a GDP growth rate at 7 to 8 percent. Another is the privatization of all public enterprises by 2002. The government has identified services, energy, agriculture, industry (high tech development), infrastructure projects and information technology as national priorities.

Key Economic Indicators

Income, Production and Employment *(billions of U.S. dollars unless otherwise indicated)*			
	1997	1998	1999[1]
GDP (current prices)	76.2	83.8	89.7
Real GDP Growth (pct)[2]	5.3	5.7	6.0
GDP by Sector			
Agriculture	17.6	17.5	17.4
Manufacturing	31.8	32.2	31.5
Services	42.6	42.3	43.3
Government	7.8	7.8	7.9
Per Capita GDP (US$)	1,260	1,310	1,406
Labor Force (millions)	17.36	17.0	18.3
Unemployment Rate (pct)	8.8	8.9	8.3

1. 1999 figures are all estimates based on Egypt's fiscal year starting 7/1 and ending 6/30.
2. Percentage changes calculated in local currency.
Source: Bureau of Economic and Business Affairs; U.S. Department of State

- **Infrastructure**
  Egypt has excellent infrastructure. Investments in the 1970s and 1990s resulted in dependable electricity, clean water, significantly improved health care, more schools, reliable telecommunications, improved village infrastructure and services, new technologies, a more efficient and diversified agriculture base, and expanded farmer access to credit, seeds and fertilizer.

- **Labor**
  Egypt's workforce is estimated to grow at an annual rate of 2.7 percent. The abundance of labor creates low wages and the necessity of labor-intensive technologies. The government's labor laws are in need of reform; in particular, there are often legal difficulties when dismissing employees. Furthermore, workers are not legally allowed to strike; child labor abuses remain a concern; workers are not knowledgeable about market-based economies; and qualified specialists are needed. Legislation has been drafted to tackle such concerns, but the law has been held up in the People's Assembly since 1996. For government and public-sector employees, the minimum wage is approximately $33 (about 113 Egyptian pounds) a month for a six-day, 42-hour workweek. Base pay is supplemented by a complex system of benefits and bonuses that may double or triple a worker's otherwise insufficient take-home pay. The Ministry of Labor sets worker health and safety standards, but enforcement and inspection are uneven.

Money and Prices
(annual percentage growth)

	1997	1998	1999[1]
Money Supply Growth (M2)	15.1	12.3	11.4
Consumer Price Inflation (period average)	6.2	4.0	2.9
Exchange Rate (£E/US$ annual average)			
Market Rate	3.39	3.39	3.396

1. 1999 figures are all estimates based on on Egypt's fiscal year starting 7/1 and ending 6/30.
Source: Bureau of Economic and Business Affairs; U.S. Department of State

Balance of Payments and Trade
(millions of U.S. dollars unless otherwise indicated)

	1997	1998	1999[1]
Total Exports FOB[2]	5,345	5,128	4,445
Exports to U.S.[2]	694	698	660
Total Imports FOB[2]	15,565	16,899	16,969
Imports from U.S.[2]	3,840	3,060	3,000
Trade Balance[2]	-10,2	-11,7	-12,5
Balance with U.S.	-3,146	-2,361	-2,360
External Public Debt	28,8	28,1	28,2
Fiscal Balance/GDP (pct)	-0.9	-1.0	-1.3
Current Account Balance/GDP (pct)	0.7	-3.4	-1.9
Debt Service Payments Ratio[3]	16.0	13.0	11.0
Gold and Foreign Exchange Reserves	20,2	20,3	18,0
Aid from U.S.	2,115	2,115	2,075

1. 1999 figures are all estimates based on on Egypt's fiscal year starting 7/1 and ending 6/30.
2. Merchandise trade. 3. Ratio of external debt service to current account receipts.
Source: Bureau of Economic and Business Affairs; U.S. Department of State

- **Merchandise Trade**
  Egypt's merchandise trade deficit is continuing to grow and contributed to a deteriorating current account.

- **Balance of Payments**
  See **Key Economic Indicators.** According to the Central Bank of Egypt, the country's balance of payment turned negative in FY 1997/98 due to deteriorating current account and a growing merchandise trade deficit. Government policies such as tightly managing the local supply of foreign currency, emphasizing export growth and implementing measures to moderate import growth contributed to a decrease in trade and current account deficits in the first half of 1999/00. The Egyptian pound has remained steady against the dollar at a rate of £E 3.4:US$ 1.

Government Influence on Business

The course of economic reform will be of significant importance in the near term. Top officials emphasize their commitment to pushing aggressively ahead; however, there are signs that the privatization program is slowing, and several recent government decrees have sent mixed messages. Both a large public bank and an insurance company are slated for privatization, but the actual timing of these transfers is yet to be determined.

TRADE
4

Leading Imports and Exports

Imports: Medical equipment, packaging equipment, oil and gas field machinery, automotive parts and maintenance equipment, construction equipment and building materials, computers and peripherals, paper and paperboard, agricultural equipment, telecommunications equipment and services, environmental equipment and services, franchising, electrical power systems, plastic materials and resins, food processing equipment, architectural, construction and engineering services

Exports: Crude oil and petroleum products, cotton yarn, raw cotton, textile, metal products, chemicals, spices, processed fruit and vegetables, fruit and vegetable juices, and some other high-value food products

Foreign Trade *(Exports and Imports in US$M)*			
	1997	1998	1999[1]
Total Exports FOB[2]	5,345	5,128	4,445
Exports to U.S.[2]	694	698	660
Total Imports FOB[2]	15,565	16,899	16,969
Imports from U.S.[2]	3,840	3,060	3,000

1. 1999 figures are all estimates based on Egypt's fiscal year starting 7/1 and ending 6/30. 2. Merchandise trade
Source: Bureau of Economic and Business Affairs; U.S. Department of State.

Best Prospects Analysis

Best Prospects for Nonagricultural Goods and Services

Environmental Equipment & Services (ENV)

	1998 $M	1999 $M	2000E $M
Total Market Size	856	942	1,038
Total Local Production	82	90	99
Total Exports	0	0	0
Total Imports	774	851	937
Imports from the U.S.	310	341	375

IT Equipment and Services (CPT)

	1998 $M	1999 $M	2000E $M
Total Market Size	520	630	693
Total Local Production	104	114	125
Total Exports	3	3.3	3.63
Total Imports	416	457	502
Imports from the U.S.	332	365	401

Telecommunications Equipment & Services (TEL)

	1998 $M	1999 $M	2000E $M
Total Market Size	1,028	1,130	1,244
Total Local Production	182	199	219
Total Exports	88	97	107
Total Imports	847	931	1,024
Imports from the U.S.	733	806	887

Oil and Gas Field Machinery (OGM)

	1998 $M	1999 $M	2000E $M
Total Market Size	772	926	1,111
Total Local Production	120	144	173
Total Exports	0	0	0
Total Imports	650	780	936
Imports from the U.S.	199	236	283

Electrical Power Systems (ELP)

	1998 $M	1999 $M	2000E $M
Total Market Size	912	1,003	1,102
Total Local Production	50	55	60
Total Exports	0	0	0
Total Imports	862	948	1,042
Imports from the U.S.	530	583	641

Medical Equipment (MED)

	1998 $M	1999 $M	2000E $M
Total Market Size	392	431	474
Total Local Production	20	22	24
Total Exports	0	0	0
Total Imports	372	409	450
Imports from the U.S.	103	113	124

Franchising (FRA)

	1998 $M	1999 $M	2000E $M
Total Market Size	565	593	615
Total Local Production	260	273	286
Total Exports	0	0	0
Total Imports	33	35	35
Imports from the U.S.	272	285	293

Packaging Equipment (PCK)

	1998 $M	1999 $M	2000E $M
Total Market Size	577	721	901
Total Local Production	139	173	216
Total Exports	0	17	21
Total Imports	323	404	505
Imports from the U.S.	16	20	25

Drugs and Pharmaceuticals (DRC)

	1998 $M	1999 $M	2000E $M
Total Market Size	1,000	1,280	1,400
Total Local Production	970	1,000	1,250
Total Exports	89	100	113
Total Imports	166	1110	1302
Raw Materials	88	1,020	1,200
Finished Products	78	90	102
Imports from the U.S.	33	38	43

Construction Equipment & Building Materials (CON)

	1998 $M	1999 $M	2000E $M
Total Market Size	1,030	1,200	1,400
Total Local Production	95	114	136
Total Exports	30	36	43
Total Imports	965	1,158	1,400
Imports from the U.S.	357	428	513

Paper and Paperboard (PAP)

	1998 $M	1999 $M	2000E $M
Total Market Size	746	850	765
Total Local Production	149	170	153
Total Exports	2	3	3
Total Imports	599	683	615
Imports from the U.S.	60	68	61

Agricultural Construction and Engineering Services (AGE)

	1998 $M	1999 $M	2000E $M
Total Market Size	730	811	892
Total Local Production	130	156	172
Total Exports	30	35	39
Total Imports	600	690	759
Imports from the U.S.	300	315	347

Hotel and Restaurant Equipment (HTL)

	1998 $M	1999 $M	2000E $M
Total Market Size	125	250	375
Total Local Production	31	62	93
Total Exports	0	0	0
Total Imports	125	250	375
Imports from the U.S.	25	50	100

Plastic Materials and Resins (PMR)

	1998 $M	1999 $M	2000E $M
Total Market Size	1,265	1,518	1,670
Total Local Production	253	304	334
Total Exports	0	0	0
Total Imports	1,072	1,286	1,415
Imports from the U.S.	535	642	730

Food Processing Equipment (FPP)

	1998 $M	1999 $M	2000E $M
Total Market Size	376	402	430
Total Local Production	41	44	47
Total Exports	29	31	33
Total Imports	364	389	416
Imports from the U.S.	22	24	26

Agricultural Equipment (AGE)

	1998 $M	1999 $M	2000E $M
Total Market Size	475	543	558
Total Local Production	90	100	105
Total Exports	25	15	17
Total Imports	400	460	470
Imports from the U.S.	25	28	29

Automotive Parts and Maintenance Equipment (APS)

	1998 $M	1999 $M	2000E $M
Total Market Size	290	319	350
Total Local Production	50	55	60
Total Exports	0	0	0
Total Imports	240	264	290
Imports from the U.S.	55	60	65

Best Prospects for Agricultural Products

Marketing Year Data: 1997 = Oct 1997 - Sept 1998, etc.

Wheat

	1997 MT ('000)	1998 MT ('000)	1999 MT ('000)
Total Consumption	13,100	13,070	12,550
Total Local Production	6,000	6,093	6,550
Total Imports	7,120	6,300	6,000
Imports from the U.S.	4,850	4,200	4,147

Corn

	1997 MT ('000)	1998 MT ('000)	1999 MT ('000)
Total Consumption	9,400	9,340	10,188
Total Local Production	6,300	5,760	5,678
Total Imports	3,010	3,230	4,500
Imports from the U.S.	1,847	1,950	3,800

Soybean Meal

	1997 MT ('000)	1998 MT ('000)	1999 MT ('000)
Total Consumption	787	713	820
Total Local Production	200	133	90
Total Imports	580	570	760
Imports from the U.S.	220	180	190

Beef and Veal

	1997 MT ('000)	1998 MT ('000)	1999 MT ('000)
Total Consumption	496	520	513
Total Local Production	425	440	400
Total Imports	100	80	113
Imports from the U.S.	25	20	29

Vegetable Oils

	1997 MT ('000)	1998 MT ('000)	1999 MT ('000)
Total Consumption	799	855	787
Total Local Production	94	90	80
Total Imports	705	854	707
Imports from the U.S.	50	35	44

Egyptian Imports of High Value Products
January - December 1999*
Total Import Value, U.S. Import Value, Market Share (%)

	Total Import $M	U.S. Import $M	Market Share %
Prepared meat	5.7	0.032	1
Prepared sauces & dressings	1	0.280	28
Nuts	21	5	23
Dried fruits	6 0.	0.401	6
Canned fruit & vegetables	12	0.462	3
Breakfast cereals	0.918	0.125	7
Juice	2.6	0.207	7

*Source: Central Agency for Public Mobilization and Statistics

The above statistics are unofficial estimates.

Exchange rate (1999): US$ 1 = £E 3.4
Exchange rate (2000): US$ 1 = £E 3.6
N/A - Not Available, E - Estimate
Note: MT = Metric Tons

Extracted from the U.S. Department of Commerce USA Trade 2000 Country Commercial Guide for Egypt.

Import and Export Tips

- ## Regulations

Red tape remains a key business impediment in Egypt. There are a multiplicity of regulations and regulatory agencies. Other problems include delays in clearing goods through customs, arbitrary decision-making processes, high market entry transaction costs, and a generally unresponsive commercial court system. However, at cabinet levels, the government is willing to promote private sector concerns. Furthermore, when onerous regulations are brought to the attention of senior officials, the government has taken steps to make them less burdensome. A strategic alliance between the U.S. Embassy, American exporters, and their Egyptian importers has proved successful in combating unfair bureaucratic practices.

Customs: Procedures are complicated and decisions can be subjective. The tariff category in which a commodity will be placed is not always clear. Under-invoicing is a common practice by local businesses; customs officials will add 10 to 30 percent to invoice values when under-invoicing is suspected. However, recent developments have been promising. Compensatory and replacement shipments, for instance, are now freed from full custom fees. Further, a Computerized Customs Declaration Form (Bill of Entry) has been applied. The goal is to simplify and standardize customs processes.

Tariffs: Egypt has received a waiver and thus does not abide by the lower tariff rates as outlined by the WTO. The economic reform program has reduced tariff rates to a maximum of 40 percent, with exceptions for powerful cars, alcoholic beverages, and some luxury items. The program was developed in conjunction with the IMF and the World Bank.

Import Taxes: The government levies a service fee on the value of imported shipments to counterbalance the reduction in tariffs. The fee is in return for inspection, listing, classification, and reexamination. In February 1994, this surcharge was raised. If the customs-duties rate is between 5 and 30 percent, the surcharge is 3 percent. If the rate is over 30 percent, the surcharge is 6 percent. However, these surcharges were reduced twice to 2 and 4 percent, respectively. In addition, a sales tax of between 5 and 25 percent is added to the final customs value of imported items. A number of further taxes and fees were canceled in 1986 and 1998.

Exchange Rate: Foreign Currency Law 38 of 1994 and the executive regulations issued under Ministerial Decree 331 of 1994 regulate foreign exchange operations in Egypt. Responsibility for exchange rate policy lies with the government of Egypt (GOE) and is administered by the Central Bank of Egypt in consultation with the minister of economy and foreign trade.

Central bank foreign exchange reserves stood at $17.4 billion in August 1999. The GOE notes officially that the free market guides the rates of exchange set by the Central Bank of Egypt, other approved banks, and dealers. However, the central bank appears to actively monitor the exchange rate in order to assure the Egyptian pound's stability. According to the Central Bank of Egypt, the value of the Egyptian pound averaged around £E 3.39 per $US 1 in 1999. Rates offered by major commercial banks reflected only a modest spread over this average, in the range of 3.4 to 3.41 £E per $US 1. The rates offered by bureau of exchange, which account for approximately 6 to 10 percent of daily foreign exchange transactions, ranged up to 3 percent above the standard commercial rate.

The intervention currency is the US dollar. There are no exchange or currency controls, and foreign currency transfers are in principle unrestricted. In the last year, however, firms reported frequent delays in the processing of their requests to convert Egyptian pounds to foreign currency. Exports in recent years may have been affected by the real appreciation of the Egyptian pound since economic reform was initiated in 1991.

• **Documentation**

Exports: Exporters should possess the following documents:

a. Export card, issued by the General Authority for Import/Export Quality Control at the Ministry of Trade and Supply.
b. Taxation card, obtained from the Taxation Authority or any of its offices.
c. Original invoice.
d. Custom procedural certificate, a customs form that lists information and date on the exported goods.

Contact the Department of Commerce, for additional information on export controls and other requirements.

Imports: Import licenses are no longer required and most goods can be imported freely. Importers should possess the following documents:

a. An Import Card which is issued by the General Authority for Import/Export Quality Control at the Ministry of Trade and Supply.
b. Taxation Card, which is obtained from the Taxation Authority or any of its offices.
c. Three forms of Annex (11) of the import/export executive regulations issued by Ministerial Decree 275/91. Annex (11), the application to finance imports with convertible currencies, includes information on the type, quantity, price and country of origin

of the imported commodities. The importer retains one copy which he/she submits to Customs to release the shipment, the second copy is submitted to the Foreign Trade Department at the Ministry of Trade and Supply and the third copy is kept with the bank to follow-up on payment. The pro-forma invoice or final invoice should be stamped by the bank.

The following documents should be presented to Customs to release imports:

a. Bill of landing, which should contain the terms Consignee and Notify Party.
b. Original invoice.
c. Packing lists.
d. Certificate of origin, authenticated and legalized. A minimum of three copies are required.
e. Form (EX), a bank form, which is applicable when the bank finances the importation transaction.
f. Content analysis of the commodity, if required.
g. Delivery order from the carrier in return for the bill of landing.
h. Custom procedural certificate, a customs form that lists information and date on the imported goods.

Labeling: Details must be printed or sealed with indelible ink on the packages directly or on the original card of the producer. Labels must also be inserted inside the carton or package. The information on the label may be in two or more languages, as long as one is Arabic. The label must include the following information: the country of origin, the name of the manufacturer (and trademark, if any), the type and brand of product (and trademark, if any), technical data, international marks for handling and transportation, and production and expiration dates. There are several further labeling requirements for food products, meat, and poultry. Food products must be packed in sealed bags. If the product contains preservatives or artificial colors, the percentage of each must be indicated on the Analysis Certificate. All flavorings that conform under CODEX or WHO are approved in Egypt. In 1994, the government decreed that all food products should have at least 50 percent of the established shelf-life remaining at the time of importation into Egypt. Shipping documents must be authenticated at an Egyptian embassy or consulate in the country of origin. Contact the Commercial Office of the Egyptian Embassy (or Consulate) for details and update on labeling requirements.

Standards: Egypt is a member of ISO and adherence to ISO 9000 specifications is recommended. Import and export in Egypt are regulated by Law 118 of 1995. Annex (8) of the import/export regulations provides a lists of commodities subject to quality control inspection prior to admittance into Egypt. The list consists of about 135 product categories including foodstuffs, spare parts, construction products, electronic devices, appliances, and many consumer goods. Despite their earnest claims, Egyptian authorities are more strict in enforcing product standards on imported food products than on local food products. Importers face the problems of unclear product standards, and backlogs result from authorities having limited resources to conduct quality inspections. Contact the Commercial Office of the Egyptian Embassy (or Consulate) for details and update on product standards and requirements.

- **Payment**

Terms: The usual credit term is 30 to 60 days. A letter of credit is recommended.

Currency Exchange: Egypt operates a free-floating exchange-rate policy regime. There are no restrictions on fund conversion and transfer once there is supporting documentary evidence. Egyptian pounds are easily exchanged for dollars and most major European currencies.

Fund Transfer: Liberalized foreign exchange regulations since 1991 permit the free transfer abroad of profits and dividends. Invested capital may be repatriated without prior approval of the government's investment authority.

MARKETING TIPS

⑤

Mere selling or even waiting for customers is more familiar in Egypt than "marketing" as practiced in the U.S. However, there are a growing number of good Egyptian marketing firms. Although foreign firms may sell directly within Egypt, if they are registered to do so, most companies work with Egyptian firms. There are a wide variety of distributors, dealers, and agents from which to choose.

Agents and Distributors

A resident agent or distributor is strongly recommended. Egyptian law places a number of restrictions on commercial agents and importers. They must have Egyptian nationality. If the agent is a company, it must be 100 percent Egyptian owned. The commercial agency law is the most liberal in the Middle East from a foreigner's perspective. The law does not require exclusivity, however, most

Egyptians expect it. The law is also neutral about dispute settlement procedures and on the amount of commission due an agent. It is up to the parties to decide at the time of appointment of the agent and in advance of a dispute. Commission rates vary from 1 percent to 15 percent according to the type of product or service, volume of sales, and effort needed by the agent. To bid on civilian government tenders, an Egyptian commercial agent is typically required. To bid on military tenders, Egyptian "consultants" may be used if the arrangement is properly done. To bid on government tenders, only registered commercial agents can be used. Often these agents have retired from the government agency to which they now sell. When selecting a partner, also keep in mind that this is a culture in which age and experience are venerated. For help selecting a partner, contact the nearest Department of Commerce Export Assistance Center in the United States, or the Commerce Department's Trade Information Center at 1-800-USA-TRADE.

Establishing an Office

Because the newer laws have not wholly transformed the cumbersome bureaucracy of Egypt's past, the advice of legal and accounting firms is necessary. The biggest, ongoing challenge will be to learn what laws affect you and how you can cope with them. A list of legal, accounting, and auditing firms is available from the Commerce Department's stat-usa.gov online service.

Distribution and Sales Channels

Wholesalers, retail outlets, and agents or distributors are available to U.S. goods and services suppliers. There are a growing number of Egyptian firms with expertise in marketing products in which they specialize.

Direct Marketing

Foreign firms can sell directly within Egypt if they are registered to do so. Many do so as part of a manufacturing or assembly operation. A few foreign firms store their goods and

hire employees to sell door to door. However, other forms of direct marketing such as catalog sales or television sales are still problematic. The use of credit cards or checking accounts drawn on foreign banks is not common (though it is increasing). There is also the potential that goods will be stolen in the mail, lost in the airport warehouse, and subject to prohibitive customs duties.

Leasing/Joint Ventures

Egyptian entrepreneurs tend to welcome foreign partners in joint ventures, particularly since the foreign firm is seen to provide security and respectability. Legally, foreign equity in joint ventures may be set at any amount. The details of joint venture or licensing agreements are defined by contract, not special law. Profits, dividends, and invested capital can be freely repatriated. The biggest barrier to licensing in Egypt has been inadequate patent protection. However, this may change if a new patent law is passed. A draft of the law has been under debate within the government for several years.

Franchising

Franchising is an area of significant opportunity. The concept has gained acceptability, yet it is only in the fast-food sector that foreign firms have established many chains. Other areas of franchising are still largely unexplored. Furthermore, franchise representatives have unified under The International Franchise Committee in order to promote their industry and overcome bureaucratic barriers.

Advertising and Promotion

Newspaper and TV advertisements are typically effective. Other popular mediums for advertising are billboards, signs, mass mailings, and faxes. Trade shows are common and important, although most are often hastily organized, which causes difficulty for foreign firms. The grandfather of trade promotion events is the Cairo International Fair, held annually in the spring. See **Contacts** for a list of Egyptian marketing and advertising firms.

Selling

Traditional negotiations follow the Egyptian conventions of momarsas, the Arabic form of a Dutch auction. Under such conventions, it is assumed that the initial asking price will be high and that there is always room for further price reductions. Egyptians will often take pride in their ability to get the very best price from a buyer. However, the companies subjected to these negotiations often view them as opaque and unfair. Business groups and the U.S. Embassy succeeded in obtaining a ban on momarsas in June 1999. However, traditional conventions and assumptions remain. Comprehensive directories to goods and services are not widely available in Egypt's major cities. Thus it can be difficult for buyers to find what they want. In Cairo, for example, the size of the city, both in terms of population and area, can make it difficult for buyers to find sellers and vice versa. Trade shows and fairs are often the most convenient way for two parties to do business. However, the number of trade and commercial directories is on the rise.

Selling to the Government

Foreign firms deal directly with the client agency, which will use funds either from the national budget or from USAID and other international donors. For USAID-funded procurement, project announcements are made in the U.S. Commerce Business Daily, published in Chicago. Foreign bidders must submit public-sector tenders through an Egyptian commercial agent, except in the case of Ministry of Defense tenders. The tender regulations are written for the government's benefit and detailed obligations and responsibilities of the suppliers are provided. Thus foreign firms must negotiate a contract that provides necessary safeguards and specific information on the buyers' needs. Dispute resolution, in particular, should be negotiated before a contract is signed. Further, according to Tenders Law, the time limits for decisions and final payments are often vague or nonexistent.

Pricing

Price rather than quality is what tends to sell in Egypt, although this bias is changing, in part due to the recent revisions of tender law. It is often best to keep costs down by tailoring a product to a purchaser's specific needs. Quality is of more consideration with consumer goods. Further, for sales that are financed by USAID and other international donors, quality is often of high consideration.

Customer Support

A strong sales and service network is necessary. Without an effective support network, improper use or maintenance may cause the foreign supplier to be blamed. Recently, interest in total quality management has grown sharply.

Intellectual Property Rights (IPR)

The protection of intellectual property rights continues to be a concern for many U.S. businesses. Although the strengthening of IPR and the passage of a new patent law are expected, Egypt remains on the U.S. trade representatives' priority watch due to a lack of progress in these areas. Meanwhile, the U.S. provides significant support for Egypt's efforts, primarily through USAID-funded programs. Egypt is a signatory to the GATT TRIPS Agreement, the Bern Copyright Convention, the Paris Patent Convention, the Paris Convention for Protection of Industrial Property of 1883, the Madrid Convention of 1954, and the Nice Convention for the classification of goods and services.

Attorney

A local attorney is advisable to ensure compliance with employment laws and other matters. Contact the Commercial Office of the Egyptian Embassy (or Consulate) or the U.S. Department of Commerce Commercial Service for list of approved attorneys.

FOREIGN INVESTMENT
6

Openness: Sharp advancements have been made in recent years, and the encouragement of foreign investment is integral to Egypt's foreign policy and economic reform program. Procedures have been streamlined, and many limitations on foreign ownership have been relaxed. Law 95 of 1992 did much to modernize Egypt's capital markets. Further, many sharp legal distinctions between Egyptian and foreign firms have been eliminated. In response, foreign investment has grown strongly. However, obstacles to investment include bureaucracy, a shortage of skills in midlevel management, periodic shortfalls in credit facilities, inadequate property-rights protection, and nontariff trade barriers.

Regulatory System: Recent reforms have been promising, and investment procedures have been simplified. However, bureaucratic obstacles remain. Regulatory agencies often have overlapping areas of authority, and the enforcement of regulations can be uneven.

Investment Agreements: The U.S. and Egypt implemented a Bilateral Investment Treaty in 1992, which provides for fair treatment for investors of both nations. The treaty also includes provisions for international legal standards on expropriation and compensation, free financial transfers, and procedures for the settlement of investment disputes. On July 1, 1999, Egypt and the U.S. signed the Trade and Investment Framework Agreement (TIFA), which aims to create freer trade and to increase the amount of investment that flows between the two countries. Egypt also has signed investment agreements with a large number of developed and developing countries.

Trade Zones and Free Ports: There are eight active free zones, as established by the Council of Ministers: Nasr City (near Cairo Airport), Alexandria, Damietta, Ismailia, Suez, Port Said, Safaga, and Sohag. New extensions are being added to Port Said and Damietta, and new zones are planned in North Sinai and the Red Sea. Companies operating in free zones are exempt from customs duties, sales taxes, or taxes and fees on capital assets and intermediate goods.

Performance Requirements/Incentives: Performance requirements are not specified by Investment Law 8 of 1997. Assembly industries must meet a minimum local content requirement of 40 percent in order to benefit from customs tariff reductions on imported industrial inputs. The same law provides for a number of tax incentives to foreign companies, including a 5-, 10-, or 20-year tax exemption for many projects. Tax holidays are also granted for investments in designated areas. Because of heavy congestion in Cairo and other major centers, government officials often provide incentives to projects based outside major cities. Export subsidies do not exist, and the GOE does not impose export performance requirements.

Capital Markets and Investment: In 1998, the market capitalization of the Cairo and Alexandria Stock Exchange (CASE) was approximately US$ 26.9 billion, with 925 companies listed. These numbers are a testament to the considerable progress that has been made in modernizing Egypt's capital markets since the passage of Law 95 of 1992. In March 1999, Moody's Investors Service assigned a Baa1 rating to the domestic currency bonds issued by the GOE. In 1997, Standard and Poor's gave Egypt an investment grade rating of BBB-9. USAID/Cairo is working with GOE authorities and CASE in an ambitious, four-year, $32-million program for the development of the Egyptian capital market. The program's four major areas of concern are legal and regulatory reform, automation, institutional development, and debt market development.

Private Ownership: Investment Law 8 of 1997 allows 100 percent foreign ownership of the businesses under the scope of the legislation. The law also guarantees the right to remit income earned in Egypt and to repatriate capital.

Property Rights: Chattel and real property are legally supported, but with often thorny questions of land-ownership proof due to poor records. Mortgages exist. Ghana is implementing the WTO TRIPS (Trade-Related Aspects of Intellectual Property Rights) agreement.

Expropriation and Compensation: There have been no expropriation actions on the part of the government since the 1960s. Law 8 of 1997, section A1, provides guarantees against many types of confiscation, seizure, sequestration, and expropriation. The U.S.–Egypt Bilateral Investment Treaty also provides protection against expropriation.

OPIC and Investment Insurance: The U.S. Overseas Private Investment Corporation (OPIC), the U.S. Export-Import Bank (EXIM), and the U.S. Trade and Devel-

opment Agency are focusing increased attention on supporting U.S. trade and investment in Egypt. The U.S. Trade and Development Agency (TDA) has provided $35 million in funding for feasibility studies, orientation visits, training grants, and conferences. The U.S. Export-Import Bank is an independent U.S. government agency that finances the overseas sales of U.S. goods and services. USAID's Commodity Import Program (CIP) is a substantial source of support for U.S. imports.

Dispute Settlement: Recent laws and amendments have streamlined the rules for dispute settlement. Egyptian law recognizes the right of investors to settle disputes within the framework of bilateral agreements, the International Center for the Settlement of Investment Disputes (ICSID), or through arbitration before the Regional Center for International Commercial Arbitration in Cairo. The U.S.–Egypt Bilateral Investment Treaty also provides for nonbinding, third-party arbitration in investment disputes. Disputes involving U.S. individuals or companies do exist. These cases can involve lengthy court proceedings and negotiations. The government has not always honored compensation requirements.

FINANCE

⑦

Key aspects of the economic reform plan are the privatization of banks and insurance companies. An upgrading of the Egyptian stock market has also been a priority. The banking system is highly liquid, and this is the major source of financing for projects in Egypt. Four state-owned commercial banks continue to dominate the banking market, while several U.S. banks have offices in Egypt. Financing may also be available from the emerging securities market and from a number of donor-

assistance credit lines. Loan rates averaged between 12 and 14 percent in 1996. Small investors without the right business connections and collateral have found it difficult to start up projects in Egypt. The Social Fund for Development provides banks with funds for loans to small-scale enterprises. The Credit Guarantee Company also assists small enterprises, and the World Bank offers opportunities to U.S. companies with projects in developing countries.

Export Financing: U.S. exporters typically rely on letters of credit from Egyptian buyers. These letters are arranged by the buyers through Egyptian banks and are confirmed irrevocably by a U.S. bank. Other financing sources include USAID's Private Sector Commodity Import Program. PSCIP makes available dollars to Egyptian banks, which then lend to Egyptian importers, to the U.S. Export-Import Bank (EXIM), and, for investors, to the U.S. Overseas Private Investment Corporation (OPIC). Multilateral banks and funds do not provide export financing to Egyptian exporters. An African Export-Import Bank (AFREXIM) began operation in early 1995 and offers low-cost financing for foreign and intra-African trade.

Project Financing: Banks are the main source of project finance, although investors have also

begun to consider the stock and bond markets. Banks are highly liquid in both the local currency and in foreign exchange. Banks do compete to finance credible, well-known clients. Although loan demand is high, actual borrowing is low because of restrictive collateral requirements and high loan rates. Egyptian pound lending rates have fallen considerably from a peak of 22 percent in 1991 and 1992 to an average of 12 to 14 percent in 1996, while the prime lending rate is much lower. The securities market began its revitalization in the early 1990s. Wider use of bonds is further expected in the coming year. U.S. Export-Import Bank loans and guarantees are available although rates are comparatively high. Smaller investors without strong business connections may turn to the Social Fund for Development.

COMMUNICATIONS ⑧

Phone

The telecommunications network offers many services, including cellular, paging, videoconferencing, voice mail, and Internet services. Total telephone lines number some 3,168 million in 1996; 70,000 digital cellular subscribers in 1998; and 7,400 analog cellular phone subscribers, large by third-world standards but inadequate for present-day requirements. From the United States, dial the international long-distance access code (011), then the country code (20). The city codes for some of the major cities are Cairo (2), Alexandria (3), Aswan (94), Port Said (66), Mahalla Al Kubra (40), Tanta (40), Luxor (95). Seek operator assistance for other city routing codes.

Internet

The number of subscribers is rapidly increasing. According to a USAID study: "The Internet as a Tool for Egypt's Economic Growth," the estimated number of users increased from 40,000 in 1997 to 100,000 in 1998. Currently, there are an estimated 50,000 Internet subscribers and 250,000 Internet users. The government hopes to increase the number of users to one million in the near future. Contact the Commercial Office of the Egyptian Embassy (or Consulate) for additional information.

Mail

The postal mailing system is reasonably well developed although some street names and numbers may not be well defined. Express mail international services are available between Egypt and the U.S.

TRANSPORTATION

Land

Alexandria and Cairo are connected by the Western Desert Highway, a high-speed toll road, as well as by the busier Delta Road. Buses take three-and-a-half hours. A nonstop Turbino train takes just over two hours. Cairo's Metro is a light rail that runs partially underground and consists of three main lines. Cairo's black-and-white taxis are inexpensive although it takes some practice and basic Arabic phrases to use them well. It may help to carry a map. The cost is better negotiated beforehand, and the age and size of the taxi does matter.

Sea

Shipping lines that serve Port Said and Alexandria (the largest port on the Mediter-ranean) are Adriatica, Ferrel, Lykes, Ogden, Prudential, and American President Lines. Egypt has its own merchant fleet.

Air

Egypt is an important air terminus for the Middle East, and Cairo is served by many major airlines. Major airports are in Alexandria, Aswan, Cairo, Hurghada, Luxor and Sharm al-Sheikh. TWA flies direct to and from the U.S. Northwest, United, and Delta have code-sharing agreements with European airlines. Other major international airlines represented in Cairo include: Air France, Alitalia, British Airways, Egypt Air, Japan Airlines, and Swissair.

WORK WEEK

Business Hours: The workweek runs from Saturday through Wednesday. No business is conducted on Friday, the Muslim holy day. Most Egyptians also do not work on Thursdays. Although business hours vary widely, a typical schedule would be 8 a.m. to 2 p.m. in the summer, and 9 a.m. to 1 p.m. and 5 p.m. to 7 p.m. in the winter

Government Hours: Government hours are 8 a.m. to 2 p.m. Government offices are closed on either Thursday and Friday or Friday and Saturday. (The variation is meant to help with traffic congestion.)

Bank Hours: Banks are typically open from 8:30 a.m. to 1:30 p.m. Monday through Thursday, with some banks keeping Sunday morning hours from 10 a.m. to 12 a.m. Most international hotels offer 24-hour banking services.

During the month of Ramadan, working hours are shortened for businesses, banks, and government offices.

HOLIDAYS 2001

New Year's Day, January
Christmas (Eastern Orthodox), January 7
Wakfet Arafet/First Day of Eid al Adha,
  March 4*
Islamic New Year, March 26*
Easter (Eastern Orthodox), April 15
Sham El Nessin (Welcoming Spring Day),
  April 16**
Sinai Liberation Day, April 25
Labor Day, May 1
Mawled El-Nabi (Prophet's Birthday), June 4*
Bank Holiday, July 1
National Day, July 23
Armed Forces Day, October 6
Suez Victory Day, October 24

First Day of Eid al Fitr, December *
Eid al-Fitr (End of Ramadan Fasting Month
  2001), December 18-19*

Some holidays may be observed on different dates depending on the day of the week on which it falls. Certain holidays are based on the lunar calendar and change every year. As in most Muslim countries, business appointments are difficult to make during the month of Ramadan.

*Depends on the lunar calendar; a difference of a day may occur.

**Sham El Nessim changes with the Coptic calendar.

BUSINESS TRAVEL

Business Customs

Business in Egypt is personal. Some international executives are very familiar with Western business customs, but on the whole, business is run in a unique way. Meetings may begin late and seem to run in a disorderly fashion; they will often begin with small talk and conversation, then draw to a close after coffee is served. Some knowledge of Egyptian culture, the Islamic faith, and basic Arabic phrases is a must. It may not be wise to initiate the topics of Israel and women (even wives and daughters) as subjects of conversation. Errors for foreigners to avoid include showing the heal of the shoes; gesturing or passing something with preference given to the left hand; and causing someone public embarrassment since saving face is always a consideration. In business dealings, patience and flexibility are required. Decisions are not made quickly. Unfamiliar processes and bureaucratic procedures can slow business activities down. Egyptians can be highly expressive and talk at a close distance. A mild "yes" can often mean "maybe" or even "no." Business cards should be printed in English on one side and Arabic on the other. A good Egyptian agent would be a helpful navigator. Note that, in choosing your representatives, age and experience are respected.

Travel Advisory and Visas

Egypt is a developing country with extensive facilities for tourists. A passport and visa are required. If traveling by air, a renewable 30-day visa can be purchased on entry for US$ 15. If arriving by land or sea, the visa must be obtained in advance. Evidence of an AIDS test is required for anyone staying over 30 days. Contact the Egyptian embassy (see **Contacts**) for more information. Terrorist attacks have declined in recent years, but it is important to remain aware. In prior years, most attacks took place in the Nile Valley governates of Minya, Assiut, Sohag, and Qena. Prior to travel in these areas, U.S. citizens are urged to seek advice from the Consular Section of the U.S. Embassy. Care and advice should also be taken when traveling off-road or near Egypt's frontiers. Leftover landmines have caused several deaths. Egypt's crime rate is low. Violence is rare although petty theft is not uncommon. Unescorted women may be harassed and verbally abused. Drug enforcement is extremely strict. The possession of small quantities of drugs is a serious offence, while smuggling convictions can be met with the death penalty. Nonemergency medical facilities are adequate in popular areas although immediate payment in cash is often required. The U.S Embassy in Cairo can provide a list of local hospitals with English-speaking physicians. Emergency and intensive-care facilities are limited. It is advised that you check with your insurance company before traveling. There is some risk of infections, hepatitis, and disease from river water. There is also a small risk of Rift Valley Fever (RVF), a mosquito-borne disease. Thoroughly cooked meat in tourist hotels is considered safe. Uncooked vegetables can cause traveler's diarrhea. Tap water is not potable. Computer peripherals, such as printers and modems, are subject to customs fees. Duties on photographic and video equipment may be imposed, but this is typically done only for large quantities. The roads in Egypt can be hazardous. Be especially cautious at night outside the major cities, where vehicles often travel with few or no lights.

Business Infrastructure

Entry Requirements (personal and professional goods): Contact the Egyptian consulate for additional information.

Currency Exchange: The pound (£E) is the main currency. There are 100 piastres in a pound. The exchange rate has remained rather steady at £E 3.4 to US$ 1.

Taxes: See **Regulations.**

Hotels and Restaurants: Most of the major hotel chains have facilities in big cities.

Housing: Representative monthly costs for acceptable furnished housing in Cairo and Alexandria are: 2 bedroom apartment $1,500 and up, 3 bedroom apartment $2,000 and up 4 bedroom apartment $3,200 approx. 5 bedroom apartment $4,700 approx. Villa/house $5,200 and up.

Utilities: Electric power is 50 cycles, 1 and 3 phase, with nominal voltage of 220 volts in the largest cities.

Business Services: See **Marketing.**

Labor Costs and Legislation: See **Labor** in **Economic Outlook.**

Literacy: Age 15 and over can read and write: 51.4% (1995 est.).

Travel Notes

The following travel notes have been supplied by the U.S. government. For the most recent general travel and consular information, see the U.S. Department of State travel publications or call the Traveler's Telephone Hotline at (202) 647-5225.

Health Precautions: Nonemergency medical facilities are adequate in popular areas although immediate payment in cash is often required. The U.S Embassy in Cairo can provide a list of local hospitals with English-speaking physicians. Emergency and intensive-care facilities are limited. It is advised that you check with your insurance company before traveling. There is some risk of infections, hepatitis, and disease from river water. There is also a small risk of Rift Valley Fever (RVF), a mosquito-borne disease. Thoroughly cooked meat in tourist hotels is considered safe. Uncooked vegetables can cause traveler's diarrhea. Tap water is not potable. Current information on health matters may be obtained from the Centers for Disease Control and Prevention's international travelers' hotline at (404) 332-4559.

Embassy Assistance

To obtain additional and updated information on entry and exit requirements, travelers can contact the Consular Section of the Embassy of Egypt at 3521 International Court, N.W., Washington, D.C. 20008; Tel: (202) 966-6342. Travelers may also contact the nearest Egypt consulate. They are located in Chicago, Houston, New York, and San Francisco.

Business travelers are encouraged to obtain a copy of the Key Officers of Foreign Service Posts: Guide for Business Representatives, available for sale by the Superintendent of Documents, U.S. Government Printing Office, Washington, D.C. 20402; Tel (202) 512-1800; Fax (202) 512-2250.

CONTACTS 13

U.S. Contacts in Egypt

American Chamber of Commerce in Egypt
33 Soliman Abaza St. Mohandessin, Cairo
Tel: 338-1050
Fax: 338-1060
Email: info@amcham.org.eg

American Chamber of Commerce in Alexandria
36 Bani Abbas St.
Alexandria
Tel: 482-9904
Fax: 492-2861

American Mideast Educational & Training Services, Inc. (AMIDEAST)
23 Mossadak St., Dokki, Giza
Tel: 337-8265
Fax: 355-2946

American Research Center in Egypt (ARCE)
2 Kasr El Doubara Sq., Garden City, Cairo
Tel: 354-8239
Fax: 355-3052

American University in Cairo (AUC)
113 Kasr El Aini St.
Cairo
Tel: 354-2964 (nine lines)
Fax: 355-7565

CARE
18 Hoda Sharaawi St. (1st floor) Cairo
Tel: 393-5262
Fax: 393-5650

Catholic Relief Services (CRS)
13 Ibrahim Naguib St. (1st floor) Garden City, Cairo
Tel: 354-1360; 356-0091
Fax: 355-8034

Ford Foundation
Middle East & North Africa
1 Osiris St.
Garden City, Cairo
Tel: 355-2121; 354-4450; 354-9635
Fax: 355-4018

Fulbright Commission
1081 Corniche El Nil St., Belmont Bldg.
Cairo
Tel: 354-4799; 354-8679
Fax: 355-7893

Community Services Association (CSA)
4 Road 21, Maadi
Tel: 350-0764
Fax: 376-8319

Int'l Executive Service Corps. (IESC)
Al Boustan Commercial Center, Suite 1 (10th
   floor)
Al Boustan St.
Bab El Louk, Cairo
Tel: 390-3232
Fax: 390-2929

Project Hope
86 Mohi El Din Aboul Ezz St. Mohandessin,
   Cairo
Tel: 348-0915; 360-6295
Fax: 360-6295

Women's Association
21 Boulos Hanna St.
Dokki, Cairo
Tel: 360-3457

Egyptian Government Contacts

Minister & Minister of Planning
Magles El Shaab St.
Kasr El Aini St.
Cairo
Tel: 391-0008; 390-9749
Fax: 390-8159

Ministry of Planning
Minister of State for Planning & International
   Cooperation
Salah Salem Road
Nasr City, Cairo
Tel: 401-4615; 602-935; 601-215; 601-416
Fax: 263-4747

**Ministry of Agriculture, Animal & Fish Wealth
 & Land Reclamation**
Prime Minister & Minister
Nadi El Seid St., Dokki, Giza
Tel: 702-677; 702-596; 702-758
Fax: 703-889; 704-660

Ministry of Social Affairs and Insurance
H.E. Mrs. Mervat El Tallawi, Minister
El Sheikh Rihan St., Bab El Louk, Cairo
Tel: 354-2900
Fax: 917-799

**Ministry of Transport, Communications and
   Civil Aviation**
H.E. Eng. Suliman Metwalli, Minister
105 Kasr El Aini St., Cairo
Tel: 354-3623
Fax: 355-5564

Ministry of Electricity and Energy
H.E. Eng. Mohamed Maher Abaza, Minister
Abbassia, Nasr City, Cairo
Tel: 261-6299; 261-6514; 261-6317
Fax: 261-6302

Ministry of Information
Maspero, Corniche El Nil, Cairo
Tel: 747-193; 749-394; 747-416
Fax: 757-144

Ministry of Foreign Affairs
Maspero, Corniche El Nil, Cairo
Tel: 354-1414; 354-2215
Fax: 354-6285

Ministry of Supply and Trade
99 Kasr El Aini St., Cairo
Tel: 355-0360
Fax: 354-4973

Ministry of Finance
Lazoughly Square, Justice & Finance Bldg.,
   Cairo
Tel: 355-7027; 354-1055; 355-7136; 354-0601
Fax: 354-5433

Ministry of Awqaf (Religious Trusts)
Sabry Abou Alam St.
Bab El Louk, Cairo
Tel: 392-6163; 392-6305
Fax: 392-6305

Ministry of Justice
H.E. Counselor Farouk Seif El Nasr, Minister
Lazoughly Square, Justice & Finance Bldg.
Cairo
Tel: 355-1176; 355-7592; 355-8103
Fax: 355-8103

Ministry of Culture
2 Shagaret El Dor St.
Zamalek, Cairo
Tel: 341-5568; 341-5495
Fax: 340-6449

Ministry of Cabinet Affairs
1 Magles El Shaab St.
Cairo
Tel: 354-1722
Fax: 355-6306

Ministry of Rural Development
4 Shooting Club St.
Dokki, Cairo
Tel: 349-7470; 349-7656
Fax: 349-7785

Ministry of Education
Minister
4 Ibrahim Naguib St.
Garden City, Cairo
Tel: 355-7952; 355-2155; 354-6039; 356-8396
Fax: 356-2952; 354-2163

Ministry of Higher Education & Scientific Research
4 Ibrahim Naguib St.
Garden City, Cairo
Tel: 355-7952; 355-2155; 354-6039; 356-8396
Fax: 356-2952; 354-2163

Ministry of Petroleum
El Mokhayyam El Da'em St.
Nasr City, Cairo
Tel: 262-2268; 262-2269; 262-2237; 262-2238; 263-1000
Fax: 263-6060

Ministry of Interior
H.E. Gen. Habib El Adly, Minister
El Sheikh Rihan St., Bab El Louk, Cairo
Tel: 354-5897; 354-8307; 355-7500
Fax: 355-7792

Ministry of Economy
8 Adly St.
Cairo
Tel: 390-6796; 390-6804; 391-9661
Fax: 390-3029

Ministry of Reconstruction, Housing & New Urban Communities
1 Ismail Abaza St., off Kasr El Aini
Cairo
Tel: 354-0419; 355-3320; 355-7978
Fax: 355-7836

People's Assembly & Shura Council Affairs
Magles El Shaab St.
Cairo
Tel: 354-3000; 354-3116
Fax: 354-8977

Ministry of Tourism
Minister
Abassia Square, Borg Misr Travel Cairo
Tel: 282-8457; 282-8456; 282-9778
Fax: 282-8771

Ministry of Water Resources & Public Works
H.E. Mahmoud Abu Zaid, Minister
El Nil St., Embaba, Cairo
Tel: 354-5884; 354-1478
Fax: 355-8008

Ministry of Health & Population
Minister
Magles El Shaab St.
Cairo
Tel: 354-1076; 354-3462; 354-0426
Fax: 355-3966

Ministry of Industry & Mineral Wealth
H.E. Eng. Soliman Reda, Minister
2 Latin America St.
Garden City, Cairo
Tel: 354-3600, 355-7034, 355-4826
Fax: 354-8362

Ministry of Defense & Military Production
H.E. Field Marshal Mohamed Hussein Tantawi, Minister
5 Ismail Abaza St., Cairo
Tel: 355-3063, 354-7487, Fax: 354-8739

Ministry of Defense & Military Production
Minister of State for Military Production
23 July St., Kobri El Kobba, Cairo
Tel: 263-5681, Fax: 291-6227, 824-086

Ministry of Manpower & Immigration
3 Youssef Abbas St., Nasr City, Cairo
Tel: 260-9362; 260-9363

Ministry of Public Enterprises
Magles El Shaab St., Cairo
Tel: 355-8026; 355-0164
Fax: 355-3606

Ministry of Environmental Affairs

H.E. Nadia Riad Makram Ebeid, Minister
30 Misr Helwan Agricultural Road, Behind
  Sofitel Hotel, Maadi, Cairo
Tel: 525-6463; 525-6472; 378-5137;
351-0970; 375-3215
Fax: 375-5438; 378-4285

Cairo Governorate

Governor of Cairo
Abdin, Cairo
Tel: 590-8591; 593-7050

Alexandria Governorate

Governor of Alexandria
Alexandria
Tel: 482-5800; 482-5805

Egyptian Government Agencies

Arab Organization for Industrialization (AOI)

Ret. Marshal Salah Halaby, Chairman
2D Midan El Abbassia, Cairo
Tel: 482-3377; 932-395; 932-822; 591-8244
Fax: 482-6010

Telecom Egypt

Ministry of Transport, Communications &
  Civil Aviation
Ramses St.
Cairo
Tel: 574-4909; 777-551; 777-566; 760-333
Fax: 574-4244

Central Agency for Public Mobilization & Statistics (CAPMAS)

Salah Salem St.
Nasr City, Cairo
Tel: 402-4110; 402-3191
Fax: 604-099

Capital Market Authority

20 Emad El Din St.
Cairo
Tel: 777-774; 762-626
Fax: 575-5339

Central Bank of Egypt

31 Kasr El Nil St.
Cairo
Tel: 392-3679; 392-6211; 393-1514
Fax: 392-5045

Customs Authority

4 El Tayaran St.
Nasr City, Cairo
Tel: 260-5710; 604-402; 608-683
Fax: 261-2672

Taxation Authority

5 Hussein Hegazi St.
Cairo
Tel: 355-7784

Sales Tax Authority

4 El Tayaran St.
Nasr City, Cairo
Tel: 260-7500; 260-7501
Fax: 260-7501

Egyptian Tourist Authority (ETA)

Misr Travel Bldg.
bbassia, Cairo
Tel: 482-0283
Fax: 483-0844

New Community Authority

Housing Bldg., 1 Ismail Abaza St. Cairo
Tel: 355-7978; 355-3320
Fax: 355-7836

Egyptian General Petroleum Corp. (EGPC)

Eng. Abdel Khalek Ayad, Chairman
Palestine St. (4th sector)
New Maadi, Cairo
Tel: 353-1441; 353-1438; 353-1439; 377-1489
Fax: 353-1570 (ext. 4177)

General Authority for Export & Import Control (GOEIC)

Atlas Building, El Sheikh Maarouf &
  1 Ramses St.
Cairo
Tel: 574-2830; 575-6095; 575-6031

General Authority for Investment & Free Zones (GAFI)

Cairo
Tel: 390-0597; 390-7240; 390-3776;
  391-6029; 390-5627
Fax: 390-7315

General Authority for Int'l Fairs & Exhibitions (GOIEF)
Fair Grounds
Nasr City, Cairo
Tel: 260-7811; 260-7815
Fax: 260-7845

General Organization for Industrialization (GOFI)
Eng. Mohamed Mahmoud Farag Abdel Wahab, Chairman
6 Khalil Agha St.
Garden City, Cairo
Tel: 354-0678; 354-4640; 355-7005
Fax: 354-4984

Immigration & Egyptians Abroad Administration
Behind the Tirsana Sporting Club
Sahafeyeen, Cairo
Tel: 303-4438; 303-4439
Fax: 303-6433

Public Enterprise Office
2 Latin America St. (6th floor) Garden City, Cairo
Tel: 355-9253
Fax: 355-9233

Stock Exchange
El Borsa St., Downtown, Cairo
Tel: 392-1402
Fax: 392-8526

Egyptian Radio & TV Union (ERTU)
TV Bldg.
Corniche El Nil, Cairo
Tel: 749-508; 760-454
Fax: 574-6989

Social Fund for Development
Hussein Hegazy St. & Kasr El Nil Sts., Cairo
Tel: 354-8339
Fax: 355-0628

Information & Decision Support Center (IDSC)
Cabinet Bldg., Magles El Shaab St.
Cairo
Tel: 356-1600
Fax: 354-1222

General Authority for Supply Commodities
99 Kasr El Aini St., Cairo
Tel: 356-0766
Fax: 356-1255

Egyptian Environmental Affairs Agency (EEAA)
30 Misr Helwan Agricultural Road, behined Sofitel Hotel, Maadi,
Cairo
Tel: 375-3215
Fax: 378-4285

Egyptian Export Promotion Center (EEPC)
106 Gameat El Dowal El Arabia St. (5th floor)
Mohandessin,
Giza
Tel: 349-3919; 349-3920; 349-3921; 349-3922; 700-037; 348-4056
Fax: 348-4142

Egyptian Export Promotion Association
14 Geziret El Arab St., Mohandessin,
Cairo
Tel: 345-4277
Fax: 345-4523

Commercial Representation Office
96 Ahmed Orabi St., Mohandessin,
Cairo
Tel: 347-1892; 347-1893; 347-1894; 347-1895; 347-1896
Fax: 345-1840

Suez Canal Authority
Marshall Ahmed Ali Fadel, Chairman
6 Lazoghly St.
Garden City, Cairo
Tel: 354-0749; 354-0748; 354-0746

EgyptAir
Eng. Mohamed Fahim Rayyan, Chairman
Cairo Int'l Airport, Cairo
Tel: 245-4400; 245-5099; 245-0270; 290-9787; 267-4500
Fax: 418-3715

Egyptian Trade Associations and Chambers of Commerce

Egyptian Trade Associations

Alexandria Business Association (ABA)
C/O Ragab Exp. & Imp. Co.
18 Avenue El Horria St.
Alexandria
Tel: 20-3-482-5518
Fax: 20-3-482-9576

Assiut Business Association (ASBA)
Al Shark Insurance Tower, El Geish St.
Assiut
Tel: 20-88-341-766
Fax: 20-88-341-755

Borg El Arab Business Association
Eng. M. Faragalla Amer
First Industrial Zone
Borg El Arab
Tel: 20-3-974-040; 545-0200
Fax: 20-3-546-5200; 546-4855

Mansoura Businessmen Association
Dakahlia Governorate
Mobil Oil Station, Sabry Abu Alam St.
Mansoura
Tel: 20-50-332-347; 328-711
Fax: 20-50-332-348

Egypt–U.S. Business Council
21 Giza St., Nile Tower Bldg.
Giza
Tel: 20-2-573-6030
Fax: 20-2-573-7258

Egypt's International Economic Forum
Semiramis InterContinental Hotel, Suite 405
Tel: 20-2-357-1761
Fax: 20-2-357-1757

Egyptian American Friendship Association
83 Ramsis St. (2nd floor)
Cairo
Tel: 20-2-575-2211; 391-5627
Fax: 20-2-390-7315; 395-3322

Egyptian Export Promotion Center (EEPC)
106 Gameat El Dowal El Arabia St. (5th floor)
Mohandessin, Giza
Tel: 20-2-349-3919; 20-2-349-3920;
 20-2-349-3921
Fax: 20-2-348-4142

Egyptian Export Promotion Association
14 Geziret El Arab St., Mohandessin, Cairo
Tel: 20-2-345-4277
Fax: 20-2-345-4523

Egyptian Businessmen Association (EBA)
Secretary General
21 Giza St., Nile Tower
Giza
Tel: 20-2-573-6030
Fax: 20-2-573-7258

Egyptian Small Enterprise Development Association (ESED)
13 Salem Salem St., El Agouza
Giza
Tel: 20-2-336-3980; 336-3982; 336-3984
Fax: 20-2-336-3985

Egyptian Junior Businessmen Group
2 Sherif St., El Lewa Bldg. (5th floor) Apt. 58
Cairo
Tel: 20-2-392-4089; 393-2203
Fax: 20-2-392-4089

Egyptian Federation for Consumer Protection Associations (EFCA)
Prof. Hassan Gemei, Secretary General
Faculty of Law, Cairo University
14 Nagi Farid St., off Mohiedin Aboulezz
Mohandessin, Cairo
Tel/Fax: 20-2-360-1558; 336-8442

Sadat City Business Association
8 El Sad El Aali St., Dokki
Cairo
Tel: 20-2-360-0150; 20-2-360-7355;
049-201-614; 049-202-929

Sharkeya Business Association (SBA)
El Galaa St.
Zagazig
Tel: 20-55-326-407; 20-55-349-981;
20-55-326-408
Fax: 20-55-328-308

Sixth of October Investors Union
6th of October, First Industrial Zone
Giza
Tel: 20-22-231-590; 20-22-231-591;
   20-22-231-592; 20-11-332-555;
   20-11-330-220
Fax: 20-11-231-593

**Small Enterprise Development Association
   (SEDA)**
El Bareed Bldg., El Geish & Mohamed
   Mahmoud St.
Port Said
Tel: 20-66-336-452; 20-66-336-453
Fax: 20-66-336-454

Tenth of Ramadan Business Association
10th of Ramadan City
District 9, PO Box 73
Cairo
Tel: 20-15-340-1508; 20-15-340-5885
Fax: 20-15-363-614

**The Egyptian Exporters Association
   (EXPOLINK)**
23 El Esraa St.
Mohandessin, Cairo
Tel: 20-2-346-1482
Fax: 20-2-345-0783

Egyptian Chambers of Commerce
(Affiliated with the Federation of Egyptian
   Chambers of Commerce)

**Federation of Egyptian Chambers of
   Commerce**
4 Falaky Square
Cairo
Tel: 20-2-355-1136;
   1164; 1813; 395-8041; 395-8042
Fax: 20-2-355-7940; 395-8043

Alexandria Chamber of Commerce
31 Chamber of Commerce St.
Alexandria
Tel: 20-3-480-8434, 480-8355
Fax: 480-8993

Assiut Chamber of Commerce
El Khidewi Ismail St.
Assiut
Tel: 20-88-3220-82

Aswan Chamber of Commerce
Abtal El Tahreer St.
Aswan
Tel: 20-97-323-084; 322-983

Beni Suef Chamber of Commerce
Rayad St.
Beni Suef
Tel: 20-82-322-094; 322-090; 323-489

Cairo Chamber of Commerce
4 Midan El Falaki
Cairo
Tel: 20-2-355-8261; 20-2-355-8262
Fax: 20-2-356-3603

Dakahleya Chamber of Commerce
El Bahr St., Midan Saleh Ayoub
El Mansoura
Tel: 20-50-322-720, 320-670
Fax: 20-50-320-670

Damietta Chamber of Commerce
Saad Zaghloul St.
Damietta
Tel: 20-57-322-799; 323-177; 322679
Fax: 20-57-320-632

El Wadi El Gedid Chamber of Commerce
El Khargah
Tel: 20-88-901-528

El Arish Chamber of Commerce
El Saha El Shabiya St., El Arish
Sinai
Tel: 20-64-340-327

El Menia Chamber of Commerce
El Tegara St.
El Menia
Tel: 20-86-323-232
Fax: 20-86-323-232

El Fayoum Chamber of Commerce
El Nadi El Reyadi St.
El Fayoum
Tel: 20-84-322-148; 323-439

El Kaliobia Chamber of Commerce
El Moderia St., Midan Saad Zaghloul
Banha
Tel: 20-13-323-177

El Menofia Chamber of Commerce
Sidy Fayed St.
Shebeen El Koum
Tel: 20-48-321-511; 32-916; 321-718

El Beheira Chamber of Commerce
Midan El Seah, El Gomhouria St.
Damanhour
Tel: 20-45-322-207

El Giza Chamber of Commerce
6 El Ghorfa El Tegarya St.
Giza
Tel: 20-2-572-1761
Fax: 20-2-568-3971

Gharbeya Chamber of Commerce
Said Pasha St.
Tanta
Tel: 20-40-324-090; 33-203
Fax: 20-40-323-793

Ismailia Chamber of Commerce
163 Saad Zaghloul St.
Ismailia
Tel: 20-64-221-663; 228-700; 225-380
Fax: 20-64-322-515

Kafr El Sheikh Chamber of Commerce
El Zawy Bldg.
Kafr El Sheikh
Tel: 20-47-322-916

Kena Chamber of Commerce
El Gamil Street
Kena
Tel: 20-96-322-690; 322-656

Matrouh Chamber of Commerce
Marsa Matrouh
Tel: 20-3-935-864; 943-819; 943-887

Port Said Chamber of Commerce
Benayet Souk El Goumla
Port Said
Tel: 20-66-222-733; 236-141
Fax: 20-66-236-141

Sharkia Chamber of Commerce
El Montaza Street
El Zagazig
Tel: 20-55-322-423; 322-329; 323-332
Fax: 20-55-349-744

Sohag Chamber of Commerce
El Kesaria El Sharki Street
Sohag
Tel: 20-93-323-036

Suez and South Sinai Chamber of Commerce
47 Salah Eldin Elayoubi St.
Suez
Tel: 20-62-227-783

The Red Sea Chamber of Commerce
Old City Council Bldg.
Hurghada
Tel: 20-62-440-761

Other Chambers of Commerce in Egypt

American Chamber of Commerce in Alexandria
36 Bani Abbas
Alexandria
Tel: 20-3-482-9904
Fax: 20-3-492-2861

American Chamber of Commerce in Egypt
33 Soliman Abaza St., Zamalek Cairo
Tel: 20-2-338-1050
Fax: 20-2-338-1060

German-Arab Chamber of Commerce in Egypt
3 Abul Feda St., Zamalek
Cairo
Tel: 20-2-341-3664
Fax: 20-2-341-3663

Greek–Arab Chamber of Commerce in Egypt
17 Soliman El Halabi St.
Cairo
Tel: 20-2-392-1190
Fax: 20-2-392-4970

Italian–Arab Chamber of Commerce in Egypt
33 Abdel Khalek Sarwat St.
Cairo
Tel: 20-2-392-2275
Fax: 20-2-391-2503

Japanese Foreign Trade Organization
56 Gameat El Dowal El Arabia St.
Mohandessin, Cairo
Tel: 20-2-574-1111
Fax: 20-2-756-966

Egyptian Chambers of Industries
(Members of the Federation of Egyptian
 Industries)

Federation of Egyptian Industries
11 Akaba St.
Dokki, Cairo
Tel: 20-2-392-8366; 20-2-392-8319;
 20-2-392-8317; 20-2-348-7909
Fax: 20-2-348-8502

Chamber of Building Materials Industries
23 Sherif St.
Cairo
Tel: 20-2-392-8820

Chamber of Cereals & Products Industries
65 El Horria Avenue
Alexandria
Tel: 20-3-491-6121
Fax: 20-3-491-6121

Chamber of Chemical Industries
5 El Tolombat St., Garden City
Cairo
Tel: 20-2-356-2633; 20-2-355-4006
Fax: 20-2-356-4597

Chamber of Cinema Industry
33 Orabi St.
Cairo
Tel: 20-2-741-677; 20-2-741-638
Fax: 20-2-751-583

Chamber of Engineering Industries
13 Sherif St.
Cairo
Tel: 20-2-393-8904
Fax: 20-2-392-1238

Chamber of Food Industries
4 Gamal Eldin Aboul Mahasen St.,
Garden City
Cairo
Tel: 20-2-356-0612; 356-0659
Fax: 20-2-354-9502

Chamber of Leather Industry
26a Sherif St., Immobilia Bldg. (2nd floor)
Cairo
Tel: 20-2-393-8294
Fax: 20-2-392-8140

Chamber of Metallurgical Industries
13 Sherif St.
Cairo
Tel: 20-2-392-8238
Fax: 20-2-392-1238

Chamber of Petroleum & Mining
26a Sherif St.
Cairo
Tel: 20-2-392-6462

Chamber of Printing, Binding and Paper
 Products
19 Mariet St., Abdel Moneim Riad Sq.,
 El Tahrir
Cairo
Tel: 20-2-578-6709
Fax: 20-2-575-0419

Chamber of Tanning, Leather &
 Fur Industries
26a Sherif St., Immobilia Bldg.
Cairo
Tel: 20-2-392-8140
Fax: 20-2-393-8294

Chamber of Textile Industries
(Egyptian Textile Manufacturers Federation,
 ETMF)
14 Geziret El Arab St. Mohandessin, Cairo
Tel: 20-2-345-4277
Fax: 20-2-346-9196

Chamber of Woodworking Industries
23 Sherif St. (2nd floor)
Cairo
Tel: 20-2-392-8820
Fax: 20-2-392-8366

Egyptian Market Research Firms

Tarek Nour Communications
32h Radwan Ibn Tabib St.,
Giza, Cairo
Tel: 573-0855; 573-0602
Fax: 573-3550

Fiani & Partners
Mrs. Josse Dorra Fiani
143 Tahrir Street
Dokki, Cairo
Tel: 348-7353; 348-7354; 348-7355; 348-7356
Fax: 348-5204

Intermarkets Advertising
42 Abdel Moneim Riad St.
Dokki, Cairo
Tel: 360-3017; 360-3018
Fax: 360-3019

International Business Associates (IBA)
Mrs. Ann Marie Harrison, Chairman
1079 Corniche El Nil
Garden City, Cairo
Tel: 357-1312; 357-1372; 357-1300
Fax: 357-1317; 357-1318

Marketeers
52 Youssef Abbas St.
Nasr City, Cairo
Tel: 262-2810
Fax: 262-2810

Middle East Marketing Research Bureau
21 Dr. Mohamed Gomaa St.
Heliopolis, Cairo
Tel: 240-1799
Fax: 249-7099

Rac
39 Gameat El Dowal El Arabia St.
Mohandessin, Cairo
Tel: 360-4851
Fax: 360-8439

Rada Research & Public Relations Co.
Mrs. Loula Zaklama
1 Mostafa El Wakil St.
Heliopolis, Cairo
Tel: 291-7956; 291-5437
Fax: 291-7563

Research & Advertising Consultants
30 Gameat Al Dowal Al Arabia St.
Mohandessin, Cairo
Tel: 360-8439
Fax: 360-4815

Shortcuts - Institutional Business Development
39, Iraq Street, Mohandessein, Cairo
Tel: 336-7355
Fax 338-2370

Transcentury
20 Adly Street, Kodak Passage, Cairo
Tel: 393-6425, 393-9038
Fax: 393-6425

Wafai and Associates
El Forsan Bldg., Behind Sheraton Heliopolis,
Bldg. A, Heliopolis, Cairo
Tel: 267-6681; 267-6682
Fax: 266-9263

Multilateral Institutions Abroad

Multilateral Development Bank Office
U.S. Department of Commerce
International Trade Administration
Room 1107, 14th and Constitution, NW
Washington, DC 20230
Tel: 202-482-3399
Fax: 202-273-0927

African Development Bank
c/o The Commercial Service
U.S. Embassy
5 Rue Jesse Owens, 01 B.P. 1712
Abidjan 01, Cote D'ivoire
Tel: 225-21-46-16
Fax: 225-22-24-37

European Bank for Reconstruction and Development (EBRD)
Office of the U.S. Executive Director
One Exchange Square
London EC2A 2EH
United Kingdom
Tel: 44-71-338-6569
Fax: 44-71-338-6487

International Finance Corporation (IFC)
1818 H Street, NW
Washington, DC 20433
Tel: 202-477-1234
Fax: 202-477-6391

World Bank
Office of the U.S. Executive Director
1818 H Street, NW
Washington, DC 20433
Tel: 202-458-0120; 202-458-0118
Fax: 202-477-2967

Multilateral Institutions in Egypt

Arab League
The Arab League Bldg., Corniche El Nil, Cairo
Tel: 393-4499
Fax: 775-626

African Export Import Bank (Afrexim)
World Trade Center Bldg. (3rd and 8th floors)
1191 Corniche El Nil
Cairo
Tel: 202-578-0281 (six lines)
Fax: 202-578-0276; 202-578-0279

**Cairo Regional Center for International
Commercial Arbitration**
3 Aboul Feda St.
Zamalek, Cairo
Tel: 340-1333; 340-1335; 340-1337;
342-3691; 342-3693
Fax: 340-1336

**Commission of the European Communities
Delegation in Egypt**
Amb. Christian Falkowsky, Head of the
Delegation
6 Ibn Zenki St.
Zamalek, Cairo
Tel: 340-8388
Fax: 340-0385

International Finance Corporation (IFC)
Representative for the Middle East
World Trade Center,
1191 Corniche El Nil St. (12th floor)
Cairo
Tel: 579-6565; 579-9900
Fax: 579-2211

**United Nations Development Program
(UNDP)**
Coordinator & Representative
1191 Corniche El Nil, World Trade Center,
Cairo
Tel: 578-4840; 578-4846
Fax: 578-4847

World Bank
Country Department
1191 Corniche El Nil
World Trade Center
Cairo
Tel: 574-1670; 574-1671
Fax: 574-1676

List of Local Banks and American Correspondent Banks

American Express Bank
4 Syria St.
Mohandessin, Cairo
Tel: 360-8226; 360-8228; 360-5256; 360-5258
Fax: 570-3146

Arab American Bank
Regional Representative
6 Salah El Din St.
Zamalek, Cairo
Tel: 340-6767
Fax: 340-6753

Citibank
4 Ahmed Pacha St.
Garden City, Cairo
Tel: 355-1501; 355-1161; 355-1873; 355-1877
Fax: 355-8056

Bank of Alexandria
49 Kasr El Nil St.
Cairo
Tel: 391-9686
Fax: 390-7793

Cairo Bank
22 Adly St.
Cairo
Tel: 390-9575
Fax: 390-1735

Bank Misr
151 Mohamed Farid St., Cairo
Tel: 391-4239, 391-1159
Fax: 393-5381

National Bank of Egypt
Cairo Plaza Bldg., Corniche El Nil St.
24 Sherif St., Cairo
Tel: 574-6858
Fax: 574-6000

Arab International Bank
35 Abdel Khalek Tharwat St., Cairo
Tel: 390-5765
Fax: 391-6233

Banque Du Caire Et De Paris
Mansour/Chairman
3 Latin America St., Garden City, Cairo
Tel: 355-2906; 390-9575
Fax: 390-1735

Cairo Barclays Bank
12 El Sheikh Youssef Sq., Garden City, Cairo
Tel: 354-0686; 355-7447
Fax: 355-2746

Commercial International Bank (CIB)
Nile Tower Bldg. (4th floor). 21/23 Giza St.
Giza
Tel: 570-3172
Fax: 570-3043

Egyptian British Bank (Ex-Hong Kong Bank)
3 Aboul Feda St., Zamalek, Cairo
Tel: 340-9186; 340-9286
Fax: 341-4010

Delta Int'l Bank
1113 Corniche El Nil, Cairo
Tel: 579-6910; 579-6911
Fax: 750-904

Egyptian American Bank (EAB)
6 Hassan Sabri St., Zamalek, Cairo
Tel: 341-7330; 341-6150; 341-6157; 341-6158; 339-1572
Fax: 341-4924; 391-8601

Misr International Bank
54 El Batal Ahmed Abdel Aziz St.
Mohandessin, Ciaro
Tel: 349-4424; 349-7091; 349-0164
Fax: 349-8072

Misr America Int'l Bank
2 Nadi El Seid St.
Dokki, Cairo
Tel: 361-6634; 361-6613; 361-6623; 361-6624; 361-6627
Fax: 361-6610

Misr Exterior Bank
Cairo Plaza Bldg.
Corniche El Nil, Cairo
Tel: 778-021
Fax: 762-806

Misr Iran Development Bank
Nile Tower Bldg., Giza St.
Giza
Tel: 572-7311; 004; 890
Fax: 570-1185

U.S. Embassy Trade Personnel

The Commercial Service
American Embassy Cairo
Bobette Orr, Counselor for Commercial Affairs
Bryan Smith, Commercial Attachq
5 Latin America Street, Garden City, Cairo
Tel: 357-2330; 357-2340
Fax: 355-8368

The Commercial Service
John Abdelnour, Sr. Commercial Specialist
Heba Abdel Aziz, Commercial Specialist
3 El Pharaana Avenue
American Center Bldg.
Alexandria
Tel: (03) 482-5607; 483-6330
Fax: (03) 482-9199

USDA/Foreign Agricultural Service (FAS)
Thomas Pomeroy, Counselor for Agricultural Affairs
Hassan Ahmed, Agricultural Attachq
8 Kamal El Din Salah St.
Garden City, Cairo
Tel: 357-2388; 357-2389
Fax: 356-3989

U.S. Information Service
David Ballard, Press Attache
5 Latin America St.
Garden City, Cairo
Tel: 357-3473; 357-3474
Fax: 357-3740

American Cultural Center
Haynes Mahoney, Cultural Attachq
5 Latin America St.
Garden City, Cairo
Tel: 357-3412
Fax: 357-3740

American Cultural Center
3 El Pharaana St.
Alexandria
Tel: 482-1009; 482-4117
Fax: 483-3811

**U.S. Agency for International Development
(USAID)**
Trade and Investment Division
Zahraa El Maadi
Maadi, Cairo
Tel: 516-5505 (ext. 2143)
Fax: 516-4652

U.S. Department of State
Counselor for Political & Economic Affairs
Counselor for Political and Economic Affairs
8 Kamal El Din Salah St.
Garden City, Cairo
Tel: 357-2251
Fax: 357-2181

**Washington-Based U.S. (Egyptian)
Contacts**

U.S. Department of Commerce
Tom Sams, Egypt Desk Officer
Mac/One, Room 2029b
Washington, DC 20230
Tel: 202-482-1860
Fax: 202-482-0878

U.S. Department of Commerce
The Commercial Service
Hch Bldg., Room 1223
Washington, DC 20230
Tel: 202-482-4836
Fax: 202-482-5179

U.S. Department of Agriculture
Agexport Services Division
Room 4939-S, 14th Independence Ave., SW
Washington, DC 20250
Tel: 202-720-6343
Fax: 202-690-4374

U.S. Department of State
Office of Egyptian and North African Affairs
Nea/Ena, Room 5250
Washington, DC 20520
Tel: 202-647-7449
Fax: 202-736-4458

U.S.-Based Multipliers Relevant for Egypt

Embassy of the Arab Republic of Egypt
3521 International Court, NW
Washington, DC 20008
Tel: 202-895-5400
Fax: 202-244-4319

Office of Economic & Commercial Affairs
Embassy of the Arab Republic of Egypt
Alaa El Din Shalaby, Minister-Counselor for
  Economic & Commercial Affairs
2232 Massachusetts Ave., NW
Washington, DC 20008
Tel: 202-265-9111
Fax: 202-328-4517

Consulate General of Egypt
1110 Second Ave. (Rm. 201)
New York, NY 10022
Tel: 212-759-7120
Fax: 212-308-7643

Consulate General of Egypt
3001 Pacific Ave.
San Francisco, CA 94115
Tel: 415-346-9700
Fax: 415-346-9480

Consulate General of Egypt
1990 Post Oak Blvd., Suite 2180
Houston, TX 77056
Tel: 713-961-4915
Fax: 713-961-3868

Consulate General of Egypt
500 N. Michigan Ave., Suite 1900
Chicago, IL 60611
Tel: 312-828-9162
Fax: 312-828-9167

Permanent Mission of Egypt to The United Nations
36 East 67 St.
New York, NY 10021
Tel/Fax: 212-879-6300

American Chamber of Commerce Egypt/U.S.
815 Connecticut Ave. NW
Washington, DC 20006-4078
Tel: 202-496-9299
Fax: 202-833-6919

National U.S.–Arab Chamber of Commerce
1100 New York Avenue, NW
East Tower, Suite 550
Washington, DC 20005
Tel: 202-289-5920
Fax: 202-289-5938

U.S. Arab Chamber of Commerce (Pacific) Inc.
PO Box 422218
San Francisco, CA 94142
Tel: 415-398-9200
Fax: 415-398-7111

American Egyptian Cooperation Foundation (AECF)
330 East 39th St., Suite 321
New York, NY 10016
Tel: 212-867-2323
Fax: 212-697-0465

Egyptian American Businessmen's Association (EABA)
50 Broad Street, Suite 1609
New York, NY 10004
Tel: 212-797-3474
Fax: 212-344-1050

Arab-American Business & Professional Association
P.O. Box 700
746 Walker Road
Great Falls, VA 33066-0700
Tel: 703-759-2235
Fax: 703-759-9300

Overseas Private Investment Corporation (OPIC)
1615 M Street, NW
Washington, DC 20527
Tel: 800-424-OPIC; 202-457-7010 Fax: 202-223-3514

Export-Import Bank (EXIM Bank)
811 Vermont Avenue NW
Washington, DC 20571
Tel: 202-566-8990; 202-566-2117
Fax: 202-566-7524

U.S. Small Business Administration (SBA)
409 3rd St., SW
Washington, DC 20416
Tel: 202-205-6531
Fax: 202-205-6928

U.S. International Trade Commission (USITC)
500 E Street, SW
Washington, DC 20436
Tel: 202-252-1000
Fax: 202-252-1798

U.S. Trade and Development Agency (USTDA)
Africa & Middle East
SA-16, Room 309
Washington, DC 20523-1602
Tel: 703-875-4357
Fax: 703-875-4009

National Institute of Standards and Technology (NIST)
Int'l & Academic Affairs
Bldg. 101, Room A505
Gaithersburg, MD 20899
Tel: 301-975-2386
Fax: 301-975-3530

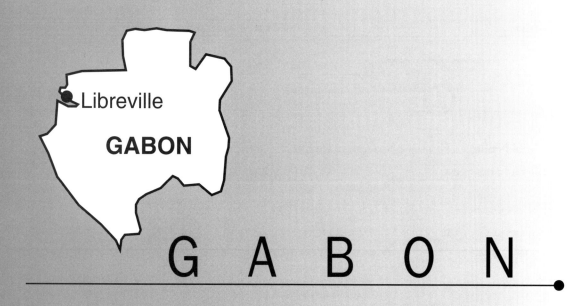

G A B O N .

TRADE AND BUSINESS GUIDE

Official Name:	Gabonese Republic
Official Languages:	French, with Bantu (Fang, Myene, Bateke, Bapounou/Eschira, Bandjabi)
Population:	1,208,436 (2000 est)
Population Growth:	1.08% (2000 est)
Age Structure:	0–14 years: 33%, 15–64 years: 61%, 65 years and over: 6% (2000 est)
Location:	Western Africa, on Atlantic Ocean between the Congo and Equatorial Guinea at the Equator
Area:	267,667 sq. km. Slightly smaller than Colorado
Type of Government:	Republic, bicameral. National Assembly, a Senate, and a Constitutional (Supreme) Court. President elected by popular vote for seven-year term (next in 2005). National Assembly and Senate elected by direct popular vote for five-year terms (next in 2001)
Head of State:	President El Hadj Omar Bongo
Cabinet:	Council of Ministers appointed by Prime Minister in consultation with president
Religion:	55% to 75% Christian, less than 1% Muslim, indigenous Animism (N/A)
Major Cities:	Capital: Libreville (350,000), Port-Gentil (123,300), Masuka (38,030), Lambarene (26,257), Mouanda (22,909)
Climate:	Tropical. Always hot and humid
Time:	The entire country is +1 GMT (Greenwich Mean Time), six hours ahead of EST (Eastern Standard Time)
GDP:	Purchasing power parity (PPP): $7.9 billion (1999 est), real growth rate: 1.7% (1999 est), per capita PPP: $6,500 (1999 est), composition by sector: agricultural= 10%, industry= 60%, services= 30% (1999 est)
Currency:	1 Communaute Financiere Africaine franc (CFAF) = 100 centimes
Exchange Rate:	CFA franc vs. US$ 1 = 593.2 (1998), 608.04 (1999), 608.04 (2000 est)
Weights & Measure:	Metric system
Natural Resources:	Oil, uranium, gold, iron, manganese, timber
Total Trade:	In millions US$ [exports (fob)/imports (cif)]: 1996 (3, 054/969), 1997 (3,042/1,018), 1998 (2,042/890)

Trade with U.S.:	In millions US$ [exports (fob)/imports (cif)]: 1997 (84/2,202), 1998 (62/1,259), 1999 (45/1,543)
Major Trade Partners:	Imports: France, Cote d'Ivoire, United States, Japan, Netherlands. Exports: United States, France, Japan, China, Spain, Germany
Membership:	AfDB, IBRD, IDB, IFC, IMF, UDEAC, UN, UNCTAD, WCO, WIPO, and WTO. See membership description in appendix

Sources: *IMF, Gabon Government Statistics, United Nations World Statistics, CIA World Factbook, U.S. Department of Commerce*

POLITICAL OUTLOOK

②

Relationship with the U.S.

The U.S. and Gabon have a good bilateral relationship.   Gabon is pro-western, and president Bongo facilitates mediating regional conflict. The U.S. encourages democratization and urges the GG (Gabonese Government) to respect human rights.   Political issues generally don't affect the climate for U.S. investors and exporters.

Influences on Business

Gabon's political parties favor a mixed economy with state playing a relatively large role.   Foreign investments are favored, especially in the minerals and agro-industrial sectors.   Structural adjustment programs, in agreement with international financial institutions, have a calendar of actions to reform and privatize inefficient parastatals, initially including the national airline (Air Gabon), the cement factory (Ciments du Gabon), the largest plywood factory (CFG), the rubber and palm companies (HEVGAB and AGROGABON), the Trans-Gabonese railway (OCRTA), and portions of the national post and telecommunications authority (OPT) and port facility (OPRAG).

Profile

System: The Legislature has a 120-member National Assembly and a 91-member Senate. The National Assembly seats by party: PDG (Gabonese Democratic Party), 100; RNB (National Rally of Woodcutters), 8; six other parties, 3 or fewer.   Senate seats by party: PDG, 61; RND, 17; remaining parties, 4 or fewer.   Smaller parties include the Gabonese Party for Progress (PGP), Gabonese People's Union (USG), African Forum for Reconstruction (FAR), Circle of Liberal Reformers (CLR), People's Unity Party. (PUP), Gabonese Socialist Union (USG), Democratic and Republican Alliance (ADERE), Rally for Democracy and Progress (RDP).

Schedule for Elections: President in 1998, 2005.   National Assembly in 1996, 2001. Senate in 1997, 2002.

Major Parties: The PDG dominates (used to be the sole party).   President Bongo is attempting to limit public-sector wage increases, and reduce some taxes and customs, duties and tariffs. However, scandals around President Bongo's personal life contributed to a unified opposite, which could block reform. To lower the cost of social services to immigrants, in early 1995, Gabon repatriated those who purchased expensive resident cards, with the rest required to leave.

Political Violence: In recent years, there has been little political violence. Gabon is generally peaceful without significant regional or inter-ethnic tensions.

Corruption: Corruption is prevalent and an obstacle for U.S. firms. Laws toward transparency and against corruption are not greatly enforced. One should seek professional assistance to negotiate agreements, select partners, and control resources. IMF and the World Bank are seeking to review public expenditures, to encourage competitive bidding, and prevent continued "sweetheart deals."

ECONOMIC OUTLOOK
③

Trends

Oil dominates the economy, so like other resource-rich countries, diversification into nonresource, intensive, tradable goods is difficult. The economy is generally subject to changes in commodity prices and exogenous shocks. Government debt hinders its power to stabilize the economy. French firms and subsidiaries are major players, receiving French government concessional finance and mixed credits. Agriculture and small to medium-sized business lack international competitiveness. Gabon lacks entrepreneurial class and educational training in business, commerce, and vocations. Labor costs are relatively high. Underdeveloped transport sector hinders development of economy, especially agriculture and forestry. Telecommunications, air and rail transports, and oil refining are managed by inefficient parastatals but are targeted for privatization. Telecommunications offer some potential for exporters.

Major Growth Sectors

Petroleum reserves are seen as flat and declining, but the oil sector will dominate the entire economy for at least four more years. Forestry is the next largest industry, with woods such as okoume and ozigo monopolized by the GG (Gabonese Government) parastatal marketing company of SNBG (Societe Nationale des Bois du Gabon). New GG codes mandate more processing investment and sustainable management to capitalize on the remaining 50 million acres of commercial wood reserves. Telecommunications are monopolized by parastatal OPT (Office des Postes et Telecommunications du Gabon). Though targeted for privatization, telecommunications have promise but also the threat of saturation. Various satellite, cellular, digital, fiber optic, and microwave technologies are expanding, influenced by French and U.S. firms. Mining is most promising in manganese, niobium, phosphates, gold, barites, talc, and possibly iron ore (uranium is nearly depleted). A GG mining code that favors mining investment has been delayed by disagreement on investor incentives.

Key Economic Indicators

Income, Production and Employment *(millions of U.S. dollars unless otherwise indicated)*			
	1996	**1997**	**1998[1]**
Nominal GDP[2]	5,646	5,149	4,480
Real GDP Growth (pct)[3]	3.8	4.1	2.1
GDP by Sector (pct)			
Agriculture	N/A	N/A	8.0
Industry	N/A	N/A	67.0
Services	N/A	N/A	25.0
Government	23.4	25.1	26.4
Per Capita GDP (US$)	5,132	4,681	4,314
Labor Force (millions)	N/A	N/A	N/A
Unemployment Rate (pct)	20.0	21.0	21.0

1. 1999 figures are all estimates based on most recent data available. 2. GDP at factor cost.
3. Percentage changes calculated in local currency.
Source: Bureau of Economic and Business Affairs; U.S. Department of State

- **Infrastructure**
  The Trans-Gabonese railway links Libreville with Franceville, offering 433 miles for travel and transport. Only 650 of 4,300 miles of roads are paved, but the main inter-city routes are being upgraded with financing from the African Development Bank and European Investment Bank. Port-Gentil, a deep-water port, handles 85 percent of the traffic by volume. Owendo, a shallow-water port, requires dredging. Together, they shipped over 21 million tons cargo in 1996. Telecommunications are fairly advanced and adequate, with direct dial from Libreville to almost anywhere. There are over 30 public airfields with some 100 private land strips and one of the largest civil aviation fleets in Africa. There are almost daily connections to Europe and Africa.

- **Labor**
  Gabon has a shortage of highly skilled managers and workers. Authorization is required from the GG to hire non-Gabonese Africans. Informal and low-skill activity is often done by non-Gabonese. Formal sector labor costs are high due to the Labor Code defending Gabonese workers' rights. Labor unions and confederations are active.

Money and Prices *(annual percentage growth)*			
	1997	**1998**	**1999[1]**
Consumer Price Inflation	2.5	2.1	2.1
Exchange Rate (CFA Franc/US$ annual average)	584	590	608

1. 1999 figures are all estimates based on most recent data available.
Sources: Bureau of Economic and Business Affairs; U.S. Department of State, IMF

Balance of Payments and Trade
(millions of U.S. dollars unless otherwise indicated)

	1997	1998	1999[1]
Total Exports FOB[2]	3,042	2,042	2,534
Exports to U.S.[2]	2,202	1,259	1,543
Total Imports CIF[2]	1,018	890	1,282
Imports from U.S.[2]	84	62	45
Trade Balance[2]	2,024	1,152	1,252
Balance with U.S.	2,118	1,197	1,498
External Public Debt	4,100	4,100	4,100
Fiscal Deficit of Public Sector/GDP (pct)	3.3	2.7	3.3
Current Account Deficit	N/A	N/A	260
Foreign Debt Service Payments/GDP (pct)	10.2	11.6	19.8
Gold and Foreign Exchange Reserves	N/A	N/A	N/A
Aid from U.S.	2.0	2.0	2.0
Aid from All Other Sources	N/A	N/A	N/A

1. 1999 figures are all estimates based on most recent data available. 2. Merchandise trade.
Sources: Bureau of Economic and Business Affairs; U.S. Department of State, IMF

- Balance of Payments
  Gabon has a favorable balance of trade because of its petroleum exports. In 1999, import and export activities resulted in a favorable trade surplus of US$ 1.25 billion. However, due to service outflows, the current account was estimated at negative US$ 260 million.

Government Influence on Business

Both the state and the private sector seek to promote greater state commitment to public goods, protect the environment, protect biodiversity, offer adequate and efficient health and education service; promote competition and efficient private markets; improve public resource management; stabilize stock of international debt and internal short-term GG debt; reform law and regulations to promote business investment. The GG realizes foreign skills, technology, and investment is needed. Practical obstacles include unfavorable codes for investment, mining, and labor; high factor costs; lack of skilled managers in some sectors; and the small population (1 million). A five-year development plan with investments made and investments desired for all sectors of Gabon is regularly published.

TRADE

④

Leading Imports and Exports

Imports: Petroleum equipment and services, mining equipment and parts, forestry equipment, telecommunications, construction

Exports: Oil, uranium, gold, iron, manganese, timber

Foreign Trade *(Exports and Imports in US$M)*			
	1997	**1998**	**1999[1]**
Total Exports FOB[2]	3,042	2,042	2,534
Exports to U.S.[2]	2,202	1,259	1,543
Total Imports CIF[2]	1,018	890	1,282
Imports from U.S.[2]	84	62	45

1. 1999 figures are all estimates based on most recent data available. 2. Merchandise trade.
Sources: U.S. Department of State, IMF

Best Prospects Analysis

Best Prospects for Nonagricultural Goods and Services

Petroleum Equipment

	1996E $M	1997E $M	1998E $M
Total Market Size	450	N/A	130
Total Local Production	N/A	N/A	N/A
Total Exports,Crude Oil	2,300	N/A	1,500
Total Imports	403	N/A	200
Imports from the U.S.	65	N/A	N/A

Estimated annual growth rate of imports: 10%
Global price fluctuations and resource depletion are variable.

Mining Equipment

	1996E $M	1997E $M	1998E $M
Total Investment	N/A	N/A	8
Total Local Production	N/A	N/A	N/A
Total Exports of Uranium/Manganese	65	N/A	165
Total Imports	45	N/A	50
Imports from the U.S.	65	N/A	N/A

Two major mining operations (COMILOG= manganese, COMUF= uranium) have large inventories of U.S. equipment. Imports include parts for manganese operation, railroad, and mineral port, as well as parts and equipment for uranium mine and treatment plant. SOMIMO (new Gabonese company) seeks phosphate in central Gabon. These statistics are unofficial estimates.

Forestry

	1996E $M	1997E $M	1998E $M
Total Investment	N/A	N/A	N/A
Total Local Production of Equipment	N/A	N/A	N/A
Total Exports	387	N/A	282
Total Imports of Equipment	34	N/A	50
Imports from the U.S.	N/A	N/A	25

1996E Timber exports: 2.4 million cubic meters
1998E Timber exports: 1.8 million cubic meters
Exploitable reserve of Gabonese wood: 400 million cubic meters. About 93% of timber by value is exported as logs, rest as plywood. Parastatal National Timber Company (SNBG) monopolizes production and marketing. Asian financial crisis decreased timber exports substantially from 1997.

Best Prospects for Agricultural Products

Gabon is a net importer of food (from South Africa, Cameroon and France) with untapped potential to grow own food.

Fishing has potential with lakes, rivers, and 800 km of Atlantic coastline. The GG is seeking to promote these activities.

Best Prospects and Investment Opportunities

Various parastatals identified for privatization. Promising: Office of Postes and Telecommunications (OPT), Air Gabon, and port facilities (OPRAG). The U.S. already provides some telecom supplies and services. French have more presence and experience in construction in Gabon. GG seeks investment in its public housing incentives and concessionary financing.

The above statistics are unofficial estimates.
N/A - Not Available, E - Estimate

Extracted from the US Department of Commerce USA Trade 2001 Country Commercial Guide for Gabon.

Import and Export Tips

- **Regulations**

  Customs: All categories of products may be imported except sugar, which has nontariff restriction to allow sugar monopoly of SOSUHO to become competitive. Gabon, in conformance with Central Africa Customs Union (UDEAC/CEMAC), offers little competition to other countries, even though a common currency and the central bank are shared. Union integration with trade and labor is slow and uneven. Duties and taxes are applied to almost all goods, in four categories. Few barriers exist in the crude oil sector. The valuation determined by cif value is stipulated on bill of lading. There is no tax on exports out of Gabon, and there are no free trade zones.

Tariffs: Category 1: basic products (medicines, vaccines, other medical supplies, rice, and wheat) at 7.2 percent of cif price. Category 2: raw materials (raw materials used in industrial sector) at 29.8 percent of cif price. Category 3: intermediate products (most food products) at 53.4 percent of cif price. Category 4: usual consumer goods (liquor, perfumes, etc.) at 99.4 percent of cif price.

Import Taxes: The value-added tax (VAT), at 18 percent, is due by all companies with turnover exceeding around US$ 330,000 on all imports except newspapers, eggs, milk, fresh fish, cooking oil, sugar, rice, and bread. Though there are no free trade zones, free trade industrial servicing centers in Port-Gentil and the island of Principe (countries of Sao Tome and Principe) are under consideration.

- **Documentation**

  Exports: No information is available at this time. Contact the commercial section of the embassy of Gabon for additional information.

  Imports: An import license is not required except for sugar. A bill of lading and invoice must accompany all goods entering Gabon.

  Labeling: Though not required by law, goods should be labeled in French if possible. Processed food and similar perishables should have an expiration date.

  Standards: Gabon generally follows French standards.

  Exchange Control: For commercial transactions inside or outside the franc zone, an import license must be presented for all imports exceeding a value of 500,000 CFA francs (about USD 833). Funds not exceeding 5 million CFA francs (USD 8,333) can be freely transferred to France or within the franc zone. A justification must be presented for all transfers exceeding this amount. Regional central banks (BEAC and BCEAO) will not honor or redeem its currency outside its own zone. The Ministry of Finance require further documentation for private transfers to points outside the franc zone.

- **Payment**

  Terms: Usual credit terms are 90 to 120 days. A confirmed irrevocable letter of credit terms is recommended for new transactions.

  Currency Exchange: Gabon is a member of the French Franc Zone and the Bank of the Central African States (BEAC), head-quartered in Yaounde. BEAC is the central bank for Gabon, Cameroon, Central African Republic, Congo, Chad, and Equatorial

New Guinea. Convertibility of CFA franc guaranteed by France through an account that links the BEAC and French Treasury. The French Treasury maintains separate reserves for each country that gives drawing rights to guarantee exchange. Interest rate structure and rules of intervention are shared by BEAC. Liquidity within zone and each country is controlled by BEAC, which grants rediscounting facilities and money market advances. The Ministry of Finance public accounts department manages public debt, and has been compelled to reschedule debt several times by either the Paris Club or the London Club.

Fund Transfer: There are no restrictions on foreign capital flow into Gabon. Transfer is free within French Franc Zone. Transfer outside Franc Zone requires proof to the Ministry of Finance that funds repatriated come from wages, salaries, or profits, and all local taxes arc paid.

MARKETING TIPS
⑤

Agents and Distributors

To find a local agent for your company, contact a U.S. Department of Commerce district office and request an agents/distributors service (ADS). If Commerce records do not already have suitable prospects, the office will acquire information from the U.S. Embassy in Libreville.

Establishing an Office

Required for business office: permit from the Ministry of Commerce; establishment of listing in the trade registry of the Ministry; fiscal statistical number from the Office of Direct Taxation of the Ministry of Finance; commercial license from the municipality.

Required to open a branch of a U.S. company: application for authorization with Ministry of Commerce, enclosing bylaws of the Gabonese company; declaration of the company to the Tax Office of the Ministry of Finance; registration with the Social Security Office (Caisse Nationale de Securite Sociale, or CNSS); preceding documents filled out with clerk of the Commercial Court, with (1) copies of parent company bylaws and minutes of the meeting of board of directors at which opening of Gabonese branch is approved; (2) certificate of appointment of general manager in Gabon; (3) copy of any agreement signed with Gabonese company or Gabonese government; (4) two copies of application to the Court for authorization to operate; (5) two photographs and copy of general manager's passport. This entire process can take up to three months. See **Contacts**.

Distribution and Sales Channels

Most U.S. products sold in Gabon are marketed through Gabonese agents. Examples include Tractafric (sells Caterpillar heavy equipment), LIFTEL (one of several firms that sells Motorola products), SOGAFRIC (sells General Electric products). Other U.S. products are sold by small local firms, often with just one outlet in Libreville.

Direct Marketing

Tenacious French-speaking representatives are recommended. Repeated visits to the country are required in order to successfully enter the market. Personal contacts and knowing the territory are important.

Leasing/Joint Ventures

Joint ventures and licensing are limited. U.S. and European beer and soft drinks are made in Gabon under license.

Franchising

See **Leasing and Joint Ventures.**

Advertising and Promotion

Daily newspaper, *l'Union*, radio, and TV channels 1, 2, 3, and 4 available for legal notices.

Selling Factors

No information is available at this time. Market survey and market research suggested.

Selling to the Government

Make sure that funds have been set aside in the Gabonese budget for the equipment you wish to sell. Credits from the U.S. Ex-Im are not available owing to the GG's poor payment record.

Pricing

Market survey and market research suggested.

Customer Support

Most successful foreign firms employ French-speaking representatives or agents and keep an inventory of spare parts. Good follow-up services and inventories give significant competitive advantage.

Intellectual Property Rights (IPR)

Gabon is a member of the African Intellectual Property Office (OAPI) based in Yaounde, Cameroon. Gabon adheres to most principles of IPR, but enforcement is weak since there is little manufacturing. Patents and copyrights are handled by the Ministry of Commerce.

Attorney

A local attorney is recommended, but if bylaws are observed or a management consultant used, one may not be necessary. The Consular Section of the U.S. Embassy maintains a list of English-speaking attorneys.

FOREIGN INVESTMENT

⑥

Openness: The Gabonese Investment Code follows the general model of French-speaking Africa, with more liberal terms than the other countries. Gabon still favors Gabonese firms, but new codes will soon liberalize this by allowing foreign companies with head offices in Gabon the same rights as Gabonese companies. With varied minimal capital and share resale requirements, Gabon allows all domestic and foreign firms to operate as branches and wholly own either Societes a Responsibilite Limitee (SARL) or Societes Anonymes (SA). IMF conditions will privatize the Transgabonese Railway (OCTRA), the electricity and water monopoly (SEEG), the international telecommunications office (OPT), and others. The World Bank has advised Gabon in hiring international consultants for needs and management of tenders. The water and electricity companies were privatized with French and Canadian firms now involved.

Regulatory System: The Gabonese economy is dominated by foreign interests. The Gabonese state reserves the right to invest in equity capital of strategic areas such as oil and mining industry sectors. As a member of Central African Customs Union (UDEAC), changed to Economic and Monetary Union (CEMAC) in 1998, Gabon is part of a free trade zone within Africa, and is virtually duty free. There are higher import duties on non-UDEAC country goods.

Investment Agreements: There is no U.S. bilateral investment and taxation agreement though one exists with France. There are agreements with other UDEAC countries also. Bilateral commercial relations with trading partners are often coordinated through bilateral "commissions" to stimulate trade and investment.

Trade Zones and Free Ports: UDEAC free trade exists only between members. Though there are no free trade zones, free trade industrial servicing centers in Port-Gentil and the island of Principe (countries of Sao Tome and Principe) are under consideration.

Performance Requirements/Incentives: French firms benefit from special agreements between France (Agence Francaise de Development) and the GG. French citizens are given free work visas, but work permits are required for other foreigners working in Gabon. There are no performance requirements for establishing, maintaining, or expanding an investment. Only small and medium-sized firms require Gabonese participation of at least 51 percent. Gabon attempts to employ its nationals. Hiring foreigners requires authorization of the Ministry of Labor. Issuing new papers to non-Gabonese has become more difficult. The Gabonese Commission on Investments is preparing a new Investment Code, in conformity with UDEAC/CEMAC (Central African Customs and Economic Union), to regulate specific activities instead of all transactions. Financial transactions within France, UDEAC members, and French Franc Zone are exempt already. Imports and exports within UDEAC trade virtually freely, whereas foreign investments must be declared to the Ministry of Finance. Oil companies and subcontractors receive preferential treatment.

Capital Markets and Investment: Gabon has a well-developed banking system with the Gabonese Development Bank (BGD) and ten commercial banks. BGD lends to small and medium-sized companies. The BEAC central bank is monitored and regulated by the French government. Local banking and credit are available to foreign and local investors on equal terms, with most banking services available or procured in Europe. Interest rate swaps and eurocurrency bonds have been used to finance oilfield development by local offices of foreign oil companies. There are no GG restrictions of foreign participation in the commercial sector. All transfers exceeding about US$ 8,300 outside the Franc Zone are subject to authorization by the Minister of Finance. Loans contracted by Gabonese companies with foreign entities subject to prior authorization by the Ministry of Economy.

Private Ownership: All investors, both nonresidents and in branches of foreign firms, have the same rights and freedom of capital transfers. Foreign investors can purchase real estate, negotiate licenses, and enter commercial agreements. Gabon's most sensitive sectors, petroleum, manganese, uranium, and forestry, are controlled by foreign interests. The GG is increasingly realizing the need for foreign investment since the GDP is too high for much foreign development assistance.

Expropriation and Compensation: Large foreign firms operate on an equal basis with national firms. There are no known cases of

discrimination or expropriation against foreign firms.

OPIC and Investment Insurance: OPIC (The Overseas Private Investment Corporation) has not been sought, but it is interested in Gabon. IMF has taken Gabon to task for slippage against economic adjustment performance criteria, mainly in privatization targets. CFA franc devaluation is seen as unlikely. Much revenue of Gabon comes from dollar-denominated exports.

Dispute Settlement: There is no track record yet for handling investment disputes. Sometimes the government has mediated commercial or labor issue settlements more in favor of U.S. firms than those obtainable through the Gabonese courts. OCTRA (parastatal railway) has been in a trade dispute with a U.S. firm around cancellation of scrap metal export contract. Most disputes are resolved before going to outside arbitration. Gabon is a member of the Multilateral Investment Guarantee Agency (MIGA). It is not a member of the International Center for Settlement of Investment Disputes or the New York Convention of 1958. Gabon is recognized as stable and a good country for doing oil and other business.

FINANCE ⑦

Gabon has a well-developed banking system, consisting of the Gabonese Development Bank (BGD) and ten commercial banks. BGD lends to small and medium-sized companies. The BEAC central bank is monitored and regulated by the French government. Local banking and credit are available to foreign and local investors on equal terms, with most banking services available or procured in Europe. Interest rate swaps and

eurocurrency bonds have been used to finance oilfield development by local offices of foreign oil companies Payment for exports is usually made by irrevocable letters of credit.

Export Financing: Credit is provided through five main commercial banks: Banque Internatiionale de Commerce d'Industrie du Gabon (BICIG), a branch of BNP France; Union Gabonaise de Banque (UGB), a branch of Credit Lyonnais; Banque

Gabonaise et Francaise Internationale (BGFI); Citibank; French Intercontinental Bank (FIBA).

Project Financing: Credit Foncier du Gabon (CREFOGA) for housing; Gabonese Development Bank (BDG); Fund for Development and Expansion (FODEX), a parastatal organization funded by the African Development Bank to finance small and medium-sized firms (PME) owned by Gabonese nationals; Banque Gabonaise de Credit Rural, which offers loans for agriculture.

COMMUNICATIONS ⑧

Phone

Local and long-distance telephone service is available 24 hours a day. Telephone rates are much higher than in the U.S. Gabon is integrated with the international calling services of AT&T and MCI. The international access code is 011, and the Gabon Republic access code is 241. City codes are not required. The local telephone number is six digits.

Internet

Local connection to the Internet is available through OPT (the telecom parastatal) or a few local providers.

Mail

Both surface and air mail (Postal Union Mail) are available. Express Mail International Service is available between Gabon and the U.S.

TRANSPORTATION ⑨

Land

Roads outside the capital are poorly developed and inadequately maintained. Taxis are available in Libreville. Main hotels offer bus service to and from Libreville Airport. Car rental is available but expensive.

Sea

The main ports in Gabon are Owendo and Port-Gentil. About 85 percent of the traffic by volume is handled by Port-Gentil. The Cape Lopez terminal near Port-Gentil is a deep-water port.

Air

International airlines serving Libreville include Air Afrique, Air France, Air Gabon, Cameroon Airlines, Equatorial Airlines of Sao Tome and Principe, Lina Congo, Royal Air Maroc, Swissair, and Sabena. There are flights six days a week to Europe, with flight time of about seven hours. There are also flights to nearby capitals and to Johannesburg. Travel to the U.S. requires a stopover (often lengthy) in Europe. Domestic flights connect Libreville with provincial capitals such as Port-Gentil, Franceville, and Oyem.

WORK WEEK

10

Business Hours: 8.00 a.m. to 12.00 p.m. and 3.00 p.m. to 6.00 p.m. Monday through Saturday, with long lunch break. Some offices are closed on Saturday afternoon.

Government Hours: 9:30 a.m. to 12:00 p.m. and 3:30 p.m. to 5:30 p.m. Monday through Friday. Some offices are open on Saturday morning.

Bank Hours: 7:45 a.m. to 11:30 a.m. and 2:45 p.m. to 4:30 p.m. Monday through Friday. Banks are closed on Saturday.

Foreign Exchange Bureaus: No information is available at this time.

HOLIDAYS 2001

11

New Year's Day, January 1
Good Friday, April 13
Easter Monday, April 16
Labor Day, May 1
Ascension Thursday, May 24
Whit Monday, June 4
Assumption, August 15
Gabonese Independence Day, August 17
All Saint's Day, November 1
Christmas, December 25
Boxing Day, December 26

Some holidays may be observed on different dates depending on the day of the week on which it falls. The two lunar Muslim holidays of Id El Fitr and Id Al Adha (the last day of Ramadan) are celebrated in Gabon, but dates are uncertain in advance.

BUSINESS TRAVEL

12

Business Customs

Guide for Business Representatives is for sale by Superintendent of Documents. See **Contacts.** For appointments with the U.S. Embassy in Libreville, contact The Commercial Section in advance.

Travel Advisory and Visas

A visa, from the Gabonese Embassy in Washington, DC or the Gabonese Mission to United Nations in NY, is advised. A visa may sometimes be obtained on arrival at the airport, but this is not recommended. Proof of yellow fever vaccination is required. Contact the Gabonese Embassy for more information.

Business Infrastructure

Entry Requirements (personal and professional goods): No information is available at this time. Contact the Gabon consulate for more information.

Currency Exchange: The CFA franc is the main currency. $1 = 735 CFAF (2000 est.)

Taxes: There is an 18 percent value-added tax.

Hotels and Restaurants: There are five main hotels in Libreville: Okoume Palace International, Meridian Re-ndama, Hotel Atlantique, Novotel Rapotchombo, Monts de Cristal. Restaurants include: L'Antre de Bacchus, Chez Marie, Le Gourmet, Michel de Gonfaron. Tipping is allowed and recommended. English is not widely spoken, but hotels can arrange for translators.

Housing: No information is available at this time.

Business Services: No information is available at this time.

Labor Costs and Legislation: No information is available at this time.

Literacy: Age 15 and over can read and write: 63.2 percent (1995 est.).

Travel Notes

The following travel notes have been supplied by the U.S. government. For the most recent general travel and consular information, see the U.S. Department of State travel publications or call the Traveler's Telephone Hotline at (202) 647-5225.

Security: Violent crime is not common but does occur. Petty thievery is common, especially in urban areas.

Health Precautions: Because malaria is endemic, begin taking Malaria suppressants prior to arrival. Drink only bottled water or bottled drinks. Restaurant hygiene is primarily good. Current information on health matters may be obtained from the Centers for Disease Control and Prevention's international travelers' hotline at (404) 332-4559.

Embassy Assistance

Travelers should contact the Embassy of Gabon for the latest information: Suite 200, 2034 20th Street, N.W., Washington, D.C. 20009; Tel: (202) 979-1000/1021/1022. Gabon Internet site: http://www.presidence-garbon.com. The U.S. Embassy in Gabon is located at Libreville, Boite Postale 4000; Tel: (241) 762-003/4 and 743-492; Fax: (241) 745-507.

CONTACTS

13

U.S. and Country Contacts

Direction Generale du Commerce
Ministry of Commerce
B.P. 561
Libreville, Gabon
Tel: (241) 760991; 745925
Fax: (241) 765838

Direction Generale des Contributions Directes
Ministry of Finance
B.P. 37
Libreville, Gabon
Tel: (241) 761644
Fax: (241) 765974

Caisse Nationale de Securite Sociale
Direction Generale
B.P. 134
Libreville, Gabon
Tel: (241) 76267

Gabonese Chamber of Commerce
B.P. 2234
Libreville, Gabon
Tel: (241) 722064
Fax: (241) 746477

Price Waterhouse/FidAfrica
B.P. 2164
Libreville, Gabon
Tel: (241) 762371
Fax: (241) 744325

Hsd - Ernst & Young
B.P. 2278
Libreville, Gabon
Tel: (241) 762067; 742168
Telefax: (241) 746130

Commercial Banks and Their Correspondents in the U.S.

BICIG
B.P. 2241
Libreville, Gabon
Tel: (241) 762613
Telefax: (241) 744034

U.S. Correspondent:
Banque Nationale de Paris
P.O. Box 127 Church Street Station
New York, NY 10008
Tel: (212) 415-9400
Fax: (212) 415-9629

Or, Citibank NA, 399 Park Avenue
New York, NY 10043
Tel: (212) 223-2681
Fax: (212) 223-2681

UGB
B.P. 315
Libreville, Gabon
Tel: (241) 777000
Fax: (241) 764616

U.S. Correspondent:
Credit Lyonnais
1301 Avenue of Americas
New York, NY 10019
Tel: (212) 261-7000; 586-2440
Fax: (212) 586-3279

Citibank-Gabon
B.P. 3940
Libreville, Gabon
Tel: (241) 730383; 731092
Fax: (241) 733786

U.S. Correspondent:
Citibank NY
399 Park Avenue
New York, NY 10043
Tel: (212) 559-1000
Fax: (212) 793-0690

Banque Gabonaise et Francaise Internationale
(former Paribas)
B.P. 2253
Libreville, Gabon
Tel: (241) 744456
Fax: (241) 760134

U.S. Correspondent:
Paribas North America
The Equitable Tower
787 7th Avenue
New York, NY 10019
Tel: (212) 841-3000
Fax: (212) 841-3555

Advertising

Publicom
B.P. 3875
Libreville, Gabon
Fax: (241) 738326

Business Travel

Superintendent of Documents
Washington, D.C. 20402
Tel: (202) 512-1800
Fax: (202) 512-2250

Hotels

Okoume Palace: Managed by Intercontinental
Hotels, the Okoume Palace is a 500-room
hotel with some apartments, located relatively
close to the airport. It has a pool, tennis, and
squash courts, and a fully equipped health spa
with aerobics classes. There are two restaurants.
Tel: (241) 732023
Fax: (241) 731629

Meridien Re-Ndama: Managed by the French
group Meridien, this hotel is near the town
center, south of the U.S. and French embassies
on the main road. It has a well-situated pool
on the beach side of the hotel and two
restaurants.
Tel: (241) 742929; 766105
Fax: (241) 742924

Hotel Atlantique: Situated on the best beach
front in Libreville, Atlantique is about 200
yards from the airport. It is known for its
sumptuous, 3-course brunches. It has a pool.
It is located about 10 km north of the U.S.
Embassy.
Tel: (241) 732446
Fax: (241) 732436

Restaurants

Novotel Rapontchombo: Only 1 block from
the U.S. Embassy, it is on the water but has no
usable beachfront. It has a pool, casino, restaurant and bar ambiance, but is less luxurious
than the Meridian and the Intercontinental.
Tel: (241) 764742
Fax: (241) 761345

Monts de Cristal: Situated in Centreville,
about 1 km from the U.S. Embassy, it is
comfortable, not ostentatious and has 49
rooms and a self-service restaurant.
Tel: (241) 762523

L=Antre de Bacchus: one of the best and most
expensive French restaurants in town, around
50 USD per person, including wine, located on
the Bord de Mer.
Tel: (241) 732161

Le Chambertin: good atmosphere, French
restaurant, decorated like a wine cellar,
complete dinner, including wine, around
40 USD per person.
Tel: (241) 737613

Chez Marie: popular place with good French
food or pizza, located on the Bord de Mer,
moderate price 25-30 USD per person.
Tel: (241) 732490

Le Gourmet: serves good French food.
Located in quartier Glass, before the SGS
office, across from the American School, price
40 USD per person.
Tel: (241) 763739

Michel de Gonfaron: delicious food, French cooking, pleasant atmosphere, on the Kango Road off the Bord de Mer after the Supergos store. 50 USD per person.
Tel: (241) 762476

La Tomate: good food at a good value, pasta and fish, quartier Louis, 20-25 USD per person.
Tel: (241) 736477

Highway Construction

Ministry of Equipment and Construction
B.P. 49
Libreville, Gabon
Tel: (241) 763856
Fax: (241) 748092

Principal Government Officials:

President of the Republic, Founder –
Gabonese Democratic Party: El Hadj Omar

Bongo Vice President: Didjob Divungi Di Ndinge

Prime Minister, Head of Government:
Jean Francois Ntoutoume-Emane

Minister of Foreign Affairs and Cooperation:
Jean Ping

Ambassador to the United States:
Paul Boundoukou-Latha

Ambassador to the United Nations:
Denis Dangue-Rewaka

Gabon maintains an embassy in the United States at 2034 20th Street NW, Washington, DC 20009 (tel. 202-797-1000).

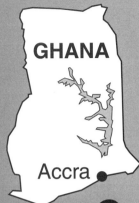

GHANA

Accra •

G H A N A

TRADE AND BUSINESS GUIDE

PROFILE

1

Official Name:	Ghana
Official Language:	English, with 75 other spoken languages and dialects
Population:	19,533,560 (2000 est)
Population Growth:	1.87% (2000 est)
Age Structure:	0-14 years: 42%, 15-64 years: 55%, 65 years and over: 3% (2000 est)
Location:	West Africa, bordering the golf of Guinea, between Cote d'Ivoire and Togo
Area:	238,540 square kilometers, about the size of Oregon
Type of Government:	Akin to the U.S. system but only one legislative arm. The president (chief executive and commander-in-chief of the armed forces), vice-president, and legislative branch (a 200-member Parliament) are elected by universal suffrage for four-year terms
Head of State:	Jerry John Rawlings. John Kuffour, President-elect
Cabinet:	President appoints and Parliament approves
Religion:	43% Christian, 38% various African, 12% Muslim; religious freedom guaranteed
Major Cities:	Capital: Accra. Principal commercial centers: Accra (867,459), Tema and Sekondi-Takoradi (400,000), Kumasi (376,246). Other centers: Ho (37,777), Tamale (135,957), Koforidua (58,731), Cape Coast (57,224), Sunyani (38,834), and Bolgatanga (32,495)
Climate:	Tropical. Accra's hottest months are February through April. Coolest months are July through September. Driest in January; wettest in June
Time:	The entire country is 0 GMT (Greenwich Mean Time), five hours ahead of EST (Eastern Standard Time), but four hours ahead during daylight savings time
GDP:	Purchasing power parity (PPP): $33.6 billion (1998 est), real growth rate: 3% (1998 est), per capita PPP: $1,800 (1998 est), composition by sector: agriculture: 41%, industry: 14%, services: 45% (1996 est)
Currency:	1 new cedi (C) = 100 pesewas
Exchange Rate:	Average exchange rate: new cedis per US$ 1 = 4410.00 (2000 est), 3,100 (1999 est)
Weights & Measure:	Metric system
Natural Resources:	Gold, timber, cocoa, industrial diamond, bauxite, manganese, rubber, fish

Total Trade: See Section 4 - TRADE

Major Trade Partners: Imports and exports: United Kingdom, Nigeria, United States, Germany, Japan, Netherlands

Membership: AFDB, ECOWAS, IBRD, IFC, IMF, ISO, MIGA, UN, UNCTAD, WCO, WIPO. and WTO

Sources: *Ministry of Finance, Statistical Service Department, Bank of Ghana, U.S. Mission estimates, CIA World Factbook, U.S. Department of Commerce*

POLITICAL OUTLOOK ②

Relationship with the U.S.

The U.S. and Ghana are bilaterally close and constructive, but disparities of size and wealth lead to divergences on global and regional political, military, economic, and trade issues. Ghana often supports third-world debt-relief and is a leader in the nonaligned movement as well as other issues of a North–South polarity. Its leaders, mostly native, often support pan-Africanism and populist African democracy. Ghana seems close to Cuba and possibly North Korea.

Influences on Business

The Government of Ghana (GOG) is pro-business. The stable, multiparty democratic environment is committed to the philosophy and practice of market liberalization. Formerly, Ghana seemed against private business and entrepreneurial development, but now it supports business environments and transactions. Since 1989, over 300 unprofitable state-owned enterprises have been in the process of privatization. Ghana's divestiture, free enterprise and private-sector initiatives, and tax incentives for foreign capital have created interest for investors.

Profile

System: December 1996 was the second multiparty election since the beginning of the 4th Republic. President Jerry John Rawlings National Democratic Congress (NDC) has been head since 1981, and won 58 percent of the vote in an election considered fair, peaceful, and free. The People's Patriotic Party (PCP) allied to a record 39.5 percent to the People's National Convention's 2.5 percent. In a 200-member Parliament, the National Patriotic Party (NPP) leads with 61 seats, the Convention Party (CP) has 5, and the People's National Convention (PNC) has 1 seat.

Schedule for Elections: Presidential and general elections take place every four years; the next was in December 2000. The leading opposition party NPP won the election. John Kuffour is the President-elect.

Major Parties: The present Parliament is mainly of the upper middle class, largely consisting of professionals in law, medicine, commerce, and industry. Increased competitiveness and debate between parties seem to encourage peaceful, democratic changes in power rather than antigovernment threats.

Political Violence: Ghana is relatively stable and predictable.

Corruption: Average. Often locally funded contracts aren't transparent, and commercial

fraud and scams are most common with gold deals.

Media: The Constitution protects the media from state control and censorship. The state media echoes official policy, but is also a watchdog over adherence to policies. The independent media is anti-Rawlings.

Trends

The Government of Ghana (GOG) is under heavy pressure from international finance sources to begin a new growth era by adhering to fiscal discipline. In 1998, macro-economic stability and resilience were encouraged by far-reaching economic initiatives. The GOG and the central bank of Ghana have lowered inflation to 9.4 percent, the lowest since 1985, and lowered interest rates. The continued fall in international cocoa and gold prices still threatens growth.

Major Growth Sectors

Gold mining is the primary industry, but has declining price problems. Cocoa looks greater than projected, due to positive crop weather. Telecommunications looks good for both equipment and service providers, especially with liberalization and the Internet's emergence. Hotels and tourism are growing in Accra and elsewhere.

Key Economic Indicators

Income, Production and Employment *(millions of U.S. dollars unless otherwise indicated)*			
	1997	1998	1999[1]
Nominal GDP[2]	6,884	7,630	N/A
Real GDP Growth (pct.)[3]	4.2	4.6	4.5
GDP by Sector			
Agriculture	2.574	3,090	N/A
Manufacturing	640	656	N/A
Services	1,976	2,220	N/A
Government	730	832	N/A
Per Capita GDP (US$)	385	415	N/A
Labor Force (millions)	8,240	8,480	8,734
Unemployment Rate (pct)	22	20	20

1. 1999 figures are all estimates based on most recent data available. 2. GDP at factor cost.
3. Percentage changes calculated in local currency.
Source: Bureau of Economic and Business Affairs; U.S. Department of State

- **Infrastructure**
  Infrastructure shortcomings have discouraged foreign investment and domestic growth. However, improvements are in progress, especially in telecommunications. Ghana Telecom privatization, Internet expansion, and wireless services have created growing voice and data transmission systems. Although the GOG is committed to road building, in the rainy season poor roads lead to slow goods delivery.

- **Labor**
  Ghana has a large pool of unskilled, cheap labor. Labor–management relations are good, and regulations and policies favor business.

Money and Prices (annual percentage growth)			
	1997	**1998**	**1999[1]**
Money Supply Growth (M)	40.8	17.6	3.9
Consumer Price Inflation (end of period)	20.8	15.7	12.6
Exchange Rate (cedis/US$ annual average)	2,250	2,346	3,100

1. 1999 figures are all estimates based on most recent data available.
Source: Bureau of Economic and Business Affairs; U.S. Department of State

Balance of Payments and Trade (millions of U.S. dollars unless otherwise indicated)			
	1997	**1998**	**1999[1]**
Total Exports FOB[2]	1,491	1,491	1,880
Exports to U.S.[2]	154	144	140
Total Imports CIF[2]	2,128	2,213	2,253
Imports from U.S.[2]	314	223	253
Trade Balance[2]	-637	-722	-373
Balance with U.S.	-160	-79	-113
External Public Debt	5,651	5,922	5,750
Fiscal Deficit/GDP (pct)	2.6	2.3	N/A
Current Account Deficit/GDP (pct)	8.5	3.5	N/A
Debt Service Payments/GDP (pct)	8.6	8.4	N/A
Gold and Foreign Exchange Reserves	508	508	364
Aid from U.S.	52	58	60
Aid from All Other Sources	N/A	N/A	N/A

1. 1999 figures are all estimates based on most recent data available. 2. Merchandise trade
Source: Bureau of Economic and Business Affairs; U.S. Department of State

Government Influence on Business

The government of Ghana continues to divest its state-owned enterprises, and take a secondary role in the economy. The government still owns Ghana Airways, and it holds a monopoly on cocoa exports.

TRADE

④

Leading Imports and Exports

Imports: Electrical power systems, telecommunications equipment, construction and earthmoving equipment, motor and heavy-duty vehicles and replacement parts, mining industry equipment, computers and peripherals, travel and tourism services, food processing and packaging equipment, second-hand clothing, medical equipment, hotel and restaurant equipment, rice, defense articles.

Exports: Cocoa, timber, and gold.

Foreign Trade *(Exports and Imports in US$M)*			
	1997	1998	1999[1]
Total Exports FOB[2]	1,491	1,491	1,880
Exports to U.S.[2]	154	144	140
Total Imports CIF[2]	2,128	2,213	2,253
Imports from U.S.[2]	314	223	253

1. 1999 figures are all estimates based on most recent data available. 2. Merchandise trade
Source: Bureau of Economic and Business Affairs; U.S. Department of State

Best Prospects Analysis

Best Prospects for non-Agricultural Goods and Services

Telecommunications Equipment (TEL)

	1997E $M	1998E $M	1999E $M
Total Market Size	44	10	80
Total Local Production	0	0	0
Total Exports	0	0	0
Total Imports	44	70	80
Imports from the U.S.	5	10	12

Electrical Power Systems (ELP)

	1997E $M	1998E $M	1999E $M
Total Market Size	40	61	64
Total Local Production	0	0	0
Total Exports	6	8	6
Total Imports	46	69	70
Imports from the U.S.	20	28	30

Computers and Peripherals (CPT)

	1997E $M	1998E $M	1999E $M
Total Market Size	15	20	25
Total Local Production	0	0	0
Total Exports	2	3	3
Total Imports	17	23	28
Imports from the U.S.	6	10	12

Automobiles/Light Trucks/Vans (AUT)

	1997E $M	1998E $M	1999E $M
Total Market Size	275	285	290
Total Local Production	0	0	0
Total Exports	0	3	3
Total Imports	275	88	293
Imports from the U.S.	28	32	33

Construction and Earthmoving Equipment (CON)

	1997E $M	1998E $M	1999E $M
Total Market Size	78	94	100
Total Local Production	0	0	0
Total Exports	0	0	0
Total Imports	78	94	100
Imports from the U.S.	23	28	32

Mining Industry Equipment (MIN)

	1997E $M	1998E $M	1999E $M
Total Market Size	86	99	80
Total Local Production	0	0	0
Total Exports	0	0	0
Total Imports	86	99	80
Imports from the U.S.	13	16	12

Hotel/Restaurant Equipment (HTL)/Household Consumer Goods (HCG)/Consumer Electronics (CEL)

	1997E $M	1998E $M	1999E $M
Total Market Size	106	122	125
Total Local Production	8	10	12
Total Exports	2	3	4
Total Imports	100	115	113
Imports from the U.S.	12	18	20

Food Processing and Packaging Equipment (FPP)

	1997E $M	1998E $M	1999E $M
Total Market Size	21.0	25.2	30.0
Total Local Production	0.1	0.2	0.3
Total Exports	0	0	0
Total Imports	20.9	25.0	29.7
Imports from the U.S.	7.6	9.1	10.0

Travel and Tourism Services (TRA)

	1997E $M	1998E $M	1999E $M
Total Market Size	297	306	386
Total Local Production	N/A	N/A	N/A
Total Exports	N/A	N/A	N/A
dTotal Imports	N/A	N/A	N/A
Imports from the U.S.	N/A	N/A	N/A

Best Prospects for Agricultural Products

Wheat

	1996E MT ('000)	1997E MT ('000)	1998E MT ('000)
Total Consumption	250	250	210
Total Local Production	0	0	0
Total Exports	0	0	0
Total Imports	225	250	270
Imports from the U.S.	190	220	250

Rice

	1996E MT (Millions)	1997E MT (Millions)	1998E MT (Millions)
Total Consumption	260	300	350
Total Local Production	110	120	130
Total Exports	0	0	0
Total Imports	150	180	220
Imports from the U.S.	45	80	100

Frozen Beef/Chicken/Turkey

	1996E MT (Millions)	1997E MT (Millions)	1998E MT (Millions)
Total Consumption	80	91	100
Total Local Production	50	55	65
Total Exports	0	0	0
Total Imports	30	36	35
Imports from the U.S.	0.5	3	15

The above statistics are unofficial estimates.
N/A - Not Available, E - Estimated
Note: MT ('000) = Thousand Metric Tons

Extracted from the U.S. Department of Commerce USA Trade 2000 Country Commercial Guide for Ghana.

The data above are estimates based on Ghana Statistical Service figures. Estimates for 1998 and 1999 take into consideration the direction of government policies, economic and political conditions, and the views of market participants.

Import and Export Tips

• **Regulations**

Customs: All imports are subject to duty taxes, except those for government, privileged people, organizations, and institution exemptions. Ghana uses the Customs Valuation Code (CVC) value assessment method of the World Trade Organization (WTO). Ghanaian agencies responsible for regulating business activities include the Internal Revenue Service (taxes); VAT service; Monetary Bank of Ghana (transactions); Ministry of Employment & Social Welfare (labor issues); Copyrights Office (copyrights); Ghana Standards Board (standards and labels); Registrar-General's Department (company registration).

Tariffs: Imports may be subject to import duties, sales tax, special duties, and import excise duty. The Harmonized Commodity Catalog (HS) is used to classify goods. Free Trade Zone companies pay no duty on imports. Companies achieve Free Trade Zone status either by exporting over 70 percent of their products or by being located in one of various industrial zones.

Import Taxes: Nearly all imports are subject to sales tax and import tax. A value-added tax of 10 percent is imposed on duty, inclusive of value. Import rates are as follows: agricultural and educational materials, 0 percent; raw materials and capital goods, 10 percent ad valorem; all other goods, 25 percent ad valorem. Sixteen categories are under additional duty to protect domestic industries. All imports are either on collection (import before paying, only with Bank of Ghana approval) or conventional, which requires a bank's letter of credit (LC) or foreign exchange provision.

Exchange Rate: The foreign exchange value of the Ghanaian cedi is established independently through the use of Interbank Market and Foreign Exchange bureaus, and currency conversion is easily obtained. The foreign exchange auction procedure was abandoned in 1992. Ghana fully accedes to Article IV of the IMF convention on free current account convertibility and transfer. Through the Bank of Ghana's intervention, the cedi depreciated by about 13 percent in 1998 compared to an annual average of about 25 percent during 1993 to 1997. Depletion of the bank's foreign exchange reserves in 1999, mainly as a result of higher oil import bills and shortfall in external program assistance, has resulted in a sharp depreciation of the cedi and a shortage of major foreign exchange. In general, the exchange rate regime in Ghana does not have any particular impact on the competitiveness of U.S. exports. This may change, however, if the euro continues its fall in relation to the dollar.

• **Documentation**

Exports: Few export controls exist. Restricted exports include military hardware, antiques and collector's items, art over 50 years old, game and wildlife, timber products, precious metals, and live plants. All require permits or certificates. Prohibited exports include narcotics, parrots, cedis in excess of ¢5,000 ($2 est), and items specified by law. The government-owned Ghana Cocoa Marketing Board (COCOBOD) monopolizes cocoa bean exportation. Agencies that require application for export permit or certificates include Ghana Museums and Monuments Board (antiques); Precious Minerals Marketing Corp. (precious minerals); Department of Game & Wildlife (wildlife); Ministry of Agriculture (live plants); and Ministry of Interior (dangerous weapons).

Imports: An Import Declaration Form (IDF) must cover most classes of goods entering Ghana. To clear customs, the importer must complete a designated Customs Entry Form, a bill of lading from the foreign exporter, a commercial invoice, an Import Declaration Form, a Bank of Ghana form (A1) and a Pre-Shipment Inspection (PSI) Certificate. Additional documents required include an income tax certificate, Shipper's Notification Form, and a packing list. No import quotas exist. Restricted imports include drugs, communications equipment, mercury, gambling machines, handcuffs, arms and ammunition, live plants, and animals. Prohibited imports include narcotics, mercuric medicated soap, toxic waste, contaminated goods, foreign cigarettes without a warning notice, foreign soil, counterfeit notes and coins of any country, and any goods prohibited by local law. Agencies that require application for import permits or certificates include Ministry of Health (drugs); National Frequency and Registration Board (communications equipment); Ministry of Finance & Economic Planning (gold coins, uncut diamonds, and goods bearing design in imitation of money); Ministry of Interior (handcuffs, machines for duplicating keys, arms and ammunition, gambling machines).

Labeling: All categories of import (except fish and petroleum) must identify in English the goods shipped, the ingredients and components, the point of origin, and the expiration date (for perishables).

Standards: The Ghana Standards Board (GSB) develops and promulgates standards and quality of imported goods. The GSB has promulgated some 160 Ghanaian standards and adopted over 300 foreign standards for certification purposes. Both manufacturers and importers must register with the GSB. The metric system of measurement and 220 V, 50 Hz electricity are used.

• Payment

Terms: Letters of credit are the minimum and recommended terms. Usual terms are for 90 days.

Currency Exchange: Ghana operates a free-floating exchange rate policy regime. There are no restrictions on fund conversion and transfer if there is supporting documentary evidence. Cedis are easily exchanged for dollars and most major European currencies. Currently, there are delays of about one month to acquire foreign exchange (for the first time since 1992).

Fund Transfer: Ghana has no restrictions on the transfer of funds associated with investment. Its investment laws guarantee the investor the transfer out of Ghana, in convertible currency, of dividends or net profits attributable to the investment; payments in respect of loan servicing where a foreign loan has been obtained; fees and charges in respect of technology transfer agreements registered under the GIPC law; the remittance of proceeds in the event of sale or liquidation of the enterprise or any interest attributable to the investment.

Offshore Loans: Offshore loans must be approved by the Bank of Ghana. It inspects the terms and interest rate. No legal parallel market exists.

MARKETING TIPS

⑤

Agents and Distributors

A resident agent or distributor is strongly recommended. The International Company Profile (ICP) is a service for checking the reputation, status, and reliability of a trading partner (at $100 per company). The U.S. Commercial Service offers the Agent Distributor Service (ADS) program and its Gold Key Service, a custom-tailored service for firms planning to visit a country. Services include office support, in-depth briefing, and potential contacts at an estimated $120 per day. Contact at least three weeks before embarking.

Establishing an Office

1. Contact the Ghanaian Investment Promotion Center (GIPC), a center for economic, commercial, and investment information for entrepreneurs and investors. It offers guidance to register, incorporate, modify, or dissolve a local company. It uses databases, documentation, formal presentations, investment missions, specific investment fora, and basic counseling.

2. To incorporate, get name availability from the Registrar of Companies.

3. Consult a local attorney before establishing a business entity in Ghana. The U.S. Commercial Service maintains updated lists.

Distribution and Sales Channels

Wholesalers, retail outlets, and agents or distributors are available to U.S. goods and services suppliers. The government and indigenous associations also buy directly. The major trading centers, with population estimates in millions, are Accra/Tema (3.5), Kumasi (1), Sekondi/Takoradi (.4), Tamale (.4), Sunyani (.2), Cape Coast (.15).

Direct Marketing

Both wholesale and retail sites are mainly concentrated in Accra, including company headquarters, branch banking, supermarkets, and specialty shops. Most small-scale retail in Ghana lacks specialization. U.S. companies require Ghanaian presence either through an agent, a distributor, or a small business.

Leasing/Joint Ventures

The Ghanaian Investment Code provides legislative support for joint ventures, but responsibilities should be well spelled out. Some local entrepreneurs expect only to sell locally, with costs borne by foreign investors. Similarly, many potential local partners have little equity and offer only local marketing knowledge.

Franchising

Franchising has growing potential, especially for smaller businesses, but is hindered by the undercapitalization of many companies.

Advertising and Promotion

Accra has over 12 advertising agencies. Larger ones provide full publicity and sales promotion. The smallest ones sometimes provide only design and printing. The U.S. Commercial Service is useful for identifying companies, publications, and media for specific marketing. Market research companies are also available. Trade fairs are popular. Eye-catching, colorful design and packaging appeal to Ghanaians. Because of warmth and humidity, shelf life is important.

Selling Factors

Though links are historically with Britain, and Britain or Asian goods had been preferred, interest is growing for American products (in part for good quality, low price, and after-sales service). A high level of personal contact and presence in Ghana are very important for sales. Traditional politeness is also important and appreciated. The pace of life is slower in Ghana than in the U.S., so adjustment may be necessary. Lebanese and Indian-Asian Ghanaians make up important business communities.

Selling to the Government

The Ghana Supply Commission (GSC) does all government purchasing. There is a typical 45-day tendering period on procurement contracts being let. Financing is often by a multilateral lending institution. Bid documents are inexpensive. Contact the GSC for additional information.

Pricing

Ghanaians are price conscious, but also aware that cheaper may mean worse quality. Local commercial credit is very limited. Most Ghanaians prefer cash, so money circulates much more than it rests in banks. U.S. exporters should have an irrevocable, confirmed letter of credit if they are new or non-resident to Ghana. The Commercial Service

provides information on sound credit policies, and the ICP (International Company Profile) program has information on specific Ghanaian firms.

Customer Support

Goods are often put to over-heavy use, so service contracts, product recalls, and warranty work are becoming more common. Low prices, high quality, and after-sales support make American goods increasingly popular. Readable service manuals, frequent personnel training, and adequate spare parts inventory are important for sales growth.

Intellectual Property Rights (IPR)

Local and international legal strides give increasing protection. Ghana belongs to the World Intellectual Property Organization (WIPO) and the English-speaking African Regional Industrial Property Organization (ESARIPO).

Attorney

Having a local attorney is advisable to ensure compliance with all employment laws, such as the Labor Decree of 1967 and the Industrial Relations Act of 1956 (Act 299), which regulate employment and collective bargaining. The Commercial Service maintains lists of local attorneys.

FOREIGN INVESTMENT
⑥

Openness: Encouraging foreign investment is integral to Ghanaian foreign policy. For privatization, two-thirds of 300 previously state-owned enterprises have been sold. For the legal environment, laws such as Ghana

Investment Promotion Center (GIPC) Act of 1994 (Act 478) secure many sectors of the economy for financial systems. Only a financial minimum is required for foreign investment, beginning at US $10,000. With money and documents, investments are registered in five working days. Areas of investing restricted to Ghanaians include taxi services under ten vehicles, pool betting and lotteries (except soccer), beauty salons, and barber shops.

Regulatory System: Trade liberalization and investment promotion are part of Ghana's move toward a clear and transparent regulatory system. The Ghana Investment Promotion Center intended to expedite various investment steps. Telecommunications, water, and power sectors are overseen by various authorities and commissions for quality and regulation.

Investment Agreements: So far, agreements with six major countries have been signed, and potentially eight more are in place. The Investment Protection Agreement and the Trade and Investment Framework Agreement (TIFA) have been signed with the U.S.

Trade Zones and Free Ports: All free zone companies (eligible by location in certain areas or by exporting over 70 percent of products) receive a ten-year corporate tax holiday and zero import duty. Work and residence permits are required, but a "one-stop approval service" by Ghana Free Zones Board assists in all formalities.

Performance Requirements/Incentives: Ghana is in compliance with the WTO Trade-Related Investment Measures (TRIM) notification. Investment levels give automatic immigration quota, with a $10,000 U.S. currency or equipment investment guaranteeing one person, and $500,000 guaranteeing four people. Many tax incentives make the effective tax rate fairly low. There is no import price control.

Capital Markets and Investment: The GOG encourages foreign investment in the private sector. The largest banks are no longer state controlled: Ghana Commercial Bank and SSB ($30 million and $80 million worth, respectively), but financing is still limited in scope. New regulatory policies are expected to enhance growth.

Private Ownership: Foreign entities are allowed ownership except for certain business activities. Private and public enterprises compete equally for access to credit, markets, licenses, and supplies.

Property Rights: Chattel and real property are legally supported, but with often thorny questions of land-ownership proof due to poor records. Mortgages exist. Ghana is implementing the WTO TRIPS (Trade-Related Aspects of Intellectual Property Rights) agreement.

Expropriation and Compensation: Ghana's laws guarantee against expropriation and nationalization, with some exceptions. The GOG may seize property when in the interest of national defense, public safety, public order, public morality, public health, town and country planning, or development for public benefit. However, fair compensation is required. No recent acquisition has happened, partly because the GOG encourages foreign investment.

OPIC and Investment Insurance: OPIC is looking to expand in Ghana. Officers visit regularly, with African Project Development Facility (APDF), African Investment Program of the International Finance Corporation, and the African Growth Fund providing investor information. Ghana is a member of Multilateral Investment Guarantee Agency (MIGA).

Dispute Settlement: The main areas of dispute for U.S. companies are rice production, agricultural trading, and telecommunications. The GOG is still discussing solutions. Foreign judgments are reciprocity based, so some are enforceable in Ghana, but not yet in the U.S. Courts do not necessarily side with the GOG. The Ghana Arbitration Center and the Mediation/Conciliation unit of the U.S. Chamber of Commerce (Ghana) provides arbitration and more security in trade and investment. A bankruptcy statute doesn't exist.

FINANCE

7

Ghana has a Central Bank, 11 commercial banks, 5 merchant banks, and 100 rural unit banks. Nonbank institutions include a stock exchange, 21 insurance companies, Social Security National Insurance Trust (SSNIT), two discount houses, the Home Finance Company, numerous building societies, a venture capital company, a unit trust, and six leasing companies. The Bank of Ghana regulates and supervises the banking and finance market. Banks have typically played it safe by investing in government securities, and nonbanks have provided little finance.

Export Financing: Letters of credit, collections, and fund transfers are available to exporters. An irrevocable, confirmed letter of credit should be chosen for reliable, speedy payment. The GSM-102 and GSM-103 Credit Guarantee Programs guarantee payment to U.S. exporters for various agricultural goods for 90 days to 1 year.

Project Financing: The International Finance Corporation (IFC) and the Overseas Private Investment Corporation (OPIC) are U.S. government sponsored and offer finance and insurance products to exporters. The Export-Import Bank of the U.S. (EXIM) supports short-, medium-, and long-term private-sector exports that create U.S. jobs. The U.S. Trade and Development Agency (TDA) offers loans to bidders of GOG-sponsored procurements and also funds for feasibility studies.

COMMUNICATIONS

8

Phone

Ghana has around 141,000 phone lines, served by Ghana Telecom & Westel (U.S. company). A new connection can take two weeks to two months. Local phone calls are 200 cedis (8 cents) per minute; to U.S. and Europe, they are US $1.10 per minute. There are three mobile cellular phone operators. Pay phone services are abundant at communication centers throughout major cities. Prepaid calling cards for local and international calls are sold by travel agents, post offices, and gas stations. For calls to the U.S., AT&T's access code is 0191. Sprint's is 01900. Globalphone and other call back services are popular. The international access code is 011, and the Ghana access code is 233. City codes are Accra (21), Koforidua (81), Kumasi (51), Takoradi (31), Tamale (71), followed by the local telephone number.

Internet

Three Internet service providers (ISPs) offer a full range of services: NCS (Network Systems), AfricaOnline, and Internet Ghana.

Mail

An ordinary airmail letter to the U.S. costs ¢1,100; up to 20 grams, ¢2,500; up to 40 grams, ¢5,000; post cards, ¢550. Big hotels sell stamps and accept mail from guests. Express Mail International Services are available between Ghana and the U.S.

TRANSPORTATION

Land

Ghana has about 40,000 km of roads, with only one-quarter paved. Accra roads are narrow, poorly maintained with daunting open gutters. Traffic is congested at peak hours, but should be lessened by current expansion and improvement projects. The buses have unreliable security, convenience, and schedules. The tro-tros are also not recommended for business travel. Taxis are abundant, but in poor condition, and fares should be negotiated before embarking. Car rentals (some chauffeured) are available for around $50 to $80 a day. Gas prices fluctuate, averaging $.35 per liter. A triangle railway connects Kumasi, Takoradi, and Accra-Tema.

Sea

The ports in Ghana are Tema and Sekondi-Takoradi. Major shipping lines with offices and agencies in Ghana are Maersk, Delmas, Liner Agencies, RoRo Services, and Torm Lines (represented in Ghana by Maritime Agencies West Africa Limited). Shipping time and costs have been lowered by the direct link offered by Maersk from Baltimore to Tema.

Air

Ghana has an international airport in Accra and three other domestic ones. Ghana Airways provides international flights, including direct ones to New York and Atlanta. The 17 other international airlines include British Airways, KLM, Swissair, Alitalia, Lufthansa, Air Afrique, Middle East Airlines, Aeroflot, and South African Airways. They connect Accra with Europe, the Middle East, and other parts of Africa. Air Link, Fanair, and Muk Airways (all private) operate internal flights to Tamale and Kumasi. The third domestic airport in Ghana, Sunyani, is not currently served.

WORK WEEK

Business Hours: 8.00 a.m. to 12.00 p.m. and 1.00 p.m. to 5.00 p.m. Monday through Friday.

Banks: 8.30 a.m. to 2.00 p.m. Monday through Thursday, and 8.30 a.m. to 3.00 p.m. on Friday.

Foreign Exchange Bureaus: 8.00 a.m. to 7.00 p.m. Monday through Friday, and 8.00 a.m. to 12.00 p.m. on Saturday.

Shops: Some are open on Saturday, but they usually close at 2:00 p.m.

HOLIDAYS 2001

New Year's Day, January 1
Eid-Ul Fitr, February*
Independence Day, March 6
Good Friday, April 21
Easter Monday, April 24
Eid-Ul-Adha, April*
Labor Day, May 1
Republic Day, July 1
Farmers' Day, December 4
Christmas Day, December 25
Boxing Day, December 26

Some holidays may be observed on different dates depending on the day of the week on which it falls.

*Business travelers should verify the dates of these holidays prior to undertaking their trip since these holidays vary from country to country and depend on the sighting of the moon. Business establishments, including the U.S. Mission, are normally closed during public holidays in Ghana. The U.S. Mission is closed on Ghanaian holidays as well as U.S. holidays.

BUSINESS TRAVEL

Business Customs

Business customs are similar to those in the U.S., but a bit more formal. Beware of excessively friendly business favors and demands (may be illegal by the 1997 U.S. Foreign Corrupt Practices Act, which can be cited). U.S. Commercial Service's Gold Key Service can arrange appointments with many local officials and businesspeople. Business cards and widely used. Most urban Ghanaians speak some English, which is the usual business language and also the official language.

Travel Advisory and Visas

A U.S. passport and international health certificate with yellow fever and cholera immunizations are required for entry to Ghana. Except for ECOWAS nationals, a visa is required. Permits for work and residence should be obtained prior to entry and are dispensed by quotas and investment level.

Business Infrastructure

Entry Requirements (personal and professional goods): Personal baggage is free of duty. Unaccompanied personal effects require Passenger Unaccompanied Baggage Declaration (PUBD) form at arrival time. Vehicles and sample goods require duty deposit, which will be refunded if re-exported within three months.

Currency Exchange: The cedi (¢) is the main currency; US $1 equals ¢2,500 (est). There are no import/export currency restrictions if it is declared upon entry, and exchanged only through banks and Forex bureaus. The cedi has been declining, but recently fairly slowly.

Taxes: A corporate tax of 35 percent exists, but there are numerous tax incentives. Nontraditional exports are taxed at 8 percent, and hotels at 25 percent. All foreign nationals are taxed at 35 percent. A customs tariff on raw materials and capital goods is at 0 percent, intermediate goods at 10 percent, and consumer goods at 25 percent. The value-added tax (VAT) is 10 percent, which includes all consumer purchases, services, hotel and restaurant bills, advertising, betting, and entertainment. There is a wealth tax of 0.05 percent on the assessed value of property.

Hotels and Restaurants: The most popular U.S. business hotels in Accra are Novotel Hotel, Labadi Beach Hotel, Shangri-La, Wangara Hotal. Cheaper popular hotels are The American Club, Esther Hotel, Frankie's Hotel, Nogahill Hotel, North Ridge Hotel, Royal Ridge Hotel, Sam's Cottages, Secaps Hotel, Sharita Lodge, Sunrise Hotel. Kumasi has City Hotel, Hotel Georgia, Stadium Hotel, Cicero Guest House, Cozylodge Guest House. Takodori has Atlantic Hotel, Hillcrest Hotel, Hotel Alrose. Obuasi has the Anyinam Lodge. Cape Coast and Elmina have Coconut Grove Hotel, Elmina Berjaya, and Savoy Hotel. CNN and Multichoice TV programs are locally available. Abundant good restaurants serve mainly European, Asian, and Ghanaian dishes.

Rent: Expatriate residential rent averages $2,000 to $3,500 per month (with often one to three years down). Commercial rent in Accra averages $7 to $25 per square foot. Purchases of land should involve careful check of ownership records.

Utilities: Power is rationed, so having a standby generator is recommended. Commercial installation ranges from $5,200 to $5,500 but costs three times that for underground cables. Average power bill per embassy house is $500 per month. Water is reliable in Accra, and costs $35 to $49 per monthly residential.

Business Services: Major cities have business centers for communication and document preparation services. Well-qualified accountants, attorneys, consultants, architects, advertisers, and managers are easily obtainable in Accra.

Labor Costs and Legislation: Minimum daily wage is 2,900 cedis (USD 1.16 est).

Transportation, rent, and meal allowances are a normal part of compensation, all of which is taxable. Monthly salary ranges (including allowances) are as follows: unskilled labor, $50 to $100; skilled labor, $200 to $600; professionals, $900 to $1,200; consultants, internationally competitive rates. Employers with over five employees must also contribute to the Social Security National Insurance Trust (SSNIT).

Education: The most popular schools for expatriates are the Lincoln Community School, Ghana International School, and Kokrobitey School. Literacy rate is 64.5%.

Insurance: Accident, sickness, liability, and medical evacuation insurance are fairly priced and should be obtained before departure to Ghana.

Travel Notes

The following travel notes have been supplied by the U.S. government. For the most recent general travel and consular information, see the U.S. Department of State travel publications or call the Traveler's Telephone Hotline at (202) 647-5225.

Security: Crime (most often, theft and scams) is a profitable growth industry, especially in urban areas. Take care even when stopped at traffic lights, don't walk alone on beaches, and stay alert. Avoid parking in unlit areas.

Health Precautions: Vaccinate against typhoid, paratyphoid, tetanus, cholera, hepatitus, meningitus, and polio before arrival. Malaria prophylaxis before and after travel is encouraged. Drink only bottled or purified water, and avoid uncooked vegetables. It is unsafe to swim in lagoons and freshwater streams. The ocean is safe, but has a strong surf and undertow. Take caution against heat, sun, and humidity. AIDS and other STDs are becoming widespread. Current information on health matters may be obtained from the Centers for Disease Control and Prevention's international travelers' hotline at (404) 332-4559.

Embassy Assistance

To obtain additional and updated information on entry and exit requirements, travelers can contact the Consular Section of the Ghana Embassy at 3512 International Drive, N.W., Washington, D.C. 20008; Tel: (202) 686-4520. Travelers may also contact the Ghana consulate, which is located in New York.

Prior to a Ghana trip, U.S. business visitors are encouraged to contact the State Economic/Commercial Office, the Foreign Agricultural Service, or the Commercial Service. The former two are located at the U.S. Embassy, Chancery, Ring Road East, near Danquah Circle. The latter is located on the grounds of the United States Information Service (USIS), at the corner of Independence and Castle Roads.

CONTACTS

13

Ministries and Other GOG Entities

Ministry of Trade and Industry
P.O. Box M47
Ministries, Accra
Tel: 233-21-665421; 663327
Fax: 233-21-668263

Ministry of Finance & Economic Planning
P.O. Box M.40
Ministries, Accra
Tel: 233-21-665421; 665441
Fax: 233-21-667069

Ministry of Foreign Affairs
P.O. Box M.53
Ministries, Accra
Tel: 233-21-664008
Fax: 233-21-664008

Ministry of Tourism
P.O. Box 3106
Ministries, Accra
Tel: 233-21-666049; 666314; 666426
Fax: 233-21-662375

Ministry of Roads & Transport
P.O. Box M. 57
Ministries, Accra
Tel: 233-21-666465
Fax: 233-21-667114

Ministry of Mines and Energy
P.O. Box 40
Stadium, Accra
Tel: 233-21-667151-3; 667090
Fax: 233-21-668262

Ministry of Works & Housing
P.O. Box M.43
Ministries, Accra
Tel: 233-21-662242; 667689
Fax: 233-21-663268

Ministry of Employment & Social Welfare
P.O. Box M.84
Ministries, Accra
Tel: 233-21-665349
Fax: 233-21-667251

Ministry of Food and Agriculture
P.O. Box M.37
Ministries, Accra
Tel: 233-21-663036
Fax: 233-21-663250

Ministry of Communications
P.O. Box M.41
Ministries, Accra
Tel: 233-21-662772
Fax: 233-21-664067

Ghana Investment Promotion Center
P.O. Box M193
Accra
Tel: 233-21-665125; 9
Fax: 233-21-663801
Email: gipc@ghastinet.gn.apc.org

Customs, Excise and Preventive Service
P.O. Box 68, Accra
Tel: 233-21-666841; 2; 662123
Fax: 233-21-660019

Divestiture Implementation Committee
P.O. Box C102
Cantonments, Accra
Tel: 233-21-772049; 773119; 60281
Fax: 233-21-773126
Email: dicgh@ncs.com.gh

Ghana Free Zones Board
Ministry of Trade & Industry Annex
P.O. Box M.47
Accra
Tel: 233-21-780532; 3; 4; 5; 7
Fax: 233-21-780536
Email: freezone@africaonline.com.gh

Ghana Supply Commission
P.O. Box M 35
Accra
The Chief Executive
Tel: 233-21-228131
Fax: 233-21-668452

**Ghana National Petroleum Corporation
  (GNPC)**
Private Mail Bag, Tema
Tel: 233-22-206020; 204654; 202823;
233-21-774234 (Accra)
Fax: 233-21-232039
Email: gnpc@ghana.com

Minerals Commission
P.O. Box M.248
Accra
Tel: 233-21-772786; 779823; 4
Fax: 233-21-773324

**Trade Associations and Chambers of
Commerce**

American Chamber of Commerce (Ghana)
P.O. CT 2869
Cantonments, Accra
Tel: 233-21-763834; 028-215372
Fax: 233-21- 771426
Email: amchamgh@ghana.com
Website: http://www.amcham-africa.org

Ghana National Chamber of Commerce
65 Kojo Thompson
P.O. Box 2325
Accra
Tel: 233-21-662-427
Fax: 233-21-662-210

The West African Enterprise Network
West Africa Headquarters
SSNIT Tower Block, 5th Block
P.M.B., Ministries Post Office, Accra
Tel: 233-21-780186
Fax: 233-21-669100
Email: ababio@ghana.com

Private Enterprise Foundation
P.O. Box C1671
Cantonments, Accra
Tel: 233-21-222313; 231488
Fax: 233-21-231487

Ghana Chamber of Mines
Minerals House
No. 10, 6th Street
Airport Residential Area, Accra
Tel: 233-21-760652; 761893
Fax: 233-21-760653
Email: chamine@ghana.com

Association of Ghana Industries (AGI)
Trade Fair Center
P.O. Box 8624
Accra-North
Tel: 233-21-777-283; 775-311, ext. 697; 723
Fax: 233-21-773143

Ghana Export Promotion Council
P.O. Box 146
Accra
Tel: 233-21-228-813; 30
Fax: 233-21-668-263

Ghana Stock Exchange
P.O. Box 1849
Accra
Tel: 233-21-669908; 669914; 669935
Fax: 233-21-669913
Email: stockex@ncs.com.gh

U.S. Embassy Trade Personnel
The local mailing address is:
Embassy of the United States of America
Ring Road East
P.O. Box 194
Accra, Ghana
Tel: (233-21) 775348; 775297; 775298
Fax: (233-21) 776008

The Commercial Service
c\o The United States Information Service
   (USIS)
Liberation and Castle Roads
P.O. Box 2288
Accra, Ghana
Tel: (233-21) 235096 (Direct)
229179 (Switchboard)
Fax: (233-21) 235096; 776008
Email: comserv@ghana.com

The Foreign Agricultural Service
Ring Road East
Embassy of the United States
P.O. Box 194
Accra, Ghana
Tel: (233-21) 775348; 775297; 775298
Fax: (233-21) 778033
Email: fasaccra@ncs.com.gh

The Diplomatic Pouch address is:
Embassy of the United States of America
Accra - Department of State
Washington, DC 20521-2020

Banks and
Financial Institutions

Commercial Banks

Commercial banks offer services such as current and savings accounts, telegraphic transfers, safe custody deposits, sale of traveler's checks and foreign transactions, including the establishment of letters of credit.

Ghana Commercial Bank Ltd.
P.O. Box 134
Accra
Tel: 233-21-666140
Fax: 233-21-662168

Standard Chartered Bank Ltd.
P.O. Box 768
Accra
Tel: 233-21-664591; 9
Fax: 233-21-667751

Barclay's Bank Ltd.
P.O. Box 2949
Accra
Tel: 233-21-667392
Fax: 233-21-667420

The Trust Bank Ltd. (formerly Meridien BIAO Bank)
P.O. Box 1862
Accra
Tel: 233-21-230486; 665562; 665605
Fax: 233-21-665710

Social Security Bank Ltd.
P.O. Box 13119
Accra
Tel: 233-21-667146; 667147; 667148
Fax: 233-21-668651

Agricultural Development Bank Ltd.
P.O. Box 4191
Accra
Tel: 233-21-662836
Fax: 233-21-662803

Bank for Housing and Construction Ltd.
P.O. Box M.1
Ministries Post Office, Accra
Tel: 233-21-220163
Fax: 233-21-229631

National Investment Bank Ltd.
P.O. Box 3726
Accra
Tel: 233-21-669301; 662629
Fax: 233-21-669307

Cooperative Bank Ltd.
P.O. Box 5992
Accra
Tel: 233-21-228735; 229438
Fax: 233-21-222292

Prudential Bank Ltd.
P.O. Box C628
Cantonments, Accra
Tel: 233-21-226322
Fax: 233-21-226803

International Commercial Bank Ltd.
P.O. Box 20057
Accra
Tel: 233-21-666190; 663429; 665779; 669572
Fax: 233-21-668221

Merchant Banks

Merchant banks offer services such as accept-
ances, new issues, private placings, and public
offers of shares for sale, underwriting of new
issues and offers of shares for
sale, corporate finance, and consulting services,
registrar's services for public and private companies, stockbroking services, management of
investment portfolios, and leasing and hire purchase services.

Merchant Bank Ghana Ltd.
P.O. Box 401
Accra
Tel: 233-21-666331
Fax: 233-21-667305

Ecobank Ghana Ltd.
Private Mail Bag
Accra
Tel: 233-21-229926; 233-28-212020
Fax: 233-21-231934

CAL Merchant Bank Ltd.
P.O. Box 14596
Accra
Tel: 233-21-231098; 231095; 231912
Fax: 233-21-231104; 231913

First Atlantic Merchant Bank Ltd.
P.O. Box C16120
Cantonments, Accra
Tel: 233-21-231433; 231435
Fax: 233-21-231399

Metropolitan and Allied Bank Ltd.
P.O. Box C1778
Cantonments, Accra
Tel: 233-21-232774
Fax: 233-21-232728

Print Media

Ghanaian Times
New Times Corporation
P.O. Box 2638
Accra
Tel: 233-21-228282 (six lines)
Fax: 233-21-229398; 220733
Email: newtimes@ghana.com

New Times Corporation
P.O. Box 2638
Fax: 233-21-229398; 220733
Email: newtimes@ghana.com

Daily Graphic
The Graphic Corporation
P.O. Box 742
Accra
Tel: 233-21-228903; 228911; 228938; 228927
Fax: 233-21-234754
Email: graphic@ghana.com

Ghanaian Chronicle
General Portfolio Limited
Private Mail Bag
Accra-North
Tel: 233-21-232713; 227789; 232608
Fax: 233-21-232608
Email: chronicl@africaonline.com.gh
Website: http://www.ghanaian-chronicle.com

Business Chronicle
General Portfolio Limited
Private Mail Bag
Accra-North
Tel: 233-21-232713; 227789; 232608
Fax: 233-21-232608
Email: chroncl@africaonline.com.gh
Website: http://www.ghanaian-chronicle.com

Business & Financial Times
Strategic Development Associates
P.O. Box 2157
Accra
Tel: 233-21-223334; 233-27-540404
Fax: 233-21-223334
Email: bft@ighmail.com

The Statesman
Kinesic Communications
P.O. Box 846
Accra
Tel: 233-21-233242
Fax: 233-21-233242

High Street Journal
Sheik Investments Ghana Ltd.
P.O. Box 588
Achimota
Tel/Fax: 233-21-500125
Email: hsjaccra@ghana.com

The Financial Post
Post Publications Limited
P.O. Box AN 8377
Accra-North
Tel: 233-21-223012; 238038-9
Fax: 233-21-238038
Email: tfnpost@africaonline.com.gh

Advertising on TV and Radio

TV

Ghana Broadcasting Corporation
P.O. Box 1633
Accra
Tel: 233-21-221107; 221161
Fax: 233-21-221149; 221153

Metro TV
P.O. Box C1609
Cantonments, Accra.
Tel: 233-21-765700; 238590-1
Fax: 233-21-765703; 234797
Email: metrotv@ighmail.com

TV3 Network
P.O. Box M. 83
Accra
Tel: 233-21-228697; 763457-8
Fax: 233-21-228629

Radio

Radio GAR (95.7 FM)
Ghana Broadcasting Corporation
P.O. Box 1633
Accra
Tel: 233-21-221147; 97
Fax: 233-21-221163
Email: gar@ighmail.com

Radio Gold (90.5 FM)
Network Broadcasting Company Limited
P.O. Box 17298
Accra
Tel: 233-21-311977; 300281; 2 ;3
Fax: 233-21-300284
Email: radiogold@africaonline.com.gh
Website: http://www.radiogold90.5fm.com

Radio Joy (99.7 FM)
Multimedia Broadcasting Company Limited
P.O. Box 17202
Accra
Tel: 233-21-233558; 233559; 233560
Fax: 233-21-224405
Email: joyfm@ghana.com
Website: http://www.joy997fm.com.gh

Radio Choice (102.3 FM)
P.O. Box CT 3032
Cantonments, Accra
Tel: 233-21-760124
Fax: 233-21-773612
Email: choicefm@ghana.com
Website: http://www.choicefm.com

Internet Service Providers

Africaonline Ghana Ltd.
2nd Floor, Rose Plaza
Kaneshie Industrial Area
P.O. Box 11241
Accra-North
Tel: 233-21-226802
Fax: 233-21-226849
www.africaonline.com.gh

Internet Ghana
Kekulasi Court, Faanofa Road
P.O. Box 6745
Accra-Adabraka
Tel: 233-21-220622; 300385
Fax: 233-21-235836
www.internetghana.com
administrator@ighmail.com

Network Computer Systems Ltd. (NCS)
7 Sixth Avenue Ridge
P.O. Box PMB
Accra-Osu
Tel: 233-21-220622; 238218; 225472; 773372;
  231191

For a good web page on doing business in
Ghana, plus rebroadcasts of all three Ghanaian
TV networks on the Internet, try going to
www.ghanaclassifieds.com. The best web pages on
tourism in Ghana are www.ncrc.org.gh and
www.landtours.com.

Advertising and Billboards

Dapeg Limited
P.O. Box 7398
Accra
Tel: 233-21-224677; 227401
Fax: 233-21-302663
Email: dapeg@africaonline.com.gh

Design & Display Publicity Ltd.
19 Ring Road East, Osu
P.O. Box 5504
Accra-North
Tel: 233-21-777827
Fax: 233-21-774205
Email: argon@ghana.com

Icon Communications
P.O. Box C878
Cantonments, Accra
Tel: 233-21-232371-2; 244405, Fax: 233-21-
  232336

Lintas Ghana Ltd.
Osu - Ako Adjei Park
P.O. Box 1262
Accra
Tel: 233-21-772321; 772324; 772481
Fax: 233-21-772498
Email: APLINTAS@ighmail.com

Media Majique & Research Systems
2nd Crescent Street, Asylum Down
P.O. Box 5893
Accra-North
Tel: 233-21-231604; 226631
Fax: 233-21224062
Email: mmrs@ghana.com

Multilateral Financial Institutions

World Bank Field Office
Mr. Peter Harrold, Country Director
69 Dr. Isert Road
North Ridge Residential Area
Accra
Tel: 233-21-229681
Fax: 233-21-227887
Email: charrold@worldbank.org

IFC Liaison Office
150A Roman Road
Roman Ridge, Accra
Tel: 233-21-778109; 779804-5; 761152
Fax: 233-21-776245
Email: ifcghana@ghana.com

Africa Project Development Facility Satellite Office
150A Roman Road
Roman Ridge, Accra
Tel: 233-21-778109; 779804-5; 761152
Fax: 233-21-776245
Email: apdf@ghana.com

Market Research Firms

Boulders Advisors Limited
No.5, 2nd Dade Walk - Labone
P.O. Box C3664
Cantonments, Accra
Mr. Reginald N. France
Tel: 233-21-775516; 771248
Fax: 233-21-771249
Email: boulders@ghana.com

CME Consulting Services
P.O. Box 9789
Airport - Accra
Mr. Y. Osafo Marfo
Tel: 233-21-773217; 776013
Fax: 233-21-773740

Databank Financial Services Ltd.
5th Floor SSNIT Tower Block
P.M.B., Ministries, Accra
Mr. Ken Ofori-Atta, Chairman
Tel: 233-21-669417; 669421; 669110; 665124
Fax: 233-21-669100
Email: databank@africaonline.com.gh

Deloitte, Haskins & Sells
4, Liberation Rd.
P.O. Box 453
Accra
Mr. Joe Forson, Managing Partner
Tel: 233-21-775355; 774169; 773761
Fax: 233-21-775480
Email: deloitte@africaonline.com.gh

J.S. Addo Consultants
P.O. Box 9820
Airport - Accra
Mr. J.S. Addo
Tel: 233-21-669342
Fax: 233-21-226803

KAB Marketing Associates
1st Floor, Glemin House, Osu
P.O. Box 01854
Osu, Accra
Mr. Kofi Adom-Boakye
Tel: 233-21-302850
Tel: 233-27-557132; 557512
Fax: 233-21-773279

Media Majique & Research Systems
P.O. Box 5893
Accra-North
Mr. Reginald Laryea
Tel: 233-21-226631; 231604
Fax: 233-21-224062
Email: mmrs@ghana.com

Peat Marwick, Okoh & Co.
Mobil House, Liberia Rd.
P.O. Box 242
Accra
Mr. E.O. Asiedu, Partner
Tel: 233-21-664881-4
Fax: 233-21-667909
Email: asiedu@kpmg.africaonline.com.gh or
kpmg-gh@kpmg.africaonline.com.gh

Plan Consult
P.O. Box C1367
Cantonments, Accra
Mr. Ebow Bannerman
Tel: 233-21-669165
Fax: 233-21-667141
Email: plancons@africaonline.com.gh

PriceWaterhouseCoopers
4th Floor, Gulf House, Legon Rd.
P.O. Box C1535
Cantonments, Accra
Ms. Victoria Cooper, Resident Partner
Mr. Felix Addo, Resident Partner
Tel: 233-21-506217; 506218; 776027
Fax: 233-21-506216; 772137
Email: pwc@ghana.com

Research International Ghana Ltd.
Osu Ako Adjei Park
P.O. Box 1262
Accra
Mr. Attafuah, Technical Director
Tel: 233-21-776637; 761141-3
Fax: 233-21-776711
Email: righana@ghana.com

Research Marketing Services
Mr. W. A. Krosah, Managing Director
Tel: 233-21-779731; 2
Fax: 233-21-773928

Washington, D.C. Contacts for Ghana

U.S. Government Agencies

U.S. Department of Commerce
International Trade Administration/Office of Africa
14th Street and Constitution Ave., NW
Washington, DC 20230
Tel: (202) 482-4388
Fax: (202) 482-5198
Email: Douglas_Wallace@ita.doc.gov

The Trade Information Center (TIC)
Department of Commerce
Office of Export Promotion Coordination
International Trade Administration
14th Street and Constitution Ave., N.W. HCHB 7424
Washington, DC 20230
Tel: (202) 482-0543
Fax: (202) 482-4473
Website: http://www.ita.doc.gov/tic

Multilateral Development Bank Operations
Tel: (202) 482-3399
Fax: (202) 482-5179

U.S. Department of Agriculture
U.S. Foreign Agricultural Service
Trade Assistance and Promotion Office
14th and Independence Avenue, NW
Washington, DC 20250-1052
Tel: (202) 720-7420
Fax: (202) 690-4374; 205-9728
Email: tapo@fas.usda.gov
Website: http://www.fas.usda.gov

U.S. Department of State
Africa Bureau-AF/W
Room 4250
Washington, DC 20520
Tel: (202) 647-3391
Fax: (202) 647-4855

U.S. Department of Treasury
1500 Pennsylvania Avenue, NW
Washington, DC 20220
IDB Room 5400
Tel: (202) 622-1231
Fax: (202) 622-1228

U.S.A.I.D. (United States Agency for International Development) AFR/ONI
Agribusiness Advisor
1111 N. 19th Street, Rm. 210
Rosslyn, VA 22209
Tel: (703) 235-9082
Fax: (703) 235-5423

Overseas Private Investment Corporation (OPIC)
1100 New York Avenue, NW
Washington, DC 20527
Tel: (202) 336-8799
Fax: (202) 336-8700

U.S. Trade and Development Agency
1621 N. Kent Street
Suite 300
Arlington, VA 22209-2131
Tel: (703) 875-4357
Fax: (703) 875-4009
Email: info@tda.gov
Website: www.tda.gov

Export-Import Bank of the United States
Coordinator for Africa
811 Vermont Avenue, NW, 7th Floor
Washington, DC 20571
Tel: (202) 566-8008
Fax: (202) 566-7524
Email: Annmarie.Emmet@exim.gov

TPCC Trade Information Center
Tel: (800) USA-TRADE

U.S.-Based Multilateral Financial Institutions

The World Bank
1818 H Street, NW
Washington, DC 20433
Tel: (202) 477-1234
Fax: (202) 477-6391

The International Finance Corporation
1818 N Street, NW
Washington, DC 20433
Tel: (202) 477-1234
Fax: (202) 477-3112

Multilateral Investment Guarantee Agency (MIGA)
1818 H Street, NW
Washington, DC 20433
Tel: (202) 473-3075
Fax: (202) 872-1521

Africa Growth Fund
1850 K Street, NW, Suite 390
Washington, DC 20006
Tel: (202) 293-1860
Fax: (202) 872-1521

The Corporate Council on Africa
1660 L Street, NW, Suite 301
Washington, DC 20036
Tel: 202-835-1115
Fax: 202-835-1117

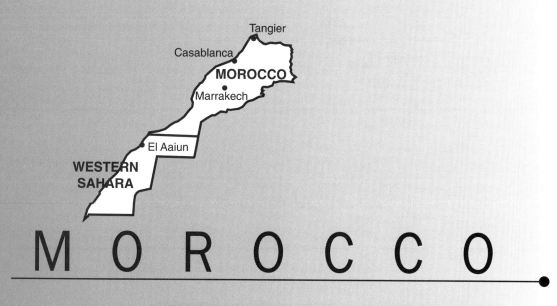

M O R O C C O

TRADE AND BUSINESS GUIDE

Official Name:	Kingdom of Morocco
Official Languages:	Arabic, with French common in business, government, diplomacy; Berber dialects, Spanish in north
Population:	30.1 million (2000 est)
Population Growth:	1.74% (2000 est)
Age Structure:	0–14 years: 35%, 15–64 years: 60%, 65 years and over: 5% (2000 est)
Location:	Northern Africa, bordering the North Atlantic Ocean and Mediterranean Sea, between Algeria and Western Sahara
Area:	446,550 square kilometers. Slightly larger than California
Type of Government:	Constitutional monarchy. Bicameral Parliament with Chamber of Counselors (by indirect vote for nine-year terms) and Chamber of Representatives (by popular vote for five-year terms). Monarch hereditary
Head of State:	King Mohammed VI
Cabinet:	Council of Ministers appointed by monarch
Religion:	99% Muslim, 1% Christian, .2% Jewish
Major Cities:	Capital: Rabat (518,616), Casablanca (2.1 million), Fez (448,823), Marrakech (439,728), Meknes (319,783), Sale (289,391), Tangiers (266,346), Oujda (260,082), Tetouan (199,615), Safi (197,616), Kenitra (188,194)
Climate:	Mediterranean in north (similar to San Diego), more extreme in the interior (similar to Phoenix)
Time:	The entire country is 0 GMT (Greenwich Mean Time), five hours ahead of EST (Eastern Standard Time)
GDP:	Purchasing power parity (PPP): $108 billion (1999 est); real growth rate: 0% (1999 est); per capita PPP: $3,600 (1999 est); composition by sector: agricultural = 16%, industry = 30%, services = 54% (1998 est)
Currency:	1 Moroccan dirham (DH) = 100 centimes
Exchange Rate:	US$ 1 = 10.80 DH (2000 est), 9.75 DH (1999 est), 9.65 (1998 est)
Weights & Measure:	Metric system
Natural Resources:	Phosphates, iron ore, manganese, lead, zinc, fish, salt
Total Trade:	In billions US$ [exports (fob)/imports (cif)]: 1997 (6.96/9.45), 1998 (7.28/10.26), 1999 (7.35/10.77)
Trade with U.S.:	In millions US$ [exports (fob)/imports (cif)]: 1997 (164/509), 1998 (198/643), 1999 (251/703)
Major Trade Partners:	Imports: European Union countries, United States, Saudi Arabia, Brazil. Exports: European Union countries, Japan, United States, Libya, India

Membership: AfDB, EBRD, IBRD, ICC, IDB, IFC, IMF, MIGA, ISO, UN, UNCTAD, WCO, WIPO, and WTO. See membership description in appendix

Sources: CIA World Facts, United Nations World Statistics, Moroccan Foreign Trade Statistics, U.S. Department of Commerce, U.S. Department of State

POLITICAL OUTLOOK ②

Relationship with the U.S.

The U.S. and Morocco enjoy close ties. Morocco is fairly active in seeking peace in the Middle East. King Mohammed VI has expressed appreciation for continuing American "solidarity and support."

Influences on Business

The Western Sahara dispute could affect business. The national liberation force, the Polisario, is based in Algeria and requires a UN peacekeeping presence in the region until a permanent settlement is achieved by the UN referendum. Islam extremism and unrest in Algeria have not spread to Morocco. Economic disparity has led to social strains and a growing Islam movement. Cannabis production in northern Morocco generates regional income, and concerns nearby European countries, but has not created instability.

Profile

System: The prime minister, chosen by the king, is affiliated with USFP (socialist party), but the Minister of Interior is independent of parties. The Minister of Interior picks officials who govern provinces, prefectures, and regions. Cities and communes have elected councils who choose presidents. Parliament has a 270-member Chamber of Counselors (elected by local councils, professional organizations, and labor syndicates), and a 325-member Chamber of Representatives (elected by popular vote). The Chamber of Counselors seats by party:

RNI (National Rally of Independents), 42; MDS (Social Democratic Movement), 33; UC (Constitutional Union), 28; MP (Popular Movement), 27; PND (National Democratic Party), 21; IP (Istiqlal Party), 21; and over 11 other parties. The Chamber of Representatives seats by party: USFP (Socialist Union of Popular Forces), 57; UC, 50; RNI, 46; MP, 40; MDS, 32; IP, 32; and nine other parties.

Schedule for Elections: The last election for members of the Chamber of Counselors was scheduled for 2000. The next elections for members of the Chamber of Representatives are scheduled for 2002.

Major Parties: Opposition: USFP, IP, PPS, OADP, PSD, FFD, MPCD. Pro-government: UC, MP, PND, MNP, MDS. Independents: RNI, PDI, PA, UT, CDT, UGTM, UTM, CS, SD, ADP, USND, UNMT, Party of Shura and Istiqla.

Political Violence: The last instance of mass violence occurred during the Fez riots of 1990. Morocco is generally insulated from the politics in nearby countries.

Corruption: A broad body of laws, regulations, and courts fight corruption. The government of Morocco (GM) has worked with Moroccan societies, the World Bank, and foreign donors to fight corruption. But U.S. companies have still named it as problem, especially in customs practices and government procurement. Bribes are illegal, but Morocco has not yet signed the OECD Convention on Combating Bribery.

ECONOMIC OUTLOOK

③

Trends

The government of Morocco (GM) seeks infrastructure development, trade, and investments. Resources include the largest phosphate reserves in the world, rich fisheries, a large tourist industry, and an inflow of funds from Moroccans abroad. Illegal cannabis exports also play an economic role. Most Moroccan trade is with Europe, with France accounting for one-fourth of imports and one-third of exports. Among the GM's problems, there is no government agency for foreign investment, and there are layers of bureaucracy.

Major Growth Sectors

Packing and assembling are promising growth sectors (Morocco has a great location for exporting into the EU). Other principal growth sectors include tourism (great natural and cultural riches), telecommunications and air industries (privatization of national operators), utility distribution, waste management, electricity generation, agriculture, fishing, industry (phosphate derivatives, processed agricultural products, and clothing), and mining (phosphate, copper, flourine, lead, barite, iron, anthracite, and base metals).

Key Economic Indicators

Income, Production and Employment (millions of U.S. dollars unless otherwise indicated)			
	1997	1998	1999[1]
Nominal GDP[2]	33,160	36,179	34,871
Real GDP Growth (pct)[3]	-2.2	6.3	-0.7
GDP by Sector			
Agriculture	5,093	5,911	5,161
Manufacturing	5,857	6,040	6,033
Services	6,451	6,833	6,520
Government	4,428	4,378	5,022
Per Capita GDP (US$)	1,218	1,303	1,235
Urban Labor Force (millions)	5,068	5,137	5,263
Urban Unemployment Rate (pct)	16.9	19.1	22.4

1. 1999 figures are all estimates based on available monthly data. 2. GDP at factor cost.
3. Percentage changes calculated in local currency.
Source: Bureau of Economic and Business Affairs; U.S. Department of State

- **Infrastructure**
  Morocco is making the development of communication and transportation networks a top priority. The infrastructure is sound for goods and services distribution, and it is improving. See **Communications** and **Transportation**.

- Labor

Labor law limits firms' ability to dismiss workers. Five percent of the workforce is unionized (roughly 450,000 workers). The Constitution guarantees the right to organize trade unions, political parties, commercial councils, and professional organizations. However, unions complain of being suspended or fired for union activity. Morocco has ratified the ILO convention, which grants right to bargain collectively. The Ministry of Interior intervenes in strikes. The Ministry of Labor is overtaxed by dispute settlements between labor and management. Unemployment problems weaken labor. See **Business Infrastructure (Labor Costs and Legislation)**.

Money and Prices *(annual percentage growth)*			
	1997	1998	1999[1]
Money Supply Growth (M2)	9.2	7.7	10.2
Consumer Price Inflation	1.0	2.7	0.7
Exchange Rate (DH/US$ annual average)			
Official	9.60	9.59	9.84
Parallel	N/A	N/A	N/A

1. 1999 figures are all estimates based on available monthly data.
Source: Bureau of Economic and Business Affairs; U.S. Department of State

Balance of Payments and Trade *(millions of U.S. dollars unless otherwise indicated)*			
	1997	1998	1999[1]
Total Exports FOB[2]	6,985	7,279	7,346
Exports to U.S.[2]	164	198	251
Total Imports CIF[2]	9,449	10,255	10,765
Imports from U.S.[2]	509	643	703
Trade Balance[2]	-2,464	-2,976	-3,419
Balance with U.S.[2]	-345	-445	-452
External Public Debt (US$ billions)	19.1	19.3	17.5
Fiscal Deficit/GDP (pct)[3]	3.3	3.5	2.3
Current Account Deficit/GDP (pct)	1.1	3.1	0.8
Debt Service Payments/GDP (pct)	8.5	8.3	8.4
Gold and Foreign Exchange Reserves	4,234	4,450	6,005
Aid from U.S.[3]	13.5	17.6	16.3
Aid from All Other Sources	1,750	N/A	N/A

1. 1999 figures are all estimates based on available monthly data. 2. Merchandise trade 3. Fiscal year basis.
Source: Bureau of Economic and Business Affairs; U.S. Department of State

- **Merchandize Trade**
  The trade deficit remained steady at 36.6 billion Dirhams in 1999. Citrus fruit and phosphates and its derivatives led export growth. Crude oil import increased by 65.4 percent in dirham terms, reflecting the increases in world oil prices. Due to a second successive year of drought, food imports are expected to increase in 2000.

- **Balance of Payments**
  See **Key Economic Indicators**. The perpetual Moroccan trade deficit in merchandise is usually offset by receipts from tourism, workers remittances, and foreign investment.

Government Influence on Business

The GM, working with the IMF, has reduced its role in the economy and has ceased direct credit and foreign exchange allocations, reduced trade barriers, restrained government spending, and begun a privatization program. Monetary growth is steady at about 6 percent, inflation is below 3 percent, and the deficit is below 3 percent. The GM is privatizing (and has already sold 56 of 114 state-owned enterprises), arguing against devaluation, reducing trade tariffs, especially with the EU. Trade and Investment Framework Agreement (TIFA) establishes and encourages bilateral trade between Morocco and the U.S. Officials and private-sector representatives from both countries meet in TIFA talks, which include reduction of tariffs, streamlining customs and bureaucratic procedures, and tackling specific problems of U.S. firms.

TRADE
④

Leading Imports and Exports

Imports: Telecommunications equipment, electrical power systems, environmental equipment and services, water resources equipment, tourism, franchising (hotels and motels, auto repair, toys, convenience stores, dry cleaning, office supplies, hardware, and printing), wheat (including durum), feed grains (including corn, sorghum, and barley), crude vegetable oil, oilseeds, soybean meal, purebred pregnant breeding heifers, milk powder and unsalted butter, pulses (lentils, garbanzos, and green split peas), dried fruit and nuts (prune, raisins, and almonds)

Exports: Food and beverages (fruits, vegetables, citrus, tomatoes), semiprocessed goods, consumer goods, phosphates and derivatives, clothing, copper, fluorine, lead, barite, iron, anthracite, base metals

Foreign Trade *(Exports and Imports in US$M)*			
	1997	1998	1999[1]
Total Exports FOB[2]	6,985	7,279	7,346
Exports to U.S.[2]	164	198	251
Total Imports CIF[2]	9,449	10,255	10,765
Imports from U.S.[2]	509	643	703

1. 1999 figures are all estimates based on available monthly data.   2. Merchandise trade.
Sources: U.S. Department of Commerce, U.S. Department of State

Best Prospects Analysis

Best Prospects for Nonagricultural Goods and Services

Telecommunications Equipment (TEL)

	1998 $M	1999 $M	2000E $M
Total Market Size	812	974	1,040
Total Local Production	16	20	27
Total Exports	0	0	0
Total Imports	796	1,042	1,013
Imports from the U.S.	159	80.9	200

(Sources: Maroc Telecom, Trade Association of Telecom Companies in Morocco,Moroccan Foreign Trade Statistics, National Telecom Regulatory Agency (ANRT)

Electrical Power Systems (ELP)

	1998 $M	1999 $M	2000E $M
Total Market Size	166	188	372
Total Local Production	0	0	0
Total Exports	0	0	0
Total Imports	166	188	372
Imports from the U.S.	42	75	115

(Sources: National Office of Electricity)

Environmental Equipment & Services (POL)

	1998 $M	1999 $M	2000E $M
Total Market Size	197	223	238
Total Local Production	0	0	0
Total Exports	0	0	0
Total Imports	197	91.4	238
Imports from the U.S.	35	11.6	48

(Sources: 1. Ministry of Environment; 2. L.P.E.E. Pollution Control NationalLaboratory)

Water Resources Equipment (WRE)

	1998 $M	1999 $M	2000E $M
Total Market Size	258	288	1,883
Total Local Production	30	35	150
Total Exports	0	0	0
Total Imports	228	253	1,733
Imports from the U.S.*	1.7	1.8	2,200

(Sources: National Office of Potable Water [ONEP], Ministry of Equipment [Direction de l'Hydraulique])

*Total import figures in this sector reflect equipment. Engineering services by foreign firms represent at least 50% of the market. Figures for U.S. imports should increase in the future when services can be reflected in statistics and present interest by U.S. firms in the water sector results in contracts.

Tourism (TRA)

	1998 $M	1999 $M	2000E $M
Number (# in millions) of Visitors	2	2.5	3
Tourist Receipts	1.678	1.875	2
Investments	500	700	900

(Sources: The Ministry of Tourism, Morocco)

Franchising (FRA)

There are over 43 different franchise operations. The most popular are fast food, clothing, cosmetics, auto repair, computer training, and industrial cleaning. Additional franchising opportunities include hotels and motels, auto repair, toys, convenience stores, dry cleaning, office supplies, hardware, and printing. Fast-food franchises expected to grow 35% to 50% within the next five years. Moroccan consumer tastes and habits are increasingly open to the fast-food franchising concept, especially among the younger generation. Foreign franchisers already operating in Morocco are McDonald's, Pizza Hut, Dairy Queen, Subways, Domino's Pizza, Hollywood Tex Mex, Schotzsky's Deli,

Benetton, Chevignon, Naf Naf, Jacadi, Yves Rocher, Futurkids, The Fourth R, Midas, Dunkin Donuts. The generation of young Moroccan entrepreneurs often schooled in the U.S. are especially receptive to franchising. Accustomed to franchises through their schooling or visits in the U.S., these Moroccan investors have the financial resources to establish foundations before the individual franchises are marketed to a larger public. See **Franchising**.

Best Prospects for Agricultural Products

Total Wheat

	1998 MT ('000)	1999 MT ('000)	2000 MT ('000)
Total Market Size	5,800	5,850	5,950
Total Local Production	4,378	2,154	1,600
Total Exports	N/A	N/A	N/A
Total Imports	2,735	2,900	3,200
Imports from the U.S.	227	350	700

Soybean Oil

	1998 MT ('000)	1999 MT ('000)	2000 MT ('000)
Total Market Size	245	250	250
Total Local Production	35	44	47
Total Exports	N/A	N/A	N/A
Total Imports	190	190	190
Imports from the U.S.	50	60	60

Soybean Meal

	1998 MT ('000)	1999 MT ('000)	2000 MT ('000)
Total Market Size	232	280	300
Total Local Production	160	200	215
Total Exports	N/A	N/A	N/A
Total Imports	70	80	85
Imports from the U.S.	40	40	40

Corn

	1998 MT ('000)	1999 MT ('000)	2000 MT ('000)
Total Market Size	850	880	850
Total Local Production	200	137	120
Total Exports	N/A	N/A	N/A
Total Imports	683	750	720
Imports from the U.S.	497	500	500

Vegetable Oil

	1997 MT ('000)	1998 MT ('000)	1999 MT ('000)
Total Market Size	350	362	360
Total Local Production	82	64	65
Total Exports	N/A	N/A	N/A
Total Imports	221	270	240
Imports from the U.S.	47	40	400

Oilseed Protein Meals (CAKES)

	1997 MT ('000)	1998 MT ('000)	199 MT ('000)
Total Market Size	232	255	264
Total Local Production	197	205	160
Total Exports	N/A	N/A	N/A
Total Imports	66	80	80
Imports from the U.S.	32	40	50

Best Prospects for Investment

Energy sector, utility distribution, and solid waste management are promising. Also promising are the tourism industry, including hotel and restaurant construction and management, information services, water and waste water treatment, resort and athletic facilities development, eco-tourism, historic preservation, and theme parks. A $700 million fund has been dedicated to infrastructure improvement. Related investment opportunities include housing, renewable energy, water treatment, telecommunications, and equipment for road construction.

The above statistics are unofficial estimates.
N/A - Not Available, E - Estimated
Note: MT ('000) = Thousand Metric Tons

Extracted from the U.S. Department of Commerce USA Trade 2001 Country Commercial Guide for Morocco.

Import and Export Tips

- **Regulations**

   Customs: Arbitrary customs regulations, and changes in them (local protections), are often a problem for U.S. exporters. Contraband of competitive products is also a threat to U.S. exports and U.S. goods produced in Morocco. The GM is battling contraband. Foreign companies also complain of government procurement irregularities. The GM is modernizing the customs administration. Computerization will manage and integrate key information such as movement of goods, processing the declarations, assessing tariffs, and payment of obligations. Goods temporarily exported to Morocco for further processing abroad are taxed only on value added outside Morocco, and the temporary admissions process is being streamlined. Customs personnel are being trained to work more efficiently. Morocco will not give binding ruling on customs classification in advance. See **Tariffs and Exchange Rate.**

Tariffs: Custom duties on goods range from 2.5 to 300 percent, though most are about 35 percent. The Free Trade Zone in Tangiers has many foreign investors and businesses. Companies in the Zone have 100 percent duty-free imports and exemption of most taxes for export production. Tariffs for raw materials, spare parts and products not manufactured locally, will be reduced by 25% per year over the next four years. There will be a three-year grace period until 2003 followed by a 10% reduction in tariffs each year over the next 10 years for imported goods that are manufactured locally. See **Trade Zones and Free Ports.**

Import Taxes: There is an additional import tax at 15 percent. Yet another value-added tax (VAT) rate is 0 to 20 percent. This VAT is not always paid on locally produced goods (like corn). Food products are subject to an average of 80 percent of cumulated duties and taxes. Consumer-oriented food products are hence prohibitive for the average Moroccan.

Exchange Rate: The Moroccan dirham is convertible for all current transactions (as defined by the International Monetary Fund's Article VIII) as well as for some capital transactions, notably capital repatriation by foreign investors. Foreign exchange is routinely available through commercial banks for such transactions on presentation of documents. Moroccan companies may borrow abroad without prior government approval. Investment abroad by Moroccan individuals or corporations is subject to approval by the Foreign Exchange Board. Approval is routinely denied for projects that do not directly benefit Morocco. Private Moroccans continue to face several foreign exchange restrictions, notably against use of international credit cards. This makes it nearly impossible for Moroc-

cans to use e-commerce to purchase goods internationally. The central bank sets the exchange rate for the dirham against a basket of currencies of its principal trading partners, particularly the French franc and other European currencies. The rate against the basket has remained steady since a 9 percent devaluation in May 1990, with changes in the rates of individual currencies reflecting changes in cross rates. Since Morocco's average inflation rate throughout the 1990s has been greater than the other currencies, many economists believe that the dirham is now overvalued. The government argues consistently against devaluation. The large weight given to European currencies in the basket results in a greater volatility of the dollar than the European currencies against the dirham. This increases the foreign exchange risk of importing from the U.S. compared to importing from Europe. The IMF has urged the GM to introduce greater flexibility into its exchange rate regime so as to help boost exports and promote growth.

- **Documentation**

Exports: There are no specific export controls. Export licenses are required for antique articles older than 100 years; historical and archaeological artifacts; specimens of anatomy, botany, mineralogy, zoology; charcoal and flour made from cereals (except rice). There are restrictions on goods exported to be sold in consignment (except fruits, vegetables, flowers, and handicraft); goods exported by individuals not registered with the Trade Registration Authority; goods valued at over $300 not exported for sale; samples valued at more than $1,000 exported without payment; exports whose payments exceed 150 days.

Imports: A commercial invoice is required on exports and imports, but no special form, consular visa, or consular certification is required. Goods must be described in

French. Certification of country of origin is required. Invoices should be on company letterhead, needed for both import licenses and foreign exchange transfers. "To order" bills are accepted as bills of lading. All promotional material, especially videos, must state in French "Promotional Use Only. No Commercial Value." There are import restrictions on firearms, explosives, used clothing, and used tires.

Labeling: There are no special regulations on exterior markings of containers for import. However, indication of net weight (kilos) with other identifications speeds up customs clearance and location of goods. Food labels can be in French or Arabic and must show country of origin. Both local and imported canned goods and beverages must print date of production and expiration date. The metric system is mandatory. Date format must be (dd/mm/yy), which is different from the U.S. (mm/dd/yy). A Food and Agricultural Import Regulations and Standards (FAIRS) report has been prepared by the agricultural attaché's office in Rabat.

Standards: Usually a one-year warranty is given to end users for products and equipment purchased.

• **Payment**

Terms: Usual terms are 90 to 120 days. Payments made on imports and exports are made via bank-to-bank irrevocable letters of credit. Pro-forma invoices must usually be provided.

Currency Exchange: DH is convertible for all current transactions and some capital transactions. If original investment is registered with foreign exchange office, foreigners can repatriate capital. The central bank sets the exchange rate against the currencies of principal trading partners. No government approval is required for foreign exchange. Currency exchange is routinely available at commercial banks with documentation for repatriation of dividends and capital; remittances by foreign residents; payments for foreign technical assistance, royalties, and licenses.

Fund Transfer: Expatriates can repatriate 100 percent of their salaries.

Offshore Loans: No information is available at this time.

MARKETING TIPS ⑤

Agents and Distributors

Foreign manufacturers and exporters are represented either through branch offices or through authorized agents and distributors. Distributors often give technical support to end users and often have contractual arrangements with their principals under which the local importers provide in-bond warehousing. Agents and distributors are often necessary for help with French documentation. Some U.S.

firms supply Morocco directly through regional distribution centers in Europe. (This is good for language and shipping, but bad because too many distribution channels raises prices.) Volume is key to success. Large-scale stores, based on Costco stores, are a good new source for direct distribution of consumer goods. German-owned Makro stores are in Casablanca, Rabat, Fes, and soon, Agadir. The Foreign Commercial Service (FCS) at the American Consulate in Casablanca sells two services to help identify agents, distributors, or potential partners. The Agent/Distributor Search (ADS) is done via a district office of the Department of Commerce. FCS in Morocco operates a Gold Key Service that arranges one-on-one meetings with potential partners, agents, or distributors. See **Contacts.**

Establishing an Office

An accounting or law firm is recommended to prepare the registration documents. Foreign investors may establish a wholly owned company in Morocco without a local partner. The registration procedures are as follows: Stock companies must file their articles of association, signed by all shareholders, with the local trade registration office (Registre Local du Commerce). An announcement of the company's formation is then published in a newspaper of legal announcements. The company must then file a registration request with the registration's office of the local court. This must include an account of the company's activities, its address, the names of managers and directors, and the amount of paid-in capital. These documents should be filed in Arabic, but French is also accepted. A company may not begin business operations until it obtains a registration number (about six weeks after filing all registration documents). Limited liability companies must first register their signed articles of association with the trade register, and then file the articles with the registration office of the local court. After the articles of association are filed at the local court, announcement of the formation is published in a newspaper of legal announcements. The limited company then files with the trade register a request for a company registration number.

Distribution and Sales Channels

Casablanca is main entry point of foreign-made goods for distribution to public, wholesalers, distributors, or retailers. Ferry service between Morocco and Spain and France allows goods to be imported or exported by truck.

Direct Marketing

Marketing services and advertising agencies are focusing more on direct marketing. Common forms of direct marketing in Morocco are point-of-sale promotions, games, moving billboards, direct mail, and door to door. Avon and Oriflame are active in door-to-door cosmetic sales.

Leasing/Joint Ventures

Moroccans are increasingly interested in joint ventures with American partners to modernize their factories or license a technology. Moroccan manufacturers want to improve production quality and efficiency. For interested American firms, Morocco provides an ideal geographic location for exporting to the EU.

Franchising

With more than 43 franchises, Morocco is open to this business model. Franchises are popular for their marketing image and the financial security of well-known American brands and products. Franchises are operated primarily by young, well-funded entrepreneurs. The challenge is to sell individual franchises to an expanding middle class with more disposable income. See **Trade (Best Prospects Analysis - Franchising).**

Advertising and Promotion

Several Moroccan advertising agencies exist, mainly on a small scale. McCann Erickson has an office in Morocco, and recently a joint operation of Leo Burnett and Darcey Masius. Benton & Bowles has begun offering resources for product launches. Television generates over 70 percent of advertising returns. Food, hygiene, and beverages are most common. Newspapers and periodicals provide ad space, but verification of subscriptions and circulation is difficult. More small and medium-sized companies use Internet and web pages for inexpensive marketing. The number of subscribers is rapidly increasing (though only 50,000, the figures are expanding geometrically, and Internet cafes are extremely popular).

Selling Factors

Most local distributors of imported merchandise expect their suppliers to provide them with substantial advertising and promotional support, particularly when introducing a new product or brand name. All sales promotional material and technical documentation should be in French. Clear and simple French-language operating instructions, plus, where possible, illustrations, help the consumers, not to mention the sales force. U.S. firms often need to train local staff, provide full documentation of products in French, supply spare parts in adequate supplies, and cooperate in advertising and marketing. Direct mail is becoming very popular.

Selling to the Government

Selling to the GM is handled mainly through government tenders. The GM is changing the public procurement system to enhance transparency, accountability, and competitiveness. The GM decree mandates public bid-opening sessions, substantially narrows the scope of restricted bidding or sole sourcing, extends the period of bid submissions, and provides for mandatory special controls and audits for contracts valued at over $500,000. The decree has created trends away from direct negotiation and toward open tenders in public procurement. Tenders are published in newspapers, and announcements are sent to embassies. Each Ministry issues its own tenders. Deadlines range from 30 to 90 days. Bidding documents are published in French, and replies must be in French using French or European standards (i.e., metric, 50/60 Hz). FCS Morocco transmits notice of GM tenders likely to be of interest to U.S. companies to the U.S. Department of Commerce for listing in the Commerce

Business Daily through the Economic Bulletin Board (EBB).

Pricing

The average sales margin for wholesalers is 5 to 10 percent; for retailers, 25 percent, depending on the product; for luxury products, 30 percent; for high-turnover products such as food products, 15 percent.

Customer Support

U.S. firms must supply their local distributor with customer and internal manuals and documentation in French. Simple maintenance and care instructions, after-sales service, and product guarantees are important for consumers. Training in the U.S. or in Morocco of management, sales, and service personnel helps build good business relationships and product loyalty.

Intellectual Property Rights (IPR)

Morocco has a relatively complete regulatory and legislative system for the protection of intellectual property, but enforcement is needed. A new single agency has been created for the registry of intellectual property rights (for patents and trademarks in the industrial and commercial sectors). Morocco is a member of the World Intellectual Property Organization (WIPO); party to the Bern Copyright Convention (the 1948 convention, not the more recent 1971 convention); Paris Industrial Property; Universal Copyright Conventions; Brussels Satellite Conventions; and the Madrid, Nice, and Hague agreements for the protection of intellectual property. According to BSA, Morocco is far from compliance with TRIPS. However, the Moroccan government affirms intention to meet TRIPS commitments. With a mainly bilingual population, Morocco has the potential to attract software developers to localize their software in French or Arabic. However, IPR laws in software may not be strong enough. The GM is more aggressively enforcing against video, CD, and audiotape piracy. Counterfeiting of clothing, luggage, and other consumer goods is more common for the domestic market than for exported goods.

Attorney

No American law firms have a practice in Morocco, but there are English, French, German, and Moroccan firms with strong international expertise. New-to-market U.S. firms are strongly advised to use a law firm or the legal department of one of the multi-national accounting or consulting firms. A complete list of recognized Moroccan law firms is available through the U.S. Commercial Service at the U.S. Embassy in Rabat or the Consulate General in Casablanca. Six new commercial courts and three new commercial courts of appeal help judicial reform. Casablanca Commercial Arbitration Center (CCAC), a nongovernmental body, and the GM are creating a Commercial Arbitration Code that will integrate arbitration laws.

Due Diligence and Bona Fides: All potential investors in Morocco, exporters of goods, and service providers are strongly recommended to perform due diligence on, and check the "bona fides" of, their Moroccan agents, partners, and customers (when extending credit). Moroccan banks supply credit information to selected recipients. U.S. firms should consider using the U.S. Department of Commerce's International Company Profile (ICP) service before signing any agreements with new partners. Via a U.S. Department of Commerce District Office, a U.S. exporter can obtain information on the reputation, reliability, and financial status of a potential partner in a confidential report, along with a recommendation from commercial officers at the U.S. Embassy about the suitability of the company as a trading partner.

FOREIGN INVESTMENT

6

Openness: The GM encourages foreign investment and is trying to improve the investment climate with regulatory changes. Investment code applies equally to Moroccans and foreigners, except in foreign exchange where foreigners are favored. The Ministry of Economy and Finance's investment promotion office is trying to reduce paperwork involved with investments. Repatriation of foreign exchange from investments is essentially free (except state-reserved agricultural land, phosphate mining, and tobacco).

Regulatory System: Morocco has liberalized its foreign exchange allocation system, import regime, and financial sector. The government's role in the economy is shrinking. Problems remain, such as regulations are sometimes not practiced, government procedures are not always transparent or efficient, and routine permits can be tough to obtain, especially from local governments.

Investment Agreements: A bilateral agreement with the USA exists. U.S. investors are treated at least as favorably as other nationals, expropriation claims will be handled promptly, and disputes may be referred to international arbitration. Morocco has similar agreements with 29 other countries.

Trade Zones and Free Ports: Morocco has signed free trade arrangements with members of Maghreb Arab Union (UMA). However, the union is stalled. Free trade has been established with Saudia Arabia though an import tax (PFI) and VAT are still applied. Morocco-EU Free Trade Agreement gives favored treatment to Moroccan exports to the EU, duty free with no quantity caps. Some agricultural goods and agribusiness products are subject to some restrictions. Tariffs on EU industrial goods will be phased out by 2011.

Performance Requirements/Incentives: There are no foreign investor performance requirements or requirements on local value-added, local equity, substitution of imports, or employment of Moroccan workers. See **Trade Zones and Free Ports.**

Capital Markets and Investment: The banking system is being liberalized. However, in practice, banks don't compete on deposit and lending rates. Credit is given on market terms. The GM seeks out participation of foreign investors. Moroccan banks are mainly sound, complying with the Basle standards, and must provide statements audited by CPAs. The Casablanca Stock Exchange has been growing larger, more efficient, and more transparent.

Private Ownership: Private entities are free to establish, acquire, and sell business interests (except for some state sectors such as phosphates). The GM welcomes foreign participation in privatization via tenders, direct negotiation, or stock exchange. In a few

instances, the GM has limited participation.

Expropriation and Compensation: The U.S. Embassy in Rabat knows of no significant expropriation of U.S. or other foreign firms since the early 1970s.

OPIC and Investment Insurance: Morocco has signed the OPIC (Overseas Private Investment Corporation) agreement. Similar agreements have been signed with agencies of France, Sweden, the United Kingdom, and Switzerland. Morocco is a member of the Multilateral Investment Guarantee Agency (MIGA), and the Kuwait-based Arab Investment Guarantee Organization (OAGI).

Dispute Settlement: The U.S. Embassy in Rabat knows of no current cases of U.S. or foreign firms seeking arbitration. Morocco is a member of International Center for the Settlement of Investment Disputes (ICSID) and party to the 1958 Convention on the Recognition and Enforcement of Foreign Arbitral awards (with reservations) and the 1965 convention on the Settlement of Investment Disputes Between States and Nationals of Other States. Minor disputes are generally resolved with the relevant government agency. The judicial system is regarded as inadequate, but new commercial courts are regarded as positive by business leaders. See **Attorney.**

FINANCE
⑦

Morocco is still developing its banking system: there are 16 major banks, 5 government-owned financial institutions, 15 credit agencies, and 10 leasing companies. The banking sector is strong, with more of a private-sector role than most African countries. Banks are eager to work with The U.S. Export-Import Bank

(EXIM) and IFC, and offer financing to foreigners (high interest, though). The Casablanca Stock Exchange is the third largest in Africa, after Johannesburg's and Cairo's. Foreign investors can own at most 49 percent of insurance companies. Advance payments to foreign exporters are prohibited.

Export Financing: The Trade Promoting Coordinating Committee (TPCC) includes the Commerce Department, EXIM Bank, Small Business Administration, Overseas Private Investment Corporation, and the Trade Development Agency. TPCC offers financial consulting. International Finance Assistance Section gives information on USG financing and multilateral development banks. TPCC agencies include The U.S. Small Business Administration (SBA), The U.S. Export-Import Bank (EXIM), The U.S. Trade and Development Agency (TDA), The Overseas Private Investment Corporation (OPIC), and the USDA Credit Guarantee Program.

Project Financing: Principal multilateral financial institutions (World Bank, African Development Bank, IFC, European Investment Bank) all lend to Morocco for infrastructure development. The Commerce Department's office of Multilateral Development Bank Operations (MDBO) has one-stop shopping for U.S. businesses that want to do business with MDBs. Projects receiving support in Morocco include infrastructure (telecommunications, fishing), environment (park management and social assessment), health management (health infrastructure), structural adjustment (telecommunications, postal and information technology). The International Finance Corporation (IFC) and Multilateral Investment Guarantee Agency (MIGA) are both part of World Bank. See **Contacts**.

COMMUNICATIONS ⑧

Phone

The national telecommunications network offers services including cellular, paging, videoconferencing, voice mail, and Internet services. Total telephone lines number some 2 million in 1998, still low per capita. There are 173,000 cellular subscribers, mainly in the Rabat–Casablanca corridor. A second GSM license will improve the telecommunications structure. A rural telephone project is under tender via the operator, Itissalat Al Maghrib. The international access code is 011, and the Moroccan access code is 212. City codes for major cities are Rabat (7 + 6 digits or 77 + 5 digits), Casablanca (2), Fez (5), Marrakesh (4), Meknes (55), Tangiers (99), Oujda (668), Tetouan (996), and Kenitra (73). Seek operator assistance for other city routing codes.

Internet

The number of subscribers is rapidly increasing (though only 50,000, the number is expanding geometrically, and Internet cafes are extremely popular).

Mail

The postal mailing system is reasonably well developed although street names and numbers may not be well defined. Express mail international services are available between Morocco and the U.S.

Land

Morocco's 60,000-km road network is among the best in Africa. Most of Morocco is accessible by well-surfaced roads. Almost all agricultural and manufactured goods are transported by road. Morocco has 466 kilometers of highways that join the coastal cities of Casablanca, Rabat, and Assilah, and the inland cities of Fez and Meknes. Traffic on the highway between Casablanca and Marrakech is frustrating to residents, tourists, and distributors. The road between Casablanca and Jorf Lasfar (through the resort town of El Jadida) has many traffic accidents with fatalities. Casablanca is congested with insufficient signaling, a shortage of pedestrian overpasses, and a lack of parking and traffic enforcement. The Office National des Chemins de Fer (ONCF) rail company is important for the economy. It employs 13,820 people and operates some 2,000 km of track. ONCF handles transport of phosphates, fertilizers, chemical products, and other minerals. Plans to modernize and extend it are being made.

Sea

The National Port Authority, Office d'Exploitation des Ports (ODEP), manages the shipping network. The port infrastructure handles 98 percent of foreign trade. Morocco's 24 ports handled 48.2 million tons in 1998, 5.8 percent more than in 1997. The port of Casablanca, the second largest in Africa, handled 41 percent of goods exported and imported. Morocco's shipping costs are high compared to Mediterranean competitors. There is frequent ferry service between Spain and between France for tourists.

Air

There are 11 major airports. The largest international airport, Mohammed V, offers 50 or more flights a day to Europe, the U.S., Canada, the Middle East, and several African cities. Merchandise can be transported to and from the airport by truck or train. All airports have modern equipment to increase traffic security and safety, and airspace radio coverage. The Moroccan Airport Authority, Office National Des Aeroports (ONDA), is planning to modernize the infrastructure of all national airports. Royal Air Maroc, Morocco's national airline, has a well-developed route structure, especially to Europe and the Middle East. RAM has a code share agreement with TWA and marketing agreements with Air France and Iberia. Regional Airlines have domestic and short-haul international routes from many Moroccan cities, Malaga, Lisbon, and the Canary Islands.

WORK WEEK

Business Hours: 8:00 a.m. to 12:30 p.m. and 2:00 p.m. to 6:30 p.m. Monday through Friday, with summer variation. During Ramadan, the day ends at mid-afternoon but with no break.

Government Hours: 8:30 a.m. to 12:00 p.m. and 2:30 p.m. to 6:00 p.m. Monday through Friday, with summer variation. During July and August, the hours are 8:30 a.m. to 12 p.m. and 4:00 p.m. to 7:00 p.m.

Bank Hours: 8:00 a.m. to 12:30 p.m. and 2:00 p.m. to 6:30 p.m. Monday through Friday, with summer variation. During Ramadan, the day ends at mid-afternoon but with no break.

HOLIDAYS 2001

New Year's Day, January 1
January 11 Presentation of Independence
  Proclamation
March 4/5 Aid El Adha (*)
April 1 Moslem New Year (*)
April 25/26 Moroccan Labor Day
May 23 Moroccan National Day
June 2/3 Prophet's Birthday (*)
July 30 Feast of the Throne
August 14 Oued Eddahab Allegiance
August 20 Revolution of the King and
  the People
August 21 King's Birthday
November 6 Green March Day
November 18, Moroccan Independence Day
December 2001, Aid El Fitr (*)

Note: Holidays with (*) are based on the lunar calendar and change every year. Dates shown are those projected for the year 2001. As is the case in most Muslim countries, it may be more difficult to make business appointments and contacts in Morocco during the month of Ramadan, which will start this year in early December.

BUSINESS TRAVEL
12

Business Customs

Moroccan business customs have a mix of Arab and Mediterranean influences, rather than African. Lunches tend to be late and long. Business meetings are most often held in offices, not over meals. Moroccan hospitality is world renowned, and business contacts enjoy entertaining in lovely homes. Reconfirm appointments and determine meeting language in advance. Get an interpreter if needed. Arrive at appointments on time, but account for possible delays. Young Moroccan entrepreneurs with American degrees often do business in English. Moroccan women are increasingly involved with business though still on a small scale. Foreign women can conduct business freely in Morocco. Morocco is a Muslim country. Alcohol consumption during fasting month of Ramadan is prohibited for Muslims. Business dress is similar to warmer climates in U.S. "Key Officers of Foreign Service Posts" and "Guide for Business Representatives" are for sale from the Superintendent of Documents and recommended. See **Contacts**.

Travel Advisory and Visas

U.S. citizens and EU members do not need entry visas. Entry visas are required for nationals of some countries, including: Egypt, Iran, Sudan and Syria. Tourist visa, valid for 3 months, is the type of temporary visa issued for Morocco. Residence permit is needed to stay in Morocco over 3 months. Resident foreigners who wish to leave Morocco and return must apply for return visa. Some expatriate business people have complained of delays in getting return visas.

Business Infrastructure

Entry Requirements (personal and professional goods): Goods imported under a temporary entry provision must be approved by decree of the Finance Ministry. Customs may authorize entry of goods on an individual basis. The limit for temporary entry is 6 months, renewable for up to one year. To obtain additional and updated information on entry and exit requirements, travelers can contact the Consular Section of the Embassy of Morocco at 1601 21st Street, N.W., Washington, D.C. 20009; Tel: (202) 462-7979.

Currency Exchange: The dirham is the main currency. US$ 1 = 10.80 DH (2000 est). Bank notes are in 200, 100, 50, 20, and 10 dirhams. See **Trade (Currency Exchange)**.

Taxes: See **Regulations**.

Hotels and Restaurants: Morocco has lodging varying from inexpensive guest houses to deluxe hotels. Most of the major hotel chains have facilities in big cities.

Rent: No information is available at this time.

Utilities: Electric power is 50 cycles, 1 and 3 phase, with nominal voltage of 220 volts in the largest cities.

Business Services: See **Advertising and Promotion**.

Labor Costs and Legislation: Industrial sector workers (except garment assembly) earn more than minimum wage (10 DH or $1 per hour). Workers paid generally for 13 to 16 months per year. Occupational health and safety standards are basic and difficult to enforce. National Social Security Fund (CNSS) provides payments for disability, pensions, diseases, and accidents not covered by workers' compensation, and benefits for leaves. CNSS covers 800,000 workers. Government employees have their own pension and insurance systems. See **Labor** and **Performance Requirements and Incentives.**

Literacy: Age 15 and over can read and write: 43.7% (1995 est.)

Travel Notes

The following travel notes have been supplied by the U.S. government. For the most recent general travel and consular information, see the U.S. Department of State travel publications or call the Traveler's Telephone Hotline at (202) 647-5225.

Security: Pick-pocketing, mugging, assaults, and scams of all types are common in urban areas.

Health Precautions: Adequate medical services are available although specialized care and treatment may not be. Hospitals and doctors expect immediate cash payment for services. U.S. travelers may want to consider supplemental medical insurance to cover medical evacuation as well as care outside the U.S. Current information on health matters may be obtained from the Centers for Disease Control and Prevention's international travelers' hotline at (404) 332-4559.

Embassy Assistance

To obtain additional and updated information on entry and exit requirements, travelers can contact the Consular Section of the Embassy of Morocco at 1601 21st Street, N.W., Washington, D.C. 20009; Tel: (202) 462-7979. Travelers may also contact the nearest Morocco consulate.

CONTACTS

13

U.S. and Country Contacts

U.S. Embassy Trade-Related Contacts

American Consulate General Casablanca
Commercial Counselor
The U.S. Commercial Service
8, Bd. Moulay Youssef
Casablanca, Morocco
Tel: (212) (2) 26-45-50
Fax: (212) (2) 22-02-59

American Embassy Rabat
Economic Counselor
Economic Officer
Agricultural Attache
Director USAID
2 Avenue de Marrakech
Rabat, Morocco
Tel: (212) (7) 76-22-65
Fax: (212) (7) 76-56-61

American Chamber and Bilateral Business Councils

American Chamber of Commerce
Hyatt Regency Hotel
Place Mohammed V
Casablanca, Morocco
Tel: (212) (2) 29-30-28
Fax: (212) (2) 48-15-97

U.S.- Morocco Council on Trade & Investment
5 Bd. Abdellatif Benkadour, 4eme etage
Casablanca, Morocco
Tel: (212) (2) 39-04-12
Fax: (212) (2) 39-04-06

Morocco-U.S. Council on Trade & Investment
Watergate Building
600 New Hampshire Ave., NW (6th Floor)
Washington, D.C. 20037
Tel: (202) 965-2380
Fax: (202) 337-0301

U.S.-Morocco Council on Trade & Investment
Rockfeller Plaza (8th floor)
New York, NY 10020
Tel: (212) 218-5750
Fax: (212) 218-5751

Country Government Offices Relating to Key Sectors

Direction Des Douanes et Impots Indirects
(Customs Office)
Avenue Hassan II (ex rue Essafi)
Rabat, Morocco
Tel: (212) (7) 26-90-01
Fax: (212) (7) 73-09-85
E-mail: adii@douane.msie.gov.ma

Director des Douanes
Boulevard Rachidi
Casablanca, Morocco
Tel: (212) (2) 22-41-16
Or, for information on specific products, U.S. exporters can consult the Moroccan Customs Web site: http://www.mfie.gov.ma.adii

Direction de la Statistique
(Department of Statistics)
Bd. Mohamed Bel Hassan El Ouazzani
Haut Agdal-Rabat, Morocco
Tel: (212) (7) 77-36-06
Fax: (212) (7) 77-30-42
E-mail: webmaster@statistic.gov.ma

Ministere de L'economie et des Finances
(Ministry of Economy and Finance)
Ancien Quartier Administratif
Rabat, Morocco
Tel: (212) (7) 76-06-61
Fax: (212) (7) 76-40-81

Direction des Investissements Exterieurs
(Foreign Investment Office)
32 Rue Honain, Angle rue Michlifen
Agdal-Rabat, Morocco
Tel: (212) (7) 67-33-75
Fax: (212) (7) 67-34-17
E-mail: die@msie.gov.ma

Ministere de L'industrie, du Commerce et de L'artisanat
(Ministry of Industry, Trade and Handicraft)
Quartier des Ministeres
Rabat-Chellah, Morocco
Tel: (212) (7) 76-18-78
Fax: (212) (7) 76-62-65

Direction du Commerce Exterieur
(Foreign Trade Office)
63 Avenue Moulay Youssef
Rabat, Morocco
Tel: (212) (7) 70-33-63
Fax: (212) (7) 70-32-31

Ministere de la Privatisation
(Ministry of Privatization)
47, Ave. Ibn Sina - Agdal
Rabat, Morocco
Tel: (212) (7) 67-19-63
Fax: (212) (7) 67-58-98

Office National de L'electricite (ONE)
(National Office of of Electricity)
65 Rue Othman Ben Affane
Casablanca, Morocco
Tel: (212) (2) 66-80-80
Fax: (212) (2) 22-00-38
E-mail: elbada@one.org.ma

Agence Nationale de Reglementation des Telecommunications (ANRT)
(National Regulatory Agency for Telecommunications)
Rue Al Khalil, Imm. A (3rd floor)
Rabat, Morocco
Tel: (212-7) 20-38-69
Fax: (212-7) 30-38-62
E-mail: benlema@anrt.net.ma

Ittissalat Al Maghrib (IAM)
(National Telephone Company)
Avenue Annakhil, Hay-Riad
Rabat, Morocco
Tel: (212) (7) 71-41-41
Fax: (212) (7) 71-33-00
E-mail: ahizoune@iamdg.net.ma

Office National de L'eau Potable (ONEP)
(National Office of Potable Water)
6 Bis Rue Patrice Lumumba
Rabat-Chellah, Morocco
Tel: (212) (7) 72-65-15
Fax: (212) (7) 72-67-07

Office Cherifien des Phosphates (OCP)
(National Office of Phosphates)
Bd. de la Grande Ceinture
Route d'El Jadida
Casablanca, Morocco
Tel: (212) (2) 23-01-25
Fax: (212) (2) 25-09-99
E-mail: s.sibaoueih@ocpgroup.com

Office d'Exploitation des Ports (ODEP)
(Moroccan Ports Authority)
175 Bd. Mohamed Zerktouni
Casablanca, Morocco
Tel: (212) (2) 23-23-24
Fax: (212) (2) 25-81-58

Royal Air Maroc
(National Airline Company)
Aeroport d'Anfa
Casablanca, Morocco
Tel: (212) (2) 91-20-00
Fax: (212) (2) 91-20-95

Country Trade Associations

Confederation Generale des Entreprises du Maroc (CGEM)
(Moroccan Employers Association)
Angle Rue de la Plage, Avenue des FAR
Casablanca, Morocco
Tel: (212) (2) 25-26-96
Fax: (212) (2) 25-38-39
E-mail: cgem@mail.cbi.net.ma

AFAC
(Feed Millers Association)
c/o Inam-Provimi
151 Route Ouled Ziane
Casablanca, Morocco
Tel: (212) (2) 31-12-49; 44-22-76
Fax: (212) (2) 31-12-49; 44-22-76

Apebi
(Telecommunications and Computers Association)
Place Zellaqua, Tour Atlas
Casablanca, Morocco
Tel: (212) (2) 45-00-54
Fax: (212) (2) 45-00-60

Federation de L'industrie Miniere
(Mining Industry Association)
1 Place de l'Istiqlal
Casablanca, Morocco
Tel: (212) (2) 30-68-98
Fax: (212) (2) 31-99-96

Association des Marchands et Importateurs de Materiel Agricole
(Association of Moroccan Importers of Agricultural Equipment)
c/o Comicom
9 Bd. d'Oujda
Casablanca, Morocco
Tel: (212) (2) 30-22-11
Fax: (212) (2) 30-60-82

Association Marocaine du Conseil et de L'ingenierie
(Engineering Association)
10 Avenue Alaouine, Imm. ONEP
Rabat, Morocco
Tel: (212) (7) 70-42-24
Fax: (212) (7) 20-03-47
E-mail: fmciass@maghrebnet.net.ma

Office des Foires et Expositions de Casablanca
(Trade Shows and Exhibitions Office)
11, Rue Boukraa (ex Jules Mauran)
Casablanca, Morocco
Tel: (212) (2) 22-28-16
Fax: (212) (2) 26-49-49

Specialized Agricultural Trade Associations

Federation Interprofessionnelle du Secteur Avicole (FISA)
(Poultry Feed, Poultry, and Eggs Federation)
123 Boulevard Emile Zola
Casablanca, Morocco
Tel: (212-2) 311249
Fax: (212-2) 311249

Lesieur
(Vegetable Oil Refiner, Oilseed Crusher)
1, Rue Caporal Corbi
Casablanca, Morocco
Tel: (212-2) 354636; 354327; 354327
Fax: (212-2) 268957; 354097

Association Nationale des Cereales et Legumineuses (ANCL)
(Grain Importers Association)
c/o COPRAGRI km 6,3, Boulevard My Ismail, Ain Sebaa
Casablanca, Morocco
Tel: (212-2) 353141; 352489
Fax: (212-2) 350869

Federation Nationale de La Minoterie (FNM)
(Wheat Millers Federation)
Angle Ibn Majid Bahar & Brihmi El Idrissi
  (Ex Girardot/Havre)
Casablanca, Morocco
Tel: (212-2) 301801; 301158
Fax: (212-2) 306551; 305913

Association Nationale des Eleveurs de Bovins de Races Pures (ANEB)
(Purebred Dairy Cattle Association)
Residence Essabah, Ilot 10, Im.Al Houceima, Apt. 5
Rabat, Morocco
Tel: (212-7) 791923
Fax: (212-7) 791924

Country Market Research Firms

Semma
18, Rue Ibn Sina
Casablanca, Morocco
Tel: (212-2) 39-60-30
Fax: (212-2) 39-60-33

Amer
Immeuble El Ouahda, Entrée A No.126
Bd. Lahcen ou Idder
Casablanca, Morocco
Tel: (212-2) 44-92-53; 54
Fax: (212-2) 44-19-17

Creargie
34 Rue de la Convention
Residence El Alami
Casablanca, Morocco
Tel: (212-2) 99-98-42; 46
Fax: (212-2) 94-98-41

Country Commercial Banks

Banque Centrale Populaire
Director Int'l Affairs
101 Bd. Mohammed Zerktouni
Casablanca, Morocco
Tel: (212) (2) 20-25-33
Fax: (212) (2) 22-26-99

Banque Commerciale du Maroc
Head of Int'l Department
2 Bd. Moulay Youssef
Casablanca, Morocco
Tel: (212) (2) 47-64-39
Fax: (212) (2) 47-64-29; 30

Banque Marocaine du Commerce Exterieur
Head of Int'l Department
140 Avenue Hassan II
Casablanca, Morocco
Tel: (212) (2) 20-04-20
Fax: (212) (2) 22-05-23

Banque Marocaine Pour Le Commerce et L'industrie
26 Place Nations Unies
Casablanca, Morocco
Tel: (212) (2) 22-41-61
Fax: (212) (2) 20-89-78
E-mail: bmcifg@casanet.net.ma

Citibank-Maghreb
Managing Director
52 Avenue Hassan II
Casablanca, Morocco
Tel: (212) (2) 22-41-68
Fax: (212) (2) 20-57-23

Credit Agricole (CNCA)
Tahar Daoudi
Head of International Division
28, Rue Abou Farris El Marini
Rabat, Morocco
Tel: (212-7) 08231; 208220; 208221
Fax: (212-7) 208267

Credit Du Maroc
Director Int'l Affairs
48-58 Bd. Mohammed V
Casablanca, Morocco
Tel: (212) (2) 22-41-42
Fax: (212) (2) 27-71-27

Societe Generale Marocaine De Banques
55 Bd. Abdelmoumen
Casablanca, Morocco
Tel: (212) (2) 20-09-72
Fax: (212) (2) 20-09-52
E-mail: yberrada@sgmaroc.com

Wafabank
Head of Int'l Department
163 Avenue Hassan II
Casablanca, Morocco
Tel: (212) (2) 22-41-05
Fax: (212) (2) 29-72-72

Abn-Amro Bank
47, Rue Allal Ben Abdallah (4th floor)
Casablanca, Morocco
Tel: (212) (2) 49-73-04
Fax: (212) (2) 20-91-45

Multilateral Development Bank Offices in Country and Trade Assistance Offices in the U.S.

For the address and phone number of the nearest Department of Commerce domestic office, call (800) USA-TRADE (800-872-8723). Contact FCS Morocco directly for the Gold Key Service by fax at 011-2122-22-02-59 at least one month in advance.

International Finance Corporation
Regional Representative for North Africa
8 Rue Kamal Mohamed (ex 30 Avenue des F.A.R.)
12eme etage
Casablanca, Morocco
Tel: (212) (2) 48-46-87
Fax: (212) (2) 48-46-90

World Bank Representation
7, Rue Larbi Benabdellah
Rabat, Morocco
Tel: (212) (7) 63-60-50
Fax: (212) (7) 63-60-51

Washington-Based U.S. Country Contacts

U.S. Department of Commerce
Regional Director
OIO/ANESA, US&FCS
U.S. Department of Commerce
Washington, D.C.
Tel: (202) 482-4836
Fax: (202) 482-5179

Office of the Near East
Morocco Desk Officer
U.S. Department of Commerce Washington, D.C.
Tel: (202) 482-1860
Fax: (202) 482-0878

Multilateral Development Banks Office
U.S. Department of Commerce
Tel: (202) 482-3399
Fax: (202) 482-5179

TPCC Trade Information Center in Washington
Tel: (800) USA-TRADE

U.S. Department of State
Morocco Desk Officer: NEA/ENA Washington, D.C.
Tel: (202) 647-4675
Fax: (202) 736-4458

Office of the Coordinator for Business Affairs
Tel: (202) 746-1625
Fax: (202) 647-3953

U.S. Department of Agriculture, Foreign Agriculture Service
Trade Assistance and Promotion Office
Director Grain & Feed Division
Washington, DC
Tel: (202) 720-6219
Fax: (202) 720-0340

U.S. Export Import Bank (EXIM)
North Africa Desk Officer,
Tel: (202) 565-3911
Fax: (202) 565-3931

Overseas Private Investment Corporation (OPIC)
North Africa Desk Office
Tel: (202) 336-8799

U.S. Trade Development Agency
Regional Director Africa/Middle East
Tel: (703) 875-4357
Fax: (703) 875-4009

Moroccan Embassy in Washington
1601 21 Street, NW
Washington, DC 20009-1002
Tel: (202) 462-7979
Fax: (202) 265-0161

Marketing

Economic Bulletin Board (EBB).
Tel (202) 482-1986 or (800) STAT-USA
  (800-782-8872)
Fax: (202) 482-2164

Diplomats

Diplomatic representation in the US:
Chief of mission: Ambassador
Chancery: 1601 21st Street NW, Washington,
  DC 20009
Tel: (202) 462-7979 through 7982
Fax: (202) 265-0161
Consulate(s) general: New York

Diplomatic representation from the U.S.:
Chief of mission: Ambassador
2 Avenue de Marrakech
Rabat
PSC 74, Box 3, APO AE 09718
Tel: (212) (7) 76 22 65
Fax: (212) (7) 76 56 61
Consulate(s) general: Casablanca

Business Travel

Superintendent of Documents
U.S. Government Printing Office
Washington, DC 20402
Tel: (202) 512-1800
Fax: (202) 512-2250

Project Financing

U.S. Small Business Administration
409 Third Street, SW
Washington, DC 20416
Office of International Trade
Tel: (202) 205-6720
Fax: (202) 205-7272
Or call (800) USA-TRADE for the location of
  your nearest U.S. Export Assistance Center.

The USDA Credit Guarantee Programs: USD
75 million (GSM-102/3) is made available to
Morocco to purchase various agricultural
commodities from the U.S. For more
information about this program, contact the
office of the Agricultural Attache in Rabat.
Tel: (212-7) 765987
Fax: (212-7) 765493

**Multilateral Development Bank Operations
  (MDBO)**
Tel: (202) 482-3399
Fax: (202) 273-0927 or the
Commercial Service Liaison Staff
Office of the U.S. Executive Director, the
  World Bank
1818 H Street NW
Washington DC 20433
Tel: (202) 458-0118; 0120
Fax: (202) 477-2967

Contact: Multilateral Investment Guarantee
  Agency
1818 H Street, NW Washington, DC 20433
Guarantees Dept.
Tel: (202) 473-6168

Projects Receiving Support in Morocco

Agriculture
Pilot Fisheries Development: The objectives of
this project are to test and implement options
to enhance value-added and competitiveness of
the fisheries sector and promote exports, while
encouraging rural employment in the coastal
areas. 5.0 million (IBRD). Consulting services
to be determined.

**Ministry of Marine Fisheries Office National
  des Peches**
66 Avenue Moulay Youssef
Rabat, Morocco.
Tel: (212-7) 77-05-48
Fax: (212-7) 77-10-61

Environment

Protected Areas Management: The overall project objectives are to establish a system of protected areas in Morocco and promote sustainable conservation management with the participation of the local population in the ecosystems of the project areas. US$ 10.1 (IBRD). Short-term consultants will be required in the areas of protected areas management and park management and social assessment.

Administration des Eaux et Forets et de la Conservation des Sols
Ministry of Agriculture
Cite Administrative
Rabat, Morocco
Tel: (212-7) 76-44-46
Directeur General de l'Administration.

Population, Health and Nutrition

Health Management: The project will support the development and implementation of new financing mechanisms, mainly health insurance; support hospital management reforms; and improve the quality of services provided through priority rehabilitation of health infrastructure, training of relevant personnel and maintenance programs. $66.0 million (IBRD). Consulting services to be determined.

Ministry of Health
335 Avenue Mohammed V, BP 812m
  Mechanar
Rabat, Morocco
Tel: (212-7) 76-16-75
Fax: (212-7) 76-38-95

Structural Adjustment

Telecommunications, Post and Information Technology Structural Adjustment: The loan will support Treasury reforms in the telecommunications, postal and information technology sectors. $100.0 million (IBRD). Consultants will be required.

Agence Nationale de Reglementation des Telecommunications
2 Rue Al Khalil
Rabat 10000, Morocco
Tel: (212-7) 20-38-69
Fax: (212-7) 20-73-73

Ittissalat Al Maghrib (IAM)
Fax: (212-7) 71-33-00

Ministry of Post and Information Technology
Fax: (212-7) 70-56-41

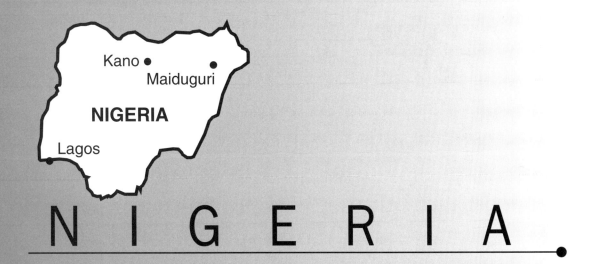

NIGERIA

TRADE AND BUSINESS GUIDE

Official Name:	Federal Republic of Nigeria
Official Languages:	English, Hausa, Yoruba, Ibo, and Fulani
Population:	123.3 million (2000 est)
Population Growth:	2.67% (2000 est)
Age Structure:	0–14 years: 44%, 15–64 years: 53%, 65 years and over: 3% (2000 est)
Location:	West Africa, bordering the North Atlantic Ocean to the south, Cameroon and Chad to the east, Niger to the north, and Benin to the west
Area:	923,768 square kilometers, slightly more than twice the size of California
Type of Government:	Based on a federal structure, Nigeria adopted a presidential system of government headed by a civilian President, with State Governors in 36 states.
Head of State:	President Olusegun Obasanjo
Cabinet:	Federal Executive Council
Religion:	50% Muslim, 40% Christian, 10% indigenous beliefs
Major Cities:	Capital: Abuja (305,900). Principal commercial centers: Lagos (1.3 million), Ibadan (1.2 million), Kano (699,900), Ogbomosho (660,000), Oshogbo (441,600), Ilorin (430,600), Abeukuta (386,800), Port Harcourt (371,000), Zaria (345,200)
Climate:	Varies: equatorial in the south, tropical in the center, and arid in the north. The rainy season lasts from March to November in the south and from April to September in the north
Time:	The entire country is +1 GMT (Greenwich Mean Time), six hours ahead of EST (Eastern Standard Time). Nigeria does not follow daylight savings time
GDP:	Purchasing Power Parity (PPP): $110.5 billion (1999 est); real growth rate: 2.7% (1999 est); per capita PPP: $970 (1999 est); composition by sector: agriculture = 33%, industry = 42%, services = 25% (1997 est)
Currency:	1 naira (N) = 100 kobo
Exchange Rate:	Average exchange rate: naira per US$ 1 = 105 (2000 est), 99.00 (1999 est), 86.8 (1998 est)
Weights & Measure:	Metric system
Natural Resources:	Petroleum, tin, columbite, iron ore, coal, limestone, lead, zinc, natural gas
Total Trade:	In billions US$ [exports (fob)/imports (cif)]: 1997 (15.2/10.3), 1998 (9.0/9.9), 1999 est (12.9/8.6), 2000 est (18.7/12.5)

Trade with U.S.:	In millions US$ [exports (customs value)/imports (fas value)]: 1997 (6,349/813), 1998 (4,194/817), 1999 (4,385/628)
Major Trade Partners:	Imports: Germany, France, Netherlands, United Kingdom, United States. Exports: Spain, Italy, France, United States
Major Trade Partners:	AfDB, ECOWAS, IBRD, ICC, IFC, IMF, ISO, MIGA, OPEC, UN, UNCTAD, WCO, WIPO, and WTO
Sources:	Nigerian-American Chamber of Commerce, World Trade Center of Nigeria, Lagos Chamber of Commerce and Industry, CIA World Factbook, United Nations World Statistics, U.S. Department of Commerce, U.S. Department of State

POLITICAL OUTLOOK

②

Relationship with the U.S.

With the return of civilian rule, the U.S., England, and the EU lifted almost all of the sanctions that were imposed against the Abacha regime. Washington's decertification of Nigeria—due to a lack of cooperation on the problem of narcotics trafficking—was waived for one year in 2000. Furthermore, the U.S. Embassy has sought to work with community leaders, the private sector, and government officials in order to bring an end to regional conflicts within Nigeria. Several delegations of U.S. Government and private-sector officials have visited Nigeria to reopen channels of communication. Progress has been made in restoring respect for basic human rights, addressing the chronic underdevelopment of the Niger delta region and combating corruption. The stock of U.S. foreign direct investment in Nigeria is estimated at around $4 billion, the far majority of which is based in the petroleum sector.

Influences on Business

Ethnic tensions in the oil-producing region of the Niger Delta present one of the most serious issues facing Nigeria's new government. Despite the removal of Abacha's regime, which did much to promote violence,

high unemployment levels among young men in this vital area serve to keep tensions high. Agricultural development and the creation of new jobs are seen as priorities in any comprehensive plan to stabilize the region. Nigeria witnessed an increase in ethnic and religious-based violence during the last year due to plans to expand the application of Sharia (Muslim) law in the northern states. A mass exodus of Christians from the north could cause severe disruptions in business and trading. Relationship with organized labor has also been troublesome over the last year, especially over the issues of increased fuel prices and minimum wages. Progress has been made through contentious negotiations to address disagreements.

Profile

System: The country is still going through a transition from military to civilian rule. Under the republic, the president is elected by popular vote for no more than two, four-year terms. The National Assembly is the country's bicameral, legislative branch. The Senate consists of 109 seats: three from each state and one from the Federal Capital Territory. The House of Representatives consists of 360 seats. Members from both houses are elected by popular vote to seven-year terms. The Provisional Ruling Council appoints judges to the Supreme Court. For the Federal Court of Appeal, judges are appointed on the advice of the Advisory Judicial Council.

Schedule for Elections: The next presidential election is scheduled for 2003. The next legislative election (House and Senate) is scheduled for 2006.

Major Parties: In July 1998, political parties that were suppressed under military rule were allowed to form. Three parties were then registered: the All People's Party (APP), the People's Democratic Party (PDP), and the Alliance for Democracy (AD).

Political Violence: Sporadic incidents have occurred, particularly with local, ethnic communities targeting foreign firms in Eastern Nigeria's oil-producing regions. These incidents have involved violence, hostages, extortion, and destruction of property. Sabotage of pipelines/installations, and kidnapping of Nigerian and expatriate oil workers are on the rise. In 1999 during communal fighting in Warri, over 400 people lost their lives. President Obasanjo's administration announced a 13 percent revenue allocation to the oil

producing areas from the federation account. In addition, the Niger delta development commission bill forwarded by the executive to the national assembly was passed into law in May 2000. The Government of Nigeria (GON), with some help from the U.S. Embassy, is working to stabilize the region. Meanwhile, incidents of civil strife have decreased from the levels of 1993 and 1994.

Corruption: Fraud and corruption are widespread, despite recent government attempts to check many dubious practices. A number of scams are targeted at foreigners. Limited progress has been made in combating corruption. Persons contemplating business deals are strongly urged to check with the U.S. Department of State, the U.S. Department of Commerce, or the U.S. Secret Service before providing any information, making any financial commitments or traveling to Nigeria. Under no circumstances should foreigners travel to Nigeria without a valid visa.

Media: The News Agency of Nigeria (NAN) is the government's voice for news and opinion. There are also a number of state government presses as well as a variety of independent publications.

Trends

Oil-rich Nigeria has suffered from years of mismanagement, political instability, and corruption. In 1999, GDP grew in real terms by only 2.7 percent, while inflation rose to an estimated rate of 12 to 15 percent. Unemployment, infrastructure, and corruption are major concerns, as are the inter-ethnic conflicts in the oil-producing Niger Delta. These political tensions pose a significant threat to Nigeria's lifeline, the petroleum industry. However, within this difficult economic environment, genuine business opportunities do exist. The IMF has approved a $1 billion standby credit facility for Nigeria to enable the nation to pursue priority projects. Nigeria is well supported by many of the world's major democracies, and if the reform efforts of Nigeria's recently elected government have any success, the rewards could be impressive.

Major Growth Sectors

In many areas, imports are a necessity due to difficulties within Nigeria's own manufacturing industries. Promising sectors for U.S. businesses include oil and gas equipment, computer hardware and software, telecommunications equipment, automotive parts and accessories, construction and earthmoving equipment, and various agricultural and agribusiness products and equipment. Approximately 70 percent of the nation's population works in agricultural production at the subsistence level. The sector grew at 4.95 percent in 1998, compared with 4.2 percent in 1997. Meanwhile, the petroleum sector dominates the economy. Oil exports accounted for over 97 percent of export earnings and 80 percent of federal government revenues. Nigeria recently began exporting Liquefied Natural Gas (LNG), an increasingly important sector which at some point may surpass oil as the nation's main revenue source. The manufacturing sector recorded a marginal 1.1 percent growth rate during 1999 after increasing 0.8 percent in 1998. Manufacturing capacity utilization rose from 34 percent in 1998 to 36 percent in 1999. Growth in the sub-sector was impaired by the low demand for local manufactured goods against cheaper imported products. The poor state of social and economic infrastructure such as power generation and water supply are notably constraints on manufacturing. The banking sector is showing signs of growth. The number of commercial banks rose from 51 in 1998 to 57 following the conversion of 5 merchant banks and the licensing of one commercial bank in 1999. On the other hand, the number of merchant banks declined from 38 to 33. The assets of 3 major banks (First Bank, Union Bank, and United Bank for Africa) represent over 70 percent of total assets of banks in Nigeria. More foreign banks have acquired licenses and are likely to begin operations before the end of the year 2000.

Key Economic Indicators

Income, Production and Employment *(billions of U.S. dollars unless otherwise indicated)*			
	1997	1998	1999[1]
Nominal GDP[2]	50.1	33.2	34.4
Real GDP Growth (pct)[3]	3.2	2.4	2.7
GDP by Sector (pct)			
Agriculture	31.5	32.3	N/A
Manufacturing	6.3	6.1	N/A
Services	9.7	9.6	N/A
Per Capita GDP (US$)	250	250	260
Labor Force (millions)	43.0	40.0	N/A
Unemployment Rate (pct)	2.6	3.9	3.9

1. 1999 figures, except exchange rates, are all estimates based on available data.
2. GDP at factor cost. Conversion to U.S. dollars done with official exchange rate of 82 naira to the dollar for 1998–1999.
3. Percentage changes calculated in local currency.
Sources: Bureau of Economic and Business Affairs; U.S. Department of State. IMF, World Bank

- **Infrastructure**

  Nigeria's extensive infrastructure is generally in a state of disrepair. Roads and bridges are crumbling; telephone service is erratic; and there are often fuel, water, and electricity shortages. Movement of goods through major ports is frustratingly slow, and the public transportation system is inadequate. Infrastructure improvements are a key aspect of the country's development program. A Chinese civil engineering company is working to rehabilitate Nigeria's rail system; the state-owned airline, Nigeria Airways, is tentatively slated for privatization; and the government intends to install three million telephone lines by 2005.

- **Labor**

  Nigeria offers a large pool of low-cost labor. Collective bargaining is common in many sectors of the economy although the rights of labor unions are greater in theory than in practice.

Money and Prices *(annual percentage growth)*			
	1997	1998	1999[1]
Money Supply Growth (M2)	15.0	23.3	31.4
Consumer Price Inflation	8.5	10.0	6.6
Exchange Rate (DH/US$ annual average)			
Official	22	82	98.2
Parallel	55	85	101

1. 1999 figures, except exchange rates, are all estimates based on available data.
Sources: Bureau of Economic and Business Affairs; U.S. Department of State. IMF, World Bank

Balance of Payments and Trade *(billions of U.S. dollars unless otherwise indicated)*			
	1997	1998	1999[1]
Total Exports FOB[2]	15.2	9.0	12.9
Exports to U.S.[3]	6.3	4.2	4.4
Total Imports FOB	10.3	9.9	8.6
Imports from U.S.[3]	0.8	0.8	0.6
Trade Balance	4.9	-0.9	4.3
Balance with U.S.[3]	5.5	3.4	3.8
External Public Debt	28.1	28.7	28.0
Fiscal Deficit/GDP (pct)	0.2	4.7	N/A
Current Account Deficit/GDP (pct)	1.2	-11.6	0.4
Debt Service Payments/GDP (pct)	1.8	1.4	N/A
Gold and Foreign Exchange Reserves	7.6	7.1	5.5
Aid from U.S. (US$ millions)	N/A	N/A	N/A
Aid from All Other Sources	N/A	N/A	N/A

1. 1999 figures, except exchange rates, are all estimates based on available data. 2. Merchandise trade.
3. Source: U.S. Department of Commerce and U.S. Census Bureau; exports (fas), imports (customs basis).
Sources: Bureau of Economic and Business Affairs; U.S. Department of State. IMF, World Bank

- Balance of Payments
  See **Key Economic Indicators**.

Government Influence on Business

Over 15 years of continuous, military dictatorship came to an end on May 29, 1999, with the inauguration of President Obasanjo. His government has taken steps to fight corruption and improve economic performance. More specific goals are to improve infrastructure, diversify the economy, and promote a business-friendly environment for domestic and foreign investment. After years of mismanagement, any transformation of government and economic practices will be difficult. Nonetheless, because Nigeria is a country with substantial natural resources, an entrepreneurial population, and a productive agricultural sector, the potential for growth is substantial.

TRADE
(4)

Leading Imports and Exports

Imports: Oil and gas machinery, computers, software and peripherals, telecommunications equipment, automotive parts and accessories, medical equipment, aviation services, cosmetics and toiletries, construction equipment, textiles and fabrics

Exports: Petroleum and petroleum products (95 percent), cocoa, rubber

Foreign Trade *(Exports and Imports in US$B)*			
	1997	1998	1999[1]
Total Exports FOB[2]	15.2	9.0	12.9
Exports to U.S.[3]	6.3	4.2	4.4
Total Imports FOB	10.3	9.9	8.6
Imports from U.S.[3]	0.8	0.8	0.6

1. 1999 figures are estimates based on available data. 2. Merchandise trade.
3. Sources: U.S. Department of Commerce and U.S. Census Bureau; exports (fas), imports (customs basis).
Sources: Bureau of Economic and Business Affairs; U.S. Department of State. IMF, World Bank

Best Prospects Analysis

Best Prospects for Nonagricultural Goods and Services

Oil and Gas Machinery (OGM)

	1999 $M	2000 $M	2001 $M
Total Market Size	550	575	700
Total Local Production	0	0	0
Total Exports	0	0	0
Total Imports	550	575	700
Imports from the U.S.	320	350	415

Computers, Software and Peripherals (CPT)

	1999 $M	2000 $M	2001 $M
Total Market Size	350	450	910
Total Local Production	0	0	0
Total Exports	0	0	0
Total Imports	350	450	910
Imports from the U.S.	250	318	636

Telecommunications Equipment (TEL)

	1998 $M	1999 $M	2000 $M
Total Market Size	300	405	1,215
Total Local Production	0	0	0
Total Exports	0	0	0
Total Imports	300	405	1,215
Imports from the U.S.	40	122	244

Automotive Parts and Accessories (APS)

	1999 $M	2000 $M	2001 $M
Total Market Size	500	500	550
Total Local Production	100	120	150
Total Exports	15	15	15
Total Imports	385	365	385
Imports from the U.S.	80	80	120

Medical Equipment (MED)

	1999 $M	2000 $M	2001 $M
Total Market Size	600	570	600
Total Local Production	170	170	170
Total Exports	20	20	20
Total Imports	450	400	450
Imports from the U.S.	20	15	20

Aviation/Avionics (AVS/AIR/APG)

	1999 $M	2000 $M	2001 $M
Total Market Size	250	300	1,000
Total Local Production	N/A	N/A	N/A
Total Exports	N/A	N/A	N/A
Total Imports	250	300	1,000
Imports from the U.S.	150	180	600

Construction Equipment (CON)

	1999 $M	2000 $M	2001 $M
Total Market Size	180	200	300
Total Local Production	50	80	80
Total Exports	10	10	20
Total Imports	120	110	200
Imports from the U.S.	75	80	100

Cosmetics (COS)

	1998E $M	1999E $M	2000E $M
Total Market Size	80	93	100
Total Local Production	12	13	15
Total Exports	N/A	N/A	N/A
Total Imports	68	80	85
Imports from the U.S.	15	22	28

Textile and Fabrics (TXF)

	1998E $M	1999E $M	2000E $M
Total Market Size	118	142	172
Total Local Production	25	24	29
Total Exports	5	6	8
Total Imports	93	118	143
Imports from the U.S.	15	23	34

Best Prospects for Agricultural Products

Wheat PS&D - NI0011

	1999 $M	2000 $M	2001 $M
Total Market Size	1,520	1,500	1,645
Total Local Production	20	40	45
Total Exports	0	0	0
Total Imports	1,500	1,460	1,600
Imports from the U.S.	1,200	1,200	1,300

Dairy PS&D - NI 3028

	1999 MT ('000)	2000 MT ('000)	2001 MT ('000)
Total Market Size	350	360	360
Total Local Production	68.5	69	69.5
Total Exports	0	0	0
Total Imports	281.5	291	291
Imports from the U.S.	18.5	20.5	21

Rice PSD: NI0011

	1999 MT ('000)	2000 MT ('000)	2001 MT ('000)
Total Market Size	2,650	2,700	2,900
Total Local Production	1,850	1,850	1,900
Total Exports	0	0	0
Total Imports	800	850	1,000
Imports from the U.S.	0.30	0.50	1

Wines and Spirits PS&D (Only FAS estimates)

	1999	2000	2001
	(1,000 cases of 12 x 70 cl)		
Total Market Size	4,000	4,000	4,010
Total Local Production	2,900	2,950	3,000
Total Exports	300	300	300
Total Imports	1,000	1,050	1,150
Imports from the U.S.	200	205	225

The above statistics are unofficial estimates.
Exchange Rates US$1 = Naira 90 (1999), 105 (2000), 110 (2001)
N/A - Not Available, E - Estimated
Note: MT ('000) = Thousand Metric Tons

Extracted from the U.S. Department of Commerce USA Trade 2001 Country Commercial Guide for Nigeria.

Import and Export Tips

- ## Regulations

Customs: Official corruption and long delays have been problems in the past. In 1998, the GON appointed private auditing and accounting firms to collect duties on imports. Duties are to be paid through one of a select group of banks. In 1999, significant port reforms were enacted. A computerized central clearing system (CCS) has also been introduced to help speed and simplify the customs process. Despite such efforts, significant progress has not yet been made in reducing red tape and corruption.

Tariffs: A new tariff structure was established in March 1995, one that is to be reviewed in 2002. Import tariffs are structured to be nonpreferential and applied equally to all countries. The Nigerian Customs and Excise Tariff uses the Customs Cooperation Council Nomenclature (CCCN). Importers shall pay a CISS Administrative charge of 1 percent of fob value of all imports assessed. Nigeria is a signatory to the Lome Convention, which allows duty-free entry into the European Union (EU) for certain exports. Nigeria is also a member of the General Agreement on Tariffs and Trade (GATT), which requires a nondiscriminatory import tariff. There have been frequent complaints, however, that

Nigeria does not fully meet its obligations under such agreements.

Import Taxes: Import taxes range from 5 to 60 percent and are payable upon entry. Depending on the commodity, duties are either specific or ad valorem. The government may impose a special duty on goods that, in its determination, are unfairly subsidized or are being dumped on the Nigerian market. Patterns or samples can be imported duty free although customs officials tend to follow their own discretion in allowing such duty-free admissions. Duties may be refunded on goods that have been abandoned, re-exported, damaged, or destroyed although particular procedures must be followed. Nigeria is a signatory to the United Nations International Convention to Facilitate the Importation of Commercial Samples and Advertising Material.

Exchange Rate: In 1999, the autonomous foreign exchange market (AFEM) was fully deregulated. Dual exchange rates were scrapped, and only AFEM rate prevails. Companies can now hold domiciliary accounts in private banks, with unfettered use of the funds. Foreign investors may bring capital into the country without Finance Ministry approval, and may service foreign loans and remit dividends. Bureau de Change offices are functioning, and transactions in the Bureau de Change offices have been increased to $10,000 per transaction. In addition, oil companies are allowed to sell foreign exchange directly to interested banks and private organizations. The Central Bank has continued to intervene at the weekly AFEM.

- ## Documentation

Exports: The Nigerian government prohibits the exportation of the following items: raw hides and skins, timber (whether processed or not) and wood in the rough, raw palm kernels, unprocessed rubber, and rubber lumps.

Imports: The GON's 23-point "Guidelines for Imports into Nigeria" went into effect on April 1, 1996. These new guidelines require that all imports carry a Clean Report of Finding (CRF) and an Import Duty Report (IDR). In order to facilitate the customs process and avoid penalties, it is crucial that these documents are available and in good order. In general, exporters should comply with a shipper's or importer"s instructions and requests for copies of documents. To claim any goods at Nigerian ports, the following documents must be presented to officials of the Customs and Excise Department:

a) Bill of lading
b) Bill of entry
c) Six copies of the approved, revised Form "M," which is available at inspection offices, Nigerian embassies, local banks, and some overseas banks. Three copies of the form are sent to the Reshipment Inspection Agents. One copy each is sent to the importer's bank, the Nigerian Customs Service, and the National Maritime Authority
d) Marine insurance policy, issued by a Nigerian insurance firm
e) Certificate of quality from the exporting country (for food and drugs)
f) Evidence of payment of value-added tax (VAT)
g) Approved product quality and release certificate from the Standard Organization of Nigeria (SON)

For more information on import documentation specifics, contact Intertek Testing Services. See CONTACTS. Duties are not waived for "temporarily imported" goods. Letters of credit or cash payments are mandatory. Checks must be cleared through one of the designated banks before goods are released to the importers. When all guidelines are properly followed, the Customs Service, in theory, must release the goods within 48 hours. The following are prohibited from importation:

a) Live or day-old chicks
b) Maize, sorghum, millet, and wheat flour
c) Vegetable oils, excluding linseed and castor oils used as industrial raw materials
d) Gypsum
e) Mosquito repellant coils
f) Domestic articles and wares made of plastic materials
g) Retreaded or used tires
h) Matches made with white phosphorous.
i) Pistols disguised in any form
j) Gaming machines
k) Weapons of any description

Labeling: All items entering the country must be labeled exclusively in metric terms. Products with dual or multimarkings will be confiscated or refused entry. A Certificate of Analysis from the manufacturer and country where the goods were manufactured is required for all imports of food, drugs, cosmetics, and items such as pesticides. Sanitation Certificates from the exporters are required for certain animal products, plants, seeds, and soils. The U.S. Department of Agriculture may issue these certificates for American exporters. Before the shipping manifests are submitted to the Nigeria Customs Service, the shipping line must ensure that Import Duty Report (IDR) numbers have been stated continuously on these manifests. For air cargo, the airline must do the same in regard to the airway bill. Packages or containers of sales samples should be marked "Free Sample" or "Free Specimen."

Standards: The Standards Organization of Nigeria is charged with the responsibility of ensuring that international standards are met. The SON has developed standards based on the ISO 9000. Importers are to apply for SON examination of imported goods immediately upon their arrival. According to SON guidelines, most inspected goods shall be granted provisional release. The importer must agree not to dispose of such goods until the SON has the results of laboratory tests and the importer receives the SON's final release letter. The National Agency for Food and Drugs Administration and Control (NAFDAC) provides testing and certification of imported and domestically produced products in the areas of food, drugs, cosmetics, medicine, water, and chemicals. The metric system of measurement is used exclusively. Electric standards are 50 cycles, 230/415 volts, 1,3 phases, 2,4 wires.

• Payment

Terms: The usual term is 90 to 180 days. The method of payment is a confirmed, irrevocable letter of credit. This method was made compulsory by the GON in 1994. Payment is made by the overseas correspondents on behalf of Nigerian banks, on presentation of the specified documents to the overseas correspondents. However, such payment is made on the understanding that the goods paid for will arrive in Nigeria and that importers submit all necessary shipping documents to the authorized dealer as agents of the Nigerian government within 21 days of negotiation of the specified documents. Bills of entry (for imports covered by confirmed letters of credit) must be submitted to the authorized dealer within 90 days of negotiation and payment by overseas correspondent banks.

Currency Exchange: The autonomous foreign exchange market began operation in 1995. The current rate of exchange is approximately 110 naira to US$ 1. The controlled rate of 22 naira to $1 is available only to the government. All applications for foreign exchange must be channeled through selected banks (all licensed commercial and merchant banks) to the Central Bank of Nigeria (CBN). In theory, the CBN will release the forex in three business days. In practice, the process takes up to three weeks.

Fund Transfer: It is now possible to remit dividends and repatriate capital although approval can take up to 18 months after the submission of paperwork. Most proceeds (other than oil and inter-bank inflows) must be held in domiciliary accounts, maintained with authorized banks in Nigeria. Local currency and foreign exchange bank delays can take up to 4 months.

Offshore Loans: No information is available at this time.

MARKETING TIPS

Agents and Distributors

The use of one or more resident agents or distributors is strongly recommended. Nigeria does not have specific laws to regulate foreign agency and distributorship agreements. Thus individual contracts and Nigeria case law govern the principal–agent relationship. In this complicated environment, all relevant terms and conditions must be carefully specified.

The assistance of experienced commercial lawyers is strongly recommended, and U.S. firms should fully investigate the reputations of potential candidates. The Department of Commerce's Agent/ Distributor Service and its Customized Market Analysis (CMA) program both aim to identify reputable and capable agents and distributors. The American Embassy in Lagos also keeps a database of agents and distributors although these potential partners have not been screened. The Commercial Service's U.S. Export Assistance Centers can also provide assistance in finding one or more partners.

Establishing an Office

No information is available at this time. Contact the commercial section of the Embassy of Nigeria and the U.S. Commercial Service (CS) at the American Embassy in Nigeria for more information. The assistance of experienced local commercial lawyers preferably through CS Nigeria database of service providers is strongly recommended.

Distribution and Sales Channels

No information is available at this time. Contact the commercial section of the Embassy of Nigeria and the U.S. Commercial Service (CS) at the American Embassy in Nigeria for more information.

Direct Marketing

No information is available at this time. Contact the commercial section of the Embassy of Nigeria and the U.S. Commercial Service (CS) at the American Embassy in Nigeria for more information.

Leasing/Joint Ventures

Foreign firms cannot operate merely through a Nigerian branch office. Instead, firms must incorporate in Nigeria and establish a place of business. In the private sector, companies, partnerships, and sole proprietorships are the three forms of legally recognized businesses. The establishment of a joint venture by itself is not legally valid. A foreign firm can participate as a shareholder only in a local company incorporated for the purpose of the joint venture.

Franchising

No information is available at this time. Contact the commercial section of the Embassy of Nigeria and the U.S. Commercial Service (CS) at the American Embassy in Nigeria for more information. The assistance of experienced local commercial lawyers preferably through CS Nigeria database of service providers is strongly recommended.

Advertising and Promotion

Advertising plays a significant role in the Nigerian market. Radio broadcasting, which reaches 12 million listeners, is the most reliable way of reaching the Nigerian people. The national network, the Federal Radio Corporation (FRC), dominates the airwaves throughout the country. FRC programs are in English, and they concentrate on domestic news. Many firms find sales promotions such as gifts and discounts to be effective. Trade shows are also a common means of spreading the word although such shows are not often geared toward technical or highly specialized products. The Nigerian Association of Chambers of Commerce, Industry, Mines and Agriculture (NACCIMA) publishes an annual directory of trade shows in Nigeria. Other helpful publications may include *Who Makes What*, printed by the Manufacturers Association of Nigeria (MAN); *The Nigerian Economist*; *The Businessman Journal*; and the *African Technical Review of Business and Technology*. See **Contacts** for a list of government and independent publications.

Selling Factors

Personal ties, flexibility, and patience are necessary for successful business activity in Nigeria. Demand for American products is growing. Owing to Nigeria's geographic size and ethnic complexities, a variety of marketing methods may be required.

Selling to the Government

A "tenders board" makes purchases for the GON. The board comprises senior government officials and may also include local consultants or the Nigeria-based representatives of foreign firms. Historically, the GON has used consultants, such as the British Crown Agents, to procure goods and services. The GON typically uses one of three procurement methods. For open tendering, advertisements are published in national daily newspapers as well as in state and local papers. For selective tendering, which is the dominant method of procurement for state and local government entities, the relevant Ministry sends bid invitations to a list of known and approved companies. The GON uses nominated tendering only for what it deems to be emergency situations; the minister or director general of the relevant Ministry nominates only one company to submit a bid. In nearly all cases, to qualify to bid, construction firms must be incorporated in Nigeria and have a Nigerian partner that holds at least 60 percent equity. Firms arc advised to establish a local company early on in order to take advantage of opportunities as they arise. As always in Nigerian business dealings, beware of fraud. The Central Bank of Nigeria (CBN), for example, does not buy products and services for the Nigerian government or its agencies.

Pricing

Nigerians are price conscious although some sectors are much more price sensitive than others. Cash is the dominant mode of payment. Because the largest bank note is valued at approximately $0.50, buyers and sellers must carry large wads of bills. U.S. exporters must use irrevocable, confirmed letters of credit.

Customer Support

No information is available at this time. Contact the commercial section of the Embassy of Nigeria and the U.S. Commercial Service (CS) at the American Embassy in Nigeria for more information.

Intellectual Property Rights (IPR)

Copyright laws and official proclamations aim to protect intellectual property, but enforcement is weak. The Standard Organization of Nigeria (SON) is charged with the responsibility of issuing patents, trademarks, and copyrights on a domestic level, whereas the Nigerian Copyright Commission (NCC) has jurisdiction at the international level. The Patents and Design Decree of 1970 governs the registration of patents. However, few companies register patents because the law is not effectively enforced. The Trade Marks Act of 1965 governs the registration of trademarks. Nigeria, as a signatory to the Universal Copyright Convention (UCC), provides national treatment for the holders of copyrights of all other signatories of the UCC. The Copyright Decree of 1988 provides an improved copyright regime, based on the World Intellectual Property Organization (WIPO) and U.S. copyright law. However, the law does not specifically cover computer programs or databases. Nigeria is a signatory to the Universal Copyright Convention and the Berne and Rome conventions. In early 1995, Nigeria became a member of the World Intellectual Property Organization (WIPO), thereby becoming party to most major international agreements on intellectual property rights.

Attorney

The assistance of experienced commercial lawyers is strongly recommended. Because of Nigeria's complicated environment, all relevant terms and conditions must be carefully delineated when important agreements are reached.

FOREIGN INVESTMENT
6

Openness: The 1995 Nigerian Investment Promotion Commission (NIPC) decree liberalizes foreign investment regimes, allowing 100 percent foreign ownership of firms in Nigeria, excluding firms in the petroleum sector. In 1996, the NIPC was authorized to help facilitate foreign investment in Nigeria, but by mid-1998, it had not begun full operation. Foreign investment is an important component of the young, civil government's development plan. The GON has expressed a willingness to assure the safety of foreign investment, particularly by entering into Bilateral Investment Protection Agreements with foreign countries. Significantly, certain sectors such as the airline industry are tentatively scheduled for privatization.

Regulatory System: There are promising signs of deregulation in the telecommunications industry, the foreign exchange market, and other sectors. Overall, Nigeria has moved to check the flow of red tape, but confusing and inconsistent regulations are still the norm. Considerable amounts of time, money, and managerial effort are needed to overcome these difficulties and establish a successful business presence.

Investment Agreements: The GON has expressed some desire to enter into Bilateral Investment Protection Agreements with foreign countries whose nationals reside in Nigeria. Until now, the list of reserved sectors (a holdover from the Enterprises Promotion Decree, which recently was repealed) has been one factor preventing the conclusion of a Bilateral Investment Treaty between Nigeria and the United States.

Trade Zones and Free Ports: Calabar, Nigeria's premier Export Processing Zone (EPZ), is in the final stages of completion. To attract foreign investments, increase exports, and thus increase foreign exchange earnings, the GON is planning an EPZ for Port Harcourt in the Rivers States of Eastern Nigeria. Many international companies have expressed their interest in operating in the EPZ. The minimum capital investment to conduct business in an EPZ is US$ 500,000.

Performance Requirements/Incentives: No information is available at this time. Contact the commercial section of the Embassy of Nigeria and the U.S. Commercial Service (CS) at the American Embassy in Nigeria for more information.

Capital Markets and Investment: In 1996, interest rates were deregulated and prices on the stock market were allowed to fluctuate freely. In 1999, the government promised to move toward privatization in the petroleum, airlines, energy, and telecommunications sectors. However, concrete steps in this direction remain elusive.

Private Ownership: Foreign firms may now establish up to 100 percent foreign ownership of firms in Nigeria, excluding firms in the petroleum sector.

Expropriation and Compensation: No information is available at this time. Contact the commercial section of the Embassy of Nigeria and the U.S. Commercial Service (CS) at the American Embassy in Nigeria for more information.

OPIC and Investment Insurance: OPIC, the U.S. Export-Import Bank (EXIM), and EXIM's insurance affiliate, the Foreign Credit Insurance Association (FCIA), have financed and insured a number of programs in Nigeria. Many of these programs were put on hold when the U.S. decertified Nigeria in 1994. However, with the return to civil rule, these programs have again looked to expand in Nigeria.

Dispute Settlement: No information is available at this time. Contact the commercial section of the Embassy of Nigeria and the U.S. Commercial Service (CS) at the American Embassy in Nigeria for more information.

FINANCE

7

The Central Bank of Nigeria (CBN) formulates and monitors a fairly open banking system. There are 90 commercial, merchant, and industrial or development banks. There is also large number of smaller finance houses and community banks. Local financing can be obtained through any of these banks and through some insurance, development, and other companies. However, some banks recently have been designated as "distressed."

Export Financing: Export loans, managed by the CBN, are available through licensed banks for the importation of raw materials, spare parts, and capital equipment. The African Development Bank (ADB) grants export-stimulation loans to exporting companies for certain operations. The ADB channels these loans through the CBN to the Nigerian Export-Import Bank (NEXIM), to NERFUND, and to licensed exporting banks. The aim of NEXIM is to facilitate export financing.

Project Financing: No information is available at this time. Contact the commercial section of the Embassy of Nigeria and the U.S. Commercial Service (CS) at the American Embassy in Nigeria for more information.

COMMUNICATIONS

8

Phone

The telephone service is erratic, with 700,000 lines serving a growing population of 110 million. Deregulation of the industry began in 1993, and a priority of the Nigerian government's development program is the replacement of the country's outdated telecommunications infrastructure. The government plans to install three million telephone lines by the year 2005. To dial Nigeria directly, dial the international access code (011), the Nigerian access code (234), the city routing code, and the local telephone number. City routing codes for major Nigerian cities are as follows: Badagry (1), Kaduna (62), Lagos (1), Port Harcourt (84). For other areas, seek operator assistance.

Internet

The telecommunications market has doubled in size since 1998. Providers of Internet and other telecommunications services should grow rapidly since the Nigerian Communications Commission (NCC) has approved about 200 operating licenses.

Mail

Service is notoriously slow. Reputable couriers such as DHL or UPS should be used for important documents. A private mail bag (PMB) or post office box (P.O. Box) should be used along with the street address. When shipping from the U.S. to Nigeria, the U.S. Postal Service provides both surface and airmail services. U.S. Postal Service parcel rates for surface shipment are $9.00 for the first two pounds and $1.92 for each additional pound or fraction. Airmail rates are as follows: first pound, $9.75; each additional pound up to four pounds, $5.28; each additional pound up to 10 pounds, $4.32; each additional pound up to 20 pounds, $4.00; each additional pound up to 30 pounds, $3.84; each additional pound thereafter, $3.68.

Nigeria

done below.

TRANSPORTATION

Land

It is better to hire a car and driver through a hotel or car rental agency than it is to use Nigeria's taxis, which can be old, unreliable, and unsafe. If a taxi is required, negotiate the fare in advance. General road conditions are poor. Maintenance is wanting; roads flood in torrential rains; there are no traffic lights or stop signs; gridlock is common; and night driving is particularly risky because of a lack of street lighting. In rural areas, the lack of paved roads can cause substantial delays. Nigeria's rail system, which includes 3,500 kilometers of track, is in a state of disrepair. The rehabilitation of the country's infrastructure is a major component of Nigeria's development plan. Nigeria also has 8,575 km of inland waterways mainly consisting of the Niger and Benue rivers and smaller rivers and creeks.

Sea

Principal ports are located in Lagos (Apapa and Tin Can Island), Warri, Sapele, Port Harcourt, and Calabar. The following steamship lines provide ocean cargo service: AAA Nordstar Line, ConFlo Lines, Direct Container Line, Interglobal Shipping, Maersk, SafBank Line Ltd., Target Shipping Inc., Torm Lines, Troy Catucci Line Inc., and Zim Container Service.

Air

The Nigeria Airport Authority oversees 15 airports, with Abuja, Kano, Lagos, and Port Harcourt handling most of the traffic. A number of international passenger and cargo airlines serve Nigeria. The domestic airline industry faces serious difficulties although upgrades over the entire system are scheduled. Safety is a concern. Some facilities are congested, whereas others are disabled. Overbooking and a lack of aviation fuel can cause delays. The state-owned Nigeria Airways is slated tentatively for privatization. Many of the private, domestic airlines have suspended operations owing to obsolete equipment. Of course the same problems do not face most of the international airlines that serve Nigeria, but when departing the country, it is recommended that you get to the airport two hours in advance of your flight time.

WORK WEEK

Business Hours: 8.00 a.m. to 1:00 p.m. and 2:00 p.m. to 4:00 p.m. Monday through Friday. In the Muslim north, all establishments close at 1:00 p.m.

Government Hours: 8.00 a.m. to 3.30 p.m. Monday through Friday. Many government and business officials are held up in staff meetings on Monday and Friday mornings.

Bank Hours: 8:00 a.m. to 3:00 p.m. on Monday and 8:00 a.m. to 1:30 p.m. on Tuesday through Friday. Some banks are open on Saturday from 10.00 a.m. to 2.00 p.m.

HOLIDAYS 2001
11

Eid-El Fitr, February*
Eid-El-Kabir*, March 5
Eid-El-Adha, April*
Good Friday, April 13
Easter Monday, April 16
Workers Day, May 1
Children's Day, May 27
Eid-El-Malud* , June 3
Nigerian National Day, October 1
Christmas Day, December 25
Boxing Day, December 26
Id-el-Fitr*, December 26

Some holidays may be observed on different dates depending on the day of the week on which it falls.

*Holidays falling on Saturdays are observed on Saturdays, and Sunday holidays on Sundays. The Muslim holidays of Eid-El-Fitri and Eid-El-Kabir are usually celebrated for two consecutive workdays. No permanent dates exist for these Muslim holidays. They are observed as announced by the Ministry of Internal Affairs.

*Business travelers should verify the dates of these holidays prior to undertaking a trip to Nigeria.

BUSINESS TRAVEL
12

Business Customs

Patience, flexibility, and the cultivation of personal ties are required to conduct business in Nigeria. Important proceedings are always conducted face to face, often over several meetings. Because deferrals and revisions typically precede any final agreement, company representatives should be empowered to negotiate. Business visitors should be well dressed. Business appointments tend to be made through personal calls or hand-delivered messages since the telephone system is unreliable and the mail is slow. Do not depend on Nigerians to be punctual. English is both the common language of business and the official language of the country.

Travel Advisory and Visas

Visas are required for stays of up to 60 days (except for nationals of ECOWAS countries). U.S. citizens may apply for a visa through either the Nigerian Embassy in Washington, D.C., or the Nigerian Consulate in New York City. Visas may be issued in 48 hours if the proper documents are submitted. Do not attempt to enter Nigeria without a valid visa. Suggestions that you may do so are normally indicative of illegal activity. A certificate of yellow fever vaccination is required at the port of entry for passengers arriving from infected areas.

Business Infrastructure

Entry Requirements (personal and professional goods): Personal baggage is free of duty although such items may be searched. Expect a $35 departure tax at the airport. Current information on entry requirements can be obtained at the Embassy of the Republic of Nigeria or at the Nigerian Consulate General in New York. See **Contacts**.

Currency Exchange: The naira is divided into 100 rarely used kobo coins. The largest bank note in circulation is worth only a small fraction of a dollar. Thus it is necessary to carry large wads of cash. Transactions through Bureaux de Changes are limited to $2,500 (per transaction), with a profit margin of 2 percent.

Taxes: Hotels charge a 5 percent value-added tax (VAT) and a 10 percent service charge. See **Regulations** for additional information.

Hotels and Restaurants: Although deluxe accommodations are quite rare, many hotels in major Nigerian cities are adequate. Reservations must be made well in advance. Up-front cash payment, often in a foreign currency, is demanded. Air conditioning, hot water, and elevator service can be a problem. Room laundry service is usually available.

Rent: No information is available at this time.

Utilities: Electric power is 50 cycles, 1 and 3 phase, with nominal voltage of 220 volts in the largest cities. Power is rationed, so having a standby generator is recommended. Commercial installation ranges from $5,200 to $5,500 but costs three times that for underground cables Service can be erratic. Water, fuel, and electricity shortages are not uncommon.

Business Services: Major cities have business centers for communication and document preparation services. Well-qualified accountants, attorneys, consultants, architects, advertisers, and managers are easily obtainable in Nigeria. The Commercial Service aids with recommendations.

Labor Costs and Legislation: President Obasanjo recently announced a new monthly minimum wage of 5,500 naira (approximately $55) for state civil servants and 7,500 (approximately $75) for those in the federal government. Labor unions and state workers expect their wages to be the same as those of federal workers.

Literacy: Age 15 and over can read and write: 57.1 percent (1995 est).

Insurance: Accident, sickness, liability, and medical evacuation insurance are fairly priced and wisely obtained before departure to Nigeria.

Travel Notes

The following travel notes have been supplied by the U.S. government. For the most recent general travel and consular information, see the U.S. Department of State travel publications or call the Traveler's Telephone Hotline at (202) 647-5225.

Security: Most U.S. citizens who travel to Nigeria do so without incident. However, violent crime is a serious problem, especially in Lagos and the southern half of the country. Armed muggings, assault, burglary, carjackings, and extortion are increasingly widespread. Pickpockets and confidence artists are especially common at Murtala Muhammad Airport. Police or military harassment is not uncommon. Further, credit cards are rarely accepted, and their use is not recommended because of the risk of fraud. To ensure safe travel to your destination, it is best to be met at the airport by a trusted associate or by a person whose identity can be verified. Upon arrival U.S. citizens should register at the U.S. Embassy in Lagos, where they may obtain current information and advice on minimizing risks. For example, Nigerian business, charity, and other scams have targeted foreigners worldwide in recent years. These scams pose dangers of financial loss, physical harm, and even imprisonment. Authorities have treated foreign "victims" as accomplices of the crime. Unsolicited offers should be avoided, as should be any offer to travel to Nigeria without a visa.

Health Precautions: A number of infectious diseases are prevalent in Nigeria. Avoid untreated water and ice as well as peeled fruits and raw vegetables. Proof of current immunization against yellow fever is required at your port of entry if you are arriving from infected areas. Regular use of malaria suppressants is strongly recommended, as are vaccinations for cholera, typhoid, tetanus, meningitis, and hepatitis. Travelers should consult their physician or local health authorities before departure. Medical facilities in Nigeria are readily available, but private clinics in large urban areas are often preferred. Common household medicines and some prescription drugs are available. Current information on health matters may be obtained from the Centers for Disease Control and Prevention's international travelers' hotline at (404) 332-4559.

Embassy Assistance

To obtain additional and updated information on entry and exit requirements, travelers can contact the Consular Section of the Nigerian Embassy at 1333 16th Street, N.W., Washington, D.C. 20036; Tel: (202) 986-8400. Travelers may also contact the Nigerian consulate, which is located in New York.

Business travelers should consult with their nearest U.S. Department of Commerce Export Assistance Office. Upon entry into Nigeria, U.S. citizens should immediately register with the American Citizens Division of the Consular Section at the U.S. Embassy in Lagos.

CONTACTS
13

GON Ministries

Federal Ministry of Agriculture
Federal Secretariat
Area II Garki, Abuja
Tel: 234-9-234 1458;
234-9-234 1572

Federal Ministry of Aviation
New Secretariat
Shehu Shagari Way, Abuja

Federal Ministry of Commerce in Africa
Federal Secretariat, Block H
Area II, Garki, Abuja
Tel: 234-9-234 1884

Federal Ministry of Communications
New Secretariat
Shehu Shagari Way, Abuja

Federal Ministry of Culture and Tourism
Federal Secretariat
Area II, Garki, Abuja

Federal Ministry of Defence
c/o New Secretariat
Shehu Shagari Way, Abuja

Federal Ministry of Education
New Secretariat
Shehu Shagari Way, Abuja

Federal Ministry of Environment
New Secretariat
Shehu Shagari Way, Abuja

Federal Ministry of Federal Capital Territory
c/o New Secretariat
Shehu Shagari Way, Abuja

Federal Ministry of Finance
Ahmadu Bello Way, Maitama, Abuja
Tel: 234-9-234-0932; 234-0936

Federal Minister of Foreign Affairs
New Secretariat
Shehu Shagari Way, Abuja
Tel: 234-9-523 0576

Federal Ministry of Health
New Secretariat
Shehu Shagari Way, Abuja

Federal Ministry of Industry
Federal Secretariat
Area II Garki, Abuja
Tel: 234-9-234 1690

Federal Ministry of Information
Radio House, Abuja
Tel: 234-9-234 6351
Fax: 234-9-234 4106

Federal Ministry of Internal Affairs
New Secretariat
Shehu Shagari Way, Abuja
Tel: 234-9-234 1145; 234 1873

Federal Ministry of Justice
New Secretariat
Shehu Shagari Way, Abuja
Tel: 234-9-523 5194

Federal Ministry of Labour and Productivity
New Secretariat
Shehu Shagari Way, Abuja

Federal Ministry of Power and Steel
New Secretariat
Shehu Shagari Way, Abuja
Tel: 234-9-523 7064
Fax: 234-9-523 6652

Federal Ministry of Police Affairs
c/o Federal Secretariat
Abuja

Federal Ministry of Science and Technology
New Secretariat
Shehu Shagari Way, Abuja
Tel: 234-9-523 3397

Federal Ministry of Solid Minerals
New Secretariat
Shehu Shagari Way, Abuja
Tel: 234-9-523 3528

Federal Ministry of Sports and Social
   Development
New Secretariat
Shehu Shagari Way, Abuja
Tel: 234-9-5235902-7

Federal Ministry of Transport
New Secretariat
Shehu Shagari Way, Abuja
Tel: 234-9-523 7053, 523 7051

Federal Ministry of Water Resources
New Secretariat
Shehu Shagari Way, Abuja
Tel: 234-9-234 1572-7

Federal Ministry of Works and Housing
New Secretariat
Shehu Shagari Way, Abuja
Tel: 090-801-449

Special Ministries posted to the Presidency,
   Aso Rock, Abuja.
Ministry of Civil Service
Ministry of Cooperative and Integrated Rural
   Development
Ministry of Economic Matters
Ministry of Special Projects
Ministry of Inter-governmental Affairs

Other GON Entities

Intertek Services International
(Inspectors of Imports to the U.S.)
3741 Red Bluff Road
Houston, Texas 77503
Tel: (713)-475-2082
Fax: (713)-475-2083

Standard Organization of Nigeria
Federal Secretariat
Phase 1 (9th floor)
Ikoyi, Lagos
Tel: (234 1) 68 26 15
Fax: (234 1) 68 18 20

National Center for Standards and
   Certification Information
(nonagricultural standards)
National Institute of Standards and
   Technology,
TRF Building #411, Room A-163
Gaithersburg, MD 20899
Tel: (301) 975-4040
Fax: (301) 926-1559

The American National Standards Institute
(for more information on foreign standards)
11 W. 42nd St. (13th floor)
New York, NY 10036
Tel: (212) 642-4900
Fax: (212) 398-0023

U.S. Embassy Offices

American Embassy
2, Eleke Crescent
Victoria Island
Lagos, Nigeria
Tel: (234-1) 261-0078
Fax: (234-1) 261-2218

Abuja Office
9 Mambilla Street
Maitama District
Abuja, Federal Capital Territory
Tel: (234)(9) 523-0960; 523-5839; 523-5857;
   523-5227
Fax: (234)(9) 523-0353
Travel advisory phone nos.:
(202) 647-5225; (202) 647-9225

Trade Associations and Chambers
   of Commerce

Computer Vendors Association of Nigeria
84 Opebi Road
Ikeja, Lagos
Tel: 01-965-750; 9620230
Fax: 01-962-657

Computer Association of Nigeria
5, Akinhanmi Street
P.O. Box 4800
Surulere, Lagos

Nigerian Society of Engineers
National Engineering Centre
1, Engineering Close
P.O. Box 72667
Victoria Island, Lagos
Tel: 01-261-749
Fax: 01-261-7315

Manufacturers Association of Nigeria
77 Obafemi Awolowo Way
Ikeja, P.O. Box 3835
Lagos
Tel: 01-967-482; 932-343

Nigerian Export Promotion Council
15 A&B Ladipo Oluwole Road Apapa
P.M.B. 12776
Lagos
Tel: 803-001

Nigerian Institution of Structural Engineers
64/66 Ojuelegba Road, Surulere
P.O. Box 7496
Lagos
Tel: 01-836622

Nigerian Institute of Building
1B, Market Street
Oyingbo, Ebute-Metta
P.O. Box 3191
Lagos

Nigerian Insurers Association
Nicon House, 1st Floor
5, Customs Street
P.O. Box 9551
Lagos
Tel: 01-264-0825

Assoc. of Advertising Practitioners of Nigeria
47 Old Yaba Road
Yaba, Lagos
Tel: 01-860-672; 865-126

Pharmaceutical Society of Nigeria
52A, Ikorodu Road
Lagos
Tel: 01-862-907

Association of Nigerian Co-Op Exporters Ltd.
17, Wharf Road
Apapa, Lagos
Tel: 01-870-347

Nigerian Textile Manufacturers Association
51 Remi Fani-Kayode Avenue
GRA, Ikeja, Lagos
Tel: 01-497-0499

Nigerian-American Chamber of Commerce
Marble House (8th floor)
1, Kingsway Road, Falomo
Ikoyi, Lagos
Tel: 01-269-3041; 269-2088
Fax: 269-3041

**Lagos State Chamber of Commerce
& Industries**
Commerce House
1, Idowu Street, V/Island
P.O. Box 109
Lagos
Tel: 01-610-391; 613-911; 613-917
Fax: 01-610-573

Nigerian-South African Chamber of Commerce
80 Allen Avenue, Ikeja
P.O. Box 389
Shomolu, Lagos
Tel: 01-965-002; 965-009
Fax: 01-493-6758; 967-418

Nigerian-British Chamber of Commerce
Ebani House (4th floor)
149/153, Broad Street
Lagos

**Nigerian-South American Chamber of
Commerce**
Lagos International Trade Fair Complex
Admin. Block, Badagry Expressway
Lagos

Nigerian-Asean Chamber of Commerce
11 Awolowo Road
South West, Ikoyi
Lagos
Tel: 01-269-0428
Fax: 01-684-713

**Nigerian-Brazilian Chamber of Commerce
& Industry**
Western House (6th floor)
8/10 Broad Street
Lagos
Tel: 01-631-328

Franco-Nigerian Chamber of Commerce
NISSCO House (1st floor)
Plot 232A, Adeola Odeku Street
P.O. Box 70001, Victoria Island
Lagos
Tel: 01-618-825, 610-071

Nigerian-Belgian Chamber of Commerce
12 Adeleke Adedoyin Street
off Kofo Abayomi Road
Victoria Island, Lagos
P.O. Box 50190, Falomo
Ikoyi, Lagos
Tel: 619-230; 613-135

**Nigerian Association of Chambers of
Commerce, Industry**
Mines And Agriculture (NACCIMA)
15A, Ikorodu Road, Maryland
P.M.B. 12816, Lagos
Tel: (234-1) 496-4727
Fax: (234-1) 496-4737

Nigerian-German Business Council
Walter Carrington Crescent
Victoria Island
Lagos, Nigeria
Tel: (234-1) 619-751

Nigerian-Japan Association
Ebani House
149/153 Broad Street
P.O. Box 2508
Lagos
Tel: (234-1) 660-387; 661-744

Nigerian-Netherlands Chamber of Commerce
Regency Suites, Apartment 204
17, Ahmed Onibudo Street
Victoria Island, Lagos
P.O. Box 55042, Falomo
Ikoyi, Lagos
Tel: (234-1) 614-619

Nigerian-Portuguese Chamber of Commerce
73 Iwaya Road, Onike
P.O. Box 623
Yaba, Lagos
Tel: (234-1) 860-602

Nigerian-Soviet Trade Council
60 Old Yaba Road, Ebute-Metta
P.M.B. 1065
Apapa, Lagos
Tel: (234-1) 880-527

Nigerian-Swedish Chamber of Commerce
Regency Suites, Suite 206
17 Ahmed Onibudo Street
Victoria Island
P.O. Box 4253
Lagos
Tel: (234-1) 613-396

Note: Each state in Nigeria has a Chamber of
  Commerce and Industry.
For more information, consult the U.S.
  Commercial Service,
Nigeria
Tel: 234-1-261-0050; 261-0078
Fax: 234-1-261-9856

Banks and Financial Institutions

Nigeria International Bank Limited
Commerce House
1, Idowu Taylor Street
Victoria Island
P.O. Box 6391
Lagos
Tel: (234-1) 262-2000-9; 262-2024-32
Fax: (234-1) 618-916

U.S. Affiliate: Citibank
Nigerian-American Merchant Bank Limited
10/12 McCarthy Street
P.M.B. 12759
Onikan, Lagos
Tel: (234-1) 260-1080-4; 260-0360-9
Fax: (234-1) 263-1712

U.S. Affiliate: Bank of Boston
World Bank Resident Mission
Plot 433 ECOWAS Road
Opposite ECOWAS Secretariat
Asokoro, Abuja
Resident Representative
Tel: (234-9) 234-5274; 234-5275; 234-5262
Fax: Abuja (234-9) 234-5267

International Finance Corporation
Plot PC 10, Engineering Close
off Idowu Taylor Street
Victoria Island, Lagos
Tel: (234-1) 611-400; 612-081
Fax: (234-1) 261-7164

The Multilateral Development Bank Office
14th & Constitution Avenue
Washington, DC 2007
Tel: 202-482-3399
Fax: 202-482-5179

Print Media

The Manufacturers Association of Nigeria
  (publishers of the journal "Who Makes What")
72 Obafemi Awolowo Way, Ikeja
Lagos, Nigeria
Tel: (234-1) 266-0756; 266-8992; 266-8985

The Nigerian Economist
c/o Sahel Publishing and Printing Co. Ltd.
71 Oregun Road
P.M.B. 21268, Ikeja
Lagos, Nigeria
Tel: (234-1) 496-5411, 496-5979
Fax: (234-1) 269-3532

The Businessman Journal
White House
23 Falomo Close, Ikeja
P.O. Box 72269, Victoria Island
Lagos, Nigeria.
Tel/Fax: (234-1) 523-299
Marketing
10 Awofeso Street
Honesty House, Palmgrove
P.O. Box 256, Oshodi
Lagos, Nigeria
Tel: (234-1) 821-008

**African Technical Review of Business and
  Technology, through Mercury Airfreight
  Anthill Ltd.**
323 Randolph Avenue
Avenel, NJ 07001
Tel: (908) 396-9555
Fax: (908) 396-1492

News Agency of Nigeria (NAN)

New Nigerian
Daily Times
Abuja Times
West Africa Magazine
State Government Press:
Sketch (Ibadan)
Triumph (Kano)
Nigerian Standard (Jos)
Chronicle (Calabar)
Observer (Benin City)
Tide (Port Harcourt)
Ambassador (Umuahia)
Independent Publications:
Vanguard (Lagos daily)
Champion (daily, pro-Eastern Nigeria)
Sunray (daily, Eastern, partly American-owned)
The Democrat (daily, Northern
Islamic, pro-Government)
The Weekly Business Times (weekly,
 pro-business)
Thisday (daily, pro-business)
Tempo (weekly magazine)
Tell (weekly magazine)
Newswatch (weekly magazine)
The Guardian (daily, pro-business)
The Diet (daily, pro-business)
The Post Express (daily, pro-business)
Business Concord (weekly, pro-business)
Tribune (Ibadan daily)
The Week (weekly magazine)
The News (weekly magazine)
The Source (weekly magazine)

International Economic Organizations

Economic Community of West African States (ECOWAS)
6, King George V Road, Onikan
P.O. Box 2745
Lagos
Tel: 01-636-841; 636-064

European Economic Community (EEC)
Committee of Vice-Chancellors Building
Engineering Close, off Idowu Taylor Street
Victoria Island
Lagos
Tel: 01- 617-852; 610-857; 617-248

World Bank
Plot PC 10, Engineering Close
Victoria Island,
P.O. Box 127
Lagos
Tel: 01- 616-0016; 616-041; 616-196

Market Research Firms

CMW (Communications Ways & Means)
15, Biaduo Street,
S.W. Ikoyi
P.O. Box 75423, Victoria Island
Lagos, Nigeria
Tel: 234-1-2693165; 234-1-684864
Fax: 234-1-685752

Strategic Analysis Limited
53A Akinola Crescent
Ikeja, Lagos Nigeria
Tel/Fax: 234-1-960521

Datapro Limited
Bata House
81/87 Broad Street
Lagos, Nigeria
Tel: 234-1-2661782; 234-1-2660191;
 234-1-2644043
Fax: 234-1-2621008

Research International
2, Sere Close, Ilupeju
P.O. Box 1360
Lagos. Nigeria
Tel: 234-1-493-7421
Fax: 234-1-493-7421

U.S.-Based Multilateral Financial Institutions

The World Bank
1818 H Street, NW
Washington, DC 20433
Tel: (202) 477-1234
Fax: (202) 477-6391

The International Finance Corporation
1818 N Street, NW
Washington, DC 20433
Tel: (202) 477-1234
Fax: (202) 477-3112

Multilateral Investment Guarantee Agency
  (MIGA)
1818 H Street, NW
Washington, DC 20433
Tel: (202) 473-3075
Fax: (202) 872-1521

Africa Growth Fund
1850 K Street, NW, Suite 390
Washington, DC 20006
Tel: (202) 293-1860
Fax: (202) 872-1521

The Corporate Council on Africa
1660 L Street, NW, Suite 301
Washington, DC 20036
Tel: 202-835-1115
Fax: 202-835-1117

Contacts in the U.S.A.

Embassy and Consular offices

New York, NY: Consulate General, 828 2nd
  Ave., 10017,
Tel: (212) 808-0301
Fax: (212) 687-1476
Hours: 9 a.m. to 1 p.m., 2 p.m. to 5 p.m. Closed
  Saturday. Jurisdiction, entire United States.

Washington, DC: Embassy of Nigeria to the
  United States,
2201 M St., N.W., 20037
Tel: (202) 822-1500
Fax: (202) 775-1385
Hours: 9.00 a.m. to 1.00 p.m. and 2.00 p.m. to
  5.00 p.m.
Passport and Visa Hours: 9.00 a.m. to 1.00 p.m.
Consular office
Tel: (202) 822-1538 and Commercial Office
Tel: (202) 986-8400
are also resident at the Embassy.

Business Information Sources

Commerce Section,
Consulate General of Nigeria
828 2nd Ave.
New York, NY 10017
Tel: (212) 808-0301
Fax: (212) 687-1476

Nigeria-United States Trade Council
214 Massachusetts Ave.
Suite 300
Washington, DC 20002
Tel: (202) 293-9433

Contacts in Nigeria

U.S. Foreign Service
Embassy, with a U.S. Foreign Commercial
  Service
Post and a Consular Section
Lagos: 2 Eleke Crescent
Victoria Island
P.O. Box 554
Tel: (234-1) 261-0078
Fax: (234) (1) 261-9856
Telex: 23616 AMEMLA NG Consular Section
Fax: (234) (1) 261-2218
COM Fax: (234) (1) 261-9856
USIS Fax: (234) (1) 263-5397
AID Fax: (234) (1) 261-4698

Nigerian Government Offices

Federal Institute of Industrial Research
Private Mail Bag 1023
Ikeja Airport

Federal Ministry of Industries
Private Mail Bag 12614 Ikoyi
Lagos

Federal Ministry of Trade
Secretariat Complex Abuja, Federal
Ministry of Industries
Federal Secretariat Complex 1 Ikoyi
Lagos

Information Division, Federal Ministry of
  Information and Culture
15 Awolowo Road (4th floor) S.W., Ikoyi
Lagos

Ministry of Finance and Economic Planning
Garki, Area 2
Abuja

Nigerian Enterprises Promotions Board
19 Keffi St, Ikoyi
Lagos

Nigerian Industrial Development Bank
  Limited (NIDB), 96/102
Yakubu Gowon St.
Lagos

Nigerian Tourist Association
47 Marina, P.O. Box 2944
Lagos

Business Information Sources

Kaduna Chamber of Commerce, Industry
  and Agriculture
24 Waff Road, P.O. Box 728 Kaduna
Tel: (234-62) 211-216
Telex: 71325

Kano Chamber of Commerce, Industry, Mines
  and Agriculture
138 Ibrahim Taiwo Road
P.O. Box 10 Kano City
Kano State
Tel: (234-64) 620165
Fax: (234-64) 620165

Lagos Chamber of Commerce and Industry,
  Commerce House
1st Floor, 1 Idowu Taylor St.
Victoria Island, P.O. Box 109 Lagos
Tel: (234-1) 613-898; 613-911; 610-533
Telex: 21368 CHACOMNG

Nigerian-American Chamber of Commerce
Marble House
1 Kingsway Road
Ikoyi, Lagos
Tel: (234-1) 269-2088
Fax: (234-1) 269-3041

Nigerian Association of Chambers of
  Commerce, Industry, Mines & Agriculture
15A Ikorodu Road, Maryland
PMB 12816
Lagos
Tel: (234-1) 964-727
Fax: (234-1) 964-737
Telex: 21368 CHACOMNG

Nigerian Tourism Development Corp.
Block 2 Sefadu Street
PMB 167, Zone 4, Wuse, Abuja
Tel: (234-9) 523-0418-420; 523-3191-3
Fax: (234-9) 592-30962

World Trade Center of Nigeria, Western
  House (9th floor)
8-10 Broad St., P.O. Box 4466 Lagos
Tel: (234-1) 263-5276
Fax: (234-1) 683-981

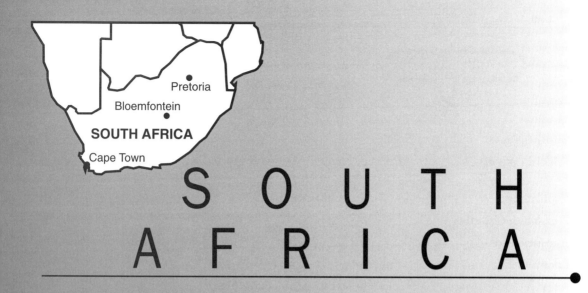

SOUTH AFRICA

TRADE AND BUSINESS GUIDE

PROFILE

①

Official Name:	South Africa
Official Languages:	Afrikaans, English, Ndebele, Sotho, Tsonga, Swati, Tswana, Venda, Pedi, Xhosa, Zulu
Population:	43,421,021 (2000 est)
Population Growth:	0.5% (2000 est)
Age Structure:	0–14 years: 32%, 15–64 years: 63%, 65 years and over: 5% (2000 est)
Location:	Southern tip of Africa
Area:	1,219,912 square kilometers. Slightly less than twice the size of Texas
Type of Government:	Republic, with central government and nine provincial governments
	Bicameral parliament elected every five years, with National Assembly (which elects chief executive president) and National Council of Provinces
Head of State:	Thabo Mbeki (African National Congress)
Cabinet:	Appointed by president
Religion:	Christian 68%, Muslim 2%, Hindu 1.5%, traditional and animistic 28.5%
Major Cities:	Capital: Pretoria (1 million). Principal commercial centers: Cape Peninsula (2.3 million), Johannesburg /Randburg (1.9 million), East Rand (1.3 million), Durban/Pinetown/Inada/Chatswort (1.3 million), West Rand (870,066), Vanderbijlpark/Vereeniging/ Sasolburg (773,594)
Climate:	Mostly semiarid; subtropical along east coast; sunny days, cool nights
Time:	Entire country is +2 GMT (Greenwich Mean Time), seven hours ahead of EST (Eastern Standard Time). Clocks are not advanced during summer.
GDP:	Purchasing power parity (PPP): $296.1 billion (1999 est); real growth rate: 0.6% (1999 est); per capita PPP: $6,900 (1999 est); composition by sector: agricultural: 5%, industry: 35%, services: 60% (1999 est)
Currency:	1 rand (R) = 100 cents
Exchange Rate:	Rand (R) per US$ 1 = 6.97 (2000 est), 6.14 (1999 est), 5.06 (1998 est)
Weights & Measure:	Metric system
Natural Resources:	Gold, chromium, antimony, coal, iron ore, manganese, nickel, phosphates, tin, uranium, gem diamonds, platinum, copper, vanadium, salt, natural gas
Total Trade:	In billions US$ [exports (fob)/imports (cif)]: 1997 (30.4/28.4), 1998 (28.2/27.2), 1999 est (29.6/27.8)

Trade with U.S.:	In billions US$ [exports (fob)/imports (cif)]: 1997 (2.5/3.0), 1998 (3.0/3.6), 1999 est (3.2/2.6)
Major Trade Partners:	Imports: Germany, United States, United Kingdom, France and Japan. Exports: Italy, Japan, United States, Germany and United Kingdom
Membership:	AfDB, CAIRNS, IBRD, ICC, IFC, IMF, ISO, MIGA, SACU, SADC, UN, UNCTAD, WCO, WIPO, and WTO

Sources: CIA World Fact Book, United Nations World Statistics, U.S. Department of Commerce, U.S. Department of State, The South Africa Reserve Bank, World Bank, IMF

POLITICAL OUTLOOK ②

Relationship with the U.S.

U.S.–South African relations are strengthening steadily now. The first multiracial and multi-party elections occurred in 1994, and the 1999 elections were even more peaceful. The U.S.–South African Binational Comission (BNC), created in 1994, promotes relations with committees in multiple areas: trade and business develop-ment, agriculture, defense, energy, environ-ment, housing, human resource development, science and technology, justice, and anticrime coordination. The U.S. Munitions list defense trade may open up to South Africa as well. South Africa is now a member of United Nations, Commonwealth, Organization of African Unity, Indian Ocean Rim Association for Regional Cooperation, Non-Aligned Movement (serves as chair), and SADC.

Influences on Business

The African National Congress (ANC) has increasingly moved away from centralized statism and nationalization toward privati-zation of some parastatal firms and greater market-driven competition. Violence was a problem around the 1994 transition out of apartheid, but is now waning. Violence still exists in some areas between ANC, Inkatha

Freedom Party (IFP), and United Democratic Movement (UDM), but a 1999 peace pact was signed between ANC and IFP. Criminal violence is still fairly high while the country moves to social stability. New government programs attack crime, and the government of South Africa (SAG) is working closely with donor countries to tackle crime. The govern-ment is expected to shift focus from political considerations to speeding up delivery of goods and services to the majority of the population. Economic growth and develop-ment agendas as well as crime reduction should benefit bilateral U.S.–South Africa trade and investment.

Profile

System: Parliament has two chambers: the National Assembly and the National Council of Provinces. The 400 seats in the National Assembly are allocated along party's vote percentages. The African National Congress (ANC) holds 66.35 percent of the vote and Assembly seats, and the Democratic Party (DP) holds 10 percent; the 90-member National Council of Provinces (NCOP) has 10 delegates from each of South Africa's 9 provinces, elected by provincial legislators. The ANC also controls the voting majority. The members of the National Assembly elect the President who is vested with broad executive powers, including the power to appoint a cabinet.

Schedule for Elections: The national elections took place in 1994 and 1999; the local elections, in 1996 and 2000.

Major Parties: Thirteen parties are represented in the National Assembly after the 1999 elections. The ANC dominates, with primarily black membership with white liberal support, and all races are represented in leadership and cabinet positions. The ANC is trying to provide adequate employment, education, health care, and housing to the apartheid-era disenfranchised majority. The Democratic Party (DP) is the second largest and is mainly white, socially liberal, and economically conservative. The National Party (NP) ruled pre-1994, and created then abandoned apartheid policies. Nine other parties range from far right to far left, economically, religiously, and otherwise.

Political Violence: Political violence is increasingly rare. Foreigners are not targeted.

Corruption: Next to crime, corruption is the largest problem, but it is not identified as a business obstacle. A new FBI-type agency will target violent and commercial crime. Anti-bribery laws are in place, but there have been few convictions.

Media: Major media outlets include television, radio, newspapers and magazines, outdoor advertisements, cinema and the Internet. The deregulation of the airwaves has introduced more competition through another independent television channel and independent radio stations.

ECONOMIC OUTLOOK ③

Trends

The government of South Africa (SAG) has been restructuring its economy for global markets with trade and industrial development initiatives, trade and industrial policy reform, and organizational and regulatory changes in financial markets; it has also been relaxing exchange control measures. Exports, capital expenditure, and joint ventures are seen as promising. Because of economic standards, size, and sophistication similar to developed countries, and easy access to areas such as Southern African Development Community (SADC), South Africa is seen as a good stepping stone to business in Africa. Threats to growth include residual import substitution, industrial protection, government bureaucracy and lack of transparency, including corruption. Skilled labor at many levels is needed.

Major Growth Sectors

Agriculture plays a larger role in the economy than the 5 percent GDP contribution indicates and has been beset by droughts. Air pollution and waste management, cellular telephony, computer software and services, (eco) tourism, and electronic commerce are all part of expansion into the global economy. Mining has some setbacks (falling gold prices and competition), but expansion from primary commodities into related processing industries such as minerals processing, petrochemicals, jewelry, and metal fabrication has potential for further growth. Security and safety equipment is growing in response to criminal activities. Large-scale SAG development initiatives target a wide range of industries in various regions. See **Contacts**.

Also promising for U.S. exports are managed health care, airports, cosmetics and hair care products, infrastructure, project finance and management. Because of SAG's income redistribution, some high-end products are on the wane, but basic needs for less prosperous demographics have potential.

Key Economic Indicators

Income, Production and Employment[1] *(billions of U.S. dollars unless otherwise indicated)*			
	1997	1998	1999 (est)
Nominal GDP (at nominal prices)	147.9	134.5	146.0
Real GDP Growth (pct)	2.5	0.5	0.9
GDP by Sector:			
Agriculture	5.2	4.3	4.6
Mining and Quarrying	8.9	7.7	8.3
Manufacturing	27.5	23.0	25.1
Wholesale and Retail Trade	18.5	15.7	17.1
Financial Services	20.6	18.5	20.1
Government	17.6	15.0	16.3
Per Capita GDP (US$)	2,987	2,525	N/A
Labor Force (millions)	9.8	13.8	N/A
Unemployment Rate (pct)	22.9	23.0 (est)	N/A

1. The following exchange rates were used in the calculations: $1:R4.61 for 1997, $1:R5. for 1998, and an estimated $1:R6.15 for 1999.
Sources: Bureau of Economic and Business Affairs; U.S. Department of State, U.S. Department of Commerce

- **Infrastructure**
  International trade transport in air and sea is well developed for bulk. Freight transport in general is not sufficient in cost and service, but the physical and service infrastructure was recently enhanced by trade support services such as cargo inspection, standards information and certification, and credit insurance. The major ports (Durban, Cape Town, Richards Bay, Port Elizabeth) are well equipped for all cargo types. For the developing world, the international trade structure is seen as excellent. Rural, township, and former homelands (prior ethnic statehoods) vary in quality of infrastructure. A series of initiatives such as Spatial Development Initiatives (SDIs), other country partnerships, public transportation in urban and rural centers, and support for provincial roads departments for restructuring and rationalization are all attempting to reduce overhead and revitalize roads. Some of the most important developments with regard to the restructuring of state assets will relate to "Transnet" (the transportation parastatal). According to President Mbeki, "the priority given to this corporation arises from the fact that the transport and logistic system it contains underpins the success of other major investment projects."

- **Labor**
  South Africa has a large pool of unskilled, cheap labor. The government is perceived as supporting labor to some degree with protective legislation.

Money and Prices *(annual percentage growth)*			
	1997	1998	1999 (est)
Money Supply Growth (M2)	18.7	13.6	10
Consumer Price Index	8.6	6.9	5.5
Exchange Rate (rand/US$ annual average)[1]			
Unified	4.6	5.5	6.2

1. The following exchange rates were used in the calculations: $1:R4.61 for 1997, $1:R5. for 1998, and an estimated $1:R6.15 for 1999.
Source: Bureau of Economic and Business Affairs; U.S. Department of State

Balance of Payments and Trade *(billions of U.S. dollars unless otherwise indicated)*			
	1997	1998	1999 (est)
Total Exports FOB[1]	30.4	28.2	29.6
Exports to U.S.[2]	2.5	3.0	3.2
Total Imports CIF[1]	28.4	27.2	27.8
Imports from U.S.[2]	3.0	3.6	2.6
Trade Balance[1]	2.0	1.0	-1.8
Trade Balance with U.S.[2]	-0.5	-0.6	0.6
External Public Debt[3]	3.3	2.7	N/A
Fiscal Deficit/GDP (pct)	4.2	5.5	N/A
Current Account Deficit/GDP (pct)	1.5	-1.6	-0.5
Debt Service Payments/GDP (pct)	6.1	6.7	N/A
Gold and Foreign Exchange Reserves	3.7	7.6	6.5
Aid from U.S. (US$ millions)[4]	110.5	71.3	53.4
Aid from Other Countries[5]	N/A	N/A	N/A

1. All South African trade statistics include export and import data for the five members of the Southern African Customs Union (Botswana, Lesotho, Namibia, South Africa, and Swaziland) up to December 1997.
2. Source: U.S. Department of Commerce and U.S. Census Bureau; exports FAS, imports customs basis.
3. From IMF Yearbook, September 1999.
4. The figures represent aid from USAID only.
5. South Africa has received substantial aid from all over the world. However, there is no comprehensive audit of the total aid given to South Africa to date.
Sources: Bureau of Economic and Business Affairs; U.S. Department of State, U.S. Department of Commerce and U.S. Census Bureau

- Balance of Payments
  See **Key Economic Indicators.** Rand versus dollar decline: In 1997, the rand declined by 10 percent, and in 1998, it declined by another 10 percent. Reasons for this decline include a 7 percent inflation rate, any unseen political factors, balance of payment accounts, currency speculation, BEM (Big Emergent Market Malaise) affecting international perceptions, and reluctance of SAG to intervene in forex operations.

Government Influence on Business

There are many incentives toward more global business. These incentives include, lower import tariffs and local firm subsidies, no more nonresident shareholders tax, corporate earnings tax rate lowered to 30 percent, and reduced tariff rates (though still a complex and volatile system). All of these incentives are part of its GEAR (Growth, Employment, and Redistribution) macroeconomic policy, designed to increase investment, privatize government enterprises, and restructure industry toward global competitiveness. Privatization can be slow because the government seeks consensus of business, government, and labor. Some of the most important developments with regard to the restructuring of state assets will relate to "Transnet" (the transportation parastatal). According to President Mbeki, "the priority given to this corporation arises from the fact that the transport and logistic system it contains underpins the success of other major investment projects."

Leading Imports and Exports

Imports: Machinery, transport equipment, chemicals, petroleum products, textiles, scientific instruments, air pollution and waste management, cellular telephony, computer software and services, (eco) tourism, electronic commerce, security and safety equipment, managed health care, airports, cosmetics and hair care products, infrastructure, project finance and management.

Exports: Gold, minerals, metals, food, chemicals.

Foreign Trade *(Exports and Imports in US$Billions)*			
	1997	1998	1999 (est)
Total Exports FOB[1]	30.4	28.2	29.6
Exports to U.S.[2]	2.5	3.0	3.2
Total Imports CIF[1]	28.4	27.2	27.8
Imports from U.S.[2]	3.0	3.6	2.6

1. All South African trade statistics include export and import data for the five members of the Southern African Customs Union (Botswana, Lesotho, Namibia, South Africa, and Swaziland) up to December 1997.
2. Sources: U.S. Department of Commerce and U.S. Census Bureau; exports FAS, imports customs basis.
Source: Bureau of Economic and Business Affairs; U.S. Department of State, U.S. Department of Commerce and U.S. Census Bureau

Best Prospects Analysis

Best Prospects for Nonagricultural Goods and Services

Telecommunications Equipment (TEL)

	1998E $B	1999E $B	2000E $B
Total Market Size	2.1	4.1	5.1
Total Local Production	1.8	2.0	2.1
Total Exports	.16	18	.19
Total Imports	1.2	1.3	1.4
Imports from the U.S.	.16	.16	.18

Includes fixed lines, cellular and broadcasting equipment. Local equipment production includes foreign parts and components. May also include components used in other sectors such as IT.

Computers Software and Services

	1998E $M	1999E $M	2000E $M
Total Market Size	455	546	682
Total Local Production	22	26	29
Total Exports	7	9	12
Total Imports	364	437	546
Imports from the U.S.	302	358	447

Airports Company South Africa (ASCA)

	1997 $M	1998 $M	1999* $M
Turnover	125	129	141
Operating Income	49	51	63
Other Income	16	15	10
Income Before Tax	64	66	73
Income After Tax	38	41	47
Net Income	30	33	37

*Year ending 3/31/99

Air Pollution and Waste Management (Equipment Only)

	1998E $M	1999E $M	2000E $M
Total Market Size	14	15	21
Total Local Production	5	6	9
Total Exports	1	3	5
Total Imports	8	9	14
Imports from the U.S.	4	5	6

Security and Safety

	1997 $M	1998 $M	1999E $M
Total Market Size	257	380	710
Total Local Production	124	146	238
Total Exports	14	17	20
Total Imports	109	128	186
Imports from the U.S.	12	15	17

Cosmetics Industry by Market Segment

	1998E $M	1999E $M	2000E $M
Perfumes and Fragrances	N/A	69	71
Color Cosmetics	N/A	25	26
Skin Care Products	N/A	53	54
Bath and Shower Products	N/A	56	57
Deodorants	N/A	49	50
Oral Hygiene	N/A	58	59
gMen's Shaving Products	N/A	44	45
Total	N/A	426	435

Best Prospects for Agricultural Products

Market Segment

	1997 $M	1998 $M	1999E $M
Consumer-oriented Products	77	59	50
Poultry Meat	44	30	20
Processed Fruits and Vegetables	4	3	3
Pet Food	7	6	7
Soybean Meal	11	12	12
Forest Products	34	21	20

Major Projects and Significant Investment Opportunities

Major Capital Projects and Fixed Investment Activity

Company	Project	Completion Date	$M
Telkom	Talkom's Vision 2000	2000	6,300
Eskom	Mjuba Power Station	2001	2,400
Foskor	Phlogopite Plant	2001	890
Durban Metro Water	Metro Water Scheme	2005	297
BP	Shell Refinery Expansion	2001	257

Consultancies Identified by U. S. Trade and Development Agency (TDA)

Environmental Projects
Telecommunications
Energy Development
Food Production
Minerals Development
Industry
Transportation
Air Traffic Control

Grants Approved for TDA Feasibility Studies (FS), Technical Conferences and Seminars (TS), and Orientations "Reverse" Trade Missions (OV)

Fluidized Bed Combustion Project (FS)
Petroleum Storage and Tanker Mooring Project (FS)
Bagasse Hydrolysis Project (FS)
Light Rail Transportation Orientation Visit (OV)
Digital Satellite Service Study (FS)
Peacock Bay Industrial Waste Incineration Project (FS)
Gauteng Province Solid Waste Management and
　Recycling (FS)
South African Trade and Investment Conference (OV)
Johannesburg-Metropolitan Area-Airport Transport
　Linkages (FS)
Dredging Orientation Visit (OV)
Glycol Processing Facility (FS)
Healthcare Orientation Visit (OV)
Bakery and Milling Project (FS)
Durban Solid Waste (OV)
Illovo Sugar (FS)

The above statistics are unofficial estimates.
Exchange Rates : US$ 1 = R4.61 (1997), R5.5 (1998),
R6.0 (1999)
N/A - Not Available, E - Estimated
Note: MT ('000) = Thousand Metric Tons

Extracted from the U.S. Department of Commerce USA Trade 2000 Country Commercial Guide for South Africa

Import and Export Tips

- **Regulations**

  Customs: South Africa is a member of the WTO and follows the Harmonized System of Classification for imports (HS). There is virtually free exchange with other members of South African Customs Union (Botswana, Lesotho, Namibia, Swaziland). U.S. shipments to South Africa qualify for MFN (Most Favored Nation) rates. The dutiable value of imported goods to South Africa and Southern African Customs Union (SACU) is calculated on the fob price in the export country, in accordance with GATT Customs Valuation Code. Dutiable weight is the legal weight, plus the weight of the product's immediate sale container, unless otherwise specified in the tariff.

  Tariffs: With World Trade Organization (WTO) commitments, SAG is reforming complex tariffs left over from apartheid-era

regimes. Tariff rate goals of 2002, for SAG and WTO are as follows: 0 to 10 percent for primary and semi primary products; 0 to 10 percent for capital products; 10 to 15 percent for components; and 15 to 30 percent for consumer products. Automobile and textile industries are more sensitive because years of import substitution render them less globally competitive, so tariffs will decline less quickly than for other sectors. Goals for 2002 are as follows: 40 percent for passenger and light commercial vehicles; 45 percent for clothing; 25 percent for yarn; 10 percent for fibers; and 30 percent for household textiles. The Board on Tariffs and Trade is a statutory body that advises the SAG on tariffs, WTO compliances, and tariff protections. All applications to the board are published for six week of comment and consultation.

Import Taxes: A VAT (value-added tax) of 14 percent is due on all imports except some goods for manufacturing or resale by registered traders. There are excise duties on alcoholic and nonalcoholic beverages, tobacco and tobacco products, mineral waters, some petroleum products, and motor vehicles. Ad valorem duties are levied on office machinery, photographic film, and luxury consumer goods such as cosmetics, home entertainment products, and motorcycles. Consult schedules in the Customs and Excise Act (not the Import Control Act) to determine imports eligible for duty rebates. Duties for bona fide unsolicited gifts entering South Africa consigned by individuals in South Africa can be fully rebated if both he or she does not receive more than two parcels per calendar year, and the value of each parcel doesn't exceed R400 (excluding baggage items, wine spirits, and manufactured tobacco). No import surcharges exist in accordance with WTO.

Exchange Rate: The South African Reserve Bank (SARB) has substantial control over foreign currency. The SARB's Exchange

Control Department administers exchange controls through commercial banks that have been authorized to deal in foreign exchange. All international commercial transactions must be accounted for through these"authorized foreign exchange dealers." The SARB is also a marketing agent for gold, which accounts for about 18 percent of export earnings. This provides the SARB wide latitude for determining short-term exchange rates. Monetary authorities usually allow the rand to adjust in an attempt to stabilize external accounts. Although the SARB recognized that the low level of hard currency reserves required continued inflow of long-term capital, the government of national unity eliminated the previous dual exchange rate and established a unified exchange rate in March 1995. Nonetheless, South Africa still maintains several capital controls to prevent large capital outflows. The government is more likely to approve foreign exchange purchases for investment abroad if the foreign partner of the South African party conducts an asset swap, whereby the foreign partner invests an equivalent amount of foreign exchange in South Africa. Although domestic as well as foreign business concerns have lobbied hard for the lifting of the asset swap requirement, it is unlikely that the government will do so until foreign reserve levels approach the three-month coverage level. While foreign reserves are currently at about $6.5 billion, the SARB maintains a large net open forward position of $15.6 billion as of the end of September 1999.

- **Documentation**

Exports: Products subject to export licenses and controls include strategic goods (exhaustible resources), metal waste, and scrap. Diamonds for export must be registered with the Diamond Board. Prohibited from export are price-controlled petroleum products from local synfuel plants, ostriches and their fertilized eggs.

Metal scrap is subject to an export permit, which is issued 5 days after the application is made, thus giving time and opportunity to local users to negotiate for the purchase price.

Imports: Goods requiring permits include fish and dairy products (health concerns), petroleum products (strategic concerns), Montreal Protocol chemicals (international obligations), pneumatic tires (quality specifications), footwear (WTO quotas), firearms and ammunition (safety concerns). The Department of State can consider requests for licenses for the export of items on the U.S. Munitions List to South Africa. Exporters should call the Bureau of Export Administration at telephone 202-482-4830 for an update on "dual use" export controls. Simplification and WTO cooperation continues.

Labeling: All items entering the country must conform to the metric International System of Units (SI). The country of origin must be identified on imported goods. Products with dual or multi markings may be refused entry. Special labeling requirements apply to all imports of foodstuff, drugs, cosmetics and toothpaste, and powder and mouthwashes containing fluorides. Some products require labels in both English and Afrikaans. Packaging and marking of commodities for local sale (including imports) are regulated by the Agricultural Product Standards Act of 1990.

Standards: The South African Bureau of Standards (SABS) is charged with the responsibility of ensuring that international standards are met. The SABS has developed standards and publishes a bulletin listing suppliers that comply with the ISO 9000 series. The Ministry of Trade may set additional safety and health standards. Additional up-to-date information can be obtained from the Department of Trade and Industry in Pretoria. See **Contacts**.

- Payment

Terms: Payment terms are commonly 60 to 90 days, but can vary from 30 to 120 days or even more for large orders of capital equipment. Letter-of-credit terms are recommended for new transactions.

Currency Exchange: Exporters should offer quotations in the currency of origin country, including fob value, freight, insurance, and additional charges. Shipping on a letter of credit (LC) basis is advised to expedite payment. Some 24 to 48 hours is typical for payment transfer upon presentation to the bank with proper import permit / documents. Currently, the South African Reserve Bank (SARB) does not provide foreign exchange in payment of goods prior to shipment or dispatch to South Africa. Foreign exchange currency payments for imports may be made only against the following documents: received for ship-ment bills of lading; on-board bills of lading; air waybills of lading; parcel post receipts; carrier's receipts or railroad bills of lading; arrival notifications issued by Ellerman and Bucknall (Pty) Limited, Safmarine Limited, the Transatlantic Shipping Agency (Pty)

Limited, or Nedloyd Agency Cies SA (Pty) Limited. Foreign exchange can be provided for advance payments of up to 33 1/3 percent of ex-factory cost of goods, or on a cash-with-order basis, but only under certain conditions. Under the conditions, authorized dealers must demand original bills of entry or local parcel post receipts as evidence of goods transfers, which are then stamped "Exchange Provided," with date and amount paid. Customers should retain documents for two years for inspection purposes.

Fund Transfer: Up to R200,000 ($33,333) in investment transfers by individuals are not controlled. SARB administers exchange controls, which authorizes commercial banks. Foreign exchange delays averages about one month. All international com-mercial transactions must be accounted by these "authorized foreign exchange" dealers. Toward globalization, further relaxation of exchange controls and foreign investment ceilings is expected.

Offshore Loans: No information is avail-able at this time.

MARKETING TIPS

⑤

Agents and Distributors

A wide variety of methods are available for product sales and distribution. Foreign suppliers can use agents or distributors, sell through wholesalers or dealers, sell directly to department stores or retailers, or establish a branch or subsidiary with its own sales force. The Ronald H. Brown Commercial Center in Johannesburg (U.S. Commercial Service) offers customized market research, market analyses, the Agent/Distributor Service program (ADS), and Gold Key Service, a custom-tailored service for firms and indivi-duals planning to visit a country (arranges

appointments and other services). Market research and then a visit to contacts are advised. Thorough research on potential agents or distributors and clear responsibility agreements are recommended. In South Africa, an agent works on commission after obtaining orders from customers, and a distributor buys and sells products directly to customers. When working with a local agent representing foreign principals, it is important to work closely to track import procedure changes and ensure that the agent effectively represents one's sales interest.

Establishing an Office

The Registrar of Companies administers the Companies Act of 1973, which regulates formation, conduct of all affairs, and liquidation of all companies. The act covers local and foreign-owned companies, both private and public. Foreign companies must register all South African subsidiaries in accordance with the act. Local branch offices must be registered with the Registrar of Companies and file annual financial statements, but do not need government approval and pay no withholding tax on remitted profits. Private companies are designated by "Proprietary Limited" (Pty) in the title, and public companies by "Limited" (Ltd.), and "Close Corporations" (CC), which are uniquely for South Africans and limited to a maximum of ten people. Contact the Registrar of Companies for additional information. See **Contacts.**

Distribution and Sales Channels

Ninety percent of the population lives in areas around Johannesburg, Cape Town, Durban, Pretoria, and Port Elizabeth, the major areas of economic activities and consumer markets. The Gauteng region (previously the Pretoria area) generates 37 percent of GDP (28 percent of aggregate SADC GDP, 9 percent of Africa's GDP). Johannesburg, located in the center of Gauteng, is the commercial and financial hub of South Africa. Johannesburg is home to industries that emphasize steel, petrochemicals, and manufacturing. As the country's transportation hub, it is the center for all rail and road connections and has the country's major international airport. Johannesburg is 456 miles from Durban and 954 miles from Cape Town. The following nine provincial authorities are increasingly important for business: Northern Transvaal, North-West Province, Guateng, KwaZulu-Natal, Mpumalanga, Free State, Eastern Cape, Western Cape, and Northern Cape.

Direct Marketing

Due to South Africa's foreign exchange controls and import documentation requirements, It is recommended that overseas firms contract with a South African partner responsible for marketing the product, holding stock, fulfilling purchasing transactions, and remitting revenue to U.S. base.

Leasing/Joint Ventures

The South African Reserve Bank (SARB) Exchange Control must approve all royalty payments. Royalty fees are a percentage of ex-factory sales, with maximum of 4 percent for consumer goods and 6 percent for intermediate and final capital goods. Minimum or annual payments are not acceptable to SARB. Contracts involving obligatory purchasing and pricing agreements and licensing sole articles from licenser are prohibited For a foreign license to manufacture a product in South Africa, apply to the Industrial Development Branch of the Department of Trade and Industry.

Franchising

Franchising is increasingly popular, with 10,000 franchise outlets and $6.8 billion of sales during 1996/97. The Franchise Association of Southern Africa (FASA) has 150 of 300 franchisers, with almost all outlets. Fast food encompasses 29 percent of all franchises, with service industries becoming prominent. Promising industries include automotive, educational training, building and home services, business services, health and beauty services, printing, real estate, and leisure services. The Department of Trade and Industry (DTI) suggests informal areas such as spaza stores, shebeens, and flea markets could be improved by franchising. Contact the Franchise Association of Southern Africa (FASA) for additional information.

Advertising and Promotion

The advertising industry is sophisticated. A full range of services in all media is available. Airwaves have been deregulated with new competition from independent radio and TV stations. The Freedom of Commercial Speech Trust promotes free commercial speech and self-regulation. Ad agencies increasingly take fees as well as commissions, which were typically 16.5 percent. Four key players are the Association of Advertising Agencies (AAA), the Association of Marketers (ASOM), the National Association of Broadcasters (NAB), and the Print Media Association (PMA). Names and addresses of major advertising agents, newspapers, magazines, market research companies, and public relations consultants along with their current rates, can be found in the Advertising and Press Annual of South Africa available from the National Publishing Company (Pty) Ltd. See **Contacts**.

Selling Factors

Wholesalers (for goods requiring industrial raw materials and maintenance of stocks) and retailers (consumer corporations, department stores, chain stores, and cooperative retailer groups) are both commonly used for wholesale buying, selling, and warehousing. A full spectrum of consumer retailers is available, and 90 percent of their trade inventories are domestically sourced. Hypermarkets have emerged in huge suburban malls for self-servicing customers. These markets disrupt the traditional distribution chain by bypassing wholesalers, for low-profit margins with high turnover, placing price pressure on competitors.

Selling to the Government

Government purchasing is a significant factor. Nearly all purchasing is done through competitive bidding on invitations for tenders in the official State Tender Bulletin, and sometimes in the newspapers. Local agents are typically paid for bidding. For bids, remember the government priority on accelerating black participation in the economy. To encourage local industry, centralization of all government-level purchasing involves all bids estimating their percentage of local content, with higher ratios earning

higher price preference on a scale of 1 to 10. Various bonus percentage points may also apply.

Pricing

Except for some petroleum and agricultural goods, prices are determined by the market. The Sales and Service Matters Act assures that auctions cannot be used to evade price marking, and persons offering goods or services for resale must retain records for possible recall with purchase costs, manufacturing costs, and selling prices.

Customer Support

There is a general lack of customer service mentality in South Africa. The legacy of economic isolation, private and parastate monopolies, and collusion still hinder customer service. Firms with strong customer support attitude will find themselves with a competitive advantage.

Intellectual Property Rights (IPR)

An independent judiciary enforces increasing property rights. Various laws include the Patents Act of 1978 (20-year grants), the Trademarks Act of 1993 (10-year, renewable), the Design Act of 1967 (5 years), and the Copyright Act of 1978 (culture, entertainment, and software). South Africa is a member of the Paris Union and WIPO (World Intellectual Property Organization). South African IPR laws and regulations are in line with TRIPPS (Trade Related Aspects of Intellectual Property). Since there is a growing concern and awareness of piracy, the Counterfeit Goods Bill and Intellectual Property Laws Amendment Bills of 1997 were implemented. The South African Medicines Act raised questions of regulation of pharmaceutical patents.

Attorney

Commercial Service in Johannesburg should be contacted for legal representation. The Law Society of the Transvaal also has information. See **Contacts**.

FOREIGN INVESTMENT
⑥

Openness: Since sanctions were lifted, and the GEAR adopted, SAG has become very appealing for foreign investment. Positive SAG actions include reducing tariffs and local subsidies, eliminating nonresident share-holders tax, removing some limits on hard currency repatriation, halving secondary tax on corporate dividends, lowering corporate tax to 30 percent, allowing foreign investors 100 percent ownership, no foreign company performance requirement, and rarely screening foreign investment. Drawbacks include the complexity and changeability of the tariff system, and sometimes there are delays or rejections in receiving work permits for proposed expatriate employees.

Regulatory System: South Africa's Companies Act provides for clear, transparent regulation regarding business establishment and operations. The Competition Commission, Tribunal, and Court implements the new Competition Act, which prohibits resale price maintenance, horizontal price fixing, horizontal collusion on condition of supply, horizontal collusion on market sharing, and collusive tendering or "bid rigging." South Africa is known for "cozy" business owner relations, with questionably extended favor systems. Tax, health, safety, laws, and regu-lations are fairly simple and transparent.

Investment Agreements: Many countries have entered into investment agreements with South Africa. The Trade and Investment Framework Agreement (TIFA) has been signed with the U.S.

Trade Zones and Free Ports: There are several Industrial Development Zone (IDZ) initiatives aim to create areas of export-oriented production and services for domestic and foreign investors, with world-class infrastructure, local and cost advantages, fiscal incentives, linkage to local markets, expedited customs procedures, and a one-stop regu-latory authority. These duty-free areas are chosen near ports and airports. A National Development Zone Authority (NDZA) is to be responsible for the regulation, facilitation, and administration of the IDZs. Contact the Department of Trade and Industry for more information on IDZs.

Performance Requirements/Incentives: There are no performance requirements for establishing, maintaining, or expanding investments. South Africa is in compliance with WTO Trade-Related Investment measures (TRIM) notification. The Small/Medium Manufacturing Development Program (SMMDP) gives an initial tax-free establishment grant for the first three years at 10.5 percent per year on qualifying assets of up to R3 million (US$ 500,000) per enterprise per project, for new manufacturers (post-1996) of final products. An additional profit and output incentive of 25 percent profit before tax (PBT) per year, for up to six years, is available under some conditions. The incentive package also provides for a foreign investment grant of up to US$ 50,000. Multiple "Spatial Development Initiatives" (SDISs), or "investment corridors," accelerate large-scale development between industrial centers by matching government information and pledges with mainly private investments. Many other programs exist, including the Motor Industry Development Program (MIDP), Black Economic Empowerment (BEE), and Industrial Participation (IP).

Capital Markets and Investment: SARB oversees South Africa's financial markets. South Africa's sophisticated non-bank finance services industry is governed by the Financial Services Board Act, which regulates pension funds, mutual funds, participation bond schemes, portfolio management, and finan-cial markets (Johannesburg Stock Exchange, Bond Exchange of South Africa, South African Futures Exchange). The Johannes-burg Stock Exchange (JSE) is the principal center for raising equity capital in South

Africa. Total capitalization value of JSE firms was over R1.3 trillion (approximately USD 216 billion as of July 1999. About 34.4 billion shares were traded in 1998 with turnover (total value of shares traded) of R319.3 billion (approximately USD 53.22 billion). The Venture Capital Market (VCM) of the JSE consist of joint ventures between listed and non-listed companies and the Development Capital Market (DCM) permits the listing of smaller companies on simplified terms at far less cost.

Private Ownership: Private property is protected equally whether it is foreign or domestic. The government does not compete with private entities, but some firms still maintain monopolies or a competitive advantage from statism days as well as some form of government allowances. These firms include ADE (diesel engines), SASOL (synthetic fuels, petrochemicals), IDC (industrial development corporation), CSIR (scientific and industrial research and marketing innovation), Central Energy Fund family of companies, Telkom (telecommu-nications), Transnet (transports and port services), Eskom (electricity).

Expropriation and Compensation: There is no record of U.S. investment having been expropriated or nationalized. The state may expropriate for public necessity or public utility, with fair market value compensation. Due process and transparency are established, but the legal process of determining compensation can last up to three years, with no interest payable.

OPIC and Investment Insurance: OPIC (Overseas Private Investment Corporation) supports, finances, and insures investment, and offers over US$ 0.5 billion in African investment funds. South Africa is a member of the Multilateral Investment Guarantee Agency of the World Bank.

Dispute Settlement: South Africa is a member of the New York Convention of 1958 regarding foreign arbitral awards, but is not a member of the International Center for the Settlement of Investment Disputes (Washington Convention).

FINANCE

South Africa's well-developed banking system resembles Britain's more than America's. Three components are the central South African Reserve Bank, private-sector banks (commercial, merchant, and general), and mutual banks. Fifty-six fully licensed banks and 60 foreign bank offices operate in South Africa, but Citibank is the only fully licensed U.S. commercial bank. Banks hold R540 billion in assets, and can broker securities, with banking regulations on the verge of inter-national "best business" standards.

Export Financing: The Export-Import Bank of the U.S. (EXIM Bank) makes all services available for U.S. sales to South Africa, including insurance, loans, guarantees, and letters of interest.

Project Financing: The U.S. Trade and Development Agency (TDA) funds many feasibility studies, consultancies, training programs, and project planning services to promote and identify development for export potential. The Development Bank of Southern Africa (DBSA) functions as a "banker's bank" for soft loans. The Industrial Development Corporation of South Africa, Ltd. (IDC) offers credit, guarantee, and other enterprise finance services. Numerous multi-lateral agencies offer financing for projects in South Africa.

COMMUNICATIONS

Phone

The telecommunications network is advanced, and telephone service in general is reliable. Cellular and data transmission services are also available. The South Africa country code is 27. City codes are Johannesburg (11), Pretoria (12), Cape Town (21), Durban (31), Sasolburg (16). Contact operator assistance for additional city codes. The United States can be dialed directly from South Africa using the country code 091. Peak rate calls (called standard time) to the U.S. are from 07:00 a.m. to 07:00 p.m., Monday to Friday and discount rate calls (called callmore time) are from 07:00 p.m. to 07:00 a.m. Monday to Friday. All weekend calls are at discount (callmore) rates.

Internet

Use of the Internet has grown rapidly, and strong growth rates are expected to continue.

Mail

DHL and Federal Express offer express air to South Africa. Airmail from the U.S. can take two or three weeks. State post office mail is slow and unreliable, so courier and Postnet service are recommended for mail within South Africa. Express mail international services are available between South Africa and the U.S.

TRANSPORTATION

Land

The road network is extensive. Road and rail links provide infrastructure deeply into even neighboring regions.

Sea

Major ports (Durban, Cape Town, East London, Mossel Bay, Richards Bay, Port Elizabeth, and Saldanha) are well equipped for all cargo types. For the developing world, the international trade structure is considered excellent.

Air

South African Airways (codeshare partner with American Airlines) is sole provider of direct flights to South Africa (from Kennedy and Miami International airports). Northwest/KLM (via Amsterdam) and United/Lufthansa (via Frankfurt) codeshare flights to the U.S. A civil aviation agreement allows up to 16 direct U.S. flights per week, so more carriers are expected. Over 50 foreign carriers service South Africa, including most European, Asian, and African airlines.

WORK WEEK

Business Hours: 8.00 a.m. to 1.00 p.m. and 2.00 p.m. to 4.30 p.m. Monday through Friday.

Government Hours: 8.00 a.m. to 5.00 p.m. Monday through Friday.

Bank Hours: 9.00 a.m. to 3.30 p.m. Monday through Friday, and 8.30 a.m. to 11.00 a.m. Saturday.

HOLIDAYS 2001

New Year's Day, January 1
Human Rights Day, March 21
Good Friday, April 13
Family Day, April 16
Freedom Day, April 27
Worker's Day, May 1
Youth Day, June 16
National Women's Day, August 9

Heritage Day, September 24
Day of Reconciliation, December 16
Christmas Day, December 25
Day of Goodwill, December 26

U.S. government offices in South Africa are closed on U.S. legal holidays.

BUSINESS TRAVEL

Business Customs

Business customs are similar to U.S. and Western Europe practices. Conservative dress is recommended (men: woolen suits year-round, with some summer linen or cotton suits; women: woolen or cotton-blend suits). South Africans are very punctual. Be sure to make an appointment in advance of a business call. The populations ethnic composition is quite complex, but "black" can refer to traditionally African, dark-skinned, or various nonwhite people in general, depending on varying contexts. Commonly, "black" excludes East Indians and people of mixed race.

Travel Advisory and Visas

A U.S. passport is needed. A yellow fever vaccination is required if arriving from an infected area. For stays of over 90 days (in business, employment, or study), visas are required, as they are for diplomatic and official passport holders. See the South African Embassy, South African Consulate, or U.S. Consular Officer for detailed visa information.

Business Infrastructure

Entry Requirements (personal and professional goods): All goods except personal clothing, essential toiletry, and used sporting goods must be declared. All gifts and articles for others must be declared. Vehicles require valid carnet and import duty deposit, to be refunded if re-exported within 12 months. Before sale of a vehicle, an import permit and duty are required.

Currency Exchange: U.S. Dollars cannot be used in South Africa. The South African rand is the main currency; US$ 1 equals 6.97 rands (2000 est). Unlimited U.S. dollars can be imported, but for all commercial and private use, the rand must be used. The rand may be exchanged only at authorized foreign exchange dealers, hotels, commercial banks, and some travel agencies. It is illegal to convey foreign currency to anyone else and Dollars may not be used in commercial or other private transactions. Rand inflation (roughly 7 percent) is relatively high.

Taxes: See **Government Influence on Business** and **Regulations**.

Hotels and Restaurants: There are over 1,500 licensed hotels. See the South African Tourism Board for guides. Rates are generally modest, and reservations are recommended, especially in resort areas in December and January. For long-term housing, plan for an initial four to eight weeks in hotels. Drinking water is ample and safe. Tipping is generally 10 percent (porters, taxi drivers, waiters, stewards).

Rent: No information is available at this time.

Utilities: Electricity ac 50 cycles, 220/380 or 230/400 volts; 1, 3 phases; 2, 4 wires (240/15 volts for Pretoria, 250/433 volts for Port Elizabeth). Industrial use currently uses 525 volts at 50 cycles.

Business Services: See **Marketing Tips** and **Contacts.**

Labor Costs: Labor costs and productivity are lower compared to western industrialized countries.

Literacy: Age 15 and over can read and write: 81.8 percent (1995 est).

Travel Notes

The following travel notes have been supplied by the U.S. government. For the most recent general travel and consular information, see the U.S. Department of State travel publications or call the Traveler's Telephone Hotline at (202) 647-5225.

Security: Political violence has significantly decreased in most areas of South Africa since the establishment of a democratically elected government in May 1994. Some public gatherings, however, have provoked violent clashes between political factions, resulting in casualties. The highest incidence of such political violence has occurred in the province of Kwazulu/Natal. Although foreigners have not been specifically targeted

in these attacks, some have been caught up in general disturbances. Some townships in the vicinity of major cities, most notably Durban, Johannesburg, and Cape Town, have been scenes of violent demonstrations and factional conflict. Areas most frequented by tourists, such as major hotels, game parks, and beaches, generally have been unaffected by political or factional violence.

Health Precautions: Medical facilities are good in urban areas and in the vicinity of game parks and beaches, but may be limited elsewhere. U.S. medical insurance is not always valid outside the U.S Hospitals often expect immediate cash payment for health services, but usually do accept credit cards. Uninsured travelers who require medical care overseas may face extreme difficulties. Check with your own insurance company to confirm whether your policy applies overseas, including provision for medical evacuation and for adequacy of coverage. Serious medical problems requiring hospitalization or medical evacuation to the U.S can cost tens of thousands of dollars. Ascertain whether payment will be made to the overseas hospital or doctor or whether you will be reimbursed later for expenses you incur. Current information on health matters may be obtained from the Centers for Disease Control and Prevention's international travelers' hotline at (404) 332-4559.

Embassy Assistance

To obtain additional and updated information on entry and exit requirements, travelers can contact the Consular Section of the Embassy of the Republic of South Africa at 3051 Massachusetts Avenue 16th N.W., Washington, D.C. 20008; Tel: (202) 232-4400. Travelers may also contact South African consulates located in New York, Chicago, and Los Angeles.

CONTACTS
13

American Chamber of Commerce and Bilateral Business Councils

American Chamber of Commerce in Southern Africa
PO Box 1132
Houghton 2041
Tel: (27 11) 788-0265
Fax: (27 11) 880-1632
E-mail: amcham@yebo.co.za

South African Chamber of Business (SACOB)
PO Box 91267
Auckland Park 2006
Tel: (27 11) 482-2524
Fax: (27 11) 359-9773
Web site: http://www.sacob.co.za

Johannesburg Chamber of Commerce and Industry (JCCI)
Private Bag X34
Auckland Park 2006
Tel: (27 11) 726-5300
Fax: (27 11) 482-2000
Web site: http://www.jcci.co.za

Durban Chamber of Commerce and Industry
PO Box 1506
Durban 4000
Tel: (27 31) 335-1000
Fax: (27 31) 304-5255
Web site: http://www.durbanchamber.co.za

Cape Town Regional Chamber of Commerce and Industry
PO Box 204
Cape Town 8000
Tel: (27 21) 418-4300
Fax: (27 21) 418-1800
Web site: http://www.capechamber.co.za

Port Elizabeth Regional Chamber of Commerce and Industry
PO Box 2221
Port Elizabeth 6056
Tel: (27-41) 484-4430
Fax: (27-41) 487-1851
Web site: http://www.pechamber.org.za

Country Trade or Industry Associations in Key Sectors

Western Cape Investment and Trade Promotion Agency
PO Box 1678
Cape Town 8000
Tel: (27 21) 418-6464
Fax: (27 11) 418-2323

Chamber of Mines
PO Box 61809
Marshalltown 2107
Tel: (27 11) 498-7100
Fax: (27 11) 834-1884
E-mail: webmaster@bullion.org.za

Agricultural and Veterinary Chemicals Association (Plant Protection and Animal Health Association of South Africa)
PO Box 1995
Halfway House 1685
Tel: (27 11) 805-2000
Fax: (27 11) 805-2222
E-mail: accasa@pixie.co.za

Information Technology Users Council
PO Box 1688
Halfway House 1685
Tel: (27 11) 805-3151; (27 11) 805-3152
Fax: (27 11) 315-7341
E-mail: ituc@mweb.co.za

Electrical Engineering and Allied Industries Association
SA Engineers and Founders Association
Electronics and Telecommunications Industry Association
Ferro Alloy Production Association
Iron & Steel Producers Association
Non-Ferrous Metal Industry Association
Materials Handling Association
All found at:
PO Box 1338
Johannesburg 2000
Tel: (27 11) 833-6033
Fax: (27 11) 838-1522

Motor Industries Federation
PO Box 2940
Randburg 2125
Tel: (27 11) 789-2542
Fax: (27 11) 789-4525
E-mail: tina@samiea.org.za

The Exhibition Association of South Africa
(EXA)
Private Bag X07
Bertsham 2013
Tel: (27 11) 494-9193
Fax: (27 11) 494-1506

Information Technology Association
PO Box 3277
Randburg 2125
Tel: (27 11) 789-3805
Fax: (27 11) 789-3805

National Clothing Federation of South Africa
PO Box 75755
Gardenview 2047
Tel: (27 11) 622-8125
Fax: (27 11) 622-8316

The S.A. Association of Consulting Engineers
PO Box 1644
Randburg 2125
Tel: (27 11) 787-5944
Fax: (27 11) 789-5264
E-mail: saace@iafrica.com

The Grocery Manufacturers' Association of
South Africa
PO Box 34
Randburg 2125
Tel: (27 11) 886-3008
Fax: (27 11) 886-5375

South African Black Business Organizations

Black Management Forum (BMF)
PO Box 781220
Sandton 2146
Tel: (27 11) 784-4407
Fax: (27 11) 784-4644
Web site: http://bbn.co.za/bmf/

Foundation for African Business & Consumer
Services (FABCOS)
PO Box 8785
Johannesburg 2000
Tel: (27 11) 333-3701
Fax: (27 11) 333-1234

National African Federated Chamber of
Commerce & Industries (NAFCOC)
PO Box 61213
Marshalltown 2107
Tel: (27 11) 336-0321
Fax: (27 11) 336-0420

Country Government Offices Relating to Key
Sectors or Significant Trade-Related
Activities
(Links to each of these offices can be
found on the Internet at
http://www.gov.za/ministry/index.html)

Trade and Industry
Private Bag X274
Pretoria 0001
Tel: (27 12) 322-7677
Fax: (27 12) 322-7851

Department of Trade and Industry
Private Bag X84
Pretoria 0001
Tel: (27 12) 310-9791
Fax: (27 12) 322-2701

Water Affairs & Forestry
Private Bag X313
Pretoria 0001
Tel: (27 21) 338-7500
Fax: (27 21) 328-4254

Housing
Private Bag X644
Pretoria 0001
Tel: (27 12) 421-1311
Fax: (27 12) 341-2998

Agriculture & Land Affairs
Private Bag X844
Pretoria 0001
Tel: (27 12) 323-5212; (27 12) 323-5213;
(27 12) 323-5214
Fax: (27 12) 321-1244

Land Affairs
Private Bag X833
Pretoria 0001
Tel: (27 12) 312-8911
Fax: (27 12) 323-7124

Agriculture
Private Bag X250
Pretoria 0001
Tel: (27 12) 319-6000
Fax: (27 12) 326-3454

Finance
Private Bag X115
Pretoria 0001
Tel: (27 12) 315-5111
Fax: (27 12) 323-3262

Minerals & Energy
Private Bag X646
Pretoria 0001
Tel: (27 12) 322-8695
Fax: (27 12) 322-8699

Minerals & Energy
Private Bag X59
Pretoria 0001
Tel: (27 12) 317-9000
Fax: (27 12) 322-3416

Environment Affairs & Tourism
Private Bag X447
Pretoria 0001
Tel: (27)(12) 321-9587
Fax: (27 12) 323-5181

Public Works
Private Bag X65
Pretoria 0001
Tel: (27 12) 337-2000
Fax: (27 12) 323-2856

Posts, Telecommunications & Broadcasting
Private Bag X860
Pretoria 0001
Tel: (27 12) 427-8000
Fax. (27 12) 427-8026

Transport
Private Bag X193
Pretoria 0001
Tel: (27 12) 309-3000
Fax: (27 12) 324-3486

Sports & Recreation
Private Bag X896
Pretoria 0001
Tel: (27 12) 334-3100
Fax: (27 12) 321-6187

Education
Private Bag X603
Pretoria 0001
Tel: (27 12) 326-0126
Fax: (27 12) 323-5989

Public Enterprises
Private Bag X15
Hatfield, 0028
Tel: (27 12) 342-7111
Fax: (27 12) 342-7226

Welfare & Population Development
Private Bag X885
Pretoria 0001
Tel: (27 12) 328-4600
Fax: (27 12) 325-7071

Health
Private Bag X399
Pretoria 0001
Tel: (27 12) 328-4773
Fax: (27 12) 325-5526

Department of National Health
Private Bag X828
Pretoria 0001
Tel: (27 12) 312-0000
Fax: (27 12) 325-5706

Country Market Research Firms

South African Market Research Association (SAMRA)
P O Box 91820
Auckland Park, 2006
Tel: (27 11) 482-1419
Fax: (27 11) 726-3639

SAMRA will be happy to refer U.S. companies to an appropriate market researcher depending on subject matter and type of study required.

Institute of Marketing Management South Africa (IMM)
PO Box 91820
Auckland Park 2006
Tel: (27 11) 482-1419
Fax: (27 11) 726-3639
Web site: http://www.imm.co.za

Country Commercial Banks

There are over 40 banks registered in South Africa; however, 4 commercial banking groups have traditionally dominated the industry:

Amalgamated Banks of South Africa (ABSA)
International Banking Division
PO Box 62238
Marshalltown 2107
Tel: (27 11) 833-5800
Fax: (27 11) 833-1171
Web site: http://www.absa.co.za

Standard Bank Group
International Business Center
PO Box 3720
Johannesburg 2000
Tel: (27 11) 636-9112
Fax: (27 11) 636-6062
Web site: http://www.sbic.co.za

First National Bank Holdings
1 First Place
Bank City
PO Box 1153
Johannesburg 2000
Tel: (27 11) 371-2111
Fax: (27 11) 371-2257
Web site: http://www.fnb.co.za

Nedcor Bank Limited
PO Box 1144
Johannesburg 2000
Tel: (27 11) 630-7111
Fax: (27 11) 630-7810
Web site: http://www.nedcorgroup.co.za

Financial Services Board
PO Box 35655
Menlo Park
Pretoria 0102
Tel: (27 12) 428-8000
Fax: (27 12) 347-0221

Multilateral Development Bank Offices

U.S. Department of Commerce Liaison Office
African Development Bank
01 B.P. 1387
Abidjan 01, Cote D'Ivoire
Tel: (225) 21-46-16
Fax: (225) 22-24-37

World Bank Resident Mission in South Africa
IBRD Section:
PO Box 12629
Hatfield 0028
Tel: (27 12) 342-3111
Fax: (27 11) 342-5511

U.S. Department of Commerce
Liaison to the U.S. Executive Directors Office
International Bank for Reconstruction and Development
1818 H. St., NW
Washington DC 20433
Tel: (202) 458-0118
Fax: (202) 477-2967

Office of Multilateral Development Banks
U.S. & Foreign Commercial Service
U.S. Department of Commerce
Room H-1806
Washington, DC 20230
Tel: (202) 482-3399
Fax: (202) 482-3914

Major Trade and Business Journals

Computer Week
Systems Publishers Pty Limited
Private Bag X8
Craighall 2024
Tel: (27 11) 789-1808
Fax: (27 11) 789-4725

Computing South Africa
Thomson's Publications
PO Box 182
Pinegowrie 2123
Tel: (27 11) 789-2144
Fax: (27 11) 789-7194

The SA Association of Consulting Engineers Directory
PO Box 1644
Randburg 2125
Tel: (27 11) 787-5944
Fax: (27 11) 789-5264

Engineering News
Martin Creamer Publications
PO Box 75316
Gardenview 2047
Tel: (27 11) 622-3744
Fax: (27 11) 622-9350

South African Builder
Melnor (Pty) Ltd
Private Bag X20
Auckland Park 2006
Tel: 27 (11) 726-3081
Fax: 27 (11) 726-3017
Cell: 083 268 0397

Financial Mail
Times Media House
PO Box 1744
Saxonwold 2132
Tel: (27 11) 280-3000
Fax: (27 11) 280-3337

Finance Week
Private Bag X786466
Sandton 2146
Tel: (27 11) 884-7676
Fax: (27 11) 884-0468 (advertising)

Franchise Digest
Franchise Association of Southern Africa (FASA)
Postnet Suite 267
Private Bag X30500
Houghton 2041
Tel: (27 11) 484-1285
Fax: (27 11) 484-1291
E-mail: fasa@faso.co.za
Web site: http://www.fasa.co.za

Enterprise Magazine (Black Business)
PO Box 2185
Houghton 2041
Tel: (27 11) 483-3863
Fax: (27 11) 783-5496

Franchising
Franchise Association of Southern Africa (FASA)
Postnet Suite 267
Private Bag X30500
Houghton 2041
Tel: (27 11) 484-1285
Fax: (27 11) 484-1291
E-mail: fasa@faso.co.za
Web site: http://www.fasa.co.za

Direct Marketing
South African Direct Marketing Association
P.O. Box 977
Auckland Park, 2006
South Africa
Tel: (27 11) 482-6440
Fax: (27 11) 482-1200

Joint Ventures and Licensing
Department of Trade and Industry
Directorate: Technology Promotion
Private Bag X84
Pretoria
South Africa 0001
Tel: (27 12) 310-9839
Web site: http://wwwdti.pwv.gov/dtiwww

Steps to Establishing an Office

Registrar of Companies
PO Box 429
Pretoria 0001
Tel: (27 12) 310-9791
Fax: (27 12) 328-3051

Advertising and Trade Promotion

Association of Marketers (ASOM)
PO Box 98859
Sloane Park 2152
Tel: (27 11) 706-1633
Fax: (27 11) 706-4151
E-mail: asom@pixie.co.za

Association of Advertising Agencies (AAA)
PO Box 2289
Parklands 2121
Tel: (27 11) 781-2772
Fax: (27 11) 781-2796

The National Publishing Company (Pty) Ltd.
IHS South Africa
PO Box 8147
Johannesburg 2000
Tel: (27 11) 835-2221
Fax: (27 11) 835-2631
Email: natpub@lia.co.za

Newspapers

Newspapers Press Union of South Africa
PO Box 47180
Parklands 2121
Tel: (27 11) 447-1264
Fax: (27 11) 447-1289

Major Newspapers in South Africa Include:

Business Day
PO Box 1746
Saxonwold 2132
Tel: (27 11) 280-3000
Fax: (27 11) 280-5600
Daily (Monday to Friday); Circulation: 44,042
Web site: http://www.bday.co.za

The Star
PO Box 1014
Johannesburg 2000
Tel: (21 11) 633-2417
Daily (Monday to Saturday); Circulation:
 166,962
Saturday Star circulation: 145,250
Web site: http://www.star.co.za

The Citizen
PO Box 7712
Johannesburg 2000
Tel: (27 11) 402-2900
Fax: (27 11) 402-6862
Daily (Monday to Saturday); Circulation:
 117,398
Saturday circulation: 112,016

The Sowetan
PO Box 6663
Johannesburg 2000
Tel: (27 11) 474-3740
Fax: (27 11) 474-8834
Daily (Monday to Saturday); Circulation:
 209,855

City Press
P.O. Box 3413
Johannesburg 2000
Tel: (27 11) 402-1632
Fax: (27 11) 402-6501
Daily circulation: 293,258

Sunday World
P.O. Box 30315
Wibsey 1717
Tel: (27 11) 471-4200
Fax: (27 11) 474-8834
Sunday circulation: 26577

Sunday Tribune
P.O. Box 47548, Greyville 4023
Tel: (27 31) 308-2911
Fax: (27 31) 308-2715
Daily circulation: 111,198

The Mail & Guardian
PO Box 32362
Braamfontein 2017
Tel: (27 11) 727-7000
Weekly; circulation: 36,555
Web site: http://www.mg.co.za

The Sunday Times
PO Box 1742
Saxonwold 2132
Tel: (27 11) 280-3000
Fax: (27 11) 280-3200
Weekly; circulation: 476,034

The Sunday Independent
PO Box 1014
Johannesburg 2000
Tel: (27 11) 633-9111
Fax: (27 11) 836-8398
Weekly; circulation: 42,628
Web site: http://www.iol.co.za

Beeld
PO Box 5425
Johannesburg 2000
Tel: (27 11) 406-4600
Fax: (27 11) 406-4643
Daily; circulation: 105,210
Saturday: 91,533

Rapport
PO Box 28052
Sunnyside 0132
Tel: (27 12) 341-0981
Fax: (27 12) 341-4620
Weekly (Sunday); Circulation: 361,666

Sales and Customer Support

The Consumer Council
Private Bag X091
Marshalltown 2107
Tel: (27 11) 355-8008
Fax: (27 11) 355-8019

Selling to the Government

Department of State Expenditure
Office of the State Tender Board
Private Bag X845
Pretoria 0001
Tel: (27 12) 315-5111
Fax: (27 12) 325-4533

Protection of Property Rights

Department of Trade and Industry
Trademarks, Patents, Design and Copyright
Private Bag X84
Pretoria 0001
Tel: (27 12) 310-8700; (27 12) 310-8707
Fax: (27 12) 323-4257

Law Society of the Transvaal
PO Box 1493
Pretoria 0001
Tel: (27 12) 323-0400
Fax: (27 12) 323-2606

**The following attorneys' firms offer useful
information on their Websites:**
http://www.werkmans.co.za
http://www.gjw.co.za
http://www.alevy.co.za
http://www.ir-net.co.za

Trade and Project Financing

South African Reserve Bank
Head, Exchange Control Department
PO Box 8432
Pretoria 0001
Tel: (27 12) 313-3911
Fax: (27 12) 313-3197
Web site: http://www.resbank.co.za

**A list of authorized dealers in foreign exchange
can also be found on the Internet at**
http://www.resbank.co.za/Exc/authdel.html

**South African Association of Airfreight
Forwarders**
Private Bag X89
Bryanston 2021
Tel: (27 11) 463-4131
Fax: (27 11) 463-1367

Development Bank of Southern Africa
PO Box 1234
Halfway House 1685, MidRand
Tel: (27 11) 313-3911
Fax: (27 11) 313-3086
Web site: http://www.dbsa.org

IDC
PO Box 784055
Sandton 2146
Tel: (27 11) 269-3000
Fax: (27 11) 269-3116
Web sites: http://www.mbendi.co.za/coid.htm;
   http://www.idc.co.za

USAID/South Africa
PO Box 55380
Pretoria 0007
Tel: (27 12) 323-8869
Fax: (27 12) 323-6443

Enterprise Development Unit
Department of Management
University of the Western Cape
Private Bag X17
Bellville 7535
Web site: http://www.uwc.ac.za/ems/ems.htm

Office of the U.S. Executive Director
African Development Bank
01 B.P. 1387
Abidjan 01, Cote D'Ivoire
Tel: (225) 20-40-15
Fax: (225) 33-14-34

Office of Multilateral Development Banks
U.S. & Foreign Commercial Service
U.S. Department of Commerce
Room H-1806
Washington, DC 20230
Tel: (202) 482-3399
Fax: (202) 482-3914

World Bank Resident Mission in South Africa
IBRD Section:
PO Box 12629
Hatfield 0028
Tel: (27 12) 342-3111
Fax: (27 11) 342-5151

IFC Section:
PO Box 41283
Craighall 2024
Tel: (27 11) 325-0720
Fax: (27 11) 325-0582

U.S. Department of Commerce
Liaison to the U.S. Executive Directors Office
International Bank for Reconstruction and
  Development
1818 H. St., NW
Washington, DC 20433
Tel: (202) 458-0118
Fax: (202) 477-2967

Office of Multilateral Development Banks
U.S. & Foreign Commercial Service
U.S. Department of Commerce
Room H-1107
Washington, DC 20230
Tel: (202) 482-3399
Fax: (202) 482-3914

Africa Project Development Facility
1818 H St., NW
Washington, DC 20433
Tel: (202) 473-0508
Fax: (202) 522-3204

United Nations Development Program
(UNDP). The United Nations' Development
Program (UNDP) is also represented in South
Africa.

UNDP
PO Box 6541
Pretoria 0001
Tel: (27 12) 320-4360
Fax: (27 12) 320-4353

Initiatives

The Lubombo Initiative
The Lubombo Initiative is a concerted program by the governments of Swaziland, Mozambique, and South Africa to ensure that new investment occurs rapidly in the area. An essential infrastructure project is the upgrade of secondary roads and construction of a tar road through the SDI to link the major South African coastal road, the N2, to Maputo, the capital of Mozambique. Tourism anchor projects being proposed are the Ponta to Puro-Kosi Bay and Futi/Tembe/Usuthu transnational tourism nodes, the Greater St. Lucia Wetland Park, a tourism cluster at Lake Sibayi, an integrated Mlawula-Hlane wildlife project, the Lavumisa-Pongola Trans-Frontier Complex and the Lubombo tourism train route. In all, 694 projects have been identified to the estimated value of R 148 billion in the tourism, education, craft, commercial, and agriculture sectors, including substantial opportunities for communities and small businesses.

Additional information can be found on the Internet at http://www.lubombo.org.za.

West Coast Initiative
The West Coast Investment Initiative is focused on the opportunities created by the mini mill of Saldanha Steel as well as underused opportunities in agriculture, tourism, manufacturing, and fishing in the region. This initiative opens a window of opportunity to potential investors in an area with a significant resource base, and adequate and improving infrastructure. In addition, an investor-friendly package of incentives and institutional arrangements is in place to enhance innovative and sound investments. One hundred and twenty investment projects were launched at the investment conference held in Saldanha Bay on the West Coast from 25 to 27 February 1998.

Additional information can be found on the Internet at http://www.westcoast.org.za.

The Fish River Initiative
The Fish River initiative has evolved to promote employment in the Port Elizabeth and East London parts of the Eastern Cape. The primary

focus of the Fish River SDI is on "crowding in" new investment from the private sector. Sectors under consideration include the automobile industry, supplier development, agro processing, and forestry. The Fish River Initiative offers exciting opportunities for investors and has been designed to provide local entrepreneurs, international and national investors, and fledgling businesses with a broad range of investment options.

Additional information can be found on the Internet at http://www.fishriver.org.za.

The Maputo Corridor

The Maputo Corridor, a development axis between Johannesburg and the city and port of Maputo, Mozambique, has seen considerable success since its launch in 1998 and is the most widely known development initiative. There has been a continual process of identifying investment opportunities in the following sectors: infrastructure, agriculture, mining, energy, chemicals, tourism and manufacturing. There are currently 180 projects under consideration with a total value estimated at approximately R42 billion (US$ 7 billion).

Additional information can be found on the Internet at http://www.dbsa.org/Corridors/Maputo.

Wild Coast Initiative

The Wild Coast is a stretch of approximately 280 kilometers (174 miles) situated between the Mtamvuna River in the north and the Great Kei River in the south. The lull of perfect beaches attracts the majority of visitors to the resorts along the coastline, and the Wild Coast Initiative builds on this attraction through agri-tourism projects. Forestry and agriculture projects are also in development.

Additional information can be found on the Internet at http://www.wildcoastsdi.org.za.

Rustenburg (Platinum) Initiative

The Platinum SDI forms part of the Coast2Coast SDI that links Maputo Port in Mozambique to Walvis Bay in Namibia. Most of the Platinum SDI falls inside South Africa's North West Province, with direct links to import tourism, industrial and agriculture processing activities in the North West Province, and to the Mabopane-Centurion Development Corridor around Pretoria. The region has a wealth of raw materials, which can be used in processing and manufacturing industries. It also has tremendous potential to develop a tourist industry considering its existing tourism infrastructure and attractions, including five big nature reserves. An appraisal of the economic potential of this area has identified approximately 200 potential projects and project opportunities in tourism, manufacturing, agriculture, and mining.

The Platinum SDI management team will provide additional information upon request.

Rustenburg (Platinum) SDI Project
Tel: (27 11) 313-3331
Fax: (27 11) 313-3000

Phalaborwa SDI

The Phalaborwa Initiative, broadly covering the Northern Province and Mpumalanga, is in the process of identifying and preparing attractive projects and investment opportunities in agriculture, forestry, tourism, mining, and mineral processing. The region is a significant supplier and processor of wood fiber in South Africa and internationally; it also includes a wide range of tourist attractions centered primarily in and adjacent to the famous Kruger National Park. The Phalaborwa SDI is linked to Maputo Development Corridor, and therefore has access to Maputo and international markets.

The Phalaborwa SDI management team will provide additional information upon request.

Phalaborwa SDI Project
Tel: (27 11) 313-3518
Fax: (27 11) 313-3086

Richards Bay Initiative

The Richards Bay Investment Center officially opened its doors in October 1998 to assist companies that want to establish a presence in the region. Industrial projects identified by the Industrial Development Corporation include opportunities in aluminum, heavy minerals, chemicals, wood, and sugar clusters. Tourism is also expected to become a key industry for the region. Richards Bay acts as a gateway to the Lubombo region, and the harbor is within a 45 minute drive of "big five" game viewing opportunities.

Additional information can be found on the Internet at http://www.richardsbay.org.za.

KwaZulu-Natal SDI

One of nine provinces of South Africa, KwaZulu-Natal stretches over 57,000 square miles on South Africa's eastern seaboard. KwaZulu-Natal is a competitive region for the attraction of foreign investment and nine target areas have been identified for this purpose. These areas include textiles, clothing, plastic products, chemicals, fabricated metal products, automotive components, wood and wood products, footwear, machinery, and appliances. During the three-year period ending March 1998, 47 foreign companies established operations in the region, primarily in four sectors: textiles, clothing and leather (38.3%), chemicals and plastics (21.3%), fabricated metal products and machinery (19.2%), and paper and paper products (17.0%).

Additional information can be found on the Internet at http://www.kmi.co.za.

COSTA RICA

TRADE AND BUSINESS GUIDE

Official Name:	Republic of Costa Rica
Official Language:	Spanish. English is commonly spoken around Puerto Limon and by many business leaders
Population:	3,710,558 (2000 est)
Population Growth:	1.69% (2000 est)
Age Structure:	0–14 years: 32%, 15–64 years: 63%, 65 years and over: 5% (2000 est)
Location:	Middle America, bordering both the Caribbean Sea and the North Pacific Ocean, between Nicaragua and Panama
Area:	51,100 square kilometers, slightly smaller than West Virginia
Type of Government:	Democratic republic
Head of State:	President Miguel Angel Rodriguez
Cabinet:	Selected by the president
Religion:	85% Roman Catholic, 14% Protestant, 1% other
Major Cities:	Capital: San Jose (1.2 million). Other major cities: Alajuela (250,000), Puntarenas (300,000), Limon (150,000), Cartago (150,000)
Climate:	Tropical. The dry season is from December to April; the rainy season is from May to November
Time:	The entire country is -6 GMT (Greenwich Mean Time), one hour behind EST (Eastern Standard Time). Costa Rica does not follow daylight savings time
GDP:	Purchasing power parity (PPP): $26 billion (1999 est); real growth rate: 7% (1999 est); per capita PPP: $7,100 (1999 est); composition by sector: agriculture = 14%, industry = 22%, services = 64% (1998)
Currency:	1 Costa Rican colon (C) = 100 centimos
Exchange Rate:	Costa Rican colons per US$ 1 = 311.00 (September 2000 est), 282.00 (1999), 257.14 (1998)
Weights & Measure:	Metric system
Natural Resources:	Hydropower
Total Trade:	In millions US$ [exports (fob)/imports (cif)]: 1997 (4,335/4,953), 1998 (5,528/6,230), 1999 est (6,634/6,541)
Trade with U.S.:	In millions US$ [exports (fob)/imports (cif)]: 1997 (2,200/2,600), 1998 (2,674/3,000), 1999 est (3,000/3,200). Note: Includes trade with Puerto Rico. Merchandise trade statistics were revised in 1998 to include goods processed in free trade zones. Prior year statistics have been updated. Publication of imports by country is pending; statistics on imports from U.S. are estimates

Major Trade Partners:	Imports: United States, Japan, Mexico, Guatemala, Venezuela, and Germany. Exports: United States, Germany, Italy, Guatemala, El Salvador, Netherlands, United Kingdom, and France
Membership:	IADB, IBRD, IFC, IMF, ISO, MIGA, OAS, UN, UNCTAD, WIPO, and WTO. See membership description in appendix

Sources: *Directorate General of Statistics and Census, 1998 Household Census, CIA World Factbook, Central Bank of Costa Rica, USAID, U.S. Department of Commerce*

POLITICAL OUTLOOK
②

Relationship with the U.S.

The U.S. and Costa Rica enjoy excellent bilateral relations. There are some disputes, however; most involve expropriation, squatters on U.S.-owned properties, and trade in textiles and bananas. Occasional disputes over the extradition of fugitives were quieted in 1996, when Costa Rica's Supreme Court supported the bilateral Extradition Treaty between the two countries.

Influences on Business

Costa Rica's democratic political environment generally is stable. The Rodriguez administration's privatization efforts remain controversial within the legislature. The government's expropriation of private land without compensation has been a problem. In many of these seizures, the land was taken to create national parks. However, in recent years, outstanding disputes have been resolved, and a 1995 expropriation law explicitly requires the GOCR to compensate owners adequately. Another area of concern stems from liberal squatter regulations. Costa Rican laws may encourage organized and sometimes violent

groups to claim land ownership. The Costa Rican police and judicial system have not always responded effectively to squatter disputes. In November 1997, a U.S. citizen and a Costa Rican squatter died during a confrontation over land ownership. In the area of workers' rights, the Rodriguez administration promised to respond to frequent complaints, but little progress has been made to date. Finally, the protection of intellectual property rights has been a problem. Abuse is widespread among pharmaceutical and agricultural chemical products as well as in the piracy of video recordings, audio recordings, and computer software. The government has proposed new legislation to address these problems.

Profile

System: Costa Rica enjoys a stable, long-standing, Constitutional democracy. Military forces were abolished in 1948. The Constitution provides for a powerful body to oversee elections. Members of the unicameral Legislature are elected every four years. The Supreme Court consists of 22 magistrates, who are divided into four Chambers. The

Constitutional Chamber (Sala IV) decides on the constitutionality of the country's laws

Schedule for Elections: The next round of elections for president and the Legislative Assembly is scheduled for February 2002. A 1969 Constitutional amendment prevents the president from seeking re-election. Deputies must sit out for one term before running again in legislative races.

Major Parties: The two major parties—the Social Christian Unity Party (PUSC) and the National Liberation Party (PLN)—both tend toward centrist platforms. The ruling PUSC leans toward the Christian democratic right, whereas the opposition PLN leans toward the moderate Social Democratic left. Miguel Angel Rodriguez of the PUSC won the February 1998 presidential election, and his party won 27 of the 57 seats in the Legislative Assembly. The PLN won 23 seats, whereas various minority parties won the remaining 7 seats.

Political Violence: Costa Rica enjoys a relatively stable political situation, and politically motivated acts of violence are uncommon. Many Costa Ricans are active political critics, but most restrain their activities to democratic channels. However, some groups block roads to publicize their grievances, and some of these demonstrations have turned violent. Violence has also occurred over confrontations with squatters. Another area of concern has been the hundreds of thousands of Nicaraguans who have migrated illegally into Costa Rica. The largest influx followed the devastation of Hurricane Mitch in 1998. Recently, the GOCR followed an ambitious plan to legalize much of this otherwise illegal workforce. Some Nicaraguan immigrants have contributed to common crimes, but few have committed significant acts of political violence. The one exception occurred in January 1996. A small group of Nicaraguans kidnapped two foreigners and held them captive for 71 days. The group's demands had political overtones. Relatives paid a ransom; the hostages were released, and the police later arrested the group leader and several others.

Corruption: U.S. firms have not found corruption to pose a substantial obstacle to doing business in Costa Rica. The country has sufficient legal regulations and penalties to combat corruption, but the resources to enforce these laws are lacking. The Costa Rican press, however, does expose corruption and force judicial action against offenders. Immediately after his 1998 inauguration, President Rodriguez directed the entire government to implement anticorruption measures. Recent exposures have occurred in the Civil Aviation Directorate, the Ministry of Public Works and Transportation, the state-owned banks, the public housing authority, and the Pacific Ports Authority.

Media: Costa Rica has an active, independent media. Journalists have been effective in exposing official corruption.

ECONOMIC OUTLOOK ③

Trends

Costa Rica has successfully transformed itself from an agricultural nation to one that is highly attractive to foreign investments, particularly in the high-technology sector. About 85 U.S. Fortune 500 companies operate in the country, many of which established operations 10 to 25 years ago. In 1998, Intel opened a US$ 200 million microprocessor finishing and testing facility, due in part to the country's agreeable business climate, political stability, skilled workforce, central geographic location, absence of capital controls, and pleasant living conditions. State monopolies in critical sectors and certain failures in the protection of intellectual property rights are the only significant barriers to investment. In recent years, the government has had some success with its privatizing attempts. These efforts, however, have met with significant opposition from the general population and the legislature. The government also faces the challenges of controlling the public-sector deficit and managing the accumulated public debt, most of which is financed domestically. Inflation was at 12.4 percent in 1998, and the unemployment rate remains around 5.6 percent.

Major Growth Sectors

Costa Rica offers a market of sophisticated consumers who are attracted to U.S. goods and services. Some of the best opportunities for U.S. exporters exist in the areas of equipment for telecommunications and power generation, restaurants and hotels, construction, health care, water resources, recreation, and sports. There is also a growing demand for paper products, computer equipment, plastic materials and resins, agricultural chemicals and automotive parts. In the agricultural sector, strong demand exists for corn, soybeans, wheat, fresh fruit (apples, grapes, peaches, and pears), processed fruits and vegetables, juices, snack foods and specialty meat products. With the recent boom in new shopping malls, franchising and retailing have been successful. Costa Rica is more attractive to companies seeking skilled labor rather than low-cost, unskilled labor. Accordingly, growth in the apparel industry has stagnated, whereas growth has been robust in industries such as electronics assembly, health-care products, upscale tourism, and regional management or service centers for multinational corporations.

Key Economic Indicators

Income, Production and Employment			
(millions of U.S. dollars unless otherwise indicated)			
	1997	1998	1999[1]
Nominal GDP[2]	9,730	13,889	15,404
Real GDP Growth (pct.)[3]	3.8	8.0	8.0
GDP by Sector (pct.)			
Agriculture	18.0	11.4	11.0
Industry	21.5	22.4	26.0
Services	53.1	43.1	39.9
General Government	7.4	23.1	23.1
Per Capita GDP (US$)	2,790	3,769	3,856
Labor Force (000)	1,377	1,377	1,383
Unemployment Rate (pct.)	5.7	5.6	6.0

1. 1999 figures are all estimates based on most recent data available. 2. GDP at factor cost.
3. Percentage changes calculated in local currency.
Source: Bureau of Economic and Business Affairs; U.S. Department of State

- **Infrastructure**
  Costa Rica still has the best transportation, energy, telecommunications, health care, and education infrastructures in Central America. However, owing to recent cutbacks in public

spending, many of these facilities are deteriorating. Specific problem areas include the main cargo port on the Pacific coast as well as a good portion of the country's roads and highways. Projects are underway to update San Jose's Juan Santamaria International Airport and the country's capacities in electric power generation.

- Labor

  Costa Rica offers a relatively well-educated and skilled workforce. Many workers seek additional specialized training, often through the National Vocational Training Institute (INA) and private-sector groups. At the same time, more specialized means of on-the-job training are still needed. Costa Rica also offers one of the largest and most diversified pools of well-educated professionals in Latin American and the Caribbean. The high skill level of many employees and the availability of vocational training have caused problems for some domestic and foreign companies. Many textile manufacturers, for example, have moved to other

Money and Prices *(annual percentage growth)*			
	1997	1998	1999[1]
Money Supply Growth (M2)	21.0	17.5	16.4
Consumer Price Index	12.0	12.4	10.1
Exchange Rate (Colones/US$ annual average)			
Official	None	None	None
Parallel	232.37	267.10	282.00

1. 1999 figures are all estimates based on most recent data available.
Source: Bureau of Economic and Business Affairs; U.S. Department of State

Balance of Payment and Trade *(millions of U.S. dollars unless otherwise indicated)*			
	1997	1998	1999[1]
Total Exports FOB[2]	4,335	5,528	6,634
Exports to U.S.[2]	1,266	2,674	3,200
Total Imports CIF[2]	4,953	6,230	6,541
Imports from U.S.[2]	1,534	1,784	2,000
Trade Balance[2]	-618	-702	93
Balance with U.S.	-268	890	1,200
External Public Debt	2,640	2,872	3,042
Fiscal Deficit of Public Sector/GDP (pct.)	3.3	2.7	3.3
Current Account Deficit/GDP (pct.)	2.2	4.4	3.0
Foreign Debt Service Payments/GDP (pct.)	6.1	5.0	4.9
Gold and Foreign Exchange Reserves	1,141	991	1,200
Aid from U.S.	5.0	18.0	15.0
Aid from All Other Sources	N/A	N/A	N/A

1. 1999 figures are all estimates based on most recent data available. 2. Merchandise trade
Source: Bureau of Economic and Business Affairs; U.S. Department of State

Central American countries to take advantage of lower wage rates. Nonetheless, the GOCR continues to promote more technologically advanced industries and workers.

- **Merchandise Trade**
  Nontraditional exports continue to record strong growth rates. Free-trade-zone and export-processing companies recorded strong demand for the import of capital goods and industrial inputs; 1998 was the first year in which these activities were counted in merchandise trade statistics.

- **Balance of Payments**
  Costa Rica recorded a surplus in its merchandise trade balance in early 1999, due in part to Intel exports and increased tourism revenues.

Government Influence on Business

The domestic public-sector debt increasingly limits the role of the government of Costa Rica (GOCR). Profits from state-owned enterprises go toward the financing of fiscal deficits, and the results can be seen in much of the country's infrastructure. Public and legislative resistance slows the progress of privatization although significant steps have been made.

TRADE
(4)

Leading Imports and Exports

Imports: Raw materials, consumer goods, capital equipment, petroleum.

Exports: Manufactured products, coffee, bananas, textiles, sugar.

Foreign Trade *(Exports and Imports US$M)*			
	1997	1998	1999[1]
Total Exports FOB[2]	4,335	5,528	6,634
Exports to U.S.[2]	1,266	2,674	3,200
Total Imports CIF[2]	4,953	6,230	6,541
Imports from U.S.[2]	1,534	1,784	2,000

1. 1999 figures are all estimates based on most recent data available. 2. Merchandise trade
Source: U.S. Department of State

Best Prospects Analysis

Best Prospects for Nonagricultural Goods and Services

Paper and Paperboard (PAP)

	1997E $M	1998E $M	1999E $M
Total Market Size	230	231	242
Total Local Production	50	53	56
Total Exports	30	32	34
Total Imports	200	210	220
Imports from the U.S.	140	147	154

Plastic Materials and Resins (PMR)

	1997E $M	1998E $M	1999E $M
Total Market Size	121.2	126.1	133.7
Total Local Production	N/A	N/A	N/A
Total Exports	20.8	21.6	22.9
Total Imports	142.0	147.7	156.6
Imports from the U.S.	92.6	96.3	102.1

Computers and Peripherals (CPT)

	1997E $M	1998E $M	1999E $M
Total Market Size	91.8	103.7	119.3
Total Local Production	N/A	N/A	N/A
Total Exports	N/A	N/A	N/A
Total Imports	91.8	103.7	119.3
Imports from the U.S.	84.5	95.5	109.8

Agricultural Chemicals (AGC)

	1997E $M	1998E $M	1999E $M
Total Market Size	211	221	231
Total Local Production	110	115	120
Total Exports	53	56	59
Total Imports	154	162	170
Imports from the U.S.	61	64	67

Automotive Parts (APS)

	1997E $M	1998E $M	1999E $M
Total Market Size	111.4	118.1	127.6
Total Local Production	35.5	36.9	38.4
Total Exports	32.5	33.7	34.9
Total Imports	108.4	114.9	124.1
Imports from the U.S.	45.2	48.8	53.7

Telecommunications Equipment (TEL)

	1997E $M	1998E $M	1999E $M
Total Market Size	84	92	101
Total Local Production	N/A	N/A	N/A
Total Exports	N/A	N/A	N/A
Total Imports	84	92	101
Imports from the U.S.	31	34	38

Construction Equipment (CON)

	1997E $M	1998E $M	1999E $M
Total Market Size	36	41	48
Total Local Production*	N/A	N/A	N/A
Total Exports	N/A	N/A	N/A
Total Imports	36	41	48
Imports from the U.S.	24	28	32

Medical Equipment (MED)

	1997E $M	1998E $M	1999E $M
Total Market Size	12.7	14.6	17.1
Total Local Production*	N/A	N/A	N/A
Total Exports	N/A	N/A	N/A
Total Imports	12.7	14.6	17.1
Imports from the U.S.	6.1	7.0	8.2

*Costa Rica's local production and exports are principally in-bond operations performed within Free Trade Zone facilities. These statistics are unofficial estimates.

Best Prospects for Agricultural Products

Soybeans

	1997E MT (000)	1998E MT (000)	1999E MT (000)
Total Consumption	170	175	185
Total Local Production	0	0	0
Total Exports	0	0	0
Total Imports	170	175	185
Imports from the U.S.	160	165	170

Corn

	1997E MT (000)	1998E MT (000)	1999E MT (000)
Total Consumption	456	460	470
Total Local Production	24	25	25
Total Exports	0	0	0
Total Imports	432	435	445
Imports from the U.S.	416	410	415

Wheat

	1997E MT (000)	1998E MT (000)	1999E MT (000)
Total Consumption	187	190	195
Total Local Production	0	0	0
Total Exports	0	0	0
Total Imports	187	190	195
Imports from the U.S.	166	170	170

Rice

	1997E MT (000)	1998E MT (000)	1999E MT (000)
Total Consumption	217	220	225
Total Local Production	157	160	175
Total Exports	0	0	0
Total Imports	67	40	N/A
Imports from the U.S.	36	67	27

Fresh Fruit*	1997E MT (000)	1998E MT (000)	1999E MT (000)
Total Consumption	N/A	N/A	N/A
Total Local Production	N/A	N/A	N/A
Total Exports	730	800	850
Total Imports	19	9.5	11
Imports from the U.S.	8	8.5	10

*Includes exports of bananas, pineapples, and melons (the three largest categories of fruits exported). Based on GOCR statistics for 1997.

Processed Fruits and Vegetables

	1997E MT (000)	1998E MT (000)	1999E MT (000)
Total Consumption	N/A	N/A	N/A
Total Local Production	N/A	N/A	N/A
Total Exports	33	35	38
Total Imports	17	19	20
Imports from the U.S.	5	5.5	7

Total exports and imports based on GOCR data.

Snack Foods

Complete data are not available. The U.S. exported US $5.0 million of snack foods to Costa Rica in 1997. Exports increased by 45% in January through April of 1999 compared to the same period in 1998. Total exports are expected to continue to rise. Competing products are exported from Chile, Argentina, and Europe. Domestic products also offer some competition.

The above statistics are unofficial estimates.
N/A - Not Available, E - Estimated
Note: MT (000) = Thousand Metric Tons

Extracted from the U.S. Department of Commerce USA Trade 2000 Country Commercial Guide for Costa Rica.

Import and Export Tips

- Regulations

    Customs: Involved bureaucratic procedures have caused significant delays. A 1995 General Customs Law reduced processing times through electronic procedures and "one-stop" export and import windows. However, significant room for improvement remains.

    Tariffs: Costa Rica continues to move toward trade liberalization and unified lowered tariffs with the Central American Common Market. In accordance with Uruguay Round negotiations, the GOCR agreed to eliminate all import quotas and to limit tariffs to a maximum of 52 percent on most goods. Exceptions are made for selected agricultural commodities, which are protected by unusually high tariff rates. For example, dairy products face a 106 percent tariff; poultry products face a 262 percent rate, and automobiles are also heavily taxed. The GOCR provides much lower, variable rates for the importation of product amounts that are less than 3 percent of national consumption.

    Import Taxes: The value-added or sales tax rate is 13 percent. This tax applies to most goods, including imported goods, but the tax does not apply to certain basic products, such as staple foods and school uniforms; nor does it apply to goods destined for official use by the central government or local governments. Selective consumption or excise taxes have been reduced or eliminated for many imported and domestic products. Excise taxes remain on about half of all imported products. Heavily taxed items include arms and munitions (75 percent); costume jewelry, fireworks, and whiskey (50 percent); new and used vehicles (varied); and wine and beer (40 percent). A 1 percent surcharge applies to most imports, except medicines and most raw materials. Central Bank taxes and surcharges also apply to some goods, whether they are imported or produced locally.

    Exchange Rate: The current exchange rate policy, originally devised in 1993, is of the "crawling peg" variety employing small daily changes. The rate of devaluation, indirectly set by the Central Bank, is driven by the market and is adjusted by the Central Bank through its sale or purchase of foreign currency. Virtually all private business is transacted at the same rate. All foreign transactions by state institutions are channeled through the Central Bank at that rate. Commercial banks are free to negotiate for-

-eign exchange prices, but must liquidate their foreign exchange positions daily with the Central Bank. The colon-to-US dollar exchange rate varied 10.7 percent during 1998, a rate similar to the change in the aggregate price level. This maintained a foreign trade-neutral exchange rate. The government has projected a devaluation of about 10.8 percent and a CPI increase of 10 percent for 1999. Thus, the rate of exchange of the colon with respect to the U.S. dollar should not have a significant impact on the importation of U.S. goods and services. Freely traded dollars from tourism and capital investment continue to flow into Costa Rica. The free and sufficient supply of foreign currency allowed imports to continue to grow during 1998 and 1999.

- **Documentation**

  Exports: The Central Bank requires export registration, which allows the government to maintain some export controls, particularly on staple goods and goods that are subsidized or are under price controls. The export of livestock, wood, and ornamental plants requires a license from the Ministry of Agriculture. The export of metal scrap requires a license from the Ministry of Economy, Industry, and Foreign and Internal Commerce. Coffee exports are regulated by ICAFE, the National Coffee Institute. Sugar exports are regulated by LAICA, a producers' organization. The Textile Quota Office, a producer's organization, allocates export amounts for textile and garment exports to the U.S. Particular producers' organizations do the same for coffee, sugar, banana, and beef exports

  Imports: The Central Bank no longer requires licenses for imports. Most exports and imports are registered for statistical purposes only. Pharmaceuticals, drugs, cosmetics, and some chemical products require an import permit and

registration from the Ministry of Health. Registration is valid for five years. Food products require registration when they are imported for the first time. The Ministry of Agriculture requires animal health certificates and phytosanitary certificates for bulk grain and horticultural products. Fresh and frozen meats require zoosanitary certificates. The Costa Rican importer must obtain the permits. Surgical and dental instruments may be sold only to licensed importers and health professionals. Arms and munitions require an import license from the Costa Rican Ministry of Public Security's Department for the Control of Weapons and Explosives. The GOCR prohibits the importation of used tires without rims (mosquitoes carrying yellow or dengue fever may breed in rimless tires). Weapons imports are closely regulated.

Labeling: Generally, there are no labeling or marking requirements. The food labeling regulations of the GOCR follow the Codex Alimentarius. All domestic and imported food products must be labeled in Spanish and must include the following: product name, list of ingredients in order by quantity, nutritional content, name and address of the importer, weight, and expiration or best-used-by date. There are further, special labeling requirements for pharmaceuticals, fertilizers, pesticides, hormones, veterinary preparations, vaccines, poisonous substances, and mouthwashes. Violations of documentation laws carry heavy fines.

Standards: A lack of equipment and funding keeps the GOCR from enforcing standards requirements. By law, the metric system must be used exclusively, but in practice, customs accepts U.S. and European standards. Only four local companies have obtained ISO 9000 certification.

- **Payment**

  Terms: Irrevocable letters of credit often

are used for purchases of over US$ 4,000. Payment for small purchases is usually direct. Only well-known and well-established customers typically receive open-account payment terms. Insurance on accounts receivable is available through the Export-Import Bank of the U.S.

Currency Exchange: There are no difficulties or unusual delays in obtaining foreign exchange. The 1995 Financial Reform Law guarantees the free conversion of the Costa Rican colon. Those who earn foreign exchange are guaranteed the right to keep 100 percent of their foreign exchange earnings.

Fund Transfer: There are no limitations on the transfer of funds associated with investments. The Central Bank does not place limitations on the remittance of investment returns. Investors are also free to remit through a legal parallel market (i.e., dollar bonds) in lieu of immediate payment in dollars.

Offshore Loans: Offshore entities may not capture deposits or lend money.

MARKETING TIPS ⑤

Establishing an Office

1. Obtain the assistance of a notary public, the only professional authorized by law to register a company.

2. Register with the Costa Rican Mercantile Registry to become a legal, authorized entity. Registration requires all information related to the new company and the persons who will administer the company. This information includes full name, nationality, occupation, civil status, domicile, the legal form of the business being organized, the purpose of the company, the amount of capital and the manner in which this capital is to be paid, the time limits for payments, the domicile of the company, and any other agreements made by the founders. An extract of the registration is then published in *La Gaceta*, the official legal journal.

3. Deposit a nominal payment (usually between US$ 100 and $1,000) on initial equity; payment must be expressed in local currency and deposited with a local bank of the Costa Rican National System until registration is completed.

4. Acquire a municipal patent or permit. (This is not required for all types of business.)

5. Appoint and retain a legal representative with full power of attorney if you have opened or intend to open branches in Costa Rica.

Note: Foreigners must become residents to work in Costa Rica. For support, information, and detailed information on establishing a particular business in Costa Rica, contact CINDE (Costa Rican Coalition for Development Initiatives) or PROCOMER (Costa Rican Foreign Trade Corporation). See CONTACTS.

Agents and Distributors

U.S. companies may export directly to Costa Rican companies, but the use of a qualified representative is strongly recommended. Local representation often is necessary to bid successfully for government tenders and to market successfully in the private sector. Costa Rica is a small country, and thus many

U.S. firms require only one distributor or representative. However, local attorneys recommend against contracts that provide for exclusive representation. Costa Rican law requires that foreign companies provide compensation when breaking an agreement with an agent or distributor. Thus it is important to have a written agreement, approved by a competent Costa Rican lawyer, with any agent or distributor. Lists of Costa Rican attorneys may be obtained from the Commercial Section and from the Consular Section of the Embassy. The U.S. Department of Commerce offers U.S. companies a range of assistance in identifying potential business partners. Contact the nearest U.S. Export Assistance Center in one of the many U.S. Department of Commerce offices, which are located in over 100 U.S. cities. For initial assistance, call (800) USA-TRADE (872-8723). The Department of Commerce offers the following services: For a nominal fee, the Gold Key Service screens potential business partners, arranges appointments, offers a market briefing, and provides an interpreter where necessary. The Agent/Distributor Service (ADS) particularly assists U.S. firms that are unable to travel immediately to Costa Rica. ADS provides a U.S. firm's literature to prospective representatives, who then may express interest in further communications.

Distribution and Sales Channels

Local representation or a local sales office is often required to market aggressively and successfully. For the different food products, distribution channels are not significantly varied. Private firms import consumer foods. A list of such firms may be obtained from the Office of Agricultural Affairs. Foreign companies must do business through distributors or representatives, unless the foreign company uses a branch or agency to manufacture within Costa Rica. Representatives must have resided in Costa Rica for ten continuous years and have done business in the country for three years.

Direct Marketing

Direct marketing is not common in Costa Rica. The mailing system does not have well-defined street names and numbers, and thus client lists with reliable addresses are rare. Costa Rican law regulates direct marketing not through specific legislation but through general laws that apply to publicity and publicity agencies.

Leasing/Joint Ventures

Licensing is not widespread in Costa Rica. Traditionally, foreign companies have exported to Costa Rica or have set up manufacturing or assembly operations in the country, either independently or through joint-venture arrangements. Foreigners may own up to 100 percent of Costa Rican companies, and foreigners may invest in all areas not expressly reserved for state or parastatal entities. Foreign corporations may be organized in several ways: as branches (except for banks), joint ventures, wholly owned subsidiaries, or locally incorporated companies.

Franchising

The franchise market is developing at a steady pace throughout much of the region, although the fast food sector is becoming saturated in Costa Rica. McDonald's entered the market in 1970, and Pizza Hut followed in 1972. Consumers in Costa Rica's franchise sector are price sensitive and highly knowledgeable. Prospective franchisers must select their franchisees carefully. Local business knowledge and contacts can be crucial. Most prospective franchisees use the internet to gather information on opportunities. The Commercial Section of the U.S. Embassy can also assist with introductions and information on tactics used to reach potential franchisees. Franchise marketing must remain sensitive to the Latin culture. Franchise royalties are taxed a 25 percent withholding tax, although the U.S. gives a foreign tax credit for this expense.

Advertising and Promotion

Costa Rican newspapers are one of the best ways to promote many products and services. Depending on the market, specialized magazines published by organizations such as the Costa Rican–American Chamber of Commerce (AmCham), the Chamber of Commerce of Costa Rica, and others may be effective. The U.S. Department's Commercial Section in San Jose can assist U.S. firms through trade missions, participation in local trade shows, matchmaker events, seminars, conferences, catalog shows, and business receptions. All these services are conducted periodically on a cost-recovery basis with preapproved budgets. There are a few privately organized trade promotion events in Costa Rica. FERCORI has at least one international trade fair every two years. Sistema Empresarial organizes FERCOMPTO, a computer-oriented event. The Costa Rican Chamber of Hotels organizes EXPO-HOTEL. The Costa Rican Association of Professionals in the Tourism Sector organizes Expotur to promote Costa Rican tourism, facilities, and sites among foreign wholesalers and travel agents. "Visit USA Costa Rica" promotes travel and tourism to the U.S. and also hosts a trade event each year. See CONTACTS for more information about these events.

Selling Factors

Costa Rican consumers are not unlike U.S. consumers. Purchasing decisions are based on price, quality, technical specifications, convenience, and the availability of local product support or after-sale service. Owing to the size of Costa Rica's population and GDP, U.S. exporters must be willing to make sales of relatively small sizes in comparison with other markets. Sales catalogs and brochures should be in Spanish. Personal relationships with buyers and representatives are crucial. A patient sales approach is preferable.

Selling to the Government

Most government entities acquire their goods and services by publishing tenders in major newspapers as well as in the official newspaper, *La Gaceta*. Some purchases are made directly from prequalified and preregistered suppliers. The Costa Rican Finance Administration Law governs the government's procurement system. Foreign companies may want to establish a representative through a power of attorney for one or more tenders. This representative should be able to translate tender documents from Spanish into English and assist in preparing bid offers in Spanish. To compete successfully for government contracts, a well-established and reputable representative is often required. In June 1995, Law No. 7494 was passed, which establishes new procedures for public procurement. Government entities or ministries with regular annual budgets of more than US$ 200 million now may issue public tenders only if purchases are above US$ 2.3 million. Tenders below this amount but above $130,000 will be circulated among a list of registered suppliers. For tenders below $130,000, bids may come from either preregistered or preselected companies. The aim of the new legislation is to speed up the bidding and procurement process. U.S. firms should register their firms with the relevant Costa Rican government institutions. More important, interested U.S. firms should contract a local representative to facilitate registration and tender processes.

Pricing

Costa Ricans are price conscious and savvy shoppers. They will pay slightly more for the perceived quality of U.S. products, but many are restricted by tight budgets. Costa Ricans often compare what items cost in the U.S. with how they are priced in Costa Rica. Even in the face of tariffs and taxes, most U.S. products are competitively priced, particularly due to savings on marketing costs compared with those expenditures in the U.S. The GOCR does not regulate the prices of goods and services. However, the government does monitor prices for products that fall within the "Canasta Basica." This "basket of consumer goods" is deemed essential to the traditional household. The basket includes foods, household consumables, school uniforms, shoes and school supplies, basic construction products, agricultural chemicals, tools, and medicines. The prices of these goods are monitored to judge if price increases are reasonable.

Customer Support

State institutions and private purchasers expect product support and after-sale service. Maintenance contracts, the identification of convenient repair facilities, and technical support are important. Service and support are usually provided through a local representative with the support of the U.S. exporter. Service literature and contracts should be written in Spanish. The proximity of the U.S. to Costa Rica provides U.S. exporters with added flexibility in arranging efficient service

and support arrangements.

Intellectual Property Rights (IPR)

Patent protection is inadequate. The services of an attorney experienced in Costa Rican intellectual property protection are recommended. Software distributors, music composers, cable TV entities, authorized video distributors, and others have had some recent success in encouraging the GOCR to step up its enforcement efforts.

Attorney

As mentioned, the services of competent, local, legal representation is critical for many aspects of business in Costa Rica. Unlike the U.S. legal system, Costa Rica's legal system is based on Roman law rather than English common law. Preferably, the attorney should be completely bilingual to avoid potentially grave misunderstandings. Frequent communication and effective oversight of legal representatives are also recommended. The Commercial Section and the Consular Section of the U.S. Embassy provide a referral list of Costa Rican attorneys.

FOREIGN INVESTMENT

6

Openness: Since 1982, the GOCR has worked successfully to open its trade and investment regime, in large part through the Ministry of Foreign Trade (COMEX). The Costa Rican Coalition for Development Initiatives (CINDE), a private nonprofit organization, also has worked successfully to attract foreign direct investment. There are few limits on the ways in which foreign companies may operate in Costa Rica or on the roles foreigners may play within such companies.

There is little or no discrimination against foreign private investments. The GOCR has a legal monopoly, however, in certain sectors such as telecommunications, insurance, public health, electrical generation and distribution, petroleum, and port and airport operations. Foreign equity in power-generating projects is limited to 65 percent.

Regulatory System: Transparent regulations and practices tend to facilitate private-sector investment. There are often one or more independent avenues to appeal regulatory decisions. Many domestic and foreign companies thrive in Costa Rica despite problems with bureaucratic red tape. The government has had some success in streamlining customs and judicial proceedings, but much remains to be done in these areas. Expertise is required to supply goods and services to the government. Officials have annulled proceedings when the prospective supplier or contractor has not followed the specifics of all regulations.

Investment Agreements: Costa Rica has reached agreements with a number of Latin American and European countries. After a six-year hiatus, the U.S. and Costa Rica resumed negotiations over a bilateral investment treaty in 1996. These negotiations were suspended again, however, in 1997.

Trade Zones and Free Ports: FTZs are located near the port cities of Lemon and Puntarenas and in several Central Valley locations. FTZ companies, whether domestic or foreign, enjoy simplified investment, trade, and customs procedures. Further benefits include 100 percent exemption from import duties on raw materials and parts; 100 percent exemption from all export taxes associated with the export or re-export of products; 100 percent exemption from sales, consumption, and remittance taxes; 100 percent exemption from income tax for the first eight years of operation; and credits for job creation in rural areas.

Performance Requirements/Incentives: Most investment incentives were terminated in 1996. The incentives still in effect are the Free Trade Zone (FTZ) system, Tourist Infrastructure Law 6990, and the Active Finishing Regime. See FOREIGN TRADE ZONES AND FREE PORTS. The Tourist Infrastructure Law offers import tax exemptions to hotels, air carriers, car rental companies, and sports-fishing operators. The Active Finishing Regime suspends and then exonerates import taxes for certain companies that import parts and then export finished goods.

Capital Markets and Investment: There are no capital controls in Costa Rica. However, the financial system is constrained by the small size of the economy, the small size the banking system, and the large size of the domestically financed public-sector debt. Long-term capital is scarce owing to high inflation and currency-devaluation rates. The Securities Exchange (Bolsa Nacional de Valores) handles 96 percent of Costa Rican securities trading. Daily volume averages US$ 30 million. In practice, the Exchange is more a forum to trade government bonds than a viable source of investment or equity capital. The three state-owned banks supply 80 percent of domestic credit. Private banks are becoming increasingly competitive. Foreign investors often obtain financing by forming joint ventures or by borrowing from abroad. Regulatory and accounting systems are transparent and sound. Most well-known accounting firms are subsidiaries of U.S. firms.

Private Ownership: Foreign and domestic individuals and entities may own business enterprises and engage in all forms of remunerative activity. The only exceptions are those sectors described earlier that are reserved for the state or that require Costa Rican citizenship or residency. Private banks have been permitted to compete for banking services since September 1996. Domestic and foreign entities are free to establish, acquire, and dispose of interests in business enterprises.

Expropriation and Compensation: In the past, the GOCR expropriated large amounts of land for national parks, biological refuges, indigenous reserves, and public infrastructure projects. Recent expropriations are relatively rare, and new legislation in 1995 explicitly defines the government's behavior in all cases of expropriation. Despite these recent improvements, several U.S. firms continue to seek resolutions to expropriation disputes that began 15 or more years ago. Landowners of beachfront property and in rural areas face particular risks. The Maritime Zone Law, which governs the use of the first 200 meters of beachfront property, is not strong. In rural areas, squatters have gained rights to property by occupying land in an open manner for over one year.

OPIC and Investment Insurance: U.S. investors in Costa Rica may receive OPIC financing and OPIC insurance coverage against expropriation, war, revolution, insurrection, and inconvertibility. Recently, OPIC has insured between three and five projects per year in Costa Rica. Financing involves up to 50 percent of initial investments between US$ 250,000 and US$ 200 million. OPIC may not offer insurance to projects that have a detrimental effect on the U.S. balance of payments or employment. OPIC-insured projects must also be approved by the GOCR, which takes into account its own balance of payments and employment. OPIC also offers the services of its computerized Opportunity Bank, which identifies and matches potential foreign investment projects

with prospective U.S. investors. See CONTACTS. Costa Rica has also been a member of the Multilateral Investment Guarantee Agency (MIGA) since 1993.

Dispute Settlement: Most investment disputes have involved expropriation. Some have involved squatters in the southern Pacific Pavones area. A major dispute involved the Millicom cellular telephone concession, which the Supreme Court ruled to be unconstitutional. Generally, in cases of investment disputes, local arbitration has produced mixed results, while resolution through the courts can take years. There is no pattern of discrimination against U.S. or other foreign investors in investment disputes. The local courts often accept and enforce the judgments of foreign courts. Costa Rica joined the International Centre for the Settlement of Investment Disputes (ICSID) in 1993. To date, only one expropriation case has been submitted to this forum.

FINANCE

The three state-owned commercial banks—Banco Nacional de Costa Rica, Banco de Credito Agricola de Cartago, and Banco de Costa Rica—continue to dominate the country's banking system. A fourth state-owned bank failed in 1994; legislative and judicial bodies continue in their attempts to determine the reasons for the bank's failure. In 1996, the state-owned banks lost their exclusive right to offer demand deposits (checking and savings accounts). Over 50 private banks and financial groups now exist in Costa Rica, and these have become increasingly competitive since 1996. Central Bank and monetary laws were significantly amended with Law

No. 7558 of 1995. The law redefined the role and structure of the Central Bank of Costa Rica, in part by creating a General Superintendent of Financial Entities (SUGEF) to expand supervision and control over financial institutions. The law also guaranteed the free exchange of foreign currency and liberalized the capital markets.

Export Financing: A variety of foreign sources make export financing available through private and state-owned commercial financial intermediaries. U.S. lenders often will undertake the credit risk only if an organization like OPIC or MIGA provides insurance against the sovereign risk. The U.S. Export-Import Bank (EXIM) has guaranteed credit to finance a large number of U.S exports. However, EXIM has not been active recently in Costa Rica. The U.S. Department of Agriculture (USDA) offers a regional GSM-102 export credit guarantee program to encourage imports of U.S. farm products. The U.S. Small Business Administration (SBA) offers loans, loan guarantees, and business development assistance to small businesses that are looking to develop export markets. The U.S. Trade and Development Agency (TDA) provides grant loans for prefeasibility studies on overseas projects that would have a high U.S. product and service export potential.

Project Financing: The foreign share of international projects is generally financed from U.S. private banks, guaranteed by EXIM, OPIC, or MIGA. Financing is available for most activities, but lenders often give preference to export or tourist service industries. Multilateral development banks such as the Inter-American Development Bank (IDB) and the World Bank provide funding for most government projects. It is recommended to have a local representative when bidding on such projects. Companies with majority Costa Rican ownership may receive project financing from the local banking system.

COMMUNICATIONS ⑧

Phone

The telecommunications network is advanced and telephone service in general is reliable. Cellular and data transmission services are also available. The Costa Rican Institute of Electricity (ICE) retains a monopoly on telecommunications. The Costa Rican Supreme Court already struck down a move to privatize a portion of the telecommunications network. ICE union workers and some political leaders oppose privatization although a constitutional amendment to open the sector to private competition stands a reasonable chance of approval. Currently, the ICE does accept private investment through joint ventures and other arrangements. AT&T, Sprint, and MCI all operate within Costa Rica. The

international access code is 011, and the Costa Rican access code is 506. City codes are not required.

Internet

Use of the Internet has grown rapidly, and strong growth rates are expected to continue. RACSA, an ICE subsidiary with responsibility for nonvoice communications, recently won the right to install 100,000 Internet lines.

Mail

The postal system is reasonably well developed although street names and numbers are not well defined. Express mail international services are available between Costa Rica and the U.S.

TRANSPORTATION ⑨

Land

The road network is extensive although lately many stretches of road and highway have fallen into a state of disrepair. Railway transport is uncommon. San Jose offers good public bus services, but taxis are recommended for business visitors. Car rental services are also available.

Sea

Costa Rica's ports are in need of modernization. The main Pacific Coast ports are Caldera and Puntarenas. The Puerto Limon/Moin port complex serves the Caribbean coast.

Air

Sixteen international passenger airlines and 19 cargo airlines serve San Jose's Juan Santamaria International Airport. Recent construction at Juan Santamaria should produce substantial improvements in the landing and terminal facilities. The Liberia International Airport serves the tourist areas of Guanacaste and the Gulf of Papagayo. Regional airports offer regularly scheduled flights to Limon, Golfito, Quepos, and Tamarindo. There are also more than 100 small private landing fields, which serve approximately 300 registered aircraft. According to the U.S. Federal Aviation Administration (FAA), Costa Rica's civil aviation authority is not in compliance with international aviation safety standards. The GOCR has worked successfully to improve its oversight of air carrier operations. For further information, contact the Department of Transportation at (800) 322-7873, or visit the FAA Internet website at http://www.faa.gov/avr/iasa.htm. The U.S. Department of Defense (DOD) assesses some foreign air carriers. Contact the Pentagon at (703) 697-7288.

WORK WEEK ⑩

Business Hours: 8.00 a.m. to 12.00 p.m. and 2.00 p.m. to 6.00 p.m. Monday through Friday.

Government Hours: 7.30 a.m. to 4.00 p.m. Monday through Friday.

Banks: 9.00 a.m. to 3.00 p.m. Monday through Friday and closed on Saturday.

HOLIDAYS 2001

New Year's Day, January 1
Juan Santamaria, April 11
Holy Thursday, April 20
Good Friday, April 21
Labor Day, May 1
Annexation of Guanacaste, July 25
Our Lady of the Angels, August 2
Mother's Day, August 15
Independence Day, September 15
Columbus Day, October 12
Christmas Day, December 25

Some holidays may be observed on different dates depending on the day of the week on which it falls. The U.S. Embassy will be closed on U.S. and Costa Rican holidays. It is recommended that business travelers do not schedule trips to Costa Rica immediately before or immediately after local or U.S. holidays.

BUSINESS TRAVEL

Business Customs

Personal contacts with Costa Rican business executives are highly important. Appointments should take place in the host's facilities rather than in a hotel room unless a special meeting place has been arranged. Costa Rica is a Spanish-speaking country although many business professionals speak English. Business suits are appropriate for most business meetings.

Travel Advisory and Visas

According to Costa Rican law, travelers must have a valid passport, and the use of a passport is highly recommended. However, for tourist or business visits of less than 90 days, Costa Rican authorities often admit travelers over the age of 17 who have only a photo ID and an original or certified U.S. birth certificate. In such cases, a tourist card is issued at the airport. An onward or return ticket is necessary to obtain the tourist card. A US$ 17 airport tax is charged upon departure. U.S. passports are a particular target of pickpockets and

other thieves. The loss or theft of a U.S. passport should be reported immediately to the local police and the U.S. Embassy.

Business Infrastructure

Entry Requirements (personal and professional goods): Contact the Consular Section of the Embassy of Costa Rica to obtain updated information on entry and exit requirements.

Currency Exchange: The Costa Rican colon is divided into 100 centimos. The exchange rate, which has been declining at a rate of about 10 percent per year, currently stands at approximately 311 colons per U.S. dollar. The colon is freely exchanged for all major foreign currencies, and exchange delays are rare.

Taxes: The 13 percent value-added tax (VAT) applies to most goods; only some staple goods are exempt.

Hotels and Restaurants: Travelers to San Jose and neighboring cities may stay in a wide variety of modern hotels and bed-and-breakfast facilities. Prices tend to be reasonable. Larger hotels typically offer business services such as telephone, fax, conference rooms, computer equipment, and audiovisual equipment. Numerous restaurants specialize in local, Oriental, American, and Continental cuisine.

Rent: Housing costs are not inexpensive although living conditions are excellent, particularly due to the climate, food, housing, and ancillary services. Modern shopping centers and supermarkets, along with traditional open-air markets, provide a complete variety of goods and services.

Business Services: San Jose and the surrounding area provide a wide range of business services. There are numerous professionals with advanced degrees, including lawyers, notaries, and business and public administrators.

Labor Costs and Legislation: The National Wage Council—comprising government, labor, and private-sector representatives—establishes minimum wage rates on a semiannual basis. Minimum monthly salaries in U.S. dollars at the end of 1999 were as follows: unskilled worker, $231; semiskilled worker, $251; skilled worker, $269; technician with a high school diploma, $290; specialized worker, $310; technician (tertiary studies), $357; bachelor degree, $438; licentiate degree, $525. Worker benefits are costly, but productivity and skill levels are high. In accordance with the 1943 Labor Code, employers pay mandatory payroll taxes, which cover INA vocational training and social security (health, maternity, disability, old age, and death benefits). All workers are entitled to a two-week paid vacation and a Christmas bonus equal to one month's salary. Workers employed for less than one year receive prorated bonuses. Female workers are entitled to four months of maternity leave. The Labor Code also requires that at least 90 percent of employees must be Costa Rican. The Labor Ministry may lower this limit to 80 percent under certain conditions during a five-year period. Foreigners cannot occupy jobs for which Costa Rican workers are available without the Labor Ministry's approval. Only 15 percent of the workforce belongs to unions, most of which are in the public sector. In the private sector, Solidarity Associations are more common. Under these associations, employers provide access to credit unions and savings plans in return for agreements to avoid strikes and other types of confrontation.

Education: The country enjoys a literacy rate of 94 percent, and many workers seek and absorb additional specialized training.

Insurance: Accident, sickness, liability, and medical evacuation insurance are fairly priced and wisely obtained before departure to Costa Rica.

Travel Notes

The following travel notes have been supplied by the U.S. government. For the most recent general travel and consular information, see the U.S. Department of State travel publications or call the Traveler's Telephone Hotline at (202) 647-5225.

Security: Pick-pocketing and thefts from cars are common in urban areas. Some remote trails in national parks have been closed because of reports of robberies. Visitors should check with forest rangers for current park conditions.

Health Precautions: In San Jose and neighboring cities, medical services are good, and specialists are widely available. In other areas, medical care is more limited. Visitors should avoid tap water and untreated fruits and vegetables. The Costa Rican Social Security Fund covers medical expenses for all Costa Rican workers and their dependents. U.S. travelers may want to consider supplemental medical insurance to cover medical evacuation as well as care outside the U.S. San Jose de Dios Hospital and Hospital Mexico are the best equipped in Central American although they are also overcrowded. Many doctors, whether in the public system or in private clinics, are trained abroad and are fluent in English. Mosquitoes in San Jose do not carry malaria. In low-lying areas along both coasts, dengue mosquitoes have been identified. Numerous eradication programs are underway. Current information on health matters may be obtained from the Centers for Disease Control and Prevention's international travelers' hotline at (404) 332-4559.

Embassy Assistance

To obtain additional and updated information on entry and exit requirements, travelers can contact the Consular Section of the Embassy of Costa Rica at 2114 S Street, N.W., Washington, D.C. 20008; Tel: (202) 328-6628. Travelers may also contact the nearest Costa Rican consulate. They are located in Los Angeles, San Diego, Tampa, Atlanta, Miami, Chicago, New Orleans, New York, Philadelphia, San Juan, Puerto Rico, Austin, San Antonio, and Houston.

CONTACTS

U.S. Embassy Commercial, Agricultural and Trade-Related Contacts

U.S. Department of Commerce Commercial Service
Unit 2508
APO, AA 34020 9508
Tel: (506) 220-3939 ext. 2203, 2207; 220-2454
Fax: (506) 231-4783

U.S. Department of Agriculture Foreign Agricultural Service (FAS)
Unit 2507
APO AA 34020
Tel: (506) 220-3939 ext. 2333
Fax: (506) 232-7709

Animal and Plant Health Inspection Services (APHIS)
USDA APHIS IS
Costa Rica
Unit 2522
APO AA 34020 9522
Tel: (506) 290-4297; 290-4309
Fax: (506) 296-3556

APHIS Screwworm Program
USDA APHIS IS
Unit 2524
APO AA 3402 9524
Tel: (506) 290-4114
Fax: (506) 220-3275

U.S. Department of State Economic Section
Unit 2501
APO AA 34020-9501
Tel: (506) 220-3939
Fax: (506) 220-2305

AMCHAM (Local American Chamber of Commerce)

Costa Rican-American Chamber Of Commerce (AMCHAM) (Camara Costarricense-Norteamericana de Comercio—AMCHAM)
U.S. Mailing Address:
1576 P.O. Box 025216
Miami, FL 33102-5216

International mailing address to Costa Rica:
Apdo 4946-1000
San José, Costa Rica
Tel: (506) 220-2200
Fax: (506)220-2300
Website: http:\\http://www.amcham.co.cr

Country Trade and Industry Associations

**Costa Rican Chamber of Commerce
Camara de Comercio de Costa Rica**
Apartado 1114
1000 San José, Costa Rica
Tel: (506) 221-0005;221-0124
Fax: (506) 233-7091

**Chamber of Representatives of Foreign
Firms Camara de Representantes de
Casas Extranjeras (CRECEX)**
Apartado. 3738
1000 San José, Costa Rica
Tel: (506) 253-0126
Fax: (506)234-2557
Website: http://www.infoweb.co.cr/crecex

**Costa Rican Chamber of Industries
Camara de Industrias de Costa Rica**
Apartado 1003-1000
San José, Costa Rica
Tel: (506) 256-2826; 283-3779
Fax:(560) 222-1007
Website: http://www.cicr.co.cr

**National Chamber of Agriculture
And Agro-Industry
Camara Nacional de Agricultura
Y Agro-Industria**
Apartado 1671-1000 San José, Costa Rica
Tel: (506) 280-2173; 233-8567
Fax: (506) 233-8658

**Chamber of Food Industry of Costa
Rica/Camara Costarricense De La
Industria Alimentaria (CACIA)**
Apartado 7097
1000 San Jose, Costa Rica
Tel: (506) 234-1127
Fax: (506) 234-6783

**Costa Rican Chamber of Textiles
and Apparel
Camara Textil y de Confeccion (CATECO)**
Apartado 1512 1002 Paseo de Estudiantes
San José, Costa Rica
Tel: (506) 220-2981
Fax: (506)220-1424

**Chamber of Highway &
Bridge Construction
Camara de Constructores de
Carreteras y Puentes**
APDO. 3803, 1000
San José, Costa Rica
Tel: (506) 221-9418
Fax: (506) 258-2824

**Chamber of Architects and Engineers
Camara de Consultorese en Arquitectura
e Ingenieria**
Apartado 1151-1002
San Jose, Costa Rica
Tel/Fax: (506) 283-7698
Tel: (506) 257-7067

**Chamber of Construction of Costa Rica
Camara Costarricense de la Construccion**
Apartado 5260-1000
San José, Costa Rica
Tel: (506) 253-5757; 381-3614
Fax: (506) 221-7952
Website: http://www.construccion.co.cr

**Costa Rican Association of the
Plastic Industry
Asociacion Costarricense de la Industria
del Plastico (ACIPLAST)**
Apartado 8247-1000 San Jose, Costa Rica
Tel: (506) 255-0961
Fax: (506) 255-0961

**Costa Rican Chamber of Restaurants
& Related Affairs
Camara Costarricense de Restaurantes
y Afines**
Apartado 113-2150 San Jose
Tel: (506) 283-2579
Fax: (506) 283-2580

Chamber of Automotive and Related
Topics of Costa Rica (CCA)
Apartado 425-1002 Paseo de los Estudiantes
San José Costa Rica
Tel: (506)233-3331
Fax: (506) 257-7432

Costa Rican Association of Importers
of Automotive Parts
Asociacion de Importadores de Partes
Automotrices (AIPA)
Apartado 242-1002 Paseo de Estudiantes
San José, Costa Rica
Tel/Fax: (506)222-8168

Costa Rican Association of Importers
of Vehicles, Equipment &
Machinery/Asociacion de Importadores
de Vehiculos, Equipo, Maquinaria y Afines
(AIVEMA)
Apartado 84040-1000 San Jose, Costa Rica
Tel: (506) 222-5513
Fax: (506) 233-5432

Federacion de Camaras de Ganaderos
Federation of Chambers of Livestock
Breeders
Apdo. 6464-1000 San Jose
Tel: (506) 221-9268
Fax: (506) 233-2180

Country Government Offices/Agencies

Costa Rican Customs Office/Dirección
General de Aduanas
San Jose, Costa Rica
Tel: (506) 255-3011; 233-9525
Fax: (506) 223-7334
Website: http://www.aduanas.go.cr

Ministry of Economy, Industry and
Commerce and Foreign Trade
Apartado 96-2050 San Pedro Montes de Oca
San Jose, Costa Rica
Tel: (506) 256-7111; 222-5910
Fax: (506) 233-9176

Labeling and Norms Department
Apartado 10216-1000
San Jose, Costa Rica
Tel: (506) 283-6580
Fax: (506) 283-5133

Consejo Nacional de Produccion - Cnp
(National Production Council)
Apdo. 2205-1000, San Jose
Tel: (506) 257-9355; 255-4283
Fax: (506) 255-4729

Ministerio de Agricultura Y Ganaderia
Y Ciencia Y Tecnologia
(Ministry of Agriculture and Livestock
and Science and Technology)
Apartado 1094-1000, San Jose
Tel: (506) 231-2344; 232-9420
Fax: (506) 232-2103

Direccion De Proteccion Agropecuaria
(Agricultural Protection Department)
Tel:(506)260-8300; 260-8647; 260-8296;
260-6190
Fax: (506) 260-8294

Instituto Costarricense De Electricidad (Ice)
(Costa Rican Institute of Electricity and
Telecommunication)
Apartado 10032-1000
San Jose, Costa Rica
Tel: (506) 220-7422; 220-7720
Fax: (506) 220-1555
Website: http://www.ice.go.cr

Instituto Costarricense De Acueductos
Y Alcantarillado (Aya)
(Costa Rican Institute Of Aqueducts
And Sewage)
Apartado 5120-1000
San Jose, Costa Rica
Tel: (506) 223-6103; 223-5012
Fax: (506) 233-7552
Website: http://www.aya.ca.cr.

Ministry Of Public Works And
Transportation
(Ministerio De Obras Públicas Y
Transportes)
Apartado 10176 - San Jose, Costa Rica
Tel: (506) 257-7798
Fax: (506) 255-0242

National Concessions Council
Apartado 10724-1000
San Jose, Costa Rica
Tel: (506) 223-9668
Fax: (506) 257-5247

Costa Rican Civil Aviation Directorate
Apartado 5026-1000
San Jose, Costa Rica
Tel: (506) 231-3666
Fax: (506) 231-2107

Tourism Institute
(Instituto Costarricense De Turismo)
Apartado 777-1000
San Jose, Costa Rica
Tel: (506) 233-9605
Fax: (506)223-5107; 255-4997
http://www.tourism-costarica.com

Ministry Of Health
(Ministerio De Salud)
Unidad de Denuncias (Former Food
Registration and Control Department)
Apdo. 10123-1000 San Jose
Tel: (506) 255-4426
Fax: (506) 256-4800

Ministry of the Environment and Energy
(Ministerio Del Ambiente Y Energía -Minae)
Apartado 10104-1000
San Jose, Costa Rica
Tel: (506) 233-4533; 223-2124
Fax: (506) 257-4580

Joint Implementation Projects:
Apartado 7170-1000
San Jose, Costa Rica
Tel: (506) 220-0036
Fax: (506) 290-1238

Ministry of Justice
Apartado 5685-1000
San Jose, Costa Rica
Tel: (506) 280-7794
Fax: (506) 234-7959

Costa Rican Correctional Institution
Tel/Fax: (506) 222-0661

Costa Rican Foreign Trade Corporation
(PROCOMER)
Apartado 1278-1007
San Jose, Costa Rica
Tel: (506) 256-7111
Fax: (506)233-5755; 233-4655
Website: http:\\http://www.procomer.com

Procomer
Free Trade Zone Division
Apartado 1278-1007
San Jose, Costa Rica
Tel: (506) 256-7111, ext. 266; 279
Fax (506) 223-5722
Website: http://www.procomer.com

CINDE/Costa Rican Investment and
Trade Development Board
Apartado 7170-1000
San Jose, Costa Rica
Tel: (506) 220-0036
Fax: (506) 220-4754
Website: http://www.cinde.or.cr

CINDE/Costa Rican Investment and
Trade Development Board
90 West Street, Suite 614
New York, NY 10006
Tel: (212) 964-1867
Fax: (212) 964-1969
Email: cinde.ny@aol.com

List of In-Country Market Research Firms

AMCHAM/Costa Rican American Chamber of Commerce should be consulted about their ability to conduct market research.

Costa Rican-American Chamber of
Commerce (AMCHAM)
(Camara Costarricense-Norteamericana
De Comercio—AMCHAM)
USA Mailing Address:
1576 P.O. Box 025216
Miami, FL 33102-5216
Within Costa Rica: Apdo 4946-1000
San José, Costa Rica
Tel: (506) 220-2200
Fax: (506) 220-2300
Website: http://www.amcham.co.cr

Grupo Hay De Centroamerica
P.O. Box 103-2300 Curridabat
Tel: (506) 220-0533
Fax: (506) 231-4520

KPMG
Peat Marwick
P.O. Box 10208-1000 San Jose
Tel: (506) 220-1366
Fax: (506) 220-0408; 220-0411
Website: http://www.kpmg.co.cr

Multivex, S.A.
P.O. Box 107-1007 Centro Colon
San Jose, Costa Rica
Tel: (506) 290-2417; 290-2418
Fax: (506) 290-2419
Email: multivex@sol.racsa.co.cr

Protrade
International Trade and Consulting Co.
Apartado 802-1002 Paseo de los Estudiantes
San Jose, Costa Rica
Tel: (506) 253-0820
Fax: (506) 283-9749

Consultores De Credito Internacionales,
S.A.
(Credit Reporting)
Apartado 1103-1000
San Jose, Costa Rica
Tel: (506) 232-0443 / (506) 296-0195
Fax: (506) 231-0929

Veritas De Centroamerica, S.A.
(Credit reporting)
Apartado 11421-1000
San Jose, Costa Rica
Tel: (506) 224-7232; (506) 253-8132;
223-9102
Fax: (506) 234-1581
Website: http://www.veritas-usa.com

Multilateral Finance Organizations
in Costa Rica

Asesoria Empresarial Centroamericana
(Business Advisory Services) (affiliated
with the World Bank)
Apartado 98-1250 Escazú
San José, Costa Rica
Tel: (506) 228-4124
Fax: (506) 228-6963

Inter-American Development Bank (IDB)
Apartado 1142-1007 Centro Colón
San José, Costa Rica
Tel: (506) 233-3244
Fax: (506) 233-1840
Website: http://www.iadb.org

Multilateral Development Bank Offices
Within The U.S.

Inter-American Development Bank
US&FCS Liaison Office
1300 New York Ave, N.W
Washington, DC 20005
Website: http://www.iadb.org
Tel: (202) 623-1000
Fax: (202) 942-8275

Multilateral Development Bank Office
14th and Constitution, NW
Washington, DC 20007
Tel: (202) 482-3399
Fax: (202) 482-5179; (202) 273-0927

Export-Import Bank of the United States
(EXIM)
811 Vermont Avenue, N.W.
Washington, DC 20571
Export Credit Insurance for one year or less
Tel: (202) 565-3911
Fax: (202) 565-3380; 565-3931
Website: http://www.exim.gov

Overseas Private Investment Corporation (OPIC)
1100 New York Avenue, N.W.
Washington, DC 20527
Insurance Department
Tel: (202) 366-8663
Fax: (202) 408-5142
Finance Department
Tel: (202) 336-8472
Fax: (202) 408-5142
Website: http://www.opic.gov

U.S. Trade and Development Agency (TDA)
Regional Director for Latin America
Room 309, SA-16
Department of State
Washington, DC 20523-1602
Tel: (703) 875-4357
Fax: (703) 875-4009
Website: http://www.tda.gov

The World Bank
1818 H Street, N.W.
Washington, DC 20433
Tel: (202) 473-4271
Fax: (202) 477-6391
Website: http://www.worldbank.org

Other Entities to Consult in Reference to
Doing Business in Costa Rica

Trade Information Center (TCI)
(800) USA-TRADE (872-8723)
Fax: (202) 482-4473
U.S. Department of Commerce
Room 7424-HCHB
14th and Constitution Avenue, N.W.
Washington, DC 20230
Website: http://www.ita.doc.gov/tic
Email: tic@ita.doc.gov

U.S. Department of Commerce
Mr. Mark Siegelman, Desk Officer
Desk Officer for Costa Rica, Room H3033
14th & Constitution Ave., N.W.
Washington, DC 20230
Tel: (202) 482-0704
Fax: (202) 482-0464

U.S. Department of State
Officer in Charge, Costa Rican Affairs
2201 C Street, N.W.
Washington, DC 20520
Tel: (202) 647-4980; 647-4000
Fax: (202) 647-2597
Website: http://www.state.gov

U.S. Department of Agriculture
Trade Assistance and Promotion Office
Foreign Agricultural Service
Stop 1052
Washington, DC 20250-1052
Tel: (202) 720-7420
Fax: (202) 690-0193
Website: http://www.fas.usda.gov

Embassy of Costa Rica
1825 Connecticut Ave., N.W., Suite 211
Washington, DC 20009
Tel: (202) 234-2945
Fax: (202) 265-4795
Email: embassy@costarica.com
(The government of Costa Rica has
consulate offices in the largest cities in
the U.S.)

CINDE/Costa Rican Investment
and Development Board
90 West Street, Suite 614
New York, NY 10006
Tel: (212)964-1774 Fax: (212)964-1969

Major Costa Rican newspapers
(in order of circulation)

La Nacion
Apartado 10138
1000 San Jose, Costa Rica
Tel: (506) 247-4747
Switchboard (506) 247-4949 Advertising
Fax: (506) 247-4849
Website: http://www.nacion.co.cr

Al Dia
Apartado 7-0270
1000 San Jose, Costa Rica
Tel: (506) 247-4666
Fax: (506) 247-4669

DOMINICAN
REPUBLIC

TRADE AND BUSINESS GUIDE

Official Name:	Dominican Republic
Official Language:	Spanish. English is widely spoken in the business community
Population:	8,442,533 (2000 est)
Population Growth:	1.64% (2000 est)
Age Structure:	0–14 years: 34%, 15–64 years: 61%, 65 years and over: 5% (2000 est)
Location:	Caribbean, eastern two-thirds of the island of Hispaniola, between the Caribbean Sea and the North Atlantic Ocean, east of Haiti
Area:	48,730 square kilometers, slightly more than twice the size of New Hampshire
Type of Government:	Representative democracy
Head of State:	President Leonel Fernandez Reyna
Cabinet:	Nominated by the president
Religion:	Predominantly Catholic
Major Cities:	Capital: Santo Domingo (1.3 million). Principal commercial centers: Santiago de los Caballeros (278,638), La Romana (91,571), San Pedro de Macoris (78,562), San Francisco de Macoris (64,906)
Climate:	Tropical maritime; little seasonal temperature variation; seasonal variation in rainfall
Time:	The entire country is -4 GMT (Greenwich Mean Time), one hour ahead of EST (Eastern Standard Time). The country does not schedule for daylight savings time
GDP:	Purchasing power parity (PPP): $43.7 billion (1999 est); real growth rate: 8.3% (1999 est); per capita PPP: $5,400 (1999 est); composition by sector: agriculture = 13.6%, industry = 30.8%, services = 55.6% (1996 est)
Currency:	1 Dominican peso (RD$) = 100 centavos
Exchange Rate:	RD$ per US$ 1 = 15.85 (2000 est), 15.73 (1999 est)
Weights & Measure:	Metric system
Natural Resources:	Nickel, bauxite, gold, silver
Total Trade:	In billions US$ [exports (fob)/imports (cif)]: 1997 (4.8/6.6), 1998 (5.0/7.6), 1999 (5.1/7.7)
Trade with US:	In billions US$ [exports (fob)/imports (cif)]: 1997 (4.4/3.9), 1998 (3.6/4.0), 1999 est (3.7/4.1)

Major Trade Partners: Imports: United States, European Union countries, Venezuela, Netherlands Antilles, Mexico, Japan. Exports: United States, European Union countries, Canada, South Korea

Membership: IADB, IBRD, IFC, IMF, MIGA, OAS, UN, UNCTAD, and WTO. See membership description in appendix

Sources: *CIA World Factbook, United Nations World Statistics, U.S. Department of Commerce, Central Bank of the Dominican Republic*

POLITICAL OUTLOOK

②

Relationship with the U.S.

The two countries have a long-standing, close relationship. The Dominican Republic is the Caribbean's largest democratic country, and the U.S. is the Dominican Republic's principal trading partner and its largest market. Political and economic nationalists sometimes revive anti-American slogans, but the great majority of Dominicans have a positive view of the U.S.

Influences on Business

Business is impeded by a poorly run, highly centralized regulatory and administrative system. Foreign and domestic business leaders complain that laws and regulations are not applied in a consistent or predictable way. Problems arise from corruption, and poor dispute settlement processes have been a source of frustration. Recently, however, the Fernandez administration has taken some steps to improve the business climate, particularly by working to reduce corruption and apply regulations more carefully.

Profile

System: The executive branch dominates the political system. The president and members of congress are elected by popular vote. Congress comprises 30 senators and 149 national deputies. An overhaul of the judicial system began in 1997. New supreme court members were appointed, and the court then appointed new judges throughout the system.

Schedule for Elections: Congressional and municipal elections were held in May 1998. Free and fair presidential elections were held on May 16, 2000. The president may not serve consecutive terms.

Major Parties: The main parties are the Partido Reformista Social Cristiano (PRSC), the Partido Revolucionario Dominicano (PRD), and the Partido de la Liberacion Dominicana (PLD). Each of the three tends toward centrist platforms.

Political Violence: There has been no recent political violence directed at foreign firms.

Corruption: At most levels of government, corruption remains a problem. President Fernandez has made anticorruption efforts a hallmark of his administration, and the court system was overhauled in 1997. However, the enforcement of court rulings must be further strengthened before corruption can be greatly reduced.

ECONOMIC OUTLOOK

③

Trends

For several years, the economic and political situation in the Dominican Republic has been healthy. GDP and per capita income have grown steadily, and inflation rates have been kept in the single digits. According to the Dominican Central Bank, the economy grew 7.3 percent in 1998 despite the ravages of Hurricane Georges. It grew 8.4 percent during 1999 with the Central Bank estimating that growth will again exceed 8 percent in 2000. The political elections of 1996 were a cause of concern among foreign investors, but after a successful and peaceful transfer of power, President Fernandez quickly launched programs to modernize the judiciary, maintain macroeconomic stability, identify government debts and capitalize state-owned enterprises. The 2000 Presidential election and transition also proceeded smoothly without a disruptive effect on the economy. Currently, the Dominican Republic is the seventh largest export market for U.S. goods and services. However, U.S. investors must be prepared to face strong competition, corruption, substantial tariff and nontariff barriers, and a cumbersome regulatory system. The increasingly popular free trade zones are exempt from many international trade restrictions, but to date the government has allowed only the limited sale of free-trade-zone output on the domestic market.

Major Growth Sectors

Sector	Real Growth in 1999 (%)
Communications	15.6
Construction	18.2
Commerce	9.1
Free trade zones Manufacturing(FTZ)	-2.5
Manufacturing (non FTZ)	6.7
Hotels, bars, and restaurants	10.0
Finance	4.2
Overall growth	8.4

Source: Dominican Central Bank

According to a number of analysts, the Dominican Republic has two sets of business sectors. One has strong growth rates, significant foreign investment, and close ties to international markets; the other has slower growth rates and ties predominantly to domestic markets. In telecommunications, the sector's boom was further fueled in May of 1998 with the passage of important, modernizing legislation. In the construction sector, the damage left behind by Hurricane Georges gave further impetus to an already strong area. The tourism sector, by comparison, is still struggling to recover from the 1999 storm. Dominican agriculture is worse off since the sector was only beginning to recover from a two-year drought when Georges hit. Dominican Government officials and free trade zone businesses were concerned that the textile industry would be adversely affected by a lack of tariff parity with Mexico. These concerns were largely laid to rest with the passage of U.S. legislation in 2000 that enhanced the benefits available under the Caribbean Basin Economic Recovery Act, bringing them into line with NAFTA treatment for many textile and other products.

Key Economic Indicators

Income, Production and Employment (billions of U.S. dollars unless otherwise indicated)			
	1997	1998	1999[1]
Nominal GDP[2]	15.0	15.9	18.5
Real GDP Growth (pct)[3]	8.2	7.3	8.4
GDP by Sector			
Agriculture	1.9	2.1	2.1
Manufacturing	2.7	2.9	3.1
Services	4.7	5.2	6.8
Government	1.0	1.1	1.4
Per Capita GDP (US$)	1,882	1,942	2,219
Labor Force (millions)	3,614	3,697	N/A
Unemployment Rate (pct)	15.7	14.3	13.8

1. 1999 figures are all estimates based on most recent data available. 2. GDP at factor cost.
3. Percentage changes calculated in local currency.
Source: Bureau of Economic and Business Affairs; U.S. Department of State

- **Infrastructure**
  The Dominican Republic's infrastructure systems are generally strong. The road and high-way network is adequate and improving. The country has seven international airports and several modern port facilities. Telecommunications are highly advanced. Radio, television, and cable TV reach wide audiences. The one major shortfall comes in the area of electric power. The state-owned supplier, Compania Dominicana de Electricidad (CDE), is not able to meet the country's demands. Most industrial enterprises have their own backup power systems, and some large firms maintain completely independent electricity supplies. Substantial improvements in the power sector may come as the CDE undergoes further privatization.

- **Labor**
  Businesses often find that the labor force is cooperative but untrained. There is no pattern of discrimination against foreign employers in response to labor complaints. The standard work-week is 44 hours. Most jobs pay salaries based on the minimum wage. According to the Central Bank, the unemployment rate is approximately 16 percent. Other sources estimate a much lower rate. Unionized workers compose about 10 percent of the nation's workforce. To enter into collective bargaining or to call a strike, a union must have the support of 51 per-cent of the company's workers. The 1992 Dominican Labor Code establishes policies and procedures for many aspects of employer–employee relationships.

Money and Prices			
(annual percentage growth)			
	1997	1998	1999[1]
Money Supply Growth (M2)	24	16	17
Consumer Price Inflation	8.3	7.8	7.5
Exchange Rate (DR Peso/US$ annual average)			
Official	14.01	14.71	15.89
Parallel	14.27	15.27	16.15

1. 1999 figures are all estimates based on most recent data available.
Source: Bureau of Economic and Business Affairs; U.S. Department of State

Balance of Payments and Trade			
(billions of U.S. dollars unless otherwise indicated)			
	1997	1998	1999[1]
Total Exports FOB[2]	4.8	5.0	5.1
Exports to U.S.[2]	4.4	3.6	3.7
Total Imports CIF[2]	6.6	7.6	7.7
Imports from U.S.[2]	3.9	4.0	4.1
Trade Balance (US$ millions)[2]	-1.8	-2.6	-2.6
Trade Balance with U.S.[2]	0.5	-0.4	-0.4
External Public Debt	3.5	3.5	N/A
Fiscal Surplus/GDP (pct)	1.6	-1.2	N/A
Current Account Deficit/GDP (pct)	-1.5	-2.4	-3.1
Debt Service Payments/GDP (pct)	1.5	2.3	2.5
Gold and Foreign Exchange Reserves[2]	0.5	0.7	0.8
Aid from U.S. (US$ millions)[2,3]	11.6	60.4	10.4
Aid from All Other Sources[2]	N/A	141.0	N/A

1. 1999 figures are all estimates based on most recent data available. 2. Central Bank; exports (fas),
imports (customs basis); 1999 figures are estimates based on data available through September. 3. Military aid
equaled US$ 800,000 in both 1998 and 1999.
Source: Bureau of Economic and Business Affairs; U.S. Department of State

- **Balance of Payments**
  For years growing surpluses in tourism have financed the country's merchandise trade deficit. Further support now comes from free-trade-zone earnings and from the substantial remittances sent by the country's expatriate population (remittances totaled US$1.3 billion in 1998). The merchandise trade balance will continue to deteriorate over the short and medium term. See **Key Economic Indicators.**

Government Influence on Business

The government's large presence can create bureaucratic and political disadvantages for foreign companies. The government owns the public utilities (except telecommunications), an insurance company, the country's largest bank (Banco de Reservas), and a number of factories. Most state enterprises are unprofitable. Legislation to allow privatization or "capitalization" was passed in June 1997. The Commission for the Reform of Public Enterprises (CREP) has since privatized a flour mill and units of the electricity company. Further transfers are scheduled for the next few years.

Leading Imports and Exports

Imports: Electrical power systems, telecommunications equipment, construction and earthmoving equipment, motor and heavy-duty vehicles and replacement parts, mining industry equipment, computers and peripherals, travel and tourism services, food processing and packaging equipment, secondhand clothing, medical equipment, hotel and restaurant equipment, rice, defense articles

Exports: Ferronickel, sugar, gold, coffee, cocoa

Foreign Trade *(Exports and Imports in US$B)*			
	1997	1998	1999[1]
Total Exports FOB[2]	4.8	5.0	5.1
Exports to U.S.[2]	4.4	3.6	3.7
Total Imports CIF[2]	6.6	7.6	7.7
Imports from U.S.[2]	3.9	4.0	4.1

1. 1999 figures are all estimates based on most recent data available. 2. Central Bank; exports (fas), imports (customs basis); 1999 figures are estimates based on data available through September.
Source: U.S. Department of Commerce

Best Prospects Analysis

Best Prospects for Nonagricultural Goods and Services

Computers and Peripherals (CPT)

	1998 $M	1999 $M	2000E $M
Total Market Size	53.7	76.8	106.5
Total Local Production	14.0	20.0	27.0
Total Exports	0	0	0
Total Imports	39.72	56.8	79.5
Imports from the U.S.	23.8	34.1	47.7

Air Conditioning and Refrigeration Equipment (ACR)

	1998 $M	1999 $M	2000E $M
Total Market Size	54.5	85.5	113.6
Total Local Production	10.0	13.0	16.0
Total Exports	2.1	3.7	5.2
Total Imports	46.6	76.2	102.8
Imports from the U.S.	32.6	49.5	66.8

Telecommunications Equipment (TEL)

	1998 $M	1999 $M	2000E $M
Total Market Size	139.4	173.9	216.8
Total Local Production	6.3	6.3	6.5
Total Exports	3.7	4.0	4.2
Total Imports	136.6	171.6	214.5
Imports from the U.S.	102.5	128.7	160.9

Engineering/Architectural Services (ACE)

	1998 $M	1999 $M	2000E $M
Total Market Size	254.63	408.20	497.9
Sales by local firms in the DR:	241.90	387.79	473.01
Sales by local firms in foreign markets:	N/A	N/A	N/A
Sales by foreign firms:	12.73	20.41	24.89
Sales by U.S.-owned firms:	10.18	16.32	19.91

Advertising Services (ADV)

	1998 $M	1999 $M	2000E $M
Total Market Size	47.0	54.0	62.1
Total Local Production	14.1	16.2	18.6
Total Exports	N/A	N/A	N/A
Total Imports	32.9	37.8	43.5
Imports from the U.S.	29.6	34.8	40.0

Food Processing and Packaging Equipment (FPP)

	1998 $M	1999 $M	2000E $M
Total Market Size	28.6	42.0	44.5
Total Local Production	1.6	2.0	2.5
Total Exports	0	0	0
Total Imports	27.0	40.0	42.0
Imports from the U.S.	18.9	24.4	28.0

Building Products (BLD)

	1998 $M	1999 $M	2000E $M
Total Market Size	233.50	294.78	338.64
Total Local Production	13.32	15.45	17.30
Total Exports	2.78	3.82	4.28
Total Imports	222.96	283.15	325.62
Imports from the U.S.	95.86	111.59	124.98

Franchising (FRA)

	1998 $M	1999 $M	2000E $M
Total Market Size:	74	80	89
Sales by local firms in the DR:	2	3	5
Sales by local firms in foreign markets:	N/A	N/A	1
Sales by Foreign firms:	72	77	85
Sales by U.S.-owned firms:	69	73	81

Automotive Parts and Services (APS)

	1998 $M	1999 $M	2000E $M
Total Market Size	148.0	158.8	171.4
Total Local Production	2.0	2.1	2.2
Total Exports	N/A	N/A	N/A
Total Imports	146.0	156.7	169.2
Imports from the U.S.	58.9	62.7	67.7

Electrical Power Systems (ELP)

	1998 $M	1999 $M	2000E $M
Total Market Size	243	254	268
Total Local Production	60	56	60
Total Exports	57	52	52
Total Imports	240	250	260
Imports from the U.S.	120	126	133

Best Prospects for Agricultural Products

Wheat

	1998 MT ('000)	1999 MT ('000)	2000E MT ('000)
Total Market Size	211	298	307
Total Local Production	0	0	0
Total Exports	0	0	0
Total Imports	211	298	307
Imports from the U.S.	211	298	307

Soybean Meal

	1998 MT ('000)	1999 MT ('000)	2000E MT ('000)
Total Market Size	221	309	324
Total Local Production	0	0	0
Total Exports	0	0	0
Total Imports	221	309	324
Imports from the U.S.	221	309	324

Corn

	1998 MT ('000)	1999 MT ('000)	2000E MT ('000)
Total Market Size	757	936	894
Total Local Production	44	44	44
Total Exports	0	0	0
Total Imports	713	893	850
Imports from the U.S.	601	893	850

Rice

	1998 MT ('000)	1999 MT ('000)	2000E MT ('000)
Total Market Size	411	414	414
Total Local Production	340	340	340
Total Exports	0	0	0
Total Imports	71	74	74
Imports from the U.S.	71	74	74

Beef

	1998 MT ('000)	1999 MT ('000)	2000E MT ('000)
Total Market Size	84	88	83
Total Local Production	77	77	77
Total Exports	0	0	0
Total Imports	6	6	6
Imports from the U.S.	1	4	4

Fresh Apples and Other Deciduous Fruits

	1998 MT ('000)	1999 MT ('000)	2000E MT ('000)
Total Market Size	7	8	9
Total Local Production	.005	.005	.005
Total Exports	0	0	0
Total Imports	7	8	9
Imports from the U.S.	7	8	8

Wine

	1998 MT ('000)	1999 MT ('000)	2000E MT ('000)
Total Import Market	6,850	6,970	7,300
Total Local Production	0	0	0
Total Exports	0	0	0
Total Imports	6,850	6,970	7,300
Imports from the U.S.	1,147	1,170	1,200

Softwood and Treated Lumber

	1998 MT ('000)	1999 MT ('000)	2000E MT ('000)
Total Import Market	58.1	71.7	73.0
Total Local Production	N/A	N/A	N/A
Total Exports	0	0	0
Total Imports	58.1	71.7	73.0
Imports from the U.S.	43.6	53.8	55.0

Detail of Major Consumer-Oriented Products

	1997 MT ('000)	1998 MT ('000)	1999 MT ('000)
Snack Foods	11.8	10.4	13.1
Breakfast Cereals and Pancake Mix	3.5	4.1	4.2
Poultry Meat	9.2	12.8	6.0
Dairy Products	15.5	15.5	13.5
Fresh Fruit and Vegetables	9.7	11.1	13.1
Processed Fruits and Vegetables	8.1	10.9	12.2
Fruit and Vegetable Juices	3.8	6.0	5.8
Pet Food	1.4	2.2	3.4

Pine Lumber

	1997 MT ('000)	1998 MT ('000)	1999 MT ('000)
Total Import Market	97.0	100.0	110.0
Total Local Production	N/A	N/A	N/A
Total Exports	0	0	0
Total Imports	97.0	100.0	110.0
Imports from the U.S.	73.2	75.2	78.0

The above statistics are unofficial estimates.
Exchange rate: US$1.00 = RD$16.12
N/A - Not Available, E - Estimate
Note: MT ('000) = Thousand Metric Tons

Extracted from the U.S. Department of Commerce USA Trade 2001 Country Commercial Guide for Dominican Republic.

Import and Export Tips

- ## Regulations

Customs: Officials have shown a strong desire to modernize the various clearance and verification procedures. The new customs law will provide more continuity, transparency, and predictability within the customs process. Dominican Customs is also moving toward the implementation of the Customs Valuation Code set forth in the WTO agreement. This code establishes in principle the acceptance of the invoice value. The temporary entry of imports is permitted for exhibition or demonstration purposes. A security must be posted at the port of entry. There are no provisions for the temporary entry of agricultural products, which may be imported under bonded warehousing and for trans-shipment.

Tariffs: Little progress has been made to date in reducing tariff rates in accord with Uruguay Round commitments. The Dominican Republic continues to use discretionary licenses to protect domestic producers from foreign competition.

Import Taxes: Taxes and duties are calculated upon the ad valorem price. Generally three taxes on imports are not subject to exemptions: (1) a basic import tax of between 0 and 35 percent; the Dominican Congress has proposed to cap this tax at 20 percent although little progress has been made to date; (2) a luxury tax of 30 percent for items such as wine, beer, cigars, and cigarettes; the tax is between 10 and 60 percent for nonagricultural, "nonessential" goods; (3) an 8 percent tax on industrialized goods and services for processed agricultural goods and all nonagricultural goods. This tax—referred to as Impuesto de Transferencia a los Bienes Industrializados y Servicios (ITBIS)—is based on the cif price plus the amount paid for other taxes and duties. The Dominican Congress may raise the ITBIS rate to 12 percent. Many domestic products are exempt from ITBIS by law or practice, meaning it is sometimes another form of tariff.

Exchange Rate: The official exchange rate is set by the Central Bank. On July 2, 1998, the peso was devalued 9 percent from 14.02 pesos per dollar to 15.33 pesos per dollar. It has continued to devalue slowly since then with the most recent official rate (November 1999) set at 15.93 pesos per dollar. The unofficial rate has also devalued and is currently in the range of 15.90 pesos to the dollar. An October 1999 increase in the fee for purchasing foreign currency to 5 percent (up from 1.75 percent) has effectively further devalued the peso. Traditional exporters such as sugar, cocoa, and coffee producers, credit card companies, and airlines are still required by law to sell foreign exchange to the Central Bank at the official rate, but most businesses and individuals are free to carry out foreign exchange transactions through the commercial bank system. The market rate is influenced by Central Bank activities such as dollar sales and the use of its considerable regulatory discretion to "jawbone" banks.

• **Documentation**

Exports: In the area of commerce and industry, no export licenses are required. However, the sworn declaration of exports (Declaracion Jurada de Exportacion) should be presented at the port of departure. Free-trade-zone companies must only submit the certifications from the National Free Zone Council to CEDOPEX (a government organization) to declare and register exports. In the area of agriculture, CEDOPEX trusts the quantity and price that exporters declare on its export declaration form.

Imports: All imports, with the exception of free-trade-zone imports, require a consular invoice from a Dominican overseas consulate. There are no legal prohibitions to imports. The Secretariat of Agriculture protects domestic production by requiring discretionary import licenses for most agricultural products. Licenses are not required for most commerce and industry products. For each pharmaceutical trademark or product, a five-year license must be obtained at the Secretariat of State for Public Health. For agro-chemicals and fertilizers, an import license must be obtained from the Secretariat of State for Agriculture. Phytosanitary certificates from recognized authorities in the country of origin must accompany live plants and agricultural materials used in planting. Imports of animals normally require certificates of origin and other veterinarian documentation to assure disease-free status.

Labeling: ISO 9000 standards are required and followed. Products meeting U.S. standards should have little difficulty in meeting Dominican regulations. DIGENOR (Direccion General de Normas y Sistemas de Calidad) itself admits that it lacks the resources necessary to thoroughly enforce the regulations on marking, labeling, and quality controls.

Standards: The Dominican Republic tends to follow U.S. standards and requirements. The government has also agreed to replace arbitrary determinations of phytosanitary risk levels with scientific standards of measurements. The Dominican Republic has formally subscribed to ISO 9000. It is also a member of COPAN, the Panamerican Convention on Norms and Standards..

- **Payment**

  Terms: Usual terms are 90 to 120 days. The most common forms of payment are letters of credit, cash (most Dominican companies maintain dollar accounts abroad), and supplier credit when a trading relationship has been established.

  Currency Exchange: With some exceptions, the Central Bank uses the market-determined rate of exchange. Importers may obtain hard currency directly from commercial banks or from the Central Bank. By law, the Central Bank must receive all dollars resulting from exports of goods manufactured by non-free-trade-zone companies. However, in practice, the dollars are turned into the commercial banking system. For exporters of nontraditional products (i.e., manufactured goods, processed agricultural goods) and for those in the tourism sector, the dollars can be sold at the free-market rate rather than the Central Bank rate.

  Fund Transfer: The foreign investment law allows for remittance of all capital and profits.

MARKETING TIPS

⑤

Agents and Distributiors

For U.S. exporters wishing to establish an ongoing presence in the Dominican Republic's market without opening offices or a joint venture, the use of an agent or distributor is recommended. Dominican Law 173 (April 1966), which protects Dominican agents or distributors, is complicated and potentially costly. Legal counsel should be sought before appointing an agent or distributor. The U.S. Commercial Service (USCS) in Santo Domingo provides the following four services to help U.S. exporters find agents and distributors: (1) Agent/Distributor Service (ADS): for a $250.00 fee, USCS staff will conduct a search and report on firms that have agreed to consider a business relationship; (2) Gold Key Service: this service offers to survey potential partners, arrange appointments, and provide a bilingual trade aide-interpreter-secretary. The fee is $300 for the first day and $200 for each additional day; (3) Expo USA is an exhibition of U.S. firms seeking agents, representatives, distributors, licensees, and franchises in the Dominican Republic and Haiti; (4) CaribExpo is an exhibition of U.S. goods and services for U.S. firms seeking agents, representatives, distributors, licensees, and franchises in the Caribbean.

Establishing an Office

1. Articles of incorporation, signed by company founders, are the basic document of Dominican companies.

2. A certification from the Trademark Department at the Secretariat of Industry and Commerce should be obtained for the use of a trademark in the country.

3. Issued shares must be fully subscribed and paid. The founder must make a sworn declaration of receipt of the payments before a notary public.

4. Founders must prepare a written list of the initial shareholders. The list includes the names, personal circumstances, residences, number of shares, and price of shares for each shareholder.

5. Payment of the capitalization tax should be made at the Department of Internal Revenue (Direccion General de Impuestos Internos).

6. A first shareholders meeting must be held. A written list of shareholders in attendance is prepared. The articles of incorporation and the declaration made to the notary are formally approved. If share payments in kind are involved, an inventory and estimate are approved, and an appraiser is appointed to verify the estimate. The board of directors and officers of the company are elected. If no payments in kind are involved, the shareholders authorize the deposit of documents and the publication of a notice announcing the company's formation.

7. When payments in kind are made for shares, a second shareholders meeting must be held not earlier than five days after the first. At this meeting, the appraiser's report is approved.

8. The articles of incorporation, the list of shareholders, and the minutes of the first (and second) shareholders meetings are registered at the Civil Registry (Oficialia Civil). Evidence that the capitalization tax has been paid must be presented and filed.

9. An authorization for the deposit of documents is required from the Gift and Estate Tax Section of the Income Tax Department (la Seccion de Impuestos a la Propiedad y Obsequios del Departamento de La Direccion General de Impuestos Internos). Internal Revenue stamps a copy of the articles of incorporation; the list of shareholders must accompany this request.

10. The Civil and Commercial Court of First Instance (Corte Civil y Comercial de Primera Instancia) and the Justices of Peace (Juzgados de Paz), having jurisdiction over the domicile of the company and any of its branches, must receive the following documents: the articles of incorporation, the list of shareholders, a copy of the receipt of payment of the capitalization tax, an abstract of the sworn

declaration made to the notary, the list of shareholders present at the shareholders meeting(s) together with the resolutions adopted, and the letter of approval from the Income Tax Department.

11. A notice of formation of the company containing the required information must be published in a general circulation newspaper.

12. Prior to commencing operations, the company must obtain an authorization to start business and, in the case of an industrial operation, obtain a certificate of industrial registration from the Secretariat of State for Industry and Commerce (Secretaria de Estado de Industria y Comercio). Prior to commencing operations, the company must also register the name of the company in the Business Registry (Registro Mercantil) maintained by the Official Chamber of Commerce, Agriculture, and Industry.

Distribution and Sales Channels

U.S. exporters typically use local distributors, a wholly-owned subsidiary, joint-venture partners, or Dominican importers and wholesalers with their own retail outlets. A distribution agreement is not required for any of these methods.

Direct Marketing

Low-cost, locally produced services have had some success in direct marketing. Avon, Jafra, and Amway have established successful, foreign-owned organizations.

Leasing/Joint Ventures

Joint venture and licensing activity is not uncommon. Legal counsel is recommended for such ventures to minimize potential conflicts, unexpected taxes, withholding expenses on royalties and contributions to capital, and related aspects of these ventures.

Franchising

Franchising is a new and rapidly growing sector. A large number of fast-food chains are in operation, as are franchises such as Radio Shack, GNC Vitamin, Alphagraphics, Sir Speedy, Dry Clean USA, Mr. Movies, Ethan Allen, Meineke Mufflers, Benetton, Liz Claiborne, and Versace. Dominican entrepreneurs are looking toward services franchises such as printing and auto service as a growth sector.

Advertising and Promotion

Businesses advertise through newspapers, television, and radio. For some products, television and radio advertisements are preferred because of high illiteracy rates. Local exhibition and trade promotion shows offer many benefits, and specialized expositions have flourished. The U.S. Embassy's Commercial Service, Santo Domingo, stages major regional exhibitions of U.S. products and services. See **Contacts.**

Selling Factors

Dominicans often prefer to actually see a product. Strong after-sales service is increasingly important. Dominicans often rely on networking and close personal relationships. It is thus necessary for local agents, distributors, or direct, in-country operations to make and sustain such contacts.

Selling to the Government

With some exceptions, foreign individuals or firms must be associated with Dominican or "mixed capital" enterprises to either bid on Dominican government-funded projects or execute them. Many direct opportunities for foreign bidders exist when project financing is from multilateral banks or foreign government aid sources, where the bidding process is open and transparent, and when payment is guaranteed by the outside sources. The Dominican government's creditworthy reputation has been suspect; payment disputes and irregularities in public contracting have not been uncommon. Since August 1996, the Fernandez administration has had some success in improving on such areas.

Pricing

The market is price sensitive, and Dominicans are often familiar with U.S. pricing practices. Successful retail outlets now cater to more affluent and sophisticated buyers, who tend to concentrate on quality and service support.

Customer Support

The concepts of service and customer support are still developing, but Dominican customers increasingly demand consistent, quality service. Several companies with good reputations for service and support are able to maintain sales without discounting.

Intellectual Property Rights (IPR)

Protection and enforcement are weak. The Office of the U.S. Trade Representative upgraded the Dominican Republic to the Priority Watch List in 1998. This status was maintained in 1999. Recently, the Dominican government has taken some steps, including several seizures of pirated goods. The U.S. Embassy also has successfully helped to resolve several IPR infringement cases. Products should be registered at the Legal Department of the Secretariat of State for Industry and Commerce. If approved, further processing should be done through a lawyer, and a notice should be published in a local newspaper. The Dominican Republic is a member of the World Trade Organization and signatory of both the Berne and Paris Conventions on Copyrights and Patents and Trademarks.

Attorney

The assistance of a lawyer is recommended to establish operations and to provide advice on doing business. See **Contacts** for a list of lawyers known to have dealt with U.S. businesses.

FOREIGN INVESTMENT
6

Openness: The foreign investment law of 1995 allows unlimited foreign investment in nearly all sectors of the economy. The Office for Investment Promotion (OPI), established in 1997, is now an important contact for potential investors. The country's free trade zones provide 100 percent exemption on all taxes, duties, charges, and fees affecting production and export activities in the zones for a period of 15 or 25 years. The zones are administered by the Free Trade Zone National Council (CNZF in its Spanish acronym). See **Contacts.**

Regulatory System: Red tape and the efficient enforcement of existing laws are still problems. However, during the last few years, the government has carried out a major reform effort to improve the transparency and effectiveness of the laws affecting competition. Legislation has been passed to update customs regulations, the labor code, and major elements of the tax laws. A telecommunications law was passed in May 1998. Furthermore, major legislative proposals are still pending in the Congress. The laws would pertain to the financial sector, the electricity sector, and various areas of commercial law, including industrial property.

Investment Agreements: The U.S. and the Dominican Republic do not have a bilateral investment agreement. The Dominican Republic is a member of the World Trade Organization. The ratification of a Central American–Dominican Republic Free Trade Area is expected, as is an agreement with CARICOM. At the Second Hemispheric Summit in Santiago, Chile, in 1998, the Dominican Republic committed itself to establishing a free-trade agreement for the hemisphere by the year 2005.

Trade Zones and Free Ports: Free trade zones are regulated by Law Number 8-90. This legislation is managed by the Free Trade Zone National Council (CNZF in its Spanish acronym), which is a joint private sector–government body. Free-trade-zone companies receive 100 percent exemption on all taxes, duties, charges, and fees affecting production and export activities in the zones. These incentives are good for 15 years. In zones near the Dominican–Haiti border, the incentives are good for 25 years. The CNZF may extend the time limits on these incentives. The free foreign exchange market handles hard currency flows from the free trade zones. Foreign and Dominican firms have the same investment opportunities by law and in practice. The CNZF reports a total cumulative investment of approximately US$ 735 million by the end of 1997. Of this investment, 30 percent is domestic. Half of all foreign investment (50 percent) came from the U.S., followed by investments from Korea and Taiwan. In comparison with firms operating outside the zones, firms operating in the free trade zones tend to have far fewer bureaucratic and legal problems. See **Contacts for CNZF Information.**

Performance Requirements/Incentives: There are few performance requirements and, outside the free trade zone, few incentives.

Capital Markets and Investment: The GOG encourages foreign investment in the private sector. The largest banks are no longer state controlled: Ghana Commercial Bank and SSB ($30 million and $80 million worth, respectively), but financing is still limited in scope. New regulatory policies are expected to enhance growth.

Private Ownership: Foreign investors are only somewhat restricted. Domestic investors have a wider range of enterprise possibilities. Foreign investment is not permitted in the areas that would affect the public health or the environment.

Investment is also not allowed in areas related to national defense or security production without authorization from the office of the president.

Expropriation and Compensation: A number of U.S. investors have outstanding disputes with the Dominican government. Compensation payment has been extremely difficult to receive, even when the government or a Dominican court has recognized the U.S. investor's claim.

OPIC and Investment Insurance: OPIC is active with both insurance and loan programs in the Dominican Republic. The Dominican government is a party to the Multilateral Investment Guarantee Agency (MIGA) Agreement.

Dispute Settlement: The government generally refuses to engage in international commercial arbitration or to negotiate a settlement directly with foreign firms. Rather, commercial disputes must be settled in the courts of the Dominican Republic. U.S. firms bound by the Foreign Corrupt Practices Act have particular difficulty defending their interests in court. Both free-trade-zone and non-free-trade-zone companies face dispute resolution problems. Although not specified in law, the government can take land without compensation.

FINANCE 7

Commercial banks, mortgage banks, development banks, and savings and loan associations make up the country's financial system. The Central Bank regulates the money supply and controls official foreign exchange reserves. There is no deposit insurance at Dominican financial institutions. However, in 1996, new management at the Central Bank declared ad hoc that it would guarantee the funds of all depositors. The government has begun to modernize the Dominican financial system, with the support of multilateral organizations such as the World Bank, the International Monetary Fund, and the Inter-American Development Bank. The government is also restructuring and revising the operations of Superintendencia de Bancos, the government office in charge of supervising banking operations. The project's goal is to maintain better control and supervision of the new financial regulations.

Export Financing: The U.S. Export-Import Bank and OPIC financing may be available to the U.S. private sector. Local financing is generally not available to foreign investors.

Project Financing: Commercial banks are the main formal sources of private-sector financing. Most commercial lending is in the form of short-term lines of credit. Private and public development banks offer medium- and long-term loans to finance projects in priority sectors (agriculture, tourism, industry, services, and transportation). Finance companies (financieras) provide short- and medium-term loans to commercial and industrial sectors. These companies provide loans when commercial banks are unable or reluctant to do so. Financing is available for specific projects from the Inter-American Development Bank, the World Bank, and OPIC. Section 936 financing from Puerto Rico is also available. The Inter-American Development Bank (IDB) provides funding primarily to public sector entities for the design and execution of projects. The International Bank for Reconstruction and Development (IBRD), a member of the World Bank Group, gives long-term loans at market-related rates.

COMMUNICATIONS ⑧

Phone

The country's telecommunications systems are among the most advanced in Latin America. Codetel, Tricom, and All American Cables and Radio are the competing firms. Services include direct distance dialing, international direct distance dialing, line 800, electronic mail, telenet, cellular mobile phones, facsimile, national paging services, and Internet services. Two private firms provide local service. Calls to the Dominican Republic can be dialed in the same manner as long-distance calls within the U.S. (1 + area code (809) + local number).

Internet

With several competing Internet service providers (ISPs), use of the Internet is rather well developed in the Dominican Republic.

Mail

The postal system is reasonably well developed although street names and numbers may not be well defined. Express mail international services are available between the Dominican Republic and the U.S.

TRANSPORTATION ⑨

Land

The country's road network is well developed by regional standards, and the government continues to invest in improvements. However, some roads and highways, particularly in rural areas, are in poor and dangerous condition. Over-the-road truckers belong to syndicates that regulate haulage prices, keeping prices artificially high.

Sea

The Dominican Republic has six ports: Santo Domingo, Haina, La Romana, Boca Chica, San Pedro de Macoris, and Porta Plata. There are modern port facilities in Santo Domingo and other major cities. Haina, located just outside the capital city, has a 2,600-foot-long,

35-foot draft wharf, a 40-ton container crane, and a 60-acre container yard. Transportation runs to more than a dozen U.S. ports on a weekly basis. A daily freight service runs to Puerto Rico. Since June 1998, a passenger-car ferry has shuttled between Santo Domingo and Mayaguez, Puerto Rico.

Air

The Dominican Republic has seven international airports. They are located in Santo Domingo (two), Puerto Plata, La Romana, Punta Cana, Santiago, and Barahona. An eighth, the Arroyo Barril Airport, is under construction in Samana. An international consortium, which includes U.S. participation, recently won a bid to upgrade and operate four of the airports.

WORK WEEK

Business Hours: 9.00 a.m. to 5.30 p.m., with lunch from 12.00 p.m. to 1.00 p.m. or from 1.00 p.m. to 2.00 p.m. Monday through Friday. Some companies also work on Saturday morning.

Bank Hours: 8.30 a.m. to 3.00 p.m. Monday through Friday.

Government Hours: 8.30 a.m. to 4.00 p.m. Monday through Friday.

HOLIDAYS 2001

New Year's Day, January 1
Day of the Epiphany, January 6
The Virgin of Altagracia, January 21
Duarte's Birthday, January 26
Dominican Independence, February 27
Good Friday, April 13
Labor Day, May 1
Election Day, May 16
Corpus Christ, June 22
Dominican Restoration Day, August 16
The Virgin of Mercies, September 24
Constitution Day, November 6
Christmas Day, December 25

Some holidays may be observed on different dates depending on the day of the week on which it falls. The U.S. Embassy will be closed on U.S. and Costa Rican holidays. It is recommended that business travelers do not schedule trips to Costa Rica immediately before or immediately after local or U.S. holidays.

BUSINESS TRAVEL

Business Customs

Many Dominican businesspeople speak English though Spanish is desirable. Normal business attire is the rule, and an exchange of business cards is the norm. Meetings often take place over lunch and, increasingly, over breakfast. Business appointments are typically required, but punctuality is not expected as it is in the U.S.

Travel Advisory and Visas

Visas are available at any Dominican consulate or at the Dominican Embassy in Washington. However, visas are not necessary. U.S. citizens may purchase a $10.00 tourist card at the airport either before departure in the U.S. or upon arrival in the Dominican Republic. There is also a Dominican departure tax of $10.00.

Currently, no travel advisories are in effect. Travelers should call the U.S. Department of State at (202) 647-5225 for up-to-date information.

Business Infrastructure

Entry Requirements (personal and professional goods): Personal baggage is free of duty. Temporary entry is permitted for exhibition or demonstration purposes.

Currency Exchange: An official exchange rate is used for traditional exports. A market-determined rate (RD$ 16.001 = US$ 1) is available from the Central Bank and from commercial banks. Recently, the Dominican peso has been declining steadily but slowly against the U.S. dollar.

Taxes: Import tax is 0 to 35 percent; luxury tax, 30 percent, 10 to 60 percent for nonagricultural, "nonessential" goods; ITBIS, a tax on industrialized goods and services for processed agricultural goods and all nonagricultural goods, 8 percent.

Labor Costs and Legislation: The Dominican Labor Code establishes policies and procedures for many aspects of employer–employee relationships, ranging from minimum wage levels, hours of work, overtime and vacation pay to severance pay, causes for termination, and union registration. Eighty percent of a foreign company's nonmanagement and non-administrative labor force must comprise Dominican nationals. The requirement applies to companies both in and out of the free trade zones. Twenty percent or more of the workers in a company may form a union. Before a union may enter into a collective bargaining agreement or call a strike, it must have the approval of 51 percent of the company's workers. Foreign employers have not been singled out when labor complaints are made.

Literacy: Age 15 and over can read and write. The literacy rate is 82.1 percent.

Travel Notes

The following travel notes have been supplied by the U.S. government. For the most recent general travel and consular information, see the U.S. Department of State travel publications or call the Traveler's Telephone Hotline at (202) 647-5225.

Security: Petty street crimes involving U.S. citizens occur infrequently. Normal precautions should be taken. Valuables left unattended on the beach, in parked cars, or in other public places are subject to theft.

Health Precautions: The Dominican government manages 146 public hospitals and health centers. These hospitals are not able to provide sufficient care to the country's eight million inhabitants. The private sector has been active in attempts to cope with the high demand for medical-care services. Current information on health matters may be obtained from the Centers for Disease Control and Prevention's international travelers' hotline at (404) 332-4559.

Embassy Assistance

To obtain additional and updated information on entry and exit requirements, travelers can contact the Consular Section of the Embassy of Dominican Republic at 1715 22nd Street, N.W., Washington, D.C. 20008; Tel: (202) 332-6280. Travelers may also contact the nearest Dominican Republic consulate. They are located in San Francisco, Miami, Jacksonville, Tampa, Boston, Chicago, New Orleans, New York, Philadelphia, San Juan, Puerto Rico, and Houston. Travelers should call the U.S. Department of State at (202) 647-5225 for current information.

CONTACTS
13

U.S. Embassy Trade-Related Contacts

U.S. Dept. of Commerce/Commercial Service Counselor
U.S. Embassy
Corner of Cesar Nicolas Penson and Leopoldo Navarro
Santo Domingo, Dom. Rep.
Tel: (809) 221-2171 ext. 356
Fax: (809) 688-4838

U.S. Dept. of Agriculture/Foreign Agricultural Service
U.S. Embassy
Corner of Cesar Nicolas Penson and Leopoldo Navarro
Santo Domingo, Dom. Rep.
Tel: (809) 688-8090
Fax: (809) 685-4743

Dominican Republic Government Offices

Secretaria De Estado De Industria Y Comercio
Ave. Mexico
Edificio Gubernamental
Juan Pablo Duarte, Piso 7
Santo Domingo, Dom. Rep.
Tel: (809) 688-2449;
685-5171
Fax: (809) 686-1973
(Secretariat of State for Industry and Commerce)
E-mail: ind.comercio@codetel.net.do
Web site: http://www.seic.gov.do

Secretaria De Estado De Agricultura
Secretary of State for Agriculture
Kilometro 6 1/2
Autopista Duarte
Jardines Del Norte
Santo Domingo, Dom. Rep.
Tel: (809) 547-3888
Fax: (809) 549-3907
(Secretariat of State for Agriculture)

Direccion General de Aduanas
Ave. Mexico
Santo Domingo, Dom. Rep.
Tel: (809) 688-7070
Fax: (809) 687-3486
(Customs Office)
E-mail: aduana.dga@codetel.net.do

Instituto de Estabilizacion de Precios (INESPRE)
Plaza Independencia
Santo Domingo, Dom. Rep.
Tel: (809) 530-0871
Fax : (809) 530-0343
(Price Stabilization Institute)

Corporacion De Empresas Estatales
Ave. Winston Churchill
Santo Domingo, Dom. Rep.
Tel: (809) 535-4291
Fax: (809) 533-5522
(Corporation of Government-Owned Enterprises)

Instituto Azucarero Dominicano
Ave. Winston Churchill No. 606
Santo Domingo, Dom. Rep.
Tel: (809) 532-9226
Fax: (809) 533-2402
(Dominican Sugar Institute)

Patronato Nacional De Ganaderos
Ciudad Ganadera
Santo Domingo, Dom. Rep.
Tel: (809) 535-7165
Fax: (809) 535-7167
(National Livestock Patronage)

Instituto Interamericano De Ciencias Agricolas (IICA)
Republica del Labano
Centro De Los Heroes
Santo Domingo, Dom. Rep.
Tel: (809) 533-2797
Fax: (809) 532-1253
(Interamerican Institute for Agricultural Sciences)

Banco Agricola
Ave. Independencia
Santo Domingo, Dom. Rep.
(Development Bank)
Tel: (809) 535-8088
Fax: (809) 532-4645
(Dominican Private Enterprise Council)
E-mail: bagricola.refor@net.do

Fundacion Dominicana De Desarrollo
Mercedes No. 4, Zona Colonial
Santo Domingo, Dom. Rep.
Tel: (809) 688-8101
Fax: (809) 686-0430
(Dominican Development Foundation)

Fundacion De Desarrollo Agropecuario, Inc. (FDA)
Jose A. Soler 50
Santo Domingo, Dom. Rep.
Tel: (809) 544-0616
Fax: (809) 544-4727
(Agricultural and Livestock Development Foundation)

Consejo Nacional de Zonas Francas
Leopoldo Navarro No. 61
Edif. San Rafael, piso no. 5
Santo Domingo, D.R.
Tel: (809) 686-8077
Fax: (809) 686-8079; 688-0236
Contact: Lic. Gabriel Castro Gonzalez, Executive Director

Chambers of Commerce

Camara De Comercio Y Produccion Del Distrito Nacional
Arzobispo Nouel No. 206
Santo Domingo, Dom. Rep.
Tel: (809) 682-2688
Fax: (809) 685-2228
(Santo Domingo Chamber of Commerce)
Web site: http://www.ccpsd.org.do

Camara Americana De Comercio De La Republica Dominicana
Ave. Winston Churchill Esq. Luis F. Thomen
Torre BHD, 4to. Piso
Santo Domingo, Dom. Rep.
Tel: (809) 544-2222
Fax: (809) 544-0502
(American Chamber of Commerce of the D.R.)
E-mail: amcham@codetel.net.do

Country Trade Associations or Industry Associations in Key Sectors

Junta Agroempresarial Dominicana (JAD)
Euclides De Morillo No. 51, Arroyo Hondo
Santo Domingo, Dom. Rep.
Tel: (809) 563-6178
Fax: (809) 566-7722
(Dominican Agribusiness Council)
E-mail: jad@codetel.net.do

Asociacion Nacional De Importadores
Roberto Pastoriza No. 16
Condominio Diandi XIII
Santo Domingo, Dom. Rep.
Tel: (809) 562-6909
Fax: (809) 541-2574
(Dominican Importers' Association)

Asociacion Dominicana De Exportadores (Adoexpo)
Winston Churchill No. 5
Santo Domingo, Dom. Rep.
Tel: (809) 532-6779
Fax: (809) 532-1926
(Dominican Exporters' Association)

Asociacion de Industrias de la Republica Dominicana
Calle Virgilio Diaz O. No. 54, Ens. Julieta
Santo Domingo, Dom. Rep.
Tel: (809) 562-9443
Fax: (809) 562-9368
(Association of Industries of the Dominican Republic)
E-mail: aird@codetel.net.do

Consejo Nacional De La Empresa Privada
Ave. Abraham Lincoln Esq. John F. Kennedy
Santo Domingo, Dom. Rep.
Tel: (809) 562-1666
Fax: (809) 540-5502
(Dominican Private Enterprise Council)

Fundacion Dominicana De Desarrollo
Mercedes No. 4, Zona Colonial
Santo Domingo, Dom. Rep.
Tel: (809) 688-8101
Fax: (809) 686-0430
(Dominican Development Foundation)

Fundacion De Desarrollo Agropecuario, Inc.
  (FDA)
Jose A. Soler 50
Santo Domingo, Dom. Rep.
Tel: (809) 544-0616
Fax: (809) 544-4727
(Agricultural and Livestock Development
  Foundation)

Country Market Research Firms

Ecocaribe, S.A.
Av. John F. Kennedy Esq. Lope De Vega
Edif. Scotiabank
Santo Domingo, Dom. Rep.
Tel: (809) 541-1090
Fax: (809) 567-7661
E-mail: ecocarib@tricom.net

Proinversion
Ave. Tiradentes with Gustavo Mejia Ricart
Santo Domingo, Dom. Rep.
Tel: (809) 562-7666 and 562-6212
Fax: (809) 562-4833

Sistemas Mercadologicos, S.A.
Ave. Romulo Betancourt No. 1302
Santo Domingo, Dom. Rep.
Tel: (809) 532-5769
Fax: (809) 532-0723
E-mail: a.asencio@codetel.net.do

Read and Associates
San Martin De Porres No. 8-b, Naco
Santo Domingo, Dom. Rep.
Tel: (809) 566-4157
Fax: (809) 562-4321
E-mail: read.asocf@codetel.net.do

Market Probe
Av. Bolivar Esq. Churchill
Edificio Bienvenida (2nd floor)
Santo Domingo, Dom. Rep.
Tel: (809) 535-0280
Fax: (809) 535-0250

Gallup Dominincana
Winston Churchill Esq. Charles Summer
Edif. Plaza Paraiso, Apt. 201
Santo Domingo, Dom. Rep.
Tel: (809) 567-5321
Fax: (809) 544-2503
E-mail: gallup@tricom.net

Despradel & Asociados, S.A. (DASA)
Av. Abraham Lincoln esq. John F. Kennedy
Edificio Ambar
Santo Domingo, Dom. Rep.
Tel: (809) 540-4540
Fax: (809) 541-0221
E-mail: c.despradel@codetel.net.do

Centro de Investigacion y Asesoria
  Empresarial, C. por A.
(CIMAECA)
Calle Alvarez Guzman No. 24, Herrera
Santo Domingo, Dom. Rep.
Tel.: (809) 537-8099
Fax: (809) 537-8099

Country Commercial Banks

ComCitibank, N.A.
Ave. John F. Kennedy No. 1 Esq. San Martin
Santo Domingo, Dom. Rep.
Tel: (809) 566-5611
Fax: (809) 685-7535

The Bank of Nova Scotia
Ave. John F. Kennedy Esq. Lope De Vega
Ens. Naco
Santo Domingo, Dom. Rep.
Tel: (809) 544-1700
Fax: (809) 567-5732

Banco Comercial BHD, S.A.
Luis F. Thomen Esq. Winston Churchill
Torre BHD
Santo Domingo, Dom. Rep.
Tel: (809) 243-3232
Fax: (809) 541-4949
Web site: http://www.bhd.com.do

Banco De Reservas De La Republica Dominicana
Avenida Winston Churchil
Esq. Porfirio Herrera
Santo Domingo, Dom. Rep.
Tel: (809) 227-2277
Fax: (809) 562-8151
E-mail: hazouri@brrd.com

Banco Dominicano Del Progreso, S.A.
Ave. John F. Kennedy No. 3, Miraflores
Santo Domingo, Dom. Rep.
Tel: (809) 563-3233
Fax: (809) 563-2455

Banco Gerencial Y Fiduciario Dominicano, S.A.
Ave. 27 De Febrero No. 50, El Vergel
Santo Domingo, Dom. Rep.
Tel: (809) 473-9400
Fax: (809) 473-2531

Banco Intercontinental, S.A.
Ave. 27 de Febrero esq. Winston Churchill
Santo Domingo, Dom. Rep.
Tel: (809) 535-5500/02
Fax: (809) 544-1298

Banco Mercantil, S.A.
Avenida Roberto Pastoriza 303
Gazcue
Santo Domingo, Dom. Rep.
Tel: (809) 221-7151
Fax: (809) 549-6509
Web site: http://www.mercantil.com.do

Banco Metropolitano, S.A.
Ave. Lope De Vega Esq. Gustavo Mejia Ricart
Edif. Goico Castro, Ens. Naco
Santo Domingo, Dom. Rep.
Tel: (809) 562-4242
Fax: (809) 540-1566
E-mail: bmetropolitan@codetel.net.do

Banco Nacional de Credito, S. A.
Ave. John F. Kennedy esq. Ave. Tiradentes
Santo Domingo, Dom. Rep.
Tel: (809) 540-4441
Fax: (809) 685-8588
Web site: http://www.bancredito.com

Banco Global
Ave. Romulo Betancourt No. 1
Santo Domingo, Dom. Rep.
Tel: (809) 532-3000
Fax: (809) 535-7070

Banco Popular Dominicano
Av. John F. Kennedy No. 20
Esq. Maximo Gomez, Torre Popular
11avo. Piso
Santo Domingo, Dom. Rep.
Tel: (809) 544-5900
Fax: (809) 544-5999

Multilateral Development Bank Offices in Country

Interamerican Development Bank (IDB)
Banco Interamericano de Desarrollo
Ave. Winston Churchill esq. Luis F. Thomen
Edificio BHD
Santo Domingo, Dom. Rep.
Tel: (809) 562-6400; 562-1547
Fax: (809) 562-2607

U.S. Trade-Related Offices

Multilateral Development Bank Office
MLDA-USA Trade Center Ronald Reagan
  Building
14th and Constitution, NW
Washington, DC 20007
Tel: (202) 482-3399
Fax: (202) 482-3414

TPCC Trade Information Center
Tel: (800) USA-TRADE
(800-872-8723)

U.S. Department of Agriculture
Foreign Agriculture Service
Trade Assistance and Promotion Office
Tel: (202) 720-7420

List of Major Newspapers and Publishers

Editora El Listin Diario
Mr. Adolfo Rodriguez Valenzuela,
  International Editor
Calle Paseo De Los Periodistas No. 52
Ensanche Miraflores
Santo Domingo, Dom. Rep.
Tel: (809) 686-6688 ext. 2082
Fax: (809) 686-8951
E-mail: el.dinero@listin.com.do

Editora Ultima Hora (part of the Listin Diario group)
Mr. Jose Mercedes Feliz
Economic Editor
Calle Paseo De Los Periodistas No. 52
Ensanche Miraflores
Santo Domingo, Dom. Rep.
Tel: (809) 688-3361 ext. 2232
Fax: (809) 688-3019

Periodico Hoy
Mr. Mario Mendez, Economic Editor
Ave. San Martin No. 236
Ensanche La Fe
Santo Domingo, Dom. Rep.
Tel: (809) 567-5442; 566-1147; 541-5967
  ext. 254
Fax: (809) 683-6803
E-mail: periodico.hoy@codetel.net.do

Periodico El Nacional (part of the Periodico Hoy group)
Mr. Emilio Ortiz, Economic Editor
Av. San Martin No. 236
Santo Domingo, Dom. Rep.
Tel: (809) 565-5581 ext. 368
Fax: (809) 565-1336

Editora El Caribe
Mr. Javier Valdivia, Economic Editor
Autopista Duarte km. 7 1/2
Santo Domingo, Dom. Rep.
Tcl: (809) 566-8161; 566-0059 ext. 306
Fax: (809) 544-4003

Periodico El Siglo
Editora El Golfo, S.A.
Mr. Claudio Cabrera, Economic Editor
San Anton No. 2
Zona Industrial de Herrera
Santo Domingo, Dom. Rep.
Tel: (809) 530-1000 ext. 261 or 262
Fax: (809) 530-8412

Periodico El Nuevo Diario
Ms. Jaqueline Morrobel, Economic Editor
Av. Francia No. 41 esq. Rocco Cochia
Santo Domingo, Dom. Rep.
Tel: (809) 687-7450; 686-1541
Fax: (809) 687-3205

Lawyers Known to Have Dealt with U.S. Business Enterprises

Aristy & Asociados
Esther Aristy, Principal Attorney
Avenida Anacaona No. 31
Edificio Maria Jesus 2c
Santo Domingo, Dom. Rep.
Tel: (809) 533-8728
Fax: (809) 533-2020
E-mail: e.aristy.asoc@codetel.net.do

Mejia-Ricart y Asociados
Mr. Marcio Mejia-Ricart
Ave. Bolivar No. 74
Gazcue
Santo Domingo, Dom. Rep.
Tel: (809) 687-3353; 685-8446
Fax: (809) 682-0791

Oficina de Abogados Dr. Carlos Cornielle
Lic. Carlos Radhames Cornielle M.
Ave. Pedro Henriquez Urena No. 55
Esq. Maximo Cabral, Gazcue
Santo Domingo, Dom. Rep.
Tel: (809) 688-3818; 689-3624
Fax: (809) 685-3096
E-mail: c.cornielle@codetel.net.do

Grisolia & Bobadilla
Mr. Andres E. Bobadilla
Av. John F. Kennedy and Lope De Vega
Edif. Bank of Nova Scotia
Santo Domingo, Dom. Rep.
Tel: (809) 562-6100
Fax: (809) 562-7609

Headrick, Rizik, Alvarez Y Fernandez
Mr. William Headrick
Elvira De Mendoza No. 51
Zona Universitaria
Santo Domingo, Dom. Rep.
Tel: (809) 686-0404; 685-4137; 8
Fax: (809) 685-2936
E-mail: hraf@codetel.net.do

Pellerano & Herrera
Mr. Juan Manuel Pellerano Gomez, President
Av. John F. Kennedy No. 10, Ens. Miraflores
Santo Domingo, Dom. Rep.
Tel: (809) 541-5200
Fax: (809) 567-0773
E-mail: lpellerano@codetel.net.do

Russin, Vecchi & Heredia Bonetti
Dr. Luis Heredia Bonetti, Owner and Manager
El Recodo No. 2
Edif. Monte Mirador, 3er. Piso
Bella VistaSanto Domingo, Dom. Rep.
Tel: (809) 535-9511
Fax: (809) 535-6649/7517
E-mail: hbonetti@rvhb.com

Dominex
Dr. Hugo J. Ramirez Risk
President
Calle La Cantera No. 10
Zona Universitaria
P.O. Box 22319
Santo Domingo, Dom. Rep.
Tel: (809) 535-5540
Fax: (809) 533-3215
E-mail: dominex@codetel.net.do

Steel Hector & Davis Llp.
Alejandro Pena Prieto
Managing Partner
Ave. Pedro Henriquez Ureña No. 157
Santo Domingo, Dom. Rep.
Tel: (809) 472-4900
Fax: (809) 472-4999
E-mail: apena@steelhector.com

List of Banks That Maintain Correspondent U.S. Banking Arrangements

Banco Comercial BHD, S.A.
Luis F. Thomen Esq. Winston Churchill
Torre BHD
Santo Domingo, Dom. Rep.
Tel: (809) 243-3232
Fax: (809) 541-4949
Web site: http://www.bhd.com.do

Banco de Reservas de La Republica Dominicana
Avenida Winston Churchill
Esq. Porfirio Herrera
Santo Domingo, Dom. Rep.
Tel: (809) 227-2277
Fax: (809) 562-8151
E-mail: mhazouri@brrd.com

Banco Gerencial & Fiduciario Dominicano, S.A.
Ave. 27 De Febrero No. 50, El Vergel
Santo Domingo, Dom. Rep.
Tel: (809) 473-9400
Fax: (809) 473-2531

Banco Intercontinental, S.A.
Ave. 27 de Febrero Esq.Winston Churchill
Santo Domingo, Dom. Rep.
Tel: (809) 545-5500; 02
Fax: (809) 544-1298

Banco Mercantil, S.A.
Roberto Pastoriza No. 303
Santo Domingo, Dom. Rep.
Tel: (809) 567-4444
Fax: (809) 549-6509
Web site: http://www.mercantil.com.do

Banco Metropolitano, S.A.
Ave. Lope De Vega Esq. Gustavo Mejia Ricart
Edif. Goico Castro, Ens. Naco
Santo Domingo, Dom. Rep.
Tel: (809) 562-4242
Fax: (809) 540-1566
E-mail: b.metropolitan@codetel.net.do

Banco Nacional de Credito
Ave. John F. Kennedy esq. Ave. Tiradentes
Santo Domingo, Dom. Rep.
Tel: (809) 540-4441
Fax: (809) 685-8588
Web site: http://www.bancredito.com

Banco Popular Dominicano
Av. John F. Kennedy No. 20
Esq. Maximo Gomez, Torre Popular
11avo. Piso
Santo Domingo, Dom. Rep.
Tel: (809) 544-5900
Fax: (809) 544-5999

Citibank, N.A.
Ave. John F. Kennedy No. 1 Esq. San Martin
Santo Domingo, Dom. Rep.
Tel: (809) 566-5611
Fax: (809) 685-7535

The Bank of Nova Scotia
Ave. John F. Kennedy Esq. Lope De Vega
Ens. Naco
Santo Domingo, Dom. Rep.
Tel: (809) 544-1700
Fax: (809) 567-5732

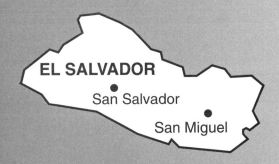

EL SALVADOR
• San Salvador
• San Miguel

EL SALVADOR

TRADE AND BUSINESS GUIDE

PROFILE

Official Name:	Republic of El Salvador
Official Languages:	Spanish, with English, Nahua
Population:	6,122,515 (2000 est)
Population Growth:	1.87% (2000 est)
Age Structure:	0–14 years: 38%, 15–64 years: 57%, 65 years and over: 5% (2000 est)
Location:	Middle America, bordering the North Pacific Ocean between Guatemala and Honduras
Area:	21,040 square kilometers. Slightly smaller than Massachusetts
Type of Government:	Republic with president (by popular vote for five-year terms) and unicameral Legislative Assembly (by popular vote for three-year terms)
Head of State:	President Francisco Flores, Perez
Cabinet:	Council of Ministers elections
Religion:	Roman Catholic 75%, Protestant N/A
Major Cities:	Capital: San Salvador (422,570), Santa Ana (202,337), San Miguel (182,817), Nueva San Salvador (116,575)
Climate:	Tropical. Rainy season is May to October, and dry season is November to April
Time:	The entire country is -6 GMT (Greenwich Mean Time), one hour behind EST (Eastern Standard Time). El Salvador does not follow daylight savings time
GDP:	Purchasing power parity (PPP): $18.1 billion (1999 est); real growth rate: 2.2% (1999 est); per capita PPP: $3,100 (1999 est); composition by sector: agricultural= 12%, industry= 22%, services= 66% (1999 est)
Currency:	1 Salvadoran colon (C) = 100 centavos
Exchange Rate:	US$ 1 = 8.75 Salvadoran colons (2000 est), 8.70 (1999 est), 8.76 (1998 est)
Weights & Measure:	Metric system
Natural Resources:	Hydropower, geothermal power, petroleum
Total Trade:	In billions US$ [exports (fob)/imports (cif)]: 1998 (2.45/3.96), 1999 (2.50/4.08), 2000 est (2.63/4.02)
Trade with U.S.:	In billions US$ [exports (fob)/imports (cif)] 1998 (1.45/2.03), 1999 (1.58/2.11), 2000 est (1.65/2.16)

Major Trade Partners:	Imports: United States, Guatemala, Mexico, Panama, Venezuela, Japan. Exports: United States, Guatemala, Germany, Costa Rica, Honduras
Membership:	IADB, IBRD, IFC, IMF, MIGA, OAS, UN, UNCTAD, WIPO, and WTO. See membership description in appendix

Sources: CIA World Fact Book, Central Bank, United Nations World Statistics, U.S. Department of Commerce, U.S. Department of State.

POLITICAL OUTLOOK
②

Relationship with the U.S.

Bilateral relations between El Salvador and the U.S. are excellent. The FMLN (an ex-guerilla organization) has close relations with the U.S. government. About 1 million Salvadorans live in the U.S., which improves Salvadoran attitudes toward the U.S. El Salvador is expected to remain politically stable.

Influences on Business

Economic policies are market oriented, and moving toward privatization. See **Political Violence.**

Profile

System: El Salvador has a presidency, an 84-member unicameral Legislative Assembly, and a Council of Ministers. Major political parties are the National Republican Alliance (ARENA, with the president and 28 Congress seats), the Farabundo Marti National Liberation Front (FMLN, 27 seats), and the National Conciliation Party (PCN, 9 seats). Figures are based on the 2000 elections.

Schedule for Elections: Presidential elections are held every five years (last in March 1999). Next presidential election is scheduled to be held in March 2004. Legislative assembly elections are held every three years, and were last held in March 2000.

Major Parties: The National Republican Alliance (ARENA) party is right of center and has a slight majority. The FMLN is left of center and seeks a mixed economy with private enterprise and investment balanced by government regulation. This policy takes social interests more into account. Smaller parties include the far right National Conciliation party (PCN), the centrist Christian Democratic Party (PDC), and the leftist Democratic Convergence Party.

Political Violence: Since 1994, there have been few confirmed acts of political violence. Crime levels are generally high, but no political violence has been aimed at foreign investors, their businesses, or their property.

Corruption: Corruption has been a problem, but reform is in process.

ECONOMIC OUTLOOK ③

Trends

Positive factors for growth are a stable currency; growing international reserves; a low debt burden; continuing tariff reductions; streamlined customs procedures; and progress toward the privatization of telecommunications, energy distribution, and pension fund administration. The Government of El Salvador (GOES) is also making needed investments in infrastructure and social services. Structural, market-oriented reforms and continued political stability make El Salvador appealing to U.S. exporters and investors.

Major Growth Sectors

The financial sector is expected to grow at 9.4 percent according to the Central Bank. El Salvador's banks are expanding and are the largest of the five Central American nations. Industrial and retail are growing and are the largest sectors for the GDP. Thirty percent growth in credit for consumer goods and 10 percent growth in national consumption strengthen those two sectors. Structural problems and the weather of "El Nino" harm the agricultural sector, the third largest GDP sector. Nontraditional and maquila exports are expected to grow 25 percent.

Key Economic Indicators

Income, Production and Employment (millions of U.S. dollars unless otherwise indicated)			
	1998	1999	2000[1]
Nominal GDP	11,864	12,380	13,120
Real GDP Growth (pct)	3.4	2.6	3.5
GDP by Sector			
Agriculture	1,432	1,475	N/A
Manufacturing	2,629	2,760	N/A
Services	6,878	7,290	N/A
Government	800	848	N/A
Per Capita GDP (US$)[2]	1,968	2,025	2,096
Labor Force (millions)[3]	2,305	2,350	2,395
Unemployment Rate (pct)[4]	7.7	7.8	7.7

1. 2000 figures are central bank estimates based on August data. 2. Per capita growth based on 1992 census data. 3. Economically active population (i.e., all those over age 15). 4. Figures do not include underemployment.
Source: Bureau of Economic and Business Affairs; U.S. Department of State

- **Infrastructure**
  The infrastructure is adequate, except for the money-losing rail system, and telecommunications. Insufficient telecommunications has been one of the main obstacles to doing business, but it has been improving through new lines and expanding cell phone services. Infrastructure problems and weather conditions have interrupted power service, but backup power generators and power expansion have lessened power problems. See COMMUNICATIONS and TRANSPORTATION.

• Labor
El Salvador's workforce is estimated at 2.2 million, with 36 percent in agriculture, 21 percent in services, 18 percent in commerce, and 16 percent in manufacturing. Unemployment was officially 7.7 percent in 2000. The minimum wage in the commerce and industry sectors is 1,260 colones or US$ 144 per month. Underemployment is higher, but unmeasured. The labor pool is seen as hard working and trainable. Education levels are mainly low, so skilled, educated labor may be needed. Middle management is sometimes scarce, so foreigners are brought in for tasks. Construction contractors are sometimes short of skilled workers. Employees have the right to form associations and unions. Closed shops are illegal. Around 20 percent of the labor force belongs to unions or collective associations. Separate stages of collective bargaining, conciliation, and arbitration are required before a strike can be legally declared. See LABOR COSTS AND LEGISLATION.

Money and Prices
(annual percentage growth)

	1997	1998	1999[1]
Money Supply Growth (M2)	20.0	12.0	9.0
Consumer Price Inflation	2.0	4.2	4.0
Exchange Rate (Colon/US$)	8.75	8.75	8.75

1. 1999 figures are central bank estimates based on August data.
Source: Bureau of Economic and Business Affairs; U.S. Department of State

Balance of Payments and Trade
(millions of U.S. dollars unless otherwise indicated)

	1997	1998	1999[1]
Total Exports CIF[2]	2,425	2,446	2,400
Exports to U.S.[2]	1,312	1,454	1,555
Total Imports FOB[2]	3,740	3,959	4,150
Imports from U.S.[2]	1,975	2,028	2,150
Trade Balance	-1,315	-1,513	-1,750
Balance with U.S.	-663	-574	-595
External Public Debt	2,680	2,630	2,500
Fiscal Deficit/GDP (pct)	2.0	2.0	2.5
Current Account Deficit/GDP (pct)	-1.9	-0.7	-0.9
Debt Service PaymentsGDP (pct)	3.0	3.0	3.0
Gold and Foreign Exchange Reserves	1,462	1,765	1,840
Aid from U.S.	38.0	38.0	56.8
Aid from All Other Sources[3]	38.0	38.0	38.0

1. 1999 figures are all estimates based on most recent data available. 2. Including gross maquila.
3. Grants only; figures do not reflect NGO assistance and bilateral loan programs.
Source: Bureau of Economic and Business Affairs; U.S. Department of State

- **Balance of Payments**
  See KEY ECONOMIC INDICATORS. Total exports are expected to grow to $2.66 billion. Central Bank figures project a widening of the trade deficit. Some $1.45 billion in family remittances and export growth have more than offset the deficit. The Central Bank projected 17 percent increase in total exports and expects remittances to continue growing at 5 to 6 percent for the next two to four years. Nontraditional and maquila exports are expected to grow more than 15 percent and Reserves are projected to reach $1.94 billion by the end of 2000.

Government Influence on Business

The GOES has shifted from direct involvement in production to macroeconomic stabilizing and promoting private market-based investments. The budget is shifting from military spending to social spending. One third of the GOES budget goes to social development, including health, education, and public works. Tax collecting and tracking have improved. The value-added tax (VAT) was about 55 percent of total revenue in 2000, and income tax was about 30 percent. Import and excise taxes will contribute 13 percentage of total revenue in 2000. The budget deficit will be about 2.6 percent of GDP.

TRADE
④

Leading Imports and Exports

Imports: Raw materials, consumer goods, capital goods, fuels

Exports: Coffee, sugar, shrimp, textiles (maquila processing products)

Foreign Trade *(Exports and Imports in US$M)*			
	1998	1999	2000[1]
Total Exports FOB[2]	2,446	2,400	2,625
Exports to U.S.[2]	1,454	1,555	1,650
Total Imports CIF[2]	3,959	4,150	4,015
Imports from U.S.[2]	2,028	2,112	2,158

1. 1999 and 2000 figures are all estimates based on most recent data available. 2. Including gross maquila.
Source: U.S. Department of State

Best Prospects Analysis

Best Prospects for Nonagricultural Goods and Services

Automotive Parts and Service Equipment (APS) (US$M)

	1997	1998	1999
Total Imports	200	N/A	264
Imports from U.S.	80	N/A	100

In 1999, over $260 million worth of vehicles (new and used) were imported into El Salvador, with $100 million from the U.S. This sector is expected to register strong growth as the economy continues to grow. Vehicle fleet from two to three thousand used vehicles is projected to enter the country each month, almost all coming from the U.S. There is a high demand for replacement parts and service, and the market is not yet saturated.

Foods Processed (FOD) (US$M)

	1996	1997	1998	1999
Total Imports	174	234	N/A	281
Imports from U.S.	N/A	N/A	N/A	N/A

Imports of consumer-ready foods and food products increased to US$ 281 million in 1999. Mexican, Guatemalan and Costa Rican products compete against U.S. goods. An expansion of foreign chains and a consolidation of local and foreign supermarkets are expected to take place as the market grows. The U.S. has advantages of scale and creative merchandising.

Architecture and Construction and Engineering Services (ACE):
International development institutions have lent hundreds of millions of U.S. dollars for infrastructure projects in El Salvador. The GOES in 2000 had about US$ 310 million earmarked for infrastructure works. El Salvador is expected to receive US$ 1.6 billion out of US$ 8 billion in financial assistance promised by developed countries for post-Mitch reconstruction in Central America. In 2000, US$ 110 million from electric distributor sales were used to upgrade urban infrastructure. Factors encouraging growth include several major projects underway, tendencies to form joint ventures or subcontract out large parts of projects, and the good reputations of U.S. firms.

Telecommunications (TEL) (TES):
ANTEL, the phone company, is being privatized. Services and equipment will be needed by companies that buy a portion. Wireless and wired companies expect a growth market in services and equipment for U.S. and international suppliers of equipment, fiber optics, and internet. There are back orders for 400,000 phone lines, with an average wait of 6.2 years. An estimated 400,000 persons would also purchase lines if the wait times were reduced.

Environmental Technologies:
The GOES law requires environmental impact studies, with civil and penal penalties for violators. Ninety percent of rivers are contaminated, and cities have air pollution problems. Water delivery, water pollution control, solid waste treatment, sanitary landfills, air pollution controls, energy conservation, auto emission reduction and testing equipment all look promising.

The market was US$ 180 million in 1999 and has been growing rapidly after the 1998 environmental law went into effect and Presidential approval of environmental regulations in May 2000.

Electric Power Generation and Distribution Equipment (ELP):
The electric company, CEL, is being privatized. In 1998, U.S., Venezuelan, Chilean and Central American investors bought four distribution companies. In 1999, an American investor bought three thermal plants, which represent approximately 30 percent of the country's total generating capacity. The break up of CEL should create demand for generating equipment, transformers, wire-related computer hardware and services, financial services, and consulting services.

Plastic Materials and Resins (PMR):
As manufacturing, maquila, processing, and packaging industries grow, more plastics are needed for bags and containers. In 1996, El Salvador's 14th largest and 22nd largest imports by values were various grades of polyethylene.

Paper and Paperboard (PAP):
Almost all newsprint and paper for school and offices is imported. In 1999, imports of paper and paperboard or carton products were US$ 165 million. With increase in newspaper readership, advertising to compete for increased consumer spending is rising. As manufacturing, maquila, processing, and packaging industries grow, demand for paperboard for packaging is also increasing. Finished paper sales have a high-profit margin.

Best Prospects for Agricultural Products

Rice.
The local demand is estimated at 2.1 million quintales of rough rice. In 1997–1998, an estimated 60,000 metric tons of rough rice was needed. In 1999/2000, the Salvadoran Rice Millers Association (ASALBAR), estimated that approximately 50,000 was needed to fulfill local demand.

Cotton:
In 1999/2000, an estimated 27,500 metric tons of cotton was needed. The U.S. supplies almost all of El Salvador's cotton.

Soybean Meal:
El Salvador produces no soybean meal for itself. It is used mainly as poultry and livestock feed, so those markets create its growing demand. Commercial trade is growing at a rapid rate due to the high demand for poultry products.

Corn:
The annual imports of U.S. yellow corn average 150,000 metric tons and represent approximate 100 percent of local demand. It is used almost only as animal feed.

Wheat:
The annual imports of U.S. wheat average 160,000 metric tons. Wheat is the main agricultural commodity imported from the U.S.

The above statistics are unofficial estimates.
N/A - Not Available

Extracted from the U.S. Department of Commerce USA Trade 2001 Country Commercial Guide for El Salvador.

Import and Export Tips

• Regulations

Customs: El Salvador has signed the Agreement on Central American Tariffs and Duties, which regulates imports, exports, and regional trade. The "autoliquidation" customs procedure permits importers to declare themselves the valuation of the goods and the import duties to be paid. For tax purposes, the commercial invoice is typically used. Fifteen percent of autoliquidations are randomly rechecked. Customs assesses its own value when there are any doubts. For used cars, customs uses *NADA*, *Edmund's*, and the Truck Blue Book.

Tariffs: Tariffs range from 0 to 30 percent. Capital goods are 0 percent; intermediate goods, 5 percent; raw materials, 10 percent; final goods, 15 percent. A few other non-essential products including textiles, agricultural products, vehicles, are charged higher tariffs, that range from 15 to 30 percent. Tariffs are based on the Common Duty System (SAC) of the Central American Common Market (CACM). For investors in industrial activities, raw materials are imported duty free.

Import Taxes: A value-added tax (VAT) of 13 percent is added to the purchase price of all products except basic foods such as medicines, corn, rice, beans, and fluid milk. The VAT is applied each time the goods change hands, from producer to wholesaler to consumer. The tax rate is charged only against the additional value, including costs and profit margin.

Exchange Rate: The exchange rate has been informally pegged at 8.75 Salvadoran colons per dollar since 1994. Large inflows of dollars from Salvadorans working in the U.S. offset a significant trade deficit. At the end of September 1999, net international reserves at the Central Bank were approximately $1.8 billion, one of the highest levels in history.

• Documentation

Exports: All exporters must register in the Centro de Tramites de Exportacion (Export Procedures Center) of the Banco Central de Reserva. Exporters of certain products must also be registered: the Consejo Salvadoreno del Café (for coffee), the Centro de Desarrolllo Pesquero CENDEPESCA (for seafood), the Inspeccion de Productos de Origen Animal-IPOA (animal products), and the Direccion de Defensa Agropecuaria (for live animals). For export, all items must have: an export license, an application for export registry, a commercial invoice, and the authorization of the Ministry of Finance and the Ministry of Labor (for machinery and industrial equipment), or the Ministry of Agriculture (for some agricultural products). The iguana-export industry is regulated by CITES, which oversees endangered species trade. Some pre-Hispanic archaeological materials are restricted from export to the U.S.

Imports: Documents required for imported goods include an import license (only for animals, vegetables, and firearms), a commercial invoice, and a bill of lading, airway bill, or carta de porte. Goods from the Central American Region require only a customs form (Formulario Aduanero). Prohibited or restricted goods include weapons; drugs; books, booklets, budgets, emblems, posters of subversive political, economic, or social content; figures, statues, books, booklets, almanacs, magazines, or other materials of an obscene nature; movies contrary to ethics or good behavior; gambling items; nonstamped cigarette papers; coin-making tools or equipment; counterfeit money; tokens of metals or alloys usable for counterfeiting; coffee trees and coffee seeds for planting. The customs administrator decides on the spot whether an item is in one of the preceding categories. Before importing any of these items, check for exemptions and permits with the relevant GOES regulatory agency.

Labeling: Consumers typically look for U.S. standard marking on imports. The Law for the Protection of the Consumer requirements include (1) retailers must have prices either on the product packaging or in a visible place; (2) products sold by weight, volume, or measure must have that measure on its label; (3) labels on frozen or canned foods must have expiration dates; (4) pharmaceuticals must have ingredients, expiration dates, dosage, contraindications, risk, residual effects, and so on, on the label as per the Ministry of Health.

Standards: There is no legislation on standards usage. The National Council for Science and Technology (CONACYT) will develop international standards and norms for El Salvador. Multinational firms usually use ISO 9000 standards, but local companies usually do not.

- **Payment**

  Terms: Letters of credit are the minimum and recommended terms for all transactions. Usual credit terms of 90 to 120 days apply. See FINANCE

  Currency Exchange: Profits by foreign businesspeople may be repatriated freely. See BUSINESS INFRASTRUCTURE (CURRENCY EXCHANGE).

  Fund Transfer: Foreign businesses freely repatriate capital and bring in investment capital.

  Offshore Loans: No information is available at this time.

MARKETING TIPS

⑤

Agents and Distributors

U.S. firms usually use agents or distributors to sell in El Salvador. Information can be obtained by purchasing the Agent/Distributor Service (ADS) of the U.S. Department of Commerce District Office; contacting the Commercial or Agricultural Section of the embassy; or contacting the PRIDEX division of Fusades, a private trade-promotion organization. The Salvadoran Commercial Code defines extensively the role of representative agents and intermediary agents. The Commercial Code also gives justified causes to terminate, not modify, or not renew the contract. If the principal terminates, modifies, or does not extend representation without meeting any of the Article 398 conditions of the Commercial Code, the agent or distributor is entitled to various compensations. Disputes over these articles are to be resolved by a commercial court in the jurisdiction of the agent or distributor.

Establishing an Office

- Find a legal representative or lawyer.
- Request a permit to operate in El Salvador from the Superintendencia de Empresas y Sociedades Mercantiles.
- Find out the minimum starting capital required for businesses to begin operations. These start at approximately US$ 25,000. The Superintendencia de Empresas y Sociedades Mercantiles determines this amount, and regulates all types of commercial activity.

- Get an income and property clearance (this includes an income tax contributor number and a value-added tax collector number from the Direccion General de Impuestos Internos at the Ministerio de Hacienda).
- Request a license at the Commerce Registry (Registro de Comercio), in the Commerce and Industry License Registry Department. The Registry must approve a Spanish version of the accounting system, and also approve the accounting books. Industrial or commercial patent registry is also obtained from this office.
- Register both the firm's board of directors and administrative personnel at the Commerce Registry.
- Get a municipal services clearance from the appropriate township or city.
- Get certification that the firm is properly registered in the Industrial and Commercial National Establishments Directory at the Direccion General de Estadistica y Censos.

- If the firm sells or manufactures pharmaceuticals, obtain a permit from the Consejo Superior de Salud Publica.
- Publish the firm's license in a local newspaper.
- Register the investment at the Foreign Capital and Technology Transfer Department of the Ministry of Economy.
- Hire both an accountant and an external auditor who have been certified by the government of El Salvador.

Distribution and Sales Channels

Most products, especially well-known ones, are directly imported by distributors. These distributors have a wide range of products and networks of buyers. They often don't have time to promote new or lesser-known products. Large department stores also import directly. U.S. distributors also sell well-known products directly to El Salvador, so many U.S. products have name recognition even before supplier–distribution relation-

ships are formal. Small retailers often travel to the U.S. to take back goods themselves, especially for used vehicles, auto parts, computers, and household goods. See **Business Travel (Business Customs)**.

Direct Marketing

Direct marketing is hindered by limited telecommunications and mail delivery capacity. As these infrastructures improve, direct marketing may grow. Direct-from-TV sales and door-to-door sales in U.S. cosmetics and household products firms are increasing.

Leasing/Joint Ventures

Joint ventures and the use of U.S. licenses must be legally established in a contract signed by both parties. The Salvadoran Commercial Code regulates both types of relationship. The Commercial Section of the American Embassy in San Salvador gives regular reports on Salvadoran firms seeking joint ventures and licensing agreements.

Franchising

U.S. franchises have been increasing in El Salvador. Several fast-food franchises and a video rental franchise now exist. Franchise opportunities are expected to rise with consumer spending.

Advertising and Promotion

Advertising is mainly done via radio, television, billboards, leaflets, and newspapers. Typical budgets spend 50 percent on TV, 30 percent on radio, 20 percent on newspapers and billboards. Three TV stations have about 70 percent of the viewers. Radio time is cheap, around US$ 3.40 for a 30-second ad, but TV time is around US$ 115 to 450 for a 30-second ad on a major station. The chamber of commerce and trade association publications usually accept ads. See **Contacts**.

Selling Factors

Sales and marketing have recently developed in El Salvador. Offers of good service and follow-up are helpful. Contests, drawings, raffles, and creative sales promotions are becoming more common. New products often have billboard ads and newspaper campaigns with an introductory reception at an upscale hotel.

Selling to the Government

Sellers generally need to speak Spanish to succeed. For small government purchases, contact the procurement office of the specific government ministry or institution. The GOES publishes tenders or contacts embassies for sales greater than US$ 10,000 to 20,000 (depending on the ministry or agency). The law requires that GOES-funded civil engineering and construction projects must go to Salvadoran companies. However, most projects receive some funding from other sources, and so the law is not seen as a trade barrier. GOES bids given to the U.S. Embassy are put on the Department of Commerce's National Trade Data Bank or online electronic bulletin board as "Foreign Government Tenders." El Salvador is a member of the WTO and is waiting to sign the international Government Procurement Treaty.

Pricing

There are generally no controls on prices in El Salvador, except for liquid propane gas and public transport rates. These are subsidized through a subsidy on diesel fuel used by public transport buses. See **Business Infrastructure (Taxes).**

Customer Support

Firms that sell equipment, machines, or electric appliances should provide good customer support. Good service and support strongly influence buyers, especially for government orders.

Intellectual Property Rights (IPR)

El Salvador IPR laws are considered world class, including their enforcement. El Salvador law provides explicit protection for copyrights, trademarks, trade secrets, and patents. It implicitly protects for semiconductor chip layouts and more sophisticated properties. El Salvador has signed the Geneva Phonograms Convention; the Convention for the Protections of Performers, Producers of Phonograms, and Broadcasting Organizations (Rome Convention); the Berne Convention for the Protection of Literary and Artistic Works; and the Paris Convention for the Protection of Industrial Property. El Salvador has agreed to conform to the TRIPS agreement of the World Trade Organization. Software has been a deficient area, but a joint GOES–U.S. software campaign is underway to protect it. Music and videocassettes, as well as apparel, shoes, and consumption product trademarks are well protected. To seek redress for IPR violations, present a completed case with a judicial order to the police and the Attorney General's Office. The National Commercial Registry has a one-stop window for registrations that speeds up routine application processing.

Attorney

Hiring a lawyer is recommended for several tasks, including opening a business in El Salvador, preparing contracts, and avoiding or resolving business disputes.

FOREIGN INVESTMENT
6

Openness: The GOES is committed to attracting foreign investment in most sectors. Many laws facilitate and regulate investment in key sectors. Special legislation also encourages portfolio investment in the privatization of telecommunications, electricity, and pensions. The primary laws for foreign investment are the Free Zones Law, the Export Reactivation Law, and the Foreign Investment Promotion and Guarantee Law. Other laws include the Banking Law, Insurance Firms Law, the Mining Law, the IPR Law, and the Stock Exchange Law. See **Establishing an Office** and **Trade (Exports, Imports).** Also see **Private Ownership** and **Trade Zones** and **Free Ports.**

Regulatory System: El Salvador has relatively streamlined and transparent laws and policies. Gasoline prices are controlled by the GOES, but are based on an average of U.S. Gulf Coast refinery prices.

Investment Agreements: El Salvador has a framework agreement with the U.S. for a bilateral Trade and Investment Council (TIC). A Tax Information Exchange Agreement is being negotiated. El Salvador belongs to the Central American Common Market, with 50 commercial and technical cooperation treaties. Investment promotion treaties exist with Mexico, Spain, and Venezuela. See **Expropriation** and **Compensation.**

Trade Zones and Free Ports: Firms in export processing zones or in bonded warehouses that export 100 percent of production outside Central America get several benefits: (1) up to 20 years exemption from income tax; (2) duty-free importing of machinery, equipment, tools, spare parts, furniture, and other operational goods; (3) duty-free importing of raw materials, semimanufactured and inter-

mediate products; and (4) duty-free importing of fuels and lubricants. Firms not in the free zones or that export less than 100 percent of production can apply for rebates of 6 percent of the fob value of exports. These rebates are exempt from income tax.

Performance Requirements/Incentives: El Salvador has no performance criteria for investors. It has no requirements for investors to export specific amounts, transfer technology, or incorporate specific levels of local content. See **Trade Zones** and **Free Ports.**

Capital Markets and Investment: Interest rates are set by market forces, and the Superintendent of Banks supervises the banking system. El Salvador has a stock exchange. Foreign and domestic financial companies are regulated by the Organic Law for the Financial System Regulatory Agency. All financial institutions are audited, authorized, and supervised by the Superintendencia del Sistema Financiero and an autonomous agency. See **Openness.**

Private Ownership: Foreign citizens and private entities can freely establish businesses in El Salvador. Foreigners must start up small businesses that have a minimum of US$ 25,000 startup capital. This minimum is not strictly enforced. Artesanal fishing within 12 miles of the coast can be done only by Salvadorans. Fishing from 12 to 200 miles off the coast can be done by Salvadorans, foreigners with legal residence, or joint ventures registered with the GOES. Fishing licenses are required from CENDEPESCA, a GOES entity.

Property Rights: El Salvador laws protect property rights, and enforcement is increasing. The legal and regulatory system can act arbitrarily, so caution should be taken to protect property and investments. El Salvador is making progress toward full TRIPPS compliance. See **Intellectual Property Rights (IPR).**

Expropriation and Compensation: The U.S. and El Salvador have an investment guarantee treaty that protects U.S. investors against losses from currency inconvertibility or expropriation. A more broad bilateral investment treaty is being negotiated.

OPIC and Investment Insurance: The Overseas Private Investment Corporation (OPIC) has a bilateral agreement with El Salvador. OPIC insures banks, currency inconvertibility, expropriation, civil strife, and corporate financing. El Salvador participates in the Multilateral Investment Guarantee Agency (MIGA).

Dispute Settlement: El Salvador is a member of the International Center for Settlement of Investment Disputes (ICSID). Resolving business disputes through the domestic legal system can be expensive and ineffective. Enforcement can be a problem, and bribery has been alleged. Arbitration clauses, with a foreign venue, should be included in contracts to resolve disputes.

FINANCE

⑦

The Salvadoran banking system is controlled by private investors. There are 14 commercial banks, 9 savings and loans banks, and some smaller institutions resembling credit unions. Interest rates and service fees are set by the market, and services are offered both in local currency and in U.S. dollars (and often Guatemalan quetzales and Honduran lempiras). Banks offer the same services and operations as U.S. banks. Financing is available for business, but it is expensive. Local currency interest rates are 16 to 22 percent for one- to ten-year terms. The financial capital base was about US$ 3.38 billion in 1997. Large Salvadoran firms prefer to borrow from U.S. funds. Credit policies favor consumer finance, agriculture, and manufacturing over trade. See **Capital Markets and Investments.**

Export Financing: U.S. exports are usually financed by loans from local banks to importers. For terms less than one year,

finance for consumption goods is 17 to 19 percent. Intermediate goods have more favorable rates and terms. Local banks offer various letters of credit, sight drafts, and other payments for competitive prices. The U.S. Embassy recommends using confirmed irrevocable letters of credit for all commercial transactions in El Salvador. See **Payment Terms.**

Project Financing: The Inter-American Development Bank (IDB) has approved loans of over $US 600 million over four years. Projects range from electric plants to highway construction to health care. Financing can also come from the Central American Bank for Economic Integration (CABEI), or USAID, or other donors. The Investment Finance (IFC–World Bank Group) has approved US$ 30 million as part of an $80 million project to Cemento de El Salvador (CESSA) for modernization. See **Contacts.**

COMMUNICATIONS

Phone

Local telecommunications are inadequate. Cell phones are typically used for business since new phone lines are hard to obtain. AT&T, MCI, and Sprint offer international phone services. Direct dialing, fax, and telex facilities connect to most countries in the world. The international access code is 011, and the El Salvadorian access code is 503. City codes are not required.

Internet

Wireless and wired companies expect a growth market in services and equipment for U.S. and international suppliers of equipment, fiber optics, and internet providers. No additional information is available at this time.

Mail

The postal system is reasonably well developed although street names and numbers are not well defined. Express mail international services are available between El Salvador and the U.S.

TRANSPORTATION

Land

A U.S. driver's license is valid for three months. Taxi service is good from major hotels. Buses run throughout the country, but are often targets for crime and often in accidents. The Pan American Highway connects most Salvadoran cities and runs from Guatemala to the Honduran border. Of the 12,500 kilometers of roads, 2,000 are paved. The Inter-American Development Bank (IDB), the GOES and Japanese governments, and the Central American Bank for Economic Integration (CABEI) have given funds and loans to maintain and develop roads. U.S. and Canadian government studies recommend that parts of the rail system be repaired and modernized. The most active lines connect Matazoan to Apogee/San Salvador (cement freight) and Acujutla/Nejapa to Sonsanate (general freight).

Sea

Acujutla has the major port. It is considered expensive, and tidal conditions hinder loading and unloading. Refrigeration cargo is limited, and most cargo in containers is dry. A telescopic unloader, a clam ladle, 2 3-ton (metric) capacity cranes, a platform scale, five tugboats, roofed storage modules and a 55-ton (metric) truck overturner-platform are available for use. A rail link connects Acukutla to Sonsonate and San Salvador. Cargo ports exist in Puerto Barrios, Puerto Quetzal (in Guatemala), and Puerto Cortes (in Honduras). Cutuco has a minor cargo port.

Air

The International Airport is 25 miles (45 minutes) from San Salvador. American Airlines, United Airlines, Continental Airlines, Delta, and TACA International Airlines connect El Salvador with Miami, Atlanta, New York, Los Angeles, Houston, New Orleans, Newark, and Washington D.C. Comalapa International Airport handles over 35 million kilos of cargo per year, 89 percent being with the U.S. (1997). Fine, Challenge, Florida West, Emery Transcontinental, and all passenger airlines offer frequent cargo service with the U.S. Ilopango, a small airport, is used by military and small craft but may be developed.

WORK WEEK

Business Hours: 8.00 a.m. to 12.00 p.m. and 2.00 p.m. to 6.00 p.m. Monday through Friday.

Government Hours: 9.00 a.m. to 5.00 p.m., continuously, Monday through Friday.

Bank Hours: 9.00 a.m. to 1.00 p.m. and 1.45 p.m. to 4.00 p.m. Monday through Friday, and closed on Saturday.

HOLIDAYS 2001

New Year's Day, January 1
Variable Holy Thursday, April*
Variable Good Friday, April*
Labor Day, May 1
Corpus Christi, June 14
Bank Holiday, last Friday in June
Feast of San Salvador, August*
Independence Day, September 15
Columbus Day, October 12
All Souls Day, November 2
Day of First Cry of Independence, November 5
Christmas Day, December 25

Some holidays may be observed on different dates depending on the day of the week on which it falls. The U.S. Embassy will be closed on U.S. and El Salvador holidays. It is recommended that business travelers do not schedule trips to El Salvador immediately before or immediately after local or U.S. holidays.

*These holidays vary from year to year.

BUSINESS TRAVEL

Business Customs

Salvadoran business manners are formal at first. Shake hands before and after meetings, use proper titles with last names, and do not use first names until relationships have been solidified. Salvadorans typically use titles such as Licenciado (college graduate), Ingeniero (engineering graduate), or Doctor (for both physicians and lawyers). Business cards are very common. On first meeting, exchange business cards. Have a supply in Spanish as well as in English. Business is increasingly done over meals. Breakfast begins around 7:30 a.m., lunch around 12:30 p.m., and dinner around 8 or 9 p.m. Lunch and dinner can last two to three hours.

Travel Advisory and Visas

Exercise caution because of the high crime rates. Contact the Travel Advisory Service of the U.S. State Department. A passport and either a visa or tourist card are required for entry. Visas can be obtained at Salvadoran consulates in Washington D.C., New York, Los Angeles, San Francisco, Chicago, New Orleans, Dallas, Houston, Miami, and San Juan, Puerto Rico. Tourist cards cost $10 and are good for one stay of up to 90 days. They can be obtained before departure at Salvadoran consulates, major airlines servicing El Salvador, and after departure at El Salvador International Airport. Temporary residency or residency is needed for extended stays. The procedures and paperwork for both can be very demanding, so hiring a lawyer or another expert is recommended.

Business Infrastructure

Entry Requirements (personal and professional goods): Items brought in temporarily may be authorized by Customs if they are re-exported without modification within a specified time frame. A bond is required to guarantee timely re-exportation. Goods imported for transformation, manufacture, or repair are regulated by Free Trade Zone laws.

Currency Exchange: The colon is the main currency. US$ 1 = 8.75 colons (average in 1994–1998). Foreign exchange is traded actively at banks and foreign exchange houses. See **Payment Terms.**

Taxes: A value-added tax of 13 percent is added to the purchase price of all products except basic foods such as medicines, corn, rice, beans, and fluid milk. See **Regulations.**

Hotels and Restaurants: El Salvador has lodging varying from inexpensive guest houses to deluxe hotels. See **Contacts.**

Housing: No information is available at this time.

Utilities: The Superintendency of Electricity and Telecommunications (SIGET) regulates telecommunications and electricity tariffs, and the distribution of electromagnetic frequencies. See **Key Economic Indicators (Infrastructure).**

Business Services: See **Advertising and Promotion** and **Performance Requirements /Incentives and Labor.**

Labor Costs and Legislation: The unemployment rate is 7.7 percent (2000 est). Minimum wage (in urban areas) is $144 per month. According to a 1993 study, urban unskilled workers earn 20 percent over the minimum wage. Labor laws require that 90 percent of the labor force at plants and clerical jobs be Salvadoran. Professional and technical jobs have few restrictions on foreigners. See **Labor.**

Literacy: Age 15 and over can read and write. 78.5 percent (1995 est).

Travel Notes

The following travel notes have been supplied by the U.S. government. For the most recent general travel and consular information, see the U.S. Department of State travel publications or call the Traveler's Telephone Hotline at (202) 647-5225.

Security: Petty and violent crimes are common. Travelers should avoid carrying valuables in public places. Pick-pocketing and thefts from cars are common in urban areas. Avoid traveling after dark on unpaved roads, and always keep car windows closed and doors locked. See **Travel Advisory and Visas.**

Health Precautions: San Salvador has many U.S.- or European-trained doctors, but treatment for complex procedures or illnesses is often below U.S. standards. Pharmacies have most medicines. Volcanoes and earthquakes can sometimes be very destructive. Water pollution is also a danger.

Current information on health matters may be obtained from the Centers for Disease Control and Prevention's international travelers' hotline at (404) 332-4559.

Embassy Assistance

To obtain additional and updated information on entry and exit require-ments, travelers can contact the Consular Section of the Embassy of El Salvador at 1416 16th Street, Suite 200, N.W., Washington, D.C. 20008; Tel: (202) 265-9671. Travelers may also contact the nearest El Salvadorian consulate. They are located in Los Angeles, San Francisco, Santa Ana, Miami, Chicago, New Orleans, New York, Boston, Dallas, and Houston.

CONTACTS
13

U.S. and Country Contacts

Country Government Agencies

Ministry of Economy Ministry of Public Works
Complejo Plan Maestro Edif.
  Dirección General de
Centro de Gobierno Caminos.
  Final Avenida Peralta
San Salvador, El Salvador, C.A.
Tel: (503) 281-0531; 293-6585
Fax: (503) 221-2797; (503) 293-6583

Ministry of Finance Ministry of Public Health
Condominio Las Tres Torres Calle Arce
  No. 827
Torre 2 San Salvador, El Salvador, C.A.
Avenida Alvarado, Diagonal
Tel: (503) 271-0008
Centroamerica Fax: (503) 221-0985
San Salvador, El Salvador, C.A.
Tel: (503) 225-7487; 225-5500
Fax: (503) 225-7491

Ministry of Agricul. & Livestock Alcaldia Municipal de San
Final 1a. Av. Norte 9a. Calle Oriente No. 320
Santa Tecla, La Libertad San Salvador,
  El Salvador, C.A.
Tel: (503) 288-9983; 222-1788; 221-1579
Fax: (503) 288-5040; 222-8670

General Directorate of Ministry of Environment
Alameda Roosevelt y 55 Av. Nte.
Aeropuerto de Ilopango Torre El Salvador,
  Edif. IPSFA
San Salvador, El Salvador, C.A.
Tel: (503) 295-0265; 260-8900
Fax: (503) 295-0345; (503) 260-3117

Country Trade Associations and Chambers of Commerce

American Chamber of Commerce of El Salvador
87 Avenida Norte No. 720
Apto. A, Colonia Escalón
San Salvador, El Salvador, C.A.
Tel: (503) 263-3262
Fax: (503) 263-3237

Cámara Salvadoreña de la Industria de la Construcción (CASALCO)
Paseo General Escalón No. 4834, Col. Escalón
Tel: (503) 263-5349; 263-6521
Fax: (503) 263-6518

Cámara de Comercio e Industria de
El Salvador
(Salvadoran Chamber of Commerce and
Industry)
9a. Avenida Norte y 5a. Calle Poniente
San Salvador, El Salvador, C.A.
Tel: (503) 271-2055
Fax: (503) 271-4461

Asociación Nacional de la Empresa Privada
(Salvadoran National Association of Private
Enterprise)
1a. Calle Poniente y 71 Avenida Norte 204
San Salvador, El Salvador, C.A.
Tel: (503) 223-3893
Fax: (503) 223-8932

Asociación Salvadoreña de Industriales
(Salvadoran Association of Industrialists)
Calles Roma y Liverpool, Colonia Roma
San Salvador, El Salvador, C.A.
Tel: (503) 279-2488
Fax: (503) 279-2070

Corporación de Exportadores de El Salvador
(COEXPORT)
(Salvadoran Exporters Corporation)
Condominios del Mediterraneo
Edificio A-23, Jardines de Guadalupe
San Salvador, El Salvador, C.A.
Tel: (503) 243-3110; 243-1329
Fax: (503) 243-3159

Fundación Salvadoreña para el Desarrollo
Económico y Social (FUSADES)
Edificio FUSADES
Blvd. y Urb. Santa Elena
Antiguo Cuscatlan
San Salvador, El Salvador C.A.
Tel: (503) 278-3380
Fax: (503) 278-3366

Country Market Research Firms

CCM
Calle El Progreso, Pasaje El Rosal No. 23
P.O. Box 2790 (CG)
San Salvador, El Salvador, C.A.
Cesar Chicas
Tel: (503) 224-4374

Goodman
89 Av. Nte. No. 4610, Apto. No. 5
Col. Escalon (Frente a Hotel El Salvador)
Tel: (503) 263-2512
Fax: (503) 263-2513

Pridex
Enma Arauz
Edificio Fusades
Blvd. y Urb. Santa Elena
Antiguo Cuscatlan
San Salvador, El Salvador C.A.
Tel: (503) 278-3380
Fax: (503) 278-3366

Procisa De C.V.
Paola Castaneda
Residencial Altos de Montebello
Calle Paracutin, Grupo 2 No. 22
San Salvador, El Salvador, C.A.
Tel: (503) 274-1976

Rimo, S.A. De C.V.
Rigoberto Monge
Centro Profesional Presidente
Edificio A, Local 31
Avenida Revolución y Calle Circunvalación
Col. San Benito
San Salvador, El Salvador, C.A.
Tel: (503) 279-0679
Fax: (503) 279-0725

A.C. Nielsen has announced that it is
expanding its retail tracking services for
food and drug products throughout
Central America. For more information,
call (708) 605-5120.

Main Commercial Banks and Financial Institutions

Banco Cuscatlan, S.A.
Edificio La Pirámide
Km. 10 Carretera a Santa Tecla
La Libertad, El Salvador, C.A.
Tel: (503) 228-7777
Fax: (503) 228-9999

Banco Salvadoreno
Alameda Dr. Manuel Enrique Araujo
San Salvador, El Salvador, C.A.
Tel: (503) 298-4444
Fax: (503) 298-0102

Banco de Comercio de El Salvador
25 Av. Nte. Antiguo Edif. Embajada Americana
San Salvador, El Salvador, C.A.
Tel: (503) 2264577
Fax: (503) 25-7767

Banco Agricola Comercial
Paseo General Escalón No. 3625
Colonia Escalón
San Salvador, El Salvador, C.A.
Tel: (503) 224-0283
Fax: (503) 224-3948

Banco de Desarrollo E Inversion
67 Avenida Norte, Plaza Las Americas
San Salvador, El Salvador, C.A.
Tel: (503) 298-0924
Fax: (503) 298-1022

Banco Hipotecario
Pje. Senda Florida Sur, Paseo General Escalón
San Salvador, El Salvador, C.A.
Tel: (503) 223-3753
Fax: (503) 298-0447

Citibank, N.A.
Edif. B, Edificio Century Plaza, Frente a Canal
  4 de TV
San Salvador, El Salvador, C.A.
Tel: (503) 224-3011; 245-1850
Fax: (503) 224-2906

**Bancasa — Banco de Construccion y
  Ahorro S.A.**
75 Avenida Sur No. 209
Colonia Escalón
San Salvador, El Salvador, C.A.
Tel: (503) 263-5508
Fax: (503) 263-550

Grupo Capital
1a. Calle Poniente 3649
Colonia Escalon
San Salvador, El Salvador, C.A.
Tel: (503) 298-5777
Fax: (503) 298-0772

Financiera Credisa, S.A.
Edificio Credisa
Alameda Juan Pablo II Pte.
San Salvador, El Salvador, C.A.
Tel: (503) 260-5633
Fax: (503) 260-3711

Atlacatl, S.A.
Alameda Roosevelt y 55 Avenida Sur
Centro Comercial Roosevelt
San Salvador, El Salvador, C.A.
Tel: (503) 279-0033

Ahorromet Scotiabank
Av. Olímpica y 63 Av. Sur No. 129
Edificio Ahorromet
San Salvador, El Salvador, C.A.
Tel: (503) 245-1211
Fax: (503) 224-2884

U.S. Embassy Trade Personnel
All located at:
U.S. Embassy - San Salvador
Econ/Commercial Section, Unit 3112
APO AA 34023
Tel: (503) 278-4444
Fax: (503) 298-2336
Email: econcomm@embsansal.usinfo.org.sv
Website: http://www.usinfo.org.sv

Washington-Based USG Country Contacts

**Overseas Private Investment Corporation
(OPIC)**
1100 New York Ave., NW
Washington, DC 20527
Tel: (202) 336-8685
Fax: (202) 408-5142

U.S. Trade and Development Agency
Room 309, S.A. - 16
Department of State
Washington, DC 20523-1602
Tel: (703) 875-4357
Fax: (703) 875-4009

Export-Import Bank of the United States
811 Vermont Ave., NW
Washington, DC 20571
Tel: (202) 565-3921
Fax: (202) 565-3380

U.S. Agency for International Development
Center for Trade and Investment Services
  (CTIS)
Room 100, SA-2
Washington, DC 20523-0229
Tel: (202) 663-2663
Fax: (202) 663-2670

U.S. Treasury Department
Desk Officer for El Salvador
1500 Pennsylvania Avenue, NW
Washington, DC 20523
Tel: (202) 622-1740
Fax: (202) 622-1273

Office of the U.S. Trade Representative
Latin America and the Caribbean
600 17th Street, NW
Washington, DC 20506
Tel: (202) 395-5190
Fax: (202) 395-3911

US Department of Agriculture
Foreign Agricultural Service
12th and Jefferson Street, NW
Washington, DC 20250
Tel: (202) 720-1340
Fax: (202) 690-2079

U.S. Department of Commerce
International Trade Administration
OLA/CBD
Room HCHB 3025
14th and Constitution Avenue, N.W.
Washington, D.C. 20230
Tel: (202) 482-1685
Fax: (202) 482-0464

U.S. Department of State
Office of Central American Affairs, El Salvador
  Desk, ARA/CEN
U.S. INTERNATIONAL Department of State
Washington, D.C. 20250
Tel: (202) 647-3681
Fax: (202) 647-2597

Steps to Establishing a Business Office

**Superintendencia de Empresas y Sociedades
  Mercantiles,**
Ministerio de Economia,
Complejo Maestro, Centro de Gobierno
San Salvador, El Salvador, C.A.
Tel: (503) 281-1122

**Direccion General de Impuestos Internos
  from:**
Ministerio de Hacienda
Avenida Alvarado y Diagonal Centroamerica
Condominio Las Tres Torres No. 2
San Salvador, El Salvador
Tel: (503) 225-1022
Fax: (503) 226-7170

**The Industrial and Commercial National
  Establishments Directory** at:
Direccion General de Estadistica y Censos
Av. Juan Bertis No. 79, Ex-Instituto
  Geográfico Nacional
Ciudad Delgado
Tel: (503) 276-5900
Fax: (503) 276-5900

Consejo Superior de Salud Publica
Paseo General Escalón No. 3551
San Salvador, El Salvador
Tel: (503) 245-3885; 245-3886
Fax: (503) 245-3886

Newspapers

La Prensa Grafica
Tel: (503) 289-1800
Fax: (503) 289-1800

El Diario de Hoy
Tel: (503) 271-0122
Fax: (503) 271-2270

Diario El Mundo
Tel: (503) 271-4400
Fax: (503) 271-4342

Free Trade Zones

San Bartolo - currently being privatized, located 10 kms. east of San Salvador on Boulevard del Ejercito.
Tel: (503) 224-6677
Fax: (503) 224-4956
El Progreso Industrial Park - located on the road to La Libertad, about seven miles west of San Salvador. It has 12,000 square meters of space in ten buildings.
Tel: (503) 228-5075
Fax: (503) 228-3492

El Pedregal - located five miles from El Salvador's International Airport and 23 miles from San Salvador.
Tel: (503) 334-6011
Fax: (503) 334-6060

Exportsalva - located 15 miles from San Salvador and 35 miles from the international airport, on the Santa Ana - San Salvador highway.
Tel: (305) 591-1844
Fax: (503) 593-0498

San Marcos Free Zone - located three miles from San Salvador, on the road to El Salvador International airport.
Tel: (503) 220-2333
Fax: (503) 220-1012

American Park - located on the road to Santa Ana 24 km from San Salvador.
Tel: (503) 228-5075
Fax: (503) 228-3492

Project Financing

U.S. Department of Commerce Liaison to the Inter-American Development Bank
U.S. Executive Directors Office
1250 H Street, NW, 10th Floor
Washington, DC 20005
Tel: (202) 942-8260
Fax: (202) 942-8275

or in El Salvador:
Luis Vergara
Condominio Torres del Bosque
10 Piso, Colonia La Mascota
Apartado Postal No. (01) 199
San Salvador
Tel: (503) 263-8300
Fax: (503) 263-7915

Travel Advisory

Bureau of Consular Affairs, Office of Overseas Citizen Services (CA/OCS)
Tel: (202) 647-5113
or the El Salvador Desk, U.S. Department of State
Tel: (202) 736-4985; 647-3505.

Also, the Travel Advisory Service of the Department of State can provide information in recorded and fax form for any travel warnings on traveling to foreign countries.
Tel: (202) 647-5225
Fax: (202) 647-3732

Hotels

Hotel Camino Real
Boulevard de Los Heroes y Avenida Sisimiles
San Salvador, El Salvador, C.A.
Tel: (503) 260-1333
Fax: (503) 260-5660

Hotel El Salvador
89 Avenida Norte y 11 Calle Poniente
Colonia Escalon
San Salvador, El Salvador, C.A.
Tel: (503) 263-0777
Fax: (503) 263-2583

Hotel Presidente El Salvador
Avenida La Revolucion
Colonia San Benito
P.O. Box 888
San Salvador, El Salvador, C.A.
Tel: (503) 243-4444
Fax: (503) 243-2020

Hotel Princess,
Zona Rosa,
Colonia San Benito
Tel: (503) 2984545
Fax: (503) 298-4500

Car Rentals

Avis
43 Avenida Sur 137
Tel: (503) 261-1212
Fax: (503) 260-7165

Hertz Rent A Car
Calle Los Andes J-16
Colonia Miramonte
Tel: (503) 260-8099
Fax: (503) 260-1351

Budget
79 Avenida Sur No. 6
Colonia La Mascota
Tel: (503) 263-7782

Sure Rent
Boulevard de Los Héroes y 23 Calle Poniente
Tel: (503) 225-1810
Fax: (503) 225-7766

Dollar
Avenida Roosevelt No. 3119
Tel: (503) 224-4385

Diplomatic Representation in the U.S.

Chief of Mission:
Chancery: 2308 California Street NW,
   Washington, DC 20008
Tel: (202) 265-9671
Consulate(s) general: Chicago, Dallas,
   Houston, Los Angeles, Miami, New Orleans,
   New York, and San Francisco consulate(s):
   Boston

Chief of Mission:
Embassy: Final Boulevard Santa Elena, Antiguo
   Cuscatlan, San Salvador
Mailing address: Unit 3116, APO AA 34023
Tel: (503) 278-4444
Fax: (503) 278-6011

Flores

Coban

GUATEMALA

Puerto Barrios

Guatemala City

GUATEMALA

TRADE AND BUSINESS GUIDE

Official Name:	Republic of Guatemala
Official Languages:	Spanish, with 23 Mayan languages (Quiche, Cakchiqueland Kekchi)
Population:	12,639,939 (2000 est)
Population Growth:	2.63% (2000 est)
Age Structure:	0-14 years: 42%, 15-64 years: 54%, 65 years and over: 4% (2000 est)
Location:	Middle America, bordering the Caribbean Sea between Honduras and Belize, bordering the North Pacific Ocean between El Salvador and Mexico
Area:	108,890 square kilometers, slightly smaller than Tennessee
Type of Government:	Constitutional Democratic Republic with president (by popular vote for four-year terms) and unicameral congress (by popular vote for four-year terms)
Head of State:	President Alfonso Antonio Portillo Cabreras
Cabinet:	Council of Ministers appointed by president
Religion:	Roman Catholic, Protestant, Traditional Mayan
Major Cities:	Capital: Guatemala City (2 million). Puerto Barrios (338,000), Quezaltenango (246,000), Coban (120,000), Mazatenango (38,319), Zacapa (35,769)
Climate:	Tropical. Hot and humid in lowlands, cooler in highlands
Time:	The entire country is -6 GMT (Greenwich Mean Time), which is 1 hour behind EST (Eastern Standard Time). The country does not schedule for daylight savings time.
GDP:	Purchasing Power Parity (PPP): $47.9 billion (1999 est); real growth rate: 3.5% (1999 est); per capita PPP: $3,900 (1999 est); composition by sector: agricultural: 23%, industry: 20%, services: 57% (1999 est)
Currency:	1 quetzal (Q) = 100 centavos
Exchange Rate:	Quetzal per US$ 1 = 7.88 (2000 est), 7.17 (1999 est), 6.27 (1998 est)
Weights & Measure:	Metric system
Natural Resources:	Petroleum, nickel, rare woods, fish, chicle
Total Trade:	In billions US$ [exports (fob)/imports (cif)]: 1997 (2.39/3.85), 1998 (2.56/4.65), 1999 est (2.26/4.41)
Trade with U.S.:	In millions US$ [exports (fob)/imports (cif)]: 1997 (840/1,585), 1998 (837/1,931), 1999 (742/1,767)
Major Trade Partners:	Imports: United States, Mexico, Venezuela, Japan, Germany. Exports: United States, El Salvador, Costa Rica, Germany, Honduras

Membership: IADB, IBRD, IFC, IMF, OAS, UN, UNCTAD, WCO, WIPO, and WTO. See membership description in appendix.

Sources: CIA World Fact Book, Central Bank of Guatemala, Government of Guatemala, United Nations World Statistics, U.S. Department of Commerce, U.S. Department of State

POLITICAL OUTLOOK
②

Relationship with the U.S.

Bilateral relations between Guatemala and the U.S. are excellent. U.S. policy toward Guatemala includes (1) supporting institutionalization of democracy, (2) encouraging respect for human rights and the rule of law, (3) supporting implementation of peace, (4) supporting sustainable broad-based economic growth with U.S. trade and investment, and (5) helping the Government of Guatemala (GOG) fight the illegal drug trade and international criminal activity, including illegal immigration transit.

Influences on Business

For about ten years, foreign investors have usually not been a target for political violence. The U.S. Department of State's travel warning for Guatemala was lifted on August 19, 1996. See **Political Violence.**

Profile

System: Guatemala has a one-term presidency, an 80-member (113-member congressional seats for the November 1999 election) unicameral congress, and municipal officers. Voter participation is low (over 50 percent abstention in the 1995–1996 elections). Major political parties are the Guatemalan Republican Front (FRG, with the president and 63 seats), the National Advancement Party (PAN, 37 Congress

seats), the New Nation Alliance (ANN, 9 seats), the Christian Democratic Party (DCG, 2 seats), the Democratic Union (UD, 1 seat), the Green party (LOV, 1 seat), and the Progressive Liberator party (PLP, 1 seat). Figures are based on the 1999 elections.

Schedule for Elections: Presidential and congressional elections are held every four years, and were last held in November 1999. The next elections are scheduled for November 2003.

Major Parties: The PAN is conservative and business oriented. The FRG is conservative and populist. The FDNG is democratic and left-of-center. The Guatemalan National Revolutionary Union (URNG) is made up of former guerilla revolutionaries.

Political Violence: Armed bands, some with political claims, commit acts in the countryside. Some unsolved murders may have political origin, but political violence is generally low. Only southern Mexico instability may affect Guatemala's border areas. Foreigners do not seem singled out as crime targets, but should be watchful.

Corruption: Bribery is illegal by penal code. However, corruption is a serious problem at nearly every level. Corruption has been most pervasive in customs transactions, especially at ports and borders far from the capital.

Trends

Available economic data indicate that real GDP grew by about 3.5 percent in 1999, a decrease compared to the 4.7 percent real growth in 1998. The economy had been on track to exceed 6.0 percent growth, but the combination of a domestic financial sector crisis and the destruction caused by Tropical Storm Mitch was a setback. Inflation, as measured by the official Consumer Price Index, is under control at 5.0 percent in 1999. The Central Bank and the Ministry of Finance have been mainly prudent in economic management, but have allowed some unregulated financial intermediaries to fail. Two factors hindering growth are that interest rates have been raised, and demand for foreign currency has gone up. Agriculture dominates the local economy with one-fourth total output and 70 percent of exports. Overall, Guatemala is dependent on a few agricultural commodities such as coffee, sugar, and bananas. Growing exports are cut flowers, specialty fruits and berries, shrimp, and textile assembly.

Major Growth Sectors

The financial services industry has been deregulated, which has led to great growth. However, the elements of the industry have not been adequately monitored and regulated. Efficient capital markets, such as an equities market, may be needed. Insufficient infrastructure and low training and education discourage higher value-added industry investments. However, one foreign investor has employed over 600 workers in a satellite-linked data processing center.

Key Economic Indicators

Income, Production and Employment (millions of U.S. dollars unless otherwise indicated)			
	1997	1998	1999[1]
Nominal GDP[2]	17,427	19,016	17,826
Real GDP Growth (pct)	4.3	4.7	3.5
GDP by Sector (pct):			
Agriculture	24	24	23
Manufacturing	21	21	21
Services	47	47	47
Government	8	8	8
Per Capita GDP (US$)[2]	1,603	1,793	1,635
Labor Force (millions)[3]	3,320	3,416	4,208
Unemployment Rate (pct)[4]	5.2	5.2	5.2

1. 1999 figures are all estimates based on available data in October.
2. Depreciation of local currency results in apparent decline in GDP expressed in U.S. dollars.
3. 1999 Labor Force Data from 1999 Survey of Family Income and Expenditures.
4. Does not reflect estimated 40 to 50 percent underemployment.
Source: Bureau of Economic and Business Affairs; U.S. Department of State

- Infrastructure

  The underdevelopment of the Guatemalan infrastructure is a large obstacle to economic growth and investment. Railroads have been rehabilitated, and highways and electrification have received investment, but on the whole, investment remains too much in the Guatemala City area. See **Communications** and **Transportation**.

- Labor

  The formal workforce is estimated by GOG at 3.5 million, and 1 million informal. Collective bargaining and unions have labor code rights. Less than 15 percent of the workforce is unionized. Input choice varies, but the large, unskilled, inexpensive workforce leads many construction and agricultural firms to use labor-intensive production means. Skilled and semiskilled workers are sometimes in shortage, especially in construction and management or information-processing professionals. See **Labor Costs** and **Legislation**.

Money and Prices (annual percentage growth)			
	1997	1998	1999[1]
Money Supply Growth (M2)	21.2	14.4	10.0
Consumer Price Inflation[2]	7.1	7.4	5.0
Exchange Rate (quetzal/US$ annual average)	6.00	6.27	7.17
Financial Market Rate (1999 data is unofficial Embassy estimate)	6.10	6.40	7.50

1. 1999 figures are all estimates based on most recent data available.
2. The official CPI is not regarded as an accurate measure of price movements.
Source: Bureau of Economic and Business Affairs; U.S. Department of State

Balance of Payments and Trade (millions of U.S. dollars unless otherwise indicated)			
	1997	1998	1999[1]
Total Exports FOB[2]	2,391	2,562	2,262
Exports to U.S.	840	837	742
Total Imports CIF[2]	3,852	4,651	4,409
Imports from U.S.	1,585	1,931	1,767
Trade Balance[2]	-1,461	-2,089	-2,147
Balance with U.S.[2]	-745	-1,094	-1,025
External Public Debt[3]	2,200	2,368	2,600
Fiscal Deficit/GDP (pct)[3]	1.0	2.9	3.0
Current Account Deficit/GDP (pct)[3]	3.6	5.4	5.4
Debt Service Payments/GDP (pct)[3]	2.4	3.0	2.4
Gold and Foreign Exchange Reserves (millions net)[3]	1100	1,400	1,100
Aid from U.S.	64	77	N/A
Aid from All Other Sources	N/A	N/A	N/A

1. 1999 figures are all estimates based on most recent data available.
2. Merchandise trade data from Guatemalan customs and central bank. Trade data does not include approximately $250 million in value added by the apparel assembly industry.
3. Data from the Guatemalan government's preliminary 2000 budget projection and Guatemala's Central Bank.
Source: Bureau of Economic and Business Affairs; U.S. Department of State

- **Balance of Payments**

    Guatemalan national income accounts excludes value added from textile assembly industry exports. With this value, and invisible inflows (mainly from nationals abroad sending home income), the official current account deficit in 1998 was $1,031 million, 62 percent higher than in 1997.

Government Influence on Business

The total tax collections are below 10 percent of GDP, so a new Tax Administration Agency and increased collections are in process by the government of Guatemala (GOG). The GOG has had too few funds to invest in infrastructure and needed social programs. The Foreign Investment Law makes trade and investment freer. However, implementation has been slow, and a new Tax Administration has created some initial bottlenecks. The GOG has sold the telephone company and the largest electricity distribution company, and given concession of the portal system to a private firm.

TRADE

④

Leading Imports and Exports

Imports: Fuel and petroleum products, machinery, grain, fertilizers, motor vehicles

Exports: Coffee, sugar, bananas, cut flowers, specialty fruits and berries, shrimp, petroleum, cardamom, textile assembly

Foreign Trade *(Exports and Imports in US$M)*			
	1997	1998	1999[1]
Total Exports FOB[2]	2,391	2,562	2,262
Exports to U.S.[2]	840	837	742
Total Imports CIF[2]	3,852	4,651	4,409
Imports from U.S.[2]	1,585	1,931	1,767

1. 1999 figures are all estimates based on most recent data available.
2. Merchandise trade data from Guatemalan customs and central bank. Trade data does not include approximately $250 million in value added by the apparel assembly industry.
Source: U.S. Department of State

Best Prospects Analysis

Best Prospects for Nonagricultural Goods and Services

Telecommunications Equipment

	1997 $M	1998 $M	1999E $M
Total Market Size	86.1	112.1	146.2
Total Local Production	N/A	N/A	N/A
Total Exports	2.7	3.3	4.0
Total Imports	88.8	115.4	150.2
Imports from the U.S.	46.9	61.0	79.3

Drugs and Pharmaceutical Products

	1997 $M	1998 $M	1999E $M
Total Market Size	67.5	135.0	155.2
Total Local Production	28.0	30.0	32.0
Total Exports	65.2	30.5	31.0
Total Imports	104.7	135.5	155.8
Imports from the U.S.	8.3	12.3	14.1

Automotive Parts and Service Equipment

	1997 $M	1998 $M	1999E $M
Total Market Size	129.0	160.0	195.1
Total Local Production	20.5	23.5	27.0
Total Exports	26.6	25.8	27.0
Total Imports	136.0	162.6	195.1
Imports from the U.S.	67.3	80.6	96.7

Electric Power Generation and Distribution

	1997 $M	1998 $M	1999 $M
Total Market Size	55.8	89.4	109.0
Total Local Production	19.3	21.0	24.0
Total Exports	1.4	2.0	3.0
Total Imports	46.9	70.4	88.0
Imports from the U.S.	30.9	41.4	51.7

Construction Equipment

	1997 $M	1998 $M	1999E $M
Total Market Size	63.0	100.6	105.9
Total Local Production	N/A	N/A	N/A
Total Exports	1.4	2.5	3.1
Total Imports	65.0	103.1	109.0
Imports from the U.S.	37.6	73.5	82.0

Food Processing and Packaging Equipment

	1997 $M	1998 $M	1999E $M
Total Market Size	58.9	72.9	86.3
Total Local Production	22.6	26.0	29.9
Total Exports	2.8	1.8	2.0
Total Imports	39.1	48.7	58.4
Imports from the U.S.	20.2	22.7	25.4

Hotel and Restaurant Equipment

	1997 $M	1998 $M	1999E $M
Total Market Size	25.9	33.8	40.8
Total Local Production	14.4	17.3	20.8
Total Exports	3.4	3.9	4.5
Total Imports	14.9	20.4	24.5
Imports from the U.S.	10.6	12.9	15.5

Best Prospects for Agricultural Products

Apples

	1997 $M	1998 $M	1999 $M
Total Market Size	N/A	N/A	N/A
Total Local Production	N/A	N/A	N/A
Total Exports	0	0	0
Total Imports	5.3	5.8	6.3
Imports from the U.S.	5.1	5.6	6.0

Cotton

	1997 $M	1998 $M	1999 $M
Total Market Size	N/A	N/A	N/A
Total Local Production	N/A	N/A	N/A
Total Exports	0	0	0
Total Imports	50.2	52.7	55.3
Imports from the U.S.	42.6	45.6	49.0

Planting Seeds

	1997 $M	1998 $M	1999 $M
Total Market Size	N/A	N/A	N/A
Total Local Production	N/A	N/A	N/A
Total Exports	0	0	0
Total Imports	4.6	4.8	5.1
Imports from the U.S.	3.7	4.1	4.4

Poultry

	1997 MT ('000)	1998 MT ('000)	1999 MT ('000)
Total Market Size	129	135	142
Total Local Production	117	123	129
Total Exports	0.6	0.6	0.6
Imports from the U.S.	12	13	14

Red Meats

	1997 MT ('000)	1998 MT ('000)	1999 MT ('000)
Total Market Size	56	52	50
Total Local Production	54	49	47
Total Exports	1.6	0	0
Total Imports	4.2	5.2	5.5
Imports from the U.S.	0.72	2.1	2.5

Fruit and Vegetable Juices

	1997 $M	1998 $M	1999 $M
Total Market Size	N/A	N/A	N/A
Total Local Production	N/A	N/A	N/A
Total Exports	N/A	N/A	N/A
Total Imports	6.6	7.0	7.5
Imports from the U.S.	1.0	1.5	2.0

Grapes

	1997 $M	1998 $M	1999 $M
Total Market Size	N/A	N/A	N/A
Total Local Production	N/A	N/A	N/A
Total Exports	N/A	N/A	N/A
Total Imports	5.4	5.1	5.6
Imports from the U.S.	4.5	4.5	5.0

Dairy Products

	1997 $M	1998 $M	1999 $M
Total Market Size	N/A	N/A	N/A
Total Local Production	N/A	N/A	N/A
Total Exports	N/A	N/A	N/A
Total Imports	53.4	55.0	56.6
Imports from the U.S.	3.8	4.2	4.6

Best Prospects for Investment

The frozen food industry stores and distributors agree that the infrastructure needs improvement. They would like to partner with U.S. firms to build facilities to handle, store, and transport frozen products.

The power industry is being privatized with many U. S. companies already involved.

Telecommunications is being privatized and is a prime foreign investment area.

The above statistics are unofficial estimates.
Exchange rate 6.20 (1997), 6.73 (1998), 7.50 (1999E)
N/A - Not Available, E - Estimated
Note: MT ('000) = Thousand Metric Tons

Extracted from the U.S. Department of Commerce USA Trade 2000 Country Commercial Guide for Guatemala.

Import and Export Tips

- **Regulations**

Customs: Trade with Guatemala is increasingly open. The GOG applies the Common External Tariff schedule of the Central American Common Market (CACM) to almost all agricultural and industrial goods. See **Contacts**.

Tariffs: Tariffs range from 0 to 15 percent. Capital goods and industrial goods are the main 0 percent items. Tariffs on textiles are up to 26 percent, which will decrease by 2005 to 10 to 15 percent. Shoe tariffs are currently up to 28 percent but will decrease by about 1 percent per year. Tariffs are based on the Common Duty System (SAC) of the Central American Common Market (CACM). Tariff Rate Quotas (TRQs) are tariffs adjustable by the GOG seasonally according to variable quota limits. TRQs exist for corn, wheat and wheat flour, apples, pears, poultry meat and byproducts, and fresh and frozen red meat. However, since U.S. prices have been high, TRQs have not been levied, so Guatemala has technically met WTO obligations.

Import Taxes: A 10 percent value-added tax is collected on entry. See **Trade Zones and Free Ports**.

Exchange Rate: Guatemala's trade deficit and capital flight have put pressure on the foreign exchange market. Though Guatemala sold an additional $400 million in foreign reserves in 1999, the local currency still depreciated by approximately 13 percent. Access to foreign exchange is unrestricted, and there are no reports of foreign exchange shortages. Though the government in 1998 passed legislation to permit banks and financial institutions to offer dollar-denominated accounts, enabling regulations have not been issued. A number of local banks currently offer dollar-denominated accounts in which the funds are actually held in offshore accounts.

- **Documentation**

  Exports: Standard export restrictions apply to Guatemala. Export license or exceptions are required for controlled items. For license exceptions eligibility, please contact the Bureau of Export Administration, U.S. Department of Commerce in Washington, D.C.

  Imports: Import licenses are not required for most products. The Ministry of Economy requires and issues licenses for various restricted goods, including lead, poultry, milk, eggs, sugar, coffee, bean and coffee plants, wheat flour, cottonseed, and others.

  Labeling: All domestic and imported food products must be labeled in Spanish and must include the following: product name, list of ingredients in order by quantity, nutritional content, name and address of the importer, weight, and expiration or best-used-by date. There are further, special labeling requirements for pharmaceuticals, fertilizers, pesticides, hormones, veterinary preparations, vaccines, poisonous substances, and mouthwashes. Violations of documentation laws carry heavy fines.

  Standards: There are no set product standards or requirements. There has not been full enforcement of requirements that all products sold in the domestic market be registered and tested. In practice, custom accepts U.S. and European standards.

- **Payment**

  Terms: Usual terms are 30 to 120 days. Payments are usually made on imports and exports via cash in advance or irrevocable letters of credit. Long-term clients sometimes finance with 60-day lines of credit to large Guatemalan importers. This may be leveraged by Guatemalan capital abroad. Be cautious before extending credit to Guatemalan firms. See **Exchange Rate and Finance (Exports and Projects)**.

  Currency Exchange: Foreign exchange is bought and sold freely in national markets. There are no foreign exchange controls. Profits by foreign businesspeople may be repatriated freely. See **Business Infrastructure (Currency Exchange)**.

  Fund Transfer: There are no restrictions on remittances or any other capital flow. Remittances can be in dollar-denominated GOG bonds, but their supply is limited. Some banks offer "pay through" dollar-denominated accounts, in which a local bank maintains an account for a U.S. bank. There is an estimated one month foreign exchange bank delay.

  Offshore Loans: No information is available at this time.

MARKETING TIPS (5)

Agents and Distributors

Choosing a good sales representative or distributor is crucial. Guatemala has many qualified and competent people for this role. Being able to speak English is not the most important factor. Look for reputation, product and industry knowledge, track record, enthusiasm, and commitment. Get to know partners well both in business and socially. Generally, foreign firms seek non-exclusivity and well-defined, renewable time periods with agent or distributors. Written agreements should be made for all agency and distribution deals, and the terms should be well explained. Referring frequently to the agreement later is a bad sign for the relationship. A Guatemalan attorney should review any agreements. Registering any intellectual property should always be done directly with the help of a Guatemalan attorney.

Establishing an Office

Foreign entities that want to operate in Guatemala must register with the same set of documents to the Mercantile Registry and the Guatemalan Internal Revenue Service (DGRI). The documents are (1) proof that the entity is legally constituted in accordance with the laws of the country (state) in which it is organized or registered; (2) a certified copy of the deed of incorporation (charter), the bylaws and modifications thereto; (3) proof that the board of directors has duly resolved to operate in Guatemala and has authorized the legal procedure to obtain permission to do so; (4) a power of attorney in which the person named is given ample powers to act and to represent the entity in all legal matters; (5) a document in which an amount is assigned as capital with reference to the entity's operations in Guatemala and in which it is expressly stated that the entity will be responsible for its obligations in Guatemala with all its assets both in Guatemala and abroad; (6) a declaration that the entity recognizes the jurisdiction of the courts and laws of Guatemala with respect to its activities and operations in the country and that neither the entity nor its representatives and employees will seek special rights as foreigners; (7) a declaration that the entity, prior to concluding operations in Guatemala will fulfill all legal requirements in connection therewith; (8) certified copies of its latest financial statements (balance sheet and income account). The documents must be certified by an authorized official in the country (state) of origin and must be authenticated by an appropriate Guatemalan Consular Official. To the DRGI, one should add a copy of the Ministry of Government authorization to operate. One must also register under the value-added tax.

Distribution and Sales Channels

Guatemalan businesspeople are used to doing business with the U.S., and many speak English. However, to maximize success, it is good to know local business practices. About one-half of the firms selling to Guatemala sell via an agent or distributor. Loosely, the more presales marketing and after-sales support and service are needed for a product, the more one needs a local agent or distributor. Personal contact is important. See **Business Customs.**

Direct Marketing

Half of all imports from the U.S. are from direct sales, primarily from Guatemalan businesspeople getting suppliers from their typical U.S. cities. Direct marketing works best when the product is well known or the buyer group is very specific. Preferably, send the same salesperson all the time to develop personal relationships with customers. Direct sales to government usually requires an authorized local representative. Telemarketing and mail order are not common.

Leasing/Joint Ventures

Joint ventures are regulated by the Guatemalan Commercial Code as contracts, not as companies or juridical persons. Trade names that include first and family names of participants make those people legally responsible if they consented to the usage. In joint ventures, an "active partner" shares profits and losses with one or more parties, the "participants," who provide goods and services. The active partner operates in his or her own name, and assumes legal relationships with third parties. The Guatemalan Development Foundation (FUNDESA) is a private organization that provides information to foreign firms on investment and joint ventures. A U.S. company may be authorized by the GOG to be established in Guatemala. Required are proof of legal constitution and a remunerated local agent with all general and special power. For purposes of the law, the agent presumably has such powers even if the agency agreement does not specify them.

Franchising

Guatemalan entrepreneurs are very receptive to U.S. firms offering franchising deals. A Guatemalan franchising association exists. Many U.S. firms already have franchises operating, especially in fast-food services, hotel operations, physical fitness facilities, and car rentals. All types of franchise look promising, especially in nonfoods.

Advertising and Promotion

Advertising is mainly done via local media such as radio, television, and the press. Billboards have been increasing along highways as well. See **Contacts**.

Selling Factors

Price, service, and quality are the deciding factors for Guatemalan customers. Products "Made in the USA" have an advantage. Direct sales go well with local advertisements, promotion campaigns, technical and illustrative brochures, sales visits, and sometimes, samples. Sometimes agents or distributors are the best means of market growth. Sales on commission or reselling are both used by local agents and distributors. If exclusive representation is given to an agent or distributor, the Agency, Distribution, and Representation Law governs how it can be transferred to someone else. End users and retailers usually do not have the time or experience to import directly or gain customs clearance.

Selling to the Government

Sales to the GOG and its corporations is best done by a local representative, who is usually required. The Government Procurement Law requires GOG purchases of over $151,000 to be open to at least five bidders (except in emergencies). Some prequalifications are required, and bidding time windows may be fairly short.

Pricing

Price is an important factor for Guatemalan businesses seeking suppliers. When local prices seem too high, many buy from abroad. Local merchants consider several factors in their pricing: (1) product fob cost, (2) product freight or transportation cost, (3) product insurance cost, (4) consular fees, and (5) import duties.

Customer Support

Sales service and support are important to Guatemalan buyers. U.S. firms have a good reputation, so service and support commitments should be made and explained to agents and distributors. Word spreads quickly about firms with poor service or support. Most retailers provide some guarantees for appliances, electronic consumer goods, telecommunications and computer equipment, electronic equipment, and industrial machinery.

Intellectual Property Rights (IPR)

Guatemala has signed the Central American Agreement for Industrial Protection. Trademarks, trade names, expressions, and publicity are covered. Intellectual property should be registered or protected directly with a Guatemalan attorney, and never with an agent or distributor. The industrial property registrar handles registration. Protection of intellectual property rights is weak. Penalties and enforcement are insufficient, and the judiciary has insufficient means to handle the issue. Guatemala has established a TRIPS mailbox, in accordance with TRIPS, and mainly pharmaceutical applications have been received. New laws for IPR are underway.

Attorney

A lawyer is recommended for many tasks: (1) preparing agent or distributor agreements, (2) registering a new company, (3) registering patents or trademarks, (4) debt collection, (5) property rights, (6) power of attorney, (7) trade arbitration. As a good business practice, do not use the same attorney as local business associates.

Due Diligence and Bona Fides: Performing due diligence and bona fides in Guatemala is difficult. Much information is private or unavailable. Bank and trade references should be obtained from potential agents and customers. U.S. banks, especially in Florida, should be asked for Guatemalan bank information. The International Company Profile Service can be obtained from the U.S. and Foreign Commercial Service. See **Contacts**.

FOREIGN INVESTMENT ⑥

Openness: Foreign investment is hindered by bureaucratic procedures and occasional arbitrary obstacles. The absence of an equities market for public trading in firms makes acquisitions and takeovers nearly impossible. All firms operating in Guatemala must formally incorporate, publish an intent to conduct business, and register with the Ministry of Economy. Foreign firms must meet additional registration requirements, including (1) demonstrating solvency, (2) depositing operating capital in a local bank, (3) supplying financial statements, (4) agreeing to fulfill all legal obligations before departing Guatemala, and (5) appointing a citizen or foreign resident with a work permit as a representative. Concessions are being granted to share production of petroleum and subsurface minerals. Only domestic airlines and ground transport must be mainly Guatemalan owned, but ground transport will be made available to full foreign ownership. The Caribbean Basin Initiative (CBI) and the Generalized System of Preferences (GSP) help the growth of some Guatemalan exports. See **Establishing an Office, Trade,** and **Private Ownership.**

Regulatory System: Bureaucratic hurdles are common for domestic and foreign firms. Regulations are often ambiguous and applied inconsistently. The Superintendency of Tax Administration (SAT) is meant to clarify import classifications, reduce delays, and reduce corruption in customs administration.

Investment Agreements: Guatemala has a framework agreement with the U. S. with a bilateral Trade and Investment Council (TIC). Inadequate intellectual property rights and other factors have delayed a bilateral investment trade treaty. Guatemala has bilateral or generally negotiating trade/investment treaties with Chile, Mexico, and Panama.

Trade Zones and Free Ports: Guatemala has eight authorized free trade zones. Free trade and maquiladora laws typically benefit textile assembly operations. Changes to free trade zone laws may occur to attract investors.

Performance Requirements/Incentives: Guatemala has no performance, purchase, or export requirements. It also has no requirements for local content in production. Investment incentives are specified in law and available to local and domestic investors without discrimination. The Drawback Industry Law helps maquiladoras (manufacturing and assembly operations). These firms get a one-year suspension of duties and value-added tax on importation of machinery and production inputs, and a ten-year income tax exemption. Incentives are also given to some forestry, mining, tourism, and petroleum investments.

Capital Markets and Investment: Guatemala has 35 banks with US$ 5 billion (est) in assets. The Superintendency of Banks regulates the financial services industry, but there is wide latitude in evaluating the value, performance, and quality of assets. There is also a lack of accepted accounting practices or procedures and standards for independent audits of banks and businesses. Real interest rates are 12 to 15 percent. Monetary policies are uncertain. Stock exchanges trade only commercial paper and government bonds. Foreigners usually don't rely on local credit to finance investments. Except for some industries, there are no restrictions on foreign control or investment in domestic enterprises.

Private Ownership: Foreign investors enjoy the same rights of use, benefit, and ownership of property as Guatemalans, according to foreign investment law. Only the Guatemalan constitution limits these rights.

Property Rights: Foreigners can have few restrictions on ownership and sale of real and personal property. Land adjacent to rivers, oceans, and international borders cannot be owned by foreigners. Legal discrimination does not exist on the surface. However, "home team" advantage makes it crucial for investors to have reliable local counsel. See **Intellectual Property Rights (IPR).**

Expropriation and Compensation: Expropriation is permitted only in cases of eminent domain, national interest, or social benefit. Advance compensation must be given for expropriation according to foreign investment law.

OPIC and Investment Insurance: The GOG signed the Multilateral Investment Guarantee (MIGA) in 1996. The Overseas Private Investment Corporation is active in Guatemala in insurance and investment financing. Foreign Government Approval (FGA) for OPIC applicants is usually fast.

Dispute Settlement: Guatemala has signed the United Nations convention on the recognition and enforcement of arbitral awards. It has not signed the convention on the settlement of investment disputes between states and nationals of other states (ICSID). Guatemalan procedures resemble those of the U.S., but are also more cumbersome, less transparent, and poorly implemented. Delays can be created by the party being accused.

FINANCE

⑦

Capital markets are still fairly shallow. There are over 35 banks, but the 5 largest control 40 percent of total assets. There are also investment firms, bonded warehouses, and some exchange houses. Many cooperatives supervised by the Ministry of Economy give credit to small and large businesses. Except for some small lending subsidies, the government does not ration or direct credit. Informal, unregu- lated institutions exist, such as money-changers, rural moneylenders, and informal investment firms. Most credit is given by commercial banks on market terms. Small and medium-sized businesses sometimes complain that commercial lending is focused on a small group of large borrowers. Foreign borrowers have equal access. The GOG Financial Modernization Program (FMP), with the Inter-American Development Bank (IADB), is intended to (1) make credit more available, (2) stretch out lending terms, and (3) make interest rates more competitive. The FMP is also (1) improving prudential regulation and information disclosure, (2) increasing the number of financial instruments available, and (3) removing some of the restrictions on types of services offered by banks and financial institutions. Almost all Guatemalan banks maintain correspondent relations with U.S. banks. See **Capital Markets and Investment.**

Export Financing: The Export-Import Bank (EXIM) is very active in Guatemala with various services. With the Central American Economic Integration Bank (BCIE), it operates a US$ 50-million credit facility to support U.S. exports to Central America. The U.S. Department of Agriculture has implemented a regional Credit Guarantee Program for Central America (GSM-102/103) and a Supplier Credit Guarantee Program for Guatemala (SCGP). The GSM 102/103 covers products from basic grains to poultry and red meats. The SCGP can eliminate the

need for letters of credit and U.S. bank transaction fees. The SGCP covers some high-value consumer-ready products. See **Trade (Payment Terms).**

Project Financing: Many sources offer project financing in Guatemala, including OPIC, EXIM, and the U.S. Trade and Development Agency. Internationally, active sources include the International Finance Corporation (IFC–World Bank Group), the Multi-Lateral Investment Guarantee Agency (MIGA), the World Bank, and the Inter American Development Bank (IADB). Many projects coincide with priorities related to Guatemala's peace accords. The Central American Economic Integration Bank (BCIE) is important, especially for projects related to public service and infrastructure. Types of projects being insured or supported include a credit facility, franchises, a jewelry factory, a financial group, electric power projects, road construction, and general infrastructure. Often joint support is offered by consortia of public, private, domestic, and international financial groups. See **Contacts.**

COMMUNICATIONS

Phone

Basic phone service is available at most hotels and offices. U.S. calls are usually no problem and can be made via the hotel operator (the Guatemalan Telecommunications Company, GUATEL), or directly (collect or calling card) by dialing AT&T (9999190), MCI (9999189), or Sprint (9999195). The international access code is 011, and the Guatemalan access code is 502 plus the local seven-digit number. City codes are not required. Telephone density is low, and it is unclear if the new privatized phone company will expand services.

Internet

There are about 7 Internet Service Providers (ISPs) in 1999. No additional information is available at this time.

Mail

The postal system is reasonably well developed although street names and numbers are not well defined. Express mail international services are available between Guatemala and the U.S.

TRANSPORTATION
9

Land

The Pan American Highway connects Guatemala with Mexico, El Salvador, and Honduras. Over 30 percent of Guatemalan trade is with neighboring countries. Cargo traffic is increasing, but intraregional commerce is threatened by poor highway conditions and lack of security.

Sea

Guatemala has five major ports. Three export ports mainly handle agricultural bulk goods. The recent railroad concession will help the flow of goods to ports, but cargo-handling facilities need more investment.

Puerto Quetzal, San Jose, and Champerico are the major ports on the Pacific coast. Puerto Barrios and Santo Tomas de Castilla are the principal ports on the Atlantic coast.

Air

Many airlines serve Guatemala. La Aurora International Airport in Guatemala City is the only airport with full passenger and freight facilities such as warehousing and refrigerated storage. It may not have the capacity and location needed for economic growth, but concessions are underway to expand La Aurora and Flores International Airport.

WORK WEEK
10

Business Hours: 8:00 a.m. to 12:00 p.m. and 1:00 p.m. to 5:00 p.m. Monday through Friday for commercial and industrial firms.

Government Hours: 8:00 a.m. to 4:30 p.m. Monday through Friday.

Bank Hours: 8:30 a.m. to 3:00 p.m. Monday through Friday. Closed on Saturday

New Year's Day, January 1
Holy Wednesday, April 11
Holy Thursday, April 12
Good Friday, April 13
Holy Saturday, April 14
Easter, April 15
Labor Day, May 1
Saint Paul's Day, June 29
Army Day, June 30
Bank Employees Day, July 1
Feast of Assumption, August 15
Jacinto Day, September 14
Independence Day, September 15
Day of the Race, October 12
Revolution Day, October 20
All Saints Day, November 1
Christmas Eve, December 24
Christmas Day, December 25
New Year's Eve, December 31

The banking sector also celebrates Bank Worker's Day on July 1 and Columbus Day on October 12.

Some holidays may be observed on different dates depending on the day of the week on which it falls. The U.S. Embassy will be closed on U.S. and Guatemalan holidays. It is recommended that business travelers do not schedule trips to Guatemala immediately before or immediately after local or U.S. holidays.

Business Customs

Most business conducted in Guatemala is based on personal relationships. Guatemalan business executives and government officials greatly value personal contacts with suppliers. U.S. suppliers should have a local representative or travel to Guatemala personally. Foreigners are often surprised at the accessibility of key decision makers and the frankness of local buyers. Promotional material should be in Spanish and emphasize U.S. origin. Technical presentations should be more educational than sales oriented.

Travel Advisory and Visas

A valid passport is required to enter and leave Guatemala. Visas are not required for stays of up to three months, which can be extended. Lost or stolen passports should be reported to the local police and the nearest U.S. consulate or embassy. A new passport should be obtained and shown to the main immigration office in Guatemala City. An exit tax must be paid when leaving the Guatemalan City Airport.

Business Infrastructure

Entry Requirements (personal and professional goods): Items to be brought in temporarily (laptop computers, cameras, cellular phones, and so on) are usually no problem. Small quantities of product samples are usually entered without difficulty. Larger quantities of products, displays for trade shows, and tools or equipment for projects should be imported temporarily with the help of a customs broker. Contact the Consular Section of the Embassy of Guatemala to obtain updated information on entry and exit requirements.

Currency Exchange: The quetzal is the main currency, and the exchange rate fluctuates very little; US$ 1 equals Q 6.7284 (January 1999). Foreign exchange is available at banks, hotels, and the airport. Major credit cards are usually accepted at major hotels, restaurants, and stores. See **Payment Terms and Currency Exchange).**

Taxes: There is a 10 percent value-added tax on all locally produced and imported goods. See **Regulations**.

Hotels and Restaurants: Hotels are abundant in Guatemala City, Antigua, and Panajachel, See **Contacts**.

Rent: Numerous real estate firms and independent agents speak English and work with business or government travelers for housing. Rents for U.S.-quality housing are relatively expensive. One should rent a place that already has phone service. Most officials and executives live in zones 10, 13, 14, 15, and on the Carretera El Salvador. The Commercial Section of the Embassy can help find real estate agents. There are many excellent and fairly priced restaurants.

Business Services: See **Advertising&Promotion** and **Investment (Performance Requirements /Incentives** and **Labor).**

Labor Costs and Legislation: Managers of Guatemalan firms must be either Guatemalan citizens or resident aliens with work permits. Both the minimum wage and maximum work week are regulated by law. Current daily minimum wage estimates are approximately US$ 3 (agriculture), US$ 3.30 (commerce), US$ 3.38 (construction), and US$ 6 (specialized labor). Workweek standard is 44 hours (8 per day) and 36 hours (6 per night) with time and a half required for overtime. The labor code requires bonuses equal to one month of salary in July and December, severance pay, and 10 percent for social security. Total benefits, bonuses, and employer contributions cost the employer about 62 percent on top of base pay. Skilled technicians charge up to US$ 20 a day.

Literacy: The literacy rate is 55.6 percent.

Insurance: Accident, sickness, liability, and medical evacuation insurance are fairly priced and wisely obtained before departure to Guatemala.

Travel Notes

The following travel notes have been supplied by the U.S. government. For the most recent general travel and consular information, see the U.S. Department of State travel publications or call the Traveler's Telephone Hotline at (202) 647-5225.

Security: Street crime is the main threat. Do not wear valuable jewelry or carry lots of cash. Valuables should be left in a hotel safty deposit box. Restaurants and night spots are best visited in groups, in taxis obtained from hotel front desks. Resistance to thieves and muggers is unwise.

Health Precautions: Drink bottled water and well-known carbonated beverages. Meals should be eaten at hotels and modern restaurants. Improperly washed or cooked foods can lead to diarrhea, food poisoning, and bacillary and amoebic dysentery. Fruits and raw vegetables should be well washed, peeled, and not had their skin broken. Current information on health matters may be obtained from the Centers for Disease Control and Prevention's international travelers' hotline at (404) 332-4559.

Embassy Assistance

The *Guide for Business Representatives* can be bought from the Superintendent of Documents. To obtain additional and updated information on entry and exit requirements, travelers can contact the Consular Section of the Embassy of Guatemala at 2220 R Street, N.W., Washington, D.C. 20008; Tel: (202) 745-4952. Travelers may also contact the nearest Guatemala consulate. They are located in Los Angeles, San Francisco, Atlanta, Baltimore, Memphis, Miami, Chicago, New Orleans, New York, Pittsburgh, Montgomery, and Houston.

CONTACTS

13

U.S. and Country Contacts

American Chamber of Commerce of Guatemala

Camara de Comercio Guatemalteco-Americana (AMCHAM)
Avenida Las Américas 18-81, Zona 14
Edificio Columbus Center, Nivel 8
01014 Guatemala, C.A.
Tel: (502) 363-17-74
Fax: (502) 363-17-74
E-mail: guamcham@ns.guate.net
Web site: http://www.guate.net/amcham

Office of Agricultural Affairs
Tel: (502) 332-4030
Fax: (502) 331-8293
Country Trade or Industry Associations in Key Sectors

Asociación de Gerentes de Guatemala – AGG (Guatemalan Managers Association)
6 Ave. 1-36, Zona 14
01014 Guatemala, C.A.
Tel: (502) 367-49-95; (502) 367-49-96;
  (502) 367-49-97; (502) 367-50-01;
  (502) 367-50-02; (502) 367-50-03;
  (502) 367-50-04; (502) 367-50-05
Fax: (502) 367-50-06; (502) 367-50-0 7
E-mail: agg@guate.net

Asociación Gremial de Exportadores de Productos No Tradicionales – AGEXPRONT
(Association of Exporters of Non-Traditional Products)
15 Ave. 14-72, Zona 13
01013 Guatemala, C.A.
Tel: (502) 362-20-02
Fax: (502) 362-19-50
E-mail: gexpron@pronet.net.gt
Web site: http://www.agexpront.com

Comite Coordinador de Asociaciones Agricolas, Comerciales, Industriales y Financieras – CACIF
(Coordinating Committee of Agricultural, Commercial, Industrial and Financial Associations)
Edificio Camara de Industria, 9no. Nivel
Ruta 6, 9-21, Zona 4
01004 Guatemala, C.A.
Tel: (502) 331-06-51; (502) 332-17-94
Fax: (502) 334-70-25
E-mail: cacif@infovia.com.gt
Web site: http://www.cacif.org.gt
Presidency rotates among the presidents of the member chambers.

Camara de Industria de Guatemala
(Guatemalan Chamber of Industry)
Edificio Camara de Industria, Nivel 12
Ruta 6, 9-21, Zona 4
01004 Guatemala, C.A.
Tel: (502) 331-91-91; (502) 334-48-48
Fax: (502) 334-10-90
E-mail: cig@ns.concyt.gob.gt

Camara de Comercio de Guatemala
(Chamber of Commerce of Guatemala)
10 Calle 3-80, Zona 1
01001 Guatemala, C.A.
Tel: (502) 232-45-45 / 253-53-53
Fax: (502) 251-41-97
E-mail: camcomgu@guate.net or
info@guatemala-chamber.org
Web site: http://www.guatemala-chamber.org

Camara Empresarial de Guatemala – CAEM
(Entrepreneurial Chamber of Guatemala)
Ruta 6 9-21, Zona 4
Edificio Cámara de Industria, 10 Nivel, Of. B
01004 Guatemala, C.A.
Tel: (502) 331-65-13; 334-68-78; 334-68-79;
  334-68-80
Fax: (502) 331-65-13
E-mail: caem@ns.concyt.gob.gt

Camara Guatemalteca de la Construccion
(Guatemalan Construction Industry Chamber)
Ruta 4, 3-56, Zona 4
01004 Guatemala, C.A.
Tel: (502) 334-48-15
Fax: (502) 334-53-08
E-mail: cgc@ns.concyt.gob.gt

Camara de Comercio Guatemalteco-
  Americana
(American Chamber of Commerce of
  Guatemala, AMCHAM)
Avenida Las Américas 18-81, Zona 14
Edificio Columbus Center, Nivel 8
01014 Guatemala, C.A.
Tel: (502) 363-17-74
Fax: (502) 363-17-74
E-mail: guamcham@ns.guate.net
Web site: http://www.guate.net/amcham

Affiliated to the Chamber of Commerce of
the United States through the Association of
American Chambers of Commerce in Latin
America (AACCLA)

Fundacion para el Desarrollo de Guatemala
  (FUNDESA)
(Guatemalan Development Foundation)
Centro Gerencial Las Margaritas, Torre I,
  Oficina 402
Diagonal 6, 10-65, Zona 10
01010 Guatemala, C.A.
Tel: (502) 332-79-52; (502) 332-79-53;
  (502) 332-79-54; (502) 332-79-55
Fax: (502) 332-79-58
E-mail: investinguat@guat.net
fundesa@gold.guat.net
Web site: http://www.fundesa.guatemal.org/

Camara del Agro
(Agricultural Industry Chamber)
15 Calle "A" 7-65, Zona 9
01009 Guatemala, C.A.
Tel: (502) 331-26-36
Fax: (502) 331-26-36
E-mail: camagro@ns.concyt.gob.gt

Asociación Nacional del Cafe – ANACAFE
(National Coffee Association)
5ta. Calle 0-50, Zona 14
01014 Guatemala, C.A.
Tel: (502) 337-00-75; (502) 333-75-35
Fax: (502) 333-77-30; (502) 373-31-38
E-mail: promocion@anacafe.org and
guatecoffe@gold.guate.net
Web site: http://www.anacafe.org

Asociación de Azucareros de Guatemala –
  ASAZGUA
(Sugar Growers Association)
6ta. Calle 6-38, Zona 9
Edificio Tívoli Plaza, 7mo. nivel
01009 Guatemala, C.A.
Tel: (502) 331-30-87; (502) 334-06-28
Fax: (502) 3318191
E-mail: asazgua@guate.net

Country Government Offices

Ministerio de Economia
(Ministry of Economy)
8va. avenida 10-43, Zona 1
01001 Guatemala, C.A.
Tel: (502) 251-86-06; (502) 251-50-86;
  (502) 253-09-03
Fax: (502) 238-0413

Ministerio de Finanzas Publicas
(Ministry of Public Finances)
8va. avenida y 21 Calle Zona 1
01001 Guatemala, C.A.
Tel: (502) 253-7072; (502) 230-5202;
 (502) 232-7939
Fax: (502) 251-0987

**Ministerio de Comunicaciones, Transporte y
 Obras Publicas**
(Ministry of Communications, Transportation
 and Public Works)
8a Avenida-15 Calle Zona 13
01013 Guatemala, C.A.
Tel: (502) 362-60-61
Fax: (502) 362-60-59

Ministerio de Trabajo y Prevision Social
(Ministry of Labor and Social Welfare)
14 Calle 5-49, Zona 1
01001 Guatemala, C.A.
Tel: (502) 238-25-22; (502) 251-56-44;
 (502) 330-13-66
Fax: (502) 230-13-63
E-mail: mintragua1@micro.com.gt

Ministerio de Relaciones Exteriores
(Ministry of Foreign Relations)
Palacio Nacional, Zona 1
01001 Guatemala, C.A.
Tel: (502) 232-67-48; (502) 221-44-44;
 (502) 238-28-27; (502) 232-67-48
Fax: (502) 251-8445
E-mail: diin@micro.com.gt

Ministerio de Energía y Minas
(Ministry of Energy and Mines)
Diagonal 17, 29-78, Zona 11
01011 Guatemala, C.A.
Tel: (502) 476-24-59: (502) 476-06-79;
 (502) 476-20-44
Fax: (502) 476-2044
E-mail: unimen1@pronet.net.yt

**Ministerio de Agricultura, Ganaderia y
 Alimentacion**
(Ministry of Agriculture, Livestock and
 Nutrition)
7ma avenida 12-90 Zona 13
Edificio Monja Blanca
01001 Guatemala, C.A.
Tel: (502) 332-3164; (502) 362-4756;
 (502) 362-4758
Fax: (502) 334-1685
E-mail: calpon@c.net.gt

Ministerio de Gobernacion
(Ministry of Government)
6a. avenida 4-64, zona 4
01004 Guatemala, C.A.
Tel: (502) 361-56-04; (502) 362-02-40;
 (502) 361-59-07
Fax: (502) 362-02-39

Ministerio de Salud Publica y Asistencia Social
(Ministry of Public Health and Social Assistance)
6ta. avenida 3-45 Zona 11
01001 Guatemala, C.A.
Tel: (502) 475-21-21; (502) 475-21-29
Fax: (502) 475-21-68
E-mail: uspas@infovia.com.gt

INGUAT - Instituto Guatemalteco de Turismo
(Guatemalan Tourism Institute)
7ma. avenida 1-17, Zona 4
01004 Guatemala, C.A.
Tel: (502) 331-1333; (502) 331-1342;
 (502) 331-1334
Fax: (502) 331-8893
E-mail: inguat@guate.net

BANGUAT – Banco de Guatemala
(Bank of Guatemala)
7ma. avenida 22-01, Zona 1
01001 Guatemala, C.A.
Tel: (502) 230-61-64; (502) 230-61-84;
 (502) 230-62-08; (502) 230-62-22
Fax: (502) 253-40-35
E-mail: webmaster@banguat.gob.gt

Registro Mercantil (Mercantile Registry)
6ta. Calle 7-57, Zona 1
01001 Guatemala, C.A.
Tel: (502) 232-0719; (502) 232-0481;
 (502) 232-0151
Fax: (502) 232-0719

Direccion General de Inversiones Y Programa de Mercadeo del Pais-PROGUAT
(Directorate General of Investment and Marketing of the Country – Ministry of Economy
8a Avenida 10-43, Zona 1
01001 Guatemala, C.A.
Tel: (502) 238-04-56
Fax: (502) 251-50-55
E-mail: vupi@ns.concyt.gob.gt

Registro Propiedad Industrial
(Industrial Property Registry – Ministry of Economy)
5ta. Calle 4-31, Zona 1
Edificio Plaza Rabi, 7o Nivel
01001 Guatemala, C.A.
Tel: (502) 230-1692; (502) 230-1822
Fax: (502) 230-1694
E-mail: repiweb@concyt.com.gob.gt

Ventanilla Unica de Inversiones – Ministerio de Economia
(One-Stop Investment Office – Ministry of Economy)
8va. avenida 10-43, Zona 1
01001 Guatemala, C.A.
Tel: (502) 238-3331; (502) 253-9640; (502) 232-0815
Fax: (502) 251-5055
E-mail: vupi@ns.concyt.gob.gt

Aduana Central
(Central Customs)
10 Calle 13-92, Zona 1
01001 Guatemala, C.A.
Tel: (502) 238-0651/3
Fax: (502) 221-4672
E-mail: aduanas@guate.net

GUATEL – Empresa Guatemalteca de Telecomunicaciones
(Guatemalan Telecommunications Company)
7ma. avenida 12-39, Zona 1
01001 Guatemala, C.A.
Tel: (502) 476-2057; (502) 238-3380; (502) 476-2371
E-mail: webmaster@ns.guate.net

INDE – Instituto Nacional de Electrificacion
(National Electrification Institute)
7 Ave. 2-29, Zona 9
01009 Guatemala, C.A.
Tel: (502) 334-57-75; (502) 334-57-76; (502) 334-57-11
Fax: (502) 334-5811
E-mail: pginde@guate.net

Business Consulting Services Firms

Aranky, Gonzales y Asociados
(Arthur Andersen)
Centro Gerencial Las Margaritas, Nivel 5
Diagonal 6, 10-65, Zona 10
01010 Guatemala, C.A.
Tel: (502) 332-7939; (502) 331-6916
Fax: (502) 331-6914
E-mail: andersenllb@gold.guate.net
Web site: http://www.arthurandersen.com

Tulischth Diaz y Asociados
Edificio El Triángulo, Nivel 17
(Ernst & Young International)
7 Ave. 6-53, Zona 4
01004 Guatemala, C.A.
Tel: (502) 332-18-67
Fax: (502) 334-70-59
E-mail: cylguatemala@guate.net
Languages: English – Spanish
Accounting Specialization:
Auditing, Financial Advisor, Consultants
Income Tax, Economic Feasibilities,
Market and Industrial

Tuncho Granados y Asociados
(BDO-Binder)
Edificio Plaza del Sol, Of. 413
12 Calle 2-04, Zona 9
01009 Guatemala, C.A.
Tel: (502) 331-9744
Fax: (502) 331-4217
E-mail: bdogua@quik.guate.com

Lizarralde, Ayestas, Asturias y Ramos
Edificio Santa Clara II, Oficina 204
13 Calle 1-51, Zona 10
01010 Guatemala, C.A.
Tel: (502) 331-5662
Fax: (502) 331-5687
E-mail: laarey@pronet.net.gt

Aldana, Salazar, Garcia y Asociados
(KPMG)
Edificio Centro Financiero, Zona 4
Torre I, Nivel 16
7 Ave. 5-10, Zona 4
01004 Guatemala, C.A.
Tel: (502) 334-2628
Fax: (502) 331-5477
E-mail: kpgm-socios@guate.net

Cordon, Parra y Cia.
(Price Waterhouse Coopers)
Edificio Tívoli Plaza, Nivel 4
6 Calle 6-38, Zona 9
01009 Guatemala, C.A.
Tel: (502) 334-50-80
Fax: (502) 331-28-19
E-mail: pw@guate.net

Lara & Coyoy
(Deloitte & Touche)
Edificio Casa, Nivel 4
7 Ave. 7-07 Zona 9
01009 Guatemala, C.A.
Tel: (502) 331-5466
Fax: (502) 332-6595
E-mail: deloitte@infovia.com.gt

Bocanegra, Cruz y Asociados
(Horwath International)
Edificio El Reformador, Nivel 4
Avenida La Reforma 1-50, Zona 9
01009 Guatemala, C.A.
Tel: (502) 334-5345; (502) 335-5349
Fax: (502) 334-5362

Country Commercial Banks

Banco Agricola Mercantil (BAM)
7 Avenida 9-11, Zona 1
01001 Guatemala, C.A.
Tel: (502) 232-16-01; (502) 232-16-02 ;
   (502) 232-16-03 ; (502) 232-16-04 ;
   (502) 232-16-05; (502) 251-95-06
Fax: (502) 232-54-06
E-mail: info@bamguatemala.com
Web site: http://www.bamguatemala.com

Banco Americano, S.A.
11 Calle 7-44, Zona 9
01009 Guatemala, C.A.
Tel: (502) 332-40-20; (502) 332-43-30
Fax: (502) 332-43-20
E-mail: grusin@infovia.com.gt

Banco Continental, S.A.
6 Avenida 9-08, Zona 9
01009 Guatemala, C.A.
Tel: (502) 339-20-01
Fax: (502) 339-20-84
E-mail: gfc@email.continet.com.gt
Web site: http://www.continet.com.gt

Banco De Comercio, S.A. (Bancomer)
6 Avenida 8-00, Zona 9
01009 Guatemala, C.A.
Tel: (502) 339-05-04; (502) 339-05-06
Fax: (502) 339-05-52

Banco De Exportacion, S.A. (Banex)
Avenida De La Reforma 11-49, Zona 10
01010 Guatemala, C.A.
Tel: (502) 331-98-61; (502) 360-12-06;
   (502) 334-69-19
Fax: (502) 332-28-79

Banco De La Construccion, S.A.
   (Construbanco)
12 Calle 4-17, Zona 1
01001 Guatemala, C.A.
Tel: (502) 230-63-82
Fax: (502) 230-61-50
E-mail: construcredit@gua.com.gt

Banco Del Agro, S.A.
7 Avenida 9-20, Zona 9
01009 Guatemala, C.A.
Tel: (502) 332-91-60
Fax: (502) 339-41-92
Web site: http://www.banagro.com.gt

Banco De La Republica, S.A.
Edifico Plaza La Repúlica
Diagonal 6,10-26, Zona 10
01001 Guatemala, C.A.
Tel: (502) 360-80-88; (502) 360-80-90
Fax: (502) 360-80-88
E-mail: brep@quik.guate.com

Banco Del Cafe, S.A. (Bancafe)
Avenida De La Reforma 9-30, Zona 9
01009 Guatemala, C.A.
Tel: (502) 331-13-11
Fax: (502) 331-14-18
E-mail: presidencia@bancafe.com.gt

Banco Del Ejercito, S.A.
7 Avenida 3-73, Zona 9
01009 Guatemala, C.A.
Tel: (502) 362-70-55; (502) 362-70-42
Fax: (502) 362-71-02
E-mail: banejer@gua.net

Banco Del Nor-Oriente, S.A. (Banoro)
Plaza Corporativa Reforma, Torre I
Avenida De La Reforma 6-64, Zona 9
01009 Guatemala, C.A.
Tel: (502) 339-08-51; (502) 339-08-63
Fax: (502) 339-08-49
E-mail: bnoro@guate.net

Banco De Los Trabajadores
8a. Avenida 10-67, Zona 1
01001 Guatemala, C.A.
Tel: (502) 232-46-51; (502) 232-46-55
Fax: (502) 251-89-02
E-mail: bantrab@infovia.com.gt

Banco Del Quetzal, S.A.
Plaza El Roble
7 Avenida 6-26, Zona 9
01009 Guatemala, C.A.
Tel: (502) 331-83-33
Fax: (502) 332-69-37

Banco De Occidente, S.A.
7 Avenida 11-15, Zona 1
01001 Guatemala, C.A.
Tel: (502) 230-58-94
Fax: (502) 261-23-40
Web site: http://www.occidente.com.gt

**Banco El Credito Hipotecario Nacional
De Guatemala**
7 Avenida 22-77, Zona 1
01001 Guatcmala, C.A.
Tel: (502) 230-65-42; (502) 230-65-62
Fax: (502) 230-22-74
E-mail: jpedchn@infovia.com.gt

Banco Empresarial, S.A.
7 Avenida 8-92, Zona 9
01009 Guatemala, C.A.
Tels: (502) 339-04-84/93
Fax: (502) 331-47-66
E-mail: empresa@c.net.gt

Banco Granai & Townson, S.A.
7 Avenida 1-86, Zona 4
01004 Guatemala, C.A.
Tel: (502) 331-23-33
Fax: (502) 334-79-13
E-mail: gt4@quetzal.net

Banco Industrial, S.A.
Edificio Centro Financiero
7 Avenida 5-10, Zona 4
01004 Guatemala, C.A.
Tel: (502) 334-51-11
Fax: (502) 331-94-37

Banco Inmobiliario, S.A.
7 Avenida 11-59 Zona 9
Edificio Galerias España
01009 Guatemala, C.A.
Tel: (502) 339-37-77
Fax: (502) 332-14-18
E-mail: info@bcoinmob.com.gt
Web site: http://www.bcoinmob.com.gt

Banco Internacional, S.A.
Avenida La Reforma, 16 Calle Zona 10
Edificio Torre Internacional
01001 Guatemala, C.A.
Tel: (502) 366-66-66
Fax: (502) 366-65-62
E-mail: gevasa@guate.net
Web site: http://www.bcointer.com

Banco Metropolitano, S.A.
5 Avenida 8-24, Zona 1
01001 Guatemala, C.A.
Tel: (502) 232-53-61; (502) 232-53-68
Fax: (502) 238-40-73
E-mail: info@bancomet.com.gt

**Banco Nacional De Desarrollo Agricola
(Bandesa)**
Avenida Reforma 2-56 Zona 9
01001 Guatemala, C.A.
Tel: (502) 332-7342; (502) 334-1383
Fax: (502) 334-1384

Banco Privado Para El Desarrollo, S.A.
(Bancasol)
7 Avenida 8-46, Zona 9
01009 Guatemala, C.A.
Tel: (502) 361-77-77; (502) 361-75-47
Fax: (502) 361-72-17
E-mail: bancasol@quick.guate.com

Banco Promotor, S.A. (Promobanco)
10a. Calle 6-47, Zona 1
01001 Guatemala, C.A.
Tel: (502) 230-53-50
Fax: (502) 251-33-87
E-mail: mensajes@promotor.com.gt
Web site: http://www.promotor.com.gt

Banco Reformador, S.A. (Bancor)
7 Avenida 7-24, Zona 9
01009 Guatemala, C.A.
Tel: (502) 362-08-88
Fax: (502) 362-08-50
E-mail: telcorgm@gold.guate.net

Banco Uno, S.A.
Blvd. Los Próceres
18 Calle 5-56, Zona 10
Edificio Unicentro
01010 Guatemala, C.A.
Tel: (502) 366-18-18
Fax: (502) 366-18-18 (ext 3421)
E-mail: msuarez@gua.pibnet.com

Citibank, N.A., Sucursal Guatemala
Avenida De La Reforma 15-45, Zona 10
01010 Guatemala, C.A.
Tel: (502) 333-65-74
Fax: (502) 333-68-60
E-mail: maya.gonzalez@citicorp.com
Web site: http://www.citicorp.com

Corporacion Financiera Nacional
11 Avenida 3-14, Zona 1
01001 Guatemala, C.A.
Tel: (502) 253-45-50; (502) 253-41-75
Fax: (502) 232-58-05

Lloyds Bank Plc, Sucursal Guatemala
Edificio Gran Vía
6a. Avenida 9-51, Zona 9
01009 Guatemala, C.A.
Tel: (502) 332-75-80; (502) 332-75-81;
   (502) 332-75-82; (502) 332-75-83;
   (502) 332-75-84; (502) 332-75-85;
   (502) 332-75-86; (502) 332-75-87;
   (502) 332-75-88; (502) 332-75-89
Fax: (502) 332-76-41

Multibanco, S.A.
7a. Avenida 6-17, Zona 9
01009 Guatemala, C.A.
Tel: (502) 332-74-74
Fax: (502) 332-74-73
E-mail: multibco@multibanco.com.gt
Web site: http://www.multibanco.com.gt

Primer Banco De Ahorro Y Prestamo Para
La Vivienda, S.A. (Vivibanco, S.A.)
6 Avenida 12-98, Zona 9
01009 Guatemala, C.A.
Tel: (502) 332-68-18
Fax: (502) 339-43-21
E-mail: sgarcia@pronet.net.gt

Multilateral Development Bank Offices

Inter-American Development Bank (IDB/BID)
12 Calle 1-25, Zona 10
01010 Guatemala, C.A.
Tel: (502) 335-2650; (502) 335-2831;
   (502) 335-2834
Fax: (502) 335-33-19
E-mail: walskap@iadb.org
Web site: http://www.iadb.org

World Bank (Wb/Bm)
13 Calle 3-40, Zona 10
Edificio Atlantis, Nivel 14
01010 Guatemala, C.A.
Tel: (502) 366-2044
Fax: (502) 366-1936
Web site: http://www.worldbank.org

Washington-Based USG Country Contacts

TPCC Trade Information Center – U.S.
   Department of Commerce
Tel: (800)-USA-TRADE

U.S. Department of Commerce
International Trade Administration
Office for Latin America and the Caribbean
14th Street & Constitution Avenue, NW,
   Room H-3203
Washington, DC 20230
Tel: (202) 482-4302
Fax: (202) 482-4726
Web site: http://www.ita.doc.gov

U.S. Department of Commerce
International Trade Administration
Multilateral Development Bank Office
14th Street & Constitution Avenue, NW,
   Room H-1806
Washington, DC 20230
Tel: (202) 482-3399
Fax: (202) 273-0927
Web site: http://www.ita.doc.gov

U.S. Department of Agriculture
Foreign Agricultural Service
Trade Assistance Promotion Office
Ag. Box 1052
Washington, DC 20250
Tel: (202) 720-7420
Fax: (202) 690-0193

U.S. Department of State
Office of Central American Affairs
2301 C Street, NW, Room No. 915 Main State
Washington, DC 20520
Tel: (202) 647-3559
Fax: (202) 647-2597
Office of Business Affairs
Tel: (202) 746-1625
Fax: (202) 647-3953

Export-Import Bank of the United States
(EXIM Bank)
International Business Development
811 Vermont Avenue, NW
Washington, DC 20571
Tel: (202) 565-3919
Fax: (202) 565-3331
Web site: http://www.exim.gov

U.S. Trade and Development Agency (TDA)
1621 N. Kent Street, Suite 300
Arlington, VA 22209-2131
Tel: (703) 875-4357
Fax: (703) 875-4009
info@tda.gov
Web site: http://www.tda.gov

U.S. Overseas Private Investment Corporation
   (OPIC)
1100 New York Avenue, NW
Washington, DC 20527
Tels: OPIC Automated Information Line:
   (202) 336-8799
OPIC Fax Line (for written inquiries):
   (202) 408-9859
Contact: Varies by OPIC program
Contact the OPIC Information Officer

Mercantile Registry
Registro Mercantil De Guatemala
6ta. Calle 7-57, Zona 1
01001 Guatemala, C.A.
Tel: (502) 253-58-19; (502) 232-07-19;
   (502) 232-04-81

Advertising and Trade Promotion

Union Guatemalteca De Agencias De
Publicidad - Ugap
(Guatemalan Union Of Publicity Agencies)
12 Calle 3-40 Zona 10
3er Nivel Local 45
Edificio Geminis 10, Torre Norte
01010 Guatemala, C.A.
Tel: (502) 367-23-01; (502) 367-23-02
Fax: (502) 367-23-03

Trade Promotion

American Chamber of Commerce of
   Guatemala
Avenida Las Américas 18-81, Zona 14
01014 Guatemala, C.A.
Tel: (502) 363-17-74
Fax: (502) 363-17-74
E-mail: guamcham@ns.guate.net
Web site: http://www.guate.net/amcham

Camara De Comercio De Guatemala
(Chamber Of Commerce)
10 Calle 3-80, Zona 1
01001 Guatemala, C.A.
Tel: (502) 232-45-45; (502) 253-53-53
Fax: (502) 251-41-97
E-mail: camcomgu@guate.net
or info@guatemala-chamber.org
Web site : http://www.guatemala-chamber.org

Camara De Industria De Guatemala
(Chamber Of Industry)
Edificio Camara De Industria, Nivel 12
Ruta 6, No. 9-21, Zona 4
01004 Guatemala, C.A.
Tel: (502) 331-91-91; (502) 334-48-48
Fax: (502) 334-10-90
E-mail: cig@ns.concyt.gob.gt

Fundacion Para El Desarrollo, S.A. - Fundesa
(Guatemalan Development Foundation)
Parque Gerencial Las Margaritas, Torre 1,
   Nivel 4, Of. 402
Diagonal 6, 10-65, Zona 10
01010 Guatemala, C.A.
Tel: (502) 332-79-52; (502) 332-79-53;
   (502) 332-79-54; (502) 332-79-55
Fax: (502) 332-79-58
E-mail: fundesa@gold.guate.net
or investinguat@guate.net

INTERFER, the Guatemalan International
Trade Fair, is held every odd year in Guatemala
City. Information on exhibiting in the "USA
Pavilion" can be obtained from the Commercial
Service Office at the U.S. Embassy
Tel: 011-502-331-15-41 (ext 259)
Fax: 011-502-331-73-73

Major Newspapers

Prensa Libre
13 Calle 9-31, Zona 1
Edificio Prensa Libre
01001 Guatemala, C.A.
Tel: (502) 230-50-96
Fax: (502) 251-87-68
E-mail: emprotec@guate.net
Web site: http://www.prensalibre.com.gt

Diario El Grafico
14 Avenida 4-33, Zona 1
01001 Guatemala, C.A.
Tel: (502) 230-50-80
Fax: (502) 251-00-14 (advertising)
E-mail: grafico@guate.net

Siglo Veintiuno
7 Avenida 11-63, Zona 9
Edificio Galerias España, Nivel 6
01009 Guatemala, C.A.
Tel: (502) 360-67-04
Fax: (502) 331-91-45; (502) 331-91-48
E-mail: buzon21@sigloxxi.com
Web site: http://www.sigloxxi.com

El Periodico
15 Avenida 24-51 Zona 13
Tel: (502) 332-1578
Fax: (502) 332-9761
E-mail: periodic@gold.guate.net

Nuestro Diario
15 Avenida 24-51 Zona 13
Tel: (502) 361-6988; (502) 361-6990
Fax: (502) 361-6988 (ext 280)
E-mail: noticia@infovia.com.gt

Al Dia [[[ED: "Al Dia" OK?]]]
Avenida Reforma 6-64 Zona 9
Plaza Corporativa, Torre Ii, Of. 203
Tel: (502) 339-0870
Fax: (502) 339-1276
E-mail: aldia@notinet.com.gt

Diario La Hora
9 Calle "A" 1-56, Zona 1
01001 Guatemala, C.A.
Tel: (502) 232-68-66; (502) 232-68-64
Fax: (502) 251-70-84
E-mail: lahora@lahora.com.gt

Afternoon Paper

Television Channels and Companies

Canal 3 De Television
Canal 7 De Television
30 Avenida 3-40, Zona 11
01011 Guatemala, C.A.
Tel: (502) 594-72-30; (502) 594-63-20
Fax: (502) 594-74-92
E-mail: informat@infovia.com.gt

Canal 5 De Television
4ta. Calle 18-38, Zona 1
01001 Guatemala, C.A.
Tel: (502) 238-17-81
Fax: (502) 232-70-03

Canal 11 De Television
Canal 13 De Television
20 Calle 5-02, Zona 10
01010 Guatemala, C.A.
Tel: (502) 368-25-32; (502) 368-25-35
Fax: (502) 333-4656
E-mail: canal13@infovia.com.gt
or canal11@infovia.com.gt

Mayacable/Comtech
23 Avenida 31-01, Zona 5
Edificio Spectrum
01005 Guatemala, C.A.
Tel: (502) 335-58-55
Fax: (502) 335-58-55 (ext 410)
E-mail: slopez@pronte.net.gt

Canal 25 De Television
3 Avenida 12-13 Zona 9
Centro Comercial Bonsai, 3 Nivel
Tel: (502) 362-0507; (502) 362-0517
Fax: (502) 362-9661
E-mail: aemundo@tikalnet.gt

Radio Stations

Radio Fabu Stereo
4ta. Calle 6-84 Zona 13
01009 Guatemala, C.A.333-4656
Tel: (502) 440-51-54
Fax: (502) 440-51-59

Radio Fabu has been incorporated by
Emisoras Unidas

Cadena Azul De Guatemala
Radio Mundial Y Radio Emperador
6ta. Avenida 2-80, Zona 1
01001 Guatemala, C.A.
Tel: (502) 253-25-52
Fax: (502) 253-25-52

Emisoras Unidas
4ta. Calle 6-84, Zona 13
01013 Guatemala, C.A.
Tel: (502) 440-51-33
Fax: (502) 440-51-59
E-mail: emisorasunidas@centroamerica.com
Web site: http://www.emisorasunidas.com

Radio Nuevo Mundo
Radio Cristal
6ta. Avenida 10-45, Zona 1, Nivel 2
Tel: (502) 230-36-18; (502) 230-46-18
Fax: (502) 232-20-36
E-mail: nuevomundo@gold.guate.net
Alfredo González Gamarra, Gerente General

Organizacion Alius
6ta. Avenida 0-60, Zona 4
Edificio Torre Profesional Ii, Nivel 3
01004 Guatemala, C.A.0
Tel: (502) 335-24-33
Fax: (502) 335-23-04
E-mail: radioactiva@guate.net

Radio Panamericana
1a. Calle 35-48, Zona 7, Col. Toledo
01007 Guatemala, C.A.
Tel: (502) 591-22-93
Fax: (502) 591-22-93

Radio Corporacion Nacional
6ta. Avenida 24 Calle Zona 9
Torre Profesional I, Nivel 9, Of 903-4
01009 Guatemala, C.A.
Tel: (502) 335-20-30
Fax: (502) 335-20-05
E-mail: rcn@starnet.net.gt
Web site: http://www.starnet.net.gt/rcn

Magazines And Business Journals

Revista Crónica
6 Avenida 0-60, Zona 4
Edificio Torre Profesional Ii
Nivel 3, Of. #312
01004 Guatcmala, C.A.
Tel: (502) 335-1693
Fax: (502) 335-2360
E-mail: cronica@guate.net

Revista Gerencia
Asociacion De Gerentes De Guatemala
6 Avenida 1-36, Zona 14
01014 Guatemala, C.A.
Tel: (502) 367-49-95; (502) 367-49-96;
  (502) 367-49-97; (502) 367-50-01;
  (502) 367-50-02; (502) 367-50-03;
  (502) 367-50-04; (502) 367-50-05
Fax: (502) 367-50-06; (502) 367-50-07
E-mail: agg@guate.net

Revista Industria
Cámara De Industria De Guatemala
Ruta 6, No. 9-21, Zona 4
Edificio Camara De Industria
01004 Guatemala, C.A.
Tel: (502) 331-91-91; (502) 334-48-48
Fax: (502) 334-10-90
E-mail: cig@ns.concyt.gob.gt
Web site: http://www.concyt.gob.gt

Mundo Comercial
Camara De Comercio De Guatemala
10 Calle 3-80, Zona 1
01001 Guatemala, C.A.
Tel: (502) 232-45-45; (502) 253-53-53
Fax: (502) 251-41-97
E-mail: camcomgu@guate.net
or info@guatemala-chamber.org
Web site: http://www.guatemala-chamber.org

Business Guatemala
Avenida Las Américas 18-81, Zona 14
01014 Guatemala, C.A.
Tel: (502) 363-17-74
Fax: (502) 363-17-74
E-mail: guamcham@ns.guate.net
Web site: http://www.guate.net/amcham

Industrial Property Registrar

Registro De La Propiedad Industrial
5ta. Calle 4-33, Zona 1
Edificio Plaza Rabi, 7o Nivel
01001 Guatemala, C.A.
Tel: (502) 230-16-92; (502) 230-16-97;
  (502) 230-18-22
Fax: (502) 230-16-94
E-mail: repiweb@concyt.com.gob.gt

Local Attorney

Beltranena, De La Cerda Y Chavez
Avenida La Reforma 12-01, Zona 10
Edificio Reforma Montufar, Torre A,
  Oficina 201
01010 Guatemala, C.A.
Tel: (502) 332-50-32; (502) 331-86-35
Fax: (502) 331-76-14; (502) 331-78-03
E-mail: fchavez@gold.guate.net

Quezada, Leonhardt, Fischer Y Asociados
13 Calle 2-60, Zona 10
Edificio Topacio Azul, Nivel 12, Ofcna. 1202
01010 Guatemala, C.A.
Tel: (502) 339-04-01; (502) 339-04-02;
  (502) 363-16-78
Fax: (502) 363-16-88
E-mail: quasoc@infovia.com.gt

Bonilla, Montano & Toriello
Avenida La Reforma 15-54, Zona 9
01009 Guatemala, C.A.
Tel: (502) 334-40-57; (502) 334-40-86;
  (502) 332-60-62
Fax: (502) 332-23-61
E-mail: ebmytlaw@guate.net

Palomo Campos Y Asociados
12 Calle 1-25, Zona 10
Edificio Gemenis 10, Torre Norte, Ofcna. 1305
01010 Guatemala, C.A.
Tel: (502) 335-33-01; (502) 35-33-04;
  (502) 35-33-05; (502) 35-33-06
Fax: (502) 335-32-97.

Soto & Soto
Boulevard Los Próceres 5-56, Zona 10
Edificio Unicentro, Oficina 702
01010 Guatemala, C.A.
Tel: (502) 366-37-35
Fax: (502) 366-45-15
E-mail: soto&soto@guate.net

Mayora & Mayora
15 Calle 1-04, Zona 10
Edificio Plaza Céntrica, Nivel 3, Oficina 301
01010 Guatemala, C.A.
Tel: (502) 366-25-31; (502) 366-25-32;
  (502) 366-25-33; (502) 366-25-34;
  (502) 366-25-36; (502) 366-25-37
Fax: (502) 366-25-40; (502) 366-25-41

Skinner Klee Y Ruiz
9a. Calle 3-72, Zona 1
01001 Guatemala, C.A.
Tel: (502) 232-61-19; (502) 251-62-35
Fax: (502) 238-34-31

Montufar International Law-Firm
Calle Montufar Y 5a. Avenida, Zona 9
Edificio El Cortez, 5o. Nivel
01009 Guatemala, C.A.
Tel: (502) 334-61-32
Fax: (502) 331-37-95
E-mail: montlawoff@pronet.net.gt

Hotel Accommodations And Housing

Hotel Clarion Suites
14 Calle 3-08, Zona 10
01010 Guatemala, C.A.
Tel: (502) 363-33-33
Fax: (502) 363-33-03
E-mail: vivaclarion@guate.net
Web site: http://www.sonda.com.gt/hotelviva

Hotel Westin Camino Real
14 Calle 0-20, Zona 10
01010 Guatemala, C.A.
Tel: (502) 333-46-33
Fax: (502) 337-43-13
E-mail: caminor@guate.net

Hotel Guatemala City Marriott
7ma. Avenida 15-45, Zona 9
01009 Guatemala, C.A.
Tel: (502) 331-77-77
Fax: (502) 332-18-77
E-mail: dorado@ns.guate.net
Web site: http://www.marriot.com

Hotel Princess Reforma
13 Calle 7-65, Zona 9
01009 Guatemala, C.A.
Tel: (502) 334-45-45
Fax: (502) 334-45-46
E-mail: princgua@guate.net

Hotel Sol Melia Guatemala
Avenida Las Americas 9-08, Zona 13
01013 Guatemala, C.A.
Tel: (502) 339-06-76
Fax: (502) 339-06-90
E-mail: guacp1@guate.net
Web site: http://www.lasamericashotel.com

Hotel Radisson Suites-Villa Magna
1a Avenida 12-46, Zona 10
01010 Guatemala, C.A.
Tel: (502) 332-97-97
Fax: (502) 332-97-72
E-mail: radisson@gold.guate.com

Hotel Hyatt Regency Guatemala
Complejo Tikal Futura
Calzada Roosevelt 22-43, Zona 11
01011 Guatemala, Guatemala, C.A.
Tel: (502) 440-1234
Fax: (502) 440-4050
E-mail: hyatt@guate.net
Web site: http://hyatt.com

Hotel Quinta Real
Km. 9 Carretera Al El Salvador, Zona 15
01015 Guatemala, Guatemala, C.A.
Tel: (502) 365-5050
Fax: (502) 365-5051
E-mail: businessguat@c.net.gt

Hotel Holiday Inn Guatemala
1era. Avenida 13-22, Zona 10
01010 Guatemala, C.A.
Tel: (502) 332-2555; (502) 332-2566
Fax: (502) 332-2578
E-mail: holidayinn@guate.net

**Diplomatic Representation in the
  United States**
Chief of Mission:
Chancery: 2220 R Street NW,
  Washington, DC 20008
Tel: (202) 745-4952
Fax: (202) 745-1908
Consulates General: Chicago, Houston, Los
Angeles, Miami, New York, San Francisco

**Diplomatic Representation from the
  United States**
Chief of Mission:
Embassy: 7-01 Avenida De La Reforma,
  Zone 10, Guatemala City
Mailing Address: Apo Aa 34024
Tel: (502) (2) 31-15-41
Fax: (502) (2) 33-48-77

Key Officers of Foreign Business Posts

Guide for Business Representatives
Superintendent of Documents, U.S.
  Government Printing Office,
  Washington, DC 20402
Tel: (202) 512-1800
Fax: (202) 512-2250

U.S. Embassy Commercial Section
Tel: (502) 334-8479
Fax: (502) 331-7373

Entry Requirements

Embassy of Guatemala
2220 R Street, N W
Washington DC 20008
Tel: (202) 745-4952; (202) 745-4953;
  (202) 745-4954
(or Guatemalan Consulate in Los Angeles, San Francisco, Miami, New Orleans, New York, Houston, Chicago)

Joint Ventures

FUNDESA (Guatemalan Development Association)
Miami Tel: (800) 741-6133
New Orleans Telephone: 504-558-3750

HONDURAS

TRADE AND BUSINESS GUIDE

PROFILE

1

Official Name:	Republic of Honduras
Official Language:	Spanish
Population:	6,249,598 (2000 est)
Population Growth:	2.52% (2000 est)
Age Structure:	0–14 years: 43%, 15–64 years: 54%, 65 years and over: 3% (2000 est)
Location:	Middle America, bordering the Caribbean Sea, between Guatemala and Nicaragua and bordering the North Pacific Ocean, between El Salvador and Nicaragua
Area:	112,090 square kilometers, slightly larger than Tennessee
Type of Government:	Democratic republic, with a unicameral National Assembly
Head of State:	President Carlos Roberto Flores Facusse
Cabinet:	Appointed by the president
Religion:	Roman Catholic, 97%, Protestant, 3%
Major Cities:	Capital: Tegucigalpa (678,700). San Pedro Sula (460,600), Choluteca (68,500), La Ceiba (68,200), El Progresso (64,700), Pueto Cortes (43,300)
Climate:	Subtropical in lowlands, temperate in mountains
Time:	Entire country is -6 GMT (Greenwich Mean Time), one hour behind EST (Eastern Standard Time)
GDP:	Purchasing power parity (PPP): $14.1 billion (1999 est); real growth rate: -3% (1999 est); per capita PPP: $2,050 (1999 est); composition by sector: agriculture = 20%, industry = 25%, services = 55% (1998 est)
Currency:	1 lempira (LP) = 100 centavos
Exchange Rate:	Average exchange rate: lempira per US$ 1 = 14.9207 (2000 est), 14.1650 (1999 est), 13,3100 (1998 est)
Weights & Measure:	Metric system
Natural Resources:	Timber, gold, silver, copper, lead, zinc, iron ore, antimony, coal, fish
Total Trade:	In millions US$ [exports (fob)/imports (cif)]: 1997 (N/A/N/A), 1998 (N/A/3,031), 1999 est (1,600/2,828)
Trade with U.S.:	In millions US$ [exports (fob)/imports (cif)]: 1997 (2,322/2,019), 1998 (2,544/2,318), 1999 est (2,713/2,370)
Major Trade Partners:	Imports: United States, Guatemala, Japan, Germany, Mexico, El Salvador. Exports: United States, Germany, Japan, Spain, and Belgium
Membership:	IADB, IBRD, IFC, IMF, MIGA, OAS, UN, UNCTAD, WIPO, and WTO. See membership description in appendix.

Sources: Honduran Central Bank, CIA World Fact Book, United Nations World Statistics, USAID, U.S. Department of Commerce, U.S. Department of State

POLITICAL OUTLOOK

②

Relationship with the U.S.

Traditionally, the two countries have had close and friendly bilateral relations. The U.S. is Honduras's most important international partner, and Honduras is the U.S's largest bilateral trading partner. The U.S. also has a large, strategic, military presence in Honduras. Honduras has complained, however, about the Helms–Burton legislation, the U.S. trade embargo against Cuba, and U.S. deportations of Hondurans. A Temporary Protected Status (TPS) was granted to Hondurans who entered the U.S. prior to December 1998 due to Hurricane Mitch disaster. The TPS was extended through July 2001. In 1998, the U.S. temporarily withdrew some trade benefits to encourage vigorous Honduran enforcement of intellectual property rights, particularly in the area of satellite TV piracy.

Influences on Business

The political situation has been relatively stable for over two decades. One recent political act of significance to the business community is President Carlos Roberto Flores's new economic plan of April 1998. The plan decreased the corporate tax from 40 to 25 percent by 1999. The economic program also increased the sales tax from 7 to 12 percent. Another recent significant political issue affecting the business community is the Hurricane Mitch reconstruction program designed to repair infrastructure damage and get the economy back on track. With elections scheduled for November 2001, presidential candidates would publicize their economic agendas.

Profile

System: The country began to move from military to democratic rule in 1980. According to its constitution, Honduras has three branches of government. The president is elected to a four-year term and is not eligible for re-election. The 128-member unicameral Congress also serves four-year terms. An independent judiciary is headed by a nine-member Supreme Court, which is elected by Congress to four-year terms. For several years, Honduras has also had a semiautonomous Public Ministry, which is headed by the attorney general.

Schedule for Elections: President Carlos Roberto Flores took office in January 1998. The next election is scheduled for November 2001.

Major Parties: Honduras has a long tradition of a two-party system. The Liberal Party (PL) is the dominant party. Since 1980, the opposition party, the National Party (PN), has won the national elections only once, in 1989. Both parties favor centrist platforms, democratic institutions, free markets, and free trade.

Political Violence: The political situation is relatively stable. Although violent crime is common, politically motivated crime is not. Peaceful protests often take place as the police stand by. There are no nascent insurrections in Honduras, and relations with the country's Central American neighbors are good.

Corruption: Corruption does pose a constraint to foreign direct investment. A team of international jurists and Public Ministry advisors, supported by USAID funds and technical assistance, has worked to improve Honduras's archaic judicial system and reduce elite immunity and corruption. Recently, there has been an increase in the number of corruption cases that have been adjudicated by the courts.

ECONOMIC OUTLOOK 3

Trends

Major steps were taken in the 1990s to open the Honduran market to foreign investment. U.S. investors and exporters responded in particular. The U.S. now accounts for about 50 percent of Honduras's foreign trade and for more than 70 percent of the country's foreign direct investment. Economic reform also led to strong GDP and export growth. Disaster struck in October 1998, however, when Hurricane Mitch took at least 5,000 lives and caused approximately US$ 3 billion in damages (equivalent to 50 percent of GDP). Recovery was impeded by another disaster: in February 1999, a major fire damaged the country's important El Cajon hydroelectric plant. Honduras under President Carlos Flores has responded well to these challenges, and the private sector has shown confidence in the government's economic guidance. In 1999, the economy showed positive signs of recovery and macroeconomic stability (see Key Economic Indicators). The Honduran Central Bank forecast fiscal deficit equal to 6 percent of GDP, inflation between 10 to 12 percent and GDP growth between 4 to 5 percent for 2001. Although full economic recovery will take some time, the economic outlook is hopeful.

Major Growth Sectors

Major business opportunities are found in tourism, computers and peripherals, medical equipment, automotive parts and service equipment, and building supplies. Strong growth was recorded in 1998 in the construction sector (up 16.7 percent), the financial services sector (up 9.9 percent), the public utilities sector (up 8.9 percent), and the Honduran maquiladora sector (precise data is not available). Honduras's major export crop, coffee, reached $430 million in exports in 1998, 32 percent higher than in 1997. The second most important export crop, bananas, fell to $176 million, 17 percent below the 1997 figure. Honduras attracts a lot of maquiladora activities especially in textile assembly. Maquiladora sector employed over 120,000 Honduran workers and provided US$ 541 million in exports and US$ 306 million in salaries and wages in 1999/2000.

Key Economic Indicators

Income, Production and Employment (millions of U.S. dollars unless otherwise indicated)			
	1997	1998	1999[1]
Nominal GDP (US$)[2]	4,386	5,135	5,346
Real GDP Growth (pct)	4.5	3.0	-1.9
GDP by Sector:			
Agriculture	1,667	1,555	1,431
Manufacturing	935	989	1,019
Services	459	475	481
Government	298	318	324
Per Capita GDP (US$)[3]	940	940	969
Labor Force (millions)	1,955	2,041	2,299
Unemployment Rate (pct)[4]	N/A	3.9	3.7

1. 1999 figures are estimates based on available data. 2. GDP at factor cost. 3. Percentage changes calculated in local currency. 4. Open unemployment is low; however, underemployment approaches 22%.
Source: Bureau of Economic and Business Affairs; U.S. Department of State

- Infrastructure

  Hurricane Mitch caused extensive damage to the country's infrastructure systems; pre-Mitch levels will not be surpassed until 2003. The government's National Reconstruction and Transformation Master Plan (PMRTN) estimates that infrastructure investments totaling US$ 1 billion will be required. Port facilities, airport facilities, and the road network are currently in good shape, but telecommunications, housing, and water and sewage infrastructure are in need of substantial improvements.

- Labor

  Though low-skilled workers are readily available, there is a shortage of skilled workers. Union officials continue to criticize the Ministry of Labor (MOL) for a failure to enforce workers' rights, particularly the right to form a union. The MOL has worked with the U.S. Trade Representative's Office to respond to such complaints, and union–employer relations have improved. Over the last several years, the number of strikes and work stoppages in manufacturing plants has dropped by more than one-third. Honduran law prescribes a maximum eight-hour workday and a 44-hour workweek, with at least one 24-hour rest period per week. The Labor Code requires 10 days of paid vacation after one year and 20 days after four years. Minors under the age of 16 may not work although 15-year-olds who have completed their compulsory schooling may work so long as they have the written permission of their parents and the MOL. Forgery of MOL permission has been a problem.

Money and Prices			
(annual percentage growth)			
	1997	1998	1999[1]
Money Supply (M2)	39.2	18.4	N/A
Consumer Price Inflation	12.8	15.7	10.9
Exchange Rate (LP/US$ annual average)			
Official	13.14	13.54	14.56
Parallel	13.05	13.41	14.42

1. 1999 figures are estimates based on available data.
Source: Bureau of Economic and Business Affairs; U.S. Department of State

Balance of Payments and Trade *(millions of U.S. dollars unless otherwise indicated)*			
	1997	1998	1999[1]
Total Exports FOB	N/A	N/A	1,600
Exports to U.S.	2,322	2,544	2,713
Total Imports CIF	N/A	3,031	2,829
Imports from U.S.	2,019	2,318	2,370
Trade Balance	N/A	N/A	-1,229
Trade Balance with U.S.	303	226	343
External Public Debt	3,455	3,489	4,383
Fiscal Deficit/GDP (pct)	2.6	1.5	N/A
Current Account Deficit/GDP (pct)	3.3	0.3	2.0
Debt Service Payments/GDP (pct)	16.6	17.3	15.0
Gold and Foreign Exchange Reserves	606	670	N/A
Aid from U.S.	36	36	556[2]
Aid from All Other Countries	116	N/A	244

1. 1999 figures are estimates based on available data. 2. Includes USAID, Department of Defense, and other agencies' disaster relief and reconstruction assistance in response to Hurricane Mitch.
Source: Bureau of Economic and Business Affairs; U.S. Department of State

- **Balance of Payments**
  Recovery of banana exports and increased activities and exports in the maquiladora sector is expected to reduce the deficit in the balance of payments. See **Key Economic Indicators.**

Government Influence on Business

The Honduran government historically has played a large and often cumbersome role in the country's economy. Since 1995, the Government of Honduras (GOH) has received more than $200 million from the Inter American Development Bank (IDB) and the World Bank to reduce the role of the state, stimulate the participation of the private sector, modernize public administration, and reorganize the executive branch. Substantial steps have been taken toward privatization and structural reform, with the pace of reform accelerating in 1998. Despite such successes, much work remains to be done, especially in reducing the size of the government workforce.

TRADE

Leading Imports and Exports

Imports: Machinery and transport equipment, industrial raw materials, chemical products, manufactured goods, fuel and oil, food stuffs

Exports: Coffee, bananas, shrimp, lobster, minerals, meat, lumber

Foreign Trade (Exports and Imports in US$M)			
	1997	1998	1999[1]
Total Exports FOB	N/A	N/A	N/A
Exports to U.S.	2,322	2,544	2,713
Total Imports CIF	N/A	3,031	2,829
Imports from U.S.	2,019	2,318	2,370

1. 1999 figures are estimates based on available data.
Source: Bureau of Economic and Business Affairs; U.S. Department of State

Best Prospects Analysis

Best Prospects for Nonagricultural Goods and Services

Textile Machinery, Equipment, and Fabrics

	1999 $M	2000 $M	2001 $M
Total Market Size	13.2	16.5	20.6
Total Local Production	N/A	N/A	N/A
Total Exports	0.8	1.0	1.25
Total Imports	13.2	16.5	20.6
Imports from the U.S.	5.2	6.5	8.1

Apparel Assembly Industry

	1999 $M	2000 $M	2001 $M
Total Investment	1082.0	1298.4	1558.0
Foreign Investment	565.5	678.6	814.3
U.S. Investment	325.0	390.0	468.0
Employment Generation	108,890	130,668	156,800

Best Sales Prospects: Spinning machines, Sewing machines, Needles, Drying machines, Bleaching or dyeing machines, Zippers, Buttons, Trims, Yarn, Boxes

Construction Machinery and Equipment

	1999 $M	2000 $M	2001 $M
Total Market Size	94.2	103.6	116.0
Total Local Production	0.0	0.0	0.0
Total Exports	0.0	0.0	0.0
Total Imports	94.2	103.6	116.0
Imports from the U.S.	78.0	85.8	96.0

Best Sales Prospects: Overall, road construction, earth-moving and road rehabilitation and maintenance equipment have the best potential; tractors, backhoes, shovel loaders, asphalt mixers, dumping trucks, move, grade, level, scrap, excavating, extracting machinery parts for machinery for public works and building, mobile crane

Telecommunications Equipment (TEL)

	1999 $M	2000 $M	2001 $M
Total Market Size	57.9	69.4	83.2
Total Local Production	0.0	0.0	0.0
Total Exports	0.0	0.0	0.0
Total Imports	57.9	69.4	83.2
Imports from the U.S.	40.7	48.8	58.5

Best Sales Prospects: Most promising sub-sectors include cellular and wireless telephone systems, data transmission equipment, trunked mobile radio systems, and paging systems.

Pollution Control/Water Resources Equipment
1994-2005

Water and sewage sector investments:	US$ 358.2 million
Environmental Technology investments:	US$ 905 million

Best Prospects: Potable water treatment equipment, Municipal waste water treatment equipment, Sewage and water treatment systems, Filtering and purifying machinery and apparatus, Solid waste handling and disposal equipment, Environmental consulting services, Pumping stations/equipment, Pumps, filters, and chemicals for water purification, Laboratory equipment, Stabilization lagoons, Home water treatment devices

Agricultural Machinery and Equipment

	1999 $M	2000 $M	2001 $M
Total Market Size	55.4	45.2	54.2
Total Local Production	0.0	0.0	0.0
Total Exports	0.3	N/A	N/A
Total Imports	55.7	61.3	70.4
Imports from the U.S.	40.7	44.7	51.4

Best Prospects: Disc plows, Disc harrows, Dump trailers, Brushcutters, Farm tractors, Row crop unit planters, Harvesting machines, Irrigation equipment, Boom sprayers

Hotel & Restaurant Equipment and Accessories

	1999 $M	2000 $M	2001 $M
Total Market Size	27.3	17.2	21.5
Total Local Production	N/A	N/A	N/A
Total Exports	3.7	4.6	5.7
Total Imports	27.3	34.1	42.6
Imports from the U.S.	13.8	17.2	21.5

New hotel projects through the year 2001: Hotels Investment in Tegucigalpa (US$3.4M), San Pedro Sula (US$10.5M), Bay Islands (US$66.9M). Total (US$ 80.8M)

Best Sales Prospects: Carpets, Comforters, Washers, Televisions, Telephones, Table Kitchenware, Air conditioning and refrigeration equipment, Electric hand-drying apparatus, Wooden Furniture, Kitchen appliances

Computers/Peripherals and Software

	1999 $M	2000 $M	2001 $M
Total Market Size	47.6	57.1	68.5
Total Local Production	N/A	N/A	N/A
Total Exports	0.0	0.0	0.0
Total Imports	48.5	58.2	69.8
Imports from the U.S.	46.1	55.3	66.3

Transshipment of equipment and parts is not reflected in data table figures.

Best Sales Prospects: Computers & Peripherals; Personal Computers, Hard disks, Keyboard units, Computer monitors, Server Systems, Modems, CD-Rom Drives, Printer Units, Computer Software/Multimedia. Computer Software; Specialized software applications (accounting, financial), General Business Application solutions for Windows, Systems supporting software, Software development/programming tools, Software games

Franchising
Over 55 Franchisors are in operation in Honduras Food sector is about 50% of total market.

Household Consumer Goods

	1999 $M	2000 $M	2001 $M
Total Market Size	125.9	151.0	181.2
Total Local Production	N/A	N/A	N/A
Total Exports	30.8	36.9	44.2
Total Imports	125.9	151.0	181.2
Imports from the U.S.	44.1	52.9	63.5

Best Sales Prospects: Soap, Plastic tableware and kitchenware, Microwaves, Food processors, Toilet paper, Glass mirrors, Drinking glasses, Cooking appliances, Stainless steel and aluminum cooking and kitchenware, Table knives, Razors, Refrigerators, Stoves, Freezers, Mowers, Juice extractors, Alarm clocks

Best Prospects for Agricultural Products

Corn

	1998 MT ('000)	1999 MT ('000)	2000 MT ('000)
Total Market Size	666	744	765
Total Local Production	595	504	625
Total Exports	5	0	10
Total Imports	66	240	130
Imports from the U.S.	63	240	130

Rice (Milled)

	1998 MT ('000)	1999 MT ('000)	2000 MT ('000)
Total Market Size	63	73	75
Total Local Production	33	13	15
Total Exports	0	0	0
Total Imports	30	60	60
Imports from the U.S.	30	50	55

Wheat

	1998 MT ('000)	1999 MT ('000)	2000 MT ('000)
Total Market Size	147	150	155
Total Local Production	0	0	0
Total Exports	0	0	0
Total Imports	147	150	155
Imports from the U.S.	140	140	145

Meal, Soybean

	1998 MT ('000)	1999 MT ('000)	2000 MT ('000)
Total Market Size	69	71	76
Total Local Production	1	1	1
Total Exports	0	0	0
Total Imports	68	70	75
Imports from the U.S.	68	70	75

Consumer-Oriented Products

	1998 $M	1999 $M	2000 $M
Total Market Size	366	388	396
Total Local Production	764	740	751
Total Exports	616	585	596
Total Imports	218	233	241
Imports from the U.S.	44	53	56

The above statistics are unofficial estimates.
Exchange Rate: 1 Dollar = 14.91 Lempiras
N/A - Not Available, E - Estimated
Note: MT ('000) = Metric Tons

Extracted from the U.S. Department of Commerce USA Trade 2001 Country Commercial Guide for Honduras

Import and Export Tips

• **Regulations**

Customs: The Honduran Customs Law regulates the normative and administrative operations of the local custom system. The Brussels Customs Value is the current method of valuation. Honduras implemented the WTO Customs Valuation Agreement on February 14, 2000, which relates to the price actually paid for the goods (invoice price). Honduras belongs to the Central American Uniform Tariff Schedule (NAUCA II) and the General Treaty for Central American Economic Integration, both of which govern imports into Honduras.

Tariffs: A great number of charges and fees have been eliminated, and further reductions are planned. Honduras is a member of the Central American Common Market (CACM). The common import tariff schedule for CACM countries (Costa Rica,

El Salvador, Guatemala, Honduras and Nicaragua) range between 5 and 20 percent. CACM countries agreed to lower the common external tariff (CET) to zero to 15 percent but allowed each country to determine the schedule of the change. In response, Honduras passed the Tariff Matching Law in April 1997. This law effectively reduced tariff rates for certain raw materials and inputs produced outside the Central American Region from 3 percent as of May 31, 1997, to 1 percent as of December 1, 1997. Tariffs on capital goods were reduced to 1 percent on January 1, 1997. The Law also established a tariff reduction schedule through 2000. According to the schedule, intermediate goods were reduced to a range between 5 and 10 percent as of December 31, 1998 and finished goods were reduced to 16 percent as of December 31, 2000. Reduction to 15% is scheduled for December 31, 2001. For selected grain products, a variable levy price band mechanism is in place. Imports of corn, sorghum, and corn meal and groats entering with prices above the band are assessed lower duties, according to a predetermined schedule; imports priced below the band are assessed higher duties, while imports within the specified band are assessed a 20 percent duty.

Import Taxes: Import duties now range between 1 and 20 percent for almost all products. Higher tariff rates will remain for some items, such as alcohol, vehicles, textiles, and petroleum-derived products. Ad valorem duties are applied to most products, as are administrative and selective consumption taxes in some cases. Duties on imports of raw materials have been reduced to 1 percent.

Exchange Rate: The central bank uses an auction system to regulate the allocation of foreign exchange. Dollar purchases, in which foreigners may participate, are conducted at 5 to 7 percent above or below the base price established every five days.

During recent auctions, the central bank has been adjudicating an average of US$ 8 million daily. Foreign exchange demand in 1998 was 96.1 percent covered. The Foreign Exchange Repatriation Law, passed in September 1990, requires all Honduran exporters, except those operating in free trade zones and export processing zones, to repatriate 100 percent of their export earnings through the commercial banking system. Until recently, commercial banks were allowed to use 70 percent of export earnings to meet their clients' foreign exchange needs. The other 30 percent had to be sold to the central bank at the prevailing interbank rate of exchange. Presently, commercial banks are required to sell 100 percent of these repatriated earnings to the central bank, which in turn auctions up to 60 percent in the open market.

- **Documentation**

Exports: The following documents are required for imports as well as exports: a commercial invoice, a bill of lading or an airway bill, a certificate of origin or title for vehicles, a phyto- or zoo-sanitary certificate (where appropriate), and a sanitary permit for foodstuffs. Exporters (except for free trade zone or export processing zone exporters) must give advanced notice to the Central Bank about the following characteristics of goods to be exported: quantity, value, destination, probable date of export, and the probable value and currency of anticipated export revenues. Exporters must also demonstrate that there are sufficient supplies to meet domestic needs prior to receiving permission to export. Price controls exist for coffee and medicines and, informally, for staple products such as milk and sugar. Export controls exist for sugar. All coffee exports must be registered with the Honduran Coffee Institute.

Imports: See **Exports** for a list of the basic, required documents. For commercial imports, documentation must also show that the dollars used to purchase such imports were acquired through the Honduran commercial banking system. Although the GOH eliminated all import-licensing requirements in accordance with GATT, Honduras uses onerous zoo-sanitary requirements to limit market access to U.S. agricultural products. The Ministry of Natural Resources issues these zoo-sanitary permits. The GOH forbids the import of items that compete with certain domestic industries. Those protected presently include cement, sugar, and rice from south-eastern Asia, and beef from South America. Import restrictions are also imposed on firearms and ammunition, toxic chemicals, pornographic material, and narcotics. Import registration procedures have been maintained only for statistical purposes.

Labeling: Processed food products must be labeled in Spanish and registered with the Division of Food Control (DFC) of the Ministry of Public Health. The GOH intends to improve their enforcement of existing regulations. The following information is currently required on labels of all food products: (1) the specific name of the product; (2) the name of the manufacturer or packaging company; (3) the country of origin; (4) a list of ingredients in descending order by initial weight (m/m) at the time the product was manufactured; (5) an indelibly marked lot number; (6) the expiration date; (7) the net content; and (8) the sanitary registration number provided by the DFC. All writing on labels must be clear and legible, and should be made in Spanish unless authorized otherwise by the DFC. If products require refrigeration, require immediate refrigeration after opening, are artificial, or have been treated with radiation, they must be labeled accordingly. The DFC does not require that samples be labeled or registered. However, all samples are subject to laboratory analysis and DFC approval.

Standards: Food and beverage products must fulfill the same registration requirements that have been established for national products in relation to residual chemical content, artificial flavoring, coloring, and preservatives. Honduras is a member of the International Standards Organization (ISO), through the Science and Technology National Council (COHCIT), since January 2000. COHCIT is in the process of establishing an Information Center to help local firms interested in obtaining details related to rules and standards for ISO certification. The Standards and Metrology division of the Ministry of Industry & Trade has established a Quality Management Technical Committee responsible for reviewing ISO 9000 and ISO 14000 technical norms before submitting a formal National Council Certification request. ISO certification for local companies is now conducted through international institutions. Local sources estimate that only a few Honduran companies have obtained ISO certification.

• **Payment**

Terms: Credit terms of 60 to 90 days apply. Due to tight financing situation, cash in advance and irrevocable letters of credit, confirmed by U.S. banks, are the most appropriate methods of payment for U.S. exporters selling to Honduran firms.

Currency Exchange: An auction system regulates the allocation of foreign exchange. Dollar purchases are conducted at 5 to 7 percent above or below the base price established every five days. The Central Bank recently has been adjudicating an average of US$ 8 million daily. All individuals, foreign or national, can participate in auction system dollar purchases. Foreign exchange demand in 1998 was 96.1 percent covered.

Fund Transfer: All foreign exchange earnings on exports from Honduras must be repatriated. This requirement does not apply to foreign currency earned by companies operating in free trade zones and industrial parks. Because of the liberalization of the Honduras foreign exchange regime, it is now much easier to remit dividends and royalties, return capital overseas, and make payments on foreign debt. Foreign debt authorizations now take less than 48 hours to obtain. It takes approximately one to two month for the Central Bank to approve remittances of dividends and royalties.

MARKETING TIPS
⑤

Agents and Distributors

Only Honduran nationals or Honduran legal entities registered with a local chamber of commerce and the Ministry of Industry and Trade may represent foreign firms. An agent or distributor is required only when selling to the government. However, a local agent or representative is strongly recommended.

When evaluating local prospects, it is advisable to consider factors such as location, financial strength, the quality of the sales force, warehousing facilities, reputation in the market, outlay on advertising, product compatibility, and overall experience. The assistance of a Honduran lawyer is recommended when drawing up the agent or distributor agreement. According to Honduran law, principals may not terminate the contract without just cause, unless they fairly compensate the agent for damages suffered. Nonexclusive, renewable relationships are thus advisable. The Embassy's Economic/Commercial Section can provide a list of lawyers. Exporters of pharmaceuticals and medicine-related products must be registered with the Ministry of Public Health. Agro-chemicals and animal feeds must be registered with the Ministry of Natural Resources. U.S. firms interested in finding a partner or distributor may make use of U.S. Department of Commerce services. The U.S. and Foreign Commercial Service (US&FCS) offers free, intensive, one-on-one counseling. The Commercial Section of the Embassy offers its Agent/Distributor Service (ADS), which locates interested, qualified representatives. The International Company Profile Report (ICP) service provides background checks on potential partners. The Gold Key Service of the Commercial Section can schedule appointments, arrange translators, and make reservations.

Establishing an Office

U.S. firms should first contact the nearest District Office of the U.S. Department of Commerce and the Economic/Commercial Section of the U.S. Embassy for counseling and advice. The Commercial Code recognizes several types of mercantile organizations: individual ownership, general partnership, simple limited partnership, limited liability company, corporation, and joint stock company. Foreign investors must become Honduran residents to work in Honduras. The necessary steps to establishing a business are relatively simple:

1. Register with the Mercantile Registry (Commerce Public Registry). The following information must be submitted: the stockholder's name, nationality, and domicile; the form of organization and the nature of business; the term of operations (usually indefinite); the authorized capital and minimum amount; a description or valuation of each shareholder's contribution in cash or other assets; the company domicile; the distribution of profits and losses among the shareholders; and any other agreements made by the founders.

2. Apply for the tax identification code (RTN) at the Ministry of Finance to use in all taxable transactions.

3. Register with local and national Chambers of Commerce. Acquire operation permit from the governmental entity dealing with the sector in which the firm will invest (if applicable).

4. Acquire a municipal patent or permit.

5. When establishing a foreign subsidiary, appoint a legal representative in Honduras, one that is fully empowered to execute all legal or other acts required by Honduran law or that may take place in Honduran territory. Once the previous legal steps have been completed, the newly formed organization must publish its registration in La Gaceta, the government's official journal.

6. Register with the Instituto Nacional de Formación Profesional (INFOP), the national institution in charge of worker instruction and qualification. The firm must contribute 1 percent of its total payroll to INFOP every month.

7. Register with the Instituto Hondureño de Seguridad Social (IHSS), the national social security hospital and out-patient care institution for workers and their dependents. The firm contributes 3.5 percent of each employee's salary to the security system.

8. Obtain an investment certificate from the Ministry of Industry and Trade. Though not necessary, the certificate can ensure compliance with all the investment protection guarantees established by the 1992 Investment Law.

A mandatory environmental impact evaluation (EIA) is required for any activity that could cause harm to the environment or historical sites. A lawyer can advise whether or not an EIA is necessary. In most areas, the time to establish an office has been reduced to a few days. The Honduran Ministry of Industry and Trade offers a one-stop service for investors and investment registry procedures. In practice, however, this office has suffered from personnel and resource constraints.

Distribution and Sales Channels

The types of distribution channels available are similar to those in the U.S. However, Honduras has fewer levels of distribution and a more limited number of specialty, chain, and department stores. Tegucigalpa and San Pedro Sula are the major distribution centers. U.S. firms also sell directly, through U.S.-based intermediaries, and through local distributors and representatives. Owing to the country's small size, a single distributor or representative is usually sufficient. Representatives and distributors often carry broad lines on a nonexclusive basis. Many local buyers make direct contacts with U.S. suppliers at the factory or warehouse level. Store owners often buy goods in small lots from stores, export brokers, or wholesalers based particularly in Miami, New Orleans, and Houston

Direct Marketing

Direct marketing is a fairly new concept in Honduras. Telecommunications, electronic commerce, mail delivery infrastructures, and credit card use are underdeveloped. Catalog and door-to-door sales are the norm. Actual sales do no occur through the mail. Local company listings and mailing information can be obtained through chambers of commerce and industry associations in Honduras.

Leasing/Joint Ventures

Joint venture initiatives offer some of the most promising opportunities. The 1992 invest-

ment law generally establishes no limits on the percentage of capital that can be owned by a foreigner. In certain industries, Honduran nationals must maintain majority control. Generally, the greatest joint venture advantages can be found in the industrial, mining, agricultural, tourism, and service sectors. The Commercial Section and the Foundation for Investment and Development of Exports (FIDE) both facilitate joint venture partnerships. For more information, visit (http:\\www.hondurasinfo.hn).

Franchising

Recently, the number of U.S. franchises in Honduras has grown rapidly. Prospects are good, particularly because of regional stability, the availability of supplies and personnel, the absence of trade barriers, and a pro-U.S. consumer market. There are now about 55 foreign firms and more than 36 U.S. franchises in operation, most of which are fast-food and casual restaurants. Other franchises operate in the areas of fast printing, movies and entertainment, automotive aftermarket services, health and fitness, electronics, cosmetics and toiletries, convenience stores, dry cleaners, and car rentals. Furthermore, several major hotel chains are constructing new facilities.

Advertising and Promotion

Newspapers are often considered the best means of advertising. Expocentro in San Pedro Sula is the only trade exposition center in the country. The center holds approximately 12 shows per year. One of the major trade promotion opportunities in the region is EXPO USA '99. See **Contacts** for a list of major newspapers and for exposition contact information.

Selling Factors

The Honduran market is divided into two regions: (1) the north coast, including San Pedro Sula, is the country's commercial and industrial capital, and (2) the central region, including the capital city of Tegucigalpa, is not as well developed. Large firms usually have offices in both major cities. The Honduran market is price sensitive. Sales promotion and customer service efforts are often extremely helpful. U.S. products compete well on the basis of quality, technology, reliability, and availability. Government and private agents often have problems securing purchasing funds due to high interest rates. Attractive financing terms allow U.S. firms to capture market share, although caution must be exercised when extending credit. Good personal relationships with prospective customers are important if not necessary.

Selling to the Government

The GOH publishes tenders in Honduras's major newspapers. U.S. businesses can access many of these bids through the services of the U.S. Department of Commerce, including the Trade Opportunities Program (TOP), the National Trade Data Bank (NTDB), and the Electronic Bulletin Board (EBB). Foreign firms must act through a local agent to submit proposals for public tenders. Foreign companies may also appoint a local representative through a power of attorney to assist with proposal submissions. Government purchases are generally exempt from import duties. Bids are often selected on the basis of cost, delivery time, firm reputation, technical support, and performance in previous contracts.

Pricing

The small Honduran market is characterized by a high elasticity of demand for consumer products. Price is one of the most important elements in determining how imports are received.

Customer Support

Service and support is often a significant consideration in purchasing decisions,

especially by the government. Distributors should offer an adequate service infrastructure. U.S. companies should consider providing training, technical assistance, and after-sales support to their local counterparts.

Intellectual Property Rights (IPR)

Honduras complied with the Trade Related Aspects of Intellectual Property Rights (TRIPS) Agreement required by January 1, 2000. The U.S. government placed Honduras on the IPR "Watch List" in 1998. The International Intellectual Property Alliance (IIPA) estimates that copyright infringements in Honduras cost U.S. firms US$ 8.3 million in 1997. Problems are especially pervasive in the areas of movie, sound recording, and software piracy. The illegitimate registration of well-known trademarks is also widespread. Certain trade preferences were suspended in April 1998 because of Honduras's failure to control broadcast television piracy. The GOH did take action against the offending stations, and trade preferences were restored in June of the same year. In December 1999, Honduras' Congress passed two new laws related to intellectual property to correct deficiencies in previous legislation concerning copyrights, patents, and trademarks. The Honduran Ministry of Industry and Trade handles the registration of patents, trademarks, and copyrights, as well as all complaints regarding IPR infringement. Patents and trademarks must be registered with the ministry to be protected under Honduran law. Patents are good for between 10 and 20 years. Trademarks are valid for up to 10 years.

Attorney

The assistance of a competent local attorney is essential to doing business in Honduras, particularly in opening a business, preparing contracts, and understanding the legal system. The Economic/Commercial Section maintains a list of attorneys who have experience assisting U.S. firms.

FOREIGN INVESTMENT

⑥

Openness: The GOH welcomes foreign investors. The 1992 Investment Law, free trade zones, low labor costs, and the reduction of trade barriers have made the Honduran market much more attractive. With a few exceptions, the GOH guarantees national treatment to all foreign private firms in Honduras. Government authorization is required for both foreign and domestic investors in a number of areas, including basic health services, telecommunications, electricity, air transport, petroleum and related substances, agricultural, insurance, and financial services. All local and foreign direct investment must be registered with the Investment Office of the Ministry of Industry and Trade. Registration provides legal investment protection and guarantees international arbitration rights. Foreign investors face some discriminatory treatment in Honduras. Foreign firms must act through a local agent to bid on public tenders. Dividends paid to foreign investors are taxed at 15 percent compared to the usual 10 percent. The GOH also uses phyto-sanitary and zoo-sanitary requirements to prevent U.S. imports of poultry, feed grains, and rice.

Regulatory System: Red tape and unclear regulations are common. The GOH has not been able to implement or enforce laws already on the books. Worse yet, many of these laws are outdated. Nonetheless, progress has been made. In particular, the Investment Law in May 1992 was a substantial step in the right direction.

Investment Agreements: The U.S. and Honduras have signed a number of bilateral investment agreements. Investors of either country receive Most Favored Nation treatment. Honduras is a member of the WTO, the Northern Triangle Honduras, Guatemala, and El Salvador, and the Central American Common Market (CACM), which includes

Costa Rica, El Salvador, Nicaragua, and Guatemala. Honduras and the rest of Central America are also negotiating a free trade agreement with Chile and Panama.

Trade Zones and Free Ports: Foreign or domestic companies that locate in free trade zones (FTZ) enjoy the following benefits: (1) duty-free import of machinery, equipment, fixtures, parts, raw materials, and supplies needed for operations (except vehicles); (2) exemption from all income, export, sales, or consumer taxes; (3) unrestricted repatriation of profits and capital; and (4) on-site customs facilities. FTZs may be managed privately or by the National Port Authority (ENP). Historically, the main FTZ is based in Puerto Cortes. In 1998, the government extended FTZ benefits to the entire country. Privately owned Tourism Free Zones (ZOLT) may be established to promote the development of the tourism industry. Furthermore, there are now at least 17 industrial parks in the country. These parks are presently dominated by the apparel assembly industry. The GOH treats parks and zones as if they were offshore operations. Import and export duties are thus applicable.

Performance Requirements/Incentives: Generally, there are no officially mandated requirements for foreign investors although the GOH demonstrates a clear preference for foreign investment in export industries. Export processing zones (EPZ) must generate at least 5,000 new permanent jobs within five years after startup. EPZ firms pay no income taxes and enjoy free repatriation of profits, but they are now required to purchase the lempiras needed for their local operations from Honduran commercial banks.

Capital Markets and Investment: Foreign investors have unlimited access to local credit markets. However, the local banking system is conservative and generally has limited credit. Two stock exchanges operate in the country: the Honduran Stock Exchange (BHV) in San Pedro Sula and the Central American Stock Exchange in Tegucigalpa. Both are supervised by the Central Bank of Honduras.

Private Ownership: The U.S. Embassy has recorded nearly 100 property dispute cases involving U.S. citizens in the past six years. Honduran laws related to property titles are neither clear nor reliable. In particular, caution should be exercised for purchases in areas along the north coast, the Bay Islands, or outside major metropolitan areas. Honduran legal advice is highly recommended.

Expropriation and Compensation: There are only a few cases in which U.S. citizens suffered possible acts of expropriation. All these cases involve the Honduran National Agrarian Institute (INA). The GOH clearly accepts its responsibilities with respect to indemnifying property owners; however, timely compensation was not received in one case.

OPIC and Investment Insurance: OPIC currently offers financing and insurance against risks of war and expropriation for U.S. citizens who invest in Honduras. Honduras is also a party to the World Bank's Multilateral Investment Guarantee Agency (MIGA).

Dispute Settlement: The Honduran legal system has been a source of complaint. The United States Agency for International Development (USAID) and other organizations are providing technical support to improve the Honduran criminal procedures code. Competent Honduran legal counsel is strongly suggested. It is sometimes advisable to establish contracts that provide for arbitration or other forms of alternative dispute resolution. Honduras is a member of the International Center for the Settlement of Investment Disputes (ICSID).

FINANCE
7

Modernization and increased competition have characterized the Honduran banking system in recent years. There are now 23 commercial banks. All Honduran banks have correspondent relations with U.S. banks. Most of these banks are associated with particular economic groups. A new banking law and a regulatory banking commission were established in 1995. The new legislation is a major step toward modernizing financial intermediation. However, bank supervision remains poor.

Export Financing: A primary obstacle to doing business in Honduras has been the scarcity of local financing. Limited, short-term trade financing is available from local commercial banks although interest rates are as high as 31 percent or more. The U.S. Export-Import Bank (EXIM Bank) offers short- and medium-term financing. These credit lines are available through U.S. commercial banks. EXIM Bank's credit facilities available to Honduras include the Working Capital Guarantee Program, Exporter Insurance Program, Bank Letter of Credit Policies, and Financial Institution Facilities.

Project Financing: Long-term financing is generally available only through special lines of credit that selected commercial banks have with Central American Economic Integration Bank (CABEI). Such financing is extended typically for export projects. The U.S. Department of Agriculture (USDA) runs its Export

Enhancement Program and its Diary Export Incentive Program. These programs provides credit guarantees for agricultural exports and export bonuses for selected products. The U.S. Small Business Administration (SBA) helps small businesses develop export markets through financial and business development assistance. The U.S. Trade Development Agency (TDA) supports overseas projects that have high U.S. products and services export potential through grant loans for prefeasibility studies. When adequate commercial financing is unavailable, OPIC provides assistance for new investments, privatization, and the expansion and modernization of existing plants sponsored by U.S. investors.

COMMUNICATIONS ⑧

Phone

Simple telephone service is adequate, but the overall Honduran telecommunications network is still underdeveloped. Honduras has only about 4.12 telephone lines per 100 inhabitants. The GOH plans to privatize 51 percent of Hondutel's stock. Direct-dial, long-distance calling is expensive. There are a number of ways to reduce costs. Nigh rates run from 10 p.m. to 7 a.m. Calls placed from the U.S. to Honduras rather than from Honduras to the U.S. are much less expensive. The international access code is 011, and the Honduras access code is 504. City codes are not required. AT&T offers its USA-Direct service, while MCI and Sprint have similar programs. Fax, e-mail, Internet, and cellular services are available. Local telegraph and telex services are commonly used. Telegraph rates run at LP. 0.35 (approximately US$ 0.02) for an ordinary, local, five-word message and at LP.1.00 (US$ 0.07) for an urgent five-word message. Additional words cost LP. 0.20 (US$ 0.01) per word. Telegraph service to the U.S. runs at LP. 3.36 (US$ 0.23) per word and LP. 6.72 (US$ 0.45) per word for urgent messages. Telegraphic service charges are subject to a 12 percent sales tax.

Internet

Internet usage and development are still at an early stage. Companies have used web pages as promotional sites but not as an additional distribution channel. The Electronic Commerce System Directorate (DISELCO)—a project of the Chamber of Commerce and Industry of Tegucigalpa (CCIT), the Chamber of Commerce & Industry of Cortés (CCIC), and the National Industry Association (ANDI)—establishes the policies and norms for electronic commerce in Honduras.

Mail

The postal system is reasonably well developed although street names and numbers are not well defined. Express mail international services are available between Honduras and the U.S.

TRANSPORTATION

Land

Hurricane Mitch did some of its worst damage to the Honduran road system, which was one of the best in Central America. The road system was the country's top reconstruction priority, and the system now can again satisfy most distribution and transportation needs. Road connections with the rest of Central America are good. Traffic delays are common in Tegucigalpa and San Pedro Sula. Taxi service in the downtown areas of is adequate although some drivers pick up as many passengers as possible along the way. Fares must be negotiated. Taxis from the major airports and hotels charge two to three times above the typical rate. Taxis can be hired on a daily or hourly basis, and car rental companies are also available.

Sea

A number of shipping companies link Honduras from both its Atlantic and Pacific coasts to major world cities. Most companies use Puerto Cortes, which is one of the three primary ports in Central America. Puerto Cortes offers no waiting time and modern Roll-on/Roll-off (Ro/Ro) and containerized facilities. Shipping time to major southern U.S. ports is approximately 48 hours. Honduran ports have recovered from much of the damage caused by Hurricane Mitch. In the short term, the ports will need to be dredged. Over the next 10 years, the National Port Authority expects that US$ 56 to 100 million will be required for seaport improvements.

Air

Passenger and air-freight services tend to be reliable. Houston, Miami, and New Orleans are only two and a half hours by air from Honduras. Honduras has international airports in Tegucigalpa, San Pedro Sula, the coastal city of La Ceiba, and the island of Roatán. The airport in San Pedro Sula is equipped with a radio-control tower, computerized customs, and a comfortable passenger terminal. The following airlines offer direct flights between Honduras and cities in North and Central America: American, Continental, COPA, LACSA, NICA, Maya World and TACA. Isleña Airlines connects Tegucigalpa with the north coast and the Bay Islands. Charter services and aircraft rentals (small single- and twin-engine equipment) out of Tegucigalpa, San Pedro Sula, and La Ceiba are also available.

WORK WEEK

Business Hours: 8.00 a.m. to 12.00 p.m. and 2.00 p.m. to 5.00 p.m. Monday through Friday, and 9.00 a.m. to 12.30 p.m. Saturday. Many shops are open from 8.00 a.m. to 12.00 p.m. and 1.30 p.m. to 6.00 p.m. on Monday through Friday, and from 8.00 a.m. to 5.00 p.m. Saturday.

Government Hours: 8.30 a.m. to 12.00 p.m. and 1.00 p.m. to 4.30 p.m. Monday through Friday.

Bank Hours: 9.00 a.m. to 4.30 p.m. Monday through Friday, and 8.00 a.m. to 12.30 p.m. Saturday.

HOLIDAYS 2001

New Year's Day, January 1
Holy Thursday, April 12
Good Friday, April 13
Holy Saturday, April 14
Honduran Labor Day, May 1
Central American Independence Day,
  September 15
Francisco Morazan's Birthday, October 3
Discovery of America, October 12
Honduran Armed Forces Day, October 21
Christmas Day, December 25

Some holidays may be observed on different dates depending on the day of the week on which it falls. The U.S. Embassy will be closed on U.S. and Honduras holidays. It is recommended that business travelers do not schedule trips to Honduras immediately before or immediately after local or U.S. holidays.

BUSINESS TRAVEL

Business Customs

Many Hondurans view U.S. citizens as reliable and trustworthy business partners. Hondurans strive for close, lifetime business relationships, in which written contracts are viewed as mere formalities in comparison with verbal agreements. Business deals are often closed with some kind of social activity; meetings move gradually into business matters, and negotiations are slower and more drawn out than in the U.S. Schedules are also more flexible, and punctuality is not as highly prized. Spanish is the official language although many Honduran professionals and businesspeople speak English. High-ranking leaders were often educated in the U.S.

Travel Advisory and Visas

A visa is not required for visits of less than 30 days. No immunizations are required for entry to Honduras. For longer stays, there are visas for investors, their dependents, and workers with specialized or technical skills.

Visas for investors and their dependents are good for three months and may be extended for up to one year. Visas for technical or specialized workers are good for one month and may be extended for up to six months. Contact the Honduran Embassy in Washington, D.C., or one of the several Honduran consulates in U.S. cities for more information. Foreigners interested in working in the country must obtain a resident visa through a Honduran consulate and a work permit from the Honduran Ministry of Labor. The resident visa must be obtained before departure, and the process may take up to four months. Visitors to Honduras should be aware that crime is a problem.

Business Infrastructure

Entry Requirements (personal and professional goods): No additional information is available at this time. Contact the Honduras consulate for additional information. See **Contacts**.

Currency Exchange: The lempira (LP) is the main currency (1 LP = 100 centavos). Currency restrictions have been liberalized. The lempira has been declining against the U.S. dollar although the rate of decline slowed in 1998.

Taxes: Corporate at 25 percent (15 percent on the first LP 200,000, which is approximately US$ 13,500). Income at 30 percent for the highest bracket (above LP 500,000 or approximately US$ 33,750). Income on profits obtained through branches, subsidiaries, or legal representatives at 15 percent. Corporate dividends and royalties on patents and trademarks at 35 percent. Sales at 12 percent, from which a number of products and services are exempt. Tourism-related services at 4 percent. Capital gains are taxed as normal income.

Hotels and Restaurants: Honduras offers a wide variety of suitable hotel and bed and breakfast accommodations in major cities and tourist areas. Major hotel construction projects are also underway. In Tegucigalpa, popular hotels include the Honduras Maya, Plaza San Martín, Princess, La Ronda, El Prado, and La Alameda. In San Pedro Sula, most business travelers stay at the Camino Real Inter-Continental, Hotel y Club Copantl, Gran Hotel Sula, and Hotel Los Próceres. The selection of restaurants is no less diverse. Options include continental, oriental, and American cuisine, local specialties, and pizza and fast-food franchises. Supermarkets and shopping malls carry products similar to those sold in the U.S.

Rent: Good residential areas offer spacious housing and apartment complexes. Domestic maid services are relatively inexpensive. Numerous real estate brokerage firms and agents offer assistance to foreigners.

Utilities: Much of the extensive damage caused by Hurricane Mitch and by a damaging fire to Honduras's electricity and water and sewage infrastructure has been repaired. The hurricane actually had a beneficial effect; it filled the reservoir of the country's main hydroelectric facility, El Cajon.

Business Services: See **Marketing Tips**.

Labor Costs and Legislation: Low-skilled labor is readily available and relatively inexpensive. The Ministry of Labor is moving to do a better job of enforcing labor rights. Regulations restrict workers to an 8-hour workday and a 44-hour workweek, with at least one 24-hour rest period per week. The Labor Code requires 10 days of paid vacation after one year and 20 days after four years.

Literacy: Age 15 and over can read and write. 72.7 percent (1995 est).

Travel Notes

The following travel notes have been supplied by the U.S. government. For the most recent general travel and consular information, see the U.S. Department of State travel publications or call the Traveler's Telephone Hotline at (202) 647-5225.

Security: Pick-pocketing and armed robberies are on the rise, and there have been incidents of armed carjackings and home invasions. Jewelry should not be worn downtown or in isolated areas. Visitors should not carry valuables or large amounts of money.

Health Precautions: Tap water is not potable. Drinking water must be boiled and filtered, and the dry season brings water shortages. Bottled water is widely available. Fruits and vegetables must be cleaned carefully, and meats must be cooked well. Significant health hazards include AIDS, malaria, dengue fever, dysentery, parasites, hepatitis A and B, typhoid, and rabies. There have been some reports of cholera as well. A malaria suppressant should be taken if traveling to coastal regions or rural areas for extended stays. There is also the risk of heat and sun exposure. Essential medical-care facilities are available in Tegucigalpa, San Pedro Sula, La Ceiba, and Choluteca. Medical centers in the countryside are limited and may be inaccessible. Current information on health matters may be obtained from the Centers for Disease Control and Prevention's international travelers' hotline at (404) 332-4559.

Embassy Assistance

To obtain additional and updated information on entry and exit requirements, travelers can contact the Consular Section of the Embassy of Honduras at 1612 K Street, N.W., Washington, D.C. Room 310, 20006; Tel: (202) 223-0185 or (202) 223-0187. Travelers may also contact the nearest

Honduras consulate. They are located in Los Angeles, San Francisco, Miami, Chicago, New Orleans, Minneapolis, New York, and Houston.

The *Foreign Service Posts: Guide for Business Representatives* is available for sale by the Superintendent of Documents, U.S. Government Printing Office, Washington, D.C. 20402; Tel (202) 512-1800; Fax (202) 512-2250. Business travelers to Honduras seeking appointments with U.S. Embassy Tegucigalpa officials should contact the Commercial Section in advance at (504) 238-5114.

CONTACTS

13

Honduran Governmental Agencies

Presidential Palace
Carlos Roberto Flores, President of the
  Republic of Honduras
Palacio José Cecilio del Valle
Blvd. Juan Pablo II
Tegucigalpa, M.D.C.
Tel: (504) 221-4545
Fax: (504) 235-6949

Central Bank of Honduras
Edif. Banco Central
Tegucigalpa, M.D.C.
Tel: (504) 237-1668; (504) 237-1677
Fax: (504) 237-6261

Ministry of Industries and Trade
Edif. Larach, 6 Piso
Tegucigalpa, M.D.C.
Tel: (504) 238-2025; (504) 237-1947
Fax: (504) 237-2836

Ministry of Finance
Palacio de Hacienda
3a. Calle
Tegucigalpa, M.D.C.
Tel: (504) 222-8701; (504) 222-2211
Fax: (504) 238-2309

Ministry of Foreign Affairs
Antigua Casa Presidencial, $^1/_2$ cuadra al norte
de la Corte Suprema de Justicia
Tegucigalpa, M.D.C.
Tel: (504) 234-3297
Fax: (504) 234-1484

Ministry of Public Works,
Transportation and Housing
Bo. La Bolsa
Comayaguela, M.D.C.
Tel: (504) 225-2690; (504) 225-0994;
  (504) 225-1993
Fax: (504) 225-2227

Ministry of Agriculture and Livestock
Col. Loma Linda Norte
Blvd. Centro America
Tegucigalpa, M.D.C.
Tel: (504) 232-8394; (504) 231-1921
Fax: (504) 232-5375

Ministry of Natural Resources and
Environment
Atras del Birichiche, carretera al estadio
Tegucigalpa, M.D.C.
Tel: (504) 235-7833
Fax: (504) 232-6250

Ministry of Labor and Social Security
Rosa América Miranda de Galo, Minister7
Calle, 2 y 3 Ave.Comayaguela, M.D.C.
Tel: (504) 237-9778
Fax: (504) 222-3220

Ministry of Tourism
Col. San Carlos, 2 Piso, Edif. Lloyd's Bank
Tegucigalpa, M.D.C.
Tel: (504) 222-4002
Fax: (504) 238-2102

Ministry of Health
3 Calle, 4 Ave.
Tegucigalpa, M.D.C.
Tel: (504) 222-5226
Fax: (504) 238-4141

Technical Ministry of International
Cooperation
1 cuadra arriba de la Procuraduría, contiguo al
Complejo Financiero Capital, P.O. Box 1327
Tegucigalpa, M.D.C.
Tel: (504) 239-5269
Fax: (504) 239-5277

Dirección General de Inversiones y
Políticas Sectoriales
Edif. Larach, 5 Piso
Tegucigalpa, M.D.C.
Tel: (504) 238-2024
Fax: (504) 237-3025

Dirección General de Gestión Empresarial
(One Stop Shop)
Edif. Larach, 7 Piso
Tegucigalpa, M.D.C.
Tel: (504) 222-0318
Fax: (504) 238-4267

Empresa Hondureña de Telecomunicaciones
(HONDUTEL)
Final Blvd. Morazan, detrás de Bigos, Edif. Los
Almendros
P.O. Box 1794
Tegucigalpa, M.D.C.
Tel: (504) 237-9802
Fax: (504) 237-1111

Servicio Autónomo Nacional de Acueductos
y Alcantarillados (SANAA)
1 Ave., 13 Calle, Comayaguela
P.O. Box 437
Tegucigalpa, M.D.C.
Tel: (504) 237-9200
Fax: (504) 237-8552

Empresa Nacional de Energia Eléctrica (ENEE)
Calle Real, Edif. Banco Atlántida, 4 Piso
Comayaguela, M.D.C.
Tel: (504) 237-8466; (504) 238-0809
Fax: (504) 237-8473

Honduran Council for Science and Technology
P.O. Box 4458
Tegucigalpa, M.D.C.
Tel: (504) 239-5186
Fax: (504) 232-5669
E-mail: gzepeda@ns.hondunet.net

Presidential Program for Investment
Edif. Banco del Pais, 6 Piso, Blvd. Suyapa
Tegucigalpa, M.D.C.
Tel: (504) 239-8613
Fax: (504) 239-8466

Municipality of Tegucigalpa
Frente al Parque Central
Tegucigalpa, M.D.C.
Tel: (504) 238-3319
Fax: (504) 222-0242

Municipality of San Pedro Sula
P.O. Box 663
San Pedro Sula, Honduras
Tel: (504) 553-4646; (504) 557-3404
Fax: (504) 557-2844
E-mail: alcaldia@netsys.hn

Honduran Fund for Social Investment (FHIS)
Edificio Ahprocafe, Col. Lara
Tegucigalpa, M.D.C.
Tel: (504) 236-6447
Fax: (504) 236-8230

Country Trade Associations and Chambers
of Commerce

Honduran American Chamber of Commerce
(AMCHAM)
P.O. Box # 1838
Tegucigalpa M.D.C.
Tel: (504) 232-7043; (504) 232-6035
Fax: (504) 232-2031
E-mail: hamcham1@netsys.hn

Foundation for Investment and Development
of Exports (FIDE)
P.O. Box # 2029
Tegucigalpa M.D.C.
Tel: (504) 232-9345;
(504) 232-9105; (504) 232-9098;
(504) 232-9099
Fax: (504) 239-0766
E-mail: fide@honduTel:hn
Web site: http://www.hondurasinfo.hn

Federation of Agricultural Producers and
Exporters (FPX)
P.O. Box # 1442
San Pedro Sula, Cortés
Tel: (504) 566-3794; (504) 566-0795
Fax: (504) 566-3852
E-mail: fpxhonduras@mayanet.hn

Honduran Council for Private Enterprise
(COHEP)
P.O. Box 3240
Tegucigalpa M.D.C.
Tel: (504) 221-0011; (504) 221-4268;
(504) 221-4272
Fax: (504) 221-0022
E-mail: cohep@hondurasnet.com

National Honduran Association of Exporters
(ANEXHON)
Local de la C.C.I.C.
San Pedro Sula, Cortes
Tel: (504) 553-3626
Fax: (504) 553-3626

Construction Industry Association (CHICO)
P.O. Box # 905
Tegucigalpa M.D.C.
Tel: (504) 232-1756
Fax: (504) 239-0973

International Chamber of Commerce
(INTERCHAM)
P.O. Box # 4548
San Pedro Sula, Cortés
Tel: (504) 557-5656
Fax: (504) 557-4994

Honduran American Chamber of Commerce
(AMCHAM)
P.O. Box # 1209
San Pedro Sula, Cortés
Tel: (504) 558-0164
Fax: (504) 558-0165
E-mail: hamcham@netsys.hn

Honduran Federation of Chambers of
Commerce (FEDECAMARA)
P.O. Box # 3393
Tegucigalpa M.D.C.
Tel: (504) 232-6083
Telefax: (504) 232-1870

Chamber of Commerce and Industry of
Tegucigalpa (C.C.I.T.)
P.O. Box # 3444
Tegucigalpa M.D.C.
Tel: (504) 232-8110, 232-8210
Fax: (504) 232-0159
E-mail: ccit@hondutel:hn

Chamber of Commerce and Industry of Cortes
(C.C.I.C.)
P.O. Box # 14
San Pedro Sula, Cortés
Tel: (504) 553-0761; (504) 553-2490
Fax: (504) 553-3777
E-mail: ccic@simon.intertel:hn

National Industry Association (ANDI)
P.O. Box # 3447
Tegucigalpa M.D.C.
Tel: (504) 232-2221; (504) 232-5731
Fax: (504) 221-5199
E-mail: andi@itsnetworks.net

Honduran Apparel Manufacturers Association
P.O. Box # 2658
San Pedro Sula, Cortés
Tel: (504) 552-4140
Fax: (504) 552-4150
Web site: http://www.netsys.hn/~ahm

Honduran Association of Banking Institutions
(AHIBA)
P.O. Box # 1344
Tegucigalpa, M.D.C.
Tel: (504) 235-6770
Fax: (504) 239-0191
E-mail: ahiba@ficohsa.hn

Honduran Mining Association (ANAMINH)
P.O. Box # 3264
San Pedro Sula, Cortés
Tel: (504) 550-1701
Fax: (504) 550-1141

Honduran Association of Importers and
Distributors of Land and Cattle Products
(ADIVEPAH)
P.O. Box # 3642
Tegucigalpa, M.D.C.
Tel: (504) 236-5115
Fax: (504) 236-5069

Honduran Association of Importers and
Distributors of Vehicles (AHDIVA)
P.O. Box # 1160
Comayaguela, M.D.C.
Tel: (504) 225-4004
Fax: (504) 225-4530
E-mail: ahdiva@optinet.hn

Honduran Association of Importers and
Distributors of Petroleum Products
(AHDIPPE)
P.O. Box # 1392
Comayaguela, M.D.C.
Tel: (504) 237-2814
Fax: (504) 237-2814

Asociación Hondureña de Compañías y
Representantes Navieros (AHCORENA)
Edif. Plaza Local 19A
1-2 Calle, 1-2 Ave, N.E.
San Pedro Sula, Cortés
Tel: (504) 552-4412
Fax: (504) 552-4412

National Aquaculture Association (ANDAH)
P.O. Box # 229
Choluteca, Choluteca
Tel: (504) 882-0986
Fax: (504) 882-3848

Honduran Chamber of Insurance
Companies (CAHDA)
P.O. Box # 3290
Tegucigalpa, M.D.C.
Tel: (504) 239-0342
Fax: (504) 232-6020

Honduran Chamber of Tourism
(CAMTURH)
P.O. Box # 5804
Tegucigalpa, M.D.C.
Tel: (504) 236-8836
Fax: (504) 221-3662
E-mail: camturh@datum.hn

National Federation of Agricultural
Producers (FENAGH)
P.O. Box # 3209
Tegucigalpa, M.D.C.
Tel: (504) 239-1303
Fax: (504) 231-1392

Honduran Entrepreneurship Association
(GEMAH)
P.O. Box # 1170
San Pedro Sula, Cortés
Tel: (504) 557-4433
Fax: (504) 557-4432

National Hotel Association (AHAH)
P.O. Box # 3574
Tegucigalpa, M.D.C.
Tel: (504) 237-0121
Fax: (504) 237-2221
E-mail: ahah@mayanet.hn

Country Market Research Firms

R. Rodríguez y Asociados
P.O. Box # 3700
Tegucigalpa M.D.C.
Tel: (504) 231-1911
Fax: (504) 231-1906
E-mail: pwc.honduras@hondudata.com

KMPG Peat, Marwick y Asociados
P.O. Box # 3398
Tegucigalpa M.D.C.
Tel: (504) 232-5907
Fax: (504) 232-5925
E-mail: kpmgtgu@hondudata.com

Ernst & Young
Morales Palao Williams y Asociados
P.O. Box # 3878
Tegucigalpa M.D.C.
Tel: (504) 231-1249
Fax: (504) 232-3709

Mercaplan
P.O. Box # 409
San Pedro Sula, Cortés
Tel: (504) 550-1992
Fax: (504) 550-1996
Web site: http://www.mercaplan.hn

C.I.D.
Consultoría Interdisciplinaria en Desarrollo,
  S.A.
(Gallup de Centroamérica)
P.O. Box # 3390
Tegucigalpa M.D.C.
Tel: (504) 232-0637; (504) 239-0993
Fax: (504) 239-0990

**The Honduran Customs Directorate operates
  under the Ministry of Finance:**
Customs and Tax Division
Address: Ave. Cervantes, Plaza Morazán,
  Tegucigalpa, Honduras 6343 Apdo. Postal
  6343, Tegucigalpa, M.D.C.
Tel: (504) 238-6790
Fax: (504) 220-0898

U.S. Embassy Trade Personnel

Economic Section
Economic/Commercial Counselor
U.S. Embassy
Avenida La Paz
Tegucigalpa, M.D.C.
Tel: (504) 236-9320
Fax: (504) 236-6836

Economic/Commercial Officer
U.S. Embassy
Avenida La Paz
Tegucigalpa, M.D.C.
Tel: (504) 236-9320
Fax: (504) 236-6836

Economic/Commercial Officer
U.S. Embassy
Avenida La Paz
Tegucigalpa, M.D.C.
Tel: (504) 236-9320
Fax: (504) 236-6836

Economic/Commercial Specialist
U.S. Embassy
Avenida La Paz
Tegucigalpa, M.D.C.
Tel: (504) 236-9320
Fax: (504) 238-2888

Legal Advisor
U.S. Embassy
Avenida La Paz
Tegucigalpa, M.D.C.
Tel: (504) 236-9320
Fax: (504) 236-6836

Foreign Agricultural Service

Agricultural Specialist
U.S. Embassy
Avenida La Paz
Tegucigalpa, M.D.C.
Tel: (504) 236-9320
Fax: (504) 236-8342

Secretary
U.S. Embassy
Avenida La Paz
Tegucigalpa, M.D.C.
Tel: (504) 236-9320
Fax: (504) 236-8342

U.S. & Foreign Commercial Service
Commercial Specialist
U.S. EmbassyAvenida La PazTegucigalpa,
  M.D.C.
Tel: (504) 236-9320
Fax: (504) 238-2888

Commercial Assistant
U.S. Embassy
Avenida La Paz
Tegucigalpa, M.D.C.
Tel: (504) 236-9320
Fax: (504) 238-2888

Commercial Assistant
U.S. Embassy
Avenida La Paz
Tegucigalpa, M.D.C.
Tel: (504) 236-9320
Fax: (504) 238-2888

Commercial Secretary
U.S. Embassy
Avenida La Paz
Tegucigalpa, M.D.C.
Tel: (504) 236-9320
Fax: (504) 238-2888
Web site: http://
  www.usia.gov/abtusia/posts/H01/wwwhce.html

Washington-Based U.S. Government, Country Contacts

U.S. Department of State
Desk Officer for Honduras
Room 4915
2201 C Street, N.W.
Washington, DC 20520
Tel: (202) 647-0087
Fax: (202) 647-2597

U.S. Department of Commerce
Office of Latin America
Caribbean Basin Division
International Trade Specialist
14th St. and Constitution Ave., N.W.
Washington, D.C. 20230
Tel: (202) 482-0057
Fax: (202) 482-0464

Office of the U.S. Trade Representative
Director for Central America and the Caribbean
600 17th Street, NW
Washington, DC 20508
Tel: (202) 395-5190
Fax: (202) 395-9675

Overseas Private Investment Corporation (OPIC)
Insurance Officer
1100 New York Avenue, NW
Washington, DC 20527
Tel: (202) 336-8572
Fax: (202) 408-5142

U.S. Trade and Development Agency
Regional Director for Latin America
Room 309, S.A.-1621 N, Kent St.
Arlington, VA 22209
Tel: (703) 875-4357
Fax: (703) 875-4009

U.S. Trade and Development Agency
Desk Officer for Honduras
Room 309, S.A.-1621 N, Kent St.
Arlington, VA 22209
Tel: (703) 875-4357
Fax: (703) 875-4009

Export-Import Bank of the United States
811 Vermont Avenue, NW
Washington, DC 20571
Tel: (202) 565-3946
Fax: (202) 566-3380

U.S. Agency for International Development
Desk Officer for Honduras
1300 Pennsylvania Ave., NW
Washington, DC 20523-5800
Tel: (202) 712-5366
Fax: (202) 216-3402

U.S. Department of Agriculture
Foreign Agricultural Service
Americas Team Leader
International Trade Policy
Washington, DC 20250
Tel: (202) 720-1325
Fax: (202) 205-3875

Office of Multilateral Development Banks
U.S. & Foreign Commercial Service
U.S. Department of Commerce
Room H-1806
Washington, DC 20230
Tel: (202) 482-3399
Fax: (202) 273-0927

U.S. Department of Commerce Liaison to the U.S. Executive Directors Office International Bank for Reconstruction and Development
1818 H Street, NW
Room MC-1-525
Washington, DC 20433
Tel: (202) 458-0118
Fax: (202) 477-2967

U.S.-Based Multipliers Relevant for Country

Embassy of Honduras
3007 Tilden Street, NW
Washington, DC 20008
Tel: (202) 966-7702
Fax: (202) 966-9751

Honduras Consulate General
80 Wall Street, Suite 415
New York, NY 10005
Tel: (212) 269-3611
Fax: (212) 509-8391

Foundation for Investment and Development of Exports (FIDE)
Miami Office
2100 Ponce de Leon Blvd.
Suite 1175
Coral Gables, FL 33134
Tel: (305) 444-3060
Fax: (305) 444-1610

Honduras Institute of Tourism
2100 Ponce de Leon Blvd., Suite 1175
Coral Gables, FL 33134
P.O. Box 140458
Coral Gables, FL 33114-0458
Toll Free: (800) 410-9608
Tel (305) 461-9608
Fax (305) 461-0602
E-mail: ihturism@honduTel:hn
Web site: www.hondurasinfo.hn

FPX International
Promoters of Agricultural Exports
2100 Ponce de Leon Blvd. Suite 1175
Coral Gables Florida 33134
Tel: (305) 471-6129
Fax: (305) 471-6140

OAS Permanent Mission
5100 Wisconsin Ave.
NW Suite 403
Washington, DC 20016
Tel: (202) 362-9656
Fax: (202) 537-7170

Advertising and Trade Promotion

Tegucigalpa Based Newspapers

Diario El Heraldo
Spanish/Daily
P.O.Box 1938
Tegucigalpa, M.D.C., Honduras
Tel: (504) 236-6000
Fax: (504) 221-0778
E-mail: heraldo2@datum.hn
Web site: http://www.heraldo.hn

Diario La Tribuna
Spanish/Daily
P.O.Box 1501
Comayaguela, M.D.C., Honduras
Tel: (504) 233-1283
Fax: (504) 234-3070
E-mail: tribuna@latribuna.hn
Web site: http://www.latribuna.hn

Semanario Tiempos Del Mundo
Spanish/Weekly
Tegucigalpa, M.D.C., Honduras
Tel: (504) 220-1336; (504) 220-1339
Fax: (504) 220-7433
E-mail: tdm@mayanet.hn
Web site: http://www.tiemposdelmundo.hn

Honduras This Week
English/Weekly
P.O.Box 1312
Tegucigalpa M.D.C. Honduras
Tel: (504) 232-8818; (504) 239-0285
Fax: (504) 232-2300
E-mail: hontweek@hondutel:hn
Web site: http://www.marrder.com/htw/

San Pedro Sula Based Newspapers

Diario La Prensa
Spanish/Daily
P.O.Box 143
San Pedro Sula, Honduras
Tel: (504) 553-3101
Fax: (504) 553-0778
E-mail: laprensa@netsys.hn
laprensa@simon.intertel:hn
Web site: http://www.laprensahn.com

Diario El Tiempo
Spanish/Daily
P.O.Box 450
San Pedro Sula, Honduras
Tel: (504) 553-3388
Fax: (504) 553-4590
E-mail: fcordon@continental.hn
Web site: http://www.tiempo.hn

Diario El Nuevo Dia
Spanish/Daily
P.O.Box 275
San Pedro Sula, Honduras
Tel: (504) 552-4013; (504) 552-4298;
  (504) 553-3740
Fax: (504) 557-9457
E-mail: dia@netsys.hn

Expos

Expo USA
Commercial Section at the U.S. Embassy
(504) 238-5114 (ext) 2245
Fax: (504) 238-2888
Web site: http://www.usia.gov/abtusia/posts/
  H01/wwwhcel12.html

Expocentro
San Pedro Sula, Cortés, Honduras
Tel: (504) 556-0345; (504) 556-0349
Fax: (504) 556-0344

List of Commercial Banks with Correspondent U.S. Banking Arrangements

Banco El Ahorro Hondureño, S.A.
P.O. Box 3185
Tegucigalpa M.D.C., Honduras
Tel: (504) 237-5161
Fax: (504) 237-4638
E-mail: bancahorro@bancahorro.hn
Web site: http://www.bancahorro.hn

Banco Atlantida, S.A.
P.O. Box 3164
Tegucigalpa M.D.C., Honduras
Tel: (504) 232-1742; (504) 232-1050
Fax: (504) 232-7860
E-mail: info@bancatlan.hn
Web site: http://www.bancatlan.hn

**Banco La Capitalizadora Hondureña, S.A.
  (BANCAHSA)**
P.O. Box 344
Tegucigalpa M.D.C., Honduras
Tel: (504) 237-1171
Fax: (504) 237-2775
E-mail: bancahsa@bancahsa.hn

Banco del Comercio, S.A. (BANCOMER)
P.O. Box 160
San Pedro Sula, Cortés, Honduras
Tel: (504) 553-3600
Fax: (504) 553-3128
E-mail: rinforma@bancomer.hn
or rinforma@netsy.hn
Web site: http://www.bancomer.hn

Banco Continental, S.A.
P.O. Box 390
San Pedro Sula, Cortés, Honduras
Tel: (504) 550-0880
Fax: (504) 550-2750
E-mail: fmendoza@continental.hn

**Banco Financiera Centroamericana, S.A.
  (FICENSA)**
P.O. Box 1432
Tegucigalpa M.D.C., Honduras
Tel: (504) 238-1661
Fax: (504) 238-1630
E-mail: webmaster@ficensa.com
Web site: http://www.ficensa.com

**Banco de las Fuerzas Armadas, S.A.
  (BANFFAA)**
P.O. Box 877
Tegucigalpa M.D.C., Honduras
Tel: (504) 232-0164
Fax: (504) 232-4210
E-mail: banffaa@simon.intertel:hn
Web site: http://www.banffaa.hn

Banco Hondureño del Café (BANHCAFE)
P.O. Box 583
Tegucigalpa M.D.C., Honduras
Tel: (504) 232-8370
Fax: (504) 232-8332
E-mail: bcafeinf@hondutel:hn

Banco de Honduras, S.A. (CITIBANK)
P.O.Box 3434
Tegucigalpa M.D.C., Honduras
Tel: (504) 232-6122
Fax: (504) 232-6167

Lloyd's Bank
P.O. Box 3136
Tegucigalpa M.D.C., Honduras
Tel: (504) 236-6864
Fax: (504) 236-6417
E-mail: lloydsbank@davidintertel:hn

Banco Mercantil, S.A. (BAMER)
P.O. Box 116
Tegucigalpa M.D.C., Honduras
Tel: (504) 232-0006
Fax: (504) 232-3137
E-mail: bamer@gbm.hn
Web site: http://www.bamernet.hn

Banco de Occidente, S.A.
P.O. Box 3284
Tegucigalpa M.D.C., Honduras
Tel: (504) 237-0310
Fax: (504) 237-0486

Banco SOGERIN, S.A.
P.O. Box 440
San Pedro Sula, Cortés, Honduras
Tel: (504) 550-0712; (504) 550-3888
Fax: (504) 550-2001
E-mail: soglalc@hondutel:hn

Banco de los Trabajadores, S.A.
P.O. Box 3246
Tegucigalpa M.D.C., Honduras
Tel: (504) 238-4342; (504) 238-0017
Fax: (504) 238-0077

Banco de la Exportación, S.A. (BANEXPO)
P.O. Box 3988
Tegucigalpa M.D.C., Honduras
Tel: (504) 239-4256
Fax: (504) 239-4265
E-mail: banexpo@netsys.hn

Banco del País, S.A.
P.O. Box 1075
Tegucigalpa M.D.C., Honduras
Tel: (504) 239-0460
Fax: (504) 239-5707; (504) 239-5707

Banco Corporativo (BANCORP)
P.O. Box 1075
Tegucigalpa M.D.C., Honduras
Tel: (504) 239-3263
Fax: (504) 239-3286
E-mail: bancorp@netsys.hn

Banco de la Producción (BANPRO)
P.O. Box 5151
Tegucigalpa M.D.C., Honduras
Tel: (504) 239-2800
Fax: (504) 239-2811
E-mail: banpro@banprohn2.com

Banco Hondureño de Crédito y Servicios (BANHCRESER)
P.O. Box 4010
Tegucigalpa M.D.C., Honduras
Tel: (504) 239-3252
Fax: (504) 239-3259

Banco Financiera Comercial Hondureña, S.A. (FICOHSA)
P.O. Box 3858
Tegucigalpa M.D.C., Honduras
Tel: (504) 239-6410
Fax: (504) 235-8114
E-mail: ficocaaf@ficohsa.hn
Web site: http://www.ficohsa.hn

Banco Futuro
P.O. Box 3325
Tegucigalpa M.D.C., Honduras
Tel: (504) 237-4000
Fax: (504) 237-1835
E-mail: cavila@futuro.hn

Banco Capital
P.O. Box 3815
Tegucigalpa M.D.C., Honduras
Tel: (504) 238-6090
Fax: (504) 238-6094
E-mail: mflores@capital.hn

Banco Credomatic
P.O. Box 3725
Tegucigalpa M.D.C., Honduras
Tel: (504) 238-7220
Fax: (504) 237-5113; (504) 237-5222
E-mail: mscomh@ns.gbm.hn

Major Hotels

Hotel Honduras Maya
Ave. República de Chile, Col. Palmira
P.O. Box 1856
Tegucigalpa, Honduras
Tel: (504) 220-5000
Fax: (504) 220-6000
E-mail: hondurasmaya@globalnet.hn

Hotel Princess
Col. Alameda Ave. Juan Manuel Galvez, #1521
P.O. Box 808
Tegucigalpa, Honduras
Tel: (504) 220-5088; (504) 220-4500
Fax: (504) 220-5087
E-mail: princessteg@datum.hn

Hotel Plaza San Martín
Fte. Plaza San Martín, Col. Palmira
P.O. Box 864
Tegucigalpa, Honduras
Tel: (504) 232-2928
Fax: (504) 231-1366
E-mail: hpsmresv@ns.gbm.hn

Hotel Plaza Libertador
Fte. Hotel Plaza San Martin
Plaza San Martin
Tegucigalpa, Honduras
P.O. Box 3983
Tel: (504) 220-4141
Fax: (504) 222-4242
E-mail: libertad@netsys.hn

Hostal Las Lomas
Col. Lomas del Guijarro, costado norte
  de FIDE
Tegucigalpa, Honduras
P.O. BOX 3319
Tel: (504) 232-0477; (504) 235-6844;
  (504) 235-6845
Fax: (504) 232-3344
E-mail: hlaslomas@david.intertel:hn

Hotel y Club Copantl
Col. Los Arcos, Blvd. del Sur
P.O. BOX 1060
San Pedro Sula, Cortés
Tel: (504) 556-8900; (504) 556-6412
Fax: (504) 556-7890
E-mail: copantl2@copantl.hn

Hotel Camino Real Inter Continental
Centro Comercial Multiplaza 7 ave.,
  12 cll-A, SO
San Pedro Sula, Cortés
Tel: (504) 553-0000
Fax: (504) 550-6255
E-mail: sanpedrosula@interconti.com

Hotel Los Próceres
17-18 Ave., 2 cll. Bo. Rio de Piedras
San Pedro Sula, Cortés
Tel: (504) 557-4457; (504) 550-3636
Fax (504) 555-3620
E-mail: proceres@netsys.hn
Web site: http://www.losproceres.com

Hotel Princess
10 Calle Ave. Circunvalación, S.O.
San Pedro Sula, Cortes
P.O. Box 4861
Tel: (504) 556-9600
Fax: (504) 550-9595
E-mail: hotelprincess@globalnet.hn

J A M A I C A .

TRADE AND BUSINESS GUIDE

Official Name:	Jamaica
Official Language:	English, with Creole
Population:	2,652,689 (2000 est)
Population Growth:	0.46% (2000 est)
Age Structure:	0–14 years: 30%, 15–64 years: 63%, 65 years and over: 7% (2000 est)
Location:	Island in the Caribbean Sea, south of Cuba
Area:	10,990 square kilometers. Slightly smaller than Connecticut
Type of Government:	Parliamentary democracy. Bicameral Parliament with Senate (by governor general on recommendations of prime minister and opposition leader) and House of Representatives (by popular vote for five-year terms)
Head of State:	Prime Minister Percival James Patterson. Queen Elizabeth II represented by governor general Sir Howard Felix Cooke
Cabinet:	Appointed by governor general on advice of prime minister
Religion:	Protestant 61%, Roman Catholic 4%, others including spiritual cults 34.7%
Major Cities:	Capital: Kingston and St. Andrew (587,789), Spanish Town (92,383), Portmore (90,138), Montego Bay (83,446), May Pen, (46,785), Mandeville (36,430)
Climate:	Tropical (hot and humid). Temperate interior
Time:	The entire country is -5 GMT (Greenwich Mean Time), which is EST (Eastern Standard Time). The country does not follow daylight savings time
GDP:	Purchasing power parity (PPP): 8.8 billion (1999 est) ; real growth rate: -0.5% (1999 est); per capita PPP: $3,350 (1999 est); composition by sector: agricultural: 7.4%, industry: 42.1%, services: 50.5% (1997 est)
Currency:	1 Jamaican dollar (J$) = 100 cents
Exchange Rate:	US$ 1 = 41.2 (2000 est), 37.3 (1999 est), 35.57 (1998 est)
Weights & Measure:	Metric system
Natural Resources:	Bauxite, gypsum, limestone, marble, silica sand, clays
Total Trade:	In billions US$ [exports (fob)/imports (cif)]: 1997 (1.4/3.1), 1998 (1.3/3.0), 1999 (1.2/2.7)
Trade with U.S.:	In millions US$ [exports (fob)/imports (cif)]: 1997 (463/1,504), 1998 (520/1,523), 1999 (469/1,364)

Major Trade Partners: Imports: United States, European Union countries, Caricom countries, Latin America, United Kingdom.
Exports: United States, United Kingdom, Canada, Norway, European Union countries, Caricom countries

Membership: CARICOM, IADB, IBRD, IFC, IMF, ISO, MIGA, OAS, UN, UNCTAD, WCO, WIPO, and WTO. See membership description in appendix.

Sources: Statistical Institute of Jamaica (STATIN), Bank of Jamaica (BOJ), Planning Institute of Jamaica, CIA World Fact Book, United Nations World Statistics, U.S. Department of Commerce. U.S. Department of State

POLITICAL OUTLOOK

②

Relationship with the U.S.

Bilateral relations between Jamaica and the U.S. are good. They occasionally disagree over issues, such as relations to Cuba. Most U.S. initiatives in the Caribbean, such as the return of democracy to Haiti, have Jamaica's agreement and support.

Influences on Business

All major political parties favor attracting foreign investment. No major political issues are affecting the business climate in Jamaica.

Profile

System: Jamaica belongs to the British Commonwealth and follows the Westminster Parliamentary model. The Queen is represented by the governor general, who is head of state. The prime minister, head of government, is the majority leader of the elected House of Representatives. Major political parties are the People's National Party (PNP), the Jamaica Labor Party (JLP), and the National Democratic Movement (NDM). The 21-member Senate has 13 PNP seats and 8 JLP seats. The 60-member House

of Representatives has 50 PNP seats and 10 JLP seats. The government's promotional arm, JAMPRO, is chaired by Joseph Matalon.

Schedule for Elections: The prime minister can call general elections any time up to five years from the previous one. The last were in December 1997. The next will be by March 2002.

Major Parties: Two major political parties (PNP and JLP) are virtually indistinguishable. The political pressure groups are Rastafarians (black religious–racial cultists) and New Beginnings Movement (NBM).

Political Violence: Politically motivated crime is not a great threat. No recent political vandalism has occurred. However, in 1999, islandwide riots (in response to a petroleum tax hike) damaged and temporarily shut down some businesses.

Corruption: Jamaica has signed the OECD convention combating bribery. Proposed anticorruption legislation will create harsh penalties for individuals and companies even if the act isn't committed in Jamaica.

Trends

The government of Jamaica (GOJ) keeps high interest rates to control inflation. Unemployment and underemployment are problems. Strong competition with imports and reduced commodity prices make Jamaica less competitive in the world market. The GOJ has several plans to improve the economy: (1) reduce interest rates, (2) privatize some publicly owned companies (some are financial companies and real estate), (3) restructure the financial sector, (4) raise new sovereign debt in the international financial market, and (5) boost tourism and related productive activities. The GOJ projects 2 to 4 percent annual growth for the next two years. This target appears extremely ambitious given the current situation. A slow recovery is more likely, with marginal growth.

Major Growth Sectors

Tourism is Jamaica's main foreign exchange earner, with US$ 1.2 billion earned in 1998. Port Royal, a historic site near Kingston, is being developed for tourism. Bauxite mining and processing entails 90 percent of all mining. The government, trade unions, and bauxite companies are cooperating to develop the sector for global competitiveness. A joint venture between a UK company and a Jamaican local entity will build a major lime production facility, which will generate J$ 876 million in investment. Agriculture generates 7 to 8 percent of GDP and employs one-fourth of the Jamaican work force. Jamaica has a favorable climate and varied soil types. Typical exports are sugar, spices, bananas, coffee, citrus, allspice, and pimento. Increasingly, yams, tropical fruits and vegetables, legumes, and horticulture are important. Bad weather and lower prices have reduced agricultural earnings. There is concern over banana exports to Europe on preferential terms.

Key Economic Indicators

Income, Production and Employment (millions of U.S. dollars unless otherwise indicated)			
	1997	**1998**	**1999**[1]
Nominal GDP	6,198.9	6,318.9	6,332.1
Real GDP Growth (pct)[2]	-2.1	-0.7	-0.5
GDP (at Current Prices) by Sector:			
Agriculture, Forestry, and Fishing	495.5	505.3	N/A
Manufacturing	994.2	954.6	N/A
Mining and Quarrying	344.7	309.2	N/A
Construction and Installation	717.2	717.6	N/A
Electricity and Water	136.4	145.1	N/A
Transportation, Storage, and Communication	687.8	746.7	N/A
Retail Trade	1,418.3	1,454.0	N/A
Real Estate Services	314.1	338.2	N/A
Finance	39.7	29.7	N/A
Government Services	750.5	799.5	N/A
Other	299.6	319.0	N/A
Per Capita GDP (US$)	2,440.2	2,468.4	2,465.0
Labor Force (000)	1,133.8	1,128.6	1,120
Unemployment Rate (pct)	16.5	15.5	16.0

1. 1999 figures are all estimates based on most recent data available.
2. Growth rate is based on Jamaican dollars, whereas nominal GDP is shown in U.S. dollars
Source: Bureau of Economic and Business Affairs; U.S. Department of State

- Infrastructure
  Jamaica has occasional power shortages, outages, and voltage fluctuations. The water and sewage system is antiquated and needs repair and expansion. The GOJ has protected the banking system with a special agency (FINSAC) and act amendments. These measures have safeguards (like deposit insurance) to protect depositors; give relevant agencies greater powers of supervision and auditing; and allow appropriate official intervention in the early stages of a troubled institution. See **Finance (Trade, Projects), Communications, Transportation,** and **Business Infrastructure (Utilities).**

- Labor
  The labor force is at 1,120,000 (1999 est) with 15 to 20 percent in trade unions and 15.5 percent unemployed. The GOJ adheres to ILO conventions protecting worker rights. Low cost, semiskilled, English-speaking labor is readily available. Skilled labor may be in shortage, but the GOJ has educational initiatives to remedy the problem. Unemployment and downsizing have kept labor negotiating power in check. See **Business Infrastructure (Labor Costs and Legislation).**

Money and Prices *(annual percentage growth)*			
	1997	1998	1999[1]
Money Supply Growth (M2) Dec - Dec	12.5	7.2	9.0[2]
Consumer Price Inflation	9.2	7.9	5.9
Exchange Rate (J$/US$)	35.58	36.68	39.0

1. 1999 figures are all estimates based on most recent data available. 2. January to July 1999.
Source: Bureau of Economic and Business Affairs; U.S. Department of State

Balance of Payments and Trade *(millions of U.S. dollars unless otherwise indicated)*			
	1997	1998	1999[1]
Total Exports FOB[2]	1,387.3	1,316.3	1,245.8
Exports to U.S.[2]	462.9	520.4	468.5
Total Imports CIF[2]	3,127.8	2,991.7	2,728.0
Imports from U.S.[2]	1,504.4	1,523.3	1,364.0
Trade Balance[2]	-1,740.5	-1,675.4	-1,482.2
Balance with U.S.[3]	-1,041.5	-1,002.9	-895.5
External Public Debt[4]	3,277.6	3,306.4	3,030.1
Fiscal Deficit/GDP (pct)[5]	-8.3	-7.5	-4.6
Current Account Deficit/GDP (pct)	6.0	4.7	N/A
Debt Service Payments/GDP (pct)	28.7	39.4	N/A
Net Official Reserves[6]	540.0	579.4	526.2
Aid from U.S.[7]	24.7	22.0	15.8
Aid from All Other Sources[8]	149.7	143.0	N/A

1. 1999 figures are all estimates based on most recent data available.   2. Merchandise trade   3. January-July 1999.
4. Figure as of August 1999. 5. Jamaican fiscal year (April-March) deficit. 6. Figure as of August 1999.
7. Estimates include development, food, and military assistance for FY 97, FY 98, and FY 99.
8. Estimated commitments for development assistance from Jamaica's cooperation partners.
Source: Bureau of Economic and Business Affairs; U.S. Department of State

- **Balance of Payments**
  See **Key Economic Indicators.** Balance of payments declined in 1999, and net international reserves fell due to a decline in the goods and services account. The merchandise trade balance is likely to widen in 2000 due to increasing oil prices and stiff competition for local exports. However, export competitiveness, diversification, and growth are important challenges to the medium-term viability of the balance of payments.

Government Influence on Business

As of May 2000, the GOJ has the following targets for the 2000–2001 budget: (1) GDP real growth of 2 percent for 2000/01 and 4 percent in 2002/03, (2) maintain exchange rate stability, (3) hold inflation rate to single digits, (4) reduce the fiscal deficit from 4.6 percent of GDP to a balanced budget in 2000/01 and a surplus of 2 percent in 2002/03, (5) maintain gross reserves to 15 weeks of imports, (6) reduce the growth of the money supply from 10.4 percent in 1999/00 to 7.1 percent in 2003/2003, (7) strengthen the financial sector supervision and (8) restrict the growth of new government borrowing and reduce the overall debt. The GOJ will raise revenue to cover the fiscal deficit by (1) improving tax compliance; (2) tax increases on various items, such as gasoline, cigarettes, some spirits, lotto, departure tax, and customs department processing fees; and (3) internal and external borrowing. Fiscal consolidation and restructuring the financial sector will be central for economic recovery.

TRADE
(4)

Leading Imports and Exports

Imports: Machinery and transport equipment (power-generating machinery and equipment, general industrial machinery and equipment), construction materials, fuel, food, chemicals (inorganic chemicals, medicinal and pharmaceutical products, essential oils and perfume materials, polishing and cleansing preparations), spare parts, intermediate inputs, wide variety of manufactured goods and raw materials (textiles, iron and steel, paper and paper products, furnishings, toys and gifts, telecommunications, sound recording and reproducing apparatus and equipment)

Exports: Alumina, bauxite, sugar, bananas, rum

Foreign Trade			
(Exports and Imports in US$M)			
	1997	1998	1999 [1]
Total Exports FOB [2]	1,387.3	1.316.3	1,245.8
Exports to U.S. [2]	462.9	520.4	468.5
Total Imports CIF [2]	3,127.8	2,991.7	2,728.0
Imports from U.S. [2]	1,504.4	1,523.3	1,364.0

1. 1999 figures are all estimates based on most recent data available.   2. Merchandise trade.
Sources: U.S. Department of Commerce, U.S. Department of State

Best Prospects Analysis

Best Prospects for Nonagricultural Goods and Services

Drugs/Pharmaceuticals (DRG)

	1998 $M	1999 $M	2000E $M
Total Market Size	74	80	86
Total Local Production	13	14	15
Total Exports	4	4	5
Total Imports	64	69	75
Imports from the U.S.	20	25	30

Automotive Parts and Service Equipment (APS)

	1998 $M	1999 $M	2000E $M
Total Market Size	21	14	18
Total Local Production	0.2	0.2	0.2
Total Exports	0.3	0.3	0.3
Total Imports	21	14	18
Imports from the U.S.	11	8	10

Paper/Paperboard (PAP)

	1998 $M	1999 $M	2000E $M
Total Market Size	83	86	89
Total Local Production	2	2	2
Total Exports	8	8	8
Total Imports	89	92	95
Imports from the U.S.	55	60	65

Telecommunications Equipment (TEL)

	1998 $M	1999 $M	2000E $M
Total Market Size	75	80	70
Total Local Production	0	0	0
Total Exports	0	0	0
Total Imports	75	60	70
Imports from the U.S.	40	40	45

Computers/Peripherals (CPT)

	1998 $M	1999 $M	2000E $M
Total Market Size	50	60	70
Total Local Production	0	0	0
Total Exports	0	0	0
Total Imports	50	60	70
Imports from the U.S.	39	48	60

Footwear (FOT)

	1997 $M	1998 $M	1999 $M
Total Market Size	19	23	24
Total Local Production	3	4	4
Total Exports	1.4	1.5	1.5
Total Imports	17	21	22
Imports from the U.S.	7	11	12

Best Prospects for Agricultural Products

Nuts

	1998 ('000)	1999 ('000)	2000 ('000)
	Kilograms		
Total Market Size	59	89	100
Total Local Production	0	0	0
Total Exports	0	0	0
Total Imports	59	89	100
Imports from the U.S.	42	49	75

Wines

	1998 ('000)	1999 ('000)	2000 ('000)
	Liters		
Total Market Size	1213	1238	1300
Total Local Production	500	400	450
Total Exports	688	293	400
Total Imports	1336	1131	1250
Imports from the U.S.	542	440	550

Onions

	1998 ('000)	1999 ('000)	2000 ('000)
	Kilograms		
Total Market Size	9337	9488	9800
Total Local Production	2457	1638	1800
Total Exports	0	0	0
Total Imports	6880	7840	8000
Imports from the U.S.	3846	3154	4400

Carrots

	1998 ('000)	1999 ('000)	2000 ('000)
	Kilograms		
Total Market Size	24115	26526	25000
Total Local Production	21605	24676	24500
Total Exports	0	0	0
Total Imports	2510	1850	2500
Imports from the U.S.	1465	877	1650

Apples

	1998 ('000)	1999 ('000)	2000 ('000)
	Kilograms		
Total Market Size	883	837	900
Total Local Production	0	0	0
Total Exports	0	0	0
Total Imports	883	837	900
Imports from the U.S.	816	810	850

Pasta

	1998 ('000)	1999 ('000)	2000 ('000)
	Kilograms		
Total Market Size	N/A	N/A	N/A
Total Local Production	N/A	N/A	N/A
Total Exports	15	17	18
Total Imports	747	801	850
Imports from the U.S.	280	316	350

Biscuits/Crackers/Cookies

	1998	1999	2000
	Kilograms		
	('000)	('000)	('000)
Total Market Size	N/A	N/A	N/A
Total Local Production	N/A	N/A	N/A
Total Exports	2017	2001	2005
Total Imports	3765	5065	5500
Imports from the U.S.	2244	828	850

Agricultural imports by major categories

	1997	1998	1999
	$M	$M	$M
Food and Live Animals	445	467	454
Beverages and Tobacco	52	57	33
Animal and Vegetable Oils	24	21	21
Cork and Wood Manufactures	24	24	29

Agricultural imports from the United States.

	1997	1998	1999
	$M	$M	$M
Food and Live Animals	219	232	218
Beverages and Tobacco	15	11	7
Animal and Vegetable Oil	17	19	17

Agricultural imports by major categories

	1997	1998	1999
	$M	$M	$M
Food and Live Animals	445	467	454
-Live animals chiefly for food	1	1	1
-Meat and Meat Preparations	63	68	62
-Dairy Products and Bird Eggs	47	49	43
-Fish, Crustaceans and Mollusks	53	57	59
-Cereal and cereal preparations	124	130	117
-Vegetables and Fruit	35	42	58
-Sugar, sugar preparations	41	42	38
-Coffee, Tea, Cocoa, Spices	9	10	9
-Feeding stuff for animals	32	23	22
-Miscellaneous edible products	40	44	44
Beverages and Tobacco	32	57	52
-Beverages	39	44	26
-Tobacco	13	12	7
Manufactures			
Animal and Vegetable Oils	24	27	21
-Animal oils and fats	4	3	2
-Fixed vegetable oils and fats	16	20	14
-Animal and Vegetable Oils and Fats, processed, and waxes of animal or vegetable origin	3	4	4
-Cork and Wood Manufactures	24	24	29

Source: External Trade Reports, Statistical Institute of Jamaica
* Jamaica Survey of Living Conditions 1998

The above statistics are unofficial estimates.
Statistical Institute of Jamaica estimates
N/A - Not Available, E - Estimated
Note: MT ('000) = Thousand Metric Tons

Extracted from the U.S. Department of Commerce USA Trade 2001 Country Commercial Guide for Jamaica.

Import and Export Tips

• Regulations

Customs: Customs tax is a major source of GOJ tax revenue. Jamaica is a member of CARICOM, a Caribbean customs union. A Common External Tariff (CET) applies to goods from outside CARICOM. Goods from within CARICOM are exempt from the CET. Exceptions are sometimes made to the CET under cost-of-living considerations or other sensitivities. (Basic foods, medicines, some fertilizers and insecticides, books, and agricultural inputs have before been given special low or zero duty rates.) Countries may also apply for Minimum Rate Approach, which allows them to exceed agreed minimum rates of the CET. Alcoholic beverages, tobacco products, petroleum products, jewelry, watches, and clocks are examples of goods approved for Minimum Rates. Nonbasic, finished goods and goods competing with those from CARICOM states have higher duty rates. See **Contacts, Business Infrastructure (Currency Exchange).**

Tariffs: The CET ranges usually from 0 to 20 percent. Some agricultural products (such as chicken and milk) carry higher duty rates. Exempt from the CET are goods imported under various conditions: (1) approved new investments, (2) approved substantial expansion to existing investment, and (3) development financing from countries or international institutions assisting Jamaica. See **Investment (Foreign Trade Zones and Free Ports).**

Import Taxes: Import duties are levied on the cif value of goods. A general consumption tax (GCT) of 15 percent applies to most items. Alcohol and tobacco products have additional duty of 25 to 56 percent, and a special consumption tax of 5 to 39.9 percent. Beverages, motor vehicles, and some agricultural products also have an additional stamp duty and special consumption tax.

Exchange Rate: On September 26, 1991, exchange controls were eliminated to allow for free competition in the foreign exchange market. The principal remaining restriction is that foreign exchange transactions must be done through an authorized dealer. Licenses are regulated. Any company or person required to make payments to the government by agreement or law (such as the levy and royalty due on bauxite) will continue to make such payments directly to the Bank of Jamaica (BOJ). Authorized dealers (commercial banks and cambios) are required to sell 5 percent of their foreign exchange purchases directly to the BOJ. In addition, under an agreement between the Petroleum Company of Jamaica (Petrojam) and the commercial banks, a further 10 percent of foreign exchange purchases are sold to Petrojam. In 1994, cambios were designated as authorized dealers to promote an increase in the official inflows of foreign exchange. Cambios account for over a third of total foreign exchange purchases by authorized dealers. Reportedly, cambio dealers have been lobbying for increased flexibility in doing business in order to increase their market share and be viable. In 1998, total foreign exchange inflows through commercial banks and cambios increased by 2.1 percent to US$ 3.6 billion. From January to September 1999, foreign exchange inflows into the official market declined by 1.6 percent over the corresponding period in 1998 to US$ 2.65 billion. The average weighted selling rate has been slipping. On November 5, 1998, the rate was J$ 40.42 to US$ 1.00. This decline is the result of uncertainty and speculation arising from unfavorable economic conditions, the postponement of a bond issue by the GOJ in the international market that was expected to help fund the current budget deficit, and attractive returns on U.S. dollar bonds issued locally. There is a broad perception in the market that the present exchange rate is not sustainable. However, the GOJ is committed to defending the exchange rate within a targeted band through the Bank of Jamaica's intervention.

- **Documentation**

Exports: Items requiring export licensing include ammunition, crocodiles and crocodile eggs, eggs, antique furniture and paintings, gold bullion and fully or semi-manufactured gold, minerals and metals (bauxite, alumina, gypsum, and so on), pimento, sugar, plasma, lignum vitae and log wood, petroleum products, live animals, motor vehicles (bodies and auto parts), and shells subject to the Convention of International Trade for Endangered Species administered by National Resources Conservation Administration (NRCA).

Imports: All imports require a supplier invoice, a certificate of origin, a bill of lading, an airway bill and other shipping documents, a declaration of value, and an import license, if necessary. (Certain products may also require phyto-sanitary certification). Possibly required are a tax compliance certificate for the importer, a Business Enterprise Number (BENO), and a Taxpayer Registration Number (TRN). Items requiring import licensing include milk powder, refined sugar, plants and parts of plants for perfume or pharmaceutical purposes, gum-resins, vegetable saps and extracts, certain chemicals, motor vehicles and parts, arms and ammunition, and certain toys (water pistols, gaming machines). Licenses are obtained from the Trade Board. For temporary entry (three to four months), regular import documentation and a C25 form with customs authorization are required. A deposit or place in bond of 100 to 150 percent of duties is required and refunded upon exit of items. Prohibited imports include amusement machines known as "one arm bandits"; dogs for racing and dog racing equipment; tablets containing a combination of methaqualone and diphenhydraine hydrochloride; certain brands of crayons from China and Thailand; all items banned under the Customs Act and the Plants Protection from Disease Act; all goods prohibited entry into the United Kingdom under the Anthrax Prevention Act 1919; animals and carcasses of animals prohibited under the Animals Diseases and Importation Act; arms and ammunition, except with the permission of the commissioner; brandy of a lower strength than 30 degrees per centum under proof, unless it is proved that it has been matured for a period not less than ten years; base or counterfeit imitation coin of any country; coin, silver, or any money not of the established standard in weight and fineness; opium and dangerous drugs; essence of brandy or whisky or flavoring essences except as approved by the minister; indecent or obscene prints, paintings, photographs, books, films; oil of gin or cognac, except as approved by the minister; rum coloring solutions; spirits and wine, unless specifically imported with casks or other vessels of at least nine gallons content or in glass or stone bottles with each case containing not less than one gallon; fictitious stamps and instruments; and sugar, except under license.

Labeling: The Jamaica Bureau of Standards administers the Standards Act, Processed Food Act, and Weights and Measures Act. These acts apply to all imported goods and have labeling requirements. Recognized international quality specifications also apply to all items sold in Jamaica.

Standards: Jamaica generally follows U.S. standards. Many mandatory standards must be followed, and copies of these can be bought from the Bureau of Standards. The quarantine division inspects and handles live animal cases. Meat imports may be inspected by the Ministry of Health. The Jamaica Bureau of Standards is increasingly monitoring the quality of imported items. The metric system is required.

• **Payment**

Terms: Usual terms are 60 to 90 days. Payments are usually made on imports and exports via letters of credit or bills for collection. Local banking commissions range from 1.15 to 3.45 percent. The Small Business Administration and the Export-Import Bank offer various financing programs.

Currency Exchange: Foreign exchange is available for residents and nonresidents via a network of authorized dealers. There are no foreign exchange controls. See **Business Infrastructure (Currency Exchange).**

Fund Transfer: There are no restrictions on capital outflow. Jamaican financial institutions, insurance companies, and so on must obtain prior approval (from either the Bank of Jamaica or the superintendent of insurance) before diversifying investments abroad.

Offshore Loans: No information is available at this time.

Agents and Distributors

No specific laws in Jamaica dictate contract terms for agents or distributors. Parties formulate their own terms and conditions of agreement with or without attorneys. However, the Fair Competition Act (FCA) in effect invalidates contract clauses that restrict competition. Signed agreements are legally binding, and breaches of such contracts may be contested in a court of law. The Department of Commerce (any district office) with the U.S. Embassy Foreign Commercial Service (FCS) provides the Agent/Distributor Service (ADS). For US$ 250, FCS will find suitable representatives and prepare a report that lists firms that have read client literature and have agreed to consider a business relationship. The Kingston U.S. Embassy's Commercial Section offers the Gold Key Service (GKS). GKS is a custom-tailored service (US$ 350 for day one, US$ 250 for later days) that combines orientation briefings, market research, and appointments with potential partners. The local government investment agency, the Jamaica Promotions Corporation (JAMPRO), and the American Chamber of Commerce of Jamaica (both in Kingston and Montego Bay) provide leads and sources for business partners. See **Contacts.**

Establishing an Office

JAMPRO facilitates the establishment of both productive and service-sector businesses. Potential investors should present project proposals to JAMPRO for assessment and guidance. Information should include costings, financial projections, and production levels. JAMPRO will assist with (1) obtaining applications to the income tax department (for an income tax number and for a business or trade number), (2) obtaining import licenses from the trade board, (3) identi-

fication of business location (factory space or land), (4) applications for concessions under incentive legislation, (5) applications to the revenue board for a Business Enterprise Number (BEN), (6) work permits for non-resident personnel, and (7) registration under the consumption duty or excise duty acts. Private, limited liability companies require at least 2 and at most 20 shareholders from any country. Incorporation requires two legal documents: a memorandum of association and articles of association. Register or incorporate the business (for example, sole proprietorship, partnership, or company limited by shares) with the Registrar of Companies..

Distribution and Sales Channels

Distribution and sales of imported merchandise in Jamaica are mainly done via importers, distributors, and agent representatives. End-user firms also directly import a large share of materials and supplies, including machinery and equipment. To maintain market position, one must have close contact with end users, provide excellent quality after-sales service, and competitive prices. Many importers of goods into Jamaica take advantage of the close proximity to the U.S. to maintain direct contact with manufacturers' representatives and exporters particularly in Florida.

Direct Marketing

Deregulation and liberalization in Jamaica have inspired creative thinking though catalogs and mail order so far have not been popular. Some firms have used telephone marketing and direct mailings of promotional materials. Local credit card companies sometimes offer goods and services via direct mailings to cardholders. Network marketing has been growing to promote products such as

Avon, Amway, and various health (food) supplements. However, this market is inherently fairly small and has disparity in purchasing power and income distribution. For precise information, special surveys may be needed since market statistics can be difficult to obtain. Personal contacts are very important to develop a close working relationship with a Jamaican sales representative, agent, or distributor.

Leasing/Joint Ventures

Nonresident partners (unless exempted under one of the incentive programs), including corporate partners, must pay tax on their share of partnership profits accrued in or deriving from Jamaica. Nonresident foreign corporations pay at the same rates as resident corporations. Double taxation relief is available under the Convention for the Avoidance of Double Taxation.

Franchising

In recent years, there has been substantial franchising, especially in fast foods. Usually a locally registered company manages the operation in conformity with franchise requirements. JAMPRO and the American Chamber of Commerce (AMCHAM) have organized events to explain and promote franchise operations, and are good points of contact before entering the market. JAMPRO also assists in setting out the terms of registration, trademarks, and other requirements.

Advertising and Promotion

Advertising is mainly done via radio, television, the press, and billboards. Several Internet service providers also exist. A number of advertising agencies have national coverage. Radio is the widest-ranging medium, with seven authorized stations. The two local TV networks are TVJ and the private Commu-

nication Videomax Mediamix (CVM). Several cable operators are licensed in designated cable television zones across Jamaica. Cable channels will probably carry advertising by companies through the international network. Jamaica has two morning dailies, one afternoon tabloid, and several periodicals and magazines. Trade missions and catalogue shows are excellent means of marketing.

Selling Factors

Several large, established distribution companies in Jamaica import and distribute a range of products. They usually own or arrange for their own vehicles. Demand and prices for products vary. Some companies specialize in high volume with fairly low markups, whereas others only distribute goods that offer a fairly high markup. Because of proximity and influence, strategies that work in North America usually work in Jamaica.

Selling to the Government

Government procurement is mainly done via open tenders, direct advertising, or invitation to registered suppliers. U.S. firms are eligible to bid. Manufactured goods usually aren't produced locally, so there is little domestic competition. Companies selling office supplies to the government must register with the Financial Management Division of the Ministry of Finance. Companies selling other kinds of equipment or materials should contact the National Water Commission (water), Jamaica Public Service Company (electricity), Jamaica Commodity Trading Company (for the purchase of certain basic food items and fertilizer under concessionary loan programs), Pharmaceutical Division of the Ministry of Health and Health Corporation Limited (medicines and medical supplies), or Ministry of Housing (for housing and construction materials).

Pricing

Most prices are freely determined by the market. Exceptions are in services such as telecommunications, electricity, water, and bus fares. The Office of Utilities Regulation monitors pricing and other activities for these companies. The Fair Trading Commission (FTC) and the Consumer Affairs Commission (CAC) monitor pricing of consumer items though there are no price regulations or controls. The FTC usually responds to consumer complaints. The CAC helps conduct research and informs the public of price variations. Many products, especially imports, have typically high markups. Pricing also changes with the money supply and the amount of liquidity in the system.

Customer Support

After-sales service is an important competitive advantage in the Jamaican market and is crucial for sales. If a U.S. firm has trouble setting up its own distribution system, it should either (1) use a local agent or distributor to maintain a trained service staff with a reasonable stock of spare parts, or (2) offer the customer rapid service from the U.S.

Intellectual Property Rights (IPR)

The Jamaican Constitution recognizes property rights. Property, including intellectual, is protected. Bilateral agreements also protect IPR. The U.S. and the GOJ have an Intellectual Property Rights Agreement and a Bilateral Investment Treaty. The GOJ has the Trademark Act, the Layout Designs (Topographies) Act, and an amendment to the Copyright Act that covers databases and the issue of trading in encrypted transmissions. These fulfill obligations to WTO Trade-Related Aspects of Intellectual Property (TRIPs), bilateral U.S. agreements, and potentially, the Paris Convention for the Protection of Intellectual Property. The Trademark Act meets internationally accepted standards for the protection of trademarks. It provides the owner of a registered trademark with a property right, thereby giving him or her the exclusive right to exploit the mark in the course of trade. The mark may be registered in relation to goods and services, and provision is made for the registration of both collective marks and certification marks. It protects a registered trademark for a period of ten years, renewable for another ten years. The Layout Designs Act protects layout designs embodied in integrated circuits and gives the owner of those rights the exclusive right to reproduce the layout design, import, sell, or otherwise commercially exploit it and authorize other persons to do so. That right lasts ten years and may be transferred by the owner by assignment, will, or legal methods. It also sets out means of legal redress for violations of the right. The bill amending the Copyright Act seeks to make explicit the provision of copyright protection on compilations of works such as databases. The Amendment also prohibits the manufacture or trade in decoders of encrypted transmissions. It also gives persons having rights in encrypted transmissions or in broadcasting or cable program services a right of action against persons who infringe on those rights.

Attorney

Professional advice is recommended in early stages of a business venture for smooth startup and compliance with local laws. The Jamaica Bar Association has over 550 attorneys, and provides membership lists.

FOREIGN INVESTMENT
6

Openness: The GOJ welcomes foreign investment. No policies or regulations restrict areas to Jamaicans. The GOJ's Financial Sector Adjustment Company (FINSAC) handles privatization and divestment activities, and seems to favor sale of assets to national investors. Investment proposals are also favored that increase productive output, use domestic raw materials, earn or save foreign exchange, or introduce new technology. New developments must have environmental impact assessments, but foreign and domestic investors are treated the same before and after the investment. Negotiations, acquisitions, and mergers are hindered only by antimonopoly trade barriers. They are subject to the Companies Act, Securities (Amendment) Act, and Jamaica Stock Exchange (JSE) rules. The JSE clearance and settlement procedures do not conform to international standards. The JSE is in a relationship with the Committee of Uniformed Securities Identification (CUSIP) Services Bureau to acquire International Securities Identification Numbers for Jamaican securities. Investors must generally register a branch office of a foreign-owned enterprise or establish a local company. See **Private Ownership.**

Regulatory System: The Fair Competition Act deals with consumer protection, misleading advertisements, price fixing, collusion, unfair trading practices, and interlocking directorships. Various tax, labor, health, and safety laws and policies facilitate investment processes. The Office of Utilities Regulations (OUR) acts as independent regulator of telecommunications, electricity, transport, and water utilities (in accordance with WTO). Bureaucracy has been identified as discouraging investment. Investment approval process can take 3 to 18 months, but the government has committed itself to halving approval times.

Investment Agreements: Jamaica has investment treaties with the U.S., Argentina, France, Italy, Germany, Netherlands, Switzerland, United Kingdom, and China. Jamaica is negotiating investment agreements with South Korea, Cuba, Costa Rica, Belgium-Luxembourg, Russia, and Canada.

Trade Zones and Free Ports: The Jamaican Free Zone Act allows investors to operate solely with foreign exchange in activities such as warehousing and storing, manufacturing, redistribution, processing, refining, assembling, packaging, and services such as banking, insurance, and professional services. Additional incentives are a 100 percent tax holiday in perpetuity; no import licensing requirements; and exemption from customs duties on capital goods, raw materials, construction materials, and office equipment. Manufacturing companies may sell 15 percent of their production on the local market through the Free Zone Administration. Single Entity Free Zones can be established. The Kingston Free Zone plans to extend an Informatics Park in Portmore (focused on information technology) and also a Commercial Free Zone in Kingston.

Performance Requirements/Incentives: No specific performance requirements exist for investment in Jamaica. Many incentives exist to attract currency and jobs, including the (1) Export Industry Encouragement Act (EIEA), (2) Hotel Incentives Act (HIA), (3) Resort Cottages Incentives Act (RCIA), (4) Motion Picture Industry Encouragement Act, (5) Income Tax Act (farmer status, (6) Factory Construction Law, (7) International Finance Company Act, (8) Foreign Sales Corporation Act, (9) Industry Modernization Program, (10) Moratorium on Duties, (11) Urban Renewal Act, (12) Accelerated Depreciation/ Special Capital Allowance. Lower lending rates for development and other nonfiscal incentives also exist. For incentive benefits, proposals must be made to JAMPRO, the GOJ agency that promotes and processes investment proposals. See **Trade Zones and Free Ports.**

Capital Markets and Investment: Foreigners may borrow freely at market terms from credit sources. Regulatory and accounting systems follow international norms. The GOJ Financial Sector Adjustment Company (FINSAC) is selling bank assets and merging banks that it is restructuring. See **Infrastructure and Investment (Openness).**

Private Ownership: Both foreign and domestic private entities are free to establish, acquire, and dispose of interest in business enterprises. Companies must register with the Registrar of Companies. Public and private entities (except for cable TV) have equal access to markets, credit, licenses, and supplies. Cable and Wireless of Jamaica Ltd. is being demonopolized, and cable TV licenses are given to companies incorporated in Jamaica and mainly owned by Jamaica/CARICOM. See **Communications (Phone).**

Expropriation and Compensation: The U.S. Embassy in Jamaica knows of no expropriation litigation between the GOJ and private individuals or companies. Section 18 of the Jamaican Constitution allows expropriation only for public purpose, with transparent purpose and principles of compensation.

OPIC and Investment Insurance: OPIC has insured various manufacturing, services, and hospitality industry projects in Jamaica. OPIC can insure projects up to a US$ 200 million cap. In 1998, OPIC insured seven projects for a total of US$ 76 million.

Dispute Settlement: The U.S. Embassy knows of no major investment disputes being handled by the government. Jamaica belongs to the International Center for Settlement of Investment Disputes, which will arbitrate disputes between nonresident investors and the GOJ. Disputes between enterprises are generally handled in local courts.

FINANCE

7

Jamaica has 6 commercial banks, 15 merchant banks, finance and trust companies, 6 building societies, 3 development banks, 67 credit unions, and 12 life insurance companies. Foreign investors have equal access as Jamaican investors to loan services. Total assets of commercial banks are J$ 185.1 billion (about US$ 4.75 billion), and for merchant banks, finance companies, and trust companies, J$ 11.72 billion (about US$ 300.5 billion) in March 1999. The Bank of Jamaica has a subsidiary National Export-Import Bank. GOJ has set up the Financial Sector Adjustment Company (FINSAC), a temporary agency that works under the Minister of Finance and Planning to restructure and strengthen numerous banks. See **Capital Markets and Investment.**

Export Financing: The GOJ has kept tight monetary measures, so fewer funds are expected for the private sector. Commercial interest rates were 39 percent in June 1999. The Securities Act regulates securities, and brokers and companies are also effectively regulated. From the U.S., the Small Business Administration and the Export-Import Bank offer various programs for loans, guarantees, and other finance and information needs.

Project Financing: Jamaica has three development banks: the GOJ Agricultural Bank of Jamaica ACB (assists agricultural sector), the GOJ National Development Bank (NDB) (works with industries earning hard currency such as tourism and manufacturing), and the private Trafalgar Development Bank (offers a range of loans and development services). Multilateral organizations that work in Jamaica include the European Union, the World Bank, the Organization of American States (OAS via the Inter American Development Bank (IADB), and the United Nations Development Program (UNDP). See **Contacts.**

COMMUNICATIONS ⑧

Phone

Jamaica has a complete digital network with wide range of local and international telecommunication services. International locations can be direct-dialed. Cable and Wireless of Jamaica (owned mainly by Cable and Wireless of the UK) has an agreement with the GOJ that gives it a monopoly. The monopoly affects domestic service, infrastructure provision and expansion, and international linkups. However, Jamaica has signed the WTO Basic Telecommunications Services Agreement. It will follow a schedule to open the market and allow (1) domestic and international market access to satellite services and facilities after 2004, (2) market access by control or full ownership to foreign investment after 2004, and (3) market access to international services and facilities by 2013.

Internet

Jamaica has several Internet service providers, including Cable and Wireless (CWJamaica), Infochannel, Colis, JamWeb, World Telenet, and Jamaica on Line.

Mail

Mail service is reliable, and several U.S.-owned air-courier services operate in the country. Express mail international services are available between Jamaica and the U.S.

TRANSPORTATION ⑨

Land

Jamaica has over 9,000 miles of roads, but most need repair. The new North Coast highway will link major coastal tourist areas. The GOJ has an agreement for Rail India Technical and Economic Services Ltd. (RITES, an India government agency) to rehabilitate Jamaica's railways. RITES, with the GOJ and others, will rehabilitate tracks, repair and refurbish buildings and locomotives, retool workshops, and acquire new equipment. Inland transportation within Jamaica and to and from ports needs improvement.

Sea

The Port of Kingston and the Port of Montego Bay are world-class, international seaports with 44 international shipping lines. Agricultural and bauxite and alumina industries use smaller, specialized ports as well. The National Investment Bank of Jamaica is processing proposals for a water ferry system to serve the Kingston, Port Royal, and Portmore areas.

Air

Jamaica has two major airports, both modern and well equipped: Norman Manley International Airport (in Kingston) and Sangster International Airport (SIA, in Montego Bay). They are served by ten major airlines and an international U.S. all-cargo air service.

WORK WEEK
10

Business Hours: 8:30 a.m. to 4:30 p.m. Monday through Friday, with most open Saturday and a few open Sunday.

Government Hours: : 9:00 a.m. to 5:00 p.m. Monday through Friday. Closed Saturday and Sunday.

Bank Hours: 9:00 a.m. to 2:00 p.m. Monday through Thursday, and 9:00 a.m. to 3:00 p.m. or 5:00 p.m. on Friday. Most banks are closed on Saturday.

HOLIDAYS 2001
11

New Year's Day, January 1
Ash Wednesday*, February 28
Good Friday*, April 13
Easter Monday*, April 16
Discover Day, Third Monday in May
National Labor Day, May 25
Queen's Birthday*, June (date varies)
Emancipation Day, August 1
Independence Day, August 6
National Heroes Day, October 19
Remembrance Day, November 9
Christmas Day, December 25
Boxing Day, December 26

Some holidays may be observed on different dates depending on the day of the week on which it falls. The U.S. Embassy will be closed on U.S. and Jamaican holidays. It is recommended that business travelers do not schedule trips to Jamaica immediately before or immediately after local or U.S. holidays.

*Actual dates vary from year to year.

BUSINESS TRAVEL
12

Business Customs

Jamaicans are slightly more formal than North Americans. For first meetings, a friendly and courteous, "Good Morning/Afternoon/Evening" brings more response and respect than the casual, "Hi." Jamaican business acquaintances usually welcome informality after first greeting.

Travel Advisory and Visas

U.S. citizens can enter Jamaica with proof of citizenship (birth certificate or passport) and a photo ID (like a valid driver's license). No visa is needed.

Business Infrastructure

Entry Requirements (personal and professional goods): Items to be brought in temporarily (laptop computers, exhibit material, machinery, and so on) must be identified at Customs. Also required is payment of a security deposit of the required duty and General Consumption Tax. The Customs Authority refunds the security deposit when one leaves Jamaica. When machinery is imported for three to six months, one must also complete Customs Form C23.

Currency Exchange: The Jamaican dollar is the main currency and is traded freely against other international currencies; US$ 1 equals J$ 39.35 (weighted average). Jamaican dollars and foreign exchange can be traded via both the commercial banking system and authorized foreign exchange dealers. There are no restrictions on repatriating profits. See **Payment Terms (Currency Exchange).**

Taxes: See **Trade (Regulations)**.

Hotels and Restaurants: Jamaican cuisine varies, and the most popular dishes are rice and peas (red), ackee (vegetable) and salt fish, patties (meat filled), jerk chicken, curried goat, and mackerel rundown. There are many U.S. fast-food outlets, such as McDonald's, Burger King, Kentucky Fried Chicken, Kenny Roger's Roasted Chicken, Popeyes, Wendy's, Dominoes Pizza, Pizza Hut, Taco Bell, and Subway. Food prices compared to the U.S. are marked up between 10 percent (wholesale) and 25 percent (retail), but these markups are decreasing.

Rent: No information is available at this time.

Utilities: Electric power is 110 volts. Power is sold at about US$ 0.12/kWh. Water is available from above and below ground, including Kingston reservoirs. Occasional droughts reduce water supplies and can require rationing by lock-off of residential areas. The hurricane season can bring mainly minor flooding to urban areas.

Business Services: See Advertising Promotion and **Investment (Performance Requirements and Incentives** and **Labor).**

Labor Costs and Legislation: As of 1999, the minimum wage is J$ 1,200 per week. The unemployment rate is 16.5 percent (1997 est). In 1989, the labor force was by occupation: services 41 percent, agriculture 22.5 percent, industry 19 percent.

Literacy: The literacy rate is 55.6 percent.

Travel Notes

The following travel notes have been supplied by the U.S. government. For the most recent general travel and consular information, see the U.S. Department of State travel publications or call the Traveler's Telephone Hotline at (202) 647-5225.

Security: Violent crime is a serious problem, especially in Kingston. Occasional gang violence and shootings are common in some neighborhoods but can occur elsewhere. Some of the neighborhoods are under curfew. Travelers should check with the local authorities or the U.S. Embassy for details.

Health Precautions: There is limited medical care in comparison to the U.S. Hospitals and Doctors expect cash payment for services. U.S. medical insurance may not be valid outside the U.S. Current information on health matters may be obtained from the Centers for Disease Control and Prevention's international travelers' hotline at (404) 332-4559.

Embassy Assistance

To obtain additional and updated information on entry and exit requirements, travelers can contact the Consular Section of the Embassy of Jamaica at 1520 New Hampshire Avenue, N.W., Washington, D.C. 20036; Tel: (202) 452-0660. Travelers may also contact the nearest Jamaica consulate. They are located in Boston, Chicago, Houston, Los Angeles, Richmond VA, Miami, and New York.

CONTACTS

13

U.S. Embassy Trade Contacts

Regional FCS Office
U.S. & Foreign Commercial Service
American Embassy
Santo Domingo, Dominican Republic
Tel: (809) 221-2171
Fax: (809) 688-4838

U.S. & Foreign Commercial Service
U.S. Embassy
Jamaica Mutual Life Center
2 Oxford Rd.
Kingston 5
Tel: (876) 929-4850
Fax: (876) 920-2580

Regional Agricultural Attache
Foreign Agricultural Service

United States Department of Agriculture
American Embassy
Santo Domingo, Dominican Republic
Tel: (809) 221-2171; (809) 688-8090
Fax: (809) 685-4743

Foreign Agricultural Service
United States Department of Agriculture
U.S. Embassy
Jamaica Mutual Life Center
2 Oxford Rd.
Kingston 5
Tel: (876) 929-4850
Fax: (876) 920-2580

Counselor for Economic and Political Affairs
American Embassy
Jamaica Mutual Life Center
2 Oxford Rd.
Kingston 5
Tel: (876) 935-6087
Fax: (876) 929-6029

Chambers of Commerce

American Chamber of Commerce of Jamaica
77 Knutsford Boulevard
Kingston 5
Tel: (876) 929-7866; (876) 929-7867
Fax: (876) 929-8597

Jamaica Chamber of Commerce
7E Parade
Kingston
Tel: (876) 922-0150; (876) 922-0151
Fax: (876) 924-9056

Jamaican Trade or Industry Associations

Jamaica Exporters Association
13 Dominica Drive
Kingston 5
Tel: (876) 929-1292; (876) 926-0586;
  (876) 926-7158

Jamaica Hotel & Tourist Association
2 Ardenne Rd
Kingston 10
Tel: (876) 926-3635; (876) 926-3636;
  (876) 926-2796

Jamaica Manufacturers Association Ltd.
85a Duke St.
Kingston
Tel: (876) 922-8880; (876) 922-8881;
  (876) 922-0787; (876) 922-2365

Private Sector Organization of Jamaica (PSOJ)
39 Hope Road
Kingston 10
Tel: (876) 927-6238; (876) 927-6958;
  (876) 927-6957; (876) 927-6786

Jamaica Promotions Corporation (JAMPRO)
35 Trafalgar Rd.
Kingston 10, Jamaica (W.I.)
Tel: (876) 929-7190; (876) 929-7199
Fax: (876) 924-9650

Government of Jamaica Ministries

Governor-General
King's House
Hope Road
Kingston 10
Tel: (876) 927-6424
Fax: (876) 929-0005

Office of the Prime Minister
Patterson, P.C., Q.C., M.P.
1 Devon Rd., P.O. Box 272
Kingston 10
Tel: (876) 927-9941; (876) 927-9943
Fax: (876) 929-0005

Deputy Prime Minister and Minister of Foreign Affairs and Foreign Trade
21 Dominica Drive
Kingston 5
Tel: (876) 926-4220; (876) 926-4228
Fax: (876) 929-6733

Minister of Agriculture
Hope Gardens
Kingston 6
Tel: (876) 927-1731; (876) 927-1734
Fax: (876) 927-1904

Minister of Commerce and Technology
36 Trafalgar Rd.
Kingston 10
Tel: (876) 929-8990*
Fax: (876) 929-8196*
*Currently, the same as the Ministry of Industry.

Minister of Education, Youth and Culture
2 National Heroes Circle
Kingston 4
Tel: (876) 922-1400; (876) 922-1409
Fax: (876) 926-1837

Minister of Environment and Housing
2 Hagley Park Road
Kingston 10
Tel: (876) 926-1590
Fax: (876) 926-0154

Minister of Finance and Planning
30 National Heroes Circle
Kingston 4
Tel: (876) 922-8600; (876) 922-8608
Fax: (876) 924-9291

Minister of Health
10 Caledonia Ave.
Kingston 5
Tel: (876) 926-9220; (876) 926-9220
Fax: (876) 926-9234

Minister of Industry and Investment
36 Trafalgar Road
Kingston 10
Tel: (876) 929-8990; (876) 929-8999
Fax: (876) 929-8196

Minister of Labour, Social Security and Sports
14 National Heroes Circle, P.O. Box 10
Kingston 5
or 1F North Street
Kingston
Tel: (876) 922-8000
Fax: (876) 922-6902

Minister of Legal Affairs and Attorney General
12 Ocean Blvd.
Kingston
Tel: (876) 922-0080; (876) 922-0080
Fax: (876) 922-6950
or 79-83 Barry Street (Atty. Gen. Chambers)
Kingston
Tel: (876) 922-6140; (876) 922-6148

Minister of Mining and Energy
36 Trafalgar Road
Kingston 10
Tel: (876) 926-9170; (876) 926-9179
Fax: (876) 926-2835

Minister of Local Government and Community Development
85 Hagley Park Road
Kingston 10
Tel: (876) 754-0996
Fax: (876) 960-0725

Minister of National Security and Justice
Jamaica Mutual Life Building, 7th Floor
2 Oxford Road
Kingston 5
Tel: (876) 906-4908
Fax: (876) 906-1724

Minister of Transportation and Works
140 Maxfield Ave.
Kingston
Tel: (876) 926-3111-9
Fax: (876) 929-2996

Minister of Tourism
64 Knutsford Blvd.
Kingston 5
Tel: (876) 920-4956
Fax: (876) 920-4944

Minister of Water
Island Life Bldg.
Kingston 5
Tel: (876) 754-0973; (876) 754-0974
Fax: (876) 754-0973

The Office of the Registrar of Companies
11 King Street
Kingston, Jamaica
Tel: (876) 922-0010
Fax: (876) 922-4103

Market Research Firms

Market Research Services Ltd.
75 Knutsford Blvd.
Kingston 5
Tel: (876) 929-6311

CARICOM Consultants (Ja) Ltd.
28 Derrymore Road
Kingston 10
Tel: (876) 926-2731
Fax: (876) 968-5895

Fidelity Economic Financial and Marketing
  Services Ltd.
15 Belmont Road
Kingston 5
Tel: (876) 929-0531

J.A. Young Research Ltd.
2a Kensington Cresc.
Kingston 5
Tel: (876) 926-7437
Fax: (876) 926-8529

Peter King Associates Ltd.
11 A Waterloo Road
Kingston 10
Tel: (876) 926-8257

Commercial Banks

Citibank N.A.
63 Knutsford Boulevard
Kingston 5
Tel: (876) 926-3270
Fax: (876) 929-3745

Bank of Nova Scotia Jamaica Ltd.
Scotiabank Center
Duke & Port Royal Streets
Box 709
Kingston
Tel: (876) 922-1000
Fax: (876) 967-1691

Union Bank Holding Company Limited
17 Dominica Drive (c/o Citizens Bank)
Kingston 5
Tel: (876) 929-2605
Fax: (876) 929-3129

Trafalgar Commercial Bank Limited
60 Knutsford Boulevard
Kingston 5
Tel: (876) 929-3383; (876) 929-3386
Fax: (876) 929-3654

CIBC Jamaica Limited
23-27 Knutsford Boulevard
Box 762
Kingston 5
Tel: (876) 929-9310; (876) 929-9316
Fax: (876) 960-2837

National Commercial Bank Jamaica Limited
The Atrium
32 Trafalgar Road
Kingston 10
Tel: (876) 929-9050; (876) 929-9089
Fax: (876) 968-1342

Bank of Jamaica (BOJ)
Nethersole Place
Box 621
Kingston, Jamaica
Tel: (876) 922-0750; (876) 922-0759

For divestment of public enterprises:
National Investment Bank of Jamaica (NIBJ)
11 Oxford Road
Kingston 5
Tel: (876) 960-9690
Fax: (876) 920-0907

Multilateral Development Banks

The World Bank
6 St. Lucia Ave.
Kingston 5
Tel: (876) 960-0459
Fax: (876) 960-0463

Inter-American Development Bank (IADB)
40 Knutsford Blvd.
Kingston 5
Tel: (876) 926-2342
Fax: (876) 926-2898

Washington-Based USG Country Contacts

U.S. Department of Commerce
International Trade Administration
Jamaica Desk
Washington, DC 20230
Tel: (202) 482-0704

Note: To request information on regional
business topics (NAFTA, CBI, etc.) by fax,
phone AMERIFax: (202) 482-2527or for global
topics TPCC Trade Information Center
Tel: (800) USA-TRADE

U.S. Department of State
Jamaica Desk
ARA/CAR, Room 3248 Main State.
2201 C Street, N.W.
Washington, DC 20520
Tel: (202) 647-3210

**U.S. Agency for International Development
(USAID)**
Jamaica Desk
LAC/CAR, Room 3243 Main State
2201 C Street, N.W.
Washington, DC 20520
Tel: (202) 647-4105

The Multilateral Development Bank Office
14th St. and Constitution Ave., NW
Washington, DC 20230
Tel: (202) 482-3399
Fax: (202) 273-0927

U.S. Department of Agriculture
Foreign Agricultural Service
Trade Assistance and Promotion Office
USDA/FAS/AGX AGSTOP 1052
Washington, DC 20250-1052
Tel: (202) 720-7420
Fax:(202) 690-0193

Advertising and Trade Promotion

The Gleaner Newspaper (daily)
7 North St.
Kingston
Tel: (876) 922-3400

The Jamaica Herald Newspaper (Sunday)
29 Molynes Rd.
Kingston 10
Tel: (876) 968-7721

The Jamaica Observer Newspaper (daily)
2 Fagan Ave.
Kingston 8
Tel: (876) 931-7825; (876) 931-7832

The Star Newspaper (afternoon tabloid)
7 North St.
Kingston
Tel: (876) 922-3400

Investor's Choice Magazine (monthly)
12 Merrick Ave.
Kingston 10
Tel: (876) 929-2993

Insight (twice monthly econ/comm newsletter
that takes advertisements)
7 Kingsway, Apt. 11
Kingston 10
Tel: (876) 926-5404

Attorneys

Jamaica Bar Association
78-80 Harbour St., Kingston
Tel: (876) 922-2319

Investment and Finance

Jamaican Stock Exchange
Jamstockex.com

Free Trade Zones
Zone, 27 Shannon Drive, Kingston 15
Tel: (876) 923-5274
Fax: (876) 923-6023.
Web site:
  http://www.investjamaica.com/freezone

Marketing

**Financial Management Division of the
  Ministry of Finance**
Tel: (876) 929-9330

Diplomatic Representation in the U.S.
Chief of mission:
Chancery: 1520 New Hampshire Avenue NW,
  Washington, DC 20036
Tel: (202) 452-0660
Fax: (202) 452-0081
Consulate(s) general: Miami and New York

Diplomatic Representation from the U.S.
Chief of mission:
Embassy: Jamaica Mutual Life Center, 2
  Oxford Road (3rd floor) Kingston
Mailing address: use embassy street address
Tel: (809) 929-4850; (809) 929-4851;
  (809) 929-4852; (809) 929-4853;
  (809) 929-4854; (809) 929-4855;
  (809) 929-4856; (809) 929-4857;
  (809) 929-4858; (809) 929-4859
Fax: (809) 926-6743

P A N A M A

TRADE AND BUSINESS GUIDE

PROFILE 1

Official Name:	Republic of Panama
Official Languages:	Spanish, English 14%; many Panamanians are bilingual
Population:	2,808,268 (2000 est)
Population Growth:	1.34% (2000 est)
Age Structure:	0–14 years: 31%, 15–64 years: 63%, 65 years and over: 6% (2000 est)
Location:	Middle America, bordering the Caribbean Sea and the North Pacific Ocean between Columbia and Costa Rica
Area:	78,200 square kilometers. Slightly smaller than South Carolina
Type of Government:	Constitutional Republic with president (by popular vote for five-year terms) and unicameral Legislative Assembly (by popular vote for five-year terms)
Head of State:	President Mireya Elisa Moscoso Rodriguez
Cabinet:	Cabinet appointed by president
Religion:	Roman Catholic 85%, Protestant 15%
Major Cities:	Capital: Panama City (584,803). San Maguelito (243,025), Colon (140,908), David (102,678)
Climate:	Tropical. Hot, humid, and cloudy. Rainy season is May to January, and dry season is January to May
Time:	The entire country is -5 GMT (Greenwich Mean Time), which is EST (Eastern Standard Time)
GDP:	Purchasing Power Parity (PPP): 21 billion (1999 est); real growth rate: 4.4% (1999 est); per capita PPP: $7,600 (1999 est); composition by sector: agricultural: 8%, industry: 25%, services: 67% (1997 est)
Currency:	1 balboa (B) = 100 centesimos
Exchange Rate:	US$ 1 = 1 balboa (fixed rate)
Weights & Measure:	Both U.S. and metric systems are used
Natural Resources:	Copper, mahogany forests, shrimp
Total Trade:	In millions US$ [exports (fob)/imports (cif)]: 1997 est (6,916/8,505), 1998 est (6,706/8,716), 1999 est (5,970/7,670)
Trade with U.S.:	In millions US$ [exports (fob)/imports (cif)]: 1997 est (367/1,536), 1998 est (312/1,753), 1999 est (365/1,742)
Major Trade Partners:	Imports and exports: United States, European Union countries, Central America and Caribbean, Japan
Membership:	IADB, IBRD, IFC, IMF, ISO, MIGA, OAS, UN, UNCTAD, WCO, WIPO, and WTO. See membership description in appendix.

Sources: CIA World Fact Book, Ministry of Economy and Finance, U.S. International Trade Commission, Embassy Projections, Comptroller General's Office, USDA, U.S. Department of Commerce, Department of State

POLITICAL OUTLOOK ②

Relationship with the U.S.

U.S.–Panama relations are mainly cooperative and businesslike. Relations are expected to be cordial, with cooperation on law enforcement and international issues. President Moscoso seems to want a close, mutually beneficial relationship with the U.S.

Influences on Business

President Moscoso has expressed commitment to agreements with the IMF, the World Bank, and the World Trade Organization. She also supports privatization so far. Moscoso's agenda for economic liberalization will be slowed by budget constraints, an oppositional legislature, and her attention to the short-term welfare of disadvantaged Panamanians. The Assembly has less budgetary power than the U.S. Congress, but has a large role in political, economic, and social initiatives. More persistent problems include corruption, drug trafficking, money laundering, and alien smuggling. Reform of the justice sector is being assisted by the IDB and USAID. The new state-controlled canal may present opportunities for private sector involvement in operations and maintenance. Vacated U.S. military properties may be promising for investment in tourism, transportation, and other sectors.

Profile

System: Panama has a presidency and a 72-member unicameral Legislative Assembly.

Major political parties are the Democratic Revolutionary Party (PRD, with 35 seats), the Arnulfista Party (PA, with 18 seats), Solidarity Party (PS, with 4 seats), Christian Democratic Party (PDC, with 4 seats), and the Nationalist Republican Liberation Movement (MOLIRENA, with 3 seats). Figures are based on the 1999 elections.

Schedule for Elections: Presidential and Legislative Assembly elections are held every five years (last in May 1999). Next elections are scheduled for May 2004.

Major Parties: The Arnulfista party is not ideologically driven, so it follows its politics from the top. The PRD traditionally appeals to the urban poor and youth, and has the largest base with over 385,000 registered members. The business-oriented parties, MOLIRENA, and the Democratic Change Party so far cooperate with the president. The Christian Democratic Party is center-left like the European groups, and can be a swing party in key legislature votes.

Political Violence: Political violence is rare. However, illicit drugs can be causes for crime. Colon, the second largest city, has unemployment at about 50 percent for youths. The criminal justice system can be overloaded, inefficient, and inequitable. Violent protests in 1998 over an attempt at water privatization were the most recent threat.

Corruption: Corruption has been a problem, but reform is in progress.

ECONOMIC OUTLOOK

③

Trends

The government of Panama (GP) has been liberalizing trade, restructuring debt, attracting foreign investment, lowering tariffs, and privatizing state entities. It has joined the WTO. With the transfer of the canal to Panama, 364,000 acres of new territory, including two former military bases will be open for development. Problems include population growth, income inequality, and corruption. Foreign investment, capital goods spending, and regulatory reform are keys to near-term growth. See **Trade (Exports, Imports).**

Major Growth Sectors

A well-developed services sector makes up about 75 percent of GDP, including the Panama Canal, container port activities, flagship registry, banking, insurance, government, and the Colon Free Zone. Manufacturing, mining, utilities, and construction are about 18 percent of GDP. Manufacturing mainly includes production of processed foods, clothing, chemicals, and construction materials for the domestic market. Agriculture, forestry, and fisheries are about 7 percent of GDP. Agriculture mainly includes bananas, shrimp, sugar, coffee, meat, dairy products, tropical fruits, rice, corn, and beans. The greatest growth for the medium term is in ports, maritime services, mining, telecommunications, tourism, and energy. Construction markets are expected to grow because of large public infrastructure projects. Toll revenue for the Panama Canal went up 10 percent in 1998.

Key Economic Indicators

Income, Production and Employment *(millions of U.S. dollars unless otherwise indicated)*			
	1997	1998	1999[1]
Nominal GDP (Current Prices)	8,657	9,143	9,608
Real GDP (1982 prices)	6,657	6,933	7,157
Real GDP Growth (pct)	4.5	4.1	3.2
Real GDP by Sector (1982 prices):			
Agriculture	429	445	457
Manufacturing	1,231	1,290	1,368
Services	3,964	4,185	3,935
Government	961	970	1,005
Real Per Capita GDP (US$)(1982 prices)	2,449	2,509	2,548
Real Per Capita GDP (US$)(Current Prices)	3,198	3,308	3,420
Labor Force (millions)	1,049	1,083	1,089
Unemployment Rate (pct)	13.4	13.6	11.6

1. 1999 figures are all estimates based on most recent data available.
Source: Bureau of Economic and Business Affairs; U.S. Department of State

- Infrastructure

  Panama's infrastructure is relatively well developed. Investment is planned for highways, ports, and the railroad in the Panama–Colon corridor. The GP owns and operates the power transmission utility, but generation and distribution facilities are private. More plants may be built to match the 6 percent growth forecast. Cable & Wireless (U.K.) has a multimillion-dollar investment in its ownership of the telecommunications utility. In 2003, its concessionary monopoly will end and the market will be open. See **Communications** and **Transportation**.

- Labor

  Panama's workforce is estimated at one million, with 80 percent in the private sector and 20 percent in the public sector. The labor code is fairly restricted. See **Business Infrastructure (Labor Costs and Legislation)**.

Money and Prices *(annual percentage growth)*			
	1997	1998	1999[1]
Money Supply (M2) Growth (pct)[2]	0.8	-0.1	N/A
Consumer Price Inflation	1.2	0.6	1.5
Exchange Rate (balboa/US$ annual average)	1	1	1[3]

1. 1999 figures are all estimates based on most recent data available. 2. Figure is based on IMF 9/99 International Financial Statistics. M2 = Deposit Money + Quasi Money. 3. The balboa/dollar exchange rate is fixed at 1:1. The legal tender is the U.S. dollar, so there is no parallel exchange rate.
Source: Bureau of Economic and Business Affairs; U.S. Department of State

Balance of Payments and Trade *(millions of U.S. dollars unless otherwise indicated)*			
	1997	1998	1999[1]
Total Exports FOB[2]	6,916	6,706	5,970
Exports to U.S.	367	312	365
Total Imports CIF[2]	8,505	8,716	7,670
Imports from U.S.	1,536	1,753	1,742
Trade Balance[2]	-1,589	-2,010	-1,700
Balance with U.S.	-1,169	-1,441	-1,377
External Public Debt	5,051	5,179	5,580[3]
Fiscal Deficit (-)/GDP (pct)[4]	-0.3	-4.4	-1.6
Current Account Deficit (-)/GDP (pct)	-6.6	-13.5	N/A
Debt Service Ratio (pct)	12.2	13.4	13.5
Gold and Foreign Exchange Reserves[5]	1,148	1,370	1,516
Aid from U.S.	7.2	4.8	5.3
Aid from All Other Sources	226	N/A	N/A

1. 1999 figures are all estimates based on most recent data available. 2. Trade statistics (Colon Free Zone included). The Colon Free Zone (CFZ) is the largest free trading area in the hemisphere. 3. External debt balance on 6/30/99.
4. Figures indicate deficit of the non financial public sector as percent of GDP.
5. Figure is based on IMF 9/98 International Financial Statistics. Panama reports no gold holdings.
Sources: Bureau of Economic and Business Affairs; U.S. Department of State, U.S. Department of Commerce.

- Balance of Payments

  See **Key Economic Indicators**. Panama has successfully joined international capital markets. Panama sovereign debt has the highest rating in the third world. The debt trades with less volatility and less risk premium than other Latin American issues. Moody's Investor Services rates the debt at Ba1, and Standard & Poor's rates it at BB+.

Government Influence on Business

The GP is expecting a seamless transition of the Panama Canal to Panama ownership. The Panama Canal Authority (PCA) will run the canal more like a business than before. Panama uses the U.S. dollar as currency, so fiscal policy is the GP's main policy tool. The U.S. military added $180 million in 1997 and $158 million in 1998 to Panama's economy, so its withdrawal will be a loss. The GP policies under President Moscoso are uncertain except for consistent support of tariff protection for agriculture.

Leading Imports and Exports

Imports: Consumer goods, capital goods, crude oil, foodstuffs, chemicals

Exports: Bananas, coffee, sugar, shrimp, clothing

Foreign Trade (Exports and Imports in US$M)			
	1997	1998	1999[1]
Total Exports FOB[2]	6,916	6,706	5,970
Exports to U.S.	367	312	365
Total Imports CIF[2]	8,505	8,716	7,670
Imports from U.S.	1,536	1,753	1,742

1. 1. 1999 figures are all estimates based on most recent data available.
2. Trade statistics (Colon Free Zone included).
Sources: U.S. Department of Commerce, U.S. Department of State

Best Prospects Analysis

Best Prospects for Nonagricultural Goods and Services

Building Products (BLD)

	1998 $M	1999 $M	2000 $M
Total Market Size	276	308	336
Total Local Production	113	135	150
Total Exports	0	0	0
Total Imports	163	173	186
Imports from the U.S.	106	114	121

Transportation Services: Port and Maritime Services

	1998 $M	1999 $M	2000 $M
Total Market Size	150	180	200
Total Local Production	10	12	16
Total Exports	0	0	0
Total Imports	140	168	184
Imports from the U.S.	50	60	69

Telecommunications Equipment (TEL)

	1998 $M	1999 $M	2000 $M
Total Market Size	110	120	140
Total Local Production	0	0	0
Total Exports	0	0	0
Total Imports	110	120	140
Imports from the U.S.	20	36	43

Automotive Parts and Service Equipment (APS)

	1998 $M	1999 $M	2000 $M
Total Market Size	60	67	74
Total Local Production	0	0	0
Total Exports	0	0	0
Total Imports	60	67	74
Imports from the U.S.	21	22	27

Management Consulting Services (MCS)

	1998 $M	1999 $M	2000 $M
Total Market Size	27	35	39
Total Local Production	7	8	10
Total Exports	0	0	0
Total Imports	20	27	29
Imports from the U.S.	15	20	24

Computer Software

	1998 $M	1999 $M	2000 $M
Total Market Size	17	18	26
Total Local Production	1	1	2
Total Exports	0	0	0
Total Imports	16	17	24
Imports from the U.S.	13	14	20

Water and Wastewater Treatment Equipment

	1998 $M	1999 $M	2000 $M
Total Market Size	7	8	10
Total Local Production	0	0	0
Total Exports	0	0	0
Total Imports	7	8	1
Imports from the U.S.	4	5	8

Franchising

	1998 $M	1999 $M	2000 $M
Total Market Size	5	7	9
Total Local Production	0	0	0
Total Exports	0	0	0
Total Imports	5	7	9
Imports from the U.S.	4	5	7

General Services: Warehousing and Wholesaling

	1998 $B	1999 $B	2000 $B
Total Market Size	11	9	11
Total Local Production	0	0	0
Total Exports	6	5	6
Total Imports	5	4	5
Imports from the U.S.	0.5	0.4	0.6

Security and Safety Equipment

	1998 $M	1999 $M	2000 $M
Total Market Size	3	4	6
Total Local Production	0	0	0
Total Exports	0	0	0
Total Imports	3	4	6
Imports from the U.S.	2	3	4

Automobiles and Light Trucks and Vans (AUT)

	1997 $M	1998 $M	1999 $M
Total Market Size	130	145	158
Total Local Production	0	0	0
Total Exports	0	0	0
Total Imports	130	145	158
Imports from the U.S.	21	25	28

Medical Equipment (MED)

	1997 $M	1998 $M	1999 $M
Total Market Size	24	30	33
Total Local Production	0	0	0
Total Exports	0	0	0
Total Imports	24	30	33
Imports from the U.S.	19	23	25

Hotel and Restaurant Equipment (HTL)

	1997 $M	1998 $M	1999 $M
Total Market Size	11	14	15
Total Local Production	0	0	0
Total Exports	0	0	0
Total Imports	11	14	15
Imports from the U.S.	6	7	8

Best Prospects for Agricultural Products

Consumer Oriented Agricultural Products

Best prospects are: beer, poultry and red meat (for processing), red meat preserved, snack foods, and fruits.

	1998 $M	1999 $M	2000E $M
Total Market Size	218	264	290
Total Local Production	221	309	350
Total Exports	165	231	260
Total Imports	162	186	200
Imports from the U.S.	82	89	100

Banana production recuperated with an increase of 40% over last year and total exports of $182 million in 1999.

Bulk Agricultural Products

Best prospect sub-sectors: yellow corn, wheat, and pulses

	1998 $M	1999 $M	2000E $M
Total Market Size	128	141	160
Total Local Production	101	114	120
Total Exports (1)	60	58	60
Total Imports	87	85	100
Imports from the U.S.	65	50	60

Intermediate Agricultural Products

Best prospects sub-sectors: Soybean meal to feed a fast growing animal industry, vegetable oilsand soybean oil.

	1998 $M	1999 $M	2000E $M
Total Market Size	215	216	222
Total Local Production	101	105	105
Total Exports (1)	3	3	30
Total Imports	117	114	120
Imports from the U.S.	80	48	70

Significant Investment Opportunities

Reverted Areas
Electric Power Generation
Port and Maritime Services
Water and Sewage
Forestry

Reverted Areas

Panama has 364,000 acres of land, over 4,000 buildings and other infrastructure in the formerly U.S.-occupied Canal Zone. Panama will use these resources for economic and social development. Many projects look promising. The GP's Interoceanic Regional Authority (ARI) administers the reverted resources and shapes development strategy. Projects approved or under consideration, include manufacturing, assembly, tourism, marine services, warehousing, education, scientific research, and energy generation. Tourism and marine service projects seem to have the most potential. The ex- Howard Air Force Base has opportunities as an air cargo hub or aircraft repair and maintenance facility.

Electric Power Generation

Panama's demand for electricity grows by 45 megawatts per year. After privatization, any company can participate in power generation and distribution. This commercial opportunity looks excellent for U.S. investors.

Mining Exploration and Operation

Panama has vast amounts of mineral resources, mainly in the central provinces. Gold, silver, copper, zinc, lead, and molybdenum are especially promising. The only restriction on foreign mining companies is that 90 percent of all employees be Panamanians. The Adrian Resources Corp., and Greenstone Resources, Inc. have invested over $100 million in mining exploration in the last three years. When world metal prices recuperate from current low levels, the Panamanian mining sector has great potential. For more information, contact the Ministerio de Comercio e Industrias, Direccion de Recursos Minerales.

Water and Sewage

The GP would like private involvement in the National Water and Sewer company (IDAAN). In 1997, IDAAN assets were $428.million. In 1998, IDAAN revenue was about $65. IDAAN water losses are about 50 percent (20 percent technical and 30 percent commercial). It has many problems, and will need large investments to modernize and upgrade.

Forestry

The GP is leasing over 20,000 acres of land in the water shed of the Panama Canal and in Central Provinces. The contracts last 20 years contracts (renewable for 20 additional years), and can be combined with fruit production and eco-tourism plans. Rental prices range from $8.00 to $16.00 per acre per year. Many tax incentives exist. For more information, contact the Foreign Agricultural Service.

The above statistics are unofficial estimates.
Exchange Rate: 1 U.S. Dollar = 1 Balboa (Fixed Rate)
N/A - Not Available, E - Estimated

Extracted from the U.S. Department of Commerce USA Trade 2001 Country Commercial Guide for Panama.

Import and Export Tips

- ## Regulations

    Customs: Import duties are on an ad valorum basis. In some cases, historical rice information is referenced. Any company with a commercial license can import goods into Panama, and customs processing is fast, efficient, and reliable. Panama uses the Harmonized System.

    Tariffs: Tariffs range from 0 to 15 percent, except for some goods, such as automobiles, and some agricultural products. Tariffs average 12 percent. Panama is a member of the WTO but has lower import duties than required.

    Import Taxes: A value-added tax (ITBM) of 5 percent is applied to cif value. Exempt from the ITBM are pharmaceuticals, foods, and school supplies. See **Business Infrastructure (Entry Requirements and Taxes), Investment (Trade Zones and Free Ports).**

    Exchange Rate: Panama's official currency, the balboa, is pegged to the dollar at a 1:1 ratio. The balboa circulates in coins only. All paper currency in circulation is U.S. currency. The fixed parity means the competitiveness of U.S. products in Panama depends on transportation costs as well as tariff and nontariff barriers to entry. U.S. exports have no risk of foreign exchange losses on sales in Panama.

- ## Documentation

    Exports: The Vice Ministry of Trade helps easy exporting at its "One Stop" office, which may take only a few hours. Required export documentation includes (1) a commercial invoice; (2) an export declaration (usually prepared and signed by a customs broker); (3) a certificate of origin (issued by the Panama Chamber of Commerce, Industry, and Agriculture or by the Panama Trade Development Institute); (4) a bill of lading; (5) an airway bill; (6) a veterinary, sanitary, or phyto-sanitary certificate (when applicable). The Fiscal Code regulates all exports. Prohibited from export are (1) drugs except those with scientific or pharmaceutical purpose, (2) scarce staple products according to the GP, (3) products the GP restrains for national economic interests or convenience. Bananas, metals, raw sugar, and natural resources are subject to export tax and authorization. Textiles are only subject to export authorization.

    Imports: No import licenses are required. Any individual or company in commercial or industrial activity must have a license. Required for imported goods are (1) an import declaration (prepared and signed by a customs broker), (2) a commercial invoice (four copies in English or Spanish), (3) a bill of lading (three copies), (4) a commercial license number, (5) a phyto-sanitary certificate (for meat and meat products) from the U. S. Department of Agriculture, (6) a certificate of free sale (CFS, if required). For details on CFS documentation, see the trade association that might issue it, or contact the Food and Drug Administration. If any documents are delayed, a bond equal to the import duties may be given instead, to be held for 90 days or even more. Goods that are prohibited include (1) counterfeit coins or printed material that imitates currencies; (2) equipment or instruments for manufacturing coins; (3) liquors, wines, beers or medicines with labels that falsely describe contents, or of any kind of harmful preparation; (4) certain firearms or war materials; (5) foreign lottery or raffle tickets; (6) opium in the form of gum or for smoking; (7) obscene brochures, books, newspapers, magazines, or postcards containing negative portrayals of the country's culture, civilization, or dignity; and (8) plants, seeds, or animals when determined by the Ministry of Agriculture. Special import permits from the Ministry of Government and Justice are needed for all types of firearms and ammunition. See **Marketing Tips (Establishing an Office).**

Labeling: No special regulations exist for labeling or marking. Labels require basic information such as (1) the name and address of the manufacturer, (2) expiration date, (3) list of ingredients, (4) lot number, (5) product form (powder, liquid, etc.). Labels in English are enough, but Spanish is required for medicines, household products, and foods with special instructions (dosage, usage, warnings, etc.). All goods entering Panama for re-export must have "PANAMA IN TRANSIT" on the outside of every box or container. In general, products that meet U. S. labeling and marking requirements will meet Panamanian requirements.

Standards: The Comision Panamena de Normas Tecnicas (COPANIT), an agency of the Ministry of Commerce and Industry, is the registering authority for the International Standards Organization ISO-9000 program. Many firms in Panama already have ISO-9000 certification. Panama is a member of the Pan American Standards Commission (COPAN), which is based in Venezuela.

• **Payment**

Terms: Usual terms are 60 to 90 days. A letter of credit is recommended. See **Finance (Project Financing)**.

Currency Exchange: Profits by foreign businesses may be repatriated freely. Panama uses the U.S. dollar, so currency conversion is not an issue. See **Business Infrastructure (Currency Exchange)**.

Fund Transfer: There are no restrictions on capital flow in or out of the country. There is an average of about one month foreign exchange bank delays.

Offshore Loans: No information is available at this time.

MARKETING TIPS

Agents and Distributors

Nationals and foreigners are equals by law. For retail and certain professions, foreigner activity is restricted, so a local lawyer should be contacted. Agents and distributors are regulated only by the private agreement between the two parties. In contract terminations or disputes, private contract clauses prevail over other documents or practices. Individuals can operate in their own name or through legal entities: the corporation (most common), general partnerships, joint stock partnerships, and limited liability companies.

Establishing an Office

Panama has very modern and flexible corporate laws. Some of the advantages are (1) two or more persons, even living outside Panama, can form a corporation with articles executed anywhere, in any language, and for any lawful purpose; (2) there are no capital payment requirements; (3) ownership can be by individuals or corporations, even with no capital held by a Panamanian; (4) shareholders have no nationality or residence requirements; (5) directors and officers don't need to be shareholders; (6) the board of directors requires three directors, but one person can hold more than one post; (7) meetings can be held outside Panama, and shareholders or directors can use proxies. To form a corpora-tion in Panama, one must provide the following: (1) the name of the corporation, in any language, ending in a word or abbreviation indicating that it is a corporation; (2) the objectives and purposes of the corporation; (3) the amount of the authorized capital (usually US$ 10,000 divided into 100 shares of US$ 100 each); (4) whether shares are nominative or bearer; (5) the duration of the corporation (usually perpetual); (6) the full names and addresses of three or more directors or officers; (7) the domicile of the corporation. Corporations usually take 15 days to 2 months to set up. Attorney fees usually range from US$ 600 to US$ 1,500. To operate in commercial or industrial activities, a proper license is required from the Ministry of Commerce and Industry: (1) Commercial License Class (for wholesale operations, commercial and mortgage banks, financial companies, international financial brokers, insurance and reinsurance companies, international transportation companies, mutual funds, public utilities, and high-technology service companies); (2) Commercial License Class B, granted only to Panamanians or corporations owned solely by Panamanians (for retail businesses, including repre-sentation agencies, service companies, bars, restaurants, drugstores, real estate agents, gas stations, local transportation, distributors, and others); (3) Industrial License (for extractive and manufacturing industries, as well as construction companies). Licenses cost about US$ 250 to US$ 750 to get, and must always be visible and accessible. Annual taxes are based on the net worth of the company. Over 400,000 corporations are registered in Panama. Exemptions from license requirements are persons or legal entities engaged (1) exclusively in agri-culture, cattle, bee, or poultry raising; or (2) in the manufacturing and sale of handicrafts if the work is not done by hired workers.

Distribution and Sales Channels

Business practices are similar to those in the U.S. Business is usually direct and straight-forward. Panama City sells 65 percent of con-sumer goods, with 35 percent sold in David, Santiago, Chitre, and Colon. Marketing involves mainly direct importers that act as wholesalers and sometimes retailers (especially for apparel, auto parts, and hardware products). Retail is separate from wholesale in consumer goods, food, and medicine. For industrial goods, local exclusive agents or distributors handle sales. In other cases, local firms order directly from the U.S. firms or brokers. Some large importers are also distributors in the Colon Free Zone, with retail store affiliations. See **Business Customs.**

Direct Marketing

Important for success in Panama are high quality, customer service, brand-name recog-nition, and attractive packaging. High-quality U.S. products are popular, but middle- to upper-middle income markets are often competitive. High disposable income markets follow U.S. and European consumption trends. Most high-end brand names are already represented, so aggressive marketing is needed for success.

Leasing/Joint Ventures

Joint ventures are becoming common. Large projects often contract and subcontract. Profits from joint ventures can be given annually, and are taxed the same as other incomes. License agreements are not regu-lated, but are often used. Agreements must be attached to the registered trademark and filed with the Industrial Property Department in the Ministry of Commerce and Industry. The agreement then becomes part of the trade-mark file. The Colon Free Zone has a one-step distribution center for marketing. However, before starting operations in the Zone, be aware of money laundering, intellectual property piracy, and drug trafficking risks.

Franchising

Panama is attractive for franchises, and welcomes them. Royalty payments and transfers are not controlled by Panama. The local market most needs recreation, entertainment services, automotive, hotel, and motel franchises. The U.S. Embassy recommends contacting a local attorney for details on setting up a franchise in Panama.

Advertising and Promotion

TV and newspaper ads are the promotions of choice for most U.S. distributors. Panama has a competitive advertising market with high production quality. Sales prices usually appear in weekend newspapers. Most foreign makers of consumer goods have a high profile presence in ads, billboards, and sponsored sports events. Trade show and exhibitions have also been effective. See **Contacts.**

Selling Factors

Panama has the highest per capita income of Latin America (with uneven distribution). For the more wealthy consumers, quality and trendiness are important. For the less wealthy Panamanian majority, quality, and price are key factors.

Selling to the Government

Panama has no central purchasing office. All purchases above certain values must be advertised for public bid. The Ministry of Economy and Finance and the Comptroller General's Office supervise procurements. For purchases above $250,000, the GP has company pre qualifications. Tender documents are discussed with interested companies to assure detailed understanding of terms. Lack of transparency, delays, and bureaucracy in bid selection have been obstacles for government bids.

Pricing

Pricing varies depending on competition, transport, and duties. The prices are sometimes higher than the world average. Import duties average 10 percent of cif value, and wholesale and retail each mark up around 25 percent. See **Business Infrastructure (Taxes).**

Customer Support

Distributors that succeed usually have the best training, counseling, and support from their principals. Distributors should be given U.S.-level training or assistance and after-sales support such as spare parts and service equipment.

Intellectual Property Rights (IPR)

Panama belongs to the World Intellectual Property Organization (WIPO), the Geneva Phonogram Convention, the Brussels Satellite Convention, the Universal Copyright Convention, the Berne Convention for the Protection of Literary and Artistic Works, and the Paris Convention for the Protection of Industrial Property. Panama has signed the WIPO Copyright Treaty and the WIPO Performances and Phonograms Treaty.

Attorney

Every corporation organized pursuant to the laws of Panama must have a resident agent attorney in Panama. The annual fee is about $200. An estimated 400,000 corporations are registered in Panama. Power of attorney is required to register a national trademark, patent, or a sanitary registration application. The National Data Trade Bank (NDTB) and domestic and foreign offices of the U.S. Department of Commerce maintain lists of attorneys.

FOREIGN INVESTMENT

⑥

Openness: Panama has a reputation as an international banking, trading, and services center, as well as for direct foreign investment (FDI). Panama's dollar-based currency has low inflation and no exchange risks. The Vice Ministry of Foreign Trade gives investors information and assistance. Projects being planned include (1) large tourism projects at former Fort Amador on the Pacific and former Fort Sherman on the Atlantic; (2) a multiuse facility on the Howard Air Base; and (3) an academic community (City of Knowledge) at Fort Clayton. Infrastructure is a priority for the GP. The regulatory and supervisory framework for taxes is weak. Most state enterprises have been privatized, but the current administration has promised not to privatize the water utility. Inflexible labor laws, high electricity and telecommunications, and high minimum wage discourage some investors. The Ministry of Commerce and Industry protects consumers. The Super-intendent of Banks has power in the banking sector though there is no bankruptcy law to help restructuring. Banking, legal, and financial services, and the legal regime are aimed at attracting foreign business and banking. See **Establishing an Office and Import and Export Tips.**

Regulatory System: For the past few years, several major sales of the GP have happened without incidents, including power distribution and generation facilities, and the telecom company. Before that, there were several cases of non transparency and questionable negotiations.

Investment Agreements: Panama has bilateral investment agreements with the U.S., United Kingdom, France, Switzerland, Germany, and Taiwan. Panama has preferential trade agreements with Costa Rica, El Salvador, Honduras, Guatemala, Nicaragua, Columbia, Dominican Republic, Mexico, Germany, Bulgaria, Czech

Republic, Hungary, Romania, Russia, and Poland. Panama is negotiating free trade agreements with Mexico, Chile, and the Andean Pact.

Trade Zones and Free Ports: The Colon Free Zone is second in the world only to Hong Kong. It operates as a separate GP institution with a board of directors, an executive com-mittee, and a general manager. Companies in the Colon Free Zone pay no taxes. Companies in the CFZ also have exemption from import duties, guarantees and licensing, and other import limitations. The CFZ has free goods movement with no tax or customs regulations on imports and re-exports. CFZ companies must apply, but don't need a commercial license or minimum capital. The CFZ has also been used for money laundering, drug trafficking, and trading pirated intellectual property and stolen vehicles. Export Processing Zones (EPZs, currently seven) are well-defined areas for industrial, commercial, and service facilities in a free trade system, where typically all production is exported. EPZ companies get tax-free status, special immigration and labor privileges, and customs exemptions. They are classified as either developers or tenants, which get different benefits. Petroleum Export Zones (currently seven) allow free trade, production, and refinement of petro-leum products. Petroleum Export Zone Companies are exempt from municipal and federal taxes, and not subject to local market regulations.

Performance Requirements/Incentives: Panama has no performance requirements for mini-mum export percentages or significant use of local content. There are strong incentives and support for investment in the Colon Free Zone (CFZ), the banking sector, the tourism sector, and Export Processing Zones (EPZs). Banks incentives include no tax on interest or income from outside Panama, and no tax withholding on savings or fixed time deposits. Tourism incentives include tax exemptions for vehicles, goods for use, and goods for infra-structure construction. Mining has similar incentives. For investment incentives, get legal and accounting advice. See **Trade Zones and Free Ports.**

Capital Markets and Investment: The national stock market has limited size and fluidity. In 1998, the rate for domestic commercial loans was 9.9 percent, with a six-month deposit rate of 6.7 percent. Total bank assets in 1998 were $36.6 billion. Bank and nonbank financing is at market terms for private domestic and foreign investors. Traditional bank lending is efficient and common. Company earnings on stock issues, fixed bank deposits, and some bonds are tax exempt. A 10 percent withholding tax on dividends discourages stock issues on the local market. There are no restrictions against hostile takeovers, foreign partici-pation or control, or foreign participation in industry standards setting. A well-financed, powerful Superintendent of Banks has regulatory authority and should encourage international standards. See **Foreign Investment (Openness).**

Private Ownership: Except for retail trade and some professions, foreign and domestic entities can freely establish, own, and dispose of businesses in Panama. Residency is not required, and business visas (even Panamanian passports) are available for significant in-vestors. Privatization framework laws do not distinguish between domestic and foreign investors. Technical viability involves pre-screening in some cases, but foreigners have been involved with all privatizations so far.

Expropriation and Compensation: No large enterprises are under expropriation risk. No official discrimination exists against U.S. or foreign investors in most areas. No foreigners can own land on islands or within 10 kilometers of the national border. No Panamanians or foreigners can own beaches or on river or lakeshores. The Ministry of Economy and Finance typically rents land for 20 to 30 years, or for tourism up to 40.

OPIC and Investment Insurance: The Overseas Private Investment Corporation (OPIC) has only one current investment in Panama. Panama law does not allow busi-nesses to use real property as collateral for OPIC loans or insurance, so OPIC has relatively limited involvement.

Dispute Settlement: Panama uses civil code instead of the Anglo-American system. Panama is a member of the International Center for Settlement of Investment Disputes (ICSID). Most companies choose not to resolve business disputes through the domestic legal system (cases are backlogged, and objectivity is questionable). Judicial pleadings are not always transparent or for public record. Some administrative notice and discovery rights may be less extensive than in the U.S. Foreign investors are allowed ten years to adjust to regulatory changes made after an investment. However, in these cases, their rights for support by their embassy are waived. The U.S. does not seem to accept this clause.

Protection of Property Rights: Panama has no modern bankruptcy law. A public property registry is expanding and being modernized. Local legal counsel is advised since the civil legal system is backlogged and perceived as unfair or biased. There is concern over counterfeit and pirated goods trafficking, but the CFZ IPR department has been conducting raids to lessen the problem. Laws exist to protect patents, trade secrets, and copyrights, but copyright protection enforcement is insufficient. See **Intellectual Property Rights (IPR).**

FINANCE ⑦

The Panamanian banking system is dynamic. It follows the Basle Accord Standards. Bank financial statements must meet international standards and be audited by internationally recognized auditors. There is no deposit insurance scheme. In 1998, Panamanian banks had $36.6 billion in assets, $26.8 billion in total deposits, and reached $8.7 in loans to the private sector (35 percent trade and commerce, 24 percent mortgages, 16 percent consumer banking). Banks fall into three classes: General License Banks (57 total), International License Banks ("Offshore," 27 total) that can accept deposits only from overseas, and Representational Offices that can only do representational activities (12 total). The two bank groups are the Panamanian Banking Association (ABP) and the Association of Panamanian Banks (APB). The GP also operates two deposit-taking institutions. The Banking Supervisory Authority regulates and licenses banks. Foreign and Domestic banks compete on equal terms. See **Capital Markets and Investment.**

Export Financing: Private financing is readily available. The GP is not an important lender and does not maintain statistics on sources or amounts of private investment or trade. Various local banks offer trade financing. The Latin American Export Bank (BLADEX) gives trade financing via the local banks. Panama is a center for international banking, and offers many financing options. OPIC, the Export-Import Bank, the Inter-American Development Bank, and the International Finance Corporation (IFC) of the World Bank have projects in Panama. The Commodity Credit Corporation's (CCC) GSM Credit Guarantee Program in Panama for 1998 (fiscal) was $42.3 million for U.S. exports such as rice, feedgrains, protein meals, wheat, solid wood products, and barley malt. Any CCC-approved bank credit is guaranteed. See **Trade (Payment Terms).**

Project Financing: The Export-Import Bank has financed various projects and is currently providing $121 million in insurance and guarantees. The Inter-American Development Bank has financed studies and projects that include the development strategy for the ex-U.S. military facilities. The World Bank has some small social sector projects, and recently co-financed a $406 million roads project. See **Contacts.**

COMMUNICATIONS ⑧

Phone

Panama has excellent local and international phone service, with direct dialing to over 150 countries. The telecommunications network is advanced, and telephone service in general is reliable. The international access code is 011, and the Panamanian access code is 507. City codes are not required.

Internet

Use of the Internet is growing rapidly, and strong growth rates are expected to continue.

Mail

The postal system is reasonably well developed although street names and numbers are not well defined. Express mail international services are available between Panama and the U.S.

TRANSPORTATION 9

Land

Buses and taxis are widely available in cities. Taxi fares are low, usually from $1 to $5 per trip. Car rentals are available. Transportation from the International Airport to Panama City is by special taxi only, and costs from $12 to $20. Intercity highways are mainly good. New roads will bring growth to the Bocas del Toro province. An International Development Bank loan will develop infrastructure in the Darien Province. The Panama Canal railway is being rehabilitated and will connect the ports at each end of the canal.

Sea

The Manzanillo International Terminal at the Atlantic entrance is the largest container port in Latin America, and contracted to buy two additional "super post panamax" cranes. A $150 million port project is underway at the Pacific canal entrance. Other ports are Balboa on the Pacific and Cristobal on the Caribbean.

Air

The Tocumen International Airport is the major airport, located approximately eight kilometers from Panama City. About 16 international passenger airlines and 13 cargo airlines serve the region.

WORK WEEK 10

Business Hours: Most private businesses are open 8:00 a.m. to 5:00 p.m. Monday to Friday, and 8:00 a.m. to 12:00 p.m. Saturday.

Government Hours: 8:30 a.m. to 4:30 p.m. Monday to Friday.

Bank Hours: 8:00 a.m. to 3:00 p.m. Monday to Friday, and 9:00 a.m. to 12:00 p.m. Saturday.

HOLIDAYS 2001

New Year's Day, January 1
Mourning Day, January 9
Carnival, March 6
Good Friday, April 13
Labor Day, May 1
Independence Day from Columbia,
  November 3
Flag Day, November 4
The Uprising of Los Santos,
  November 10
Independence Day from Spain, November 28
Mother's Day, December 8
Christmas Day, December 25

All private, government, municipal, and U.S. Embassy offices are closed on local holidays. The U.S. Mission observes all U.S. holidays. Many Jewish-owned businesses observe Jewish holidays.

BUSINESS TRAVEL

Business Customs

Business practices and customs mix North American methods and traditional Latin style. Foreign corporations in Panama affect business styles and manners.

Travel Advisory and Visas

U.S. citizens are subject to Panamanian law when visiting. Penalties for possession, use, and trafficking in illegal drugs are severe. Required for visiting are (1) a passport or certified copy of a U.S. birth certificate and an official picture ID, and (2) a Tourist Card ($5) purchased from an airline serving Panama. Tourist Cards are valid for 30 days and renewable for more 30-day periods. There are three visa types for extended stays: (1) Investor — at least $100,000 must be invested, with an advanced deposit of $500 with the Ministry of Government and

Justice, and $100 with the Ministry of Economy and Finance; (2) Temporary Visitor's Visa, for executives and technicians working for a company in Panama for a limited time — it is good for a one-year term and is renewable; (3) Working Permit, for professionals or skilled personnel transferred from an overseas office to work in Panama temporarily — earnings from outside Panama must be proven, and it is good for three to six months. See **Contacts**.

Business Infrastructure

Entry Requirements (personal and professional goods): The Fiscal Code allows temporary entry for up to one year with two options: (1) a deposit is put down equivalent to the import duty, and reimbursed upon exit; (2) an insurance company issues a bond covering the duty value, which is payable if the goods don't exit on time. For trade shows and exhibitions at the Atlapa Convention Center, goods enter without warranty or bond. Sometimes they can be displayed and sold duty free. Samples with commercial value follow temporary entry requirements. Samples with no commercial value are duty free unless they are in large containers.

Currency Exchange: The balboa is the main currency. U.S. currency is also legal tender and used freely. See **Payment Terms (Currency Exchange).**

Taxes: A value-added tax of 5 percent is added to the purchase price of all products. The maximum corporate tax rate is 30 percent of domestically produced earnings. The maximum personal tax rate is 35 percent. See **Regulations.**

Hotels and Restaurants: There are several international-level hotels. Typical facilities include swimming pools, tennis courts, fitness centers, clothing and souvenir shops, casinos, restaurants, coffee shops, and bars. Hotels usually offer American, European, and local cuisine. For longer stays, furnished apartments are available. A wide variety of international cuisines are available, including Chinese, Italian, Mexican, Indian, Spanish, and Japanese. Some restaurants specialize in seafood.

Rent: Permanent and temporary office space is widely available. Information on costs is not available.

Business Services: See **Advertising and Promotion,** and **Foreign Investment (Performance Requirements / Inventives) and Labor.**

Labor Costs and Legislation: The unemployment rate is 11.6 percent (1999).

Minimum wage ranges from $0.76 to $1.33 depending on location and sector. Amendments may create flexibility, easier termination of workers, and fewer constraints on productivity-based pay. See **Economic Outlook (Labor).**

Literacy: The literacy rate is 90.8 percent (1995 est).

Travel Notes

The following travel notes have been supplied by the U.S. government. For the most recent general travel and consular information, see the U.S. Department of State travel publications or call the Traveler's Telephone Hotline at (202) 647-5225.

Security: Use the same precautions as when visiting a U.S. metropolitan city.

Health Precautions: Health conditions are good, especially in urban centers. Running water is widely available and mostly potable. Use bottled or boiled water in some rural areas and small province towns. Current information on health matters may be obtained from the Centers for Disease Control and Prevention's international travelers' hotline at (404) 332-4559.

Embassy Assistance

To obtain additional and updated information on entry and exit requirements, travelers can contact the Consular Section of the Embassy of Panama at 2862 McGill Terrace, N.W., Washington, D.C. 20008; Tel: (202) 387-6154. Travelers may also contact the nearest Panama consulate. They are located in Atlanta, Houston, Miami, New Orleans, New York, Philadelphia, San Diego, San Francisco, and Tampa.

CONTACTS

U.S. and Country Contacts

U.S. Embassy Contact

The Commercial Service
U.S. Department of Commerce
Tel: (507) 227-1777
Fax: (507) 227-1713
E-mail: OfficePanama@mail.doc.gov
Web site: http://www.ita.doc.gov

Economic Unit, U.S. Department of State
Chief, Economic/Political Section
Tel: (507) 227-1777
Fax: (507) 227-1964

Foreign Agricultural Service,
U.S. Department of Agriculture
Tel: (507) 227-1777
Fax: (507) 225-4209

Embassy Mailing Address in the U.S.:
Unit 0945
APO AA 34002
Tel: (507) 227-1777
Fax: (507) 227-1964

Washington-Based USG Country Contacts

U.S. Department of Commerce
International Economic Policy
Panama Desk
14th & Constitution Ave.
Washington, DC 20230
Tel: (202) 482-4464
Fax: (202) 482-4157

U.S. Department of State
ARA (Inter American Affairs)/CEN-PAN
2201 C St. NW
Washington, DC 20520
Tel: (202) 647-4986
Fax: (202) 647-2901

U.S. Department of the Treasury
Office of Latin America & Caribbean
1500 Pennsylvania Ave. NW
Washington, DC 20220
Tel: (202) 622-1266
Fax: (202) 622-1273

U.S. Department of Commerce
Liaison Office to the Inter-American
Development Bank
1250 H Street, NW (10th floor)
Washington, DC 20005
Tel: (202) 623-3821
Fax: (202) 623-2039

U.S. Department of Commerce
Liaison Office to the International Bank for
Reconstruction and Development
U.S. Executive Director's Office
1818 H St., NW, Room D-13004
Washington, DC 20433
Tel: (202) 458-0118
Fax: (202) 477-2967

U.S. Department of Commerce
Office of Multilateral Development Banks
Ronald Reagan Building
MS/MDBO
Washington, DC 20230
Tel: (202) 482-3399
Fax: (202) 273-0927

U.S. Department of Agriculture
Foreign Agricultural Service
Trade Policy, Marsha Moke
12th and Jefferson Drive, SW
Washington, DC 20250
Tel: (202) 720-6010
Fax: (202) 690-2079

Overseas Private Investment Corporation
1100 New York Avenue, NW
Washington, DC 20527
Tel: (202) 336-8472
Fax: (202) 408-9866

Export-Import Bank of the U.S.
811 Vermont Avenue, NW
Washington, DC 20571
Business Development
Tel: (202) 565-3921 (ext 3916)
Fax: (202) 565-3931
Web site: http://www.exim.gov

U.S. Trade and Development Agency
Latin America & Caribbean
1621 N. Kent St., Suite 300
Arlington, VA 2209-2131
Tel: (703) 875-4357
Fax: (703) 875-4009

Office of U.S. Trade Representative
USTR for Western Hemisphere,
Director for Caribbean Basin Affairs
Office of the U.S. Trade Representative
600 17th Street, NW
Washington, DC 20506
Tel: (202) 395-5190
Fax: (202) 395-3911

U.S.-Based Multiplier Organizations Relevant for Country

Embassy of Panama
2862 McGill Terrace NW
Washington, DC 20008
Tel: (202) 483-1407
Fax: (202) 483-8413

Ministries and Government Owned Agencies in Panama

Ministerio de Comercio e Industrias
(Ministry of Commerce and Industry)
P.O. Box 9658
Panama 4, Republic of Panama
Tel: (507) 227-4222
Fax: (507) 227-4134
E-mail: Uti@mici.gob.pa
Web site: http://www.mici.gob.pa

Ministerio de Comercio e Industrias,
Direccion General de Registro de la Propiedad
Industrial
(Industrial Property Registry Administration)
P.O. Box 9658
Panama 4, Republic of Panama
Tel: (507) 227-3987
Fax: (507) 227-2139

Vice Ministerio de Comercio Exterior
P.O. Box 6-1897
Panama 6, Republic of Panama
Tel: (507) 236-0550; (507) 236-0347
Fax: (507) 236-0495
E-mail: secomex@mici.gob.pa

Ministerio de Desarrollo Agropecuario
(Ministry of Agricultural Development)
P.O. Box 5390
Panama 5, Republic of Panama
Tel: (507) 232-5043
Fax: (507) 232-5044

Ministerio de Economia y Finanzas
P.O. Box 7304
Panama 5, Republic of Panama
Tel: (507) 227-4998
Fax: (507) 227-2357
E-mail: mhyt@mhyt.gob.pa
Web site: http://www.mhyt.gob.pa/

Direccion Nacional de Aduanas
(Customs Service)
P.O. Box 1671 Balboa, Ancon
Panama, Republic of Panama
Tel: (507) 232-5355
Fax: (507) 232-6494
Web site: http://www.mhyt.gob.pa

Ministerio de Salud, (Ministry of Health)
P.O. Box 2048
Panama 1, Republic of Panama
Tel: (507) 262-3511; (507) 262-3510
Fax: (507) 262-5597
Web site: http://www.min-salud.gob.pa

Ministerio de Obras Publicas
(Ministry of Public Works)
P.O. Box 1632
Panama 1, Republic of Panama
Tel: (507) 232-5572
Fax: (507) 232-5776
E-mail: infomop@sinfo.net
Web site: http://www.mop.gob.pa/

Autoridad de la Region Interoceanica (ARI)
(Interoceanic Regional Authority)
P.O. Box 2097, Balboa
Panama, Republic of Panama
Tel: (507) 228-8044
Fax: (507) 228-8988
E-mail: infomop@sinfo.net
Web site: http://www.ari-panama.com

Autoridad Marítima Nacional
(National Maritime Authority)
P.O. Box 8062
Panama 7, Rep. of Panama
Tel: (507) 232-5553; (507) 232-5528
Fax: (507) 232-5527

Administracion de la Zona Libre de Colon
(Colon Free Zone Administration)
P.O. Box 1118
Colon, Republic of Panama
Tel: (507) 445-5794; (507) 445-5114
Fax: (507) 445-2165
E-mail: david@zolicol.org
Web site: http://www.zonalibre.com

Direccion de Aeronautica Civil (DAC)
(National Aeronautics Authority)
P.O. Box 7615
Panama 5, Republic of Panama
Tel: (507) 315-0210; (507) 315-0212
Fax: (507) 315-0214
E-mail: fabrega@pan.gbm.net

Instituto Panameno de Turismo (IPAT)
(Tourism Institute of Panama)
P.O. Box 4421
Panama 5, Republic of Panama
Tel: (507) 226-7414; (507) 226-3751
Fax: (507) 226-3483
E-mail: webmaster@ipat.gob.pa
Web site: http://www.ipat.gob.pa

Instituto de Acueductos y Alcantarillados
Nacionales (IDAAN),
(National Water Works Company)
P.O. Box 5234
Panama 5, Republic of Panama
Tel: (507) 223-8640
Fax: (507) 264-0034

Inter-American Development Bank
(In-country office)
Apartado Postal 7297
Panama 5, Rep. of Panama
Tel: (507) 263-6944
Fax: (507) 263-6183
Web site: http://www.iadr.org

Trade Associations

American Chamber of Commerce and Industry
P.O. Box 168, Balboa
Panama, Republic of Panama
Tel: (507) 269-3881
Fax: (507) 223-3508
E-mail: amcham@sinfo.net
Web site: http://www.panamcham.com

Asociacion de Distribuidores de Automoviles
de Panama (ADAP)
(Automobile Distributors Association)
P.O. Box 476
Panama 9A, Republic of Panama
Tel: (507) 261-1264
Fax: (507) 261-0906
E-mail: analmo@sinfo.net

Asociacion de Usuarios de la Zona Libre
de Colon
(Colon Free Zone Users Association)
P.O. Box 3118, Zona Libre de Colon
Colon, Republic of Panama
Tel: (507) 441-4244
Fax: (507) 441-4347
E-mail: au@sinfo.net

Asociacion Panamena de Exportadores (APEX)
(Exporters Association)
P.O. Box 6-6527
Panama 6, Republic of Panama
Tel: (507) 230-0284; (507) 230-0169
Fax: (507) 230-0805
E-mail: sip@sinfo.net

Camara de Comercio, Industrias y Agricultura
de Panama
(Chamber of Commerce, Industry and
Agriculture of Panama)
P.O. Box 74
Panama 1, Republic of Panama
Tel: (507) 227-1285; (507) 227-1445
Fax: (507) 227-4186; (507) 225-3653
E-mail: cciap@panama.phoenix.net
Web site: http://www.panacamara.com

Camara Panamena de la Construccion (CAPAC)
(Construction Chamber)
Apartado 6793
Panama 5, Republic of Panama
Tel: (507) 264-2255
Fax: (507) 264-2384
E-mail: capac@pty.com

Sindicato de Industriales de Panama (SIP)
(Industrialists Association of Panama)
P.O. Box 6-4798
Panama 6, Republic of Panama
Tel: (507) 230-0284; (507) 230-0169
Fax: (507) 230-0805
E-mail: sip@sinfo.net

Country Commercial Banks

Superintendencia de Bancos
(Banking Superintendency)
Lewis Romero
P.O. Box 0832-2397 WTC
Panama, Rep. of Panama
Tel. (507) 206-7800
Fax. (507) 264-9467
E-mail: superintendencia@superbancos.gob.pa
Web site: http:// www.superbancos.gob.pa

Asociacion Bancaria de Panama
(Banking Association of Panama)
P.O. Box 4554
Panama 5, Republic of Panama
Tel: (507) 263-7044
Fax: (507) 263-7783
E-mail: abp@orbi.net

Banco del Istmo
P.O. Box 6-3823, El Dorado
Panama 6A, Republic of Panama
Tel: (507) 270-0015
Fax: (507) 270-0861
E-mail: www@banistmo.com
Web site: http://www.banistmo.com

Banco General
P.O. Box 4592
Panama 5, Republic of Panama
Tel: (507) 265-0303
Fax: (507) 265-0206
Web site: http://www.banco-general.com

Banco Comercial de Panama
P.O. Box 7659
Panama 5, Republic of Panama
Tel: (507) 263-6800; (507) 263-4433
Fax: (507) 263-8033

Banco Nacional de Panama
P.O. Box 5220
Panama 5, Republic of Panama
Tel: (507) 269-2966; (507) 269-2966
Fax: (507) 264-7155

The Chase Manhattan Bank, N.A.
P.O. Box 9A-76
Panama 9A, Republic of Panama
Tel: (507) 263-5855; (507) 263-5877
Fax: (507) 263-6009

Citibank, N.A.
P.O. Box 555
Panama 9A, Republic of Panama
Tel: (507) 236-4044
Fax: (507) 236-1025

PRIBANCO, Primer Banco de Ahorros
P.O. Box 7322
Panama 5, Republic of Panama
Tel: (507) 265-3444
Fax: (507) 265-3838

The First National Bank of Boston
P.O. Box 5368
Panama 5, Republic of Panama
Tel: (507) 264-2244; (507) 264-2146
Fax: (507) 223-4089

Country Market Research Firms

Ditcher & Neira - Marketing Consultant
P.O. Box 6-7373, El Dorado
Panama, Republic of Panama
Tel: (507) 264-3466
Fax: (507) 223-1174
E-mail: d&n@pananet.com

Jaime Porcell & Asociados
P.O. Box 4760
Panama 5, Rep. of Panama
Tel: (507) 226-0438; (507) 226-0452
Fax: (507) 226-7390

Grupo Ariston
P.O. Box 944
Panama 9A, Republic of Panama
Tel: (507) 226-1276
Fax: (507) 226-5275
E-mail: mthalass@pan.gbm.net

Major Newspapers

La Prensa
P.O. Box 6-4586, El Dorado
Panama, Republic of Panama
Tel: (507) 222-1222
Fax: (507) 221-7328
E-mail:ventas@prensa.com
Web site: http://www.prensa.com
Daily circulation: 35,000
Format: standard
Advertising prices: US$ 13.00 per columnar inch, each page has 126 columnar inches.

El Panama America
P.O. Box B-4
Panama 9A, Republic of Panama
Tel: (507) 230-1666
Fax: (507) 230-1033
E-mail: clientes@epasa.com;
webmaster@epasa.com
Web site: http://www.epasa.com
Daily circulation: 22,000
Format: standard
Advertising prices: US$ 8.00 per columnar inch, each page has 126 columnar inches.

La Estrella de Panama
P.O. Box Q
Panama 4, Republic of Panama
Tel: (507) 227-0555
Fax: (507) 227-0723
Daily circulation: 20,000
Format: standard
Advertising prices: US$ 6.00 per columnar inch, each page has 126 columnar inches.

El Universal de Panamá
P.O. Box 9815
Panama 9, Rep. of Panama
Tel: (507) 225-7700
Fax: (507) 225-6993
E-mail: eluniver@sinfo.net
Daily circulation: 10,000
Format: Standard
Advertising prices: US$ 3.50 per columnar inch, each page has 126 columnar inches.

Best Prospects for Investment

Forestry
The Foreign Agricultural Service, American Embassy Panama, Unit 0945, APO AA 34002
Tel: (507) 227-1777
Fax: (507) 225-4209
E-mail: OfficePanama@mail.doc.gov

Import-Export Documentation

The Food and Drug Administration,
Division of Programs and Enforcement Policy
200 C Street, SW
Washington, DC 20204

Panamanian Banks with Correspondent U.S. Banks

Banco Comercial de Panama, S.A. (BANCOMER)
P.O. Box 7659
Panama 5, Republic of Panama
Tel: (507) 263-6800
Fax: (507) 263-8033

U.S. Correspondents:
Citibank N.A., New York
The Bank of New York, New York
The Chase Manhattan Bank, N.A., New York
Marine Midland Bank, N.A., New York
Barnett Bank of South Florida, N.A., Miami

Banco Continental de Panama, S.A.
P.O. Box 135
Panama, 9A, Republic of Panama
Tel: (507) 263-5955
Fax: (507) 264-3359

U.S. Correspondents:
Chemical Bank, New York
Citibank, New York and Miami
Credit Suisse, Miami
Nations Bank, Miami
Standard Chartered Bank PLC, Miami

Banco de Latinoamerica, S.A. (BANCOLAT)
P.O. Box 4401
Panama 5, Republic of Panama
Tel: (507) 264-0466
Fax: (507) 263-7368

U.S. Correspondents:
Banco Atlantico, New York
The Chase Manhattan Bank, New York
Extebank, New York
AmTrade Bank International, Miami
Barclays Bank PLC, Miami
Capital Bank N.A., Miami
Hamilton Bank N.A., Miami
The International Bank of Miami, Miami
Republic National Bank of Miami, Miami
Popular Bank of Florida, Miami

Banco del Istmo, S.A.
P.O. Box 6-3823, El Dorado
Panama, Republic of Panama
Tel: (507) 270-0015
Fax: (507) 270-0861

U.S. Correspondents::
Capital Bank, Miami
Nations Bank, Miami
Standard Chartered Bank, Miami

Banco Atlantico, Miami
Barclays Bank PLC, Miami
The Chase Manhattan Bank N.A., New York
Brown Brothers Hamman & Co., New York

Banco del Pacifico, S.A.
P.O. Box 6-3100, El Dorado
Panama, Republic of Panama
Tel: (507) 263-5833
Fax: (507) 263-7481

U.S. Correspondent
First Chicago International Bank, New York

Banco Disa, S.A.
P.O. Box 7201
Panama 1, Republic of Panama
Tel: (507) 263-5933
Fax: (507) 264-1084
Web site: http://www.bdisa.com

U.S. Correspondents:
The Chase Manhattan Bank N.A., New York
and Miami
Marine Midland Bank, New York
Nations Bank International, New York
Dadeland Bank, Miami
National Westminister USA International,
Miami

Banco General, S.A.
P.O. Box 4592
Panama 5, Republic of Panama
Tel: (507) 265-0303
Fax: (507) 265-0210
Web site: http://www.banco-general.com

U.S. Correspondents:
Citibank N.A., New York
The Chase Manhattan Bank N.A., New York
Marine Midland Bank, New York
Bank of America N.T. & S.A., San Francisco
Nations Bank, Atlanta
Dadeland National Bank, Miami
First Union Bank, Miami

Banco Internacional de Costa Rica, S.A. (BICSA)
P.O. Box 600
Panama 1, Republic of Panama
Tel: (507) 263-6822
Fax: (507) 263-6393

U.S. Correspondents:
Citibank N.A., New York
BankAmerica International, New York
Banco Atlantico, New York
The Bank of New York, New York

Banco Internacional de Panama, S.A. (BIPAN)
P.O. Box 11181
Panama 6, Republic of Panama
Tel: (507) 263-9000
Fax: (507) 263-9514

U.S. Correspondents:
Nations Bank International, Miami
Barclays Bank, Miami
Banco Internacional de Costa Rica, Miami

Banco Latinoamericano de Exportaciones, S.A. (BLADEX)
P.O. Box 6-1497, El Dorado
Panama, Republic of Panama
Tel: (507) 263-6766
Fax: (507) 269-6333

U.S. Correspondents:
The Chase Manhattan Bank N.A., New York
Citibank N.A., New York
Credit Lyonnais, New York
Swiss Bank Corporation, New York
Barclays Bank PLC, Miami

Banco Panamericano, S.A. (PANABANK)
P.O. Box 1828
Panama 1, Panama
Tel: (507) 263-9266
Fax: (507) 269-1537
E-mail: panabank@sinfo.net

U.S. Correspondents:
American Express Bank, New York
Marine Midland Bank, New York
Hong Kong and Shanghai Bank, New York
Popular Bank of Florida, Miami
Hamilton Bank N.A., Miami
Barclays Bank PLC, Miami
Nations Bank International, Miami

Asociacion Bancaria de Panama
(Panamanian Bank Association)
P.O. Box 4554, Panama 5,
Republic of Panama
Tel: (507) 263-7044
Fax: (507) 223-7630 or (507) 263-7783.

Certificate of Free Sale Documentation

Food and Drug Administration
Division of Programs and Enforcement Policy
200 C Street, SW
Washington, DC 20204

Travel Advisory and Visas

In 1987, the State Department's Bureau of Consular Affairs established the Consular Affairs Bulletin Board (CABB) as a means to keep the international business community informed about security and crime problems abroad. Access to the CABB is free of charge to anyone with a computer and a modem. Callers dial (202) 647-9225 from their modem. Consular Affairs and the Bureau of Diplomatic Security update the CABB daily.

Travel Advisory Service of the Department of State
Provides information in recorded and fax form for any travel warnings on traveling to foreign countries.
Tel: (202) 647-5225
Fax: (202) 647-3000.

The Consular Section of the U.S. Embassy in Panama
Unit 0945, APO AA 34002
Tel: (507) 227-6988
Fax: (507) 227-0239

"Guides for Business Representatives"
The Superintendent of Documents
U.S. Government Printing Office
Washington, DC 20402
Tel: (202) 512-1800
Fax: (202) 512-2250

Business travelers to Panama seeking appointments with U.S. Embassy Panama officials should contact the Commercial Section in advance.
Tel: (507) 227-1777 (ext 2225)
Fax: (507) 227-1713

Diplomatic Representation in the U.S.
Chief of mission
Chancery: 2862 McGill Terrace NW,
Washington, DC 20008
Tel: (202) 483-1407
Consulate(s) general: Atlanta, Houston, Miami, New Orleans, New York, Philadelphia, San Francisco, San Juan (Puerto Rico), Tampa

Diplomatic Representation from the U.S.
Chief of mission
Embassy: Avenida Balboa and Calle 38,
Apartado 6959, Panama City 5
Mailing address: American Embassy Panama,
Unit 0945, APO AA 34002
Tel: (507) 227-1377
Fax: (507) 227-1964

TRINIDAD AND TOBAGO

TRADE AND BUSINESS GUIDE

Official Name:	Republic of Trinidad and Tobago
Official Languages:	English. Hindi, French, and Spanish spoken
Population:	1,175,523 (2000 est)
Population Growth:	-0.49% (2000 est)
Age Structure:	0–14 years: 25%, 15–64 years: 68%, 65 years and over: 7% (2000 est)
Location:	Caribbean, islands between the Caribbean Sea and the North Atlantic Ocean, northeast of Venezuela
Area:	5,130 square kilometers, slightly smaller than Delaware
Type of Government:	Parliamentary democracy
Head of State:	Prime Minister Basdeo Panday
Cabinet:	Appointed by Parliament
Religion:	32.2% Roman Catholic, 24.3% Hindu, 14.4% Anglican, 14% other Protestant, 6% Muslim, 9.1% none or unknown
Major Cities:	Trinidad – capital: Port-of-Spain (64,000). Principal commercial centers: San Fernando (36,000), Arima (29,700), Point Fortin (20,000). Tobago – main town: Scarborough
Climate:	Tropical; with a rainy season from June to December
Time:	The entire country is -4 GMT (Greenwich Mean Time), which is one hour behind EST (Eastern Standard Time). The country does schedule for daylight savings time
GDP:	Purchasing power parity (PPP): $9.41 billion (1999 est); real growth rate: 5% (1999 est); per capita PPP: $8,500 (1999 est); composition by sector: agriculture = 2%, industry = 44%, services = 54% (1998 est)
Currency:	1 Trinidad and Tobago dollar (TT$) = 100 cents
Exchange Rate:	Average exchange rate: TT$ per US$ 1 = 6.30 (2000 est), 6.19 (1999 est), 6.220 (1998 est)
Weights & Measure:	Metric system
Natural Resources:	Petroleum, natural gas, asphalt
Total Trade:	In millions US$ [exports (fob)/imports (cif)] 1997 (2,542/3,036), 1998 (2,264/3,011), 1999 est (2,219/2,167)
Trade with U.S.:	In millions US$ [exports (fob)/imports (cif)]: 1997 (998/1,563), 1998 (830/12,341), 1999 est (681/1,006)
Major Trade Partners:	Imports: United States, Latin America, European Union countries, Japan. Exports: United States, Caricom countries, Latin America, European Union countries

Membership: CARICOM, IADB, IBRD, IFC, IMF, ISO, MIGA, OAS, UN, UNCTAD, WCO, WIPO, and WTO. See membership description in appendix

Sources: *Central Bank of Trinidad and Tobago: Central Statistical Office Data, CIA World Fact Book, United Nations World Statistics, U.S. Department of Commerce*

POLITICAL OUTLOOK ②

Relationship with the U.S.

Relations between the two countries have been excellent. Secretaries of State Warren Christopher and Madeleine Albright and Attorney General Janet Reno have visited since 1995. An Extradition Treaty, a Mutual Legal Assistance Treaty, a Maritime Counter-narcotics Agreement, and statements on cooperation in the areas of energy and the environment were signed.

Influences on Business

Political instability is not a great concern among businesses in Trinidad and Tobago. Trade unions have opposed the retrenchments that can occur with the government's divestments of national companies. The majority of union members and the public at large, however, do not racially oppose the government's economic reform programs. Crime and drug trafficking became major concerns in the early 1990s. The Panday government was elected in large part on an anticrime platform. The crime-suppression initiative of 1997 has had some success. Crime rates in Port of Spain are not unlike those of a similarly sized U.S. city.

Profile

System: Trinidad and Tobago is a parliamentary democracy based on the Westminster model. The United Kingdom granted the country independence in 1962. Trinidad and Tobago adopted a new constitution in 1976, establishing it as a republic within the British Commonwealth. The Cabinet is appointed and headed by the prime minister. The bicameral Parliament consists of a 36-member elected House of Representatives and a 31-member appointed Senate; the Court of Appeals is the highest level of the country's judicial system.

Schedule for Elections: Parliament's maximum term is five years. Elections may be called at any time. No additional information is available.

Major Parties: Traditionally, the two major parties are the People's National Movement (PNM) and the National Alliance for Reconstruction (NAR). The PNM generally represents urban and African voters, whereas the UNC is based more with the rural and Indian populations. There are no radical differences in their platforms. The PNM has held power for most of the past several decades. The National Alliance for Reconstruction (NAR) held a majority from 1986 to 1991. In 1995, the United National Congress (UNC) surprised many by winning nearly half of the seats in Parliament. Currently, the UNC has 17 seats, the PNM has 15, the NAR has 1, and there are 3 independents.

Political Violence: Since a 1990 coup attempt, there have been no serious cases of political violence. The current government is stable and democratic, held in check by a lively and well-functioning opposition.

Corruption: The level of corruption is moderate. Trinidad and Tobago has laws designed to combat corruption, but enforcement is lax due to a sluggish legal system. Increased drug trafficking and money laundering have the government's attention.

Most U.S. firms have not identified corruption as a major obstacle to doing business, but U.S. firms sometimes feel they are at a competitive disadvantage against local and third-country competitors that are not subject to the Foreign Corrupt Practices Act or to U.S.-type conflict of interest rules.

Media: The media often serves as a vehicle for active opposition and lively political debate.

Trends

The two-island nation of Trinidad and Tobago has earned a reputation as an excellent investment site for U.S. businesses. In 1995, after eight years of economic decline, Trinidad's implemented economic reforms. Since then, almost all investment barriers have been eliminated, and foreign investment and trade have flourished. The country's international debt rating is now one of the highest in the hemisphere. Trinidad is second only to Canada in terms of per capita U.S. direct foreign investment. A stable political system and a strategic location off the coast of South America have not hindered the country's revival. If problems lie ahead in Trinidad's otherwise hopeful economic outlook, they may be found in two areas: high unemployment rates and increased consumer demand. The latter has led to trade deficits and has put pressure on the exchange rate and the balance of payments. The Central Bank projected a real growth rate of 6.7 percent for 2000. This would make six straight years of real growth after eight years of economic decline.

Major Growth Sectors

The petrochemical sector (methanol, ammonia, urea, natural gas liquids) grew at a rate of 12.3 percent in 1996. However, that rate fell to 4.6 percent in 1997, due largely to falling prices. Oil production has declined, but natural gas production has continued to expand. The completion of the Atlantic LNG plant in 1999 was the biggest development. This plant produces 3 million metric tons of liquefied natural gas per year. Additional natural gas exploration projects have been approved. Outside the hydrocarbon sectors, distribution grew at 17.6 percent, construction at 15 percent, transport, storage, and communications at 4.7 percent, and manufacturing at 3.5 percent. The government of Trinidad and Tobago (GOTT) hopes tourism will expand, particularly the country's highly successful hosting of the 1999 Miss Universe Pageant.

Key Economic Indicators

Income, Production and Employment *(millions of U.S. dollars unless otherwise indicated)*			
	1997	1998	1999[1]
Nominal GDP	5,780	5,811	6,136
Real GDP Growth (pct)	3.4	3.2	5.6
GDP by Sector			
Agriculture	124	119	126
Manufacturing	440	480	507
Services	3,503	3,841	4,056
Petroleum	1,638	1,242	1,312
Government	477	518	547
Per Capita GDP (US$)	4,537	4,531	4,785
Labor Force (millions)	541	559	564
Unemployment Rate (pct)	14.5	14.2	14.1

1. 1999 figures are all estimates based on six months of data, except as noted. 1997 and 1998 figures have been revised.
Source: Bureau of Economic and Business Affairs; U.S. Department of State

- **Infrastructure**
  The country's infrastructure is adequate by regional standards. The network of paved roads is extensive. Utilities are fairly reliable in the cities although rural districts still suffer from water shortages, power failures, and inadequate drainage. The government has budgeted significant amounts toward infrastructure improvements, especially rural roads and bridges, rural electrification and telephone service, and drainage and sewerage. Telephone service is relatively modern, but rates are higher than in the U.S. Cellular service is available in urban areas. Tenders have been offered for new cellular carriers, a move that should expand coverage while lowering fees. Internet usage is widespread although service can be slow at peak times.

- **Labor**
  The labor market offers a high number of skilled and experienced workers, and the educational level of the population is among the highest in the developing world. The official unemployment rate at the end of 1998 was 14.1 percent.

Money and Prices *(annual percentage growth)*			
	1997	1998	1999[1]
Money Supply Growth (M2)[2]	11.6	12.3	-1.9
Consumer Price Inflation	3.8	5.6	3.7
Exchange Rate (TT$/US$)	6.29	6.30	6.30

1. 1999 figures are all estimates based on six months of data, except as noted. 1997 and 1998 figures have been revised. 2. Through July 1999.
Source: Bureau of Economic and Business Affairs; U.S. Department of State

Balance of Payments and Trade (millions of U.S. dollars unless otherwise indicated)			
	1997	1998	1999[1]
Total Exports FOB	2,542	2,264	2,219
Exports to U.S.	998	830	681
Total Imports CIF	3,036	3,011	2,167
Imports from U.S.	1,563	1,341	1,006
Trade Balance	-494	-747	52
Balance with U.S.[2]	-565	-511	-325
External Public Debt	1,541	1,430	1,420[3]
Fiscal Deficit/GDP (pct)	-0.1	-1.1	-1.3
Current Account Deficit/GDP (pct)	-6.6	-3.5	0.9
Debt Service Payments/GDP (pct)	8.0	5.0	4.6
Gold and Foreign Exchange Reserves	703	779	706[3]
Aid from U.S.[4]	3.0	3.5	3.7
Aid from Other Sources	N/A	N/A	N/A

1. 1999 figures are all estimates based on six months of data, except as noted. 1997 and 1998 figures have been revised. 2. 1999 U.S. trade with Trinidad and Tobago are estimates based on six months of data.
3. As of July 1999. 4. Represents primarily security assistance and counternarcotics program funding, training, equipment transfers, and in-kind contributions. Includes USIA and USDA exchanges.
Source: Bureau of Economic and Business Affairs; U.S. Department of State

- Balance of Payments
  See **Key Economic Indicators.** The exchange rate has hovered around TT$ 6.30 to US$ 1.00 for several years. The stability of the currency against the U.S. dollar has been maintained by the government's tight monetary policy.

Government Influence on Business

The government's economic strategy is marked by fiscal and monetary discipline, private sector investment, and export-led growth. An ambitious public-sector investment program aims particularly to improve the country's physical and educational infrastructure and its supply of water and electricity. The government's ongoing divestment program has been fairly successful. Subsidies to state enterprises have been reduced, and a respectable list of companies has been completely or partially divested since 1994.

TRADE

④

Leading Imports and Exports

Imports: Machinery, transportation equipment, manufactured goods, food, live animals

Exports: Petroleum and petroleum products, chemicals, steel products, fertilizer, sugar, cocoa, coffee, citrus, flowers

Foreign Trade *(Exports and Imports in US$M)*			
	1997	1998	1999[1]
Total Exports FOB	2,542	2,264	2,219
Exports to U.S.	998	830	681
Total Imports CIF	3,036	3,011	2,167
Imports from U.S.	1,563	1,341	1,006

1. 1999 figures are all estimates based on six months of data, except as noted. 1997 and 1998 figures have been revised.
Source: Bureau of Economic and Business Affairs; U.S. Department of State.

Best Prospects Analysis

Best Prospects for Nonagricultural Goods and Services

Equipment, Services (OGS/OGM)

	1997E $M	1998E $M	1999E $M
Total Market Size	515	630	630
Total Exports	N/A	N/A	N/A
Total Imports	N/A	N/A	N/A
Imports from the U.S.	N/A	N/A	N/A

Figures based on actual and estimated capital investment in the sector.

The energy sector accounts for approximately 23 percent of the country's GDP. Natural gas is now more important to the economy than oil. Proven natural reserves are estimated at 21.3 trillion cubic feet (tcf) as of January 1999. The *Medium Term Policy Framework* document provides U.S. companies with insights into the types of opportunities that will become available from the GOTT.

Architecture, Construction and Engineering Services (ACE/CON)

Several large construction projects are ongoing in the petrochemical and manufacturing sectors. In particular, various companies are actively bidding on the construction of one of the largest oxygen plants in the world. In the area of housing, a GOTT priority is for all its citizens to have access to acceptable and affordable shelter. Opportunities exist for home construction joint-venture projects. Opportunities also exist in the further development of the country's roads and bridges.

Engineering and Construction Services and Materials*

	1997 $M	1998 $M	1999E $M
Total Market Size	750	750	750
Total Exports	N/A	N/A	N/A
Total Imports	N/A	N/A	N/A
Imports from the U.S.	N/A	N/A	N/A

*Includes expenditures on chemical production machinery for new major industrial plant projects.

Figures based on actual and estimated private-sector capital expenditure on new facilities and planned government expenditure on construction projects.

Construction Equipment and Parts (CPT)

	1997E $M	1998E $M	1999E $M
Total Market Size	20.1	23.0	23.5
Total Exports	3.5	4.0	4.0
Total Imports	16.6	19.0	19.5
Imports from the U.S.	12.1	15.5	16.0

Water Resources Equipment (WRE)

	1997E $M	1998E $M	1999E $M
Total Market Size	15.0	25.0	45.0
Total Exports	2.5	3.0	3.0
Total Imports	10.2	15.0	30.0
Imports from the U.S.	5.0	10.0	20.0

Electrical Power Systems and Equipment (ELP)

	1997E $M	1998E $M	1999E $M
Total Market Size	57.3	66.5	70.0
Total Exports	1.1	1.5	1.5
Total Imports	56.2	65.0	68.5
Imports from the U.S.	16.3	25.0	26.0

These statistics are unofficial estimates.

Foods - Processed (FOD)

	1997E $M	1998E $M	1999E $M
Total Market Size	160.0	175.0	180.0
Total Exports	74.2	89.0	90.0
Total Imports	79.9	95.8	96.0
Imports from the U.S.	22.8	29.6	30.0

Automotive Parts and Accessories (APS)

	1997E $M	1998E $M	1999E $M
Total Market Size	17.0	21.0	25.0
Total Exports	0.9	1.0	1.0
Total Imports	16.9	20.0	24.0
Imports from the U.S.	4.1	6.0	6.0

Drugs and Pharmaceuticals (DRG)

	1997E $M	1998E $M	1999E $M
Total Market Size	39.0	43.0	45.0
Total Exports	2.5	3.0	3.5
Total Imports	36.4	40.0	41.0
Imports from the U.S.	8.5	10.0	11.0

Cosmetics, Toiletries (COS)

	1997E $M	1998E $M	1999E $M
Total Market Size	20.0	21.8	22.0
Total Exports	4.5	5.3	6.0
Total Imports	15.5	16.5	18.0
Imports from the U.S.	4.0	5.5	7.0

Consumer Electronics and Household Consumer Goods (CEL/HCG)

Household Appliances and Domestic Articles

	1997E $M	1998E $M	1999E $M
Total Market Size	13.0	14.0	15.0
Total Exports	2.5	3.0	3.5
Total Imports	10.2	11.0	12.0
Imports from the U.S.	5.1	6.5	7.0

Consumer Electronics (audiovisual only)

	1997E $M	1998E $M	1999E $M
Total Market Size	15.2	17.0	18.0
Total Exports	N/A	N/A	N/A
Total Imports	14.9	16.7	17.0
Imports from the U.S.	9.6	11.5	11.5

Computers and Peripherals (CPT)

	1997E $M	1998E $M	1999E $M
Total Market Size	25.0	41.0	45.0
Total Exports	0.5	1.0	1.0
Total Imports	24.4	40.0	44.0
Imports from the U.S.	20.1	30.0	35.0

Security and Safety Equipment (SEC)

Complete and accurate data are not available. The country recently witnessed a boom in the number of private security guards; now sales of security equipment—such as fences, burglar and car alarms, and hardware for grillwork—are on the rise. In addition, the large oil and gas sector requires fire and safety equipment and clothing for industrial employees.

Pollution Control Equipment, Environmental Consulting Services (POL)

Complete and accurate data are not available. Parliament created an Environmental Management Authority (EMA) in 1995. The EMA has stepped up publicity on environmental protection and has moved ahead on new standards and regulations. Purchases of pollution control equipment and expertise are growing accordingly. The subsectors offering the most opportunities include oil sludge and oil spill cleanup technology, sewage treatment technology, and liquid effluents control and monitoring technology.

Pleasure Boats and Accessories, Port and Shipbuilding Equipment (PLB/PRT)

Complete and accurate data are not available. The marine industry, especially yachting, has been growing rapidly. There are opportunities in the full range of sailing and motorboat supplies and spare parts. In particular, there are opportunities in the areas of hot dip galvanizing equipment, large marine hoists, welding and sandblasting, and gel-coat stripping equipment. Further demands exist in the construction of piers, docks, and related facilities to service new petro-chemical and industrial projects in Point Fortin and Point Lisas. Specific opportunities are in dredging, land reclamation, and cargo handling equipment.

Pleasure Boats

	1997E $M	1998E $M	1999E $M
Total Market Size	2.5	3.0	4.0
Total Exports	0.64	0.8	1.0
Total Imports	1.8	2.2	2.5
Imports from the U.S.	1.0	1.5	1.8

Port and Shipbuilding Equipment

Complete and accurate data are not available.

Airport and Ground Support Equipment (ARP)

Complete and accurate data are not available. Approximately $105 million will be spent to upgrade Piarco International Airport by 2001. The completed 37,000 square meter facility will have 16 gates, capacity for 1,500 passengers per hour and will be able to accommodate any type of aircraft currently used worldwide. The GOTT also plans to improve Tobago's Crown Point International Airport. Air Caribbean plans to upgrade their domestic terminal and construct new maintenance and administration buildings.

Agricultural Machinery and Equipment and Agricultural Chemicals (AGM/AGC)

Demand for chemicals, agricultural equipment and seeds is growing as efforts to increase domestic food production shows sign of success. The agricultural chemicals market is for fertilizers with potassium and phosphorus. About 40% of the market is for agricultural insecticides. U.S. suppliers have a small portion of the fertilizer market, and a 40% market share of the agricultural insecticides market segment.

Agricultural Equipment and Parts*

	1997 $M	1998 $M	1999E $M
Total Market Size	2.25	3.0	3.2
Total Exports	0.08	0.08	0.08
Total Imports	2.24	2.29	2.9
Imports from the U.S.	0.56	1.3	1.4

*Does not include food processing machinery or home gardening equipment.

Agricultural Chemicals*

	1997 $M	1998 $M	1999E $M
Total Market Size	3.7	4.8	5.0
Total Exports	0.2	0.3	0.4
Total Imports	3.5	4.5	4.8
Imports from the U.S.	0.8	1.3	1.5

*Trinidad & Tobago is a major exporter of ammonia and urea, but in raw form, not processed into final fertilizers.

Hotel and Restaurant Equipment (HTL)

Complete and accurate data are not available. The GOTT is aggressively promoting the country as a tourism destination. The government is actively courting investment in additional hotel and support infrastructure, especially in Tobago. Tourist arrivals rose from 314,045 in 1996 to 324,288 in 1997 and to 347,693 in 1998. The government acts as a facilitator for new development through the tourism and Industrial Development Company (TIDCO).

Best Prospects for Agricultural Products

Wheat

The U.S. exported just under US$ 20 million to Trinidad and Tobago in 1998. This amount comprises nearly all the country's wheat imports. The major purchaser is National Flour Mills, which is currently being divested. U.S. exporters to Trinidad frequently make use of the USDA GSM export credit guarantee program.

Soybeans

Soybeans imported from the U.S. are crushed to produce soybean meal for animal feed and edible vegetable oil. The largest importer, National Flour Mills (NFM), also exports soybean meal made from imported beans to neighboring countries. Soybean exports to Trinidad and Tobago dropped to around US$ 7 million in 1998, down significantly from the 25-year high of US$ 33.3 million in 1996. Carryover stocks and reported management and crush capacity problems at NFM may explain this drop. Imports of U.S. soybean meal, however, increased 45 percent in 1998 to over US$ 3.7 million. Other soy-related market segments that remain underdeveloped include textured vegetable protein foods, soy milk-based products, and food-grade soybeans.

Feeds and Fodders

Trinidad's thriving poultry industry requires feed corn, which is provided almost entirely by U.S. exporters. Imports of feeds and fodder, excluding pet foods, have leveled off to around US$ 12 million. Pet food sales from the U.S. continue to grow, reaching US$ 1.3 million in 1998.

Lumber and Wood Products

	1996E $M	1997E $M	1998E $M
Forest products:			
Imports from the U.S.	15	19	19
Softwood and treated lumber:			
Imports from the U.S.	N/A	10.7	9.9

The country is experiencing a mini construction boom, which should further increase demand for lumber and building products over the next two to three years.

Rice

	1997E $M	1998E $M
Imports from the U.S.	9.4	9.4

Trinidad produces about 25 to 30 percent of the rice needed for domestic consumption and imports the rest from the U.S. and Guyana. Guyana recently claimed that U.S. imports should be taxed under the Common External Tariff (CET) of CARICOM. Trinidad has successfully fought the measure. Another threat to U.S. market share is an effort by the largest purchaser, NFM, to identify lower-cost suppliers. However, NFM experimented unsuccessfully with imports from India.

Dairy Products

Total imports of dairy products rose to nearly US$ 5 million in 1998, a 20 percent jump over the previous year. The majority of these imports are for milk powder sold directly to consumers under various local brand names and used in the manufacture of UHT milk.

Pet Foods

U.S. imports increased again in 1998, growing by 25 percent to over US$ 1.25 million.

Hatchling Chicks and Hatching Eggs

Trinidad is nearly self-sufficient in poultry production, but the country imports a large number of baby chicks and hatching eggs from the U.S. Approximately 8,000 cases of U.S. hatching eggs are imported per month.

Red Meat and Poultry

U.S. sales of beef, veal, pork, lamb, and chicken meat to Trinidad and Tobago exceeded US$ 4.5 million in 1998, up 50 percent from 1997. The strong market for these U.S. exports is due largely to attractive prices, increased marketing campaigns, and a good match with consumer tastes. Furthermore, increased tourism is fueling the demand for well-priced, quality, and versatile meats from the U.S.

The above statistics are unofficial estimates.
N/A - Not Available, E - Estimate
Note: MT = Metric Tons

Extracted from the U.S. Department of Commerce USA Trade 2001 Country Commercial Guide for Trinidad and Tobago.

Import and Export Tips

- **Regulations**

  Customs: Customs clearance can be marked by bureaucratic inefficiency. Recently, the GOTT has taken several steps to streamline the customs process. For goods that are to be re-exported, temporary entry is allowed with advance arrangement. The items must be clearly identified by a mark such as a serial or part number. A deposit or bond must be posted prior to entry to cover duty liability. Ten percent of that deposit is owed for every three months the items remained in the country. Commercial samples and advertising film that are to be demonstrated and then re-exported are allowed entry without payment of duty.

  Tariffs: The customs value applied on imported goods is the price paid for goods when sold for export to Trinidad and Tobago. This is computed on the cif value and includes all other foreign costs incidental to the delivery of goods to Trinidad and Tobago. Imports are subject to the CARICOM Common External Tariff (CET). Since July 1, 1998, CARICOM tariff levels have been reduced to a targeted range of 0 to 20 percent.

  Import Taxes: A 15 percent value-added tax is collected on the retail sales of most goods, whether they are imported or produced locally. Only two items—sugar and poultry—are now subject to supplementary import surcharges of 5 to 45 percent.

Exchange Rate: In April 1993, the government removed exchange controls and floated the TT dollar. The Central Bank loosely manages the rate through currency market interventions and consultations with the commercial banks. In 1996, foreign exchange pressure mounted, and a decision by the Central Bank to allow a freer float led to a depreciation, which went as low as TT$ 6.23 to US$ 1.00 in December 1996. Since early November 1997, the rate has hovered around TT$ 6.29 to US$ 1.00. Foreign exchange supply depends heavily on the quarterly tax payments and purchases of local goods and services by a small number of large multinational firms, of which the most prominent are U.S. owned. Foreign currency for imports, profit remittances, and repatriation of capital is freely available.

• Documentation

Exports: For the export of goods on the negative list, an exporter must apply for a license from the Ministry of Trade and Industry. This list includes some marine species for the protection of local heritage, items related to foreign policy and national security, human organs, live nonlivestock animals, works of art, artifacts and archaeological findings, nonferrous metal scrap and ores, subsidized items, and firearms.

Imports: The list of the items that do still require an import license is continually revised. Prospective importers should contact the Licensing Section, Trade and Commerce Division of the Ministry of Trade and Industry. Exporters are required to have the following documents: CARICOM invoice, supplier invoice, certificate of origin, bill of lading, shipping documents, declaration of value, and an import license (for negative list items).

Labeling: Standards, labeling, testing, and certification issues do not often hinder U.S. exporters.

Standards: The Trinidad and Tobago Bureau of Standards (TTBS) is responsible for most trade standards. The Chemistry, Food, and Drug Division of the Ministry of Health monitors standards for food, drugs, and cosmetics. The TTBS uses the ISO 9000 series of standards and is a member of ISONET. The government is not a party to the WTO Standards Code.

• Payment

Terms: Exporters use all types of payment. Local banks have excellent reputations and foreign correspondent relationships.

Currency Exchange: The GOTT has removed exchange controls on foreign currency and securities. However, the Ministry of Finance has started levying a 10 percent tax on the interest earned on locally held U.S. dollar accounts and on local currency accounts.

Fund Transfer: The repatriation of capital, dividends, interest, and other distributions and gains on investment may be freely transacted without limits. Remittance usually takes 24 hours.

Agents and Distributors

The U.S. & Foreign Commercial Service at the U.S. Embassy in Santo Domingo offers guidance through the following services: The Agent/ Distributor Service (ADS) provides a search for appropriate representatives. A report is then prepared that lists firms that have agreed to consider a business relationship. The fee is US$ 250.00. The Gold Key Service surveys potential representatives or customers. The service schedules appointments with these prospects and provides the services of a trade aid. The fee is US$ 200.00 for the first day and $125.00 for each additional day. See **Contacts.**

Establishing an Office

A new Companies Act took effect in 1997. It is based largely on the Canadian model, which is similar to U.S. law. All companies must submit an annual return for each financial year to the Registrar of Companies. Public companies must also submit audited financial statements. Companies must hold at least one general meeting every calendar year to discuss the annual financial statements of the company and the appointment of directors and auditors. Common forms of business entities are as follows:

Public and Private Limited Liability Companies are the most widely used form. Nonpublic companies must have at least two directors; public companies must have at least three, at least two of whom are neither officers nor employees of the company or any of its affiliates. For nonpublic companies, the articles of incorporation restrict the right to transfer shares and prohibit any invitation to the public to subscribe for shares or debentures.

Branch Offices must be registered within 14 days of establishment. Submit constitutional and corporate information to the Registrar of Companies. The information must include the name of an attorney-in-fact resident in Trinidad and Tobago authorized to accept service for process and other notices. Filing fees and expenses total TT$ 2,000 (US$ 320). It is only slightly more difficult to incorporate a company than to register a branch, and trading branches typically have tax disadvantages.

Incorporated Companies must file Articles of Incorporation with the Registrar of Companies to receive a Certificate of Incorporation. The Registrar office must also approve the name of any proposed company with limited liability. The Articles of Incorporation include rules governing shareholder rights. Bylaws include rules and regulations governing the company's operations. Once registered, the company must (1) apply to the Value-Added Tax Office for a registration number (when applicable), (2) apply to the Board of Inland Revenue for a corporation tax file number and an employer "PAYE" number, and (3) apply to the National Insurance Board for registration as an employer for national insurance purposes. See **Contacts**.

Distribution and Sales Channels

Few restrictions are placed on the nature of relationships with representatives, distributors, or franchisers. The parties involved may freely agree upon contractual terms. Long-term distributors and agents sometimes acquire certain claims on distribution rights that go beyond contract rights under local common law interpretations. Common contracts are sales agency agreements, marketing agency agreements, and distributory agreements. In a marketing agreement, no authority is vested in the agent to contract on behalf of the principal. If the contract is drawn up properly, an overseas supplier will not be deemed to be trading within Trinidad and Tobago and incurs no tax liability on sales of the product.

Direct Marketing

Direct telephone marketing and door-to-door sales are not commonly used as marketing vehicles in Trinidad and Tobago.

Leasing/Joint Ventures

The government encourages joint ventures between foreign and local corporations. Corporate partners in a joint venture are governed by a joint-venture "partnership" agreement.

Franchising

Local and international franchises, such as fast food or Benetton clothing stores, are common. Related royalty payments are payable to a nonresident franchiser and subject to varying withholding tax rates. As an alternative to direct franchising, a franchiser may delegate responsibility for recruiting, appointing, and supervising franchisees to a "master licensee."

Advertising and Promotion

There are few laws and regulations for product advertising and trade promotion. Exceptions include a law protecting trademark use and restrictions on the advertising of professional services, such as those of doctors and lawyers.

Selling

The U.S. presence is strong in Trinidad and Tobago, and U.S. products enjoy high brand-name recognition. Many Trinidad and Tobago nationals have traveled to the U.S., and many view U.S. television programs with U.S. commercials on Trinidad and Tobago cable TV. Advertisers often target specific age, income, and ethnic groups. For many companies, radio is the preferred advertising medium, followed by print advertising (mostly newspapers) and television. Word-of-mouth advertising is also important, particularly owing to the country's small size.

Selling to the Government

An open bidding process is generally the rule, and government procurement practices are typically open and fair. U.S. firms compete successfully for many bids. The GOTT is not a party to the WTO Government Procurement Code.

Pricing

Businesses typically find they have a good deal of flexibility in the pricing of their products. It should be noted, however, that prices may be challenged under Trinidad and Tobago's antidumping laws. The Trinidad government controls the prices of sugar, schoolbooks, and some pharmaceuticals.

Customer Support

Companies doing business in Trinidad and Tobago must register an agent or representative in the country. The requirement ensures that an in-country business entity can be held liable in the event of legal disputes. No other regulations govern sales, service, or customer support.

Intellectual Property Rights (IPR)

The U.S. and the GOTT signed an Intellectual Property Rights (IPR) Agreement in 1994. The agreement and the GOTT legislation that followed provide for IPR protection similar to that in the U.S. However, enforcement is lax, particularly in the broadcast, cable, video, and entertainment fields.

Attorney

A local attorney is recommended in establishing business arrangements. The U.S. Embassy publishes a list of some of the most experienced and respected law firms that deal specifically with corporate and business law. (The U.S. Embassy assumes no responsibility for the performance of the firms listed.) See **Contacts.**

FOREIGN INVESTMENT
6

Openness: The GOTT actively encourages foreign direct investment, and generally there are no restrictions on investment. The 1996 Bilateral Investment Treaty (BIT) with the U.S. requires equal treatment in most areas for foreign and domestic investments. The government becomes involved only in foreign investments when the investor seeks government incentives or wishes to lease land in a government-owned industrial park. Telecommunications is the only sector that remains closed to new foreign investment in key areas.

Regulatory System: The regulatory system is not as large or as cumbersome in Trinidad and Tobago as it is in many other countries. Foreign investors in Trinidad do complain about delays in the investment approval process. Various ministries may be involved, sometimes causing delays of several years.

Investment Agreements: The regulatory system is not as large or as cumbersome in Trinidad and Tobago as it is in many other countries. Foreign investors in Trinidad do complain about delays in the investment approval process. Various ministries may be involved, sometimes causing delays of several years.

Trade Zones and Free Ports: The Free Zones Act of 1988 promotes export development and foreign investment projects in a bureaucracy-free, duty-free, and tax-free environment. Three multiple-user and 11 single-user zones are currently in operation or under construction. Free Zone enterprises may be established in any part of the country. They are 100 percent exempt from most customs duties; import and export licensing requirements; land and building taxes; work permit fees; foreign currency and property ownership restrictions; capital gains, income, corporation, or withholding taxes on sales or profits; VAT on goods supplied to a Free Zone; and duties on

vehicles for use only within the Free Zone. Application to operate in a Free Zone is made on specified forms to the Trinidad and Tobago Free Zones Company. Free Zone activities that qualify for approval include manufacturing for export, international trading in products, services for export and development, and management office zones. Production activity involving petroleum, natural gas, or petrochemicals, and activities involving investment in excess of US$ 50 million do not qualify for the program. See **Contacts.**

Performance Requirements/Incentives: There are no legal performance requirements. However, the GOTT uses negotiable incentives to strongly encourage certain projects. Encouraged investments typically generate employment and foreign exchange, provide training or technology transfer, boost exports or reduce imports, have local content, and generally contribute to the welfare of the country. Foreign investment is also screened for its environmental impact. The government may grant tax holidays and concessions in the manufacturing and hotel industries. Tax and nontax incentives may be negotiated for investments in manufacturing, tourism, and energy.

Capital Markets and Investment: Foreign investors have access to well-developed capital markets and a small but reputable stock market. There are no restrictions on borrowing by foreign investors although rates tend to hover around the 15 percent range.

Private Ownership: Private foreign and domestic entities have the right to establish and own business enterprises and engage in remunerative activity. Businesses may be freely purchased or disposed of. A license is required to own more than 30 percent of the share capital in a public company. Current legislation requires a license for the foreign ownership of over an acre of land for residential purposes and five acres for trade purposes. To date, however, waivers on corporate equity and land ownership restrictions have been freely granted.

Property Rights: Rights are protected under the constitution and under common-law practice. Secured interests in property are recognized and enforced. Intellectual Property Rights (IPR) enforcement, however, remains insufficient.

Expropriation and Compensation: Expropriation has not been a concern among U.S. businesses. Incidents have not occurred since the mid-1980s, and when incidents did occur, all expropriations were justly compensated. The recently signed Bilateral Investment Treat with the U.S. explicitly prohibits expropriation or nationalization of an investment without just compensation.

OPIC and Investment Insurance: OPIC, EXIM Bank, and the Multilateral Investment Guarantee Agency (MIGA) have active programs in Trinidad and Tobago.

Dispute Settlement: There are often long delays before a case will be heard before the High Court of Justice. Steps are currently underway to modernize this aspect of the judicial system. In 1996, the Chamber of Commerce launched its Dispute Resolution Center to foster mediation training and hear commercial disputes. The center has been successful and increasingly influential. The Bilateral Investment Treaty with the U.S. provides for dispute resolution alternatives, including binding arbitration. Trinidad and Tobago is a member of the International Center for the Settlement of Investment Disputes (ICSID) and is a signatory to the New York Convention on the Recognition and Enforcement of Foreign Arbitral Awards.

FINANCE ⑦

The banking system is well developed and reliable. There are five commercial banks, two merchant banks, and related financial institutions. The Central Bank does a competent job of overseeing the banking system. As of December 1998, the Central Bank estimates the total assets of the country's commercial banks at TT$ 26.5 billion. All Trinidad and Tobago banks have correspondent relationships with U.S. and Canadian banks. Citibank is the only U.S. bank with well-established offices in the country.

Trinidad and Tobago's sovereign credit risk rating is among the highest in the hemisphere.

Export Financing: Trinidad and Tobago uses all kinds of export and import financing and insurance. Bank borrowing is the most common form of financing. Interest rates, however, are high. The Agricultural Development Bank, Development Finance Limited, and the Small Business Development Company and the Venture Capital Fund are other sources of local funds for trade and investment. The U.S. Export-Import Bank, similar institutions from other countries, and OPIC guarantees may also be used. U.S. agricultural exporters should refer to the list of programs at the USDA Foreign Agricultural Service's Web site: www.fas.usda.gov.

Project Financing: Local project financing is not widely available. Most financing comes from overseas sources. Financing for some projects is available from the World Bank, the Inter-American Development Bank, and the European Union. A number of U.S. banks have been active in providing project financing, divestment brokerage, overseas bond marketing services, and acting as correspondent banks for U.S. agricultural credit programs.

COMMUNICATIONS ⑧

Phone

Telecommunications networks are reliable although costs are higher than in the U.S. Users can access the U.S. and other countries by direct dial. Simply dial the area code (868) plus the local number. International service overall is excellent, and domestic services is good. Both are provided by the majority state-owned TSTT/Cable and Wireless (UK) monopoly. Cellular service is available in urban areas. The admission of new cellular carriers should expand coverage and lower fees. Officials are considering whether or not to open up the general telecommunications sector to additional providers.

Internet

The Internet is widely used although service can be slow at peak times.

Mail

Mail service is reliable, and several U.S.-owned air-courier services operate in the country. Express mail international services are available between Trinidad and Tobago and the U.S.

TRANSPORTATION ⑨

Land

The road network is extensive, with over 4,300 kilometers of paved roads. Goods and services are regularly distributed even to the most remote parts of the country.

Driving is on the left side of the road. There is a minimal agricultural railroad system near San Fernando.

Sea

The seaports are at Pointe-a-Pierre, Point Fortin, Point Lisas, Port-of-Spain, Scarborough, and Tembladora.

Air

A US$ 105 million upgrade of Piarco International Airport has recently been completed. Loeb Partners plans to make Piarco the regional hub of its BWIA Airline. American Airlines also has established a presence in the market. Upgrades are planned for Tobago's Crown Point International Airport.

WORK WEEK

(10)

Business Hours: 8.00 a.m. to 4.00 p.m. Monday through Friday.

Government Hours: 8:15 a.m. to 4.30 p.m. Monday through Thursday, and 8.15 a.m. to 4.00 p.m. Friday.

Bank Hours: 8.00 a.m. to 2.00 p.m. Monday through Thursday, and 8.00 a.m. to 1.00 p.m. and 3.00 p.m. to 5.00 p.m. Friday. Closed on Saturday.

HOLIDAYS 2001
(11)

New Year's Day, January 1
Eid El Fitr (variable)
Carnival Monday and Tuesday, March*
Baptist Liberation Day, March 30
Good Friday (variable), April 13
Easter Monday (variable), April 16
Indian Arrival Day, May 30
Corpus Christi (variable), June 14
Labor Day, June 19
Emancipation Day, August 1
Independence Day, August 31
Divali (variable)
Christmas Day, December 25
Boxing Day, December 26

NOTE: *Carnival Monday and Tuesday (the Monday and Tuesday preceding Ash Wednesday) are not official public holidays, but almost all businesses are closed. Last year,

Carnival Monday and Tuesday were March 6&7, 2000. The Hindu and Muslim festivals of Divali and Eid-ul-Fitr, respectively, are public holidays in Trinidad and Tobago. Where the public holiday is a religious observance, the date is selected in accordance with the particular religious calendar.

Some holidays may be observed on different dates depending on the day of the week on which they fall. The U.S. Embassy will be closed on U.S. and Trinidad and Tobago holidays. It is recommended that business travelers do not schedule trips to Trinidad and Tobago immediately before or immediately after local or U.S. holidays.

*Depends on the lunar calendar; a difference of a day may occur.

Business Customs

Local business dress and customs are similar to those in the U.S. Trinidad's businesspeople are informal and friendly; they value personal contact and courtesy. First names are freely used after the initial meeting.

Travel Advisory and Visas

For travel information compiled by the Department of State's Bureau of Consular Affairs, telephone (202) 647-5225. Travel information is also available through the Consular Affairs website: http://travel.state.gov. The Guide for Business Representatives is available for sale by the Superintendent of Documents, U.S. Government Printing Office, Washington, D.C. 20402; Tel. (202) 512-1800; Fax (202) 512-2250. Business travelers to Trinidad and Tobago seeking appointments with U.S. Embassy Port of Spain officials should contact the Economic/Commercial Section in advance at (868) 622-6371 or ustrade@tstt.net.tt.

Business Infrastructure

Entry Requirements (personal and professional goods): U.S. citizens must have a passport to enter. Visas are not required for stays of less than three months. Work permits are required for some types of work, whether the worker is paid or not. A visitor may work in any area without a work permit for up to 30 days, with one entry per 12-month period permitted. Business visitors should be sure to check the "business" box rather than the "work" box on the immigration entry form, unless they are being paid in Trinidad and Tobago. For further information, travelers may contact the Embassy of Trinidad and Tobago, 1708 Massachusetts Avenue N.W. Washington, D.C. 20036; Tel: (202) 467-6490.

Currency Exchange: For several years, the Trinidad and Tobago dollar (TT$) has held steady against the U.S. dollar at an approximate rate of TT$ 6.30 to US$ 1.00. There are no exchange controls on foreign currency.

Taxes: A value-added tax of 10 percent is levied on retail sales of domestic and imported goods. The Ministry of Finance levies tax of 10 percent on the interest earned on locally held U.S. dollar accounts and on local currency accounts. No additional information is available..

Hotels and Restaurants: Many large hotels cater to business functions and needs. The country's cultural diversity is reflected in its variety of dining options, which includes East Indian, Chinese, Middle Eastern, Creole, Italian, and French restaurants.

Housing: Reputable real estate agents list everything from modern houses with large yards to condominiums or townhouse apartments. Most residential areas are within easy commuting distance from commercial and industrial areas. Rental prices have gone up significantly in the last several years. Prices for small houses in neighborhoods comparable to U.S. middle-class suburbs start at approximately US$ 1,200 per month. Executive-type houses range from US$ 2,000 to $4,000 per month.

Utilities: Much needed rehabilitation programs are underway to improve the supply of electricity and water, particularly in rural areas. Extensive repairs are also planned on wastewater treatment plants. No additional information is available.

Business Services: See **Marketing Tips.**

Labor Costs and Legislation: Salaries vary considerably between industries. The national minimum wage is TT$ 7.00 per hour (approximately US$ 1.20). The

Maternity Protection Act of 1998 provides for maternity benefits. The Industrial Relations Act governs labor relations. The IRA provides for recourse to an industrial court for resolution of disputes that cannot be resolved at the collective bargaining table or through conciliation efforts by the Ministry of Labor. Approximately 25 to 30 percent of Trinidad and Tobago's workforce is unionized.

Education: An accredited international school with a predominantly U.S. curriculum for grades K through 12 opened in Port of Spain in 1994. Enrollment is now over 250 students. Several respected private schools offer Trinidadian–British curriculums, while one private school offers a Canadian curriculum. The literacy rate is 97.9 percent.

Travel Notes

The following travel notes have been supplied by the U.S. government. For the most recent general travel and consular information, see the U.S. Department of State travel publications or call the Traveler's Telephone Hotline at (202) 647-5225.

Security: Crime rates in Port of Spain are now similar to those in U.S. cities. Crime and

drug trafficking were on the increase in the early 1990s, and these issues remain hot political topics.

Health Precautions: Tap water is potable. Medical care is good, but not up to U.S. standards. Doctors and dentists with overseas training are available in most specialties. Costs are often inexpensive. Air ambulance service is available for emergencies. Most prescription drugs can be bought locally. Current information on health matters may be obtained from the Centers for Disease Control and Prevention's international travelers' hotline at (404) 332-4559.

Embassy Assistance

To obtain additional and updated information on entry and exit requirements, travelers can contact the Consular Section of the Embassy of Trinidad and Tobago at 1708 Massachusetts Avenue, N.W., Washington, D.C. 20036; Tel: (202) 467-6490. Travelers may also contact the nearest Trinidad and Tobago consulate. They are located in Miami and New York.

Business and investment advice is available from the U.S. Embassy in Port of Spain or the American Chamber of Commerce of Trinidad and Tobago (AmCham).

CONTACTS
13

U.S. and Country Contacts

U.S. Embassy
Chief, Economic and Commercial Section
Economic Officer
U.S. Embassy
Port of Spain
15 Queen's Park West
Port of Spain
Tel: (868) 622-6371
Fax: (868) 622-2444; (868) 622-5462
E-mail: ustrade@carib-link.net

Foreign Commercial Service, U.S. Embassy
Corner of Calle Cesar Nicolas Penson & Calle
  Leopoldo Navarro
Santo Domingo, Dominican Republic
Tel. (868) 221-2171
Fax: (868) 688-4838

U.S. Dept. of Agriculture/Foreign Agricultural Service
U.S. Embassy, Caracas
Calle F con Calle Suapure
Colinas de Valle Arriba
Caracas 1060-A Venezuela
Tel: 011-582-975-8861; 011-582-975-7695
Fax: 011-582-975-7615

Registrar of Companies
34 Frederick Street
Port of Spain
Tel: (868) 625-9971
Fax: (868) 625-6530

Embassy of Trinidad and Tobago
1708 Massachusetts Avenue N.W.
Washington, DC 20036
(202) 467-6490

Washington-Based U.S. Government Country Contacts

U.S. Department of Commerce/Caribbean Basin Division
Desk Officer for Trinidad and Tobago
Department of Commerce
14th Street & Constitution Ave. Room 3203
Washington, DC 20230
Tel: (202) 482-1648
Fax: (202) 482-2218

U.S. Department of Commerce Liaison Office
Procurement Liaison Officer
Office of the U.S. Executive Director
1818 H Street, NW
Washington, DC 20433, Room MC 13525
Tel: (202) 458-0118
Fax: (202) 477-2967

U.S. Department of Commerce Liaison with the Inter-American Development Bank
Office of the U.S. Executive Director
1300 New York Ave., NW
Washington, DC 20577
Tel: (202) 623-3822
Fax: (202) 623-2039

USDA/FAS/Export Credits Program Development Division
Latin America & Caribbean Area
1400 Independence Avenue SW
AG Box 1034
Washington, DC 20520-1034
Tel: (202) 720-0625
Fax: (202) 690-3077

USDA/FAS/Export Credits/CCC Operations Division/Regulations, Procedures & Reports Branch
AG Box 1035
Washington, DC 20520-1035
Tel: (202) 720-0624
Fax: (202) 720-0938

U.S. Department of State
Desk Officer for Trinidad and Tobago
Office of Caribbean Affairs
ARA/CAR
U.S. Department of State
2201 C Street NW, Room 4908
Washington, DC 20520-4908
Tel: (202) 647-4757
Fax: (202) 647-4477

U.S. Department of State – Office of Business Affairs
Senior Coordinator
2201 C Street NW, Room 2318
Washington, DC 20520
Tel: (202) 647-1625
Fax: (202) 647-3953

TPCC Trade Information Center number in Washington:
(800) USA-TRADE

Country Government Agencies

Tourism and Industrial Development Company of Trinidad and Tobago (TIDCO)
P.O. Box 222
10-14 Philips Street
Port of Spain
Tel: (868) 623-6022; (868) 623-6023
Fax: (868) 625-7548
Web site: http://www.tidco.w.tt

Trinidad and Tobago Free Zones Company
  Limited (TTFZ)
Albion Court, 2nd Floor West
61 Dundonald Street
Port of Spain
Tel: (868) 625-4749; (868) 623-8363
Fax: (868) 625-4755

The Chaguaramas Development Authority
  (CDA)
Airway Road
Chaguaramas
P.O. Box 3162
Carenage
Tel: (868) 634-4227; (868) 634-2051
Fax: (868) 643-4311
E-mail: chagdev@tstt.net.tt
Web site: http://www.chagdev.com

The Trinidad and Tobago Bureau of Standards
Lot 1, Century Drive
Trincity Industrial Estate
Macoya
Tel: (868) 663-4835; (868) 663-4836
Fax: (868) 663-4335

The Chemistry, Food and Drug Division
Ministry of Health
92 Frederick Street
Port of Spain
Tel: (868) 623-2834
Fax: (868) 623-9528
(Monitors imports of foodstuffs, drug and
  cosmetics.)

Country Trade Associations and Chambers
of Commerce

American Chamber of Commerce of Trinidad
  and Tobago
Hilton Hotel
Upper Arcade
Lady Young Road
Port of Spain
Tel: (868) 627-8570
Fax: (868) 627-7405
E-mail: amcham@trinidad.net
Web site: http://www.amchamtt.com

Trinidad and Tobago Chamber of Commerce
  and Industry
P.O. Box 499
Columbus Circle
Westmoorings
Tel: (868) 637-6966
Fax: (868) 637-7425

The South Trinidad Chamber of Industry and
  Commerce Inc.
Cross Crossing Shopping Centre
San Fernando
Tel: (868) 657-9077; (868) 657-3008
Fax: (868) 652-5023
E-mail: secretariat@southchamber.com
Web site: http://www.southchamber.com

Trinidad and Tobago Manufacturers Association
8A Stanmore Avenue
Port of Spain
Tel: (868) 623-1029; (868) 623-1030
Fax: (868) 623-1031

Country Market Research Firms

Caribbean Market Research Ltd.
21A Marli Street
Port of Spain
Tel: (868) 622-6545
Fax: (868) 622-4924
E-mail: caribres@wow.net

Mary King & Associates – A Ham's Affiliate
The Halycon Building
112-114 E. Main Road
St. Augustine
Tel: (868) 662-9535; (868) 663-6751
Fax: (868) 663-4252
Web site: http://www.louisharris.com

Market Facts & Opinions Ltd.
37 Victoria Square South
Port of Spain
Tel: (868) 627-8417; (868) 627-8524
Fax: (868) 625-7913
E-mail: mfoserv@trinidad.net

Namdevco (National Agriculture Marketing &
   Development Company)
(research in food & agricultural sector,
   agro-industry)
Tel: (868) 647-3218
Fax: (868) 647-6087
E-mail: namdevco@tstt.net.tt

Commercial Banks

Scotia Bank Trinidad and Tobago Ltd.
Park & Richmond Streets
Port of Spain
Tel: (868) 625-3566
Fax: (868) 624-2179
Web site: http://www.scotiabanktt.com

Citibank (Trinidad and Tobago) Ltd.
12 Queen's Park East
Port of Spain
Tel:(868) 625-1046-9
Fax: (868) 624-8131; (868) 627-6128

Republic Bank Ltd.
P.O. Box 1153, Republic House
9-17 Park Street
Port of Spain
Tel: (868) 625-3611-9
Fax: (868) 624-1323
E-mail: republic@trinidad.net

Royal Bank of Trinidad and Tobago Ltd.
P.O. Box 287, Royal Court
6th Floor, 19-21 Park Street
Port of Spain
Tel: (868) 623-1322 (ext) 2606
Fax: (868) 625-3764
E-mail: royce1999@trinidad.net

First Citizens Bank
50 St. Vincent St.
Port of Spain
Tel: (868) 623-2576
Fax: (868) 624-5981

U.S.-Based Multipliers Relevant for Trinidad and Tobago

American Soybean Association
12125 Woodcrest Executive Dr.
Suite #100
St. Louis, MO 63141-9200
Washington, DC 20062-2000
Tel: (202) 463-5485
Fax: (202) 463-3126
E-mail: inbox@aaccla.org
Web site: http://www.aaccla.org

Tel: (314) 576-1770
Fax: (314) 576-2786
Web site: http://www.oilseeds.org

Association of American Chambers of Commerce of Latin America
1615 H Street, NW

Major Newspapers

Trinidad Guardian
22 - 24 St. Vincent St.
Port of Spain
Tel: (868) 623-8870
Fax: (868) 623-8871 (ext 5000)

Daily Express
35 & 37 Independence Square
Port of Spain
Tel: (868) 623-1711
Fax: (868) 627-1451

Newsday
Chacon House
19-21 Chacon Street
Port of Spain
Tel: (868) 623-4929
Fax: (868) 625-8362

Television Stations

International Communications Network (ICN)
Television House
Maraval Road
Port of Spain
Tel: (868) 622-4141
Fax: (868) 622-0344 (newsroom)

Caribbean Communications Network (CCN)
Independence Square
Port of Spain
Tel: (868) 627-8806
Fax: (868) 627-2721

The Information Channel
Lady Young Road
Morvant
Tel: (868) 674-1333
Fax: (868) 675-4286

U.S. Embassy List of Reputable Corporate and Business Law Attorneys

Ashmead Ali & Co.
21D and 21E Pembroke Street
Port of Spain
Tel: (868) 623-5200
Fax: (868) 625-7586

M.G. Daly & Partners
115A Abercromby Street, Port of Spain
Tel: (868) 623-4237; (868) 623-4239
Fax: (868) 625-0601

De Nobriga, Inniss & Company
90 Edward Street, Port of Spain
Tel: (868) 623-4802
Fax: (868) 625-0329

Fitzwilliam, Stone, Furness-Smith & Morgan
36 Pembroke Street, Port of Spain
Tel: (868) 623-1618; (868) 623-1619; (868)
  623-2425; (868) 623-2426; (868) 623-0606
Fax: (868) 623-0605; (868) 623-6524

Gittens Smart & Co
55 Edward Street, Port of Spain
Tel: (868) 623-4820
Fax: (868) 623-5077

Hamel-Smith & Company
19 St. Vincent Street, Port of Spain
Tel: (868) 623-4237; (868) 623-4239

Hobsons
13-17 Keate Street, San Fernando
Tel: (868) 652-3801; (868) 652-3803
Fax: (868) 652-1282

Mair & Company
50 Richmond Street, Port of Spain
Tel: (868) 624-0428
Fax: (868) 623-9117

Pollonais, Blanc, De La Bastide & Jacelon
62 Sackville Street, Port of Spain
Tel: (868) 623-8505; (868) 623-5461
Fax: (868) 625-8415

J.D. Sellier & Company
129-131 Abercromby Street, Port of Spain
Tel: (868) 623-4283
Fax: (868) 625-2984

Attorneys in Tobago
(Most of these firms also work in Tobago.)

Gift & Company
1 Bacolet Street, Scarborough Tobago
Tel/Fax: (868) 639-3187

Deorah More-Miggins
Young Street, Scarborough Tobago
Tel: (868) 639-3175

Abbreviations for International Organizations

African Development Bank	AfDB
Asia-Pacific Economic Cooperation	APEC
Asian Development Bank	AsDB
Association of Southeast Asian Nations	ASEAN
Central American Common Market	CACM
Caribbean Community and Common Market	CARICOM
Common Market for Eastern and Southern Africa	COMESA
European Bank for Reconstruction and Development	EBRD
Economic Community of Western African States	ECOWAS
European Economic Area	EEA
European Free Trade Association	EFTA
European Monetary System	EMS
European Union	EU
Gulf Cooperation Council	GCC
Inter-American Development Bank	IADB
International Bank for Reconstruction and Development	IBRD
International Chamber of Commerce	ICC
Islamic Development Bank	IDB
International Finance Corporation	IFC
International Monetary Fund	IMF
International Organization for Standardization	ISO
Latin American Integration Association	LAIA
Southern Cone Common Market	MERCOSUR
Multilateral Investment Guarantee Agency	MIGA
North American Free Trade Agreement	NAFTA
Organization of American States	OAS
Organization for Economic Cooperation and Development	OECD
Organization of Petroleum Exporting Countries	OPEC
South African Customs Union	SACU
South African Development Community	SADC
Central African Customs & Economic Union	UDEAC
West African Economic and Monetary Union	UEMOA
United Nations	UN
United Nations Conference on Trade and Development	UNCTAD
World Customs Organization	WCO
World Intellectual Property Organization	WIPO
World Trade Organization	WTO

Web Sites and Internet Resources

U.S Government Internet Sites

Name	Description	Address
Africa Growth and Opportunity Act (AGOA)	Trade Leads, Matchmaker Programs U.S. - trade information	www.agoa.gov
Commercial News USA	Trade Leads	www.cnewsusa.com
Infrastructure Division (USDOC)	Current infrastructure projects world-wide	www.ita.doc.gov/infrastructure
Trade Opportunities Program (TOPS)-(USDOC)	Provides companies with current sales leads from international firms seeking to buy or represent their products or services.	www.stat-usa.gov
United States & Foreign Commercial Service (US&FCS) (U.S. Department of Commerce)	Trade leads designed so that U.S. exporters can retrieve and respond to qualified international business opportunities in real-time.	www.usatrade.gov
U.S. Global Technology Network (USAID)	Operated by USAID, investment and partnerships worldwide.	www.usgtn.org
U.S Department of Agriculture (USDA)	Small Business Opportunities Agriculture trade leads, market reports, statistics, etc.	www.usda.gov/da/smallbus.html

Non-Government Internet Sites

Name	Description	Address
Africa Library and Information	Resources Africa: Selected Internet Resources	www.sul.stanford.edu/depts/ssrg/africa/africa.html
Africa Link	A USAID initiative to help link its African partners.	www.usaid.gov/alnk/site.html
Africa Online	Africa info, News, leads links, and internet communication services throughout Africa	www.africaonline.com
Alibaba	Trade Leads	www.alibaba.com
American Export Register (Thomas Publishing Co.)	Listings for 45,000 and 5,000 product categories in six languages	www.aernet.com
Buyers Guide	Trade Leads	www.buyersguide.com
ChemNet	Trade leads and directory for chemical Industry	www.chemnet.com
Clearfreight	Trade Resource Center, freight forwarder/customs brokers, industry news	www.clearfreight.com
Data Pro Business	Online Africa info, leads and links for South Africa	www.bol.co.za/
Exportall	Trade leads; Country Information; Export Information; Reference Tools; and a listing of International Organizations.	www.exportall.com
Federation of International Trade Associations	Trade leads, and directory	www.fita.org/webindex/0060.html

Name	Description	Address
Foreign Trade On-Line	Trade leads	www.foreign-trade.com
Guia Export Online	Bell South's international guide of products and services; in both English and Spanish	www.guiaexport.bellsouth.com
International Import Export Business Exchange	Trade leads; Comprehensive trade lead links	www.imex.cominternational.html
Latin-American Business Link	Latin-American Trade Leads	www.labl.com/trademall.htm
Latin Export	Trade leads for MERCOSUR countries (Brazil, Arentina, Uruguay, Paraguay, Chile and Bolivia).	www.latinexport.com
Mbendi	Africa info, leads and links	www.mbendi.com
Nigerian Business Galleria	Nigerian trade leads	www.nigeriangalleria.com/home.htm
Owens Online	Trade leads & International Credit Reports	www.owens.com
South Africa Daily Tender Bulletin	South African Government Tenders	www.tradeinfo.co.za/dtb.htm
Tradeline.com	Trade leads with an emphasis on the Mercosur countries	www.tradeline.com.ar/
Trade Submit	Global trade leads organized by industry sector	www.trade-submit.com
Trade Express	International Int'l Bulletin Board Services	www.trade-express.com
Trade Leads	Online Leads for Argentina & Mercosur	www.tradeline.com.ar/
Trading Floor	Many links to trade lead sites	www.tradingfloor.net
U.S. Dairy Export Council	Trade Leads Trade Leads for exports of U.S. dairy products	www.usdec.org/
World Access Network Directory	Global directory of manufacturers and service businesses. Provides trade opportunities and enables businesses to register services. (In 16 languages)	www.wand.com
WorldBid.com	Good source for a large number of global trade leads.	www.worldbid.com
World Trade Center Association	World Trade Center lists, Int'l trade leads	www.wtca.org
World Trade Exchange	Leads and contacts	www.wte.net/
World Trading Information Center	Trade leads; listing of import/export companies	www.world-trading.com
World Wide Government Procurement	Links to world government procurement sites	www.ctc.gov.au/links
World Trade Zone	Import/Export directory site with over 125,000 company listings, trade discussion forums, and trade lead archives	www.worldtradezone.com

Non-Government Internet Sites (Fee/Subscription)

Name	Description	Address
Center for Global Development	Trade Services	www.cgtd.com/global/ index.html
The Exporter	Monthly international trade journal	www.exporter.com
Global Textile Network	Sourcing and distribution for textiles	www.g-t-n.com/
Project Guides	Project leads for several industries, including environmental, energy, transportation, information management and engineering	www.projectguides.com
ProNet Link	Import/Export Information, Trade Leads	www.pronetlink.com/ index.asp
World Market Watch	Trade Services	www.wmw.com
World Trade	Trade Leads	www.worldtrade-sites.com